RACE AND THE OBAMA PHENOMENON

RACE
AND THE
OBAMA
PHENOMENON

★ ★

The Vision of a More Perfect Multiracial Union

EDITED BY
G. Reginald Daniel and Hettie V. Williams

UNIVERSITY PRESS OF MISSISSIPPI
JACKSON

www.upress.state.ms.us

The University Press of Mississippi is a member of the Association of American University Presses.

Copyright © 2014 by University Press of Mississippi
All rights reserved
Manufactured in the United States of America

First printing 2014

∞

Library of Congress Cataloging-in-Publication Data

Race and the Obama phenomenon : the vision of a more perfect multiracial union / edited by G. Reginald Daniel and Hettie V. Williams.
  pages cm
Includes bibliographical references and index.
ISBN 978-1-62846-021-6 (cloth : alk. paper) — ISBN 978-1-62846-022-3 (ebook) 1. Obama, Barack—Influence. 2. United States—Race relations—21st century. 3. United States—Politics and government—2009– 4. National characteristics, American—History—21st century. 5. Democracy—United States. I. Daniel, G. Reginald, 1949– II. Williams, Hettie V.
  E908.3.R33 2014
  305.80097309'05—dc23   2014005431

British Library Cataloging-in-Publication Data available

CONTENTS

Preface [IX]
HETTIE V. WILLIAMS AND G. REGINALD DANIEL

Acknowledgments [XIX]

Foreword
Race Will Survive the Obama Phenomenon [XXI]
DAVID ROEDIGER

Introduction
Understanding Obama and Ourselves [XXXIII]
GEORGE LIPSITZ

PART I
RACE, OBAMA, AND MULTIRACIALITY

1.
Race and Multiraciality
From Barack Obama to Trayvon Martin [3]
G. REGINALD DANIEL

2.
By Casta, Color Wheel, and Computer Graphics
Visual Representations of Racially Mixed People [41]
GREG CARTER

3.
Barack Obama
Embracing Multiplicity—Being a Catalyst for Change [62]
JANET C. MENDOZA STICKMON

4.
In Pursuit of Self
The Identity of an American President and Cosmopolitanism [84]
HETTIE V. WILLIAMS

PART II
OBAMA, BLACKNESS, AND THE "POST-RACIAL IDEA"

5.
Barack Hussein Obama, or, the Name of the Father [117]
TAVIA NYONG'O

6.
The End(s) of Difference?
Towards an Understanding of the "Post" in "Post-Racial" [133]
LISA ANDERSON-LEVY

7.
On the Impossibilities of a Post-Racist America in the Obama Era [147]
KARANJA KEITA CARROLL

8.
Obama, the Instability of Color Lines, and the Promise of a Postethnic Future [167]
DAVID A. HOLLINGER

PART III
RACE, GENDER, AND THE OBAMA PHENOMENON

9.
From Chattel to First Lady
Black Women Moving from the Margins [177]
MARSHA J. TYSON DARLING

10.
The "Outsider" and the Presidency
Mediated Representations of Race and Gender in the 2008 Presidential Primaries [201]
TESSA DITONTO

11.
Obama's "Unisex" Campaign
Masculinities, Race, and Law [225]
FRANK RUDY COOPER

12.
"Everything His Father Was Not"
Fatherhood and Father Figures in Barack Obama's First Term [244]
HEIDI ARDIZZONE

PART IV
RACE, POLITICS, AND THE OBAMA PHENOMENON

13.
Barack Obama's Address to the 2004 Democratic National Convention
Trauma, Compromise, Consilience and the (Im)Possibility of Racial Reconciliation [265]
DAVID A. FRANK AND MARK LAWRENCE McPHAIL

14.
Barack Obama's White Appeal and the Perverse Racial Politics of the Post–Civil Rights Era [287]
PAUL STREET

15.
Barack Obama's (Im)Perfect Union
An Analysis of the Strategic Successes and Failures in His Speech on Race [311]
EBONY UTLEY AND AMY L. HEYSE

Epilogue
Obama, Race, and the 2012 Presidential Election [329]
PAUL SPICKARD

References [339]

Contributors [385]

Index [391]

PREFACE

THE CONCEPT OF A MORE PERFECT UNION IS A CONSTANT THEME IN THE political rhetoric of Barack Obama. This is evident from his now historic race speech to his second victory speech delivered on November 7, 2012. "Tonight, more than 200 years after a former colony won the right to determine its own destiny, the task of perfecting our union moves forward," stated the forty-fourth president of the United States upon securing a second term in office following a hard fought political contest. Obama of course borrows this rhetoric from the founding documents of the United States as illustrated in the U.S. Constitution and in Abraham Lincoln's "Gettysburg Address," delivered in 1863. In this context, the term "multiraciality" has a dual significance. It is reflected in the trope of "a more perfect union" that many commentators have argued is directly connected to questions of Obama's mixed-race background as well as his views about the possibility of cross-racial coalition politics and individual transcendence despite race: "The idea that if you're willing to work hard, it doesn't matter who you are, or where you come from, or what you look like ... whether you're black or white or Hispanic or Asian or Native American," he states in his November 2012 acceptance speech. How naive or realistic is Obama's vision of a more perfect American union that brings together people across racial, class, and political lines? How can this vision of a more inclusive America be actualized in a society that remains racist at its core.

Race and the Obama Phenomenon: The Vision of a More Perfect Multiracial Union examines Obama's administration during the intervening years, while engaging the voices of some of the most preeminent race scholars writing on the topic. The previously published essays were selected for their stellar analyses in helping elucidate some critical aspect of the central theme of the book—"a more perfect union." Individually, they stand out among the myriad publications on the Obama phenomenon and will remain relevant to any future discussions; combined into an anthology their critical resonance is augmented. We sought to enhance the volume by also soliciting new original essays from race/gender scholars via a call for papers, to which we received many responses.

Although several chapters in the volume discuss the Obama administration as well as aspects of the 2012 election, many chapters cover material specifically related to the 2008 election. We do not believe the value of the book depends, however, on Obama's administration or the outcome of the 2012 election or on any election at all. In fact, the individual contributions in *Race and the Obama Phenomenon*, as well as the edited volume as a single scholarly contribution, will last beyond the "Obama phenomenon." Indeed, 2008 brought to light many issues that have been with us for a very long time and that this volume will help us understand in the future.

The scholars in *Race and the Obama Phenomenon* interrogate the connection between race, politics, gender, and the Obama phenomenon from multiple disciplinary perspectives. Some of the contributors—such as G. Reginald Daniel and David A. Hollinger—find Obama's vision of a more perfect union a viable plausibility while others—such as David Roediger, Paul Street, and Karanja Keita Carroll—are less sanguine about its viability when contemplating race and the Obama phenomenon. In fact, the essays in this collection are seemingly at odds over the meaning of the Obama phenomenon altogether. It was our intention to bring together competing perspectives on race and the Obama phenomenon given the historic significance of Obama's election and re-election. This dialogue surrounding the meaning of the Obama presidency in U.S. history and society remains ongoing and is currently without consensus. Further, we recognize that Obama's political ascendance and presidency in part represents the larger ethno-racial demographic changes that have taken place in U.S. society in the post–World War II era.

It is important to first situate the Obama phenomenon within the framework of the ever-changing ethno-racial composition of the United States. The cross-racial coalition forged by Obama to twice secure the office of the presidency is only understood through an understanding of what *Time* magazine labeled in 1993 as "the changing face of America." In many respects, the election of the first self-identified African American (with a mixed-race ancestry) to the office of president is reflective of the changing social geography of the U.S. In 1952, the U.S. Congress passed the McCarren-Walter Act, which basically stated that anyone entering the U.S. as an immigrant could apply for citizenship. In 1965, President Lyndon B. Johnson signed into law the Immigration and Nationality Act (or Hart-Celler

Act), which abolished national quotas and allowed naturalized citizens to send for relatives. Census data taken between 1965 and 2005 indicate that of the 40 million foreign-born people living in the United States, the majority came from non-Western societies such as China, the Philippines, India, Vietnam, and Mexico.

The United States is rapidly becoming a nonwhite nation as immigrants from the West Indies, Latin America, Asia, and various countries in Africa have come to populate the society. According to Pew Research polls, 82 percent of the U.S. population increase by 2050 will come from immigrants arriving after 2005 from non-Western (nonwhite) nations and their descendants. Correspondingly, the election of Obama has global implications. People of color from around the world erupted in jubilation, from California to Kenya, upon the election of the first black president in U.S. history.

Obama's mixed-race lineage (he is the son of an African immigrant, who came to the United States in the 1950s, and a white mother from Kansas) represents "the changing face of America." In 2000, the U.S. Census for the first time allowed individuals to select more than one race; the mixed-race population, based on those who opted to select "more than one" race, was calculated at roughly seven million. Interracial marriages have increased by 20 percent since 2000 to compose roughly 8 percent of the total marriages in the United States, while the most recent census (2010) indicated that the mixed-race population has increased to more than nine million. This is roughly a 32 percent gain up from the 2000 number of seven million.

The 2010 census reflects some profound demographic changes in the United States as specifically related to mixed-race Americans. The majority of those who self-identify as mixed-race are Millennials under thirty. This has prompted some pundits to refer to the year 2000 as the beginning of a mixed-race millennium. In 2010, 1.6 million people in the United States checked both black and white on their census forms, a figure 134 percent higher than a decade earlier. The largest groups of mixed-race Americans include the categories of white-black, white-some other race (typically "Hispanic"), white-Asian, white-Native Hawaiian, and white-Native American. The latest data collected by the census bureau also indicate that the majority of children younger than age one in the United States are members of diverse population groups. Some 50.4 percent of the U.S. population under age one, as of July 1, 2011, are members of ethnically diverse populations; this is up from the 49.5 percent estimate revealed in 2010. There are currently 114 million members of diverse populations in the U.S., reflecting 36.6 percent of the U.S. population.

The census data clearly reflect a United States that has become rapidly more diverse in the last few decades. This has political implications. There are five states that have significant percentages of "majority-minority" populations, including Hawai'i (77.1 percent), California (60.3 percent), New Mexico (59.8 percent), and Texas (55.2 percent). This pattern is also evident in Washington, D.C. (64.7 percent). By July 2011, 348 of the nation's 3,143 counties were listed as majority-minority. The largest ethnically diverse county in the nation is Los Angeles County. The U.S. remains the most ethnically diverse nation in the world. The abolition of anti-miscegenation laws and the increase in interracial marriages has contributed greatly to the multiracial mosaic that is the United States. The society has become increasingly multicultural with the rise in the numbers of diverse populations that reside in the nation, while at the same time becoming increasingly multiracial as individuals have begun to marry across racial boundaries. African Americans constitute 43.9 million (up 1.6 percent since 2010). Latinas/os are the most rapidly expanding "minority" group at 52 million (this population has increased by 3.1 percent since 2010). Asian Americans are the second fastest growing ethnic group in the U.S. at 18.2 million (growing by 3.0 percent since 2010). The cross-racial and cross-generational coalition of voters who secured for Obama a victory in two presidential elections included primarily Latinas/os, African Americans, Jewish Americans, women, and college-age Millennials, some of whom are of the offspring of interracial marriages.

We recognize that the Obama phenomenon is a part of the larger ethnoracial transformation of U.S. society, while at the same time understanding that racism persists in a union not yet made perfect. In his bid for re-election, most national statistics indicate that Obama's opponent Mitt Romney secured 72 percent of the white vote while Obama maintained support from roughly 38 percent of the white vote. These numbers suggest an imperfect union that remains divided by race.

The vitriolic response by some European Americans to the election of an African American president has been evident since the 2008 election. In fact, the election of the first black to the nation's highest office and the world's most powerful nation presents a challenge to both local and global hierarchies of white supremacy. This, in turn, has engendered a sea of white anxiety and, in some cases, white rage, whether implicitly or explicitly expressed in racial terms. The "birthers" (those who deny that Barack Obama was born in the United States) and the "deathers" (those who claim that Obama is a closet socialist seeking to erect death panels via healthcare reform) represent one dimension of the white racial hysteria that has swept the United State in this "age of Obama." This rage is endemic of the larger lack of civility in many sectors of U.S. society, including the political arena.

The rage we speak of reached deadly proportions on January 8, 2011, when gunman Jared Lee Loughner shot twenty people, killing six, in front of a Safeway supermarket in Casas Adobes, Arizona, during a "Congress on Your Corner" event. One of those wounded was Democratic congresswoman Gabrielle Giffords, who was shot in the head. Federal judge John Roll and a young member of the Giffords's staff were both killed. The Southern Poverty Law center is one of the only civil rights advocacy groups that have recognized a link between Loughner's ranting and the white supremacist group "American Renaissance." Peter King, Republican congressman from New York, ushered in a new era of McCarthyism with his March 2011 hearings on the Islamic community and their perceived lack of cooperation with authorities in the war on terror or the failed condemnation of Islamic extremists. Yet while his committee recounted heart-wrenching stories of victims of Islamic terrorism, King reportedly previously supported the violent actions of the Irish Republican Army (IRA) in Northern Ireland in the early 1990s. This Islamophobia is yet another dynamic of the white racial anxiety that is pervasive in the post-9/11 world.

In many respects, the old racism is the new racism, as many European Americans have simply refused to accept the legitimacy of our nation's first black president. This may indicate that the depictions of Barack Obama as a monkey in the *New York Post* and beyond, as well as pimp or gangster, coupled with denunciations of his U.S. citizenship and Christian faith, are manifestations of a growing white racial anxiety and resentment as buttressed by the nation's changing social geography. In Spring Lake, New Jersey, a few weeks before the November 2012 election, a shop owner set up a display that included a poster of the president represented as a witch doctor with a bone through his nose. Clint Eastwood in his speech delivered at the 2012 Republican National Convention, used an empty chair as a prop to represent the president as an absent leader. His address prompted some white extremists around the country to lynch chairs from trees in their front yards. There have been several incidents since the first election in 2008 of people lynching a replica of the president on their front lawns. The imagery of lynching as a symbol is a powerful reminder of the violent regime of white supremacy that once controlled the nation in the Jim Crow era.

The structural inequalities that persist in the United States, particularly in regards to the black experience, have not dissipated with the Obama presidency. The African American high school dropout rate is nearly twice the national average, as is the black unemployment rate. Black men make up roughly one half of the 2.3 million men incarcerated in the U.S. prison system. In fact, one could argue that the plight of blacks has worsened economically, particularly in terms of unemployment and the decline in black homeownership coupled with the increase in foreclosures. Clearly, the election of a mixed-race self-identified black man is not enough to alleviate structural inequality. What, then, is the significance of the Obama phenomenon beyond the symbolic? Why does the election of a black president matter if racism persists—if, in fact, it has not worsened—as compounded by profound levels of socioeconomic (or class) inequality? These questions are addressed in our text. The fact that a black man can become president of a nation that has historically been, and continues to be, profoundly racist is worthy of sustained scholarly interrogation.

Accordingly, the volume brings together a host of contributors to contemplate the theme of "race and the Obama phenomenon," along with issues that intersect with race (e.g., gender, identity, class, and privilege). The disciplines represented in this volume include sociology, history, black studies, political science, communication studies, American studies, psychology, and cultural studies more generally. This collection of analyses is unique in its substance and coverage of a wide range of issues related to race and the election of the first African American president. The sections of the book encompass discussions of multiraciality, black identity, gender, and politics in conjunction with the overarching theme of "race and the Obama phenomenon." Moreover, this is one of the first anthologies to devote complete sections to both the topics of multiraciality and gender, which should contribute meaningful points to discussions on these subjects as they relate to the Obama phenomenon.

There have been a series of books released between 2009 and 2011 comparable to our volume. Scholars and pundits alike have sought to capture the meaning of "race and the Obama phenomenon" since the 2008 election. Surprisingly, none of the earlier works delved into the multifaceted meanings of Barack Obama's biracial background. *Obama and the Biracial Factor: The Battle for a New American Majority* (2012), edited by Andrew J. Jolivétte, was the first book to explore the role of Obama's mixed-race background in his path to the presidency. It also offers a broad and penetrating view of the importance of race and multiraciality in the ongoing development of U.S. politics at home and abroad. The initial collection of serious texts on race and Obama began to appear in 2009. Prior to that, a host of scholarly journals, such as the *Black Scholar* and the *Journal of Black Studies*, among others, devoted entire volumes to the subject of race and Obama since 2004. In 2004, Obama gave a keynote speech at the Democratic National Convention and had thus been a "phenomenon" before he was elected president. Obama, likely one of the more prolific writers who ever occupied the White House, wrote two books before he became president: his memoir *Dreams from My Father: A Story of Race and Inheritance* (1995) and *The Audacity of Hope: Thoughts on Reclaiming the American Dream* (2006). The first books published about race, Obama, and the election of 2008 were written by pundits, polemicists, and journalists who followed Senator Obama along the campaign trail.

Gwen Ifill, moderator and managing editor of *Washington Week*, and senior correspondent for *The PBS News Hour*, award-winning journalist Bob Woodward, along with David Remnick, editor of *The New Yorker*, produced some of the first books written about race, the 2008 election, and Obama as president. Ifill's *The Breakthrough: Politics and Race in the Age of Obama* (2009) is an examination of the African American political structure, race, and the rise of Barack Obama in the context of the gains of the civil rights movement. Woodward's *Obama's War* (2010) is an examination of the first eighteen months of the Obama administration and policy decisions made about the war in Afghanistan. Remnick's *The Bridge: The Life and Rise of Barack Obama* (2010) concentrates less on race and more on Obama's political career, but it does explore the various racial and geographical crosscurrents in Obama's life. He argues that Obama's multiple points of origin and reference—his biracial birth and multicultural upbringing—have made him adaptable to any situation. This explains in part Obama's signature "cool." It also imbues him with the skills necessary to build a bridge between racial groups.

The focus of much of the aforementioned journalistic literature on Obama, with the exception of Ifill's work, has emphasized Obama's rise to power and his foreign and domestic policy as was also the case with *Newsweek* editor Jonathan Alter's *The Promise, President Obama, Year One* (2010). John Heilemann and Mark Halperin's *Game Change: Obama and the Clintons, McCain and Palin, and the Race of a Lifetime* (2010), although it focuses primarily on key personalities along the campaign trail of 2008, sparked a "racial" controversy by relating statements made by then-Senate majority leader Harry Reid's racially insensitive comments regarding Obama. Heilemann and Halperin reported in their book that Reid described Obama as an acceptable candidate because he was a "light skinned" black with no "Negro dialect."

The emergent scholarly literature has been more comprehensive and critical in terms of discussions of race and Obama. The topic of race and the Obama phenomenon has inspired scholars from across the disciplines, including Michael Eric Dyson, Roy L. Brooks, Denean Sharpley-Whiting, and Manning Marable. Tim Wise, polemicist, writer, and antiracist activist, has delivered a scathing critique of race in the age of Obama with his text *Between Barack and a Hard Place: Racism and White Denial in the Age of Obama* (2009). In this discourse, Wise highlights the bold reality of racial inequalities in the United States despite the election of a black president. John Kenneth White's more hopeful *Barack Obama's America: How New Conceptions of Race, Family, and Religion Ended the Reagan Era* (2009) concentrates on the demographic shift that helped create "the Obama phenomenon."

Brooks's *Racial Justice in the Age of Obama* (2009) provides a comprehensive discussion of the major theoretical approaches to civil rights and racial justice while illuminating the structural inequalities that remain in U.S. society despite the Obama election. Brooks also attempts to provide some concrete solutions to the problem of inequality in the Obama era. The text by Clarence E. Walker and Gregory D. Smither, entitled *The Preacher and the Politician: Jeremiah Wright, Barack Obama, and Race in America* (2009), situates Reverend Wright and his conflict with Obama within the larger historical context of the African American religious tradition and the history of racial politics. There has also been a proliferation of surveys and anthologies that are much more substantive and critical than the journalistic literature that emerged between the years 2009 and 2011.

Some key surveys and anthologies have been recently authored by scholars from social scientists to historians in the field of race studies. For example, John Bernard Hill's *The First Black President: Barack Obama, Race, Politics, and the American Dream* (2009) is a survey on race, identity, and the meaning of blackness in the context of the civil rights legacy, while cautioning against the misreading of Obama's significance. Thomas J. Sugrue, noted civil rights historian and sociologist, has written of the intellectual influences that have shaped Obama through the post–civil rights era. *Obama's Race: The 2008 Election and the Dream of a Post Racial America* (2010), by Michael Tesler and David O. Sears, examines the presidential contest of 2008 from an interdisciplinary perspective. More importantly, they incorporate a discussion of gender in their chapter "The Paradox of Gender: Traditionalists Support of Hillary Clinton," thereby further expanding the dialogue on race and Obama into the area of gender studies. The more recent

The Election of Barack Obama: Race and Politics in America (2010), by Jason Porterfield, places the election of Obama into the broad context of the history of slavery, race, and civil rights.

The journalistic, survey, and monographic studies of Obama have been joined by some important anthologies. One of the first notable anthologies written about race and Obama was edited by historian and political scientist Manning Marable and civil rights attorney Kristen Clarke. This volume, entitled *Barack Obama and African American Empowerment: The Rise of Black America's New Leadership* (2009), traces the evolution of black leadership and black politics since the civil rights movement, including essays that specifically interrogate the intersection of race and gender. *The Speech: Race and Barack Obama's A More Perfect Union Speech* (2009), edited by Denean Sharpley-Whiting, includes key chapters on the Obama speech by Bakari Kitwana and William Julius Wilson. Social scientists Matthew Hughey and Gregory S. Parks compiled an edited volume entitled *The Obama's and a (Post) Racial America?* (2011), which examines the unconscious anti-black bias harbored by whites in U.S. society, including commentaries by some noted race scholars. These are but a few of the torrent of scholarly publications on race and the Obama phenomenon. For an extensive list of over 400 publications on Obama see Steven F. Riley's *Mixed Race Studies* website: http://www.mixedracestudies.org/wordpress/?cat=63.

Moreover, the relevance of race and Obama as a scholarly subject is further indicated with the notion of an "Obama effect." If the election of the first black president has triggered white anxiety and, in the extreme, white rage, it has also produced an effect—particularly among black Americans who have sought political office in the face of seemingly insurmountable odds, as well as in the potentiality of a more positive level of black identity formation among young black men. The Bradley effect in black politics has been seemingly supplanted by the Obama effect given the fact that Obama has been elected more than once to the office of the presidency of the United States. The meanings and parameters of this Obama effect are contemplated in this volume through essays related to racial formation, particularly in terms of black politics and identity formation.

HETTIE V. WILLIAMS
G. REGINALD DANIEL
July 2013

ACKNOWLEDGMENTS

Neither time nor space allows us to acknowledge the many individuals who helped bring this book to fruition. This manuscript would not have been possible without the stellar editorial assistance provided by Gary L. Haddow and Alyssa Newman, outstanding research assistants who helped track down important material. David Estrin helped tighten the manuscript without sacrificing our ideas. Jennifer Burton of Columbia Indexing Group is a miracle worker when it comes to compiling an index. For technical support in completing this project, we are also indebted to Grafikart Copy Shop, particularly Nicole Allen and David Miller. We would also like to thank Dean Stan Green and the School of Humanities and Social Sciences' Travel and Grants Committee for the Grant in Aid of Creativity at Monmouth University to help complete this project.

A special thanks to Joseph and Kathryn Weber, Donnalynne Shaw, Sheila Gardette, Kip Fulbeck, Josef and Socorro Castañeda-Liles, Ivan and Gladys Garcia-Lopez, Xuan Santos, Nicholas (Nick) Hall, Rebecca Romo, James McKeever, Anthony Francoso, Patrick Lopez-Aguado, Melissa Guzman, Christopher Bickel, Alexis McCurn, Melissa McDonald, Jessie Turner, Marissa Williams, Linda Hall, Lisa Torres, Jennie Marlow, Spotted Eagle, Neda Maghbouleh, Clayton Childress, Mo Rae, Jimmy McCarthy, Adam Henry, Britta Kiefer, Gary Haddow, Melissa Cohen, Victoria Perez, Greg Tanaka, Jennifer Gong, Nina Moss, as well as Katie Swain, Alyssa Newman, Kenly Brown, Nancy Drye, Phyllis Sladick, Rafael J. Hernandez, Victoria (Vika) Stansky, Michael Bean, Maria P. P. Root, Teresa Williams-León, Jeannie and Daniel Palmer, Trica Danielle Keaton, Steven and Julia Riley, Phillip Handy, Heidi Durrow, and Fanshen Cox.

Craig Gill, editor in chief at the University Press of Mississippi, is an exemplary editor. We are grateful to him and to the readers, as well as copyeditor Peter Tonguette, who were recruited by the Press. We would also like to express our gratitude to Leila W. Salisbury, Katie Keene, Steven B.

Yates, Courtney McCreary, John Langton, Anne Stascavage, Shane Gong Stewart, Pete Halverson, and other staff at the press. In addition, there are many unnamed friends, colleagues, students, and relatives whose support contributed to making this a better book.

Santa Barbara, California, and West Long Branch, New Jersey
August 2013

FOREWORD

Race Will Survive the Obama Phenomenon

DAVID ROEDIGER

THE IDEA OF RACE EMERGED AMID EVOLVING PROCESSES IN WHICH GOVernment, economy, and society sorted people into very different relationships to property, management, punishment, and citizenship, according to fictive biological categories. Great struggles, peaking in the 1860s and 1870s, and again a century later, forced important changes. But those struggles lost momentum and unity before effecting other political economic changes that might have decisively disconnected color from degradation and suspicion, leaving even formal, legal equality fragile. They also allowed room for the development of new racial sorting by state-sponsored incarceration and deportation.

With whites today having, on average, more than nine times the household wealth of African Americans and Latinos, and with white-male incarceration rates at less than one-seventh those of African American men, desires to claim white identity and to defend the relative advantages attached to it will persist unless substantial changes occur, even in the wake of post–civil rights gains for some minority groups. That is so not only because the past of slavery and racial discrimination lingers on, but also because since the civil rights movement, deep racial inequalities have now been recreated across two generations. Only a tiny remnant of the always-inadequate palliative of affirmative action remains to address racial inequality, and that is seldom defended out loud by political leaders.

And yet we hear often that race is almost spent as a social force in the United States, eliminated by symbolic advances, demographic changes, and private choices, if not by structural transformations or political struggles. Nowhere is that argument more forcefully, or more contradictorily, made than in analyses of Barack Obama's campaign for president.

"Race Over" was the headline of the Harvard University sociologist Orlando Patterson's prognostications a few years ago in *The New Republic*. In 2050, Patterson assured readers, the United States "will have problems aplenty. But no racial problem whatsoever." Inconsistencies littered Patterson's predictions. Black people in the raceless United States would use new technologies to change their appearance. In the Northeast and Midwest, "murderous racial gang fights" would persist—but allegedly without the issue of race being involved. In the Southeast, the racial divisions of the "Old Confederacy" would continue but would somehow make no difference in the national picture. A more glaring contradiction obtruded when Patterson added another set of futurological observations in a 2001 *New York Times* article, which contested the common view of demographers that white people would become a minority in twenty-first-century America. Arguing that "nearly half of the Hispanic population is white in every social sense," Patterson forecast that the "white population will remain a substantial majority and possibly even grow as a portion of the population." Patterson's point—that some of the children of intermarriages between non-Hispanic white and Hispanic white people will identify, and be identified, as "white"—is not implausible, but the contrast between the two articles is jarring: race will vanish, but whiteness will persist.

In 2008, Patterson was back in the *Times*, analyzing Hillary Clinton's "red phone" campaign advertisement. In it, she answered an emergency 3 A.M. phone call with an assurance that, according to the implication of the ad, Obama could not provide. Patterson observed that the commercial had Clinton defending white children (and perhaps some meant to be seen as Latino) in a way that implied that the nebulous danger evoked might be a black man. Not only did the advertisement cast Obama as unfit to be the reassuring solution, but its subtext associated him with the menace itself. Race, over or almost done, still saturated public discourse.

Patterson is by no means alone in his vacillations. We are often told in the news media that race and racism are on predictable tracks to extinction. But we are seldom told clear or consistent stories why. Often multiracial identities and immigration take center stage. To take one example, a 1993 issue of *Time* magazine, on the "New Face of America," used a computer to morph into existence a new "Eve," created out of images of those migrating to and mixing in the United States. The cover girl typified a future mixed America; at the same time, she also represented an obsession with race, types, and genes.

The sunsetting of race by a fixed date acquired legal weight in the 2003 Supreme Court decision in *Grutter v. Bollinger*, in which Justice Sandra

Day O'Connor's majority opinion upheld the affirmative-action admissions policy at the University of Michigan Law School. Justice O'Connor emphasized the benefits of diversity for majority students but added that the court "expects that 25 years from now," preferences would no longer be needed. A research group on inequalities of wealth, United for a Fair Economy, reached a quite different and much better-grounded conclusion in its "Foreclosed: State of the Dream 2008" report assessing racial justice. The report estimated that existing trends would not equalize black and white median household wealth for more than half a millennium. On some measures, the report added, equality is several thousand years in the future.

The attacks on the World Trade Center and the Pentagon on September 11, 2001, solidified the perception that race was almost over: fear of a common enemy would erase divisions among Americans. Politicians, editorialists, and even comedians repeatedly emphasized the essential unity of everyone in America. However, the long aftermath of 9/11 has strongly challenged that idea.

From the outset of the war on terror, the racial profiling of Arab Americans and of Arab and Islamic travelers to the United States became a concern for many supporters of civil rights. Initially, jokes from black stand-up comics played on relief at getting to take a rest from being the subjects of suspicion. But such lines proved less funny as the broadcast faces of terror often resembled those of South Asians, African Americans, and Latinos, not simply the imagined Arab stereotype. The possibility of an Obama presidential campaign matured in a post-9/11 moment, but that moment also created the dynamics leading some conservatives to miss no opportunity to use the candidate's full name, Barack Hussein Obama. It made good political sense.

The Obama campaign itself became the alleged proof that the United States had so quickly moved beyond race that even Justice O'Connor was too gloomy in her timetable. However, that campaign has also illustrated the tenacity of old racial divisions, and the force of new ones. The conservative *Wall Street Journal* editorial page greeted the earliest of Obama's primary triumphs as proof that the nation had transcended the bad old days of racism. The misnamed and conservative American Civil Rights Institute parlayed Obama's primary successes into proof of the absence of institutional racism—and any need for affirmative action.

At the same time, the "colorblind" news media combined such assertions with strikingly reductionist resorts to race to "explain" voting patterns. Early in the campaign, for example, African Americans were said to support Clinton because of an atavistic questioning of whether Obama was "black enough," as *Time* asked in a headline.

When Obama did well among black voters, such arguments were immediately cast aside, although there was no acknowledgment in the news media that its earlier reasoning had been egregious. Nor did commentators stop to notice that African Americans were supporting a mixed-race candidate with a foreign-born father, making them perhaps the most cosmopolitan sector of the electorate. As the campaign progressed, the candidates were said to grapple over who would get the Hispanic vote or the "white male" vote, with the news media assuming simple equations between identity and voting. Crude racial profiling of voters jostled for space with extravagant claims regarding the transcendence of race. Such careening representations of the Obama campaign reflect an overwhelming desire to transcend race without transcending racial inequality—as well as the impossibility of doing so.

As Obama himself seldom tires of saying, he is the product of Kenya on his father's side and Kansas on his mother's. Thus, he evokes the promise that intermarriage will break down color lines. If his second-generation-immigrant success story has so far resonated only a little with the recent immigrant population of the United States, it is nonetheless a part of his broader appeal. His elite education typifies a stratum of a new black middle class that has matured as segregated education has partially given way. Above all, his political attractiveness to a substantial minority of white voters is unprecedented, with the support of young white voters at times especially impressive. Among much else, it underlines how much African American protest traditions, however hesitantly embraced by Obama, are associated with the possibility of change.

When Obama has deflected difficult questions regarding race with the charming response that, given his parentage, he could not be on any one side, he also reflects an increasing experience of the nation, especially its youth, with what cultural-studies scholars call "hybridity." Moreover, he appeals to a widespread sense that race is now, more than ever before, about choice. With Jim Crow illegal, with science firmly declaring against the biological import of race, with racial status on the census having for decades been determined by self-identification, and with the 2000 census offering an array of mixed-race choices for such self-identification, race is today a far more fluid category, both popularly and at law.

A huge share of the "white" population now regards itself as identifying with "non-white" peoples or culture in some way that respondents regard as central to their lives. Those identifications range from living and loving interracially, to parenting interracial children or adopted children of color, to devotion to Buddhism, intense reggae, salsa, jazz, hip-hop, blues, gospel, or world music, to wanting to be like Michael Jordan or Tiger Woods. The images are often powerfully, and at times superficially, connected with, to borrow from Yale University's Paul Gilroy, wanting to be free and to be seen as free. A mixture of the exalted, the everyday, and the fanciful—of the intimate and the commercial—informs the ways that white people identify with nonwhite cultures, figures, and products.

Fluidity and choice, however, exist within the very structures of deep contemporary inequality. Such inequality especially afflicts those readily identifiable as black and poor, or as Latino, poor, and "illegal," or as American Indians on or off reservations. Possibility and tragedy coexist, while two desirable changes remain impossible for both Obama and the larger society. The first impossibility is achieving meaningful black-immigrant unity; the second, speaking out in mainstream politics against the existence, persistence, and continued reproduction of racial hierarchies. Both of those impossibilities spawn endless discussion in the news media's coverage of Obama's campaign. Nonetheless, the full import of each goes largely unacknowledged.

It is possible that the growth of a mixed-race population and of immigrant communities divided more by nationality than race might someday simply overwhelm attempts to repackage what James Baldwin called "the lie of whiteness." But history should make us wary of predictions that demographic changes will cause race to disappear, rather than simply to be reconfigured. In any case, we are at this moment very far from such a reality, and we are not on a road that leads in any sure direction.

If we project the recent increase in births of mixed-race children over time, new patterns do emerge. However, the patterns remain contradictory. A recent study—published in a conference paper, "Recent Trends in Intermarriage and Immigration and Their Effects on the Future Racial Composition of the U.S. Population," posted online—by the population specialists Sharon M. Lee, Barry Edmonston, and Jeffrey S. Passel, who used computer modeling to project the population in 2100, concluded that, in that year, the "pure" (both parents of the same "race") and the mixed-race populations of the United States will be almost exactly equal. Hybridity will be greatly concentrated among Latinos, a group in which the "pure" would make up 30 percent of the total population, while the Latino/mixed would total 70 percent. Among white people, on the other hand, 65 percent would be "pure" and 35 percent white and mixed. Among African Americans, 63 percent would have two African American parents; 57 percent of Asian Americans would have two Asian American parents.

Interracialism, therefore, might well vary by race. Indeed, if present patterns of inequality persist, the projected 2100 population will contain 66 million "unmixed" African Americans, as well as new generations of desperately poor immigrants whose race, class, and illegality will be linked in popular perception. Those groups will almost certainly be racially despised. Offered as a serious effort at estimates, not an ironclad guide to an unpredictable future, such figures also remind us that no one knows what the racial identification of Latinos who are of mixed race, the largest single category projected, will be in 2100.

In particular, the ways in which those whom the Chicana feminist Cherrie Moraga called "21st-century mestizos" unite with other people of color, both in voting patterns and in struggles to end the material bases for thinking about race, will be key to whether the idea of race can survive.

But it is precisely on that point that Obama's candidacy has so far failed to offer hope for even symbolic change. Although he may be able to win over some voters as an African American candidate, a mixed-race candidate, and an exemplar of racelessness, Obama has not been able to gain support as a second-generation-immigrant candidate. During the 2008 election, Obama lost in the California primary, despite his great successes among black and even white voters, because of Latino and Asian American support for Clinton. Like most children of African and Afro-Caribbean immigrants, Obama is seen by those groups only as black.

The news media's drumbeat of emphasis on Obama's lack of support among Latinos says both too much and too little about race. It is manifestly false that black candidates cannot win significant majorities of Latino votes: Harold Washington did so in Chicago's mayoral election in 1983, as did David Dinkins in New York City in 1989 and 1993. In the 2005 Los Angeles mayoral election, black votes for Antonio Villaraigosa were pivotal. In most presidential elections, big majorities of African American and Latino voters unite behind white Democrats. Up against a Clinton machine very experienced in turning out Latino voters, Obama ran a relatively poor campaign among Spanish-speaking voters, producing bilingual materials only late in the day. As the University of Chicago political scientist Michael Dawson astutely remarked after Obama's Philadelphia speech on race, "Most surprising, perhaps, was the minimal acknowledgment given to the recognition that the racial landscape has fundamentally changed with the large-scale immigration of particularly, but not exclusively, Latino and Asian populations into the United States."

With neither Democratic candidate forwarding ambitious plans for immigrant rights or concrete proposals for immigration reform, exit polls in Texas showed that over half of Latino voters counted the economy the dominant issue. The votes of that large bloc of economically concerned, Democratic Latinos went overwhelmingly to Clinton, although some in her camp joined the news media in turning a particular trend into a universal truth about Hispanic hostility to black candidates.

While the reality and the "racial" character of a black/Latino electoral divide has been inflated and inflamed by the news media, the fact remains that antiracist forces face significant legislative and structural hurdles in attempting to forge a black/immigrant coalition. Perhaps least noticed are the difficulties in creating unity between immigrants and their descendants. The 1965 Immigration Reform Act passed with negligible input from people of color. Its framers paid little attention to its potential impact on patterns of immigration among, and racial hatred toward, Latin-American, Asian, and African migrants. Statutory openings to those advantaged by their professional, medical, and technical occupational status and by family networks somewhat delinked immigration and poverty for some newcomers, but imperial wars and neoliberal trade policies ensured that other sectors of the immigrant and refugee populations would be desperately poor.

At the same time, to rectify slights toward Eastern and Southern European nationalities victimized by discriminatory immigration quotas since 1924, the 1965 act applied quotas to immigration from the Americas and refused to adjust one-size-fits-all limits on legal immigration to acknowledge that Mexico, a large and nearby nation, was bound to furnish a number of immigrants far exceeding its quota. The results were predictable: 781,000 immigrants from Mexico suffered expulsion from the United States in 1976 alone. If legal status has been yet another source of division among immigrants, it has more tragically also served as the rallying point for overwhelmingly white anti-immigrant vigilante groups along the border and for political mobilizations purporting to defend the nation's racial character.

Divided as they are by class, immigration category, language, legal status, nationality, and race, migrants are very far from a unitary category. The massive 2006 immigrant-rights demonstrations in Los Angeles, the largest working-class mobilizations in American history, relied on the combination of an energized Mexican American base and grassroots leadership by many experienced in activism prior to their arrival in the United States. They succeeded in reaching across different immigrant nationalities, in uniting the undocumented minority with the "legal" majority of immigrants, giving immigrants common purpose, and in eliciting solidarity from those longer established in the country. That unity rested in no small measure on the extent to which people of color are subject to attacks based on both recognition and misrecognition: Sikhs were among those hurt in the post-9/11 "anti-Arab" assaults in the United States, while Vincent Chin, whose 1982 murder came to symbolize violence connected to resentment against Japanese, was actually Chinese. It is patterns like those that make opposition to anti-immigrant racism, often expressed as a demand for dignity, central to the immigrant-rights movement. Dramatic differences between, for example, the treatment of incarcerated Haitian refugees and Irish undocumented workers have likewise helped to make race a central part of some immigration policy debates.

So far, however, such struggles have not coalesced to produce enduring alliances. The labor movement, impressed by immigrant heroism in organizing campaigns and aware of the difficulties presented when employers can threaten union supporters with deportation, has belatedly adopted more humane positions on immigration at the national level, although in some unions the impulse to exclude immigrants remains strong. Moreover, the unions are so weak that their insistence on immigrant rights, or on prosecuting employers of undocumented labor, tends to be ignored.

The question of what could anchor meaningful black/immigrant unity goes largely unexamined amid all of the talk about racial voting blocs. Even the insight that labor lies at the heart of the question is too easily oversimplified into the question of whether "Americans" (in this context, usually meaning jobless African Americans) "want to work" in backbreaking, sub-minimum wage jobs far from their homes. The structure of the debate continues to allow African Americans to be damned as degraded if they do and as lazy if they do not.

Columbia University's Nicholas De Genova's recent study of Mexican Chicago shows how management in factories constructs a divide between immigrant unskilled labor and African Americans, with Mexican workers being told they have been given jobs as a result of their being more tractable and less union-minded than their black predecessors. In urban hotels and in packinghouses in smaller Midwestern cities, management by race and nationality (and now by legal status) is ever more apparent, with the poor of the world vying to keep jobs and avoid immigration raids. To bring those concrete realities into dialogue with the demands of black communities is critical, but so far it has proved impossible within national presidential campaigns—and largely impossible outside of them.

When Obama's primary campaign looked to be heading for victory in March, he came under sharp attack for his relationship with the Reverend

Jeremiah Wright, the former pastor of the church Obama attended. Influenced by black liberation theology, Wright's jeremiads indicted American racism in ways reminiscent of Malcolm X and Martin Luther King, Jr., After two weeks of calls to "denounce" Wright, Obama delivered his speech in Philadelphia, in which he sharply separated himself from the minister's message but did not abandon the man.

Whatever sympathy Obama professed for Wright stemmed from the latter's experience with the frustrations of Jim Crow, which had left many in Wright's generation refusing to see that the nation had changed. While Obama did call for expanded discussion of race and vigorous civil rights enforcement, the speech lacked concrete proposals for producing equality. It managed to be vague to the point of indecipherability on affirmative action, broached as a source of understandable "white resentment" rather than as a policy worth defending. By April, Obama denounced Wright more stridently, reckoning his former pastor as the polar opposite of the unifying figure that the candidate himself worked to be. He attributed his angry opposition to Wright's divisiveness to something written in his own "DNA," in a perfect illustration of how biology-based conceptions of race persist in post-racial America.

The point here is not to expect that Obama, or any mainstream politician, will take risks to aggressively defend the last fragments of affirmative action. His reticence on the issue is widely shared. When pressed, he has vaguely suggested that affirmative action be based less on race and more on poverty, allowing that his daughters should not benefit from the policy. In making the case for "class-based" affirmative action, he follows the impractical but high-sounding path of some conservative opponents of "race preferences" and of John Kerry and other Democrats. Indeed, many activists are tempted to give up the affirmative-action ghost. But it is nonetheless worth stressing that Obama does not represent the triumph of an advancing antiracist movement but rather the necessity, at the highly refracted level of electoral politics, of abandoning old agendas, largely by not mentioning them.

However, now, after the primaries, it will not be easy to avoid taking strong public positions on "divisive" racial issues like affirmative action, as Republicans aggressively raise "wedge" issues to split Democrats along racial lines. The Notre Dame political scientist Darrin Davis observes that "on every racial issue, Barack Obama is walking the tightrope." Conservatives have already organized several anti-affirmative-action referenda to coincide with the presidential election in pivotal states. "The more he supports traditional black issues like affirmative action, the more that will eat into his white base of support," Davis writes. Equally, open retreats from such issues will decrease enthusiasm among parts of his base.

Adroitly responsive to polling data, Obama's maneuverings nonetheless serve to distort how we conceptualize and address white supremacy, past and present. He moves from the casting of race as "divisive" to terming it a diversion from "real" issues affecting all Americans: the environment, war, housing, jobs, and healthcare. However, the problem with settling for that partial truth is that racial inequality itself remains a fundamental problem, both in coalition building and in everyday life. When Obama waxes nostalgic for the good old days of economic progress and calls for a focus on pocketbook issues like job training, trade policies, and gas prices, his narrative breaks faith with remembering the bitter days when Wright was growing up and likewise underplays the impact of the past on us. In critiquing race politics in his Philadelphia speech, Obama proposed a new departure based on too-easy appeals to economic unity: "This time we want to talk about the shuttered mills that once provided a decent life for men and women of every race, and the homes for sale that once belonged to Americans from every religion, every region, every walk of life."

Not only is such a departure not new—ironically, it was a staple of Bill Clinton's appeal to win back conservative "Reagan Democrats"—but it posits as the objects of its nostalgia two historical arenas most responsible for present inequalities. The closed mills Obama refers to were presumably the Southern textile factories that were long the embodiment of Jim Crow employment practices, and the steel factories in which limited, much-resisted attempts to undertake affirmative action were so long delayed that their eventual implementation coincided with the industry's decline. And the overwhelming channeling of federal subsidies to home loans for white families and the construction of infrastructure for segregated suburbs have created and increased the tremendous racial gaps in wealth that exist in the contemporary United States.

Such blind spots have far more than mere historical importance, as they call into question the very way that Obama portrays today's issues as simply cutting across racial lines. Nowhere is that more apparent than in the subprime mortgage crisis. The wholesale foreclosures accompanying that crisis fall into distinct racial patterns, reflecting the lack of resources that black and Latino home buyers bring to the market because of past discrimination, and the ways that they are still steered and preyed upon by lenders. Federal data show people of color to be more than three times as likely to have subprime loans as white people are, with a substantial majority of African American borrowers in that category (against one in six white borrowers).

The lack of an aggressive response by Obama to the subprime crisis has led some critics to propose that this issue best marks the limit of his economic populism, reflecting instead his close ties to banking and investment capital. Such critics are not wrong, but race has also mattered in the evasion of the full gravity of the crisis in home mortgages. The absence of any racial and historical framing of the subprime issue, a deficiency shared by Obama with Clinton and McCain, strengthens the tendency to rely for a cure on the same banks and investment firms that caused the problem. The subprime catastrophe was poised to serve either as a perfect vehicle to show how issues capable of dragging down much of the whole economy are about both race and class, or as an occasion for generalities, pro-mortgage-industry policy changes, and wishful thinking. The latter road is the one taken by Obama and all his major competitors.

To expect more that is concrete, forthright, and policy-oriented regarding race from Obama in the context of a presidential campaign is apparently fruitless. To sum up eloquently the ways in which the idea of race has and has not changed, the most important aspect of his campaign has been to show how much and how many people desire peace and want to find a way to move beyond race. To make their hopes and their commitments match up will require new, even unforeseeable, considerations of the role of white supremacy. It will require new alliances, especially of African Americans with immigrants, and of feminist and working-class organizations with antiracist forces, in movements seeking not only to be represented within a highly unequal order but also to transform that order. The alternative is that race-thinking will survive in new and destructive permutations, and will continue to serve as a diversion from other brutalities and as a prop on which they rest.

Note

Written in fall 2008, a version of this foreword appeared in *How Race Survived U.S. History: From Settlement and Slavery to the Obama Phenomenon* (New York: Verso, 2008).

INTRODUCTION

Understanding Obama and Ourselves

GEORGE LIPSITZ

RACE AND THE OBAMA PHENOMENON: THE VISION OF A MORE PERFECT *Multiracial Union* offers something for everyone. The seventeen essays compiled in this collection by G. Reginald Daniel and Hettie V. Williams present a broad range of perspectives, positions, ideas, and interpretations. The authors disagree with each other about the significance of the election of Barack Obama as president, and these disagreements reveal deep divisions about many of the most important issues of our time. In attempting to understand the importance of Obama, these essays demonstrate that we need to know more about ourselves and each other—about our identities and identifications, our affinities and our antagonisms, our points of connection and our points of conflict—if we are ever to live together justly and decently.

In a photograph, a sunrise and a sunset look the same. Deciding whether the present moment signals the rise of a dawn bringing justice or represents the twilight of democratic hopes is a matter of interpretation. Does the election of Obama signal the end of the white stranglehold on politics or does it prefigure the termination of race-based identity politics? Is his electoral success a victory for the black freedom struggle or a triumph of managerial multiculturalism? Will Obama's visibility promote new consciousness about multiracial identity or reinforce the black/white binary? Does the shake-up enacted on the symbolism of the social order by Obama's victory contest the hierarchies of gender or merely confirm them? Is the election of a black president proof of the progressive nature of the national project or is it evidence of the isolation of people of color in the United States from anti-imperial and anticolonial struggles? Will Obama's prominence promote a long delayed reckoning with the cumulative, collective, and continuing legacies of white supremacy or will it produce even more effective evasions of them?

Race and the Obama Phenomenon addresses these questions and contradictions by offering a seemingly freewheeling, unruly, and even ungainly dialogue among a diverse group of authors. The co-authored essay by David A. Frank and Mark Lawrence McPhail on Barack Obama's address to the 2004 Democratic Convention stages these oppositions within a single piece, offering an exemplary model of how scholars can learn from disagreements and conflicts as well as from points of agreement and coalescence. Frank and McPhail "write together separately," demonstrating in this case how the same speech can be read as either a *tour de force* that masterfully promotes racial reconciliation or as evidence of a failure of conviction that cravenly evades racial realities and social responsibilities. For some of the authors in this collection, Obama's election means that everything has changed; for others, that nothing has changed. What some discern as a politics of hope, others perceive as the politics of disavowal. Obama's election, these authors tell us collectively, is a triumph of possibility yet tragic in its limitations. Some proclaim Obama's election as a harbinger of the destabilization of black male identity while others see it as a powerful reification of blackness and masculinity. Some perceive in the Obama phenomenon popular desires for peace and justice, while others discern only a longing for peace and quiet. The wide range of topics addressed in this book testifies to the complexity of the Obama phenomenon.

Part I, "Race, Obama, and Multiraciality," points out that the election of a multiracial man as president connotes both promise and peril for the ways people understand their individual and collective identities as evidenced in the chapters by G. Reginald Daniel, Greg Carter, Janet C. Mendoza Stickmon, and Hettie V. Williams. This section opens with a comprehensive overview of Obama and the multiracial phenomenon written by G. Reginald Daniel, followed by Greg Carter's historical interpretation of mixedness in society and culture through the Obama era. Janet C. Mendoza Stickmon delivers an examination of Obama in relation to the multiracial experience while Hettie V. Williams's essay questions the very idea of multiracial identity as applied to the black-identified Obama. Daniel's more optimistic vision of Obama's race speech is later challenged by some of the contributors writing in the last section.

Part II, "Obama, Blackness, and the 'Post-Racial Idea,'" considers the notion of Obama's blackness and the "post-racial." The perception of Obama as a post-racial politician likely to usher in an era of color blindness elicits both praise and condemnation from Tavia Nyong'o, Lisa Anderson-Levy, and Karanja Keita Carroll, who directly questions the more optimistic vision of the United States as a "post-racial" society in the Obama era. Tavia Nyong'o's eclectic piece discusses Obama in relation to "the name of the father," while Lisa Anderson-Levy contemplates whiteness and the idea of the "post-racial."

Part III, "Race, Gender, and the Obama Phenomenon," includes essays by historian Marsha J. Tyson Darling, legal studies scholar Frank Rudy Cooper, as well as an essay by political scientist Tessa Ditonto. This section opens with Darling's essay, "From Chattel to First Lady: Black Women Moving from the Margins." Darling delivers a comprehensive overview of the history of black womanhood invoking the term "herstory" to write African American women into the historical record, including an examination of Michelle Obama. The focal point of Ditonto's chapter "The 'Outsider' Presidency: Mediated Representations of Race and Gender in the 2008 Presidential Primaries" is a discussion of race and gender representations of the two major candidates Barack Obama and Hillary Clinton. This section ends with Cooper's chapter entitled "Obama's Unisex Campaign: Critical Race Theory Meets Masculinities Studies." In this chapter, Cooper advances the audacious notion that Barack Obama embodied feminine qualities while steadfastly avoiding the "angry black man persona" to defeat Hillary and become the nation's first African American president. Heidi Ardizzone's "'Everything His Father Was Not': Fatherhood and Father Figures in Barack Obama's First Term" closes this section with a compelling discussion of Obama's performance as a father and the role it has also played in his political career. Ardizzone argues that Obama's ability to embody the nurturing modern father with a deep connection to his own family and a genuine ease with children is particularly significant. She also points out that these images simultaneously resonate against a complicated pattern of expectations for fatherhood, for black men and their families, and for dual-career couples and parenting. Obama's real and symbolic position as the First African American father evokes the absence of other black men from the African American family: absent fathers and endangered (or dangerous) black boys.

Part IV, "Race, Politics, and the Obama Phenomenon," includes chapters by communication studies scholars David A. Frank, Mark Lawrence McPhail, Ebony Utley, and Amy L. Heyse, as well as historian Paul Street. Frank and McPhail open this section writing together "separately." The impact of Obama's identity on the role of race as an organizing principle informing the nature of electoral politics produces heated disagreements among these authors. The section ends with the chapter written by Utley and Heyse who offer a less flattering interpretation of Obama's much lauded speech on race. In this chapter, they challenge the more celebratory analysis of Obama's race speech that appears in the Daniel chapter at the beginning of this book.

In the epilogue, Paul Spickard's "Obama, Race, and the 2012 Presidential Election" brings the story up to the dawning of Obama's second term as president. He deftly draws together strands from Obama's early life, his appearance on the national political scene, the racial content of his first presidential campaign, the ways that both supporters and opponents racialized Obama, and his performance on racial issues in office. Spickard analyzes the elements, including race, which were instrumental in creating Obama's 2012 victory.

It is always difficult to take stock of one's own time, to assess the future meanings of present events. As Roy D'Andrade noted in another context, trying to study one's own culture can be like attempting "to measure the physics of moving bodies while living in the middle of an avalanche" (Andrade 1984, 111). Yet, however imprecise the results, there is much to be gained from the attempt. Scholarship and citizenship are shared social activities. We know more together than we know separately. The conversations we share are the sources of our most profound knowledge. The fact that the authors in this volume disagree with each other about the meaning of the Obama phenomenon is the book's greatest strength. Reading these essays in succession is like attending a spirited town hall meeting, an assembly filled with debate and disagreement, passion and provocation, conflict and connection.

Authors coming from different social groups, different scholarly disciplines, different political perspectives, and different positions of privilege do not see things in exactly the same ways. Their disagreements do not stem from purely personal considerations, however. They are evidence of deep fissures and fractions in our society, chasms that cannot be bridged by glib proclamations, but rather which need to be worked out and resolved through constructive and creative political conflict. Most of all, they compel participation from each of us, reminding us at this crucial historical moment of both our civic and scholarly responsibilities.

These obligations have a particular history. They are rooted in a past that has tremendous significance for the present. *Race and the Obama Phenomenon* is a contemporary manifestation of the continuing significance of desires for democracy promoted by the various mid-twentieth century civil rights movements among communities of color. In the twelve months that preceded his assassination in 1968, Martin Luther King, Jr., increasingly identified the ability to promote engaged activism among millions of previously apolitical individuals as the African American civil rights movement's greatest success. Its collective mobilizations produced new kinds of people capable of creating new kinds of politics. Deliberative talk and face-to-face decision-making imbued participants with the dignity that comes with shaping one's own destiny. Facing danger together erased prior distinctions based on differences of color, class, and caste, replacing invidious divisions with unifying solidarity. Participatory democracy and consensus-based decision making made every voice count equally. Diffusing authority and responsibility broadly among the population lessened reliance on charismatic leaders and inhibited the development of insider cliques and bureaucratic elites. In *Where Do We Go From Here: Chaos or Community?*, the brilliant yet sadly neglected book published one year before his death, Dr. King declared that "no great victories are won in a war for the transformation of a whole people without total participation. Less than this will not create a new society: it will only evoke more sophisticated token amelioration" (King, Jr. 1969/1991, 567–78).

The participatory democracy of the civil rights movement emerged largely out of necessity rather than abstract philosophical or political predilection. Mass participation made the movement stronger in many ways. Diffusing authority and responsibility widely enabled the movement to survive the assassination and co-optation of individual leaders. A federation of semi-autonomous local chapters offered both physical proximity and political accountability to a scattered rural population. Generating projects, proposals, and programs at the grassroots wed the movement to the immediate goals of the people it most needed to recruit and spoke to alienations and indignities as they were understood consensually by a large group. Small meetings among people with personal loyalties to one another fused the personal with the political while mass meetings composed of less intimate relations (and even strangers) enacted the broader solidarities that movement ideologies could only envision. The civil rights movement succeeded largely because circumstances compelled it to trust and empower the masses, to fashion affiliations and alliances across lines of class and color, to turn radical divisiveness into exuberant solidarity, to transform radical dehumanization into liberating rehumanization. One of the factors promoting support for Obama in the 2008 election was the continuing influence of that history on the present.

Yet the civil rights project was also a knowledge project. As Michel Foucault argues in his unconventional analysis of social movements in general, the question "who are we?" does not have to be an atomized inquiry into identity isolated from considerations of social structure, power, and history. He explains that the self-activity intrinsic to the assertion of new identities often challenges the abstract identities imposed on people by economic, political, cultural, and scientific institutions. "They are an opposition to the effects of power," Foucault writes, "which are linked with knowledge, competence, and qualification: struggles against the privileges of knowledge. But they are also an opposition against secrecy, deformation, and mystifying representations imposed on people" (Foucault 1983, 212).[1] People struggling for new ways of being needed new ways of knowing, and in the process they helped democratize not only their own immediate surroundings, but also the scholarly institutions set up to study them. Yet these democratic impulses coexist uneasily with what Eduardo Bonilla-Silva and Tukufu Zuberi describe as the "white logic and white methods" that inflect the ways of knowing validated and perpetuated by academic gatekeepers across the disciplines with uninterrogated allegiances to white supremacy (Bonilla-Silva and Zuberi 2008, 3–30). As Karanja Keita Carroll shows in this volume, many of the key epistemological commitments that *enable s*cholarship in the disciplines also *inhibit* the study of race and occlude its importance as a social force. The origins of the disciplines in Europe's encounters with peoples it designated as "other" have produced deeply constrained ways of knowing.

Anthropologists, sociologists, political scientists, and psychologists have consistently studied social groups by looking for differences and then exaggerating them in order to rationalize unequal social outcomes. Scholars of music, philosophy, literature, and art, in contrast, have falsely aggregated diverse cultures and populations to make the dominant particulars of the European experience seem like universal truths, confusing *humanity* with *Eur-manity.* The impact on scholarship and social policy of the origins in eugenics of statistical research on racial groups remains underexplored and undertheorized to this day. Social scientists routinely treat race as a reliable variable, consequently attributing to race things that can really only be explained by racism. Perhaps most importantly, as Charles Mills demonstrates, the knowledge traditions of the West have taught scholars not to ask certain questions, to accept the inequalities of racist societies as baseline norms not to be challenged, and to disqualify in advance the testimony of witnesses capable of exposing the workings of whiteness (Mills 1997, 132). Knowledge projects grounded in simplistic Manichean binary oppositions—between modern and pre-modern, male and female, nature and humans, self and other, purity and pollution, writing and orality—relentlessly reinforce racial projects and racialized thinking. Sociology's commitments to social order, history's notions of evolutionary progress, literature's relationship to the individual subject formed in opposition to fear of engulfment by a threatening social aggregate, anthropology's construction of people without history, and the valorization of the market subject in economics, the rights bearing subject in law, and the interior psychic subject in psychology, all inhibit understanding of the collective, continuing, and cumulative qualities of racial formation and subordination.

The election and re-election of Barack Obama, in 2008 and 2012, as the first African American president is a product of many forces, but prominent among them are the changes in the national racial order created by decades of legislation, litigation, education, and agitation.[2] These changes have also been important to many people who are not black. Legal and social victories by African Americans have paved the way for inclusionary and egalitarian measures that have benefited citizens of every race, especially poor and working class whites, women, members of sexual and religious minorities, and people with disabilities. It is because of the mass upheavals of the mid-twentieth century that a critical mass of academics trained in critical race theory, "women of color" feminism, queer theory, and postcolonial studies exists. That is why a volume like *Race and the Obama Phenomenon* is possible. Yet while grounded in social movements forged through solidarities of sameness, the political and scholarly studies of the past half century have also established that differences can be dynamically generative, that just as there is no single way to be black, queer, or a worker, there should be no one way to study society. Our differences, which always raise the specter of division and disunity, are in fact precious resources because they call our attention to unredressed wrongs and unsolved problems. The oppressions of race, gender, sexuality, and class do not produce uniformly undifferentiated subjects, but rather a seemingly endless array of new forms of differentiation that require their own critiques grounded in diverse forms of situated knowledge. Moreover, these divisions can be useful because they hold us to a high standard and demand that our analyses and interpretations measure up to the complexity of actual lived experiences. They compel us to confront the ways power actually works, to study people as they are, not as we might wish them to be. As George P. Rawick noted more than four decades ago in an address to his fellow sociologists, true objectivity is achievable "only by being part of the struggles of *large groups of people* because these struggles arise out of *objective necessity*, not voluntary consciousness or abstract will" (Rawick 2010, 65).

It is this intellectual tradition grounded in the history of the civil rights movement that propels the most original and generative challenges articulated in *Race and the Obama Phenomenon*. These ideas and arguments emanate from scholars who feel obligations to participate in the social world their research describes. The key questions for them do not revolve around whether we like or dislike Obama, but rather about how we understand the conditions that made the Obama phenomenon possible and what additional possibilities and perils those conditions contain. The readings of politics and culture in this book are not just diagnostic, but also symptomatic. Just as Freudian psychologists long believed that every symptom contains a story, these scholars scour the Obama story for the social symptoms that it encodes. They wonder about possibilities and impossibilities ingrained in the present, about the prospects for black-immigrant unity, for openly addressing in mainstream politics the existence and persistence of white privilege, for democratizing rather than merely diversifying the social order, for deriving identities from political positions instead of deriving politics from identities, for developing fluid and flexible models of self-identity based on ongoing negotiations among multiple positions, for fusing black feminist discourses within and against U.S. national formations with postcolonial politics and practices, for refusing to grant race unchallenged status as a valid social concept without denying racism's pervasive and pernicious presence in our lives.

Our understanding of the Obama phenomenon requires us to recognize the full impact of the black freedom struggle of the twentieth century and the broad currents of anticolonialism, feminism, and queer politics that its successes drew from and helped promote. But we also need to acknowledge that victories by the forces of antiracism in the United States have always been partial, incomplete, and even ephemeral. Passing laws that proclaim equality has been difficult, but producing practices that instantiate legal equality in everyday life has proven harder still. As critical race theorist Kimberlé Crenshaw noted nearly two decades ago, a deliberate and emphatic repudiation of the aims and ideals of the civil rights movement became the dominant force in U.S. culture and politics during the last quarter of the twentieth century. This Age of Repudiation saw Supreme Court decisions, legislative initiatives, and actions by the executive branch of government designed to dismantle many of the key policies created during the civil rights era such as school desegregation and affirmative action. At the same time, municipalities, states, and the federal government largely refuse to enforce fair employment and fair housing laws. In order to protect and preserve the traditional privileges of whiteness, leaders across the political spectrum have increasingly embraced the cynical strategy of "color blindness," arguing that recognizing race for the purposes of redressing racial injustices violates the law as much as the race-based discrimination that made it necessary to pass those laws in the first place. In all areas of U.S. life, we now confront the presumption that color-bound injustices require colorblind remedies, that race-based problems should be addressed by race-blind remedies. As a result, more than four decades after the civil rights activism of the 1960s, and nearly one hundred and fifty years after the abolition of slavery, race tragically remains the most important single variable determining opportunities and life chances in the United States.

The conversation this book stages, as well as the broader dialogue of which it is a part, are more important than the preliminary conclusions we draw about Obama and ourselves. Despite their many differences and disagreements, the authors in this collection all seem to believe that the present is an important moment in history, that it is one of those times when dramatic transformations and changes are possible. Not all of these potential changes are located in the macro-social realms of state power, economics, and warfare. Some reside in formerly taken for granted assumptions about desire, domesticity, affect, identity, and interiority. The success of a political campaign that promised "change you can believe in" has clearly raised aspirations and expectations that may leave the common sense wisdom of yesterday with diminished authority and credibility tomorrow. The actions of those who came to power in the wake of that campaign, however, might be so feeble and fragmented that they destroy the dream once again. Or the revanchist reaction to the faint glimmers of hope made visible in Obama's election may usher in a nightmare of grotesque and horrible dimensions. Whether change takes place or whether the present moment is just another one of many possible historical turning points that failed to turn remains to be seen. But we are not merely spectators to these processes; we are also participants in them. The conversation started by this book is significant in itself as an example of how freewheeling open debates among people who do not agree can create a generative scholarly climate. This conversation can lead to important connections, coalitions, and creative conflicts, but only if we participate fully, honestly, and wholeheartedly.

At a crucial moment in the Montgomery Bus Boycott of 1955 and 1956, Reverend Ralph Abernathy addressed a mass meeting. Recognizing that the energy of the masses in motion had produced a turning point from which there was no turning back, Abernathy departed for a moment from his role as a leader and spokesperson. "This show," he told the people at the meeting, "is your show. And it is not only your show; it is the show of Negroes all across America. And it is not only the show of Negroes all across America; it is the show of freedom loving people all over the world."[3] If a better future for the world was to be written, Abernathy recognized, the black working class of Montgomery would be among its most important authors. In our time, the ultimate significance of Obama's victory, the eventual meaning of race and multiracial identities, the possible emergence of a post-racial United States, the final import of all the things that his victory revealed about what unites us and what divides us cannot be known now. The future always remains to be written through scholarship and civic action. But this show is not Obama's show. It is not the show of the Democratic or the Republican Party. It is not the show of the corporate media and or the entertainment industry. This show is your show, and what you make of it will do a great deal to determine our fate and the fates of freedom loving people all over the world.

Notes

1. For an analysis that blends the work of Foucault with the theories of Claus Offer, see Plate, "What's So New About New Social Movements?," 113–36.
2. The concept of a "racial order" comes from Kim, *Bitter Fruit*, 14–15.
3. Author's notes on *Eyes on the Prize* video, vol. 1, "Awakenings, 1954–1956."

PART I

RACE, OBAMA, AND MULTIRACIALITY

1. RACE AND MULTIRACIALITY

From Barack Obama to Trayvon Martin

G. REGINALD DANIEL

RACE, IDENTITY, AND THE ONE-DROP RULE:
A THEORETICAL PERSPECTIVE

THE RULE OF HYPODESCENT IS A SOCIAL CODE DESIGNATING RACIAL group membership of first-generation offspring of unions between European Americans and Americans of color exclusively based on their background of color. Successive generations of individuals who have European American ancestry combined with a background of color have more flexibility in terms of self-identification. The one-drop rule of hypodescent designates as black everyone with any African American ancestry ("one-drop of blood"). It precludes any choice in self-identification and ensures that all future offspring of African American ancestry are socially designated and self-identified as black (Daniel 2002, ix–xi, 16–17, 37; Davis 1991, 9, 15, 118).[1] Beginning in the late sixteenth century, the dominant European Americans began enforcing rules of hypodescent as part of anti-miscegenation statutes aimed at punishing and eventually prohibiting interracial intimacy, as well as defining multiracial offspring as black in an attempt to preserve white racial "purity" and privilege. By the middle of the eighteenth century, interracial marriages in the Southern and some Northern colonies (and eventually states) in Anglo-North America were proscribed and stigmatized where they were not legally prohibited (Barthé, Jr. 2012, 83–85; Daniel 2006, 89–92).

During the early seventeenth century, African Americans were comparatively small in numbers and the distinction between the white indentured servant and the black slave was less precise than that between bonded and free. There were no laws against miscegenation despite strong prejudice against interracial intimacy (Daniel 2002, 87; Hodes 1997, 1–15; Spickard 1989, 237; Tenzer 1990, 56–68). Consequently, a small, but not insignificant, number of European indentures and African slaves intermarried or formed common-law unions of some duration. They had legitimate offspring, alongside more widespread clandestine and fleeting liaisons involving births outside of wedlock. Most of the latter were between white masters and indentured or slave women of African descent, and involved coercive sexual relations as in extended concubinage or rape. The offspring of these unions were slaves contingent upon the slave status of the mother, not the rule of hypodescent. Accordingly, the rule did not increase the numbers of slaves, but rather, the numbers of blacks whether slave or free. Still hypodescent did conveniently function to exempt white landowners (particularly slaveholders) from the legal obligation of passing on inheritance and other benefits of paternity to their multiracial progeny (Davis 1991, 9, 15, 118).

The ancestral quanta defining legal blackness have varied over time and according to locale. There is evidence of perceptions and practices that were normative long before they were formalized in law. Statutes and court decisions were inevitably more precise than social custom (Jordan 2014, 73). The one-drop rule gained currency as the informal or "commonsense" (Omi and Winant 1994, 106) definition of blackness between the seventeenth and nineteenth centuries. It did not become a customary part of the legal apparatus until the early twentieth century (circa 1915) (Daniel 2002, 34–42; 2006, viii–ix; Davis 1991, 9–11, 55–58). The rule has supported legal and informal barriers to racial equality in most aspects of social life. At the turn of the twentieth century, these restrictions culminated with the institutionalization of Jim Crow segregation.

Beginning in the mid-1950s, those proscriptions were dismantled and accompanied by the passage of historic civil rights legislation in the 1960s, including the 1967 *Loving v. Virginia* decision, which removed the last laws prohibiting interracial marriage. Notions of racial purity that supported the ideology of white supremacy were increasingly repudiated. Rules of hypodescent have been removed from all state statutes. European Americans, nevertheless, have maintained identities and privileges based on white racial exclusivity originating in hypodescent. According to Lipsitz, European Americans continue to uphold a "possessive investment in whiteness" (Lipsitz 1998, 2). This manifests itself by means of a matrix of practices that leads to significantly different life chances along racial lines. These outcomes are not merely the byproducts of benign neglect. They are also the cumulation of the purposeful designs of whites that assign people of different racial groups to different social spaces. This, in turn, results in grossly inequitable access to education, employment, transportation, and housing (Lipsitz 2011, 6).

Hypodescent had unintended consequences for groups of color, especially blacks. By drawing boundaries that excluded blacks from having contact as equals with whites, it legitimated and forged group identities among the former. Consequently, blacks hold on tenaciously to the one-drop rule. It is considered a necessary, if originally oppressive, means of maintaining the integrity of the black community and mobilizing in the continuing struggle against racial inequality (Daniel 2006, 217). Yet the rule has become so accepted in the U.S. that its oppressive origins are largely obscured and its logic never questioned. It is part of what Bourdieu defines as the "doxa" (Bourdieu 1977, 159)—the sphere of sacrosanct or unquestioned social dogmas that have acquired the force of nature. Individuals reinforce, if only unwittingly, blackness and whiteness or any other racial designations as if they were mutually exclusive, if not hierarchical categories of experience, as well as objective phenomena with an independent existence of their own.

Hypodescent is the lynchpin of U.S. constructions of whiteness, including notions of white racial purity, which have been critical to maintaining white racial privilege. It is also the basis of monoraciality and its associated advantages that accrue to European Americans as well as groups of color ("monoracial privilege") (Nadal 2011, 43). Consequently, monoraciality has been internalized as the normative pattern of identification. It has suppressed a multiracial identity through macroagressions and mezzoagressions involving institutions and organizations respectively that structure the behavior of actors in the political and cultural economy. Johnston and Nadal argue that monoraciality has also sustained microaggressions in the sphere of interpersonal relations, where individuals are the perpetrators (Johnston and Nadal 2010, 123–44). Whether intentional or unintentional, these discriminatory attitudes and practices form part of what they refer to as "monoracism" (Johnston and Nadal 2011, 127; Nadal 2011, 43).

A critique of monoraciality should not be understood as a dismissal of monoracial forms of identification as illegitimate. Rather, it interrogates the external ascription of monoracial categories of identification that delegitimizes all other forms of identification. Monoraciality is itself reflective of a broader "monological" paradigm premised on an "either/or" mentation, which seeks to erase complexity, multiplicity, and ambiguity. Singularity is the norm in terms of the construction of all categories of difference encompassing race, gender, sexuality, and a host of others including one's stance on critical social issues relating to morality and politics (Colker 1996, 1–10; Daniel 2012, 244; Wilber 1997, 71–92; Wilber 1998, 141; Wilber 2000, 278).

This chapter explores several questions. First, to what extent has the U.S. racial order become more willing to bend or break the one-drop rule, as indicated by the election to the nation's highest office the first African-descent American, who is also the multiracial offspring of an African father and European American mother? In other words, to what extent does the election of Barack Obama indicate a decrease in the rigid enforcement of the one-drop rule as the primary factor determining the social location of African-descent Americans? Finally, to what extent is Obama's election emblematic of increasing inclusiveness of African-descent Americans as equals more generally in the U.S. racial order?

BLACK AND MORE THAN BLACK: TOWARD A MORE PERFECT UNION

On March 18, 2008, at the National Constitution Center in Philadelphia, Pennsylvania, presidential candidate, then senator Barack Obama delivered a speech entitled "A More Perfect Union." Since announcing his candidacy, Obama sought to maintain a "race-neutral" campaign. He was forced to address racial concerns in response to the controversy surrounding Reverend Jeremiah Wright, the pastor of his church in Chicago, Trinity United Church of Christ. In several sermons, Wright made what some considered inflammatory remarks about U.S. race relations and foreign policy (Ross and el-Buri 2008). Obama's thirty-minute speech was a persuasive piece of oratory on race relations unlike anything one customarily hears from politicians.[2] It was more analogous to a thoughtful history and sociology lesson. On several occasions, Obama addressed the topic of multiraciality (Ponder 2012, 62). He mentioned his interracial parentage and noted that some commentators questioned whether he is either "too black" or "not black enough" (Obama 2008b). He stated that Michelle Obama is the descendent of slaveowners and slaves, a heritage that has been passed on to their two daughters; and finally, Obama acknowledged his large international family that includes individuals scattered across several continents.

Obama also contextualized Wright's remarks. He discussed white racism, white privilege, racial inequality, and provided a nuanced framing of "black anger" and "white resentment" (Obama 2008b). He acknowledged these phenomena as expressions of the racial and class strife that has marred the egalitarian principles set forth in the nation's founding documents. The title and sentiment of Obama's speech were thus taken from the U.S. Constitution and, by extension, the Bill of Rights. The speech also called to mind the Declaration of Independence by symbolically offering a "Declaration of Interdependence,"[3] which could bring the nation closer to perfecting the union envisioned in its originating principles. Obama's address also hearkened back to Dr. Martin Luther King, Jr.'s "I Have a Dream" speech, which he presented at the August 28, 1963, March on Washington. King called upon the nation to live out the meaning of its founding documents and judge individuals by the content of their character rather than by the color of their skin.

Reverend Jesse Jackson's 1984 and 1988 presidential campaigns—particularly his 1984 speech, which laid the foundation for his even more successful 1988 campaign—is perhaps the most immediate precursor of Obama's Philadelphia speech. Obama distanced himself from Reverends Jackson and Al Sharpton,[4] as well as other black political figures whose worldviews were informed by the mass protests against Jim Crow segregation.[5] Yet Jackson's speech demonstrated the effectiveness of moving beyond calls simply for black mobilization to include appeals that would resonate with a substantial plurality of white voters as well as other communities of color (Walters 2005, 133–44; Walters 2007, 15–16). Obama's speech demonstrated "the transformative ability of oratory to infuse familiar ideas with new meanings" (Carson 2009).[6]

Obama's Philadelphia address, like his other speeches and writings, was a masterful example of what Frank and McPhail call the "rhetoric of consilience" (Frank and McPhail 2005, 571–94). In this strategy, "understanding results through translation, mediation, and an embrace of different languages, values, and traditions" (Frank and McPhail 2005, 578). Obama juxtaposes the trials and tribulations of blacks with those of other racial groups, including whites, but without equating them. He conceptualizes a race-neutral space where they may share common principles and the "transcendent value" of equity and justice (Shafer 2008).

Yet black public figures, particularly individuals seeking elective office, often studiously avoid or minimize the topic of race in order to appeal to a larger, particularly white, constituency (Davis 2011, 48–49). Steele refers to this racial diplomacy as "bargaining" (Steele 2004, 73). Bargaining seeks to disarm race for whites by extending them racial redemption from the historical injustices inflicted on blacks. It also holds out the promise of race-neutrality in addressing contemporary inequality and the pursuit of social justice. But bargaining trusts that whites will reciprocate by not holding the bargainers' race against them given the magnanimity of the original gesture (Steele 2004, 74–75; Wingfield and Feagin 2009, 33; Wingfield and Feagin 2012, 1–29). On the other hand, "challenging" (Steele 2004, 73), embodied in the civil rights tradition of leadership personified by Reverend Wright, confronts whites with the injustices perpetuated against blacks. An expectation is that whites take some ownership of corrective and compensatory measures, legal and otherwise, to help eliminate racial inequality (Steele 2004, 77–78; Wingfield and Feagin 2009, 4).[7]

Obama sought to differentiate himself from the civil rights tradition of leadership but conveyed respect for it. Indeed, the civil rights struggle contributed to social advances that made possible his nomination and eventual election (Sugrue 2012, 13–16). Obama provided a compassionate explanation for Wright's comments without justifying them, and denounced them without rejecting the minister himself (Obama 2008b, 17–23). Obama eventually severed ties with Wright and his church by virtue of additional controversial assertions he made in an interview on *Bill Moyers Journal* and in speeches at the National Association for the Advancement of Colored People (NAACP) in Detroit and the National Press Club in Washington, D.C. (Johnson 2008; Neumeister 2010).[8] The delicate task of bargaining, apart from Obama's intense campaign schedule, may, in part, explain why he declined to appear at Tavis Smiley's "State of the Black Union" symposium in New Orleans in February 2008 (Mitchell 2008)[9] and at the Lorraine Motel in Memphis on the anniversary of Dr. Martin Luther King Jr.'s assassination in April 2008 (MacGillis 2008).

Obama's skillful deployment of bargaining and consilience is integrally connected to his experience as the son of a white mother from Kansas, the heartland of the United States, and black father from Kenya, the African homeland of humanity. Obama has stated, "I am rooted in the African-American community. But I'm not defined by it. I am comfortable in my racial identity. But that's not all I am" (CBS 2007a). In his autobiography *Dreams from My Father: A Story of Race and Inheritance*, Obama maintains, "I learned to slip back and forth between my black and white worlds, understanding that each possessed its own language and customs and structures of meaning, convinced that with a bit of translation on my part the two worlds would eventually cohere" (Obama 1995, 82).

The immediacy of Obama's interracial parentage and rearing outside the continental United States, in Hawai'i and Indonesia, by his white mother and her relatives, along with his Indonesian stepfather (Obama 1995, xv, 23–25, 30–33), has imbued his consciousness with a broader vision and wider ranging sympathies in forming an identity. This enhances his image as the physical embodiment of the principles of inclusiveness and equity. Yet Obama has never said he *identifies* as multiracial (Dariotis and Yoo 2012, 99, 105; Jeffries 2014, 64–70; King-O'Riain 2013, 114; Miletsky 2012, 142; Ponder 2012, 76).[10] This was underscored when he checked only the "Black, African American, or Negro" box on the 2010 census race question even though, since 2000, respondents have been allowed to check more than one box (Roberts and Baker 2010). To the disappointment of MAVIN, one of the nation's multiracial advocacy groups, Obama cautioned about a multiracial identity in conversation with organization representatives who were hoping to capitalize on his celebrity for their documentary film "Chasing Day Break" (Elam 2011, 35–36).

For all his hybridity, Obama's identity is situated in the black community and extends outward from that location (Collins 2012, 169–90). This differs from a multiracial identity, which manifests itself "betwixt and between" the boundaries of traditional U.S. racial groups (Turner 1969, 97). It extends outward from this liminal location depending upon individuals' orientation toward the groups that compose their background (Anzaldúa 1987, 77–91; Daniel 2002, 93–113; Renn 2004, 67–93; Rockquemore and Brunsma 2002, 40–52; Rockquemore, Brunsma, and Delgado 2009, 13–34; Wallace 2001, 121–25, 147–52). Despite myriad backgrounds, experiences, and identities, the shared liminality based on identification with more than one racial background becomes an integral part of the self-conception of multiracial-identified individuals, and a defining component of the multiracial experience (Cornell and Hartmann 1998, 86, 96). This identity interrogates the "either/or" thinking that underpins U.S. racial formation and seeks to shift to a "both/neither" mindset (Daniel 2002, 3, 10, 111).

Since the late 1960s, growing numbers of individuals have challenged hypodescent and its proscriptions. This is related to the dismantling of Jim Crow segregation and implementation of civil rights legislation during the 1950s and 1960s. More specifically, it is attributable to the landmark 1967 decision in *Loving v. Virginia*, which overturned statutes in the remaining sixteen states prohibiting racial intermarriage. Previously, the racial state regarded interracial intimacy as a private rather than public matter. This was part of the state's tactic of deflecting attention away from the contradictions between its espousal of freedom and justice and the empirical realities of Jim Crow segregation, including anti-miscegenation statutes.

Interracial intimacy thus became central to the debate on the relationship of private matters to the public sphere of civil rights activism. Many activists wanted interracial intimacy to be considered a public matter as part of the promotion of equal rights and social justice, particularly in terms of black-white relations. They endeavored to achieve this primarily through popular culture, but also through litigation. Activists hoped to expose the pervasive racism in the legal system of a nation that trumpeted itself as the arsenal of democracy to the rest of the world (Lubin 2005, ix–xxi, 66–95, 151–59; Moran 2007, 239, 249–50). The *Loving* decision did not, however, derive from the civil rights movement itself although the changing climate engendered by the movement paved the way. It originated in a lawsuit filed by an interracial couple, Richard Loving, who was European American, and his wife Mildred Jeter, who was an African-descent American. They took their case to the Supreme Court, which ruled anti-miscegenation laws unconstitutional (Daniel 2002, 97).

In 1961, when Barack Obama was born, twenty-one states still maintained anti-miscegenation laws, the majority of whites disapproved of racial intermarriage (96 percent according to survey research), and individuals who dared cross the racial divide were considered deviants (Altman and Klinkner 2006, 299–315; Dedman 2008; Rockquemore and Brunsma, 21). Furthermore, Obama grew up in an era when a multiracial identity was not an option. This identity is more common among offspring of interracial marriages, including black-white individuals, born in the post–civil rights era. Many individuals display traditional monoracial identities. Increasing numbers exhibit a multiracial consciousness based on identification with more than one racial background (Binning, Unzueta, Huo, and Molina 2009, 36–36, 44–46; Korgen 1998, 9–56; Renn 2004, 67–94; Rockquemore and Brunsma 21, 41–48).

Beginning in the late 1970s, this consciousness emerged in a movement seeking to change official racial-data collection standards that required individuals to identify with only one racial background (DaCosta 2007, 21–46; Daniel 2002, 125–54; Williams 2006, 1–64). By the 2000 census, this movement succeeded in making it possible for individuals to express a multiracial identity by checking more than one box in the race question (DaCosta 2007, 2–4, 21–46; Daniel 2002, 125–51; Williams 2008, 39–84). Consequently, many scholars argue that the one-drop rule has less impact on identity formation of multiracials of partial African descent. Others contend it still influences identity formation through external imposition as well as self-ascription (Jeffries 2014, 64–70; Khanna 2010, 96–121; Rockquemore and Brunsma 2002, 45–46).

BLACK, WHITE, AND MULTIRACIAL: A MORE PERFECT UNION

Barack Obama's significance as the first African-descent American elected to the nation's highest office cannot be underestimated. It demonstrates the considerable gains some blacks have made since the 1960s. Obama's election has transformed the aesthetic of the nation's political landscape and instilled a sense of pride and optimism in African Americans while inspiring more black youth to realize their potential for advancement. If Obama has significance for African Americans, he has special meaning for the growing population of multiracial-identified Americans (Jeffries 2014, 64–70). Multiracials totaled 7 million on the 2000 census (Stuckey 2008; Jones 2005). Based on 2010 census data, their numbers increased to 9 million—or 2.9 percent of the population. Although they still make up only a fraction of the total population, this is a growth rate of about 32 percent since 2000, when multiracials composed 2.4 percent of the population (Humes, Jones, and Ramirez 2011, 6–7).

Although Obama does not identify as multiracial, his public success, loving extended interracial family, and comfort as an African American who acknowledges his multiracial background indicates how much things have changed since he was born (Dedman 2008). During his first news conference as president-elect, Obama conveyed this comfort with the throwaway response "mutts like me" when asked by reporters what types of puppies he would consider getting for his daughters. This was a more personalized reference to Obama's multiracial background than his typically more oblique reference to it by mentioning his parents.[11] Moreover, Obama's open discussion of his multiracial background, along with heightened interest among lay and professional genealogists, has provided the U.S. with an opportunity to embrace itself as a more complex and interconnected racial terrain. In the past, few records were available and only enthusiasts made the effort to do genealogical research. The abundance of information on the Internet, including Ancestry.com's massive data base in Provo, Utah, as well as information publically available on family genealogy websites, coupled with the ease and increased sophistication of DNA testing, now makes it possible to verify the centuries of extensive racial intermingling (Stolberg 2012).

For example, Lynne Cheney, in doing research for *Blue Skies, No Fences*, a memoir about growing up in Wyoming, discovered that Obama and then-Vice President Dick Cheney share a seventeenth-century white male ancestor, which makes them eighth cousins (Associated Press 2007). Billionaire financier Warren Buffett and Obama are seventh cousins, three times removed. Obama and the former Republican senator from Massachusetts, Scott Brown, are tenth cousins. Actor Brad Pitt and Obama are ninth cousins. Sarah Palin and Barack Obama are tenth cousins. The president is also tenth cousins (once removed) with Rush Limbaugh (Rose 2010). Obama's other distant cousins include former President George W. Bush and his father, George H. W. Bush, Gerald Ford, Lyndon Johnson, Harry S. Truman, James Madison, British prime minister Sir Winston Churchill, and Civil War general Robert E. Lee (Johnson 2010; Jones 2009; Lavoie 2008).

In September 2009, former professional African American boxer Muhammad Ali visited Ennis, Ireland, to celebrate his Irish ancestry. A plaque was unveiled in the city to honor Ali's ancestors, particularly the ancestors and descendants of his great-grandfather Abe Grady, who immigrated to the United States in the 1860s and married a black woman (Associated Press 2009a; Pogatchnik 2009). Some of Senator McCain's white male ancestors reportedly not only owned slaves but also fathered children with slave women. These individuals have living descendants as do many others who were enslaved on the McCain plantation.[12]

Michelle Obama has Native American ancestry and her maternal third great-grandfather was European American. This individual fathered a biracial son, Dolphus T. Shields, with Melvina Shields, who was the First Lady's maternal third great-grandmother. Both Melvina and Dolphus were slaves. Consequently, the latter was born outside of wedlock, and may have been the product of rape. These findings substantiate a longstanding family rumor about a white forebear (Smolenyak 2009; Swarns 2012a, 210; Swarns and Kantor 2009). Anyone familiar with U.S. history would not be startled by these revelations. While blacks are monoracially identified, most have African, European, and in many cases, Native American ancestry, although the actual combination varies from individual to individual. Furthermore, for several centuries many blacks who are predominantly European in ancestry have displayed phenotypes that have made it possible for them to "pass for white." Whites with African ancestry inherited from these individuals number in the millions (Davis 1991, 52).

The public disclosure and discussion of Michelle Obama's genealogy provides a direct link between her ancestors' journey from servitude and her seat in the Office of the First Lady (Swarns and Kantor 2009). It is also another opportunity for increased openness and honesty in discussing multiraciality as an integral part of the nation's history, which has been obscured by centuries of racism. A requisite component of this conversation would involve acknowledging that the multiracial phenomenon in the U.S. historically originated in interracial relationships largely consummated more through coercion and violence during slavery, as was most likely the case with Michelle Obama's third great-grandparents, than mutual consent and peaceful means, as in the case of Barack Obama's parents.

If Barack Obama's biography has suggested his background does not include slave ancestors, genealogists of Ancestry.com have discovered marriage and property records, which, along with DNA evidence, challenge that assumption. Their findings indicate Obama's maternal lineage may include an individual of African descent in colonial Virginia named John Punch. In 1640, Punch was an indentured servant who escaped from Virginia to Maryland. He was captured in Maryland, along with two white servants who also escaped, and was put on trial. Punch's punishment—servitude for life—was harsher than that of the white servants. This was years before Virginia legalized slavery, which held individuals in bondage in perpetuity. Historians have never been able to pinpoint an exact date for the beginning of African slavery in the U.S. Some now regard Punch as the first individual of African descent to be legally enslaved (Stolberg 2012).

Records suggest Punch fathered children with a white woman, who passed her free status on to them. This gave rise to a family with a slightly different name, Bunch, of which Obama's mother, Stanley Ann Dunham, is a descendent. The genealogists traced two major Bunch family lineages, one that migrated to North Carolina, where they were recorded as "mulatto" in early records. The other lineage remained in Virginia, continued to intermarry, became prominent landowners, and was considered white. Obama descends from the Virginia line, which eventually migrated to Tennessee, where his great-great-great-great-grandmother Anna Bunch was born. Her daughter, Frances Allred, who was born in 1834, moved to Kansas where Dunham was born in 1942. There is no indication Dunham knew about her African American ancestry. Because many records have been destroyed, researches could not make a definitive determination of whether John Punch, the slave, is a Bunch ancestor. However, the Bunch family maintains an online database that traces their genealogy. It is supplemented with DNA tests indicating the men in the family have genetic markers consistent with sub-Saharan African ancestry (Stolberg 2012).

In the media Obama is generally referred to as black or African American, less frequently as multiracial or biracial. Yet individuals have displayed varying responses in terms of how he is viewed racially. Data on these attitudes were collected for Mark Williams by Zogby International in a November 2006 Internet poll of 2,155 people. Individuals were told Obama's parents' background, and then were asked to identify Obama's race. Obama was identified as black by 66 percent of African Americans, 9 percent of Latinas/os, 8 percent of whites, and 8 percent of Asian Americans. He was designated with multiracial-identifiers by 88 percent of Latinas/os, 80 percent of whites, 77 percent of Asian Americans, and 34 percent of African Americans.[13]

Obama's multiracial background has made it possible for a wide range of individuals to feel comfortable with him, which was instrumental in building an impressive voter coalition in 2008. According to election polls, this included 95 percent of blacks and a 2-1 advantage among all other racial groups, including Latinas/os, Asian Americans, and others. In addition, Obama carried every age group other than those sixty-five and older (Mercurio 2008). Young people of all racial groups born roughly between 1982 and 2003—the "Millennial generation" (Apollon 2011, 1; Winograd and Hais 2008, 66–67)—have been among Obama's most ardent supporters. According to figures from the 2008 Current Population Survey, slightly more than half of Millennials—56 percent—are European American. The remaining 44 percent are Latina/o (20 percent), African American (15 percent), Asian American (5 percent), multiracial (3 percent), and Native American (1), with a significantly larger share of blacks and multiracials than previous generations. This population is the most racially diverse cohort in U.S. history and has been exposed to a comparatively more racially diverse society than any previous generations (Apollon 2011, 3–28; Tseng 2008).

That said, Senator McCain led Obama by twelve points among white voters. However, this is hardly the anticipated "Bradley Effect"[14] in which whites, who oppose a black politician, mislead pollsters about the candidate for whom they will vote in order to appear racially unbiased (Mercurio 2008). Obama won decisively in the electoral vote (Obama 365, McCain 173). The popular vote was considerably closer (Obama 66, 882, 230, McCain, 58, 343, 671). Obama garnered 53 percent and McCain 46 percent (CNN 2008). Pre-election polls were generally accurate in reflecting voters' preference for Obama. The recent economic crisis supplanted Iraq as the dominant campaign issue (MacAskill 2008). A candidate's perceived ability to handle that turmoil, along with widespread dissatisfaction with the Bush administration, was a deciding factor in the election. Those sentiments, apart from questions of race, gave Obama an edge over McCain despite the latter's strength in national security (Feldman 2008).

In the 2012 election, Obama's showing of 93 percent among blacks, who turned out in record numbers, was all but guaranteed. The true game changer came with garnering 73 percent of the Asian American vote and 71 percent of the Latina/o vote. Asian Americans in particular have remained an elusive voter bloc. Support from these communities is attributable in part to massive organizing in response to voter suppression efforts in more than a dozen states. Republicans passed restrictions aimed at reducing the turnout of Obama's "coalition of the ascendant"—young voters, African Americans, and Latinas/os (Berman 2012). According to 2012 exit polls, nationally Romney won 60 percent of the white vote; Obama garnered 40 percent (Scocca 2012). However, 60 percent of Obama's supporters were 18–29 years of age, and 54 percent of females voted for him (Murray 2012). A newly released voter poll found that feminists, not simply women in general, were critical to Obama's 2012 re-election (Plank 2013).[15]

RACE AND WHITENESS: HEGEMONY AND THE POLITICS OF INCLUSION

Although Obama has sought to be defined by policy positions instead of race (Inskeep 2007; Walters 2007, 13–14), the media have repeatedly referred to his candidacy and election as a milestone in the nation's racial history. Yet for the most part Obama's biography stands outside of the most poisonous aspects of the historic African American experience—slavery, Jim Crow segregation, and the emergence of urban ghettos (Dedman 2008). Moreover, Obama's ability to draw on his racial whiteness has enhanced his ability to bridge the racial divide. During the 2008 campaign, he frequently reminded us of his white mother and grandparents who raised him, as well as his white uncle, a World War II veteran. The image of Obama's white relatives sitting in support of him at the 2008 Democratic National Convention is a remarkable moment underscoring his historic significance (Dedman 2008).

This connection to whiteness was strategically emphasized in black educator, activist, political commentator, and Democratic Party affiliate Donna Brazile's appeal to whites who might not vote for Obama simply because he is an African-descent American rather than because they disagreed with his political platform. Brazile stressed that Harvard-educated Obama is "biracial" and "spent nine months in the womb of a white woman. He was raised for the first eighteen to twenty-one years by his white grandparents. He ain't spent no time in living rooms like I spent my childhood" (Brazile 2008). Black reporter Ed Gordon stated, "If ever there was an African American man who had that entrée to those folks [white voters], it would be Barack Obama. He's half-white, he's Ivy League. He's all the things that white America considers safe" (MSNBC 2008).

Similarly, a white canvasser recruiting voters for Obama in 2008 succeeded in getting many ambivalent whites to acknowledge that their hesitation to vote for him could be attributable to racial bias. Some individuals changed their opinion after she stated, "You know, Barack's mom looked a lot like me. I wish that you would take a closer look at this man and try to see deeper than just his skin color" (SuzeNYC 2008). Vice President-elect, then-Senator Joseph Biden (D-DE), said Barack Obama is "the first sort of mainstream African-American who is articulate and bright and clean and a nice-looking guy. I mean, that's a story-book, man" (Gregory 2007). Senate Democratic leader Harry Reid stated in a private conversation that Barack Obama should seek—and could win—the White House because he is a "light skinned African-American . . . with no Negro dialect, unless he wanted to have one" (Heilemann and Halperin 2010, 37). Sens. Biden and Reid later apologized for the unintended insensitivity and racist implications of these comments (Associated Press 2010b).

These statements are harsh reminders that whiteness, either explicitly or implicitly in all its code words, is still the norm against which all else is measured in terms of value. The number of blacks holding public office has increased dramatically over the years. Blacks are included in the economic mainstream in ways that were unheard of half a century ago. Absolute gains in years of formal education are significant (Daniel 2002, 162–63). Yet Hochschild and Weaver indicate that darker-skinned blacks have lower socioeconomic status, diminished prestige, and more punitive relationships with law enforcement (Hochschild and Weaver 2007, 643–70). Findings by Stanford University, the University of Colorado at Boulder, Mississippi Urban Research Center, and other institutions bolster this argument. They found that among black men pronounced West African features and darker skin tone play an important role in the perception of a link between race and criminality. Villanova University researchers studied more than 12,000 cases of black women imprisoned in North Carolina and found that lighter-skinned women were sentenced to approximately 12 percent less time than their darker-skinned counterparts. Women with lighter skin also served 11 percent less time than darker women (Price and Gyimah-Brempong 2006, 2–3; Viglione, Hannon, and DeFina 2011, 250–58).

FIGURE 1. Pluralist and integrationist dynamics

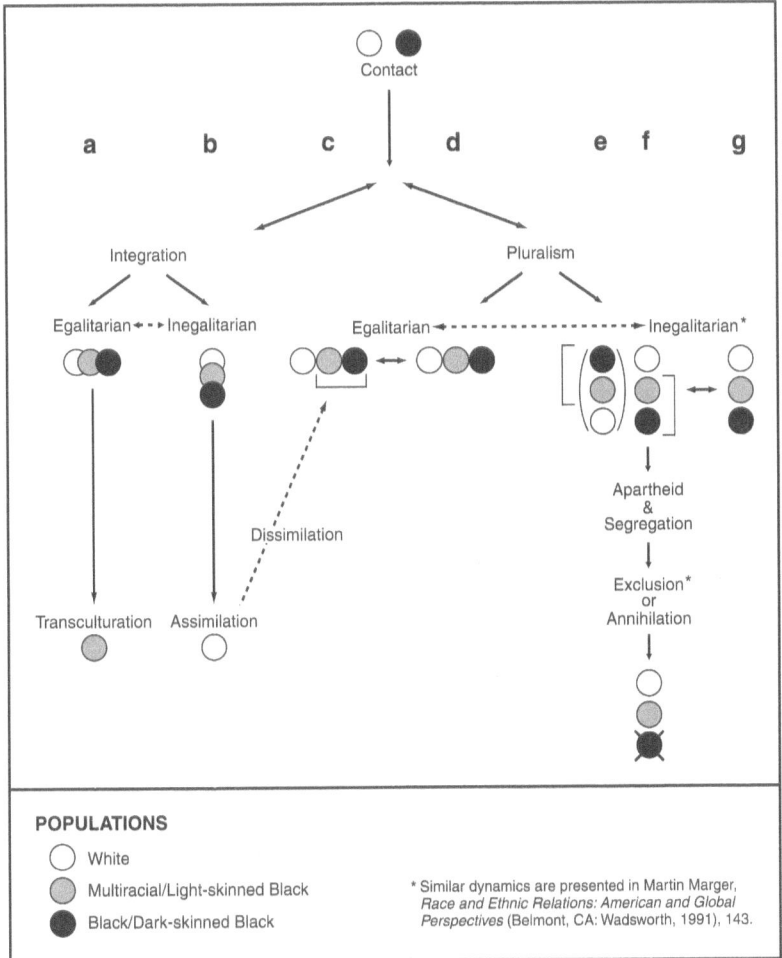

Survey research also indicates that educational attainment, occupational opportunities, and family income among blacks increases considerably with lighter skin (Russell, Wilson, and Hall 1992, 127–28, 134–62; Wade, Romano, and Blue 2004, 2550–58). Hughes and Hertel do not attribute this to intergenerational benefits passed on to individuals because of their families' higher educational and socioeconomic status. That stems from the history of previous preferential treatment of individuals who more closely approximate whites in terms of physical appearance or perceived ancestry. Instead, they conclude that skin color continues to operate as a "diffuse status characteristic" (Hughes and Hertel 1990, 1116). Whites, even if only unconsciously, thus often select individuals of color who more closely approximate them in physical appearance, believing they are making impartial decisions based on competence or other criteria.

Keith, Herring, and other scholars, by contrast, hold that whites may consciously express a preference for individuals of color who more closely approximate their phenotypical norms as well as assumed attitudinal and behavioral characteristics (Keith and Herring 1991, 760–78). Many individuals of color internalize similar biases when judging individuals in their own racial group and other groups of color (Hall 2003; Thompson and Keith 2001, 336–57).[16] Livingston and Nicholas argue that apart from "impeccable credentials, demonstrated competence, and tireless diligence, having a nonthreatening, disarming appearance—physical, psychological, or behavioral traits that attenuate perceptions of threat by the dominant group"—has been shown to be a plus, if not a necessity, for successful black leaders, and particularly men (Livingston and Pearce 2009, 1229).

Moreover, conservatives have been able to showcase "successful" blacks and other individuals of color. These individuals have supposedly overcome obstacles through sheer determination and merit alone—thus fulfilling the American dream and serving as living testaments to the much-vaunted colorblind tenets espoused in the nation's founding documents. These compelling "lift-yourself-up-by-your-bootstraps" personal narratives have made it possible for conservatives to frame liberals (particularly European Americans) as patronizing bigots (or racist "complainers"). These success stories have also allowed conservatives to frame communities of color as collective self-victimizers that bemoan racial discrimination against groups, while at best significantly underestimating and at worst undermining the power of individual agency. Conservatives have succeeded in enrolling some of these individuals in their ranks.

Conservatives have also deployed colorblind rhetoric that deflects attention away from and masks the disproportionate representation of the masses of color, particularly blacks, in the secondary labor force and among the ranks of the underemployed and unemployed. This colorblind ideology has obscured the selective nature of integration in the post–civil rights era where some individuals of color—particularly the more socioeconomically advantaged—have been allowed to gain increased access to wealth, power, privilege, and prestige. The growth, prosperity, and increased integration of more prosperous blacks does not mean racism has abated. Their partial integration into the white power structure merely furthers the illusion of power sharing without actually requiring whites to give up structural control. Even worse, it fosters the belief that the excluded majority of blacks could surmount their difficulties if only they had the character and drive to do so (Daniel 2006, 206–15; Haney López 2014, 215).

These developments indicate the post–civil rights racial order has largely shifted away from white domination. Yet the latter is not absent. Racial differences still serve as the basis of perpetuating social inequality notwithstanding the belief that civil rights and other initiatives eradicated ascribed markers such as race. Social inequities are now said to be largely attributable to other factors—class and culture—which are subject to change through effects of merit and achievement. Compensatory measures such as affirmative action are now considered part of a racial spoils system that at worst is a form of "reverse racism" against whites (Figure 1e). Even support for the concept of multiculturalism (Figure 1d) is often believed to intensify and prolong the fixation on race and racial categories, which supposedly impedes the national project of unifying individuals as Americans (Daniel 2006, 141–74, 206–15).

Accordingly, pervasive formal exclusion and coercion (or inegalitarian pluralism) (Figure 1g) have been replaced with more informal dynamics, which are increasingly juxtaposed with patterns of selective inclusion (or inegalitarian integration) (Figure 1b).[17] The increase of inegalitarian integration does not preclude the existence of more egalitarian, if considerably less pervasive, patterns of integration based on equality (Figure 1a). However, it follows that integration (inclusiveness) would continue to be deeply marked by more inegalitarian dynamics given that the larger social order is still underpinned by racial hierarchy. Drawing on the work of Gramsci, Omi and Winant encapsulate the selective nature of this form of integration (or assimilation) with the term "hegemony," which creates the illusion of equality while effectively allowing dominant groups to maintain power, control, and hierarchy. This also disguises the fact that U.S. society is still racist to the core (Gramsci 1971, 263; Omi and Winant 1996, 66–69, 84, 115, 148).

This growth of white hegemony in terms of blacks has been accompanied by a decrease in the rigid ascription of the one-drop rule in determining their social location. Skin color, along with other phenotypical features, such as hair texture, eye color, and nose and lip shape, etc. (Hagiwara, Kashy, and Cesario 2013, 892–98), working in combination with attitudinal, behavioral, and socioeconomic attributes, has increased as a form of "racial capital" (Daniel 2002, 155–57; Hunter 2005, 5, 8, 10, 46; Hunter 2011, 142–61).[18] Indeed, one is struck by the number of African American "firsts" in the post–civil rights era who display comparatively more European ancestry in terms of physical appearance. Consider, for example, Thurgood Marshall, the first black Supreme Court justice (1967); Edward W. Brooke, the first black senator to be elected since Reconstruction (1966); Patricia Harris, the first black woman cabinet member (1976) and ambassador (1965–1967); David Dinkins, the first black elected mayor of New York (1990); L. Douglas Wilder, the first black elected governor (1990); General Colin Powell, the first black Chairman of the Joint Chiefs of Staff (1989–1993) and Secretary of State (2001–2005), Vanessa Williams, the first black Miss America (1983); Halle Berry, the first black woman to receive an Academy Award for Best Actress (2002), to mention only a few (Daniel 2006, 203–204).

The strengthening of white hegemony, along with the colorblind ideology supporting the belief that the United States has transcended racism—commonly referred to as "metaracism"—became the cornerstone of U.S. race relations during the last two decades of the twentieth century (Korgen and Brunsma 2012, 191–193; Kovel 1970, xi, xxix, xxx–xxxiii, liv–lv, 211–30, 234, 247). In 2013, this was evinced in the June 24 and 25 Supreme Court decisions that undermine, respectively, the enforcement of affirmative action initiatives (Leitsinger 2013) and sections of the 1965 Voting Rights Act. The latter required federal preapproval for any changes in election procedures and were intended to prevent certain jurisdictions, primarily among the Southern (and some Western) states, from enforcing historical practices (e.g., poll taxes, literacy tests, grandfather clauses, etc.) designed to disenfranchise "racial minorities," particularly blacks.[19] Those provisions also targeted contemporary discriminatory practices, including voter ID laws and gerrymandering (or voter redistricting) aimed at minimizing the voter strength of communities of color who tend to be Democrats (A. Liptak 2013). Several states have already moved to enact new voter suppression laws and redistricting in the wake of the Supreme Court decision (Childress 2013; Williams 2013).

Many observers believe this colorblind ideology influenced the dismissal of race as a mitigating factor in the unfolding of events leading to the shooting death of Trayvon Martin by George Zimmerman as well as the July 13, 2013 not guilty verdict (by a nearly all-white jury) in the Zimmerman trial.[20] On the rainy night of February 26, 2012, Martin, an unarmed seventeen-year-old African American, was fatally shot by George Zimmerman, a neighborhood watch coordinator. Zimmerman's father, a retired Magistrate Judge, is a European American. His mother, a former deputy court clerk, is a Peruvian, who describes herself as African-descended (or Afro-Peruvian).

Zimmerman was identified as "white" in the initial police report.[21] Later it was learned he identifies as "Hispanic."

The media have variously described Zimmerman as white, Hispanic, white and Hispanic, and white Hispanic (Butera 2012; Gamboa 2012; Schmalfeldt 2012). "White Hispanic" does not necessarily indicate he is being described as "biracial" as would be the case with "white and Hispanic." Rather, it is more a reflection of official terminology used in the collection of data on race and ethnicity. For example, the census ethnicity question (question 5) asks individuals whether they are of "Hispanic origin" or "Non-Hispanic origin." Hispanic is not among the categories on the race question (question 6), which includes white, black, Indian or Alaskan Native, as well as several Asian and Pacific Islander categories. Individuals may be "white" in the race question and "Hispanic" in the ethnicity question (e.g., a white Hispanic). Respondents are allowed to check more than one race on the race question. Individuals of partial Hispanic descent, such as Zimmerman, are neither permitted to check both Hispanic and non-Hispanic origins on the ethnicity question, nor are they provided with a Hispanic identifier in the race question (Daniel 2006, 225, 234).

Zimmerman lived in a gated townhouse community (The Retreat at Twin Lakes) in Sanford, Florida, which was also the residence of Martin's father's fiancée, who Martin and his father were visiting. The community was racially diverse, but there were a proportionately larger number of whites. Over the past year, there had been a series of burglaries and attempted break-ins on the premises, several of them involving young black men (Parker 2013). Consequently, Zimmerman was wary of strangers walking about the complex. While driving through the community, Zimmerman observed Martin, who was returning from a nearby convenience store. He did not recognize Martin, felt he looked suspicious, and called the Sanford police department's non-emergency number. Subsequently, Zimmerman got out of his car and began pursuing Martin. However, the police dispatcher advised him that was not necessary (Novogrod, Winter, and Connor 2013). There was an altercation and Zimmerman shot Martin in the chest at close range with his 9mm handgun.

Following Zimmerman's earlier call, Sanford police arrived on the scene minutes after the shooting. They took him into custody for questioning and concluded Zimmerman shot Martin in self-defense. The police released Zimmerman for lack of evidence and legal grounds for an arrest (Dahl 2012). Following weeks of intense and contradictory media coverage, as well as public outcry, particularly from black public figures and leaders,

Governor Rick Scott appointed a special state prosecutor to the investigation. On April 11, after further examination of the evidence, the prosecutor charged Zimmerman with second degree murder and issued a capias for his arrest. On April 12, he pleaded not guilty and was eventually released on bail (Fausset 2012)

Zimmerman's trial began on June 10 in Sanford. During the proceedings witnesses gave conflicting accounts of what transpired before the shooting, particularly in terms of who was the aggressor (Novogrod, Winter, and Connor 2013; Prieto 2012; Schneider and Hightower 2013b). The second-degree murder charge required the prosecution to show Zimmerman displayed ill will, hatred, or spite but killed without malice aforethought. Ahead of closing remarks prosecuting attorney Richard Mantei asked that jurors be allowed to consider a verdict on the lesser charge of manslaughter. Circuit Judge Debra Nelson ruled in favor of the request. To get a manslaughter conviction, prosecutors only needed to show Zimmerman committed an unjustifiable killing but without premeditation (Yilma 2013). Manslaughter with a firearm could result in a maximum sentence of thirty years. Second-degree murder carries a maximum sentence of life in prison. The jurors had three options for their verdict: guilty of second-degree murder, guilty of manslaughter, and not guilty (Muskal and Hennessy-Fiske, 2013).

Notwithstanding the real legal challenges involved with establishing that racial animus was a factor in Zimmerman's behavior the night he shot Trayvon Marin, the judge barred the prosecution from using the term "racial profiling"[22] during the court proceedings. Yet in his closing arguments lead prosecutor Bernie de la Rionda stated Zimmerman made and acted upon "wrong assumptions" about Martin. This insinuated that Martin was racially profiled as a criminal because he was a young black male in a hoodie (MSNBC 2013a). Prosecutor John Guy made a similar allusion to racial profiling in his rebuttal to the defense's closing argument when he asked: "If the roles were reversed…and if it was Trayvon Martin who had shot and killed George Zimmerman, what would your verdict be? That is how you know it is not about race" (MSNBC 2013b). This role reversal appropriated color-blind logic to infer the case was in fact about race.

Conversely, the defense sought to imply Martin's own racial animus by capitalizing on his reported description of Zimmerman as a "creepy-ass cracker." Shortly before the shooting Martin noticed Zimmerman pursuing him and reportedly referred to the latter using the term while on his cell phone conversing with a friend Rachel Jeantel, a key prosecution witness. Cracker (or cracka) is generally an epithet for European Americans, particularly poor rural (typically racially-biased) whites in the U.S. south. At the closing of Jeantel's testimony, defense attorney Don West asked her to describe the "culture" she said uses the word "cracker" to describe white people. "The area I was raised in?" Jeantel asked, to which West replied, "Yes" (Christopher 2013).

What shocked many observers, however, was Jeantel's avowal of the term's race-neutrality although she understood Martin was using it in the common, derogatory sense. But, in Florida where Jeantel was raised, cracker has not consistently been used as a racial slur. It has often been employed self-descriptively with pride as a nod to the region's history and one's own pre–Civil War heritage as a native of Florida (or Georgia). One theory is that the term cracker refers to the original rugged colonial-era English and Anglo-American pioneer settlers of south Florida (and Georgia), many of them cattle drivers. If crackers were not known for their racial tolerance, they were renowned for their ability to handle and "crack" large leather whips ("Florida Crackers") in driving their livestock herds as well as frightening away alligators. Yet it is unclear when and how cracker evolved from a race-neutral regional colloquialism into a racial epithet (Christopher 2009; Hislop 2009).

That said, the imposition of colorblind rational not only prohibited use of the term racial profiling but also intentionally kept conversations about race off the table in court proceedings, including never overtly mentioning Martin's and Zimmerman's race. Many commentators believe this helped undermine the prosecution's ability to meet the burden of proof necessary to refute Zimmerman's account of self-defense beyond a reasonable doubt (Bloom 2013; Coates 2013; Cohn 2013; Hutchinson 2013; Muskal 2013; Peters 2013; Taylor 2013). Rosenfeld maintains that many attorneys and analysts familiar with jury trials and courtroom procedure argue this was compounded by the otherwise incoherent and indeed puzzling missteps by the prosecution. These observers have questioned whether Florida law enforcement, from the local police to the special prosecutor overseeing the Martin case, simply did not want to see Zimmerman convicted, threw away the case, and thus allowed the prosecution to crumble (Boardman 2013; Rosenfeld 2013).

This is further complicated by the problematic relationship between Florida's "stand your ground" provision and questions of self-defense. Under the "Castle Doctrine," individuals may "stand their ground" and use lethal force to defend themselves and property against home invaders without needing to retreat (Florida Senate 2011a).[23] For hundreds of years, English and U.S. common law have recognized there is nowhere to retreat when cornered in one's own "castle." Some states such as Florida go one step further, removing the duty of retreat from other, particularly public, locations. According to these "stand your ground" laws, individuals have no obligation to abandon a place in which they have a legal right to be, or to give up ground to an assailant. Moreover, they have the right to use reasonable force to defend themselves (Gasper 2012).

Prior to 2006, Florida's law required individuals to work themselves free and retreat when confronted with a threat, whether it was a deadly threat or simply the threat of violence, or even actual violence. Being wrongfully attacked did not justify the use of force likely to cause great bodily harm or death if by retreating one could have avoided the use of that force. In 2005, Florida amended its law and removed the duty to retreat provision. It implemented a stand your ground rule, which allowed individuals to defend themselves (with deadly force if necessary) to protect their lives (Gasper 2012; Hutchinson 2012). Yet Hutchinson and Gasper maintain the stand your ground rule only applies to the individual who is not the aggressor, instigator, or pursuer of the first direct personal conflict. The rule makes it irrelevant who felt threatened first or who struck the first blow. If you simply pursue someone and tell them "to do something and they refuse, and you subsequently start an argument, confrontation, or fight," you are the instigator (Gasper 2012). One does not have legal recourse to claim self-defense if one is the aggressor *unless* the victim's response was so great that one feared serious bodily injury or death, and the use of lethal force was proportional to the threat. But in such a situation, the aggressor must also exhaust every other "reasonable means to escape such danger" (Florida Senate 2011b; Hutchinson 2012).

Since Zimmerman's attorneys chose not to invoke stand your ground as a defense, some observers have characterized this as a standard "self-defense" rather than a "stand your ground" case. But Flatow notes the written jury instructions made clear that, in Florida, there is no longer an effective distinction. "Stand your ground" is incorporated in the state's self-defense law, whether or not a defendant chooses to hold a hearing specifically on the question (Flatow 2013). The instructions were as follows:

> *If George Zimmerman was not engaged in an unlawful activity and was attacked in any place where he had a right to be, he had no duty to retreat and had the right to stand his ground and meet force with force, including deadly force if he reasonably believed that it was necessary to*

do so to prevent death or great bodily harm to himself or another or to prevent the commission of a forcible felony. (Coates 2013)

That said, Juror B37, whose spouse is an attorney, and one of two jurors to speak publicly, stated that initially one juror wanted to convict Zimmerman of second-degree murder and two jurors were in favor of manslaughter. Juror B29, who is Puerto Rican, told ABC's *Good Morning America* she was originally ready to convict Zimmerman on second-degree murder. In her heart she felt he was guilty. Consequently, she was not averse to a hung jury. But she believed the evidence simply did not prove his guilt beyond a reasonable doubt. Nonetheless, she felt she owed the Martin family an apology (Voorhees 2013). The jurors eventually decided on a not guilty verdict given the legal parameters specified in the jury instructions. They reportedly never believed racial animus was a motive in Zimmerman's actions. Consequently, race was not taken into consideration in reaching a verdict (CBS News 2013).

It is one thing to say racial animus underpinned Zimmerman's actions the night he shot Trayvon Martin. It is another to say he is a racist individual. Yet proving in a court of law that racial bias influenced his behavior would not necessarily be an easy task (Hutchinson 2013).[24] Alvarado maintains, nonetheless, that race is central to this case. Notwithstanding Zimmerman's Latino background and identity, and somewhat intermediate location in the black and white racial binary, she argues "he squarely aligned himself with whiteness by virtue of acting in accordance with dominant social and legal structures" that criminalize blackness (Alvarado 2013). His European American background and surname may have leveraged him racial and cultural capital, respectively, given historical racial disparities in the application of criminal laws. Using Federal Bureau of Investigation (FBI) data on 43,500 homicides from 2005 to 2009, Roman found that whites who kill blacks in "stand your ground" states are far more likely to be found justified in their killings. In non-"stand your ground" states, whites are 250 percent more likely to be found justified in killing blacks than whites who kill other whites; in "stand your ground" states that number increases to 354 percent (Childress 2012; Roman 2013, 1).

In 2012, the Department of Justice (DOJ) initiated a federal investigation into Trayvon Martin's death. The department halted its inquiry until the state completed its criminal proceedings. Since Zimmerman's acquittal, the department has renewed its investigation. Shortly after the not guilty verdict, the NAACP, the nation's oldest and largest civil rights organization,[25] launched a MoveOn.org petition calling on the DOJ to file federal civil rights charges against Zimmerman. The petition garnered 1.5 million signatures in three days. This has been accompanied by expressions of outrage in the form of mass rallies, demonstrations, and teach-ins involving individuals across the racial spectrum. There have been calls for conferences, vacationers, and entertainers to boycott Florida (Figueroa and Hinojosa 2013; Lipton 2013; Yager and Strauss 2013).

A Pew Research Center national survey conducted on July 17–21 among 1,480 adults indicates that roughly as many respondents were satisfied with the verdict (39 percent) as dissatisfied (42 percent), with nearly one in five (19 percent) offering no opinion. More broadly, 52 percent said race is being given more attention in this case than it deserves; 36 percent believed the case raises important issues about race that need to be discussed. Blacks expressed an unequivocally strong response to the case. They were dissatisfied with the acquittal by an 86 percent to 5 percent margin (Pew Research 2013, 1). According to a *Washington Post*-ABC News poll conducted on July 18–21 among a random national sample of 1,002 adults, 86 percent of blacks, 60 percent of Latinas/os, and 33 percent of whites disapproved of the verdict (Cohen 2013).

Attorney General Eric Holder said the Department of Justice may move forward with civil rights charges against Zimmerman, but only if the evidence reveals a prosecutable violation of federal criminal civil rights statutes within its jurisdiction (Lipton 2013; Yager and Strauss 2013). Although federal prosecutors would have more resources at their disposal than state prosecutors in mounting their case, clearing the legal bar for such charges is very high. Prosecutors must prove beyond a reasonable doubt that Zimmerman "acted willfully with a seriously culpable state of mind" to violate Martin's civil rights. Holder states, "Something that was reckless, that was negligent, does not meet that standard. We have to show that there was specific intent to do the crime with the requisite state of mind" (Lipton 2013).[26]

RACE AND WHITENESS:
THE POLITICS OF ANXIETY, RESENTMENT, AND RAGE

Barack Obama is an iconic figure who embodies and at the same time seeks to transcend race and speak to the nation's common destiny (Steele 2008, 81–117; Tesler 2010, 1–4). He has strategically sought to navigate the treacherous waters of the U.S. racial divide and transform it into a metaphoric bridge that redefines the nation's civic culture and social contract in more inclusive terms (Dedman 2008). Indeed, the collateral impact of Obama's multiracial background, along with his hopeful campaign promises, generated unrealistic expectations among voters. Many of those who were desirous of change they could believe in imbued him with an almost messianic ability to cleanse the nation of its racial sins.

Obama does not feel his presidency represented the end of the U.S. racial divide. In a *Rolling Stone* magazine interview he stated, "Look, race has been one of the fault lines in American culture and American politics from the start. I never bought into the notion that by electing me, somehow we were entering into a post-racial period" (Wenner 2012). Haney López argues that even if Obama rejects postracial thinking "as a claim" that the United States is "past race," he "adopts an *approach* toward race that can be considered 'postracial'" (Haney López 2014, 195). Obama's race-neutrality has been purposely designed to downplay, if not ignore, questions of race and racial inequality, in order to appeal to a larger nonblack, particularly white constituency. Consequently, it has been catalytic in nurturing the post-racial fantasy (Logan 2011, 32; Tesler 2010, 1–4; Watkins 2013).

The Obama phenomenon's post-racial allure appeals to abstractions that obscure or ignore the empirical reality of the historical and contemporary inequities (Wingfield and Feagin 2009, 1–2, 243–44; Wingfield and Feagin 2012, 177–211) engendered by what Mills refers to as the nation's "racial contract" (Mills 1997, 130).[27] Mills describes the racial contract as an ideological predisposition that informs the beliefs whites have developed about themselves and racialized "others," and the behaviors in which they have engaged as a result of those beliefs. Unlike the social contract idealized in Western thought, the racial contract reveals the inequitable ideological presuppositions, policies, and material conditions that have sustained the U.S. racial order since its inception.

Notwithstanding Obama's race-neutrality, his campaign and election have engendered a sea of white anxiety and in the extreme, white resentment and rage, whether implicitly or explicitly expressed in racial terms (Parker and Barreto 2013, 1–19; 191–217; Tucker 2013). Stephens-Davidowitz found that a racially charged Google search was a robust negative predictor of Obama's vote share in the 2008 election. Using a new, non-survey proxy for racial animus—Google search queries that included racially charged language—his estimates implied these sentiments cost Obama 3 to 5 percentage points of the popular vote. Obama also gained some votes because of race but this effect was comparatively minor. The majority of voters for whom Obama's race was a positive factor were liberals who would have voted for any Democratic presidential candidate. Increased support from blacks added only about one percentage point to Obama's totals (Stephens-Davidowitz 2012). However, Obama would not have won the 2008 election without support from black voters and other voters of color (Feagin 2012, 165).

During the 2008 election, similar sentiments were expressed in the foiled plot by white supremacists to assassinate Obama, an Obama monkey doll, Obama waffles that parody Aunt Jemima at the Christian Right Voter Summit, and an effigy of Obama hanging from trees at the University of Kentucky and George Fox University in Oregon (Associated Press 2008a; Huckabee 2008; Stan 2008). During the 2012 election, a bumper sticker displayed a racist play on words: "Don't Re-Nig in 2012 . . . Stop repeat offenders. Don't re-elect Obama!" (Keys 2012). Chief Judge Richard Cebull of the federal district court in Montana received and forwarded an email comparing Obama's conception to sex with a dog. The email read: "A little boy said to his mother; 'Mommy, how come I'm black and you're white?' His mother replied, 'Don't even go there Barack! From what I can remember about that party, you're lucky you don't bark!'"(Mears 2012). The Kansas-based Patriot Freedom Alliance posted on its website a picture describing Obama as a skunk. The photo included the caption: *"The skunk has replaced the eagle as the new symbol for the president. It is half black, it is half white, and almost everything it does, stinks"* (Stodghill 2011).

This white anxiety is also embodied in the Tea Party movement, which voters roundly rejected in the 2012 election. A key motivation of the Tea Party's agenda, as well as that of conservative Republicans, was an adamant fear of, and contempt for, Obama with the goal of making certain he was not re-elected (Burghart and Zeskind 2010; Dolan 2010; Ostroy 2010). These sentiments are generally framed in supposedly race-neutral protests assailing big government, corporate taxation, and so on, as well as infringements on individual freedom and "traditional values"(Ostroy 2010; Parker and Barreto 2013, 102–89; Tucker 2013). So-called "birthers" claimed Obama was ineligible to be president because there is no proof he was born in the United States. Hawai'i's health director said in 2008 and 2009 she had seen and verified Obama's original vital records, and birth notices in two Honolulu newspapers were published within days of Obama's birth at Kapiolani Maternity and Gynecological Hospital in Honolulu. She confirmed that Obama's name is in its alphabetical list of names of individuals born in Hawai'i, maintained in bound copies available for public view. At Obama's request, state officials eventually made an exception to a 2001 policy that prohibited anyone from getting a photocopy of an original birth certificate. They usually hand out computer-generated versions (Niesse 2011; Waggenspack 2010, 167–68).[28]

These occurrences are largely reflective of extremist, fringe elements. As has become routine in these types of incidences, several of the perpetrators apologized for the perceived insensitivity of their commentaries, which were supposedly anti-Obama (rather than racist) in motivation. Yet since the 2008 election, authorities have noticed increased hate group membership, as well as more threatening writings, Internet postings, and other activity directed at Obama than with any previous president.[29] Moreover, this white racial hysteria is illustrative of the lack of civility endemic to U.S. society, particularly in the political arena. Notwithstanding Obama's keynote address at the 2004 Democratic National Convention, in which he stated there is only one America (Obama 2004), the 2008 and 2012 national conventions provided striking portraits of what were clearly two Americas. The Democratic conventions were noticeably more diverse. The Republican conventions were largely a sea of white faces. Republicans made a strategic effort, particularly in 2012, to include as many speakers of color as possible on stage to convey a sense of racial diversity. This has become even more evident in attempts at rebranding the party in the wake of the shellacking in the 2012 election (Healy 2008).

The racial composition of the two major parties confirms this increasing racial partisanship. From 2000 to 2012, the percentage of Republicans who are white has remained relatively steady, about 87 percent. On the other hand, the percentage of Democrats who are white has dropped from 64 percent in 2000 to 55 percent in 2012. If current trends continue, in a few years the Democratic Party will be a majority-minority party (Pew Research 2012, 1–9, 14; Pew Research 2011a, 21, 38). Tesler argues that Obama's presidency has produced a renewed alignment between political preference and "old-fashioned racism," which was long thought to have disappeared in U.S. politics. This is defined as a belief in the biological inferiority of blacks and support for racial segregation and discrimination. The Obama phenomenon also taps into the new racism, which is characterized by a moral sense that blacks violate traditional U.S. values like individualism, self-reliance, the work ethic, obedience, and discipline (Tesler 2013, 110–123).

Obama's election illustrates the tremendous gains some blacks have made since the 1960s. Yet blacks overall have higher rates of unemployment, poverty, and incarceration, fewer years of education, shorter life expectancy, and overall lesser wealth and quality of life. These social indicators were exacerbated by the "Great Recession" from 2007 to 2009, which disproportionately affected blacks and Latinas/os in terms of unemployment and foreclosures (Hudson 2013; Kennedy 2011, 7–10; Pew Research 2011b, 1–32; Smith 2012, 118–20; Wingfield and Feagin 2009, 243–44). Obama's race-neutrality in this regard was apparent at the prime-time news conference marking his first one hundred days in office. A BET (Black Entertainment Television) reporter asked Obama whether targeted programs might be needed to address depression level unemployment of black and Latino men in New York City. The president avoided endorsing race-based remedies, indicating rather, that the overall success of his "Stimulus Program" will be the rising tide "that will lift all boats" (Daniels 2009; Ford 2009). Obama's plan for universal programs, such as his American Jobs Act presented on September 8, 2011 at a rare joint session of Congress, would have had measurable benefits for blacks.[30]

Yet criticism of Obama's race-neutral approach has been voiced by Rep. Maxine Waters (D-CA) of the Congressional Black Caucus (CBC). She expressed concern about Obama's persistent refusal to implement initiatives that address the depression level unemployment among blacks. The legitimacy of addressing the particularistic concerns of blacks is not in question. However, any notion that Obama would specifically target those concerns is based on misplaced expectations (Curiel 2007; Halperin and Heilemann 2013, 39; Kennedy 2011, 7–10; York 2011).[31]

In response to such criticism, in November 2011 the Obama administration released a forty-four-page report entitled "The President's Agenda and the African American Community." It highlights policies the White House says have disproportionately benefitted blacks. These include the subsidized jobs programs, Recovery Act, Earned Income Tax Credit and Child Tax Credit, mortgage-modification plans for distressed homeowners, healthcare reform, increased funding for Pell Grants, and so on. Obama's expansion of the Child Tax Credit and Earned Income Tax Credit in 2010 benefited approximately 2.2 million black families and nearly half of all black children, while extending unemployment insurance to benefit over a million blacks. The Fair Sentencing Act of 2010 ended the racial discrepancy in punishment for crimes that involve the same amounts of crack and powdered cocaine, which disproportionately affected blacks (Alter 2013, 272–75, 313; Gordy 2011; White House 2011).[32]

Obama's race-neutral stance was also previously reflected in his response to Rep. Joe Wilson's (R-SC) unprecedented outburst during the president's September 10, 2009, speech to Congress in which Wilson shouted, "You lie."

The shout followed Obama's comment that undocumented immigrants would be ineligible for federal subsidies to buy health insurance. On March 20, 2010, demonstrators descended upon the Capitol to protest the passage of healthcare reform preceding the president's speech to an assembly of House Democrats. The gathering quickly turned into abusive heckling, as members of Congress passing through Longworth House office building were subjected to epithets and even mild physical abuse. Congressional Black Caucus member, Rep. John Lewis (D-GA) said that racial epithets, including the word "nigger," were hurled at them. One congressman, Rep. Emanuel Cleaver (D-MO), said he was spat upon. The most high-profile openly gay congressman, Rep. Barney Frank (D-MA), was reportedly heckled with anti-gay chants (Kane 2010).

Former President Carter voiced the concerns shared by many Democrats that Wilson's comments, and much of the opposition to or animosity expressed toward Obama and his agenda, is attributable to racial factors notwithstanding the nation's considerable progress toward achieving greater racial equality (Koppelman 2009; Stein 2009). Obama acknowledged that individuals may view him and his policies through the prism of race. Yet he did not believe Wilson's criticism was racially motivated, but rather, based on differences with his politics or policy (IMDb 2009). Indeed, beginning with his 2008 election campaign, Obama and his advisers have carefully avoided engaging in racial concerns (Zelney 2005, 1), much less making allegations of racism against Obama, in part to silence charges that he is "playing the race card" (Koppelman 2009; Stein 2009). As has been the tradition in other presidential campaigns, Obama's team typically deployed surrogates to mediate contentious discussions dealing with racial issues (Sinclair-Chapman and Price 2008, 740). Obama's caution surrounding engagement with racial issues is not unfounded. Although Republicans voiced disapproval of Wilson's outburst, some increasingly associated Obama with radical identity politics.

Yet in David Remnick's January 27, 2014, article in the *New Yorker*, Obama displayed a surprising and seeming about-face, at least in terms of his public statements, on the topic of race. Obama said he believes race has had an impact on his political standing since the beginning of his presidency. Moreover, Obama contended that racial tensions may have weakened his popularity among white voters during the last two years. Obama stated, "There's no doubt that there's some folks who just really dislike me because they don't like the idea of a black president." Conversely, Obama stated: "Now, the flip side of it is there are some black folks and maybe some white folks who really like me and give me the benefit of the doubt precisely because I'm a black president" (Remnick 2014).

Obama's initial cautious response to the not guilty verdict in the George Zimmerman trial was criticized by some commentators as yet another example of his failure to give voice to African American grievances. He acknowledged the tragedy that Trayon's death meant for the Martin family and the nation, as well as the strong passions his death and the Zimmerman verdict elicited. But Obama stated that "we are a nation of laws, and a jury has spoken." He called for a widening of the "circle of compassion and understanding" in the nation's communities and for national reflection on gun violence (Goff 2013). Others argued Obama's response was pitched perfectly in terms of content and tone, given the necessity of making a public statement yet also honoring the constraints of his delicate and complicated role as a president who also happens to be black (Swerdlick 2013). On July 19, in response to much public criticism by commentators and urging from some of his supporters (Prince 2013), Obama gave a more forceful and unusually personal, if measured, reply to Zimmerman's acquittal at an impromptu appearance at a White House press briefing (Benjamin 2013). He stated, "You know, when Trayvon Martin was first shot, I said that this could have been my son. Another way of saying that is, Trayvon Martin could have been me 35 years ago" (O'Brien 2013). Obama mentioned further that there are few blacks, including himself, "who have not had the experience of being followed when they were shopping in a department store" (O'Brien 2013).

Obama also addressed the perils associated with being a black male in the United States in this regard. He affirmed, "There are very few African American men who haven't had the experience of walking across the street and hearing the locks click on the doors of cars ... or getting on an elevator and a woman clutching her purse nervously and holding her breath until she had a chance to get off." Moreover, Obama said, "[there] is a history of racial disparities in the application of our criminal laws ... A lot of African-American boys are painted with a broad brush ... If a white male teen was involved in the same kind of scenario ... both the outcome and the aftermath might have been different" (O'Brien 2013). Obama also spoke out directly against the stand your ground laws.

Obama's press briefing elicited praise from many individuals (Trinko 2013). These included Senator John McCain (R-AZ), who believes all states, including his own, should review their "stand your ground" laws (Volsky 2013). Others criticized Obama's briefing as race-baiting (Kaplan 2013; Morgenstern 2013); still others criticized it for not being forceful enough in denouncing white racism (Bogado 2013a; Bratu 2013; Holloway 2013; Volsky 2013). Hutchinson points out that Zimmerman's exoneration does not, however, imply justice is colorblind or law enforcement and the criminal justice system themselves maintain an intrinsic racial animus toward blacks. Neither does it suggest race is a contributing factor in these circumstances simply because the media and civil rights activists conspired to make it so (Hutchinson 2013; Roman 2013). Rather, it is a perfect case study of the "complicated relationship between explicit racism, unconscious bias, policymaking, and culture" (Sen 2013). It indicates how race is deeply, subtly, and indeed insidiously embedded in social interactions as well as institutions of the larger society and inscribed in social geography (Bogado 2013b; Hutchinson 2013; Mock 2013; Roman 2013, 1). Consequently, individuals are conditioned "not to see what really is there to be seen" (Senna 2005, 407). This obfuscates how racism takes place and also delegitimizes the necessary tools to eradicate it (Lipsitz 2011, 15, 108).

Similarly, if Rep. Wilson's comment was racially motivated, it need not be indicative of explicit or dominative racism that is more easily verified. It could be reflective of a diffuse and largely unconscious racial animus that can unwittingly lead to a lack of deference and lapse in protocol displayed toward an individual, or negative perceptions about their competence and merit, which are nevertheless thought to be racially impartial. Caruso, Mead, and Balcetis found that individuals tend to view members of their own political party more positively than members of a competing political group, which in turn influences their perceptions of a biracial candidate's skin tone.

In three studies, participants rated the representativeness of photographs of a hypothetical (Study 1) or real (Obama: Studies 2 and 3) biracial candidate. The participants were unaware that several photographs had been altered to make the candidate's skin tone either lighter or darker than it was in the original photograph. Participants whose partisanship matched that of the candidate they were evaluating consistently rated the lightened photographs as more representative of the candidate than the darkened photographs. Participants whose partisanship did not match that of the candidate showed the opposite pattern. For evaluations of Obama, the extent to which individuals rated lightened photographs as representative of him was positively correlated with their stated voting intentions and reported voting behavior in the 2008 presidential election. This effect persisted when controlling for political ideology and racial attitudes (Caruso, Mead, and Balcetis 2009, 20168–73).

CONCLUSION:
"HYPOCRITICAL" MULTIRACIALITY AND THE CRITICAL DIFFERENCE

Even the best-intentioned efforts to eradicate racial inequality will be continually thwarted as long as the nation refuses to confront and eradicate the pathologies of white racism and privilege, however subtle these phenomena may be. Steinhorn and Diggs-Brown argue this will require a willingness to take collective responsibility for the necessary "social engineering, constant vigilance, government authority, official attention to racial behavior" (Steinhorn and Diggs-Brown 1999, 222–23) in the pursuit of greater equity in the nation's political, educational, and socioeconomic spheres. These efforts must be accompanied by a more honest assessment of the factors that keep European Americans in an advantaged position, and communities of color in a disadvantaged one, not to mention a more accurate rendering of the historical, political, social, and cultural forces that put them there in the first place. And this must be achieved without internalizing any sense of "white guilt" by whites and "victimization" by people of color (Steele 1990, 48–9, 77–109).

This transformation will necessitate programmatic initiatives in the media and educational system to disabuse the nation of the illusions and falsehoods spawned by four centuries of racism. These initiatives should include a conceptualization of multiraciality as part of U.S. history and national consciousness. That said, the impulses behind and implications of the celebration of multiraciality can themselves be mixed. For example, national racial and cultural identities in Latin America have been officially articulated as hybrid, multiracial, and egalitarian (Figure 1a). Yet they have been hypocritically multiracial ideologies based on what Bonilla-Silva refers to as "colorblind racism" (Bonilla-Silva 2006, 25). This has become a means of erasing racial distinctions that have deliberately obscured subtle hegemonies while deflecting public attention and policy away from tackling continuing racial inequities (Figure 1b) (Daniel 2006, 148).

Yet the *concept* of multiraciality, when based on egalitarian (e.g., "critical") premises, has the potential to serve as an "intellectual weapon" and "theoretical wedge" (Zack 1994, 99) in the pursuit of "colorblind antiracism" (Daniel 2012, 150). This is not to suggest that a multiracial identity, in and of itself, is the solution to racial inequality and heralds a post-racial social order (King and Smith 2009, 207–14). Any such notion is dangerously misguided and naïve. Rather, it posits critical multiraciality as a *template* for engaging in transgressive *education* (Williams, Nakashima, Kich, and Daniel 1996, 359–79) or *pedagogy* (Jolivétte 2012, 8, 28) and *praxis* that interrogates racial essentialism. This would provide the basis for more porous and inclusive collective subjectivities across all racial groups, including multiracials, which facilitate building other issue-based coalitions. The ensuing shared sense of community would embrace racial and ethnic diversity, while simultaneously working toward an intersectional politics that recognizes the complexity of various types of oppression and how each feeds on the others in order to thrive (Hutchins and Kaahumanu 1991, xxii–iv).

This posits a post-racist, if not post-racial, social order where racial distinctions would no longer determine, or at least have considerably less significance in determining, individuals' social location in terms of wealth, power, privilege, and prestige. Such politics would create a constructive and beneficial relationship between the different groups, one marked by mutual respect, interdependence, a balance of power, and a shared commitment to community and nation (Steinhorn and Diggs-Brown, 1999), as well as the greater humanity (and ultimately a more encompassing "human" identity). This would be a necessary component of a genuinely post-racial society (Iweala 2008; Smith and King 2009).[33]

Critical multiraciality could further this objective by opening up a long-overdue conversation about humanity's genetic comity, as well as shared ancestral and cultural connections, which have been ignored, obscured, and erased by several hundred years of Eurocentric thought. Indeed, given that humans first evolved in eastern Africa millennia ago, everyone shares this universal heritage that has been bequeathed to the modern world. This also means that everyone in the United States is in some sense an African-descent American, apart from those individuals who are also descendants of the West African diaspora associated with the Atlantic slave trade from the sixteenth to the nineteenth century.

Between 90,000 and 180,000 years ago, populations from an earlier African diaspora spread throughout Africa, Asia, Europe, and the Pacific; perhaps as early as 30,000 years ago, but at least as recently as 15,000 years ago, they migrated to the Americas. As they adapted to various environments they evolved into geographical populations displaying differences in various bodily features. Some of the externally visible features—skin color, hair, and facial morphology—are commonly referred to as "racial traits." Although all humans share 99.9 percent of their genes, these physical differences reflect 0.1 percent of some of the differences in genetic information that are transmitted through one's ancestors. So there are populations that, taken as aggregates, exhibit higher incidences of particular genetic and physical traits than do other populations, taken as aggregates.

Nevertheless, the boundaries delineating populations have always been eroded by contact—through migration, trade, and war. This phenomenon was shaped by new ideologies and practices that accompanied European colonial expansion beginning in the sixteenth century. Indeed, the Americas have been the site of unprecedented combinations of indigenous peoples, Africans, and Europeans, and immigrants from across the globe. Yet racial blending has existed from time immemorial. Therefore, although we recognize certain genetic markers and physical traits as delineating population aggregates as different from one another, in fact, a "multiracial" lineage is the norm rather than the exception, regardless of one's identity. If you trace back twenty generations each individual has 1,048,576 ancestors (CBS 2007b; Olson 2006). If we trace back further, the number of ancestors, as well as the myriad possibilities in terms of their "racial" composition, is staggering. This should awaken everyone to the fact that they share the gray liminal space between the extremes of black and white. Moreover, it would be a critical part of the foundation upon which to create the more perfect union that has eluded the United States throughout its history.

Notes

Earlier versions of this chapter appeared in *The Black Scholar* 39, no. 1 (Fall/Winter 2009), 51–59, and *Barack Obama and the Biracial Factor: The Battle for a New American Majority*, ed. Andrew J. Jolivétte (Bristol, UK: Polity Press, 2012), 21–59.

1. U.S. attitudes toward the offspring of unions between blacks and other groups of color (e.g., Native Americans) have varied. More often than not, these individuals have been subject to the one-drop rule.
2. Houston Baker was less sanguine about Obama's speech. He states:

Sen. Obama's race speech at the National Constitution Center, draped in American flags, was reminiscent of the Parthenon concluding scene of Robert Altman's Nashville: a bizarre moment of mimicry, aping Martin Luther King Jr., while even further distancing himself from the real, economic, religious and political issues so courageously articulated by King from a Birmingham jail. In brief, Obama's speech was a pandering disaster that threw, once again, his pastor under the bus." "What Should Obama Do About Rev. Jeremiah Wright?" (Salon.com. 2008)

Utley and Heyse in this volume argue that Obama's speech was an appropriate and successful response to a political-personal crisis. He negotiated the controversy surrounding his personal relationship with Rev. Wright by acknowledging racial disparities in the U.S. without placing blame for those disparities. Accordingly, Obama maintained a post-racial rhetorical stance that appealed to extremely diverse audiences. They argue, however, that the speech failed to accurately represent a racially differentiated United States. By sanitizing the nation's histories of chattel slavery and racism, Obama's speech reified many harmful racial tropes.

3. The Declaration of Interdependence was a movement spearheaded in the 1940s by Pulitzer Prize-winning philosopher Will Durant. A primary goal was to reduce racial hostility by promoting human tolerance, fellowship, and mutual respect. Will Durant Foundation, http://www.willdurant.com/interdependence.htm.

4. Sharpton stated he has strategically underplayed his hand, avoiding public appearances with Obama during the election campaigns since it could be used by his opponents to discredit him. However, Sharpton has been to the White House at least eight times since Obama's 2008 election. Todd Boyd, a professor of African American studies at the University of Southern California, sees a cynical ploy by Obama to use Sharpton as a foil to Jackson, embracing what he considers the lesser of two evils (Samuels and Adler 2010).

5. Yet, since 2008 the Obama administration has worked closely with the National Association for the Advancement of Colored People (NAACP) under the leadership of Ben Jealous. The organization expanded its focus to include immigration, gay rights, and voting rights, which have been among Obama's leading priorities. Jealous was instrumental in helping ex-felons, many of them African American, obtain voting rights. Jealous and his colleagues thus had ready access to Obama, which opened the door for the organization to raise money to dig out of a gaping financial hole. The group was criticized for working so closely with the Obama Administration that it was unable to effectively criticize the latter ("NAACP President Ben Jealous Abruptly Announces His Resignation," *Your Black World*, September 8, 2013. http://www.yourblackworld.net/2013/09/black-news/naacp-president-ben-jealous-abruptly-announces-his-resignation/).

6. One also hears echoes of Senator Barbara Jordon's "We the People" speech, which she delivered at the 1974 Watergate Hearings concerning the impeachment of President Nixon, as well as her keynote address at the 1967 Democratic Convention.

7. Both tactics may be employed by anyone seeking inclusion in the white male-dominated mainstream of society. Also, they are applicable to aggrieved groups besides blacks.

8. In a 2010 letter obtained by the Associated Press, Wright told a group seeking to raise funds for African relief that his pleas to release frozen funds for use in earthquake-ravaged Haiti would likely be ignored. "No one in the Obama administration will respond to me, listen to me, talk to me or read anything that I write to them." He said he is "toxic" to the Obama administration and that President Obama "threw me under the bus" (Schapiro 2010).

9. Obama asked that his wife, Michelle, be allowed to speak on his behalf.

10. Jeffries conducted in-depth interviews with multiracial-identified college students to determine their perceptions of Barack Obama. Interviews examined the influence of race on Obama's identity management and political career, the relationship between Obama and respondents' multiracial identity, and Obama's impact on U.S. race relations. Notwithstanding the fact that Obama does not embrace a multiracial identity, respondents held favorable opinions of him and respected his right to identify as black. Though sometimes

deeply disappointed in that choice, they believed emphasis on Obama's blackness, rather than his multiraciality, is the outcome of personal choice and political pressure. That said, they emphasized that racism remains a significant factor in Obama's career and in the United States more generally (Jeffries 2012, 49–79, 183–200).

11. This comment was not unanimously considered positive. Some individuals viewed it as a re-articulation of previous pathological images of multiracials as social misfits and genetically inferior (Fram 2008; Graham 2008).
12. The tradition among the black McCains is that they have biological ties to the white McCains. The latter say they are unaware of this connection (Blackmon 2008).
13. Most respondents designated Obama with multiracial-identifiers. Small percentages responded with "white," "none of the above," and "not sure." Blacks upheld the one-drop rule. See Johnson 2010; Williams 2006.
14. This trend is named after Democratic candidate Tom Bradley, a former black mayor of Los Angeles, who lost the 1982 California gubernatorial election after leading in the polls. Exit polls indicated Bradley leading by a wide margin. He thought there would be an early election night. However, Bradley lost to Republican candidate George Deukmejian. Subsequently, other black candidates who were comfortably ahead in polls lost or narrowly won the elections. For example, in the 1989 Virginia gubernatorial race, Democrat L. Douglas Wilder, who is black, won by less than half of 1 percent over Marshall Coleman, the Republican candidate, who is white. However, pre-election exit polls showed Wilder on average with a comfortable 9 percent lead over Coleman. Other elections cited as possible indications of the Bradley effect include the 1983 and 1989 mayoral elections, respectively, in Chicago and New York City (Associated Press 2008b).
15. A record number of deportations during Obama's first administration have left many immigrants, largely people of color, and others ambivalent about his policies (Shalal-Esa 2012). Obama appointed individuals of color and women to important governmental positions during his first administration, and many of his top advisers and staffers in the White House are women. Obama's cabinet has been largely composed of white males (Lawrence 2013; K. Liptak 2013).
16. See also Rondilla and Spickard 2005.
17. Blacks and other communities of color also continue to maintain a strong positive sense of identity and differentiation as collective subjectivities, which can serve as the basis for projects in the form of egalitarian pluralism (Figure 1.d).
18. Data on Latinas/os are particularly instructive. The report "How Race Counts for Hispanic Americans" indicates that white and black Hispanics—as well as Hispanics who say that they are "some other race"—work different jobs, earn different levels of pay, and reside in segregated neighborhoods in terms of skin color. The report indicates that Latinas/os who identified as white on the 2000 census (nearly 50 percent) had the highest incomes and lowest rates of unemployment and poverty and tended to live near communities of non-Hispanic whites. The 2.7 percent who described themselves as black, most of them from the Caribbean, had lower incomes and higher rates of poverty than the other groups—despite having a higher level of education. Among Latinas/os who described themselves as "some other race" (47 percent), earnings and levels of poverty and unemployment fell between black and white members of their ethnic group (Arce, Murguía, and Frisbie 1987, 19–33; Fears 2003; Gómez 2008, 193–204; Telles and Murguía 1990, 682–96).

19. This also had implications for Latinas/os, Asian Americans, and Native Americans, especially in Texas and the Southwest, where similar practices were in place.
20. Based on visual observations, the media identified five of the jurors as white. One, Juror B29, was initially identified as black or Hispanic. After the trial, it was revealed she is Puerto Rican. All of the jurors were female (Schneider and Hightower 2013a).
21. According to some reports, police in Florida routinely designate Latinas/os as whites if they do not display very dark skin even if they have other non-European features (Dahl 2012).
22. Racial profiling involves stereotyping individuals, typically by law enforcement, based on their perceived racial group membership as a key factor in determining whether to engage in investigation and enforcement. It disproportionately affects people of color and automatically ascribes criminal behavior to them without evidence justifying such attributions.
23. This can include unlawfully or forcefully entering of occupied vehicles (or carjackings).
24. As a counter to claims that Zimmerman's actions were racially motivated it has been pointed out that he has Afro-Peruvian relatives (and is of Afro-Peruvian descent through his mother's side of the family), as well as African American friends and associates, including black mentees (Yawson 2013). Also, the year before Martin's shooting, he participated in a citizen forum at the Sanford City Hall to protest the beating of a black homeless man by the son of a white Sanford police officer (Thuman 2012). Some voice forensic and audio experts disagree with allegations that Zimmerman used the racial epithet "fucking coons" commonly referring to blacks but rather "fucking punks," which he uttered under his breath during his recorded conversation with the police dispatcher leading up to the shooting (Novogrod, Winter, and Connor 2013). Yet Zimmerman displayed a pattern of making 911 calls over several years, several of them about "suspicious" black men (Lipton 2013). Earlier statements on his old MySpace account also provide ample evidence that he is capable of expressing sentiments that could hardly be described as race-neutral (McNally 2013; Political Blind Spot 2013).
25. The NAACP was formed in 1909. Its concerns encompass the civil rights of all Americans, but it has historically been considered a black organization invested in the African American struggle.
26. In a criminal trial, a not guilty verdict means the prosecution failed to prove its case beyond a reasonable doubt, not that a defendant is innocent. An individual may be acquitted of a crime but found civilly culpable in a civil case regarding that same crime because civil cases have a lower burden of proof simply based on the preponderance of evidence. Zimmerman could face a wrongful-death civil suit from Martin's parents. They would need to show he was culpable simply by the preponderance of the evidence rather than beyond a reasonable doubt. A successful outcome would allow a judge to place a lien on any proceeds from materials (e.g., book, TV, or movie deals) relating to Martin's death, causing them to be distributed to the victim's family (Reid 2013).
27. Oprah Winfrey was one of Obama's most ardent high-profile African American and celebrity campaigners in 2008. Winfrey has not been openly critical of the Obama administration. Yet she has reportedly become less enthusiastic about the White House given that the open communication with and access to the president, which she anticipated and supposedly was promised, has never materialized (Fitzgerald 2013). Two of Obama's harshest black critics, who believe he has failed to address black concerns, are commentator Tavis Smiley and Union Theological Seminary professor Cornel West although both believe the

election of Obama has been a great symbolic victory (Carnell 2013). In a 2009 interview West remarked: "Symbolically, black man breaks through makes you want to break dance ... because the hopes that were generated and the call for change, and then we end up with this recycled neo-liberalism. There's no fundamental change at all" (McNally 2009).

West is also among those individuals who have become disheartened by, if not disillusioned with, the Obama administration's track record on human rights and civil liberties. This includes what are perceived as increasing dragnet-like domestic and international surveillance policies (Greenwald 2013; McCoy 2013). Obama asserted he has the authority to carry out extrajudicial killings of U.S. citizens if they are believed to be "senior operational leaders" of al-Qaida or "an associated force" even if there is no intelligence indicating they are engaged in an active plot to attack the United States. The directive recognizes some limits on the authority it lays out. Critics argue that the limits are elastic, vaguely defined, and could easily be manipulated (Isikoff 2013). Other criticism has been directed at Obama's failure to prosecute and impose meaningful punishments on those financial institutions whose unethical decisions and management were architects of the recent financial meltdown—or even use his unilateral power to propose stringent Wall Street regulations (Sirota 2013). Some have observed an increasing and ominous intertwining of U.S. politics with business interests (Chomsky 2013).

28. Spickard in this volume points out that the birthers are either ignorant of or conveniently ignore U.S. constitutional law, which automatically makes Obama a U.S. citizen, even if he was born outside the United States, because his mother was a U.S. citizen (Spickard 2013,).
29. Obama has been protected by an increasingly over-stretched Secret Service. According to the Secret Service, Obama is the most threatened person in the United States, regardless of political party, and the most threatened president in U.S. history (Patterson 2012; E. Sullivan 2008).
30. This proposal never became law because Republicans opposed it as another "failed stimulus" that would not boost the economy.
31. According to Halperin and Heilemann, Obama reportedly has equal parts discomfort with, if not dislike for, the identity politics and agenda of the CBC as with those of the Tea Party notwithstanding the fact that the former has remained among Obama's staunchest supporters (Halperin and Heilemann 2013, 39).
32. Since the act was not retroactive, its provisions are not applicable to individuals convicted and sentenced before it was signed into law. Currently, approximately 30,000 men and women, representing roughly 15 percent of the entire federal prison population, are serving time for crack cocaine offenses. More than 80 percent of those inmates are black (Berman and Protass 2013).
33. Despite the lack of consensus on the term "post-racial," MSNBC's Chris Matthews encapsulated a common perception of its meaning in his comments about Obama's January 27, 2010, State of the Union address. Matthews stated he "forgot" Obama was black. In other words, it was noteworthy to Matthews that a black president was addressing a room of mostly whites and how the issue of race was noticeably absent as compared to the time when he was growing up in 1950s and 1960s when racial divisions were pervasive and ever-present (Associated Press 2010a).

2. BY CASTA, COLOR WHEEL, AND COMPUTER GRAPHICS

Visual Representations of Racially Mixed People

GREG CARTER

TODAY, VISUAL REPRESENTATIONS OF RACIALLY MIXED PEOPLE REFLECT a general level of acceptance greater than past periods in U.S. history. Marketing and casting executives use ambiguous-appearing bodies to reach more segments of the public, and to evoke positive notions about diversity. These images seem to praise ambiguity and the disruptive potential of mixed race. However, some reflect a long-standing obsession with percentages of racial makeup, offering a rich field for analysis. From the eighteenth century to the present, through different media, visual representations of racially mixed people in the Americas have continued a tradition of organizing bodies into stable racial hierarchies.

I begin in colonial Mexico, with the *casta* ("caste") paintings that titillated art collectors in Spain with images of mixture in the new world. These works depicted combinations of Spanish, indigenous, and African people in the distant colony. Later, eugenicist C. B. Davenport, a believer in the corrosive effects of racial mixing, studied skin complexions in Louisiana, Jamaica, and Bermuda. The book showcasing his findings in 1913 featured photos of his subjects with discrete fractions revealing their racial makeup. For their fall 1993 special issue, the staff at *Time* magazine used arbitrary percentages and Morph 2.0 software to create a cover star that lionized racial mixing, but also expressed deep ambivalence about white demographic minoritization. Most recently, Shepard Fairey's Barack Obama poster deployed certainty in a different way. By 2008, Obama's parentage was common knowledge, so there was no need to reveal it. However, the red, white, and blue spaces exist within distinct boundaries, a visual sign that negated Obama's mixture.

The actors in each of these cases differ greatly, spanning various contexts over three centuries. The greatest shift in the United States has been the rise of "colorblind racism" in the decades after the civil rights legislation of the 1960s. As Eduardo Bonilla-Silva writes, "In contrast to race relations in the Jim Crow period, however, racial practices that reproduce racial inequality in contemporary America are: (1) increasingly covert; (2) embedded in normal operations of institutions; (3) void of direct racial terminology; and (4) invisible to most whites" (Bonilla-Silva 2001, 48). Popular culture, as "a set of cultural practices that define American nationality—who 'real Americans' are in any given historical moment," does the same (Lee 1999, 6). The public readily censures hate speech, but systematic racial inequality remains. Similarly, describing mixture as a boon to the nation is common, but most prefer "separate but equal families," citing romantic individualism as a justification for staying within racial bounds (Moran 2001, 1–16). In other words, they praise ambiguity but prefer certainty. These developments complicate recent representations of racially mixed people, producing a rift between the periods before and after the end of legal discrimination, which I mark with the Supreme Court's *Loving v. Virginia* decision. My cases before 1967 operated in situations where the protection of white racial purity was explicit. Those of recent memory may openly praise mixture, diversity, and hybridity, but the desire to protect racial purity remains.

However, they all demonstrate how discourse around mixture in the Americas strives to stabilize racial identities by disaggregating backgrounds. This has happened visually, but also verbally, through the use of accompanying text. Regardless of the medium used to discipline racial mixture, they have been less than one hundred percent effective. Varieties of liaisons, changes in scientific mores, and the practices of self-identification constantly produce destabilizing matters to deal with. I provide this historical analysis to counter the notion that mixed-race visibility is a new phenomenon, and that their appearance signifies the dawn of a "post-racial" society. Ultimately, the ideologies continue to this day, even if acceptance of mixture has concealed them.

CASTA PAINTING:
THE BEGINNING OF MIXED-RACE REPRESENTATIONS

As Gary Nash wrote in "The Hidden History of Mestizo America," racial mixture has been a shaping force in the new world, even if the study of it has sidelined the array of relationships it produced. Taking place throughout the Americas, interracial intimacy generated a visual language in the

Spanish colonies as well as the Portuguese, French, and British. Regardless of the ruling nation, all of the colonies developed a system of white supremacy. In the United States, the distinction between whites worthy of privilege and all others became the most prominent. In Latin America, labels for different kinds of mixture between European colonizers, indigenous people, and African slaves arose. Instead of a dyad of white versus nonwhite, their system was more of a spectrum, appreciating many shades between white and black. Regardless, this pigmentocracy benefited those of greater European descent. Some of this verbal and visual discourse remains in Latin American vernacular to this day (Nash 1995, 941–64).

Casta paintings served three general functions: First, they documented racial mixing. Second, they illustrated the distinctive character of the colony. Third, they served as mementos for elites visiting there. It is possible that this art form began in 1711 with a portrait of a mulatto male and another of a mulatto female that belonged together. The colony's regulations regarding who could produce religious artifacts led to an abundance of artists working in the secular realm, and an increase in commissioned of portraits. Through the following decades, the style transformed, reflecting the increasing urban population, shifting marriage patterns, and changes in the mercantilist relationship between New Spain and the Bourbon ascendancy in the mother country. For them, the paintings illustrated varieties of *raza*, a term with the same roots as the English "race." However, they thought of it more as "lineage," once again emphasizing the value of Spanish descent (Carrera 2003, 1–43, García Saiz 1989; Ilona Katzew 2004, 1–63).

A quick comparison of extant samples could lead to the conclusion that the paintings became more sophisticated over time. However, a better assessment would be that their visual and verbal conventions changed with the colony more broadly. By the mid-eighteenth century, the standard form had taken root, usually consisting of sixteen tiles within a large frame, each featuring a certain racial combination. Each showed a male of one racial group, a female of another, and their child. At top were the combinations between the Spanish and the two other primary groups and between the Spanish and the first generation of mixed offspring. The remaining eleven cells varied in order, but they usually displayed the continued mixture between the already mixed. None of those remaining featured the *pura* ("pure") Spanish, and the positions farther down the piece feature more abject offspring. Across eighteenth century variations of this art, the heathen indigenous population was usually the last. Degrees of Spanish descent were a major preoccupation for the colonials, and those with more took great pride in that *calidad*, a term that translated as "quality." The term also referred to noble standing; these meanings were one and the same for the elites.

Through the decades of their popularity, the canvases varied in size. Sometimes one frame contained all sixteen, and sometimes each stood independently. Most loose cells dispersed through the years, making complete sets a rarity today. The most effective paintings would make each of the forty-eight characters distinctive through recognizable visual signs in four areas: skin color, clothing, accessories, and mannerisms. The lighter one's complexion, the more civilized one was. Coupling *calidad* with gender, the Spanish character was always male in the first five panels. The European style of their clothing showed their higher status, just as folk and indigenous styles of the others communicated theirs. Their possessions did the same, with the elite handling musical instruments, writing, or laying hands on their children, and the lower classes laboring in the market, the home, or the field. Lastly, the way the figures interacted expressed associations regarding both genealogy and gender.

The *casta* paintings provided written words with the images, naming the parents and children within each cell. Along with making figural statements about the racial hierarchy in colonial Mexico, the paintings named sixteen possible combinations of the first three generations of mixture, giving their recipes (Mörner 1967, 58):

> *Español and india beget mestizo*
> *Mestizo and española beget castizo*
> *Castizo and española beget español*
> *Española and negro beget mulato*
> *Española and mulato beget morisco*
> *Morisco and español beget albino*
> *Español and albino beget torna-atrás*
> *Indio and torna-atrás woman beget lobo*
> *Lobo and india beget zambaigo*
> *Zambaigo and india beget cambujo*
> *Cambujo and mulata beget albarasado*
> *Albarasado and mulata beget barcino*
> *Barcino and mulata beget coyote*
> *Coyote woman and indio beget chamiso*
> *Chamisa and mestizo beget coyote mestizo*
> *Coyote mestizo and mulata beget ahí te estás*

To a twenty-first-century English speaker, these names may seem nonsensical, but within their own times the meanings of these terms were part of the vernacular. This was especially true for the first seven, which appeared in everyday documents and conversations. While these were uniform, artists often differed on the other nine combinations. Similarly, just as *mulatto* subsumed *quadroon* and *octoroon* in the United States, *mulata*, *zambo*, and *mestizo* often covered specialty terms naming the more complex mixes in colonial Mexico. The conventions of the *casta* paintings called for sixteen to be present, even if some had minimal presence in the real world. Remarkably, these forms influenced later representations of mixed race in the United States, even without a direct, intellectual connection.

C. B. DAVENPORT: MILTON BRADLEY TOYS AS TOOLS FOR EUGENICS

Obsession with racial makeup was prevalent north of the border as well, even if the prominent white or not-white dyad reduced stations to just two. The meanings of race, mixture, and freedom were in flux during the period following the Revolutionary War. Perspectives on mixture reflected attitudes towards the other topics; for example, antipathy towards mixture meant antipathy towards freedom for the racially mixed. Defense of slavery meant conscribing mixed offspring to the status of their nonwhite parents. As the question of slavery became more contentious during the antebellum period, scientists defending the institution preoccupied themselves with discerning mulattoes. Defining blackness was central in four areas: First, it determined citizenship for individuals; only those who qualified as free white men could claim it. Second, as the Constitution limited the powers of the Southern plantation states by counting slaves as three-fifths a person, counting chattel determined congressional seats. Third, since offspring of slave owners could not claim their parents' estates, a strict color line protected property. Lastly, rules dictating whether one was born into slavery depended on how easily one inherited blackness from their parents. Racial mixture had always complicated all of these, and ethnologists like Samuel Morton, Louis Agassiz, and Josiah Nott relied on several ideologies to disentangle its effect. Primary was the notion that humanity consisted of different species, and procreation between them was unnatural and repugnant. Even when the continued profligacy of mulattoes showed that whites and blacks were of the same species, believers in hybrid degeneracy argued that the offspring were physically and mentally unstable; black characteristics could reappear in future generations; and mixture weakened society as a whole. It would benefit all to preserve slavery, prevent mixture, and enforce the one-drop rule (Gossett 1997, 54–83, Morton 1847, 39–50, Nott 1843; Stanton 1960, 54–81).

These beliefs withstood, even though emancipation made the counting of slaves moot. The racial aspects of social Darwinism and eugenics picked up where proslavery scientists left off, prescribing white supremacy. While social Darwinists suggested that hands-off policies would weed out the less desirable, American and British eugenicists advocated anti-miscegenation laws, sterilization, and immigration limitations to move nations to a higher level of development. According to Francis Galton, human civilization had thwarted the mechanisms of natural selection, allowing the less fit to pull societies towards a dysgenic state. This racialist work gained popular acceptance; for example Lothrop Stoddard's *The Rising Tide of Color* appeared as a conversation piece in F. Scott Fitzgerald's *The Great Gatsby*, and Madison Grant's *The Passing of the Great Race* was a major influence on Adolf Hitler's racial thought. Many geneticists like Charles B. Davenport held on to the idea of hybrid degeneracy, while a few like William E. Castle, who had introduced Mendel's ideas on heredity to the United States, argued that racial mixing could produce superior offspring. In between were many who could apply hybrid vigor to corn, mice, and livestock, but never humans (Castle 1903, 396–506; Castle 1926, 16–19; Davenport 1928, 225–38; Davenport 1930, 501–502; Fitzgerald 1925, 12–13; Kevles 1995, 41–57).

In 1913, Davenport published *Heredity of Skin Color in Negro-White Crosses*, a privately funded project investigating complexions of racially mixed people. Davenport had one research assistant who recorded subjects' parentage in distinct fractions and measured their complexions. He chose Bermuda and Jamaica, rather than the Southern states because "all matings of blacks and whites are illegal and the genealogies of 'colored' people are usually either difficult to obtain or else unreliable" (Davenport and Danielson 1913, 1). (He also included data regarding a few families in Louisiana.) Davenport had hoped to prove the theory of hybrid degeneracy through rigorous quantitative methods. Most remarkable was his methodology, which utilized a children's game of the day. In addition to recording subjects' racial makeup, his assistant compared skin color using a Milton Bradley color wheel, a toy that taught the basics of color theory. To do this, they asked subjects to reveal a light patch of skin on the upper arm and matched it as well as they could to the color wheel's combinations of red, blue, and yellow.

The resulting report, published by the Carnegie Institution of Washington, is truly fantastic. As Werner Sollors, scholar of ethnic literature, wrote, *Heredity of Skin Color in Negro-White Crosses* "looks like it was invented in a novel by Ishmael Reed or Charles Johnson" (Sollors 1997, 135). The first one hundred pages are full of charts, genealogies, and combinations of black (N), red (R), yellow (Y), and white (W). It used terms that have lost favor in recent decades, including *hybrid*, *miscegenation*, and *Negro*. They contribute to the uncanny yet familiar feeling the book gives.

Black and white photos of some of the families occupied the pages after the main body of the report. The parents and children all sat together in their everyday clothes. A few of the snapshots displayed just a couple members. Most were larger groups, with the largest being the some of the "F" family of Bermuda, with seventeen members across two generations. Covering each of these pages were sheets of translucent paper that overlaid outlines over the figures in the photographs. This allowed coding of the individuals without cluttering the reproductions. Flipping through its pages gives an experience perverting W. E. B. Du Bois's concept of "the veil." Rather than gaining the "sense of always looking at one's self through the eyes of others, of measuring one's soul by the tape of a world that looks on in amused contempt and pity" (Du Bois and Hayes Edwards 2007, 6), turning the overlay gives two versions of how Davenport saw the subjects: either impersonal labels, or poor rural families, informal yet uncomfortable, obliging to gather for a picture.

Rather than prove the threat mixture posed, the data led to three conclusions: First, the heredity of skin color came from both parents. Second, there was no evidence that dark skin would reappear after generations of mixture. Third, mulattoes were prolific. Davenport listed these in the section, "Summary of Conclusions." Even having dispelled long-standing myths about racial mixing, he dedicated little attention to the significance of these results. As with other American eugenicists who made such discoveries, he resisted taking any position that could credit minorities (Davenport and Danielson, 46–47).

THE NEW FACE OF AMERICA:
THE HAZARDS OF COVER STARDOM

During the social movements of the twentieth century, other minority groups followed African Americans in creating collective identities built on racial pride, unity, and strategic essentialism. Likewise, mass action, litigation, and executive intervention became priorities for minority groups seeking progress. "Latino" and "Asian American" solidified in the 1970s, reflecting the government's acknowledgment of the disadvantages they had faced. While these umbrella ethnicities attempted to smooth out matters of identity, they also made diverse collections of people monoracial. During the 1980s and 1990s, multiculturalism not only elevated minority experiences, but also led to a pigeonholing of race, ethnicity, and culture.

Along with the Gallup polls indicating a higher acceptance of interracial marriage, Americans have expressed greater acceptance of other ambiguities that racial mixing brought into being. However, three centuries of racial thinking that relied on firm categories conditioned them into needing to know each other's racial identity in order to process them. Since racialization by origin, appearance, and custom has exerted such a force on life in the United States, knowing a person's race can be a way to understand their background, their tastes, and their priorities. More often than not, though, it requires making generalizations. What one understands as white, black, Hispanic/Latina/o, Indian, or Asian is the product of their own perspective, which has limitations. Members of any of these groups can recount exchanges in which someone has made presumptions about them because of their physical appearance. On the one hand, these signature experiences that have risen to cliché reveal that particular individuals are ill-equipped to understand the experiences of others. But on the other, these trivial encounters reveal how deep racialization influences us.

The most prevalent of these for racially mixed people is the "What are you?" moment, in which a new acquaintance asks for one's racial background immediately upon meeting. Since physical appearance persists as the primary way Americans discern racial identity, the ambiguity of a racially mixed person can produce a mystery for many. In turn, this produces the wish to solve the mystery. The most eager of these new acquaintances holds racial identity as the primary way to understand another, and the question becomes a mystery to solve, and receiving an answer is very satisfying. The mystery is exciting, but the solution is what they really want. More often than not, the "What are you?" moment comes from a benign wish to get to know an ambiguous-looking person better. The speaker may consider blended features to be exotic and stories of mixed backgrounds especially interesting. It is always reductive, which assumes that one's makeup is the whole of one's identity. It is also dehumanizing, requiring that a mixed person justify their existence as an object. Often, the question comes out of context, with a jarring effect. Sometimes it comes right after learning one's name (or even before), revealing that the speaker cannot proceed without knowing the answer to the question (Bradshaw 1992, 77–88; Daniel 2002, 93–154; Gaskins 1999, 3–12; O'Hearn 1998, vii–xiv; Root, 1996, 3–14).

In this survey of visual representations, the reception of celebrities is useful. In the 1980s, various mixed figures achieved nationwide recognition. Figures like Lisa Bonet, Lenny Kravitz, and Mariah Carey appeared in magazines and on television. It became de rigueur for them to announce their parentage and in the press introducing them to the public. While it was possible for these figures to refuse, or to announce an alternative way to process their identities, they never did. This is because, while Americans praised ambiguity, they preferred certainty; they put public figures through the "What are you?" moment just as they did regular mixed folk. In general, Americans have settled on monoracial ways of understanding racially mixed people, rather than adopt more complex paradigms that appreciate the ambiguities they initially praise. Even though laws against interracial intimacy were a memory, acceptance surpassed past levels, and mixed figures were more visible than ever, the tensions between stabilization of racial identity and defense of racial mixing have remained relevant.

The fall 1993 cover of *Time* magazine featured one of the most famous representations of a mixed-race American. This special issue on immigration presented the bust of a young adult woman with brown eyes and hair, who smiled to the reader. The text read, "Take a good look at this woman. She was created by a computer from a mix of several races. What you see is a remarkable preview of ... The New Face of America: How Immigrants Are Shaping the World's First Multicultural Society" (*Time*, Fall 1993). Inside, *Time*'s managing editor revealed the tool that made her possible: the computer-generated image (CGI) software, Morph 2.0. He called her "a symbol of the future, multiethnic face of America" (Gaines, 2), then divulged her genealogy (ibid.):

A combination of the racial and ethnic features of the women used to produce the chart [at the center of the magazine, which places seven men and seven women of distinct ethnic backgrounds at each axis], she is: 15% Anglo-Saxon, 17.5% Middle Eastern, 17.5% African, 7.5% Asian, 35% Southern European and 7.5% Hispanic. As onlookers watched the image of our new Eve begin to appear on the computer screen, several staff members promptly fell in love. Said one: "It really breaks my heart that she doesn't exist." We sympathize with our lovelorn colleagues, but even technology has its limits. This is a love that must forever remain unrequited."

Anyone adept at genealogy could recognize these fractions as preposterous. How does someone end up with percentages like these? This write-up, along with the cover image, another CGI tour de force at the center of the magazine, and the context of the magazine's articles made this the example par excellence of the imagined mixed-race American. However, just because mixed race became a cover story does not mean racial thinking had progressed; it simply meant that it had joined the ranks of topics that were viable to sell magazines. After all, the previous issue featured downsizing and the following featured Billy Graham.

At the center of the magazine was a chart with seven women from various ethnic groups across the top and seven men from the same groups along the side—what I call "The Miscegenation Matrix." It allowed readers to pick racial types they identified with and imagine producing children with a man or woman of some other. Alternatively, exploring the spread was like visualizing another pair of adults racially different from oneself copulate. The choice of racial types subscribed to typological categories of past racial science, limiting many people to their physical features; the labels asserted that *this* was what Middle Easterners, Italians, Africans, Vietnamese, Anglo-Saxons, Chinese, and Hispanics looked like. The young men and women all had the same facial expression, as well as unremarkable hairstyles and body types.

The article accompanying the chart, "Rebirth of a Nation, Computer Style," explained how the staff created these faces, using Morph 2.0 to find a medium between points on each source face. Of physical features, eyes, skin color, and neck shape were the most crucial in producing a successful blend. Most of the "morphies" were fifty-fifty combinations between their two progenitors, but in some cases the designers used more of one feature than another to create a face that complied with notions of masculinity and femininity. The author joked, "One of our tentative unions produced a distinctly feminine face—sitting atop a muscular neck and hairy chest. Back to the mouse on that one" ("Rebirth of a Nation, Computer Style," *Time*, Fall 1993). This was an admission that their process involved conscious exclusions. Like many media producers, they described their work in terms emphasizing aesthetics, but these choices were never neutral, no matter how naïve they were. They produced faces that had no personalities, experiences, or histories that real people share with their ancestors. These were free of any struggles to come to the country, the day-to-day difficulties as minorities in the United States, or the challenges that arose when two disparate people entered into a relationship.

Time's grid replaced *casta* paintings' display of wealth with hygienic fitness. Otherwise, the concerns remained the same as in eighteenth-century casta paintings and in 1993's "Rebirth of a Nation, Computer Style": obsession with race, prurient voyeurism, and making sense of changes in diversity. The Miscegenation Matrix lacked the racial names for each of the forty-nine combinations, as well as the background, clothing, or occupations. But the homogeneity of their look made the labels unnecessary. Instead, these naked, young, and fit bodies symbolized the perpetuation of centrist values. Rather than appear in the field, villa, or wilderness, they appeared before a blank background, doing nothing. Perhaps the blankness was a conception of the blank palate of imagination. More likely, it suggested that they were *tabula rasa*, blameless, like healthy newborns of the future United States. They were born fully adult, but without any histories, participating in what David Roediger called "a multiracial denial of racial reality" (Hill 2004, 11–12; Roediger 2002, 3–26).

Like the figures from the centerfold, the New Face was fresh, clean, and symmetrical, reflecting the appealing, feminine set of features her designers had assembled. Following John Berger's maxim, "men act, women appear," the New Face did nothing but smile out to the viewer, enigmatically (Berger 1973). If we accept Laura Mulvey's assertion regarding the predominance of the male gaze in narrative film, then we can say that the New Face was available for men to ogle. However, her presentation differed from those in the grid, offering another aspect to interpret. While the others appeared on a white background, she appeared with a washed out representation of the Miscegenation Matrix behind her. Rather than "SimEve," mother of them all, as Donna Haraway described her, she was the daughter of them all, racial mixing carried to its logical end (Haraway 2003). Rather than cultural annihilation, white demographic minoritization, or strife, *Time* predicted a cheerful end result for current trends. Mixture, as symbolized by the New Face, our future daughter, would produce beauty, equality, and peace. Rather than dissolving race altogether, the New Face suggested that an abundance of race and interracial intimacy was the way of the future (Mulvey 1977, 6–18).

The use of racially mixed models to cast social change in a positive light continued through the 1990s. As Cynthia L. Nakashima wrote concerning the discursive uses of mixed people,

> *In fact, these days just about every political and ideological camp utilizes mixed-race people in support of their arguments. The single best illustration of this is golf prodigy Tiger Woods, who in 1996–97 became*

perhaps the busiest symbolic tool in the history of fictional or nonfictional mixed-race characters. (Nakashima 2001, 42)

Even without verbal cues, their appearances in print ads, commercials, and film scenarios evoked favorable associations with youth, diversity, and style. Their unconventional physical features brought an enigma to the products they represented. Racially ambiguous bodies served as riddles to solve, or exercises in reverse engineering when the answer was present. Sometimes the cipher can remain, but most often discovering the makeup is the goal. For example, Vin Diesel, star of *Pitch Black*, *XXX*, and *The Fast and the Furious*, made a point of concealing his racial makeup. Whether they knew he was mixed or not, the moviegoing public delighted in the urbane, confident, muscular values he embodied. As Rob Cohen, his director in *The Fast and the Furious* and the *XXX* franchise, says, "He's a new American. You don't know what he is, and it doesn't even matter, because he's everybody. Everybody looks at Vin and goes, 'I see myself'" (Williams 2002). However, the public withheld higher adoration from Diesel, in part, because they could not categorize him. While Americans praised ambiguity, they preferred certainty.

As Caroline Streeter suggested regarding mixed-race females appearing as symbols of racial harmony in her essay, "The Hazards of Visibility,"

Yet when we look closely, it is clear that a deep ambivalence about miscegenation undergirds these images, whether they are designed to seduce the viewer with a mixed race woman's sexual availability or to convince us that buying jeans somehow constitutes antiracist activity. (Streeter 2003, 316)

While Streeter juxtaposed power over women against desire for women, many described this ambivalence as a struggle between the acceptance of interracial relationships versus a wish to protect racial purity, or the acceptance of racially mixed people versus fear of white demographic diminution. However, it was also a conflict between fascination with ambiguity and the need for certainty.

CONCLUSION:
BARACK OBAMA—BLACK AND WHITE, BUT BLACK ALL OVER

The first decade of the twenty-first century has been a short period of time, but the fascination with racial makeup has continued, with historical roots to past expressions. The most notable, recent case arose with the emergence of Barack Obama on the national scene. His white grandparents immigrated to Hawai'i from Kansas, where their daughter met his father, an international student from Kenya. Obama was born in 1961, but his father soon left to seek a Ph.D. at Harvard and then moved back to Kenya. The boy's mother remarried a few years later, to an Indonesian businessman, and the family moved to Djakarta. She sent Barack back to Hawai'i to attend a prestigious prep school and live with his grandparents. He attended Occidental College in Los Angeles, and then transferred to Columbia University. In March 2004, journalist and novelist Scott Turow wrote, "No other figure on the American political scene can claim such broad roots within the human community. Obama is the very face of American diversity" (Turow, "The New Face of the Democratic Party—and America"). In July, Obama spoke at the Democratic National Convention supporting John Kerry's candidacy for president and offering his racial makeup as a case of the universal relevance of the American dream. Turow described his *modus operandi* as a product of his makeup, as if it is an inborn talent. Writing in 2004, before Obama's senate run, he ended his piece by suggesting that Obama may "become the embodiment of one of America's most enduring dreams" (Obama 1995; Obama 2004).

The apotheosis continued with a cover article in *Time* describing the freshman senator as "the political equivalent of a rainbow—a sudden preternatural event inspiring awe and ecstasy," praising his ability to find common ground with political opponents, but also suggesting that he brought together all colors (Klein, "The Fresh Face"). Articles like these suggested that his political method was a product of his racial makeup rather than a well-learned political strategy. "He transcends the racial divide so effortlessly," Joe Klein wrote, "that it seems reasonable to expect that he can bridge all the other divisions—and answer all the impossible questions—plaguing American public life" (Klein, ibid.). The challenges Obama faced matched the special talents his racial makeup has conferred upon him, when in fact, they surpassed him. Just as mixed-race children were supposed to fix the strife in their families, a mixed-race politician was supposed to fix the whole nation's divisions. At this time, it was not his job to fix them.

In January 2007, the senator announced that he was forming an exploratory committee to consider running for president, a customary move indicating strong intentions. Even before he announced his candidacy the following month, some declared that he was not really black. Peter Beinart, former editor of *The New Republic*, called him a "good black" with less support from most African Americans than authentic, "bad blacks" received. Stanley Crouch conceded that Obama was black, but clarified that he wasn't black like he was, a descendent of western Africans in the Atlantic slave trade. He refused to consider Obama "one of us" (Crouch 2006). Journalist and author Debra Dickerson went farther with the criteria for blackness, emphasizing this genealogical difference. She suggested that categorizing him as African American demeaned the racial experience that many true African Americans had, and allowed his supporters to disregard the legacy of slavery. He was an outsider, free of the weight of that legacy. Just three years before, she had written *The End of Blackness*, a book that argued that "'blackness' must be updated so that blacks can free themselves from the past and lead America into the future" (Dickerson 2004, 7). Now she was drawing a line between African Americans and immigrants of African descent, calling their experiences invalid because their pasts were different. By association, her view of racially mixed African Americans may have been the same (Coates 2007).

After she made this proclamation, Dickerson appeared on Stephen Colbert's news satire show, *The Colbert Report*, to defend it. His interview revealed the weaknesses of her position on four counts: First, he suggested that if Obama did not have the adequate descent to be black, that he run as a white guy. Colbert knew that Obama's physical appearance made that untenable, and the impossibility of claiming white descent only made Dickerson's protection of black descent absurd. She had to acknowledge that he was black, but a different kind of black, maybe an "African African American." Second, he pointed out that had he never heard her distinction, he might have gotten a sense of fulfillment from supporting a black candidate, without being a racist (ColbertNation.com, "Debra Dickerson"):

> Dickerson: *This is a critique of white self-congratulation, of saying we're embracing a black person when we're not really.*
> Colbert: *Listen, if you hadn't told me he wasn't black I would have thought that I was supporting a black person. And then I would have been supporting all black people. But now I won't because he's not.*
> Dickerson: *Well, then that would make you a racist.*

Colbert: If I were white. But I don't see race, because I've moved beyond that. I've developed beyond that. I'm so not a racist that I don't see race. People tell me I'm white and I believe them because I think Barack Obama is black.

Here, Colbert further showed his familiarity with Dickerson's assumptions about race, posing the notion that he did not fit within her understanding of whiteness. Her distinctions about blackness could be irrelevant to him, or any other voter who thought differently. Lastly, if the criteria for blackness in the United States arena depended on the lived experience of slavery, Colbert proposed, "What if, for just a brief period of time, he were enslaved?"—perhaps to a real black person—to gain "all the street creed he needs" (ibid.). This ruse served the coup de grace to Dickerson's narrow conception of blackness: It was easy to construct, but it excluded anyone outside of its narrow parameters. Obama would have to be a slave to satisfy it. Pieces arguing that Obama wasn't black enough became more rare, indicating that the argument had lost momentum. For the time being, it seemed that the public rejected it, rather than incorporate it into their understanding of him. His physical appearance, his dating choices, his beliefs, and his politics outweighed the arguments of naysayers.

In the weeks following his initial announcement, a few writers on race made sure to remind everyone that he was mixed. Some emphasized that even with a monoracial self-descriptor, Obama faced expectations from both blacks and whites. This created a double jeopardy where it was possible that he could disappoint more sets of constituents. Shelby Steele, the mixed, black writer and opponent of affirmative action, also argued that Obama would have to make a choice between being a bargainer or a challenger. The former (for example, Oprah Winfrey) let the public forget about racial differences. The latter (for example, Al Sharpton) always emphasized them. Steele wrote, "He has to drop all masks, all obsessions with identity, all his fears of being called a sell-out, and very carefully come to reveal what he truly believes as an individual" (Steele 2007). This was a statement on political strategy, but also advice on how to manage one's position as a racial minority. James Hannaham was one of the few writers to accent Obama's mixed identity and refuse to reduce it to one traditional label, or two warring bloods. He reminded us that Obama's racial reality was complex, even if he and others tried to simplify it. Appreciating this complexity required leaving questions unanswered, an exercise contrary to centuries of racial categorization in the Americas (Hannaham 2008).

In 2008, along with the writing about Obama's racial identity came an abundance of visual representations. At least four different action figures appeared during the presidential campaign: a six-inch caricature by Jailbreak Toys, two editions of a six-inch bobble head by Funko (including a Captain Obama variation with a costume much like Superman's), and a realistic, twelve-inch action figure by Dragon in Dream. All of these depicted the candidate in a neutral to heroic way. Over a hundred magazines placed Obama's image on their covers before Election Day. This format is significant because it both reflects and shapes discussions on whatever topic they purvey in real time. Editors and designers aim to create magazine fronts that are both easy to comprehend and compelling to purchase. Lastly, whether the producers aspire to impartiality or not, magazine covers communicate ideologies around issues of race, class, and gender.

Some of these represented Obama in visually fragmented ways. *New York* magazine headlined their August 18, 2008, issue, "Race: The Impossible Conversation (but here goes . . .)," introducing articles on post-raciality, his progress in the primaries, and his marriage. In duotone black and white, Obama filled the foreground of the cover. Behind him, the cover split between a black half on the left and a white half on the right, communicating a choice between two candidates. However, with no opponents visible, its depiction of a choice between racial groups was more obvious. Obama's warring blood could never truly blend. He had to be one or the other. Behind his shoulder on the black side was Michelle Obama, acknowledging her contribution towards his success. Born in Chicago to an all-black family with Christian values, she had a more conventional African American identity. Michelle and Barack's married life, the community organizing work, and the fact that they ended up together (rather than, say, a white woman) all contributed to his achieving a conventional African American identity for himself. Her strong presence, bold style, and physical features influenced how many saw each of them racially. Her figure's position hinted at her role as a spouse, a supporter, and a black presence in his life. *New York* evoked these themes, all within the context of a tradition of mutually exclusive, monoracial categorization. Racially mixed people were easy to understand if disaggregated into their constituent colors, and associated with particular relations. Here, Obama was literally black or white, with a black influence.

While it appeared to be a conventional portrait of the man, I found another cover especially evocative of the themes at hand, the October 20 edition of *Time*, which announced, "Why the Economy is Trumping Race: How Worried White Voters Are Turning toward Obama." This text operated on the assumption that voters considered only two issues: whether a candidate was racially similar to themselves and the economy. According to *Time*, whites were switching from one to the other. Recalling *New York*'s cover two months prior, this image split his face down the middle, with the left in black-and-white, and the right in full color, intimating a choice between seeing him as either black or white, or in full, realistic terms—in other words, focusing on the divisive issue of race, or the universal issue of the economy. Since October 2006, *Time* had favored Obama, so this cover also suggested that choosing to focus on the economy rather than his racial identity was the enhanced (full-color) way to think.

However, the most famous visual representation of Barack Obama, Shepard Fairey's poster supporting his campaign, utilized the contrast of basic colors. The visual artist first received recognition in the 1980s when he combined images of the professional wrestler, André the Giant, with the word "obey," offering a pop-art critique to celebrity, consumerism, and the cult of personality. Fairey's popularity increased through the 1990s as he expanded from decals to DJ-ing benefits, a clothing line, and marketing for clients such as Pepsi, Hasbro, and Netscape. During the same years he plied his street-art style to icons such as Darth Vader, Billy Idol, and Led Zeppelin, balancing corporate success with a countercultural ethos.

Reflecting this grasp of his own work as a marketable commodity and a willingness to use it for public suasion, Fairey created anti-Bush posters in 2000 and 2004. However, it wasn't until Obama's ascent that he felt the commitment to create an image in support of a candidate. The resulting "Hope" poster combined an image of Obama looking into the future with the word "progress" underneath, entirely in red, white, light blue, and dark blue. The candidate's campaign office thanked him for his efforts, requesting that he replace that word with "Hope." Over the coming months, the image became ubiquitous, as Fairey distributed 300,000 stickers and 500,000 prints, and the retailer, Urban Outfitter also sold t-shirts with the image. Also, two websites offered ways for visitors ways to improvise upon Fairey's creation. First was a do-it-yourself Obama poster creator that added custom slogans to the "Hope" poster ("Do It Yourself Barack Obama Poster," http://www.pentdego.com/obama.aspx). Second was a project from *Paste* magazine that allowed visitors to ply the red-white-and-blue effect to their own picture files, and then add their own slogans. The creations became public, and other visitors rated them. It was also possible to add creations to mugs, postage stamps, and other merchandise ("Obamaicon.Me," Paste Media Group, http://obamiconme.pastemagazine.com/).

The "Hope" poster followed a different model than the others I have discussed. It was a singular image, rather than a set like the *casta* paintings. It was not part of a scientific survey demonizing or praising mixed people. Still, it reflected ideologies about the figure it depicted, namely that he was a symbol of progress, hope, or change. Lastly, the poster did not reveal Obama's parentage like the others. That was public knowledge, so there was no need to. However, it did use contrasting fields of color to suggest a way to perceive Barack Obama's racial identity. Like the black-and-white half of the *Time* cover I mention above, Fairey's image constituted Obama's face out of distinct red, white, or blue spaces that never blended. Each color existed within its own boundaries. At the same time use of the star-spangled colors makes him into a symbol of the United States, they also convey a nation with systematic divisions. The background was red on one side and blue on the other, expressing the popular conception that bipartisanship had split the nation. Fairey, like the New Face's designers, probably did not intend to communicate so much about racial identity. But stabilized thinking about race runs deep throughout visual representations of mixture in the Americas. The prevalence of colorblind thinking may hide visual statements on race in the post–civil rights era, but they still become apparent when we least expect them to.

Another set of representations took a different, yet consistent, approach to dealing with Obama's mixture, blending his features with objects unrelated to his own background. This reflected the growth of audiences remixing, mashing-up, and reconfiguring existing mass media objects. This phenomenon grew with participatory technologies available on the Internet, but really started three decades earlier with the proliferation of home electronics. Tape decks, VCRs, and home computers had made remixing an accessible practice. In the visual realm, memorable images trained viewers' eyes to the shifting contours of identity. These included *Time*'s New Face, but also the shape-shifting T-1000 from *Terminator 2: Judgment Day* (1991) and the sequence of multicultural faces from the video for Michael Jackson's "Black or White" (1991). As pop culture artifacts, they hinted at mixture, casting that process as seamless, painless, and free of historical contexts. But, as the creators of the New Face revealed, to create a comprehensible morph, you have to believe in the fixity of their parent objects.

Often the effect was comical, but also uncanny, like a mad scientist's experiment gone wrong. Manipulation of DNA had advanced since Scottish scientists cloned a sheep in 1997. In the United States, the Bush administration had opposed this kind of research on moral grounds, which prevented the nation from competing in this field. Still, Americans were aware of the technology, whether they found it fascinating, promising, or unnatural. These same attitudes had been prevalent regarding interracial intimacy. In the 1850s, pro-slavery scientists obsessed with rationalizing mulatto inferiority claimed a similar feeling of repugnance towards mixture of types of mankind. In the same era, blackface minstrelsy took off as a seminal form of entertainment, poking fun at African American cultural forms, black sexuality, and mixture (judging from the popularity of all-male send-ups of *Uncle Tom's Cabin* and *The Octoroon*) to bolster white, working-class identities. Mixture on the body formed the foundation of minstrelsy; its humor relied on combining black and white elements on performers' bodies in obvious ways. In this kind of performance, verisimilitude was irrelevant; blackface (and later, yellowface for Asians) relied on audiences appreciating how shoddy the conceit was. Following the theme of certainty in identifying bodies, they enjoyed minstrelsy because they could discern the ingredients of the conceit.

Images of Obama mixed with someone else appeared over 150 years after the development of minstrelsy, but they drew on similar dynamics. Ron English's Abraham Obama planted the forty-fourth president's facial features in the middle of the sixteenth president's hair and cheekbones, resulting in a portrait that was both ludicrous and noble. They both came from Illinois; they were both freshmen on Capitol Hill before gaining their parties' presidential nominations; and they both faced expectations to unite a divided nation. But English's creation accented the impossibility of their melding. *Time*'s November 24, 2008, cover replaced Franklin Delano Roosevelt, smiling and smoking a cigarette behind the wheel of a car, with the president-elect. This joined a collection of features praising Obama in the magazine, beginning in 2006. It evoked comparisons between FDR and Obama: they were both media-savvy; they both faced economic trouble; and they both had a physical disadvantage. But Obama was out of place in FDR's clothing, as were the convertible and the 1930s onlookers. He could not exist in that context, not as a social phenomenon and definitely not as a nonwhite man. On the other hand, *Mad* magazine definitely recalled blackface minstrelsy by mixing their mascot, Alfred E. Newman, with the candidate and handing him a placard claiming, "Yes We Can't! Alfred E. Obama '08," a play on one of the campaign's slogans. Like others in their decades-long series of freckled, gap-toothed caricatures Newman-Obama imbued the Illinois senator with the character's dimwitted peace of mind.

More notorious, though, was Barry Blitt's cartoon, "The Politics of Fear," which recast the Obamas doing the fist-bump when he won the Democratic Party nomination as a secret handshake between Americans' worst fears about the couple. This image on the July 21, 2008, issue of *The New Yorker* imagined Barack and Michelle as a turban-wearing Muslim and an afro-crowned black nationalist. In Obama's Oval Office, the first couple hung a portrait of Osama Bin Laden and burned an American flag in the fireplace underneath. Many readers and viewers considered the stereotypes it conveyed offensive. Both the Obama and McCain campaigns censured it as injudicious. These responses required David Remnick, the magazine's editor, to explicate the ironies of the cover: "The fact is, it's *not* a satire about Obama—it's a satire about the distortions and misconceptions and prejudices *about* Obama." Characteristic of the post–civil rights era, Americans found this kind of humor distasteful. However, even this reaction showed that they got the joke, just as viewers of minstrelsy had in the nineteenth century. Remixing the Obamas' bodies with signs of Muslim fundamentalism and black nationalism produced something uncanny and blatant, yet useful for gleaning certainty about racial mixture. In all of these, an ambiguous body with recognizably black elements and recognizably white elements becomes a body easier to comprehend.

However, even with both the literal explanation of his mixture via his autobiography and the symbolic one through morphing caricatures, many thought of him as monoracial. Obama resisted this way of thinking by sharing his interracial background. But he also contributed to it by adopting African American idioms, styles, and values. When the polls announced a Democratic win, three forces fixed Obama as black: First was the label, "black president," a moniker that made his interracial family apocryphal. Second was the link many made between slavery and his victory; many newscasters drew a straight line from slavery to the civil rights movement to November 4, 2008, as the resolution of those difficulties. Third, and closely related, was the connection the media made between Obama and African Americans more broadly, making it their victory, rather than one any American could appreciate. A smaller set of writers reminded us of his mixed background, praising him as a bridge between all races, noting a boost in mixed-race self-esteem, and anticipating a further breakdown of predominant racial thought. Others declared his victory the arrival of post-raciality, a condition where racial difference no longer mattered and racial identity was merely descriptive. It was easier to understand Obama as black or post-racial than to understand him as mixed, even if one of these was an anti-label. More broadly, this turn showed that many settle on a monoracial (or raceless) understanding of racially mixed Americans, rather than behold the ambiguity that is so attractive to them. Because the desire for racial certainty remains, even with monumental social change, putting these cases in conversation produces a warning against taking contemporary praise of racial mixing and racially mixed people at face value.[1]

Note

[1]. For example, in *The American Prospect*, Adam Serwer asserted, "He's black, get over it," mainly citing Obama's self-identification as black as the basis for this conclusion. He expressed the common sense understanding of Obama's racial identity, which received widespread validation through the label, black president. But this position also rejected the prospect of ambiguity, even as it acknowledged the distinguishing features of Obama's experience (Serwer 2008).

3. BARACK OBAMA

Embracing Multiplicity—Being a Catalyst for Change

JANET C. MENDOZA STICKMON

INTRODUCTION

PEOPLE OF MULTIETHNIC BACKGROUNDS ARE ACCUSTOMED TO EXISTING at the intersections of multiple worlds and multiple identities, holding and juggling those spaces in tension.[1] We become adept at navigating in, out, and through numerous ethno-racial and ethno-cultural contexts. The more one enters and exits these contexts and the more one critically examines racial hierarchy and essentialism and their impact on the dynamics between racial groups, the more pronounced one's experience of multiraciality and multiethnicity becomes. An understanding of critical race theory coupled with the experience of existing within the interstices of life—surviving and thriving in a world dominated by binary thought and then being inspired to rise above the surface "unfragmented"—are vital for multiethnic individuals who seek to live out the fullness of their humanity. It requires a creativity that is prompted by the mere existence of the intersection in the road, as well as the time taken to reflect upon the ramifications of that intersection.

As a Blackapina, a woman of African American and Filipino American descent, I regularly reflect upon how truly I am embracing both sides of my heritage and how well I am serving the populations on both sides of my bloodline. Existing in this in-between space of ethnicities and critically examining this intersectionality informs and strengthens my ability to recognize the complexities and nuances that characterize life's mosaic. We, as multiethnic people, have the potential to navigate this world of complexity and nuance. And it becomes quite natural for us to relate to West African tricksters like Eshu and Ananse for this reason: they embody the multiplicity that many of us call home. Eshu creates unconventional solutions at the intersections of life. Ananse crosses the line and inspires transformation. They are unconventional and transformative because the state of being at the intersection forces them to deal with the multiple paths that come together; if those paths never meet, if the crossroads do not exist, there is almost no reason, no opportunity for creative outcomes to arise.

So what does it mean to be at the crossroads? It means to stand at any intersection, any meeting of multiple paths, and ask the question: So what do I do now?

Binary thinking would suggest selecting one of two paths. Perhaps a more nuanced way of thinking that informs the experience of many multiethnic people would suggest entertaining or exploring the possibility of taking multiple paths simultaneously. It means daring ourselves to believe that it is possible to walk multiple paths at the same time, embracing the transition, defying the conventional, the orthodox, the hegemonic, and actively walking all of those paths to become a living, breathing tapestry. As one walks the multiple paths, one clears passageways like Eshu. This means knocking down all obstacles that obstruct the flow of understanding, compassion, and cooperation. This increases the ability for humanity to co-create a world predicated on our capacity to remain in dialogue and allow our ideas to build upon each other as opposed to being combative. Consequently, any collaboration amongst human beings should reflect this spirit of interdependence, manifesting in a force that brings healing wherever there is brokenness.

President Barack Obama is one of us who lives at the interstices of life, embracing multiple perspectives and attempting to clear passageways; he challenges the citizens of the United States and people throughout the world to do the same. Being biracial, having a Kenyan father and a white mother of Irish ancestry, he has negotiated his own ethnic backgrounds, simultaneously living in various cultural contexts from Hawai'i and Jakarta as a child to Boston and Chicago as an adult.

Obama is a product of the heterogeneity of this country. In his speeches, he has spoken about how the United States has made it possible for someone like him to run for president. It is also this country's white supremacy that has prompted him to develop the very characteristics that we admire. Racism forces a biracial man who identifies as and is seen as African American to realize that he cannot afford to be mediocre. He must be eloquent at all times; he can't just be of average intelligence—he must be a graduate of Harvard Law School *and* graduate with honors; he must be well-informed about history, foreign relations, terrorist threats, economics, healthcare, education, immigration, popular culture, and prove he is "black enough" and "not too black" at the same time. I speculate that this country's embrace of binaries created enough discomfort within Obama to prompt him to make sense of the tensions of his biracial background, realizing that he is a living embodiment of the racial tension that exists between whites and African Americans in this country (not to mention the tensions between whites and other underrepresented ethnic groups and the intersections thereof).

It is this biracial experience that has also contributed to his ability to code-switch, be strategic, identify nuances, and be suave and yet down to earth. He straddles multiple worlds and holds these worlds in tension, using finesse as he maneuvers between worlds.

In this chapter, I examine Barack Obama's speeches in Cairo, Egypt, to the Muslim world, in Tucson, Arizona, at the Tucson memorial service, and in Washington, D.C., during the 2011 White House Correspondents' Association Dinner. Focus lies with these three speeches because they offer good insights into the messages he seeks to communicate to the masses. Throughout these speeches, Obama supplants misconceptions, disrupts binaries, plants new ideas, and reshapes public consciousness. In the process, he becomes a catalyst for change in the spirit of Eshu and Ananse. It is significant to note that drawing parallels between Obama and these two West African tricksters does not necessarily suggest that he is "more" African than Irish, nor does it serve to demonstrate that he consciously emulates or channels Eshu and Ananse.[2] Instead, the intent is to illustrate how such parallels are a reflection of his hybridity—Obama, like Eshu and Ananse, embodies multiplicity, intersectionality, and the effort of straddling multiple worlds simultaneously.

Secondly, the speeches reveal his flexibility, fluidity, and versatility, making him an example of how the process of psychosynthesis can manifest itself in multiethnic, multiracial individuals. He juggles his identities as mediator, minister, and subversive jokester and in the course of embracing this multiplicity works in the spirit and service of trickster deities like Eshu and Ananse.

PSYCHOSYNTHESIS AND MULTIRACIALITY

In the research of Susan Leksander, she examines the theory of psychosynthesis and applies it to multiraciality. Psychosynthesis is a process within Western psychology positing that "multiplicity within the human personality is . . . normal" (Leksander 2007, 2).³ She states that psychosynthesis draws from various traditions including an African worldview describing a human being "seen as a community in and of itself, including a plurality of selves" (Ogbonnaya 1994, 75).⁴ Furthermore, "psychosynthesis seeks to normalize the experience, familiar to many multiracial individuals, of having different personalities at different times" (Leksander 2007, 2). Each person has subpersonalities that are normal and healthy.⁵ These subpersonalities develop as a result of living in various contexts/environments. Leksander describes subpersonalities in the following fashion: "Subpersonalities are thought to form in response to a 'unifying center,' a center of meaning that evokes a deep response in us. Different subpersonalities might arise in relationship to many different unifying centers—'parents, siblings, school, profession, philosophical systems, religious environments and the natural world.'⁶ I would add to this cultural and ethnic communities. A unifying center can be contacted at any age, from our earliest relationships to experiences late in life. What one experiences as outside of oneself, with enough exposure and meaning, eventually becomes internalized as a subpersonality. This new identity internalizes and consolidates the skills, gifts, drives, qualities, beliefs and values activated and gained in response to the unifying center" (Leksander 2007, 12). In her clinical implications section, Leksander describes indicators of a healthy multiracial identity:

> *The individual has access to all ethnicities and cultures contained within; all of her/his ethnic identities are welcome within the self; s/he is aware of the needs, wants, gifts and fears of various parts of her/himself; s/he is familiar with her level of comfort, identification with and relationship to her/his multiple identities; s/he can identify internalized racism and oppression and ways in which s/he may be internally conflicted because of it; s/he can utilize her will to turn her consciousness to parts of herself that most want/need to be called forth in a given situation; s/he is free to identify her/himself in whichever way feels true and meaningful; and s/he is able to be in healthy relationship with individuals from her/his various communities as well as those from other ethnic communities. (Leksander 2007, 12)*⁷

Barack Obama exhibits the skills that are common amongst many of multiethnic, multiracial heritage who have reflected critically upon the implications of their hybridity. Experiencing the throes of essentialism and racism, negotiating various facets of his identity, and living in the in-between space informs and strengthens his potential for recognizing complexities and nuances in the process of effectively engaging the world as mediator, minister, and subversive jokester. I propose that he draws upon his multiplicity while functioning in a Western hegemonic context. Through the knowledge and wisdom imparted by his words, Obama creates bridges between communities, nations, and religions, reframing the discourse in a way that is unifying and not polarizing. Through close examination of the aforementioned speeches, we will notice how he uses his will, as Leksander describes, to turn his consciousness to the parts of himself that need to be "called forth" given the social context. Even when addressing his critics, he is neither defensive nor yielding; he acknowledges their comments just enough and then maintains focus on the issue at hand. Through these three speeches, we catch a glimpse of Obama's versatility in reaching each audience and the potential power of the Word in reshaping public consciousness.[8]

ESHU AND ANANSE—WEST AFRICAN TRICKSTERS

Eshu and Ananse are trickster deities in the West African tradition. They embody multiplicity and are catalysts for change. Eshu and Ananse do not just play tricks for the sake of playing tricks. They employ a number of qualities, such as verbal trickery, the ability to learn, the use of the unconventional, mediation, and subversion all for the purpose of bringing wisdom to humanity (Stickmon 2007, 80). Eshu, the trickster deity of the Yoruba, is respected as the god of the crossroads. He clears passageways, disturbs convention, and holds multiple perspectives in tension.

In one mythology, Eshu transforms himself (thereby revealing the multiplicity within himself), prompting two farmers to grapple with the possibility of multiple perspectives and struggle to "encompass the other's vision" (Pelton 1980, 142). As Pelton notes: "They notice Eshu's clothing, his staff, and his pipe, but neither really sees his movement—or what the other sees. They are bound by habit. It is the past that holds them, not the present. Finally, their quarrel reveals all sorts of suppressed animosity ... there was surface harmony, but underneath lay suspicion, anger, and violence. The friendship was held together by custom, not by mutual awareness and a willingness to undergo modification together" (Pelton 1980, 59). Eshu's trickery had the effect of bringing the farmers' differences to the surface, allowing them to engage in a deeper, more authentic relationship. Eshu becomes known as the god who can disrupt and expose the superficial harmony and convention undertaken by human beings in order to bring them to a deeper meaning of communal existence (Pelton 1980, 142–44).

Amongst the Yoruba, Eshu is central to their daily life and worship. Eshu is a deity known as a "divine messenger" between the gods and humans (Pelton 1980, 135). The Yoruba understand him as a "mediator between gods and men" and "always a catalyst stimulating the deeply intended relationship between gods and humans" (Pelton 1980, 128–30). Furthermore, Pelton states that according to the Yoruba, Eshu enables "both to become what they are" (Pelton 1980, 137). For example, in another story, Eshu functions as mediator, finding a solution that is mutually beneficial for the gods and humans, thereby introducing Ifa (wisdom) into the world (Ford 1999, 156). To humans, Eshu gives knowledge and therefore a degree of control over their destiny and to the gods, he gives the food that the humans have offered as sacrifice; this is done on condition that the orishas share their wisdom with the humans (Ford 1999, 156).

As mentioned earlier, Eshu is often associated with the crossroads (Hyde 1998, 116). Pelton states, "Eshu can keep peace in the market and watch over the passageways and transition points in Yoruba life because his proper place is at the transcendent center of that life" (Pelton 1980, 128). Eshu is the "god of the market, the lord of exchange, presides over the beginning of the week and also over its close in the market that begins the next week, just as he does over the beginning of the day, the beginning of the year, the beginning of the world, and the beginning of the order restored through divination" (Pelton 1980, 149).

Eshu is also known for his agility, fluidity, and ability to be at home with paradox (Hyde 1998, 114). The Yoruba view him as the "the embodiment of a paradox" (Pelton 1980, 129). For example, the Yoruba consider Eshu to be the youngest orisha, and yet also the father of all orishas (Pelton 1980, 130). Another example involves the relationship between Eshu and Ifa. Pelton asserts that the connection between Eshu and Ifa divination must be examined in order to understand how the Yoruba combine "anger and playful dancing" and "disruptive and creative sexuality" in a single figure (Pelton 1980, 133). Pelton cites Wescott who views "Eshu and Ifa as opposing principles of change and order, both needed to ensure the harmony of Yoruba society" (Pelton 1980, 135). Ifa, a deity also called Orunmilla, is understood as the personification of the Yoruba divination system (Pelton 1980, 133–35). In this relationship, Eshu is superior to Ifa though Eshu does not possess the system of divination (Pelton 1980, 135).

Eshu "sets in motion the whole divinatory process and oversees the movement from order to disorder to diagnosis to new order" (Pelton 1980, 135). Ifa also makes known to human beings what Olurun's purpose is and what sacrifices Eshu must have humans provide (Pelton 1980, 133). Finding the "ancestral guardian soul" through divination is vital to the Yoruba (Pelton 1980, 133–34). The ancestral guardian soul is the "heavenly counterpart of the person, with whom he must maintain a constant contact that he might truly exist, or 'stand forth' in his own full being according to the divine order" in which each Yoruba is believed to be "at least partially a re-emergent clan ancestor" (Pelton 1980, 133–34). Finding this counterpart reveals where the person belongs in society, as well as their "relationship to the gods" (Pelton 1980, 133–34). Pelton also describes divination as that which is "needed to prescribe remedies for many sorts of disorder, and because it touches and links the multitude of human and extrahuman forces present in Yoruba life, it is the practical center of Yoruba religion." The Yoruba turn to Ifa (the personification of divination) in times of need, being given advice by the diviner or the babalawo, offering sacrifice to Eshu, in so doing, also lifting up this sacrifice to Olurun (Pelton 1980, 133–34). Through seeking the assistance of these three deities, Bascom explains that Eshu, Ifa, and Olurun, together, help humanity "achieve the destiny which is assigned each individual before his ancestral soul is reborn" (Pelton 1980, 133–34).

Ananse, the trickster deity of the Ashanti people, is often depicted as a spider. In all the stories or anansesem, the quality of Ananse that is most prominent is ambiguity. This is evident in the following quote: "He is both fooler and fool, maker and unmade, wily and stupid, subtle and gross, the High God's accomplice and his rival. The anansesem show that this multiformity accounts for both Ananse's comic value and his mythic importance. He is a schemer and a thief, a lecher and an ingrate, yet he is, prototypically, 'wonderful'" (Pelton 1980, 28). In one story between Ananse and Hate-to-be-contradicted, they compete with their lies. Hate-to-be-contradicted had a history of telling lies, hating to be contradicted when animals became privy to his lies. Yet Ananse remains verbally engaged with him, lying as well. In this competition of lies, Ananse prevails, killing Hate-to-be-contradicted, cutting him into pieces and thereby spreading contradiction around the world. This story brings attention to two of Ananse's important skills: 1) his ability to lie with someone who is already known to be a liar, and 2) in his triumph, Ananse spreads contradiction around the world; this being attributed to him as a quality that humanity benefits from—the tolerance or ambiguity of contradiction (Pelton 1980, 29). Since Ananse brings this "disorder and opposition," Ananse must be dealt with carefully by humanity since he is a "medium of coherence and incoherence at the same moment" (Pelton 1980, 29). In another story, Ananse competes in a head-butting contest with an elephant and tricks other animals to take his place, thereby having food to eat (i.e., the other animals who are defeated by the elephant). Ultimately, he kills the elephant, eating him as well. This story, and others like it, are a testament to the "triumph of cleverness over brute strength" (Pelton 1980, 54). In a third mythology, Ananse uses unconventionality, verbal trickery, and trickery to outsmart and capture life-threatening and/or elusive creatures. Consequently, he is named the wisest one of all and the new owner of all Akan stories.[9] In the process, he uses particular strategies to appeal to natural anthropomorphic qualities of each creature. Ananse invites the snake to settle an argument by appealing to its sense of goodwill to bring peace to a conflict; to capture the lion, he uses flattery to massage the lion's ego; to capture the bees, he feigns generosity, taking advantage of their naïveté; and lastly he uses food to capture the fairy, appealing to the fairy's appetite (Stickmon 2007, 79). Moreover, Pelton points out the significance in how the stories

> rest on a central point of mythology, the contrast between the raw and the cooked, the wild and the human and also on Ananse's own metamorphic powers, which are rooted in his ability to cross, break, and recreate the ontological margins that both join and separate these parallel worlds. Laughter is somehow the key to Ananse's power . . . Within the stories, then, laughter is not the means by which Ananse transforms, but the sign of his power to transform. Ananse so links transcendence and absurdity that his presence simultaneously dissolves old boundaries, evokes laughter and foolishness, and establishes new shapes. (Stickmon 2007, 55)

Like Eshu, Ananse is "the image of the openness of the passageway to transformation—an openness that again and again brings into relationship center and boundary, source and resource, and one sort of potency with another, and thus enables human life to be made and remade. Particularly as the agent of this sort of doubleness, Ananse is an Ashanti creation" (Stickmon 2007, 67). Essentially, Ananse's humor, ambiguity, ingenuity, and wit are employed to clear obstructions from passageways in human relationships and thus allow transformative wisdom to be introduced into the natural world.

DISCUSSION OF "A NEW BEGINNING—PRESIDENT OBAMA SPEAKS TO THE MUSLIM WORLD"

June 4, 2009: Obama delivers a speech in Cairo, Egypt, to Muslims around the world. Historically, the United States has alienated the Muslim world through its policies and rhetoric, producing an extremely strained, polarized relationship. However, the message Obama brings to the Muslim community is one that is uncharacteristic of a country that has assumed the position of world police with the objective of entering countries suspected of possessing weapons of mass destruction and/or injecting its brand of democracy. Instead, Obama's speech reveals how deeply the United States is inextricably linked with Islam. He fleshes out the complexities of Islam's history, expresses a desire to dismantle misconceptions about the Islamic world, invites Islam to abandon sweeping generalizations of the United States, explores our common goals and interests, and gives a close examination of the sources of tension that lie between our country and the Muslim world. He functions as mediator and clearer of passageways, seeking to improve the flow of communication between the United States and nations in the Muslim world in hopes of effectively engaging in collaborative efforts.

Obama begins with an acknowledgment that he comes to Cairo during a time in history marred by tensions between the United States and Muslims throughout the world and carefully states his purpose for being in Cairo: "I have come here to seek a new beginning between the United States and Muslims around the world; one based upon mutual interest and mutual respect; and one based upon the truth that America and Islam are not exclusive, and need not be in competition. Instead, they overlap, and share common principles—principles of justice and progress; tolerance and the dignity of all human beings" (Obama 2009d).[10] He points out that he speaks from the perspective of a Christian who is familiar with Islam through his father, his years living in Indonesia, and his work in Chicago. Obama continues by recognizing the beauty and contributions of Muslims throughout the centuries, noting discoveries and achievements in the areas of algebra, medicine, poetry, and religious harmony.

Opening in this fashion, while also drawing upon the Qur'an, demonstrates to the audience that a wealth of knowledge about Islam's history informs his hope that a mutually beneficial alliance between the United States and the Islamic world is possible; this knowledge and experience is born from an educated point of view, as opposed to being shaped by misconceptions. This is evident when he states, "So I have known Islam on three continents before coming to the region where it was first revealed. That experience guides my conviction that partnership between America and Islam must be based on what Islam is, not what it isn't. And I consider it part of my responsibility as President of the United States to fight against negative stereotypes of Islam wherever they appear" (Obama 2009d). Similarly, he suggests that this "same principle must apply to Muslim perceptions of America" (Obama 2009d). By speaking from an informed perspective, misconceptions are discredited and passageways of communication become cleared simply because the obstacles that had long distorted the image of Islam were removed. At the same time, he challenges Muslims to confront and dismantle stereotypes of the United States. This can potentially lead to greater opportunities for dialogue and fruitful diplomatic relations between the United States and Muslims around the world.

Obama continues by pointing out an important overlap in the United States and Islam: the fact that close to seven million Americans are Muslim and there are over 1,200 mosques in the United States (Obama 2009d). Consideration of the population of Muslims who make up a sizable part of this country problematizes any efforts seeking to pit the United States and Islam against each other. When we see the intersection of the two, whether it be pointing out the number of Muslim Americans or examining the ways in which the United States is indebted to Islam, it becomes clear that "Islam is a part of America" (Obama 2009d). The two are not mutually exclusive, therefore the two should not be perceived as such. The speech closes the chasm between a nation and a religion that has long been deep and wide, portraying the two as diametrically opposed. In the spirit of Eshu, Obama further blurs the boundaries that have separated us by pointing out our common humanity, noting that our behavior toward each other should reflect that mutual recognition of this humanity: "Given our interdependence, any world order that elevates one nation or group of people over another will inevitably fail. So whatever we think of the past, we must not be prisoners of it. Our problems must be dealt with through partnership; progress must be shared" (Obama 2009d). This is once again a message communicating the spirit of interdependence, as opposed to competitiveness, encouraging us to reap the benefits of that partnership together.

Obama certainly communicates the importance of recognizing our similarities as a necessary component in the process of creating a strong, enduring relationship. However, he is explicit in stating that this cannot be done at the expense of understanding the tensions that lie between the United States and the Muslim community. He says, "Indeed it suggests the opposite: we must face these tensions squarely" (Obama 2009d). Like Eshu prompts the differences between the two farmers to surface, Obama sheds light on and confronts seven sources of tension between the United States and the Muslim world: 1) violent extremism, 2) Israelis, Palestinians, and the Arab world, 3) rights and responsibilities pertaining to nuclear weapons, 4) democracy, 5) religious freedom, 6) women's rights, and 7) economic development and opportunity. As he explores each of these tensions, he fleshes out the complexities and nuances of each of the issues. He defies binaries that tend to polarize the discussion and undermine the spirit of cooperation. He then introduces alternatives. In doing so, his vision mirrors the qualities of Eshu as he introduces wisdom into a community by encouraging society to look closely at our differences in order to have deeper, more meaningful relationships (Stickmon 2007, 79). Below, five of these issues will be examined: violent extremism, Israeli-Palestinian conflict, democracy, religious freedom, and women's rights.

As Obama discusses violent extremism, he clarifies that the United States is not "at war with Islam" (Obama 2009d). At the same time, he expresses his commitment to confront violent extremism that threatens the security of the citizens of the United States, this being his "first duty" (Obama 2009d). He makes a distinction between the war in Afghanistan and the war in Iraq, stating that the war in Afghanistan was not by choice whereas the war in Iraq was. Though truly both wars were by choice, the distinction implies that he defends the idea that the war in Afghanistan was justified since it was in response to al Qaeda's attack on the World Trade Center and the Pentagon on September 11, 2001. He notes that extremists not only kill Americans but also kill Muslims. Such a statement shows that extremists not only pose a threat to Americans, but also those of other countries, of different faiths, including Muslims "more than any other" (Obama 2009d). Given this, Obama's words suggest that all those victimized and terrorized by violent extremists, regardless of country or religion, should have a collective interest in confronting them.

It is significant that within this section on violent extremism, Obama makes two important admissions: 1) Iraq was a war of choice, and 2) the United States acted "contrary to our ideals" (Obama 2009d). Considering the former, Iraq being a war of choice translates into: "The war in Iraq was unjustified." He noted that it was a reminder that the United States "need[s] to use diplomacy and build international consensus to resolve our problems whenever possible" (Obama 2009d). In the latter, Obama recognizes that in response to 9/11, "in some cases" the United States acted "contrary to our ideals" and it is in the process of "taking concrete actions to change course" (Obama 2009d). He seeks to remove all American troops from Iraq by 2012. He had ordered Guantanamo Bay to be closed by early 2010. He sustained criticism for the fact that by October 2010, the detention camp in Guantanamo Bay was not closed. Obama's response to such criticism was the following: "When people start being concerned about, 'You haven't closed Guantanamo yet,' I say, listen, that's something I wanted to get done by now, and I haven't gotten done because of recalcitrance from the other side. Frankly, it's an easy issue to demagogue. But what I have been able to do is to ban torture. I have been able to make sure that our intelligence agencies and our military operate under a core set of principles and rules that are true to our traditions of due process" (Wenner 2010, 44).

In addressing the Israeli and Palestinian conflict, he acknowledges that the historical bond between Israel and the United States is "unbreakable" and that the United States knows the history of hatred that prompted the need for a Jewish homeland (Obama 2009d). To demonstrate how deeply he understands this need, he includes his plan to visit Buchenwald, "part of a network of camps where Jews were enslaved, tortured, shot and gassed to death by the Third Reich" (Obama 2009d).[11] At the same time, he acknowledges that Palestinians have suffered in the course of finding a homeland, as well. He states that the only solution is for there to be two states in which both can coexist peacefully. In this sense, he functions as Eshu the mediator, embracing a solution that can be mutually satisfying for both Israelis and Palestinians (Ford 1999, 156). He tells Palestinians that they must end their violence, and he warns Israel that the U.S. does not condone continuous construction of Israeli settlements. Both undermine peace efforts. He also warns Arab States to recognize the Arab Peace Initiative and remain mindful of other problems outside of the Arab-Israeli conflict. He is effective in using the story of Isra in reminding the audience that in their own scripture, there is a story where Moses, Jesus, and Mohammed pray together to point toward a vision of Judaism, Christianity, and Islam coexisting peacefully.

With regards to democracy, Obama makes explicit the significant point that "no system of government can or should be imposed upon one nation by any other" (Obama 2009d). This is in stark contrast to the message communicated by the speeches and policies under the Bush administration that clearly saw the United States as the "bringer of democracy" to Iraq. The discourse is nuanced as he adds that he favors "governments that reflect the will of the people," acknowledging that "each nation gives life to this principle in its own way, grounded in the tradition of its own people" (Obama

2009d). This reflects a degree of respect for the autonomy of other nations. Furthermore, he provides a list of universal human rights that governments should protect which includes "the ability to speak your mind and have a say in how you are governed; confidence in the rule of law and the equal administration of justice; government that is transparent and doesn't steal from the people; the freedom to live as you choose" (Obama 2009d). This list functions as a standard by which a government can be measured. He states that "governments that protect these rights are ultimately more stable, successful and secure" (Obama 2009d). Obama includes that there are various paths by which this can be achieved, which suggests an interest in the ability for countries to maintain agency; this also suggests a value for multiplicity—that there is no one system of government that can achieve the aforementioned standard and that each nation will establish a government that reflects the "will of the people" based on its own history, "grounded in the tradition of its own people" (Obama 2009d).

Concerning religious freedom, Obama highlights the richness of religious diversity, emphasizing that it need not be divisive. He draws from Islamic history, using examples of religious coexistence such as Andalusia, Cordoba, and Indonesia. He asserts that Western countries should avoid interfering with Muslims' ability to freely practice their religion. Considering an example of Western interference in the practice of Islam, he notes the Western preoccupation with what Muslim women wear and states that hostility towards any religion cannot be disguised under the pretense of liberalism (Obama 2009d). Obama's remarks are contrary to the philosophy that unity is based on conformity and uniformity. Instead, embracing religious diversity subscribes to the concept that unity can be achieved within a religiously heterogeneous society, creating opportunities for religious exchange without compromising the integrity of the various religions. Hence, embracing differences is not divisive, as long as they are viewed as opportunities for greater dialogue and collaborative service.

With regards to women's rights, he rejects Western preoccupation with viewing a woman as inferior if she chooses to wear the hijab or burqa, for example. He shifts the listeners' attention to how women are denied an education and how this leads to inequality between women and men. First and foremost, he advocates for women's agency, respecting "those women who choose to live their lives in traditional roles. But it should be their choice. That is why the United States will partner with any Muslim-majority country to support expanded literacy for girls, and to help young women pursue employment through micro-financing that helps people live their dreams" (Obama 2009d).

In short, throughout Obama's speech to the Muslim world, he speaks from an informed perspective (not crippled by Orientalist notions of Islam) as he encourages the dismantling of misconceptions on both sides. He communicates how deeply the United States and Islam are intertwined, therefore giving reason for the pursuit of greater dialogue and collaborative efforts so we can reap the benefits of interdependence and partnership together.

DISCUSSION OF PRESIDENT OBAMA'S SPEECH AT THE TUCSON MEMORIAL SERVICE

As a woman who has found solace in homilies and sermons at funeral services for my parents and other loved ones, I have experienced what it means for one's spirit to rest in the preacher's hands. I listened for words that would give me a reason to continue living and words that would allow the memory of the departed to live on. As a teacher and professor who has lost students, I learned how vital it was to ensure that my actions reflected a care and concern for those who were grieving the loss of their classmate and confronting their own mortality, allowing them the space to share their stories about the departed and stories of other losses triggered by the recent death. My responsibility was to share and demonstrate ways we could honor the departed with our lives. This is no easy task. All of this requires love, patience, and temperance—all signs of a steady spirit with its anchor resting in the Divine. Obama's speech at the Tucson memorial service on January 12, 2011 revealed signs of a steady spirit. It was pastoral in nature, exhibiting a combination of care, finesse, and spirituality as he spoke of the departed, the injured, and the heroes. In spite of months of discussion—ranging from emotionally charged rhetoric to outright hate speech in Arizona regarding healthcare, immigration reform, and Ethnic Studies—he does not use this time of mourning as an opportunity to bring attention to these issues. Instead, he allows space for contemplation and space for the survivors to grieve. Obama functions as minister and healer to the living.

He begins by honoring the six people who died, telling a brief story about each of them: how beautiful their lives were and how their lives came to a tragic end as they came to visit and listen to Congresswoman Gabrielle Giffords during what she called "Congress on Your Corner." He speaks of everyone from Judge John Roll to nine-year-old Christina Green. Including these stories demonstrates the effort made to learn who his citizens were, making the service meaningful for the survivors in the audience. During a sermon, inclusion of such details serves to assist in the healing process of the living (Obama 2011a).

This was followed by time dedicated to honoring the living: the thirteen survivors of the shooting, including Congresswoman Giffords, Daniel Hernandez, Giffords's intern who tended to her wounds, the men who tackled the gunman as he attempted to reload, the sixty-one-year-old woman, Patricia Maisch, who wrestled the shooter's ammunition away from him, and the doctors, nurses, and first responders. They were all deemed heroes as they served to save lives (Obama 2011a).

He explored the nature of heroism, which is in the heart and does not require formal training: "They remind us that heroism does not require special training or physical strength. Heroism is here, all around us, in the hearts of so many of our fellow citizens, just waiting to be summoned—as it was on Saturday morning" (Obama 2011a). From heroism, Obama asks the questions, "How can we honor the fallen? How can we be true to their memory?" (Obama 2011a). He is careful to note how the current climate has "become so sharply polarized" and warned against the public using this as an opportunity "to turn on one another" (Obama 2011a). Instead, we must "make sure that we are talking to each other in a way that heals, not a way that wounds," and use humility when we discuss this tragedy (Obama 2011a). He states, "Rather than pointing fingers or assigning blame, let us use this occasion to expand our moral imaginations, to listen to each other more carefully, to sharpen our instincts for empathy, and remind ourselves of all the ways our hopes and dreams are bound together" (Obama 2011a).

Obama introduces an alternative way of interacting with each other. Indeed, during such a devastating incident, it is natural to search for reasons and cast blame on someone or something. However, he challenges his citizens to ponder the nature of what brings about reconciliation of a nation and creates greater understanding. To "expand our moral imagination" is to think of ways we can open our listening hearts and fine-tune our propensity for empathy. Furthermore, the use of the phrase "sharpen our instincts" implies that human beings already possess this seed of empathy which just needs to be nurtured so it can manifest itself in our behavior toward one another. As he reminds us that "our hopes and dreams are bound together," we are prompted to reflect on our interdependence—how deeply our lives are inextricably linked. The incident causes us to look upon the past, present, and future, "on the manner in which we live our lives and nurture our relationships with those who are still with us" (Obama 2011a). This tragedy becomes an opportunity to reflect on the quality of time we spend with those we love.

Obama further challenges the nation to ensure that we deal with this tragedy in a way that honors the dead. He says, "If this tragedy prompts reflection and debate . . . let's make sure it's worthy of those we have lost. Let's make sure it's not on the usual plane of politics and point scoring and pettiness that drifts away with the next news cycle" (Obama 2011a). This simple statement prompts us to contemplate how our spirits are an integral part of our humanity. We, as human beings, are far more than our intellects and the political polarized debates shaped by our finite intellects. We must not forget our spirits and our capacity for generosity, selflessness, and compassion. This is best captured by the following lines: "We recognize our own mortality, and are reminded that in the fleeting time we have on this earth, what matters is not wealth, or status, or power, or fame—but rather, how well we have loved, and what small part we have played in bettering the lives of others" (Obama 2011a). Obama maintains focus on the living, particularly those who are mourning. He notes that the time we have on this earth is "fleeting" and therefore we must use this time to be a loving influence on one another's lives. He recognizes the tenderness and fragility of their hearts and emotions and speaks directly to those hearts in a way that has the potential to gently nurture and strengthen their spirits. Secondly, this reflects another quality of multiracial, multiethnic individuals who, by virtue of our hybridity, are challenged to continuously contextualize and straddle multiple worlds and reflect critically upon that experience. For us it becomes difficult to embrace binaries and think solely in terms of extremes. We are constantly forced to consider alternative ways of thinking and behaving that are not limited by the way the external mainstream forces us to frame the discourse. Obama effectively summons that ability by challenging his citizens to speak about the incident and the departed in a manner that is on a higher moral plane, one that is worthy of the lives sacrificed. Throughout this speech, as he ministers to his citizens, Obama introduces wisdom, clears the way for contemplation and dialogue, straddles multiple worlds, and blurs the boundaries that limit the "moral imagination"—all in the spirit of Eshu.

DISCUSSION OF PRESIDENT OBAMA'S SPEECH AT THE WHITE HOUSE CORRESPONDENTS' ASSOCIATION DINNER

During the White House Correspondents' Association Dinner on April 30, 2011, Obama speaks to a room full of journalists, celebrities, senators, and government employees. The elements that distinguish this speech from the other two are his clever sense of humor and the use of visual media. Obama wins the audience's laughter and applause with his verbal acumen and wit, allowing him to effectively combat critics ranging from Mitt Romney to Donald Trump. In addition to the mediator and minister, we bear witness to another facet of Obama: the subversive jokester. In this regard, his qualities bear resemblance to Ananse.

Immediately after Obama is introduced, a montage is projected on-screen: the flag of the United States flows as an image of his birth certificate explodes from its center. In the background the audience hears the opening lines of the song "Real American" by Derringer: "I am a real American, fight for the rights of every man. I am a real American, fight for what's right, fight for your life." (The birth certificate explodes as the line "fight for your life" is sung.) Following the montage, Obama addresses the crowd, "My fellow Americans. Mahalo!" He emphasizes "fellow," and many laugh and applaud (Obama 2011b).[12] His use of the Hawaiian word for "thank you" is a clever reminder of his birthplace, as well as the multiplicity integral to the American identity. Since his campaign, a vocal segment of the population, many of whom are white, had questioned Obama's American citizenship and therefore eligibility to be the president of the United States. With this imagery and brief reference to Hawai'i releasing his long-form birth certificate, he puts an end to the debate. He then says, "But just in case there are any lingering questions, tonight I'm prepared to go a step further . . . I am releasing my official birth video" (Obama 2011b). A clip from *The Lion King* is shown in which all the animals gather around to watch Mufasa raise up and present his son, Simba, atop Pride Rock in Africa. Following this clip, Obama says, "Oh well. Back to square one" (Obama 2011b).

It is significant that even after presenting the birth certificate, he is jokingly prepared to present more evidence. This points to a poignant reality of people of color in the United States who, due to racism, have been conditioned to be prepared to defend not only the authenticity of our Americanness, but also defend our intellectual prowess and moral standing. This serves as a reminder that he, like many of us people of color, is not allowed the luxury of mediocrity that often white privilege affords. Moreover, his statement "back to square one" implies, in jest, a feigned defeatism that his African ancestry has unfortunately tainted his authenticity as an American. It is fabulous that this issue is dealt with indirectly and with humor. Mel Watkins, in *On the Real Side*, notes, "Indirection which employs suggestion and innuendo rather than direct, declarative statement, not only works hand in hand with the traditional African custom of expressing protest without confrontation, but also permits cloaked or disguised conversation that only initiates can decipher" (Watkins 1994, 68).

Following the "birth video," Obama immediately makes a calculated jab at Fox News by clarifying that this was a joke, knowing their history of spinning facts. It also acts as an indirect defensive strike at those, including the Fox News staff, who may attempt to turn his facetious use of *The Lion King* clip into some grounds for serious political debate.

Obama has similar comebacks for Matt Damon, Paul Ryan, and some of the individuals who have expressed a desire to run against him in the 2012 election, like Michele Bachman, Tim Pawlenty, Mitt Romney, Jon Huntsman, and Donald Trump. For example, he pokes fun at Pawlenty's middle name, "Hosni," and remarks, "What a shame," jokingly expressing the same disappointment that some in the United States expressed about Obama's middle name being Hussein (Obama 2011b). Truly, in Obama's case, to call it disappointment would be inaccurate; for example, during the 2008 presidential campaign, some voters were outraged at the thought that someone who could potentially become president has a middle name identical to Saddam's surname. Immediately, racist, Orientalist perceptions surfaced. Such voters were overwhelmed by the fear that Obama was potentially Muslim and/or a Middle Eastern terrorist.

The highlight of the evening was how Obama confronted Donald Trump. Trump was among the more vocal "birthers" demanding to see Obama's birth certificate, and at one point expressed an interest in running for president. Obama feigns sympathy for Trump saying, "he has taken some flak lately, but no one is happier, no one is prouder to put this birth certificate matter to rest than the Donald. And that's because he can finally get back to focusing on the issues that matter like, did we fake the moon landing? What really happened in Roswell? And where are Biggie and Tupac?" (Obama 2011b).

This list of "issues that matter" is a facetious measure of what Trump might deem worthy of investigation—all of which are considered conspiracy theories. Through this use of indirection and innuendo, the implication is that if Trump believed that the authenticity of Obama's American citizenship was worth investigating, then he would invest time and effort into some of these other issues—issues popularly dismissed as frivolous. So, not only are Trump's priorities labeled ridiculous, but so is Trump himself.

Obama continues: "But all kidding aside, obviously, we all know about your credentials and breadth of experience" (Obama 2011b). Through his subtle use of sarcasm, Obama cleverly questions Trump's credentials and experience, disguising it as praise. As a former coworker of mine used to say, "You don't know whether you've been kicked or kissed!" These qualities are reminiscent of Ananse. In *The Trickster of West Africa*, Pelton states, "Laughter is somehow the key to Ananse's power . . . Within the stories, then, laughter is not the means by which Ananse transforms, but the sign of his power to transform. Ananse so links transcendence and absurdity that his presence simultaneously dissolves old boundaries, evokes laughter and foolishness, and establishes new shapes (Pelton 1980, 55). Furthermore, if we recall Ananse's use of verbal trickery in outsmarting the lion, the python, the bees, and the fairy, the trickster strategically appeals to their weaknesses in order to capture these life-threatening and/or elusive creatures. For example, Ananse captures the lion by using flattery to massage the lion's ego (Stickmon 2007, 79). If Trump were equated with the "lion," what better way to capture the "lion" than to render him ridiculous and incompetent?

Obama ends on a serious note, talking about all the soldiers serving overseas, as well as the residents of Alabama and the rest of the South suffering the storms during the previous week. He reminds all "to keep those Americans in our thoughts and in our prayers" (Obama 2011b). In contrast to the delayed and inadequate response of the Bush administration to the needs of the South after Hurricanes Katrina and Rita, Obama vows that the federal government supports them now and in the coming years as they recover from the storms. He ends with a powerful reminder of where the media's attention and energy can lie, unifying the purpose of journalists: "And I've got faith that the journalists in this room will do their part for the people who have been affected by this disaster by reporting on their progress, and letting the rest of America know when they will need more help. Those are stories that need telling. And that's what all of you do best, whether it's rushing to the site of a devastating storm in Alabama, or braving danger to cover a revolution in the Middle East" (Obama 2011b).

Sometimes communicating one's intentions indirectly and giving the sense that one is confident that the journalists already know to report on such an event is more effective than explicitly stating what they should be reporting on. This is most evident in the phrase "I've got faith." He inserts the statement "those are stories that need telling" in order to show what he wants the media to focus on. He then acknowledges how the lives of journalists have been threatened as they seek to "bring us the story, to give people a voice, and to hold leaders accountable" (Obama 2011b). He praises the journalists for risking their lives for the principles they uphold, those principles of ensuring that "no one is silenced" and remembering that "everyone deserves to know the truth" (Obama 2011b).

As Obama, throughout his speech, combats his critics using wit and humor, the audience becomes "relaxed" by their own laughter, effectively being "opened" up for sober reminders of soldiers fighting overseas and the plight of residents in the South affected by natural disaster. Like Ananse, he uses clever humor to subvert his "enemies," and like both Ananse and Eshu, he later capitalizes on his audience's attention by injecting wisdom as he prompts the audience to understand that accurate coverage of such stories is crucial and encourages them with unifying messages of praise for their dedicated service.

CONCLUSION

Whether he is speaking in Cairo to Muslims across the world, Tucson to mourning citizens of the United States, or Washington D.C., to journalists, celebrities, and politicians, President Barack Obama exhibits characteristics that are so common amongst many of multiethnic, multiracial heritage who have reflected critically upon their hybridity. His life experience of negotiating various facets of his identity and living in the in-between space informs and strengthens his potential for recognizing the complexities and nuances in the process of engaging the world as mediator, minister, and subversive jokester. His versatility in effectively juggling these multiple roles suggests that this ability is derived partially from some critical reflection on his multiethnicity and multiraciality; however, this can merit further research.

In Cairo, he functions as a mediator who imparts wisdom reminiscent of Eshu. Obama held multiple perspectives in tension and sought to dismantle misconceptions of Islam and the United States and shed light on how deeply our histories are intertwined. This served as justification for having greater dialogue absent of past obstacles and greater collaborative endeavors in order to experience the benefits of progress together. In Tucson, Obama exhibits the skills of a minister and healer to the living. He reminds us to draw from our capacity for generosity, selflessness, and compassion born from the goodness of our spirits. Obama clears the way for contemplation and dialogue, straddles multiple worlds, and blurs the boundaries that limit the "moral imagination"—all in the spirit of Eshu. In Washington, D.C., we see the subversive jokester, combating his harshest critics with a sense of humor. Throughout this speech, he wins the audience's laughter and applause, opening them up for a subtle bite of reality. He closes with praise for the work and sacrifices shared by journalists. Unbeknownst to the audience (and perhaps to Obama, as well) they have just been bitten by the spider, Ananse.

Through these three speeches, Barack Obama becomes a catalyst for change. He also displays his fluidity and versatility, demonstrating one way psychosynthesis can manifest itself in multiethnic, multiracial people. He juggles his identities as mediator, minister, and subversive jokester with finesse and in the course of embracing this multiplicity, works in the spirit and service of trickster deities like Eshu and Ananse.

Indeed, speeches of politicians should not be taken at face value, and it is crucial to examine the consistency between words and policies. However, it is also important to never underestimate the vibratory power of the Word and its ability to shift consciousness, assuming that those words resonate with the general populace and there is a strong enough commitment amongst the general populace and the executive, legislative, and judicial branches of the United States government to collectively make that shift of consciousness a lived reality. The Word has the power to bring things into existence. Amongst the Bambara, there is the belief that the universe emanates from the Cosmic Word, Yo (Ford 1999, 178). For the Yoruba, Ashe refers to the all-pervasive energy that circulates around the universe; when it said after a person speaks, it means, "It definitely shall be so" (Coleman 2002). It is important to take care of the intention that is infused in our breath which is then spoken and transmitted to the rest of the world. Barack Obama's words, like our words, have the potential to mend hearts, shift consciousness, and influence behavior.

Notes

1. The term "multiethnic" is used to denote a person who is comprised of more than one ethnicity. Based on the work of sociologist G. Reginald Daniel, I use "multiethnic," as opposed to "multiracial," considering the notion that ethnicity includes the concepts of both race and culture. Daniel states, "Ethnicity generally refers to a segment or subset of a larger society whose members are thought by themselves and/or others to share a common culture (beliefs, ideals, values, meanings, customs, artifacts), which sets them off from other groups in the society. However, these individuals also share a common ancestry or origin (real or imagined)—and thus may have similar or common geno-phenotypical traits—that distinguish them from other members of society as well. In addition, they may more or less participate in shared activities in which that common origin and culture are significant ingredients. Considering that ethnic formation includes notions of both race and culture, it might seem more appropriate in this book to use the term multiethnic, rather than multiracial" (see Daniel 2002, xv).
2. Considering the nature of collective consciousness within African-centered philosophy, it is possible that Obama is responding subconsciously to the call of Eshu and Ananse through his words and behavior. This is worthy of further investigation. Furthermore, one

could examine the degree to which the trickster spirit may lie within his ancestral memory. Given his ethnic background(s), such a study would require an examination of the qualities of Kenyan and Celtic trickster figures and an assessment of the characteristics Obama may have in common with these tricksters.

3. Firma and Gila 2002, 68, quoted in Leksander 2007, 2.
4. Ibid.
5. Ibid., 11.
6. Ibid., 12.
7. Ibid.
8. A particular coherence and framing lie in Obama's words, and it generates a power embedded in the intentions that are spoken. When an intention is clear and unwavering and the individual is highly "ordered" on a subatomic level, the greater the chance his message(s) will resonate with the public. This can find its basis in the physics concepts of resonant frequency and entrainment as discussed in the work of Lynne McTaggart entitled *The Power of Intention*. Quantifying the impact the messages have on a people's consciousness would be a challenge and would most certainly require further research. Within the cosmic realm, the Word may manifest itself immediately or gradually. Possible determining factors worthy of consideration would be: 1) how much damage must be undone in the course of making the change via the new message, 2) to what degree are the U.S. government (all branches) and the general populace open to the messages communicated, and 3) to what degree are the U.S. government (all branches) and the general populace committed to collectively bringing those messages into fruition.
9. The Ashanti are an ethnic group within the Akan family.
10. Barack Obama, "Transcript of Barack Obama's Speech at Cairo University," Cbc.ca, last modified June 4, 2009, http://www.cbc.ca/news/world/story/2009/06/04/f-obama-egypt-speech004.html.
11. It is notable that Obama chooses to visit Buchenwald given some of the controversy concerning the validity of accounts claiming that it was liberated by the 761st Tank Batallion, an all-African American unit.
12. Barack Obama, *2011 White House Correspondents' Dinner*, video, 18:54, April 30, 2011, http://www.youtube.com/watch?v=n9mzJhvC-8E; Obama, "Transcript of President Obama's Speech at the White House Correspondents' Association Dinner," April 30, 2011.

4. IN PURSUIT OF SELF

The Identity of an American President and Cosmopolitanism

HETTIE V. WILLIAMS

> What do we call a subject who is both more and less than an individual and stronger and weaker than a free agent? (Hale 1994, 445–71)

BARACK OBAMA PROJECTS AN IDENTITY THAT IS FRAGMENTED AS opposed to an identity that is essentialist or unitary. In nearly every public setting where the issue of his race has been introduced, Obama, although he routinely self-identifies (Avila 2010) as an African American, continuously acknowledges his mixed-race heritage. He rarely fails to mention the gratitude he feels towards his white grandparents for raising him. In his autobiography he states, "I can't even hold up my experience as being somehow representative of the black American experience" (Obama 1995, xvi). Obama makes this statement in the same breath in which he claims to be writing about his life as a "black American" (Obama 1995, xvi). Obama's self-identity, as based on his writings, speeches, and public statements, may be characterized as a type of hybrid fluidity as opposed to the hybrid fixity sometimes expressed in black/white multiracial identity. In other words, hybrid fixity tends to focus on one's multiraciality as the primary vehicle for self-identification and actualization. Obama's composite identity includes a mixed-race dimension as merely one component of a more encompassing hybridity, which also embraces his subjectivity as local (African American) and transnational (world citizen). Obama's hybrid fluidity is deployed in his autobiographical writings.

The mutable subjectivities, often illustrated in ethnic autobiographies, are evidenced in Obama's two books. Michael M. J. Fischer contends that ethnic autobiography helps us to better understand contemporary society, because in these autobiographies there is an illustration of a multifaceted or pluralist concept of the self that serves as a basis for a "wider social ethos of pluralism" (Fischer 1986, 194–233). This chapter presents an understanding of Obama's autobiography as a specific genre of writing often used by members of distinct ethnic groups to express the inexpressible aspects of self-identity through memoir and trauma narrative. In these narratives, the autobiography functions as a mechanism through which ethno-racial subjectivity is materialized, negotiated, and sometimes reformed. Obama's *Dreams from My Father* as a form of ethnic self-life-writing is also a *bildungsroman* (coming of age story) that details his passage into blackness. The book is also analyzed in this chapter as a form of ethnic autobiography that helps to support the notion of Obama's hybrid-fluid sense of self-awareness.

Barack Obama consistently negotiates a range of racial identity positionings that are at times reflective of the shifting understanding of race in contemporary America.[1] Obama has learned to negotiate the fluid contours of self-identity having been born and raised outside of African American culture as expressed in his "many voices." British-Jamaican novelist Zadie Smith, author of *White Teeth* (2000) and *On Beauty* (2005), in her analysis of *Dreams from My Father* describes Obama as a "many-voiced man."

> *The tale he tells is all about addition. His is the story of a genuinely many-voiced man. If it has a moral it is that each man must be true to his selves, plural. (Z. Smith 2009)*

Americans have been forced to rethink race, blackness, and multiraciality in significant ways (DaCosta 2009, 4–5) since November 4, 2008. Smith's assessment of Obama's ethnic autobiographical writing, *Dreams*, helps to demonstrate the notion of Obama as having a fluid sense of self-awareness or "selves." This hybrid fluidity is best expressed in the Obama writings and sometimes in his everyday race talk; and is reflective of what Russian literary theorist Mikhail Bakhtin referred to as "double voice."

This chapter examines Barack Obama's journey to self-identity as a racialized subject by incorporating sociological, cultural, and feminist theory with variant forms of philosophical cosmopolitanism. The core argument of this chapter is twofold in that I am asserting the notion of (1) *other black* as contingent upon and in opposition to essentialist notions of blackness, and the phrase (2) *hybrid fluidity* that incorporates multiple subjectivities such as multiraciality and cosmopolitanism. The term "other black" is borrowed from cultural studies theorist Shirley Ann Tate to illustrate the idea that Obama selects the identity category of black, and represents himself as a black man, while speaking back to blackness. The concept of *hybrid fluidity* includes multiracial identity and variant trajectories of cosmopolitanism. Taken together, these terms help to define Obama's composite sense of self-awareness as: *other black cosmopolitan*. In order to capture Obama's complex self-identity, a discussion of race and the multiracial movement, hybrid identities, linguistic subjectivity, and cosmopolitanism are necessary.

The chapter is divided roughly into six major sections. The first part is an examination of the concept of "other black" as applied to Obama's self-identity, followed by a discussion of race and the multiracial movement in section two. Obama's biography is highlighted in section three while section four concerns race, hybridity, and blackness. Obama as linguistic subject and cosmopolitan are detailed in sections five and six respectively.

OBAMA AND THE CONCEPT OF "OTHER BLACK"

Obama is best described as an "other black"[2] cosmopolitan. He may be considered a self-identified black man with a complex sense of self-awareness. This complex sense of self-awareness incorporates identities that go beyond blackness. In her book *Black Skins, Black Masks: Hybridity, Dialogism, Performativity* (2005), British cultural studies scholar Shirley Ann Tate utilizes the phrase "other black" to examine the lives of black/white biracial women in contemporary Britain. Applying the concept of "other black," Tate integrates the theories of Michel Foucault, Mikhail Bakhtin, and Homi Bhabha, among others, to advance her theory of the "hybridity of the everyday." Tate utilizes this concept to examine the daily speech patterns of black biracial women "who speak back" to blackness as illustrated in their everyday conversations about race.

Similarly, Obama's sense of self is shaped by his early social experiences, developed outside of the African American community, having been brought up by his white maternal grandparents, and Asian stepfather, along with his mother, in Hawai'i and Indonesia. He has constructed a composite self out of his mixed-race background and his transnational experiences. Obama's self-perception is also in part fashioned in reaction to how he has been/is sometimes perceived by those outside of his immediate family: as a black man and a member of the black community. Yet he occasionally speaks back to blackness.

Obama does not embrace a hybrid self that crystallizes in a multiracial identity nor does his sense of self include identification with multiracial individuals as a part of his broad subjectivity (that is to say hybrid or multiracial fixity is not the locus of his core identity). Rather, as an "other black cosmopolitan" he embraces a broader and more dynamic hybrid sense of self-awareness. He acknowledges his multiracial background but embraces an identity that encompasses his transnational experiences while at the same time being grounded in the African diasporic experience through a visceral connection with the struggles of African Americans. Obama's "other" blackness challenges essentialist assumptions about blackness, race, and multiraciality by speaking back to blackness but not against blackness as primarily illustrated in his autobiographical narrative *Dreams*. Political scientists Valeria Sinclair-Chapman and Melanye Price note that Obama's ability to articulate the self as "occupying liminal spaces" was integral to his success on the campaign trail (Sinclair-Chapman and Price 2008, 739–45).

Moreover, Obama made an explicit connection to questions of his multiraciality in the statement "A lot of shelter dogs are mutts like me" (Kornreich 2008), which he made as president-elect during his first official news conference November 7, 2008. However clumsily articulated, Obama found a way to acknowledge his mixed-race heritage. He does this in his very first official performance as the forty-fourth president of the United States of America. Obama has been continuously referred to as "no drama Obama" by his campaign team. Thus, this statement was not necessarily a "clumsy" error on the part of a man who has come to be known as a more than elegant speaker. A brief overview of Obama's biography may help provide some insight into this statement.

Obama's mother, Stanley "Ann" Dunham, is of European American descent, a white woman originally from Wichita, Kansas. He was raised by both his mother and maternal grandparents in Indonesia and Hawai'i. He has siblings that would presumably self-identify as black-African and a sister from his mother's second marriage, to an Indonesian man, who could/would easily self-identify as Asian (her husband is Chinese Canadian) but defines herself as "hybrid." In an interview with Deborah Solomon, Obama's sister Maya Soetoro-Ng was asked about her brother's race and responded in such a way:

Solomon: Do you think of your brother as black?
Soetoro-Ng: Yes, because that is how he has named himself. Each of us has a right to name ourselves as we will.

Solomon: Do you think of yourself as white?
Soetoro-Ng: No. I'm half white, half Asian. I think of myself as hybrid. People usually think I'm Latina when they meet me. That's what made me learn Spanish. (Solomon 2008)

Obama speaks quite evocatively of the brief union between his "white" American mother and his "black" African father, originally from Kenya, in *Dreams from My Father: A Story of Race and Inheritance* (1995).

The inheritance that Obama speaks of is that of a man with a mixed-race ancestry or "divided inheritance" of race bequeathed to him by both his white American mother and black African father. It is in essence the search for a way to name himself "a race." Obama found a way to "name himself" black, as his sister states, without completely relinquishing his mixed-race background. Obama explains in his memoirs how at the end of his parent's marriage he was left in the space in-between: "Even as that spell was broken and the worlds that they thought they'd left behind reclaimed each of them, I occupied the place where their dreams had been" (Obama 1995, 27). The narrative seems largely to be a story of maturation into a black identity but "the place where their dreams had been" is the sanctuary of the hybrid that struggles for actualization through the racial inheritance of his mother and father.

Barack Obama therefore embraces his blackness while at the same time consistently celebrating his multiracial background. David A. Hollinger has commented on how visible Obama's whiteness is and how Obama has made Americans aware of multiraciality:

Press accounts of Obama's life, as well as Obama's own autobiographical writings, render Obama's whiteness hard to miss. No other figure, not even Tiger Woods, has done as much as Obama to make Americans of every education level and social surrounding aware of color-mixing in general. (Hollinger 2008, 1033–37)

Obama's sense of self as understood in this examination is both fluid and contingent upon blackness while rejecting notions of essentialist hybridity (or hybrid fixity)[3] reflected in the "popular" multiracial movement. His counter to this is a hybrid fluidity that is illustrated in his autobiography, speeches, public statements, and other writings, and as a result of his lived experience.

Obama's multilayered identity is an intricate interweaving of the particular and the universal. Obama's cosmopolitanism combines cultural, political, and visceral trajectories grounded in an identity shaped by his transnational experiences and mixed-race background. He also has a sense of black cosmopolitanism or black collective subjectivity that transcends national and geographical specificity. He rejects what I call essentialist hybridity that he associates with the multiracial movement in general. Cultural and visceral cosmopolitanism (Nava 2007, 3–5) are more thoroughly examined in section six while Obama's connection to his multiracial ancestry is further developed in the next section.

RACE AND THE MULTIRACIAL MOVEMENT

The landmark text by Michael Omi and Howard Winant, *Racial Formation in the United States from the 1960s to the 1980s* (1986), introduced a contemporary concept of racial formation theory. This theory asserts that race is a multidimensional process of competing race projects, as produced in social relations, shaped by sociopolitical power structures as well as subjective phenomenon articulated in racial identities shaped by perceptions about the body (phenotype), and cultural practices. The concept of "race" today has little to do with biology given the findings of social scientists, historians, and geneticist's altogether. The race concept was initially manufactured to justify the enslavement of Africans and regulate black bodies in servitude. Historically, race has been an unstable concept. Most scholars have recognized that race continues to operate at the social level in U.S. society but not as a concrete biological reality.

There remains no consensus among the biological sciences as to what race actually is or how many races exist if human biology is to be considered in discussions about race. The genetic characteristics present in one population are not necessarily absent in another. The notion that race (or mixed race) can be simply understood as ancestry is problematical given the most recent research in human genetics. The idea of mixed race as ancestry may be explained away quite succinctly as Pilar Ossorio and Troy Duster assert:

> *People whose skin color is perceived as white can have genetic profiles indicating that 80% of their recent ancestry is West African, and people whose skin color is perceived as black can have genetic profiles indicative of predominantly European ancestry. A person with substantial, recent African ancestry may pass as White and may have medically and psychologically consequential social advantages of whiteness. On the*

other hand, a person may pass as White but possess medically relevant alleles more commonly associated with Blacks or with African ancestry. (Ossorio and Duster 2005, 116–18)

Ancestry fails to serve as a firm moniker for race or "mixed race," from one generation to the next, despite arguments to the contrary made by mixed-race studies theorists.

The case of the South African woman Sandra Laing, a woman born in 1955 with a markedly African phenotype of two white parents, was continuously reclassified as first white then as a person of color despite the circumstances of her "white" birth and European "ancestry." Her white parents fought to have her reclassified as white (her father attesting to his paternity in court) and there appeared no recent evidence of known African ancestry in her "white" parent's lineage. Scientists at the time argued the "genetic throwback" theory insisting that Laing's physical features were a result of an unknown "African" ancestor's DNA, having lain dormant for generations, manifested in Sandra, thereby explaining the difference between nearly pure white parents with an "African" child.[4] Laing eventually selected to become reclassified as a person of color upon her romantic association and subsequent marriage to a man of African descent.

Troy Duster has further argued that understanding race involves a complex interplay of social and biological realities as coupled with ideology and myths about race as word and idea:

Rather, when race is used as a stratifying practice (which can be apprehended empirically and systematically), there is often a reciprocal interplay of biological outcomes that makes it impossible to disentangle the biological from the social. (Duster 2003, 259–62)

Duster notes that the empirical biological data is not uniformly consistent with the social, ideological, or cultural assumptions about race such as with claims about ancestry.

Race operates at the social level as based on perceptions about human bodies. Race and racism operated in the life of Barack Obama as a man of mixed-race[5] ancestry with a particular phenotype who could not pass for white. He articulates this in his autobiography when he describes his life as a child not yet realizing, "I needed a race" (Obama 1995, 27). But as Omi and Winant have argued, racial projects have appeared throughout the modern history of humankind. As a result of these "projects," race, operating at both the micro level of individual social experiences, and at the macro level in racial classification systems, has become reconfigured but has not disappeared.

The 1960s activism of African Americans, coupled with changes in U.S. immigration laws, and the global migration of nonwhites into the United States, helped to produce a new "racial project" as predicated on a ternary racial order that acknowledges white, black, and other mono-racial identities as well as multiracial identities. G. Reginald Daniel, in his book *More Than Black*, contends that the emergence of the multiracial identity movement after 1967 can be understood as "a natural outgrowth" of the civil rights activism of the 1960s and is defined by individuals "who resist the one-drop rule and navigate the uncharted waters of multiracial identity" (Daniel 2002, 124). The multiracial movement as advancing a new racial project should be briefly examined here before we can discuss how, and later why, Obama incorporates his multiracial background into his complex sense of self that rests upon a foundation of blackness.

The multiracial movement is a broad-based scholarly, social, and cultural movement that includes a host of support groups, informational, and educational agencies. It engages both the scholars who have advanced mixed-race studies, the fastest growing subfield within ethnic studies, in the academy and dozens of groups such as I-Pride (Interracial/Intercultural Pride), founded in Berkeley, California, in 1979; the Biracial Family Network (BFN), established in 1980 Chicago; the Interracial Family Alliance (IFA) of Houston; the Multiracial Americans of Southern California in Los Angeles (MASC); and Project RACE (Reclassify All Children Equally). The Association of MultiEthnic Americans (AMEA) is a nationwide multiracial/ethnic organization, based on existing local groups, that was developed in 1988 and is now centered in California.

Matt Kelley, a nineteen-year-old college freshman at Wellesley University in Connecticut, created MAVIN magazine out of his college dorm room in 1999. The MAVIN Foundation, as a 501(c) 3 nonprofit group, became one of the most important associations dedicated to the support of projects and the dissemination of information related to the mixed-race experience. The first major scholarly anthologies dedicated to the study of the mixed-race experience were Maria P. P. Root's *Racially Mixed People in America* (1992), which was followed by *The Multiracial Experience* (1996). These anthologies included essays by some of the foundational scholars associated with the mixed-race studies movement in academia.

The multiracial movement is not monolithic. There have also been proliferations of online journals, blogs, and forums such as "Interracial Voice" and "Mixed Chics" that exist alongside the aforementioned associations. There are an increasing number of scholarly texts by those who seek to advance knowledge about the mixed-race experience. One of the major goals sought by advocacy groups such as the AMEA and later Project RACE was to make it possible to collect data on multiracial identified individuals on official forms such as the U.S. census. In 2000, the U.S. Census did indeed allow for "a mark more than one" option. This was a significant victory for the multiracial movement in general. Yet, in his 2010 U.S. census form, Obama did not select "more than one" but instead chose the category Black/Negro/African American.

The advocates of a multiracial identity category tend to emphasize ancestry, experience, demographics, and personal expression to determine their identity that hinges upon a *hybrid fixity* (that is, the condition of being of two or more races as the axis of identity). Scholars in support of the multiracial identity label have helped to develop a definition of multiracial identity as determined by ancestry. This definition includes the labeling of "first generation" (one parent who is socially designated as black and one parent who is socially designated as white) and "multigenerational" (those with parents or generations of ancestors with multiracial backgrounds, who have resisted identifying only with the African American community) as multiracial (Daniel 2002, 6–7).

Challengers to the multiracial identity project label these scholars "pro-identity scholars" (Spencer 2006, 91–93). Indeed, the emphasis by multiracial advocacy groups, and some scholars, on personal experience and hybrid "fixity" through ancestry (by drawing lines of delineation that create a distinct multiracial category out of ancestry and social experience) prompted Obama ultimately to reject MAVIN's overtures in such a way when meeting with the Generation Mix college students in his senate offices April 25, 2005:

> *Well, you know, I don't think that you can consider the issue of mixed race outside of the issue of race. And I do think that racial relations have improved somewhat, and I think to the extent that people of mixed race can be part of those larger movements and those larger concerns then I think that they serve as a useful bridge between cultures ... What I am always cautious about is persons of mixed race focusing so narrowly on their own unique experiences that they are detached from larger struggles, and I think it's important to try to avoid that sense of exclusivity, and feeling that you're special in some way ... ultimately the same challenges that all of you face a lot of young people face.*[6]

Obama rejects the "exclusivity" of the multiracial category as predicated upon ancestry and experience. This does not mean that he has not found a way to incorporate his own multiracial ancestry into his self-presentation. His more composite sense of self-awareness, as rooted in blackness, is made abundantly clear in his narrative writings. It has been noted by mixed-race studies scholars that individuals of mixed-race ancestry, such as Barack Obama, often, in specific situations, embrace a range of identity formations.

Sociologists David Brunsma and Kerry Ann Rockquemore have demonstrated, in their comprehensive cross-regional studies of black/white biracials in the United States, that identity formation for these individuals is customarily multidimensional. That is, black/white biracial identity has a tendency towards the interactional and situational as shaped by social perceptions, personal choice, and cultural assumptions. Brunsma has drawn a distinction between the public categories and private identities of black/white multiracials stating that "black/white biracials understand themselves in a multitude of ways that are rooted in their private and social worlds" (Brunsma 2006, 555–76).

Furthermore, Rockquemore contends that black/white biracial individual self-understanding contains a range of identity categories such as singular (monoracial), border (biracial), protean (sometimes black, white, or biracial) and transcendent (no single race identified) (Rockquemore and Brunsma 2002, 335–56). Obama's core identity is thus closest to a combined singular/border (that is at times strategically transcendent) identity as coupled with notions of cosmopolitanism. He certainly does not claim a distinct multiracial or biracial identity that supersedes his blackness. Indeed, Obama has routinely claimed to be black and writes a memoir clearly detailing his passage into a "functional" blackness despite his multiracial experience.

Consequently, the desire of many individuals associated with the multiracial movement to claim Obama as their own is at best highly speculative. This of course does not diminish the choice made by those few individuals who do indeed publically and privately embrace a multiracial identity. However, the notion that Obama is "at his core" multiracial is a gross misreading of *Dreams from My Father*. The denial of Obama's self-affirmation of blackness (in private or otherwise) seems dangerously close to white supremacist and anti-black sentiments regarding African Americans more generally. This attempt to superimpose *hybrid fixity* upon Obama tends to privilege mixed-race identity and ultimately whiteness.

Scholars and activists associated with the multiracial (identity) movement, that is, those that advance the notion of a distinct multiracial category, tend to promote a *hybrid fixity* that hinges upon bloodlines (ancestry) and personal experience. The construction of race as a stratifying practice that defines one as either "multiracial" or "monoracial" is a new race project that is both exclusionary and self-indulgent as is the nature of identity movements. Human ancestry is shared. Indeed, if ancestry overlaps with genetic inheritance (and it does), and mixed-race identity is to be understood as determined by ancestry, "mixed race" constitutes the human community as a whole. Obama's deployment of self-identity is far more progressive than what has been promulgated by the multiracial movement in that he deploys a self-awareness that is an ongoing negotiation between multiple "I" positions that have no firm axis or point of "fixity."

The only evidence we have of Obama's sense of racial self-identity is to be found in his memoirs, his political treatise, and everyday race talk. *Dreams from My Father* is the most comprehensive discussion yet delivered by Obama concerning his personal notions of racial self-identity. To label Obama at his core biracial or mixed race is to call into question the man's own words as having consistently defined himself as a black man with a mixed-race heritage or more composite sense of self-awareness (where the mixed-race component is largely muted by choice). Indeed, Obama does speak of a mixed-race experience in *Dreams* through the metaphor of "two-worlds" but it is an experience that ultimately reinforces his blackness, not a *mixed identity* private or otherwise. Obama is clearly far too self-assured an individual to lurk around in private hiding his true "self" from the world despite the hegemony of the one-drop rule.

In one instance in *Dreams*, upon telling his sister Auma the story of a romantic relationship he had with a white woman, he affirms that to continue his involvement with a white woman was to agree to live in her world stating, "I knew that if we stayed together I'd eventually live in hers. After all, I'd been doing it most of my life. Between the two of us, I was the one who knew how to live as an outsider."[7] If indeed Obama tells us of his "mixed-race experience" in *Dreams*, he also tells us of living the life of an *outsider* within that experience. Thus, what resonates with him most upon his trip to Africa and his personal connections with African Americans is the struggle of black people and blackness despite having lived outside of African American culture.

This attempt to impose a multiracial identity upon Obama hinges upon a hybrid fixity that seeks to delineate the monoracial from the multiracial as predicated upon a "feeling of in-between" and blood lines. To foist upon Obama a private multiracial identity is a form of sophistry that seeks to make of Obama a type of multiracial mascot for a new race project. The film *Invasion of the Body Snatchers* (based on the Jack Finney novel *The Body Snatchers*) comes to mind: imposter simulacrums grown from giant plant-like pods invade suburbia masquerading as the people we know. Obama has the typical experience of a mixed-race person but has repeatedly chosen to self-identify as a black man and has consistently called himself black. To believe that he is at his core, or in private, a mixed-race-identified person is tantamount to believing that he is a type of imposter black man or black simulacrum who is hiding his mixed-race identity only to be revealed in private.

If we are to believe the notion that Obama has been forced to capitulate to the one-drop rule that defines anyone as black with one drop of black blood, we must also take into account that perhaps Obama may have indeed chosen to call himself black in reaction to white racism. That is, Obama's refusal to identify with mixed-race categories might very well be a type of reactionary disassociation with whiteness (his white ancestry) and white supremacist beliefs that hold blackness in contempt. Though he does not live it, what resonates with Obama the most is the black experience. Therefore, given the disdain for blackness present in U.S. society it seems more plausible (as blackness is more often than not determined by phenotype) that Obama found community in blackness and with black people not through his mixed-race experience and does not identify himself as merely mixed race in private or public. Despite the "archetypes" and "tropes" of the mixed-race experience that appear in Obama's autobiography he found greater comfort and camaraderie with people who look like him (as he so states).

Tanya Hernandez, among others, contends that U.S. society is increasingly adopting a "multiracial matrix" similar to Latin America in which mixed-race identity serves as a moniker of racial transcendence (Hernandez 2002, 45). This is not to infer that the "multiracial matrix" present throughout Latin American countries affords equality to people of color (in other words, the myth of racial democracy in places such as Brazil has long been abandoned by scholars). One can infer though that the one-drop rule is becoming less hegemonic in U.S. society. In fact, much like the popular multiracial movement, there seems to be a fixation with mixed-race identity like never before in U.S. history while mixed-race people by the millions have begun to self-identify. This is not necessarily a climate in which a mixed-race president of the most powerful nation on the planet would hide his "true" core identity from the world.

Certainly, had Obama's phenotype been lighter or nearly white, his choice may have been different. The question of phenotype tends to complicate the whole notion of a mixed-race experience altogether for black/white multiracial individuals. Indeed, Obama embarks on a search for "his people" (African Americans that is) at an early age, feeling like a stranger in *Another Country*[8] among white people. This is the story he tells us in his own words.

Obama relates to us, in his memoirs, a story of blackness as a doing and a becoming. His own sister tells us that she considers herself "hybrid" but her brother has chosen to name himself black. For most individuals, self-identity tends to be fixed while identification is about process. At the same time, identification with one or more "selves" threatens to unseat the very notion of identity. Obama's biography is clearly the story of a man searching for a way to name himself black while maintaining a connection to his multiracial background whenever possible. The title *Dreams from My Father: A Story of Race and Inheritance* is enunciated through the story he tells us: that the racial inheritance bequeathed to him from his father is blackness. This notion of Obama as a black man is continuously reinforced in his autobiography, stating at the very end his claim to blackness: "The pain I felt was my father's pain. My questions were my brother's questions. Their struggle, my birthright" (Obama 1995, 430). Obama's personal biography is examined in the following section.

THE OBAMA BIOGRAPHY IN PERSPECTIVE[9]

Barack Obama was born August 4, 1961, in Honolulu, Hawai'i, to a white American mother, Stanley "Ann" Dunham, and a black Kenyan father, Barack Hussein Obama, Sr. His parents were students at the East-West Center of the University of Hawai'i at Manoa during the time of Obama's birth. He has seven siblings, including Maya Soetoro Ng, from his mother's second marriage to an Indonesian man, Lolo Soetoro, and a total of six more from his father's marriages to other women (one African wife and a Jewish American woman). Obama was raised primarily by his white American mother and grandparents in Hawai'i after his father left to pursue doctoral studies at Harvard, and later returned to Kenya, when Barack, Jr., was two years old. Ann Dunham married Lolo Soetoro in 1967, another student at the East-West Center, when Barack was six years old. The family relocated to Jakarta, Indonesia, after Soetoro was forced to return home due to unrest in Indonesia. Obama's sister, Maya, was born August 15, 1970, in Jakarta, Indonesia. Obama attended schools in Indonesia until he was ten years old. His mother sent him back to Hawai'i in 1971 to be raised primarily by his grandparents. He would only see his father once more, although they corresponded with one another, at the age of ten before Barack, Sr., was killed in a car accident in Nairobi, Kenya, in 1982.

Historian Paul Spickard has noted that Pacific Islander Americans who inhabit Hawai'i have complex multiethnic identities based on ancestry, family, practice, and place; and they have a "greater consciousness" than other American groups of being mixed peoples having multiple ethnicities including Samoan, Tongan, Marquesan, Tahitian, Maori, and European (Spickard and Fong 1995, 1365–83). Pacific Islanders are more successful at balancing multiple ethnicities while being "deeply involved" with more than one of these identities at the same time; therefore, Pacific Islander American identity is ultimately situational (Spickard and Fong 1995, 1365–83). In his historical and ethnographic studies of Pacific Islander ethnicity, Spickard has provided several examples of how multiple identities are balanced and negotiated in Hawai'i. Barack Obama, coming of age in Hawai'ian culture, would have learned to balance his multiple selves more proficiently as opposed to if he came of age on the U.S. mainland. Indeed, his memoir suggests that he found ways to incorporate his "multiple selves" into a composite self, including his biracial background as developed in a multiethnic setting that encourages the "balancing" of more than one ethno-racial identity.

The hybrid Obama came of age in Indonesia and the multicultural setting that is Hawai'i, where he struggled to name himself black. For Obama, becoming black in his formative years was at times a difficult process, as noted in his memoirs. On several occasions, he illustrates to his reader the process of being/becoming black out of the sometimes-awkward relationship with white people and whiteness (including the grandparents who raised him). Obama speaks of a search for self and manhood, in his early years that could not come from his grandfather but rather from "some other source."[10] He found a way to become black by watching *Soul Train* and at the basketball courts where he met a cohort of sometimes-angry black youth.

TV movies, the radio; those were the places to start. Pop culture was color coded, after all, an arcade of images from which you could cop a walk, a talk, a step, a style. I couldn't croon like Marvin Gaye, but I could learn to dance all the Soul Train *steps. I couldn't pack a gun like Shaft or Superfly, but I could sure enough curse like Richard Pryor. And I could play basketball, with a consuming passion.*[11]

Obama found camaraderie and community among his black boyhood friends in Hawaiʻi: "It was there [the basketball court near his grandparents home] that I would meet Ray and the other blacks close to my age who had begun to trickle into the islands, teenagers whose confusion and anger would help shape my own."[12]

Obama, as a college student, continued to search for a sense of self until he moved to Chicago where he became black. He was made aware at an early age that he needed both a race and a community as asserted in his autobiographical narrative *Dreams from My Father*. Two years after graduating from high school, he was still pondering the question, "Where do I belong?"[13] He articulates this upon receiving a letter from his father:

Two years from graduation, I had no idea what I was going to do with my life, or even where I would live. Hawaii lay behind me like a childhood dream; I could no longer imagine settling there. Whatever my father might say, I knew it was too late to ever truly claim Africa as my home. And if I had come to understand myself as a black American, and was understood as such, that understanding remained unanchored to place. What I needed was a community, I realized, a community that cut deeper than the common despair that black friends and I shared when reading the latest crime statistics, or the high fives I might exchange on a basketball court. A place where I could put down stakes and test my commitments.[14]

Barack Obama "named" himself black before leaving Hawaiʻi for the mainland to pursue his studies at Occidental College, but he remained "unanchored" in blackness.

In his writings, Obama trots out a succession of black friends from childhood to the college years, including Ray, Reggie, Marcus, and Regina in an attempt to legitimate to his readers, and possibly to himself, see, "I have black friends." His quest for place in blackness is at times painful during his awkward early years, from grade school through college and ultimately law school. Indeed, Obama characterizes his early college experience as a time when he, particularly in his first year at Occidental, felt as if he were "living a lie" and continuously "running around in circles" trying to "cover his tracks" when interacting with his black friends.[15] On one occasion he tells Regina, after giving a public address in association with the divestment campaign against South Africa organized by black students on campus, that he has no "business speaking for black folks."[16] It is through Regina's stories that his romanticized vision of black life and community takes shape:

> She [Regina] told me about evenings in the kitchen with uncles and cousins and grandparents, the stew of voices bubbling up in laughter. Her voice evoked a vision of black life in all its possibility, a vision that filled me with longing—for place, and a fixed and definite history. As we were getting up to leave, I told Regina I envied her:[17]
> "For what?"
> "I don't know. For your memories, I guess."[18]

Obama's quest for self seemed to be ultimately stifled at Occidental. Was he to be forever consigned to live vicariously through Regina's, and other friends, memories and experiences of blackness in his personal attainment of a black self? This pursuit of self eventually continued beyond Occidental and took him to another space.

The search for community and "place" brought Obama to New York City and Columbia University, where he began to further conceptualize himself as a black man.

> And so, when I heard about a transfer program that Occidental had arranged with Columbia University, I'd been quick to apply. I figured that if there weren't any more black students at Columbia than there were at Oxy, I'd at least be in the heart of a true city, with black neighborhoods in close proximity.[19]

It was at Columbia University that Obama became acutely aware of the structural inequalities in American society that he understood to have a deep impact on the ability of African Americans to progress.

> But whether because of New York's density or because of its scale, it was only now that I began to grasp the almost mathematical precision with which America's race and class problems joined; the depth, the ferocity, of resulting tribal wars; the bile that flowed freely not just out on the streets but in the stalls of Columbia's bathrooms as well, where no matter how many times the administration tried to paint them over, the walls remained scratched with blunt correspondence between niggers and kikes.[20]

Obama continues:

> *It was as if all middle ground had collapsed, utterly. And nowhere, it seemed, was that collapse more apparent than in the black community I had so lovingly imagined and within which I had hope to find refuge. I might meet a black friend at his Midtown law firm, and before heading to lunch at the MoMa, I would look out across the city toward the East River from his high-rise office, imagining a satisfactory life for myself—a vocation, a family, a home. Until I noticed that the only other blacks in the office were messengers or clerks, the only other blacks in the museum the blue-jacketed security guards.*[21]

Obama's musings on black people and his search for community in blackness, at times, are romanticized and paternalistic. Nonetheless, his journey into blackness is consummated in New York City. The second Obama, as a black man anchored in place, comes of age in Chicago. Indeed, he became black in Chicago, confirming his entrenchment in blackness through endogamy. He met and married a dark-skinned black woman named Michelle Robinson with roots in Chicago's Southside. The following section examines how Obama came to balance his hybrid self with a functional blackness grounded in the black community[22] but never completely dismissing his mixed-race heritage as articulated in both his memoir and his political biography, *The Audacity of Hope*.

RACE, HYBRIDITY, AND FUNCTIONAL BLACKNESS

In her book *Black Skins, Black Masks*, Shirley Ann Tate postulates a space where black as a category is constantly recouped, transformed, and reformed. Obama is both performer and producer of an "other black" identity that is sometimes in opposition to positionings within the larger discourses of blackness. The "larger" discourses about blackness are predicated upon experiences that Obama does not have before and initially after he leaves Hawai'i, beyond his friend Ray's anger or "rage at the white world"[23] on the basketball courts of Hawai'i and, later, Regina's memories of home. It is clear that Obama, with his "African" features and skin tone, could never pass for white. Obama was not completely at ease in his blackness until he learned the language, gesture, and "ways" of his two worlds in his path to self-development.

His embodiment of blackness can be seen in representations of his public self and language. Through his musical sense of language and his ability to harness the creative power of the word *nommo* (Howard 2009, 1–3), we see a black identity deeply connected to the African American experience. Yet his journey into blackness took place within a multicultural setting where he learned to appropriate the languages of his "two worlds."[24] His blackness is, in part, performance. He learned to speak, talk, and perform blackness on his journey into adulthood.[25] This homogenizing trajectory (Banita 2010, 24) into blackness has never been completely divorced from Obama's multiracial self as shaped by his upbringing in multicultural Hawai'i. Further, Obama's blackness is contingent upon, and in opposition to, essentialist concepts of race while also being connected to his hybrid cosmopolitan subjectivity.

Cultural studies theoretician Homi K. Bhabha postulates hybridity as a "third space" subject position or indeterminate space in between where a constant blurring and questioning of essentialist boundaries occurs.[26] Further, Bhabha asserts that this "third space" may be characterized as an "interruptive, interrogative, and enunciative" space where the process of identification takes shape "through another object, an object of otherness" (Bhabha 1990, 207–21). For Obama, blackness, as understood in a multicultural setting by a man with a multiracial background, is at first an object of otherness. Tate, utilizing the theories of Bhabha, has argued that the third space of hybridity is a "dialogical space where speakers thread together discourses to identify with and through objects of otherness" (Tate 2005, 59). Tate examines the discussions by mixed-race women "who speak back to their positioning within blackness" to establish her premise that hybridity is about "the ongoing assemblage of identifications" (Tate 2005, 59).

Neither Bhabha nor Tate understand hybridity as a fixed identity but rather as a process of identification. Obama's blackness is in part a type of hybrid blackness as understood in relation to his multiracial background and cosmopolitan outlook. Hybridity, as Naomi Pabst contends, "enables us to conceive of a blackness that crosscuts, overlaps, and blends with other categories, racial and otherwise" (Pabst 2009, 112–32). Obama's blackness blends with other categories.

This process of identification through dialogue is ongoing and not merely about selecting a moniker of self-identity such as "multiracial" or "black" on a public form. Obama repeatedly speaks back to his positioning within blackness from the standpoint of his biracial and multicultural experience through his memoir, political writings, and public speeches. He embodies the "experience" but not the identity of a multiracial person on many occasions.[27] He may have become black through endogamy and by situating himself within the black community, as married to a black woman with dark skin, but his composite identity is far more complex than "black," "white," or "multiracial." The self for Obama is framed broadly as opposed to unitary or essentialist. Bhabha contends that the hybrid "third space" is an ambivalent space where there exists no unity or fixity (Bhabha 1994a, 38–39, 54–56; 1994b, 269–72). This notion of the hybrid pertains to Obama's blackness, which may be seen as the foundation of the self but not the end of the self.

Indeed, blackness does not constitute the beginning, end, or composite of the self for this U.S. president. This blackness is neither unitary nor fixed given that Obama is at times in dialogue with blackness. Obama's black identity may be seen as political or public in that he does indeed situate the self as grounded in the black community and claims a black/African American identity that seems much more nuanced when coupled with his writings, speeches, and everyday race talk. Given that Americans continue to see race through a binary lens, Obama understood that he needed a race (as he states in his memoirs) to become president. This many-voiced man spoke the language of an "other black"[28] to secure the highest position in the land.

Obama's blackness has been hotly debated since he entered the political arena. Critics of his blackness have included Stanley Crouch, who wrote a piece in the *New York Daily News* detailing why he believed Obama was not "black like me"; Debra Dickerson, who insisted that Obama did not meet the proper criteria for blackness because he did not descend from African slaves; and *New Republic* columnist Peter Beinart, who defined Obama as a "good black." Questions of Obama's identity have engaged both the far right and liberal Democrats. Joe Biden (who later became Obama's choice for vice president) described Obama as "clean and articulate," while Democratic Senate Majority Leader Harry Reid defined Obama's blackness in similar ways in terms of his ability to speak as a proper "Negro."

In an interview with Charlie Rose, Obama himself commented on his blackness in such a way: "If I'm outside your building trying to catch a cab," he told Rose, "they're not saying, oh there's a mixed-race guy." It is interesting to note that Obama's critics on the far right have blackened Obama further as he has become president. Indeed, many on the far right contend that Obama is an alien non-citizen born in Africa. Yale University race scholar Naomi Pabst has noted that to question a person's blackness is to admit the very blackness of the person under scrutiny: "You have to be black by some definition in order to be "not really black" (Pabst 115). Obama's blackness may also be understood as a doing and a becoming as evidenced in his biographical narratives. One can sense this "otherness" in his memoir *Dreams from My Father* on several occasions (exemplified in his dialogue with "blackness"), and to a lesser extent, in his book *The Audacity of Hope* (through the rhetoric of racial transcendence). Though Obama consistently defines himself as an African American, it is through his writings that we see him struggle with his racial self. As Carly Fraser asserts, "Obama writes in a way that emphasizes the complexities of his background and his desire to embrace all aspects of it" (Fraser 2009, 19–40). This struggle with his racial self is an attempt by Obama to construct a composite identity that includes blackness, mixed-race ancestry, and his transnational experiences. To illustrate this further, it is necessary to examine Obama as linguistic subject.

OBAMA AS LINGUISTIC SUBJECT

Obama wrote, "I learned to slip back and forth between my black and white worlds, understanding that each possessed its own language and customs and structures of meaning, convinced that with a bit of translation on my part the two worlds would eventually cohere" (Obama 1995, 82). This statement encapsulates Obama as linguistic subject. The French linguist Emile Benveniste (1902–76) argued that it is "in and through language that man constitutes himself as a subject." The understanding of individual self-identity through the study of language has been the concern of psychology, philosophy, and literary theory for some time. Russian philosopher and literary critic Mikhail Bakhtin (1895–1975) studied literature to examine how human social identity is materialized through language and voice. Bakhtin's ideas are directly applicable to Obama as linguistic subject.

Mikhail Bakhtin's study of the philosophy of language and literature led him to coin phrases such as "heteroglossia" and "dialogism." The former is a combination of the Latin term *hetero* for different and the Greek word *glossa* for tongue/language. Heteroglossia, as utilized by Bakhtin, connotes "different-speech-ness," "another's speech in another language," or the coexistence of distinct varieties of speech within a single linguistic code. More succinctly, heteroglossia constitutes the existence of conflicting discourses within any field of linguistic activity such as with a work of literature (a novel or memoir) or a diversity of voices, styles of discourse, or point of view. The

Obama narratives *Dreams from My Father* and *Audacity of Hope* contain an often conflicting discourse on Obama's racial identity while Obama himself "speaks in tongues" throughout much of *Dreams*. Dorothy J. Hale contends that African American linguistic identity contains a powerful heteroglossia that may be equated with Du Boisian double consciousness (Hale 1994, 445–71). Hale has argued that scholars of African American literature and culture have found a way to read Du Boisian double consciousness through Bakhtinian double voice thereby "transforming the Du Boisian crisis of subaltern invisibility into a Bakhtinian triumph of self-articulation."[29] Obama's journey to self-articulation evolves in his *Dreams from My Father*.

On the one hand, *Dreams* is about Obama's journey into blackness, but on the other hand, he continuously tells his reader how he learned to appropriate the language of his two worlds while running around in circles and tripping over his tongue when lamenting the crimes of "white folks." Further, in *Audacity of Hope*, he tells us again how he has never completely harnessed a singular ethno-racial identity through which to understand himself in the world as a "black man of mixed race heritage" stating, "I've never had the option of restricting my loyalties on the basis of race, or measuring my worth on the basis of tribe" (Obama 2006, 14, 274).

Mikhail Bakhtin studied novels because it was his contention that the novelist best illustrated the social voices present in language. Bakhtin often understood voice as accent, ventriloquation (internal dialogue of voices or a process through which self-understanding of experience receive linguistic formulation), refraction, or inflection. Voice as a property of language allows for an understanding of human identity as both self-selected and socially determined (both individual and collective). For Bakhtin, human subjects are both voiced and have the ability to "voice." The quality of being "voiced" illustrates the language that speaks the subject into society while the subject's use of *voice* may be used to speak back to the dominant discourses concerning identity. Obama's use of the terms "mutt" and more recently "mongrel" could perhaps be analyzed through Bakhtinian theories of language and subjectivity. For Bakhtin, all language appears dialogic. That is, everything anyone says always exists in response to things that have been said before and in anticipation of things that will be said. Obama's thinking is highly strategic if not anticipatory on questions of race as imbued with hybrid utterances or passages that may employ a single speaker but one or more "voices."

Obama has straddled his two worlds in his early development and as a political figure, from his speech at the 2004 Democratic National

Convention to his first two years as president through 2010. It is as candidate, and later president, that we see Barack H. Obama harness the language of his "two worlds" best. There is a marked difference that speaks to the "many-voiced" man that Obama is—between a speech that he gave at the opening convocation at Howard University and the commencement address that he gave at Southern New Hampshire University while on the campaign trail. The international addresses connect us more to the cosmopolitan Obama (for obvious reasons) while in his speeches to the American public there seem to be greater variations of the black/white Obama navigating between his "two worlds" as predicated upon context and situation. Indeed, his public persona in these public forums presents a self that is at times contradictory. Zadie Smith notes Obama's talent for dialogue as evidenced in his memoir:

> In Dreams from My Father, *the new president displays an enviable facility for dialogue . . . Obama can do young Jewish male, black old lady from the South Side, white woman from Kansas, Kenyan elders, white Harvard nerds . . . This new president doesn't just speak* for *his people. He can speak them. It is a disorienting talent in a president; we're so unused to it. (Z. Smith 2009)*

Smith notes, as too few others have, that Barack Obama with his "many-voiced" narrative articulates a plural self with multiple ethno-racial and transnational allegiances. She goes on to state that because Obama is a mixed-race man, born in the space in-between where his parents dreams ended, he had no choice but to "speak in tongues" like all others born in this place "betwixt and between:"[30]

> *When your personal multiplicity is printed on your face, in an almost too obviously thematic manner, in your DNA, in your hair and in the neither this nor that beige of your skin—well, anyone can see you come from Dream City . . . You have no choice but to cross borders and speak in tongues. (Z. Smith 2009)*

Barack Obama utilizes his "many-voices" to connect with all people beyond the U.S. when he speaks. This is evidenced in Obama as linguistic subject. Obama's identity is connected to a cosmopolitanism that accepts broad notions of self-identity, but neither rejects nor discards subjective racial identities.

OBAMA THE COSMOPOLITAN

The term "cosmopolitan" is derived from the Greek word *kosmopolites* for "citizen of the world." It has been utilized in reference to a broad range of views about moral, social, and political philosophy since Greek antiquity. A central tenet of most forms of cosmopolitanism is that all human beings can belong to a single community either on political, moral, economic, or cultural terms. Moral and political cosmopolitanism are perhaps more familiar, while cultural cosmopolitanism remains the subject of great debate. The concept of moral cosmopolitanism is a legacy of antiquity that can be traced back to the Cynics and Stoics. The phrase "citizen of the cosmos" was first utilized by the Cynics. Both the Cynics and Stoics saw the world as their community on moral grounds in their appeals for universal human solidarity. The Cynic Diogenes claimed in the fourth century BCE: "I am a citizen of the world." Zeno of Citium, a Stoic, utilizes a similar phrase in his understanding of humanity as belonging to a single moral community.

The Cynics and Stoics did not envision a transnational political entity, as is the case with the type of political cosmopolitanism advanced by the German philosopher of the High Enlightenment, Immanuel Kant. In his *Perpetual Peace* (1795), Kant envisions a "cosmopolitan law" that binds together "citizens of the earth." The Scottish philosopher Adam Smith imagined a type of economic cosmopolitanism as a global free market made up of equal trading partners among all humans (or nations).

The major divergent forms of cosmopolitanism that exist today, as coupled with the aforementioned moral, political, and economic, also include cultural and visceral cosmopolitanism. Cultural cosmopolitanism emphasizes the value of cultural pluralism, the importance of some attachment to culture, and that a person's identity need not be bounded or homogenous. The term "visceral cosmopolitanism" was coined by British cultural studies theoretician Mica Nava in her book *Cultural Cosmopolitanism: Gender, Culture, and the Normalization of Difference* (2007). In this text, Nava examines gendered, imaginative, and empathetic aspects of cultural and racial difference through a discussion of the vernacular as coupled with cosmopolitanism. Nava introduced the phrase *visceral cosmopolitanism* in this study of race relations in post war Britain. She focuses on romantic relationships between British women and soldiers of African descent in wartime Britain and after, including an examination of the high-profile couple Princess Diana and Dodi Al Fayed. Diana, as world traveler and cosmopolitan, develops a "taboo" romantic connection with Al Fayed (a man of Arab descent). Her emotional connection to Al Fayed is a "structure of feeling" made possible by her transnational experiences and cosmopolitan outlook. This is not unlike Obama's (initially) largely emotional and "romanticized" connection to blackness and the black experience.

Obama's self-understanding and political philosophy is imbued with multiple trajectories of cosmopolitanism. This includes the moral, political, cultural, and visceral variations as evidenced in his speeches and writings. America as redeemer nation is a constant in the Obama speeches. American political and moral (Christian) values form the basis of the universal and global human community that is advanced by Obama in his political treatise and speeches. In his memoirs, his connection to blackness occurs at first through the visceral or it is a structure of feeling and camaraderie that he develops upon seeking out various African American "role models" and friends. He ends *Dreams* having come to the realization that "their struggle was my struggle." Several pundits, polemicists, and scholarly observers of Obama have defined him as a cosmopolitan.

Barack Obama is viewed as a cosmopolitan by several observers, from John Zogby to Mexican novelist Carlos Fuentes, and we see in Obama's own words the sentiments of a cosmopolitan. Zogby has contended that

> *Obama has much more in common with 18 to 29 year olds, a group I call the First Global Citizens . . . Having roots in Kenya, lived in Indonesia and raised in poly-ethnic Hawaii, Obama's background makes him more of a world citizen than perhaps any other president. (Zogby 2009, 45)*

This is Fuentes on Obama:

> *The historical election of Barack Obama—the first "mestizo" to the White House will go a long way toward redeeming the promise of the United States in the eyes of the world . . . For the first time, a mixed-race leader will have come to power north of the border. (Fuentes 2009, 34)*

In his first major speech abroad, as a presidential candidate in the summer of 2008, Obama described himself in such a way:

> *I come to Berlin as so many of my countrymen have come before; although tonight, I speak to you not as a candidate for President, but as a citizen—a proud citizen of the United States, and a fellow citizen of the world.*[31]

We see in Obama's speeches and writings a visceral, moral, and political cosmopolitan.

His autobiographical writings indicate notions of a *visceral cosmopolitan*. He tells us in *Audacity of Hope* that he "can't help but view the American experience through the lens of a black man of mixed heritage, forever mindful of how generations of people who looked like me were subjugated and stigmatized," while in *Dreams* he relates a story of becoming black by seeking out connections with black people, watching *Soul Train*, or finding solace in basketball. He does not have Regina's memories of home nor does he completely possess a comparable anger at whites that his friends Ray and Marcus claim. In fact, in one instance in *Dreams*, he ponders the notion that Ray's anger at white people may not always be authentic: "Sometimes, after one of his performances, I would question his judgment, if not his sincerity."[32]

Obama obviously does have his own direct experiences with racism while living with his grandparents in Hawai'i and, of course, after he leaves the island. He relates these instances in his writings. The argument here though is that his connection with blackness is at first tenuous and initially accessed largely through the visceral but grows stronger as he proactively appropriates for himself a "race." He remains uncomfortable uttering the phrase "white folks" when railing against the indignities of racism even after coming to the realization of race and racism in the early stages of his self-development. "The term itself was uncomfortable in my mouth first; I felt like a non-native speaker tripping over a difficult phrase. Sometimes I would find myself talking to Ray about *white folks* this or *white folks* that, and I would suddenly remember my mother's smile."[33] The visceral is combined with the moral and political aspects of cosmopolitanism as he becomes Obama the political candidate, and then president.

The sentiments of cosmopolitanism are present in both his national and international public addresses as a constant theme. Barack Obama delivered the commencement address at the University of Notre Dame on May 18, 2009, amid public controversy over his stance on abortion. The common human community shared by all citizens of the world (in terms of the moral and the political) resonates in Obama's words.

> *In short, we must find a way to live together as one human family. And it's this last challenge that I'd like to talk about today ... For the major threats we face in the 21st century—whether it's global recession or violent extremism, the spread of nuclear weapons or pandemic disease—*

these things do not discriminate. They do not recognize borders. They do not see color. They do not target specific ethnic groups. Moreover, no one person, or religion, or nation can meet these challenges alone.[34]

In his Cairo speech, delivered on June 4, 2009, at Cairo University, the recurrent themes of universal moral community and political cooperation are present:

I've come here to Cairo to seek a new beginning between the United States and Muslims around the world, one based on mutual interest and mutual respect, and one based upon the truth that America and Islam are not exclusive and need not be in competition.[35]

In this same speech, Obama tells his audience that "there must be a sustained effort to listen to each other, to learn from each other, to respect one another and seek common ground," and that he remains firm in his belief that "the interests we share as human beings are far more powerful than the forces that drive us apart."[36] The sentiments of a universal morality and transnational political cooperation are echoed in the Nobel Peace Prize lecture delivered by President Obama on December 10, 2009, at Oslo City Hall, in Oslo, Norway. Obama states in this address that mutual cooperation among nations is necessary to combat common global threats and that "American cannot act alone" when confronting such threats.[37] This, of course, does not mean that Obama as president has sought to radically change liberal democratic policies to alleviate the suffering of black people (in terms of social and economic disparities). Clearly, he has not. Indeed, his political character is more that of a political pragmatist as opposed to idealistic social reformer.

CONCLUSION

Barack Obama may be seen by some as a calculating individual. He is a savvy, shrewd, and pragmatic politician who gives himself to no one and everyone at the same time. Reverend Jeremiah Wright and Shirley Sherrod were unceremoniously dismissed by the Obama administration amid racial controversies. Wright, Obama's former pastor for twenty years, was discarded for his audacious articulation of black liberation theology. The now-famous Obama speech on race was delivered to specifically salvage his campaign (again, Obama responds out of necessity) after an incendiary speech by Wright "damning America" surfaced on YouTube. Obama was forced to divest himself of Wright, the quintessential "angry black man," or run the risk of irreparable damage to his carefully crafted bid for president. Sherrod, an African American Department of Agriculture administrator in Georgia, was asked to resign for her alleged mistreatment of white farmers on the basis of race.

Obama is not the first politician of African American descent to use a strategy of racial transcendence to win an election. His rhetoric of transcendence is often strategically deployed and never completely anchored in black social-justice claims (Sinclair-Chapman and Price 2008, 739–45). Of course, his campaign for president may have utilized some of the same techniques as those who came before him, including Shirley Chisholm, Harold Washington, and Jesse Jackson, in terms of his connections to the black community (through the black church and his community organizing experience) but his deployment of racial ambiguity (through his many voices) as opposed to a "black-centered" rhetoric of social justice gained him more white votes than any other black candidate on the national scene ultimately helping him to secure the highest office in the land (Sinclair-Chapman and Price 2008, 739–45).

Obama articulated, in his now-famous race speech, the grievances harbored by African Americans with the demands of "all people" or all Americans while at the same time giving voice to "legitimate" white resentment. This technique flagrantly diminishes the real structural inequalities faced by African Americans past and present but nonetheless proved successful for candidate Obama, with a campaign team that was made up of mostly white operatives of the Democratic party who were outside of the black community. The Obama campaign was not a traditional "black" campaign. His deployment of the rhetoric of racial transcendence in some respects mirrored the composite self that he has managed to forge.

Obama's nuanced and dispassionate engagement with race has been interpreted by some as a type of silence. Naomi Klein has remarked that "no matter how race-neutral Obama tries to be, his actions will be viewed by a large part of the country through the lens of its racial obsessions" (Klein 2009). The far right has fueled enough white racial anxiety about Obama since his election, including the "birthers," "deathers," and "tea-baggers," that fears about his "otherness" have not been quelled. Indeed, according to some national statistics, a large number of Americans continue to believe that Obama is a Muslim and that he was not born in the United States. Klein goes on to state that because "his most modest, Band-Aid measures are going to be greeted as if he is waging a full-on race war" (Klein 2009).

Obama has, perhaps naively, attempted to use his diverse background to engage wider questions of race, ethnicity, and community. This approach has not sustained nor assuaged white fears about his perceived "foreign" or "alien" character. Indeed, his perceived "otherness" has been exploited by extremists and the far right for the purpose of inciting white rage and personal political gain. Barack Obama occupied the space where his parent's dreams of a life-long union failed to take shape. The pursuit of self by this U.S. president reflects the nation's long struggle with race and racism. Our union remains imperfect.

Notes

Other versions of this chapter appear in *Converging Identities: Blackness in the Modern African Diaspora*, ed. Julius O. Adekunle and Hettie V. Williams (Durham: Carolina Academic Publishing, 2013), 115–38.

1. The notion of human identities as partial, contradictory, strategic and ultimately fragmented is not new and has long been associated with feminist, cultural, and postcolonial theory. The work of Donna Haraway (1991) in the "Cyborg Manifesto"; Nancy Hartsock's writings on feminist historical materialism (1983); and Chela Sandoval's work on "oppositional consciousness" (1991) engage the concept of identity as a complex affair. Haraway's assertions on identity infer that subjects negotiate a series of positionings that are never completely fixed on a given positioning (partial), that these positionings may be in conflict (contradictory), and that a subject positions herself/himself according to context or situation at a given moment. Feminist Standpoint theory, which understands knowledge as particular rather than universal, defines subjects as constructed by relational forces rather than as transcendent; Hartsock argues that some perceptions of reality are partial, and Sandoval views the world as a type of topography where groups and individuals may produce themselves as oppositional subjects.

2. In her book *Black Skins, Black Masks: Hybridity, Dialogism, Performativity* (2005), Shirley Ann Tate conceptualizes the notion of an "other black" identity in the lives of mixed-race women of black/white parentage in contemporary England through an examination of the everyday "talk" of these women. Tate utilizes the work of Mikhail Bakhtin, Homi K. Bhabha, Paul Gilroy, Stuart Hall, Franz Fanon, and Gayatri Spivak to articulate her notion of the "other black"; such as with her discussion of language as hybrid and performativity in hybridity. The women in Tate's study project a multidimensional sense of self by simultaneously deploying blackness and mixedness in an interactional "hybridity of the everyday." My use of this term advances the notion of Barack Obama as an "other black" cosmopolitan as he embraces a public blackness while his narratives and other writings

(and statements) present a more complex sense of self through a "dialogical space" (written and spoken).

3. The term "essentialist hybridity" will be defined in conjunction with my notion of "fluid hybridity" later in this chapter.
4. Sandra Laing's story has been the subject of books, documentaries, and feature films, such as the recently released movie *Skin* and the documentary *Skin Deep: The Sandra Laing Story*.
5. Here, again, I use the term "mixed-race" to connote largely the social understanding of the term as based on claims about ancestry by self-identified multiracial activists and scholars.
6. This statement was made by Barak Obama to the Generation Mix college students while on tour in 2005. They were invited to his Senate offices and the scene also appears in the film *Changing Daybreak*.
7. Obama, *Dreams*, 211.
8. Many scholars, including Zadie Smith, have remarked how Obama's own memoirs are clearly influenced by James Baldwin's *Another Country*.
9. G. Reginald Daniel, and Hettie V. Williams, "Barack Obama and Multiraciality," *Encyclopedia of African American History*, ed. Joe Trotter (New York: Facts on File, 2011), 20. Some of the information in this section, in terms of the generic biographical material on Barack Obama, was coauthored by this author and G. Reginald Daniel for a forthcoming publication that includes a biographical essay of Barack Obama in relation to his multiracial background.
10. Obama, *Dreams*, 78.
11. Ibid.
12. Ibid., 80.
13. Ibid., 115.
14. Ibid.
15. Ibid., 102.
16. Ibid., 108.
17. Ibid., 104.
18. Ibid.
19. Ibid., 115.
20. Ibid., 120–21.
21. Ibid.
22. G. Reginald Daniel makes the argument in his essay in this volume that, though Obama may be understood as hybrid, it is a hybridity that extends outward from the location of a black identity rooted in the black community.
23. Obama, *Dreams*, 81–82.
24. Ibid.
25. Ibid.
26. Homi K. Bhabha is considered one of the chief architects of understanding hybridity in postcolonial theory. He develops his notion of hybridity in an interview he gave titled "The Third Space" that appears in *Identity, Community, Culture, Difference* (1990), with such works as *The Location of Culture* (1994), and in "Frontliners/Borderposts" in *Displacements: Cultural Identity in Question* (1994).

27. In both *Dreams of My Father* and the *Audacity of Hope*, we find that Obama makes repeated inferences to his mixed heritage and multicultural experience while at the same time claiming a black identity that is not rooted in the "typical" experience of most African Americans. He does this in the opening pages of *Dreams* and once again in the early chapters of *Audacity of Hope*.
28. Shirley Ann Tate utilized the phrase "other black" as applied to her study of mixed-race women in the UK, illustrated in her text *Black Skins, Black Masks*, in the development of her important thesis of hybridity as a dialogical space where these women fashion for themselves a "hybridity of the everyday" through everyday "talk." I appropriate the phrase "other black" from Tate and apply it to the life and writings of Obama, while also understanding that hybridity is about dialogue and "dialogical space" (Tate utilizes the notion that language or dialogue is hybrid from the Russian philosopher Mikhail Bakhtin) as evidenced in Obama's writings and speeches. Further, I postulate that Obama frames the self within a transnational and cosmopolitan context, henceforth my notion of Obama as "other black cosmopolitan" is unique in that it presents Obama as having a complex multilayered sense of self that is both dependent upon a public essentialism *and* hybridity *at the same time* within a larger cosmopolitan frame.
29. Ibid.
30. The use of this phrase "betwixt and between" connotes notions of liminality first advanced by the German born French ethnographer and folklorist Arnold Van Gennep in his important text *Les Rites de Passage* (1909), later borrowed, expanded, and enhanced by anthropologist Victor Turner in his work "Betwixt and Between: The Liminal Period in Rites de Passage," which appeared in *The Forest of Symbols: Aspects of Ndembu Ritual* (1967). G. Reginald Daniel has applied the concept of liminality understood as a place "betwixt and between" to the multiracial experience in various writings such as with his landmark text *More than Black: Multiracial Identity and the New Racial Order* (2002).
31. Barack Obama, "Address to the People of Berlin," July 24, 2008, *AmericanRhetoric.com*, http://www.americanrhetoric.com/speeches/barackobamaberlinspeech.htm.
32. Obama, *Dreams*, 81.
33. Ibid., 80–81.
34. Barack Obama, "Commencement Address at the University of Notre Dame," May 18, 2009, *Americanrhetoric.com*, http://www.americanrhetoric.com/speeches/barackobama/barackobamanotredamecommencement.htm.
35. Barack Obama, "A New Beginning: Speech at Cairo University," June 4, 2009, *Americanrhetoric.com*, http://www.americanrhetoric.com/speeches/barackobama/barackobamacairouniversity.htm.
36. Ibid.
37. Barack Obama, "Nobel Prize for Peace Lecture," December 10, 2009, *Americanrhetoric.com*, http://www.americanrhetoric.com/speeches/barackobama/barackobama/barackobamanobelprizeforpeacelecture.htm.

PART II

OBAMA, BLACKNESS, AND THE "POST-RACIAL IDEA"

5. BARACK HUSSEIN OBAMA, OR, THE NAME OF THE FATHER

TAVIA NYONG'O

> But this is amazing, you know, the first black president. I know you're biracial, but, the first black president. You're proud to be able to say that: "The first black president." That is, unless you screw up. And then it's gonna be "What's up with the half-white guy? Who voted for the mulatto?"
>
> WANDA SYKES, WHITE HOUSE CORRESPONDENTS' ASSOCIATION DINNER, MAY 2009

WHILE MANY COMMENTATORS HAVE HELD FORTH ON THE POSSIBILITY that Barack Obama might be our first "post-racial" president, and while others have subjected this notion to a perhaps deserved derision, few have been as interested in contemplating another, equally likely prospect: Obama would be, and now is, our first post*colonial* president.˙ This silence bespeaks the degree to which "empire" remains a name that is still, on many public occasions, forbidden to pronounce. And Obama's relationship to the colonial-modern is so obvious, yet so hard to hold consistently in view, like the nose on one's face. Barack Hussein Obama has a Swahili first name, a Luo surname, and that notorious middle name. He was born in Hawai'i, and raised there and in Indonesia. And yet a crucial percentage of the U.S. voting public actively disattended the transnationalism and postcoloniality of this black name long enough to select him as a national surrogate. But now that American presidentialism has appropriated to itself the black male body that has so long served as its other, how is this interstice between the national and non-national to be navigated?

The "irony" of the first black president being born of a white mother and a black Kenyan father has been pointed out so often that one starts to suspect that said irony is really something else: a *point de capiton*, Lacan's term for the anchoring point in discourse "by which the signifier stops the otherwise indefinite sliding of signification" by embedding it in the real (Lacan 2005, 681). As in the joke Wanda Sykes told before a gathered press, political and celebrity corps—in which future success will determine whether Obama *will have been* black, white, or mulatto—a national racial taxonomy acts to gather up the amorphous discourses circulating around Obama's nativity, halting the ceaseless spread of their signification just before they threaten to spill over onto non-national, postcolonial terrain.[1] What could be realer, or more arbitrary, than these three choices? The subversive power of Sykes's joke lies in the unlikely proposition of success blackening and failure whitening. Within this topsy-turvy comic scenario lies the cultural logic of Sykes's half-serious threat to revoke Obama's "firstness" should he disappoint. With this performative, Sykes restages a powerful symbol in black feminist discourse: the black woman with the public capacity *to name*. Is it possible, this essay asks, to articulate this black feminist capacity against the national public discourse it occasions? Might the *point de capiton* of "black-white-mulatto" nonetheless tether another discourse that does different justice to Obama's postcolonial trajectory?

THE KENYAN FATHER AND OBAMA'S PATERNAL METAPHOR

To explore this question, we must account for how the phrase "Kenyan father" within discussions of Obama's racial heritage is both an explanation and obfuscation. It anchors him to the sign "black."[2] But paradoxically, it does so by partly obfuscating the sign "Kenya," which is wrested from its context only long enough to explain Obama's racial heritage. Stripped of its colonial historicity, the phrase "Kenyan father," is another *point de capiton* within an American discourse about race, and possesses little meaningful to link it to the history or future of the Republic of Kenya. It is quite different, for instance, from how the phrase might operate in Kenya itself, where the operative term could as easily be Obama's "Luo father" (ethnicity being a key factor meaningful to other Kenyans, less meaningful or even interpretable to Americans). The point is both that "Kenya" as geopolitical sign is polysemic and that this polysemy attaches itself in discrepant discursive configurations.

Erroneously but frequently characterized as an immigrant (even by the 2008 Obama campaign itself), Obama, Sr., was first imagined as another of the world's huddled masses gazing at America, yearning to breathe free. Subsequent revelations of a polygamist, alcoholic, and violent man fed into another set of colonialist tropes about black male primitivism and afropessimism. Anticolonial freedom dreams—however partially Obama, Sr., might have represented them—were excluded from this characterization as being of little concern. Less concern, for instance, than repeated DNA "discoveries" of both slave and slaveholding parentage on Obama, Jr.'s American mother's side. Why speculate so speciously over Obama possibly descending from a seventeenth-century slave, in order to secure him finally to a black historical narrative, unless the much more immediate and seemingly relevant black historical narrative of decolonization had not already been deemed somehow inadmissable? (Stolberg 2012). Does Obama's outer-national paternity not act here as *object a*, that little bit of the real that disrupts the narcissistic fantasy that the nation is the completely absorbing object of the other's desire?

A brief glance into the cesspool of U.S. xenophobia confirms the doubled logic of this fantasy. The conspiratorial right, determined to expose Obama as a Manchurian candidate sent to steal our national enjoyment (a mirror image of the liberal wish to see the world's admiration renewed in the election of Obama as president),[3] launched multiple lawsuits against his presidential victory. The less interesting suit claimed that Obama was secretly born in Kenya, and had forged his birth certificate.[4] But the more intriguing suit began with the claim that Obama was born with a right to Kenyan citizenship as well, and therefore could not be what the Constitution intends by a "natural-born" U.S. citizen.

In truth, Obama was born merely with a paternal relation to the status of British colonial subject, because the Republic of Kenya did not yet exist in 1961.[5] What the lawsuit missed was how Obama's father's travel to the U.S. was part of the transition from colonial rule, and participated in the *invention* of a Kenyan nationality. Not an immigrant at all, Obama, Sr., was part of the famous "airlift" spearheaded by the Kenyan nationalist and trade unionist Tom Mboya, who envisioned a cadre trained outside the colonial metropole who would return and govern the new nation (Mboya 1963). The xenophobic claims articulated in the two lawsuits missed precisely this movement of postcolonial subjects out from under the colonial-modern into an alternative modernity. The figure of the younger Obama as an alien being whose citizenship claims preyed upon the American heartland thus occludes the historical *event* of Kenya's emergence as an independent nation (Wallis 2008).

Despite the xenophobic intentions, the "birther" movement's doubling back upon the question of Obama's nativity nonetheless becomes means of plucking out the *point de capiton* that secures race and gender to nation in discourses of Obama's paternity. The argument that follows takes its shape through my selective reading of Obama's 1995 memoir, *Dreams from My Father: A Story of Race and Inheritance*. I do not believe any special acumen is required to predict that this book will, in years to come, be included among the canonical twentieth-century African American autobiographies. If it is so included, it will in part be for the unusual circumstance of its having been composed before its author settled on the political career that went on to make history. It is revealing to a degree rare in a campaign biography. Since I proceed with the aid of psychoanalytic theory, I should state up front that my intention is not to offer a psychological portrait of the president. My aim is rather to hystericize the American racial symbolic order—that is, to draw attention to its fundamental and underlying anxieties. To do so I draw upon black feminist theory, in particular upon Hortense Spillers's generative readings of the American grammar, to argue that the desire of the mother is at issue in a manner neither the national symbolic order nor traditional psychoanalysis is prepared to address. My argument runs parallel to that of Saidiya Hartman, who has insisted upon the historical, political, and discursive *non*-relation between African America and post-colonial Africa. The desire of the mother, still traceable underneath the "paternal metaphor" of Obama's title *Dreams from My Father*, returns us to the surprising ways in which the (white) American mother, as much as the (black) Kenyan father, secures a symbolic accession to the status of "first black president" (Hartman 2007, 163).

AFRICA AS AN UNCLAIMED PATERNITY

Part one of Obama's memoir, entitled "Origins," begins with news of his father's death. While a college student at Columbia University, Obama is informed by telephone that the father he hardly knew has been killed in a traffic accident in Kenya. With this news, the possibility of future rapprochement is lost, and the name of the father becomes an enigma wrapped in a permanent mystery. Here I should explain the psychoanalytic meaning of the phrase "Name-of-the-Father." For Lacan, the Name-of-the-Father is the fundamental signifier securing the entry of the subject into the symbolic order courtesy of a lineage, and instating Oedipal prohibition, the Father's Law. Its efficacy is not related to, and can indeed actually be increased by, the actual father's death or absence. *Dreams from My Father* thus becomes a memoir that is overdetermined by the Name-of-the-Father, although the biographical father is missing.[6] With the news that he will never know who his father was, and even more anxiously, that he will never know *who he was for his father*, paternity takes the shape of an "unclaimed experience" (Caruth 1996). *Dreams from My Father* thus revolves around the dilemma produced for a patriarchal culture (American, Kenyan) when patrimony goes unarticulated, but remains nonetheless of great consequence. That consequence here figures as an uncanny doubling of the name, because here the Name-of-the-Father is also the name of the son.

The title of Obama's memoir seems to suggest recourse to a quasi-mystical faith in trans-individual organic memory to recover Africa as an unclaimed paternity. When I first read the memoir in 1995, I remember that phrase "a story of race and inheritance" sticking in my craw. Why "race," and not "nation," "home," or "ethnicity"? Why was a postcolonial freedom dream presented as a racial one? Why was the name of the father being racialized through the biological metaphor of inheritance? To grasp how the metaphor of an inheritable racial dream might have served as an anchoring point to a diasporic subject such as Obama, we might usefully bring into play Lacan's distinction between the *symbolic father* and the *imaginary father*. Obama's text both exposes and seeks to resolve the non-relation between the symbolic fathers who order the American discourse of race and inheritance, and his imaginary father (who is also in this case a real, biological father, who remains "imaginary" and fantastical because he is not available to suture the child to a discursive order). The imaginary father can be thought of as a fatherly Imago, whose absence from the son's upbringing renders mythic and exterior the very Kenya the son would seek to "inherit." Instead of the Father's Law (discursive order), the son receives only his Name, and with it, the contours of an absent presence he must somehow fill. The metaphor of the inheritable dream mediates this division between symbolic and imaginary, as Obama imagines that what he can inherit is, paradoxically, the ability to interpret the dreams—the fantasies and desires—of his own parents, an idea that comes to have surprising uses in the text.[7]

Is a dream inheritable? A name certainly is. But what does a name transmit, other than itself? The hybrid Luo/Swahili/Arabic name that the younger Obama inherits from his father is a veritable palimpsest of history, archived in its very phonemes. The name engages multiple symbolic orders (Nilotic, Bantu, Semitic) and imaginary registers (fanatic terrorist, corrupt African, multicultural American, hybrid savior, etc.). Yet it also points to a bedrock anxiety in the *speaking* of language, one reflective of what Derrida terms "the originary violence of language" (Derrida 1998, 112). Derrida critiques the concept of the "proper name," which he considers an improper notion, insofar as to name is to inscribe difference, divorcing the subject from self-presence. The "proper name" can be experienced as improper, as an impropriety, to its bearer. And that impropriety opens up the name-as-archive to its other scene, that of the mother who ostensibly lacks the power to name, who seemingly has no dreams to inherit. This lack is, of course, a fiction, as every page of *Dreams from My Father*, despite its androcentric title, gives away.

It is the mother's dream that names as much as any other's. It is the mother's *desire*, her transgression of white female propriety, that delivers the son into a world in which he is a stranger to his own proper name. With that name the young Obama must perilously navigate the shifting shoals of ignorance and interpellation in Indonesia, Hawai'i, California, New York, and Chicago. In *Dreams from My Father*, he describes temporarily mitigating his awkwardness by accepting the Americanized nickname Barry from his white grandfather. But even unspoken, the name preserves an "originary violence" of impropriety, foiling any effort to seamlessly integrate paternal lineage into the symbolic order, even through belated, grand-paternal effort.

Introduced into a new class in Hawai'i after his return from Indonesia, Obama encounters a friendly teacher who tries to reintegrate him into an American classroom by paying sensitive attention to his name and identity, saying:

> "I used to live in Kenya, you know. Teaching children just your age. It's such a magnificent country. Do you know what tribe your father is from?"
>
> Her question brought on more giggles, and I remained speechless for a moment. When I finally said "Luo," a sandy-haired boy behind me repeated the word in a loud hoot, like the sound of a monkey. The children could no longer contain themselves. (Obama 1995, 60)

Here, the sound pattern of "Luo" provides a thrilling whoop of racist pleasure. As he hears the word describing his father's heritage spoken aloud, the son's shame is enhanced by the inability to either fill that sign with the proud content of cultural knowledge his teacher apparently expects. The name fails him doubly: it fails to assimilate him to his current symbolic order, and it also fails to provide an alternative one into which he might retreat.

But the name-as-archive also carries with it latent alternatives, as becomes apparent later on in the memoir, when an older Obama shares a drink with a friend and is addressed by another by a name that surprises her. After being told his given name is Barack—"my father's name"—and given its origin and meaning, his friend "repeated the name to herself, testing out the sound. 'Barack. It's beautiful.' She leaned forward across the table. 'So why does everybody call you Barry?'"[8] Here, the sound pattern of the name, its foreignness, is tested in the mouth like hot coffee and found, to a more mature palate than that of the whooping boy, beautiful. This sound of the name possesses a musical rhythm that resonates beyond mere cross-cultural appreciation. For its beauty resides in a repetition that takes place *after* the revelation of its proper meaning.

What remains consistent across both of the above examples is the fundamental ambiguity of the "vocative absolute," which alternately produces shame, hilarity, curiosity, and desire. The patronymic is present but not fully operative: it is in that sense broken. To break down is different than to fail: a broken thing persists through its inoperability, its presence urging repair, or perhaps an alternate use. As a politician, Obama learned to address this brokenness of the patronymic with self-deprecating humor. Such was the approach of the video biography introducing Barack and Michelle Obama to the Democratic National Convention in fall of 2008. They both mocked his "funny" name in the context of recalling their first dates, implicitly allowing the nation to relax and laugh about it too. The joke, we were led to believe, was that even *Obama* finds his name funny. And the scene of the African American Michelle LaVaughn Robinson meeting Barack Hussein Obama is played for mock-xenophobic laughs, as the future First Lady presents herself as initially unprepared to date someone with so strange-sounding a name. In the context of African American cultural politics—in which taking African names became an important cultural nationalist act in the 1970s—there are many layers of racial pride and class calculation in such a hesitation. But as many commentators have gone on to confirm, Michelle Obama's charisma and connections went a long way in confirming her husband's bonafides in the black American community in Chicago, Illinois, and the nation. While ostensibly accepting the patronym of her husband, Michelle Obama, like Wanda Sykes, still performs the public authority of black women to name.

INVAGINATING THE BROKEN PATRONYMIC

How is this ability of the black woman to name related, if at all, to the broken genealogy of Obama's Kenyan patronymic? Here we might relate the Luo patronymic to what performance theorist Fred Moten calls, via Derrida, an "invagination," which Moten describes as a "cut and augmented hermeneutic circle [that] is structured by a double movement." As he goes on to explain:

> *The first element [of this double movement] is the transference of a radically exterior aurality that disrupts and resists certain formations of identity and interpretation by challenging the reducibility of phonic matter to verbal meaning or conventional musical form. The second is the assertion of what Nathaniel Mackey calls "broken claim(s) to connection" between Africa and African America that seeks to suture corollary, asymptotically divergent ruptures—maternal estrangement and the thwarted romance of the sexes—that he refers to as "wounded kinship" and "the sexual cut."* (Moten 2003, 6)

The first element of invagination, as Moten describes it here, helps account for how the name as an ethnic identifier induces transference in the subject. The ethnic proper name remains a "radically exterior aurality" to its bearer—as when it is sounded in the mouths of the sandy-haired child, of Regina, even (of the then) Michelle Robinson on first being romantically approached by Barack Obama. This resounding disrupts and resists both identity and the interpretation as belonging to a patrilineal line. Elsewhere, I have reflected on Obama's public persona and the psychoanalytic concept of the *transference*.[9] Here, I want to link this transference to Moten's second element, wherein he suggests a double fold of "asymptotically divergent ruptures"—the divergent ruptures of the Middle Passage and African colonization—that manifest a wounded kinship between Africa and African America. Moten productively refigures the radical non-relation of the sexes, conveyed in the Lacanian maxim "there is no sexual relationship," into a more capacious image of the "thwarted romance of the sexes." I like this formulation because its syntax captures a crucial element, so often missed, of the American grammar book. In making "thwarted" the modifier and "romance" the noun, rather than vice versa, it better reflects the "heartbreaking" stakes of a black sentimentality.[10] Moten's formulation allows me to augment my reading of the *transference* (the projection of fantasized characteristics onto an other *as* love) with and through a reading of racial kinship *as* sexual difference.

Invagination as a challenge to the paternal symbolic order plays an important role in black feminist theory. In "Mama's Baby, Papa's Maybe: An American Grammar Book," Hortense Spillers subjects Daniel Patrick Moynihan's notorious black matriarchal thesis to a powerful genealogical and psychoanalytic critique. Moynihan's thesis purported to explain racial subjugation in America by means of the supposedly inverted gender hierarchy in African American culture produced by chattel slavery. "In essence," to quote the Moynihan report itself, "the Negro community has been forced into a matriarchal structure which, because it is too out of line with the rest of the American society, seriously retards the progress of the group as a whole, and imposes a crushing burden on the Negro male and, in consequence, on a great many Negro women as well."[11] In a telling excerpt, the report names the advantages of patriarchy precisely in terms of how the symbolic father grants, through the transmission of his name, his children's accession to the social order:

> *The white family, despite many variants, remains a powerful agency not only for transmitting property from one generation to the next, but also for transmitting no less valuable contracts with the world of education and work. In an earlier age, the Carpenters, Wainwrights, Weavers, Mercers, Farmers, Smiths acquired their names as well as their trades from their fathers and grandfathers. Children today still learn the patterns of work from their fathers even though they may no longer go into the same jobs.*[12]

The patronymic, we might say, has work to do. But the principal alibi for the white Name-of-the-Father—its archaic relation to occupational status—is dropped in the above quotation as quickly as it is raised. While this ostensibly makes the name subservient to "patterns of work," a reference to the transmitting of property is in plain sight, vouchsafing the transmission of whiteness as property in an American vernacular (Harris 1993, 1707–91). More shockingly, this passage elides the former power of the white names like Carpenter and Wainwright (as well as Robinson) to transmit enslaved black people *as property*, a power which the Moynihan report must somehow disavow if it is to maintain its tight focus on the pathology of the black family, rather than the thanatopolitics of slave life.

Spillers's work serves as a trenchant corrective to Moynihan's deployment of the patronymic as ruse. Instead of benignly attributing the cause of racial hierarchies to "patterns of work," her genealogy of race, gender, and embodiment reopens the traumatic wounds of enslavement and the Middle Passage as an alternative origin for racial capitalism:

> *The symbolic order that I wish to trace in this writing, calling it an "American grammar," begins at the "beginning," which is really a rupture and a radically different kind of cultural continuation. The massive demographic shifts, the violent formation of a modern African consciousness, that take place on the sub-Saharan Continent during the initiative strikes which open the Atlantic slave trade in the fifteenth century of our Christ, interrupted hundreds of years of black African culture. We write and think, then, about an outcome of aspects of African-American life in the United States under the pressure of those events. (Spillers 2003, 209)*

Insisting upon the historicity of the symbolic that more conservative readings of psychoanalysis might deny, Spillers here rejects a facile retroactive and compensatory gendering or naming of the enslaved African. She insists that, to the contrary, the calculus of violence and profit by which life was merchandised and consumed in the cauldron of Atlantic slavery targeted a violated, ungendered *flesh*. *Partus sequitur ventrem* was the American "innovation" that proclaimed that the child born of an enslaved mother would also be enslaved, regardless of the condition of the father. It inaugurated not an actual black matriarchy (that is, a social system in which black women dominate men) but rather, an emergent symbolic order of gender and race in which blackness and femininity repeatedly figure as excess:

> *This human and historic development—the text that has been inscribed on the benighted heart of the continent—takes us to the center of an inexorable difference in the depths of American women's community: the African-American woman, the mother, the daughter, becomes historically the powerful and shadowy evocation of a cultural synthesis long evaporated—the law of the mother.*[13]

Spillers rejects the Moynihan report's comparison between the white family and the black family as baseless in both theory and history, given the dependence of the historical production of the former on the destruction of the latter. What *partus sequitur ventrem* introduces (keeping in mind its status as a patriarchal law designed to protect the property rights of slaveholders) is not the comparability but rather an "inexorable difference" within "American women's community," an innovation upon gender Spillers calls the "shadow" or threat of a "law of the mother." That this synthesis has long since evaporated (but is perhaps still perfuming the air?) suggests a mystique that is also a mistake—the mistake, that is, of a patriarchal symbolic order, in writing into its legal codes the consequential presence of a female shadow power. As Spillers writes of the post-slave black woman:

> *This problematizing of gender places her, in my view, out of the traditional symbolics of female gender, and it is our task to make a place for this different social subject. In doing so, we are less interested in joining the ranks of gendered femaleness than gaining the* insurgent ground as female social subject. Actually *claiming the monstrosity (of a female with the potential to "name"), which her culture imposes in blindness.*[14]

This "monstrous" power surfaces in surprising locations, such as in the name of the father itself, a name that disrupts the function of the symbolic father (even the president as symbolic father) not with any given imaginary alternative, but with the "insurgent ground" of a real that traverses the fantasy of a coherent national narrative, invaginating the heteropatriarchal reproduction of racial difference with the "asymptotically divergent rupture" of black femininity.

CONCLUSION: DREAMS OF THE MOTHER

The insurgent potentiality of the black female social subject to "name" endows Barack Obama an imaginary black maternity that places the pressure of its "inexorable difference" on his actual white maternity. How might we think through this "inexorable difference" in relation to the "thwarted romance" Obama presents in *Dreams from My Father*, that between a white teenager from Kansas and a glamorous and worldly student from Africa? How are we to approach this apparent fusion or fission of the black family with the white, if not in terms that always return to the "black-white-mulatto" *point de capiton*? Where in the cut and augmented hermeneutic circle of postcolonial blackness might the white mother belong?

Katherine Bassard has employed Spillers's formulation of an "inexorable difference" in American women's community to offer a suggestive reading of one founding text of black feminist literature, Harriet Wilson's 1859 novel, *Our Nig*. To be sure, Wilson's autobiographical protagonist Frado and Barack Obama are not at all similar characters. But as the children of white mothers metonymically "blackened" by their relation to black husbands and children, their shared position within the American racial symbolic order offers the former as a suggestive intertext to the latter. Bassard reads Frado's origin story—born to a black father who dies of consumption, leaving her overburdened white mother to give her up to service in an unkind Massachusetts family home (a "Two-Story White House")—allegorically as well as autobiographically. For Bassard, Wilson's narrative of Frado's birth and childhood sets up an alternative black feminist origin myth that reroutes the imputed guilt of *partus sequitur ventrem*. If the slave law that makes the child follow the condition of the mother preserves "the vilification of black women as the originators of both 'blackness' and chattel status," then Frado's birth to a white mother dissolves this vilification, "denaturalizing the legal and discursive presumption of blackness with servitude and 'rescuing,' if you will, the black mother from originary blame" (Abel, Christian, and Moglen 1997, 197–98).

One possible implication of Bassard's reading, admittedly, is that the black mother needs to be rescued from the blameworthiness of her blackness by the intercession of white womanhood. While admitting this possibility, I am interested in pursuing the alternative implication that Frado's mother Mag is presented as *desiring* blackness—not simply accepting the stigma of racialization, but experiencing the transference of blackness as "a radically exterior aurality that disrupts and resists certain formations of (white) identity and interpretation." Since Frado is set up as the privileged interpreter of this desire of the mother, I want to use this alternative implication to read a highly suggestive moment in Obama's memoir, where he sets himself up in a similar position.

While Stanley Ann Dunham cannot in any way *stand in* for the black female experience, her Americanness is nonetheless *marked* by its non-relation to Afro-Americanness. The outer-national, antenatal, improper blackness she experiences in the following scene evades any blameworthiness passed via proper lines of descent (or, via her recently revealed imputed slave ancestry, improper ones). That she encounters this foreign blackness through a line of identification ultimately linked back to her own homeland, even to her own heartland, only reinforces the insurgency of the black female subject with the potential to name. This presence is first voiced in a space where shadows possess a particularly powerful mystique: cinema.

A final scene from *Dreams from My Father*:

> One evening, while thumbing through The Village Voice, *my mother's eyes lit on an advertisement for a movie*, Black Orpheus, *that was showing downtown. My mother insisted that we go see it that night; she said that it was the first foreign film she had ever seen....*
> *We took a cab to the revival theater where the movie was playing. The film, a groundbreaker of sorts due to its mostly black, Brazilian cast, had been made in the fifties. The story line was simple: the myth of the ill-fated lovers Orpheus and Eurydice set in the favelas of Rio during Carnival. In Technicolor splendor, set against scenic green hills, the black and brown Brazilians sang and danced and strummed guitars like carefree birds in colorful plumage. About halfway through the movie, I decided that I'd seen enough, and turned to my mother to see if she might be ready to go. But her face, lit by the blue glow of the screen, was set in a wistful gaze. At that moment, I felt as if I were being given a window into her heart, the unreflective heart of her youth. I suddenly realized that the depictions of childlike blacks I was now seeing on the screen ... was what my mother had carried with her to Hawaii all those years before, a reflection of the simple fantasies that had been forbidden to a white, middle-class girl from Kansas, the promise of another life: warm, sensual, exotic, different. I turned away, embarrassed for her, irritated with the people around me.*[15]

In this passage, Obama settles on the image of "carefree birds in colorful plumage," his simile for a degrading, almost minstrel performance. And indeed, *Black Orpheus* (a 1959 film directed by Marcel Camus) contains plenty to embarrass and irritate the contemporary viewer, including a scene centering on the black man's bottomless appetite for sex and (what else?) watermelon. But we can read this passage against the grain to reveal the musicality and rhythm of *Black Orpheus* as a "sonorous envelope" larger than the auditorium Obama would confine it to.[16] Psychoanalytic theory has theorized the sense of immersion that music can produce as related to "oceanic" fantasies of return to womb-like security. *Black Orpheus*, in which the sounds of carnival drumming are almost continuously audible throughout the film—assisting the monolingual English viewer's pleasurable immersion into the exteriority of a foreign tongue—is a powerfully seductive sonorous envelope. We can see the difficulty Obama encounters when he addresses a dream from his mother, in which he must reckon with the originary force of her desire for blackness.

This unexpected and embarrassing encounter with the cinema as a primal *screen* produces a repudiation in the young Obama, as he attempts to reduce its meanings for his mother to "the simple fantasies" of "the unreflective heart of her youth." *Black Orpheus* must be repudiated because it invaginates the paternal line of succession, around which the memoir is organized, with a blackness that evades the natal occasion with a peculiarly insistent previousness,[17] a blackness that the "mother had *carried with her* to Hawaii all those years before." Pregnant with expectations born of the womb of carnival, Stanley Ann Dunham had "named" Obama even before she knew his name. She had dreamed of blackness and, just as early modern European medical science feared she might, she gave birth to blackness (Fissell 2003, 43–74).

So, what kind of African and African American blackness irritated and embarrassed our future president in that revival theater that night? Shall we accept his *Wizard of Oz* story of a repressed Kansas girl with Technicolor dreams of the "warm, sensual, exotic, different?" Or do we also hear in this irritation and embarrassment the undoing of the patronymic name? Do we hear echoes of Derrida's "loss of the proper … in truth the loss of what has never taken place, of a self-presence which has never been given but only dreamed of"? (Derrida 1998, 112). Perhaps. If we do, we might also recognize a detail omitted from Obama's summary of *Black Orpheus* that must surely have struck him at the time. At least, it strikes me in watching the film today. Obama's generalized reference to "depictions of childlike blacks" omits the highly plausible identification his mother may have had with the lead female role Eurydice, the simple country girl who is shown, in the film's marvelous opening scene, arriving into Rio by boat. Obama never mentions that we enter into the world of Afro-Brazilian carnival through the eyes and heart of a young black woman. Neither does he name the ebullient, melancholic actress who portrayed Eurydice, born eight years prior to his mother, not in Brazil, but in Pittsburgh, Pennsylvania. If Marpessa Dawn could have shown Ann Dunham how to dance the samba, what other "broken [hearted] claim(s) to connection" might there be?

Notes

* An earlier version of this chapter appeared in *The Scholar and Feminist Online* 7, no. 2 (Spring 2009). http://sfonline.barnard.edu/africana/print_nyongo.htm. Since the original publication of this essay, "anticolonial" has indeed been introduced into the discourse surrounding Obama, albeit as a term that moves within a hostile context that employs "anticolonial" as almost a racial epithet. I refer of course to the charge leveled by the conservative ideologue, Dinesh D'Souza, and repeated by former speaker of the House Newt Gingrich, that the president displays a "Kenyan, anticolonial" worldview inherited quasi-biologistically from his (absent) father. Although a full accounting of this extended context for anti/postcolonialism in U.S. political culture would require another essay, it gives me handy evidence here to wield against critical suspicions that the term "postcolonial" is too neutral a term. The absence, even within the latest paranoid expansion of suspicions around Obama's paternity, of the *thinkability* of a postcolonial Africa, which is to say, of the *thinkability* of decolonization as an historical, if contested achievement of black power, seems to me to justify the continued merits of this term. What I mean is that if "anticolonial" is, apparently, already captured and overdetermined by a reactionary discourse as its preferred "other," the ambivalence of "postcolonial," for which it is often savagely criticized, has something left to do. D'Souza's casting, and castigating of, Obama as "the last anticolonial" evidences the rhetorical moves of a once and future colonialism that postcolonial criticism, I wager, remains positioned to deconstruct. See Dinesh D'Souza, "Obama's Problem with Business," *Fortune*, September 2010a; Robert Costa, "Gingrich: Obama's 'Kenyan, anti-colonial' Worldview," *National Review Online*, September 11, 2010, http://www.nationalreview.com/corner/246302/gingrich-obama-s-kenyan-anti-colonial-worldview-robert-costa.

1. To be sure, Lacan did not believe that a nonpsychotic subject could do without anchoring points, so simply to locate one is not in itself to launch a critique of it.
2. A sign to which other political figures of nonwhite, non-U.S. parentage, such as Republican governor Bobby Jindal, are not stably secured.
3. The contours of this national desire are drawn with remarkable economy in the title of one postelection article in a U.S. marketing publication. See Lakin 2008.
4. Why, if true, this would preclude him from being considered a "natural-born" citizen was unclear, since he would have held a claim to U.S. citizenship through his mother, regardless of his place of birth. For instance, his rival for the presidency in 2008, John McCain, was actually born of U.S. parents on a military base in Panama. See Associated Press 2009b.
5. Kenya became a republic on December 12, 1964. Barack Obama was born August 4, 1961.
6. But this without the psychosis Lacan believed would be consequent upon such a foreclosure: "For psychosis to be triggered, the Name-of-the-Father—*verworfen*, foreclosed, that is, never having come to the place of the Other—must be summoned to that place in the symbolic opposition to the subject." See Lacan 2005, 481.
7. Because Obama, Sr., cannot symbolize the American racial order within which he nevertheless positions his son, he also takes on a specific relation to the third, enigmatic role Lacan speaks of: the *real father*. This is not the "biological father," or the father in reality, but the pressure of paternity asserted as a trauma upon the child in the form of rumor and reported speech—the man "said to be" the father. When Obama returns to Africa towards the close of his memoir, in search of the real father by way of the fatherly imago in other's memories of him, he is brought face to face with this trauma of the real father through the inconsistent reports of this person "said to be" the father, and must thus confront the

possibility of his own non-relation, precisely *through* his filial connection, to this father in the real.
8. Obama, *Dreams*, 104.
9. See the conclusion of my *Amalgamation Waltz*.
10. I must again thank my anonymous reviewer for the term "heartbreaking."
11. *The Negro Family: The Case for National Action*. Office of Policy Planning and Research, U.S. Department of Labor, March 1965, http://www.dol.gov/oasam/programs/history/webidmeynihan.htm.
12. Ibid.
13. Ibid., 228.
14. Ibid., 228–29.
15. Obama, *Dreams*, 123–24.
16. On music as sonorous envelope and its relationship to oceanic fantasy, see the first chapter of Schwarz 1997.
17. My formulation here is indebted to Fred Moten's *In the Break*.

6. THE END(S) OF DIFFERENCE?

Towards an Understanding of the "Post" in "Post-Racial"

LISA ANDERSON-LEVY

DURING THE DEMOCRATIC PRIMARY, AS SENATOR BARACK OBAMA CREPT ahead in the delegate count and later in the presidential election, he was referred to as the post-racial candidate, was lauded for running a post-race campaign, and/or was described as marking the beginning of an era when race matters less—a post-race moment.[1] Of course, these usages of "post-race" mean different things to differing constituencies. On the one hand, this term was used to refer to Obama representing a new black politics and politician, one that is not seen as emerging from the civil rights movement in the same way that someone like Jesse Jackson did.[2] The term was also used to express a sort of hopefulness that the days when race operates as a marker of inequality may be coming to an end. During the presidential campaign, I asked my students, "Why has race not been so central in previous elections," and time and time again their response was: "Because there has not been a nonwhite candidate who is a serious contender." Perhaps, but we have always had raced candidates, they have just been able to ignore their raced identities and how those influence what they do in a way that Barack Obama cannot. The ability to claim whiteness is the ability to claim racelessness. It is the ability to claim a certain objectivity about race by virtue of being above, beyond, or outside of race. It is the ability to claim a certain humanity that is unencumbered by vagaries of culture and race and free to imagine and speak to the "universal condition." This privilege, white privilege, is crucial to understanding how this historical moment may be understood as post-racial. I am concerned here with troubling the notion of "post" in "post-race" and demonstrating why white privilege is an important element undergirding the tendency or ability to understand this as a particular kind of post-race moment.

In this chapter, I will argue that within the context of the operation of race in the U.S., the conceptual space inhabited by the "post" in "post-race" is only understandable through white privilege and that white privilege necessarily requires an explication of white fear, which is also evident in this post-racial moment. Before I lay out the argument for the importance of white privilege in this discussion, I will briefly comment on how this "post" is similar to, say, the "post" in "postcolonial." Despite their initial attractiveness for some, it is crucial that these ideas are critically examined because "post" talk necessarily entails the silencing of some.

ONE "POST" STORY

There is no agreement about the precise meaning of the term "postcolonial."[3] This may be a deliberate strategy on the part of its users who want the flexibility and ambiguity the term offers.[4] As a spatio-temporal phenomenon it refers to the period after the end of colonialism, usually European colonialism, and is interested in issues confronted by nascent independent states. Implicit in the relationship between colonialism and postcolonialism is a certain temporal or political progression from one way of being to another, from "bondage to freedom."[5] Spatially, it refers to much of the so-called Third World–parts of Africa, Asia, Melanesia, and the Caribbean, former sites of European colonialism. As an aspect of identity, it refers to people who call themselves postcolonial because of their relation(s) to those they perceive as colonial oppressors. The term has been used to describe marginalized people worldwide, even those who are not traditionally thought of as enmeshed in colonial relations such as white lesbian and gay communities in the United States.[6] And finally, though not exhaustively, postcolonialism has also been used as a space of critique of colonialism, of nationalist projects that emerged during anticolonial struggles, and, arguably most significantly, of Eurocentrism itself.[7]

Like other bodies of knowledge, postcolonial theory is a system of knowledge that constitutes its object in particular ways while it forecloses certain kinds of investigations.[8] That said, are there similarities between the "post" in "postcolonial" and "post-race"? While the term "post-race" is not usually understood as having an obvious geographic component, I would argue that because post-race is only understandable within the context of the United States, within the particular historical, social, and political conditions that constitute race, there is a geographic element at work here. In the

U.S., race frames every social relation, whether we choose to recognize it or not. Of course, the ability or choice to ignore race is the domain of the few and is a privilege, white privilege. It is in this sense that it may be seen as referencing the geography of the United States. Popular interpretations of the temporal dimension, which are also understandable within the frame of U.S. racial politics, refer to the end of race as a marker of inequality. In this understanding, race is seen as the domain of some but not others because it describes what is often understood as a biological condition for which a group of people were unfairly discriminated against. Because race is not viewed as being embodied in every body, and racism is seen as a character flaw of a few rather than being productive of social, political, and economic structures in the United States, change is understood as possible over time with changes in the law.

How blacks and other "people of color"[9] react to social-outcasting, to the violence, or to the general denial of rights depends on them. If some appear to succeed, particularly against incredible odds, then it must be true that all have the same opportunity. In this view there is no need to level playing fields because the bad eggs—that is, the racist individuals—have no power to institute their racism structurally. That, despite incredible odds, "people of color" have become, teachers, doctors, lawyers, generals, secretary of state, and now the president, only fuels this view. Social or political gains by "people of color" are understood as within the realm of possibility for all "people of color" and as proof that affirmative action has worked and is no longer needed. Thus, the measure of the deleterious effects of racism is based on the experiences of a few and race as an impediment to social and/or political advancement is seen as no longer relevant.

Changes in codified racist practices are understood as marking the end of racist cultural practices and when this understanding is coupled with success among the group being discriminated against race is no longer seen as a marker of inequality. It is in this conceptual space that post-race is understood as beyond race, as temporally past a time when race matters. Of course, another way to read the "post" in "post-race" is as a space for critique that may be usefully conceived of as beginning a different conversation about race. This is where I situate my own understandings of this moment and find it useful to consider how other "posts" have been re-conceptualized to address evolving or different issues.

In "Colonialism: Anthropology and Criticism," David Scott attempts to work through the question of how postcolonial theory can continue to be conceptually useful to anthropology and what sort of engagement would be most fruitful in this regard. Scott contends that non-historical critiques of the kinds of questions asked in postcolonial theory, that is, critiques that do not pay attention to the historical context in which the questions were asked and thus do not address the proposition to which the questions were to respond in the first place, are problematic. He sees this point as crucial for what he calls "historically minded anthropological understanding ... concerned with the problems of colonialism" (1997, 517).[10] This point is an important one because it takes seriously the notion that the intellectual terrain in which a particular set of questions were asked may have shifted such that these questions lose critical purchase and "remain recognizably coherent but largely academic" (1997, 518).

For Scott the problem of re-conceptualizing the work postcolonial theory can do is two-fold. The first portion involves the deconstruction (and reconstruction) of the anthropological "object" and the second a shift to what he calls "an historical anthropology of the post-colonial present" (1997, 518). Scott notes the oft-repeated, though important, point that anthropological objects are not "transparently given but are *made*—constructed ... in particular conceptual and ideological histories" (1997, 520).[11] It is his second point that I find more compelling: that the problem space of the "postcolonial present" demands that new questions are asked, which "seek to explore the new concepts and the institutions based on these concepts that colonial/ Western power introduced, and to inquire into the nature of the transformations and reorganizations that were affected by this new form of power" (1997, 523).

This means moving away from anticolonial nationalist concerns about "overcoming"[12] colonial power and away from notions of power as operating within the constraints of a binary system. In these different imaginings, power cannot continue to be seen only as shifting the "struggle between colonizer and colonized, but also [as shifting] *the terrain of the struggle itself*" (1997, 523). Scott sees this form of power as co-emergent with modernity— modern power—as "operat[ing] not so much on the details of behaviour as on the conditions in which behaviours are obliged to assume their form" (1997, 523). Scott's formulation of the "postcolonial present" is useful here if we consider his charge, insofar as it can be applied to the post-race discussion, to rethink the ways in which race as a conceptual category operates. Conversations about race in the U.S. have traditionally been limited to those who are seen to embody race, to somehow have race, to those who cannot claim whiteness.

Conversations about race that do not examine the role of whiteness in the articulation of race, and indeed in the very constitution of raced categories, are inherently limited. If we accept Scott's call for a critical "problem space" in which we imagine and ask questions about race that fundamentally refigure the rules of engagement within these conversations, the role of whiteness can no longer be ignored. Therefore, it is crucial to consider carefully the role of white privilege and whiteness in any larger discussions about race and also their role in the very conceptualization of this as a post-race moment. Conceptualizing this moment as post-racial is only useful if it allows us to engage critically with conversations about race that include critical discussions about whiteness and white privilege without privileging whiteness. What is whiteness and what do I mean by "white privilege"?

WHITE PRIVILEGE

It is worth reflecting on the ubiquity of the effects of white privilege in our national imagination and understanding of what constitutes Americanness. Here, I am referring to the great American myth that everyone has equal opportunities, that we all have the same ability to pull ourselves up, the sunny American optimism that everything will be all right if we just work hard enough, that we can do anything, that American ingenuity can solve any problem. All of these elements of our collective imagination are gendered as much as they are raced, and my point here is that these ideas are only possible because they are undergirded by white privilege. They are only understandable within the context of white privilege. How is it possible then to talk about who we are as a nation without some understanding of what white privilege is and how it operates. So, what do I mean when I use the term?

White privilege is a system of unearned advantages that benefit white people by depriviliging or not providing advantages or opportunities for "people of color." Rowe notes that "whiteness may be understood, then as a set of relational practices that circulate through institutions for the transmission of power" (2008, 98). Of course, this is not a system that benefits all white people in the same way. White lesbians, heterosexual women, and poor whites have a more complicated relationship to this privilege, though I maintain that these groups still benefit through their alignment with whiteness, according to Lipsitz, through their "investments in whiteness." As Cheryl Harris points out in "Whiteness as Property," whiteness became *the* essential property and a crucial element in claims for personhood. As whiteness came to represent the condition of freedom and blackness enslavement, one space was marked as privileged and the other as not. Whiteness and blackness thus could not be seen or understood to meet or overlap because privilege only accrues to the non-slave, or white position. Therefore, as whiteness accrued privilege, it also became normalized through these processes.

Race has always been an issue in presidential elections. Nevertheless, it has not been the kind of issue that required explanation because whiteness is not understood as paradigmatic of race as blackness often is in these United States. Because whiteness is naturalized as the "norm," it is deemed unremarkable. It is thus understandable if black voters supporting a white candidate say something about the qualifications of the candidate, but nothing about the race of the candidate. Blackness, on the other hand, is paradigmatic of race in the United States and does require explanation, as does white support for a black candidate whose qualifications are not separable from, in this case, *his* race.

Thus, Obama's candidacy is remarkable not only because he is black but also because his appeal crossed into white voting blocks and therefore had to be explained. It is at this juncture that various heuristic devices are employed to explain this phenomenon. Post-race is attractive for a variety of reasons and one facile explanation is, where conceived temporally, post-race is seen as marking a time beyond when race matters. This, of course, has consequences for affirmative action policies and is important. Yet I am more interested in understanding the terrain from which post-race emerges and how it is both produced by and is productive of white privilege.

If post-race emerged as an attempt to explain the success of Obama's blackness in the last presidential election, its continued deployment may be understood as a way to elide the role of whiteness in the business of race. Understood in this way, the term "post-race" deflects the urgency of discussion about race even as it maintains the racial paradigm that excludes whiteness as crucial to discussions of and understandings about race. Obama's candidacy in the Democratic primary (and his presidency) have disturbed the immutability and invisibility of this privilege by bringing white fear to the fore. I would argue that the general unease with which many white voters grappled had to do with the fear of the loss of white privilege, even though they may have been unaware of the language of privilege.

For those voters who were able to articulate the fear, it is described as fear of retribution by "people of color," particularly blacks. For others, the fear manifested in questions about Obama's youth, his inexperience, his otherness, his perceived connections to Islam, and about whether or not he *really* is an American citizen. My point here is that if whiteness is understood as accruing privilege and white privilege is seen as not simply benefiting some but doing so at the expense of others, it becomes easier to see how fear emerges as one response to the perception of loss. It is also crucial to recognize how this fear becomes constitutive of whiteness itself. In this iteration, understanding the role of white privilege becomes crucial to any substantive engagement with fear.

WHAT'S FEAR GOT TO DO WITH IT?

In the run-up to the presidential elections last year, National Public Radio ran a series on *Morning Edition* and *All Things Considered*[13] where reporters spent time in York, Pennsylvania, discussing the election and how, or if, race mattered to voters. In these sessions between twelve and fifteen voters who identify as black, white, Latina/o, and/or South Asian met in an informal setting and discussed their feelings and thoughts about the role of race in the presidential elections and the role of race in the Unied States more generally. In one segment of the series, a white female voter, Leah, noted that while she did not want to seem racist and that she was not in fact racist, she was afraid that if Obama won the election "black people will feel it's payback time." She worried that there would be widespread chaos and that "blacks will take over." She was careful to say that she was not talking about the blacks in the room but that she was referring to "other" blacks on the street, those looking for trouble.

In another segment, a white woman told a story about when she and her husband adopted an African American infant. She remembers looking at his feet and commenting to her husband that based on their size, he was going to be a big man, and further that "she had about a decade to build a good rapport with him." She says her husband called her on this comment and wondered if she would have said this if their son was white. She admits she would not. Her comment and the ensuing family interaction brought her fear of black men to the fore and forced her to acknowledge this fear.

These stories serve as a jumping-off point into conversations about the role of white fear in discussions about race and racism in the United States and how this fear is a constitutive element of white privilege. White fear may be understood as fear of a generalized "other," but the particular history of race in the U.S. constitutes this "other" as black. White fear, then, is of an easily recognized though largely unknown blackness (the way the woman described her fear of black men above).

A more critical look might allow us to think about what undergirds this fear of blackness. Why is blackness threatening? Why are blacks a threat? As bell hooks (1992) has pointed out, blacks have more to fear from white people, who through the structural power they possess are in a better position to inflict long term harm. Yet the idea that blacks are afraid of whites seems ridiculous, laughable even. Given U.S. history, fear of blackness is often interpreted as fear of the "chaos" that would result from "blacks taking over." In other words, what if blacks got into "power" and do what "we" did to them? What if whites were put into the socially and politically subordinate positions? Put another way, what if whites lose their privilege? I believe this to be the elephant in the room in conversations about race and about how to combat racism, yet its importance is often elided because of the fear of loss of white privilege. It is this fear that keeps whites possessively investing in whiteness. Ignoring this fear substantiates white privilege, embraces its existence, and demonstrates that whites benefit in general from it.

The fear of the loss of white privilege also undergirds this historical moment because proclaiming the end of racial inequality relieves white guilt and nullifies programs aimed at eliminating or ameliorating the effects of structural inequalities. This, in turn, ensures that structurally disadvantaged "people of color" remain disadvantaged while structures and ideologies that support white privilege remain in place even as they claim that we are all equal "under God." Understanding the role of fear in the construction of whiteness may shed some light on the operation of white fear itself, as well as how white fear and privilege operate together. To this end, I will make a brief foray into a discussion about the role of fear in the production of whitenesses in Jamaica in order to draw connections to the ways in which gated communities in the U.S. produce a very specific kind of whiteness and what this means for thinking about privilege.

Fear of crime bleeds into every aspect of life in Jamaica. Visitors to the island are warned to beware of petty thieves and "hard" criminals who not only steal your goods but will also kill you if you are not careful. For Jamaicans, especially middle and upper-class Jamaicans, fear has become a way to differentiate themselves from poor and working-class people while reinforcing the similarities among members of their own group. Rather than fear "encod[ing] other social concerns," I would say that fear is constitutive of the group that marks itself as fearers. The unrealistic dread of the poor, militant, nonwhite masses banging at the gate, seeking every opportunity to steal children and take merchandise is only possible if residents of gated communities imagine themselves and the spaces they occupy to be inherently different from those they fear.

Thus, there is a dialectical relationship between those who fear and the feared, which functions to reproduce both groups. If the fearers construct themselves as middle or upper-class, law-abiding white victims, they do so against a poor or working-class, black, lawless, and gun-toting other. If the recognition of alterity and its constitutive effects are at the center of the wheel in discussion about whiteness, then recognition of the everyday processes through which whiteness itself is constituted are the spokes. These ideas operate together and are most theoretically useful when considered as inextricable.

For instance, Claire, an upper-class Jamaican white,[14] has lived in fear of poor and black Jamaicans for most of her life. Though she feels a strong bond to Jamaica and cannot imagine living elsewhere, it is a bond to the country, the space or geography of Jamaica, rather than its people. Poverty was in the background for her because it did not affect her life. As a child and even as an adult, she lives in fear of being attacked (verbally or physically) by black Jamaicans. She believes this fear of blackness and/or poverty affects how she operates in public spaces—that is, it affects her demeanor, her public personae.

The fear Claire describes operates first to create divisions between the feared and those who fear them and also to provide a space where those in the latter group are able to represent themselves as fundamentally, perhaps even inherently, different than those who are feared. As these differences become reified through and in daily discourse, the group who fears withdraws as much as is possible, in a place as small as Jamaica, from contact with members of the feared group. This disconnection, as haphazard or uneven as it is, makes it possible for those in the group that fears to reconstruct themselves against the feared through this daily practice of fearing the other.

The conditions of possibility are thus created for both the construction or (re)construction, if you will, of a relationship that is only intelligible in the context of the feared as poor and black and the fearer as upper/middle class and brown or white. Thus, fear becomes an avenue through which different kinds of citizens are created. On the one hand are the upper-middle and upper-class Jamaican whites who construct themselves as white, disciplined, and socially responsible. This is in opposition to poor Jamaicans, who are constructed as black, undisciplined, and socially (and morally) irresponsible. Thus, the more one talks about being fearful and retreats into hiding in either private or "white" domains, the more likely it is that one will be considered a part of this white elite whatever one's color. In local parlance, one should avoid "de indiscipline ole nega dem."[15]

Similarly, in "The Edge and the Center: Gated Communities and the Discourse of Urban Fear," Setha Low tries to understand the motivations of mostly white, middle and upper-class residents of Queens, New York, and a northern suburb of San Antonio, Texas, as they retreat behind the "protected" walls of gated communities. She found that the number one reason residents gave for relocating was fear of crime and fear of how their old neighborhoods were changing. Low examines the relationship between urban and gated spaces by talking with some of the residents of gated communities as well as service providers associated with these communities. She eventually concludes that "the discourse of urban fear encodes other social concerns including class, race, and ethnic exclusivity as well as gender" (2001, 12). Low mentions that despite the walls, the surveillance, and the guards, some members of these gated communities still did not feel safe and could not articulate what it might take to make them feel safe. While I would agree with her analysis, I would argue that "safety" is not the goal here. Rather, it is segregation or differentiation.

In the United States, whites' unreasonable fear of blacks, therefore, has more to do with the maintenance of whiteness and white privilege than actual fear of harm. I have had white colleagues, friends, and students recount stories about being in social situations in the United States where they were the only white person in the room/event/bus and that this was a watershed moment when they report being uncomfortable, afraid, and aware of their whiteness. Yet black people are in these kinds of "only one" situations all the time, sometimes daily. The former situation is remarkable because it foregrounds whiteness in a way that the regular routines of most middle-class whites do not allow.

To return to thinking about white fear and its relation to white privilege, my point is that when white fear is understood as fear of the loss of privilege then its connection to white privilege becomes clearer. White fear maintains white privilege, and white privilege gives rise to white fear. Viewing this moment as a particular kind of post-racial moment is understandable through white privilege and the white fear that supports it. Understanding this as the kind of post-racial moment where racial categories are no longer seen as markers of inequality imbues a certain chaotic quality to this moment. If the racial hierarchy no longer matters, then blacks and other "people of color" are moving out of place, moving into place and spaces "we" do not belong, into spaces that make white people uncomfortable.

There is some historical precedence for thinking about this as a moment when white fear is close to the surface, recognizing that this fear is rooted in the fear of loss of privilege, and recognizing that this fear often has devastating consequences for "people of color." Smith (2002) notes that there have been moments in U.S. history when eruptions of white fear lead to the formation of social or political groups that are charged with protecting white privilege.[16] Consider, in the contemporary moment, the growth of groups like the Minutemen Civil Defense Core, the Tea Party Patriots, or the Council of Conservative Citizens. These are groups that are primarily concerned with protecting white privilege at the expense of "people of color." These groups are often dismissed by white liberals and/or academics as fringe. However, I would argue that the fear of loss of privilege is indeed mainstream and underlies much of our discussions about race even though it is not often discussed. The pervasiveness of this fear must be understood as not simply related to white privilege but as constitutive of it and must be considered in conversations about white privilege.

CONCLUSION

Peggy McIntosh's 1988 article (McIntosh 1995) lists the everyday and mostly unnoticed benefits of white privilege. Whenever I use this piece in a course, white students are routinely appalled by the benefits that have gone unnoticed in their lives and almost all focus on item twenty-one—"I am never asked to speak for the people of my racial group"—or item twenty-six—"I can easily buy posters, postcards, picture books, greeting cards, dolls, toys, and children's magazines featuring people of my race"—or item 46—"I can choose blemish cover or bandages in "flesh" color and have them more or less match my skin." While these items are important for making an argument for a "thousand cuts" each day, they distract the students from the more difficult items on McIntosh's list.

I bring this up to make the point that to attend to these items or not is itself a function of this privilege as is reframing the conversation to include the more palatable aspects of said privilege. In other words, as with racism, white privilege will cease to be a problem when a wider array of bandages and greeting cards are available, or when a "person of color" becomes president. To understand that white privilege is the foundation upon which post-race emerges is to begin a different conversation about race that is responsive to whiteness as an essential element in discussions about race. Pointing out that whiteness is an essential element in conversations about race does not mean that I am advocating that white people ought to control or determine the parameters of discussions about race. I am saying though that this historical moment is understandable as post-raced precisely because whiteness and white privilege have not been recognized as crucial elements in conversations about race.

We can benefit here from considering how postcolonial as a critical space for rethinking colonial encounters emerged. Postcolonial projects were driven by the colonized who recognized and fruitfully explored the role of the colonizers and the spaces where the two overlapped. Which voices are claiming this a post-race moment? How do we put whiteness and white privilege at the center of discussions about race without further privileging white people? Conceptually, post-race (as it is understood temporally) is a product of white privilege. Questions about the amelioration of the effects of racism can no longer only be about helping "people of color" "overcome" racism. They must also address helping white people "overcome" their privilege and divest themselves of their fear of loss of said privilege. This post-race moment has greatest theoretical purchase when it is understood as a space where according to Scott *"the terrain of the struggle itself"* (1997, 523) shifts as concerns are reconfigured to address how and why they continue to be salient.

Notes

1. See Daniel Schorr's comments in "A New 'Post-Racial' Political Era in America," January 28, 2008, http://www.npr.org/templates/story/story.php?storyId=18489466
2. See, for example, Bai, August 10, 2008. In this article, he discusses differences between "old" and "new" black politicians.
3. A colleague pointed out that, as with "anti-semitism " and "antisemitism," there may be slight differences in meaning between "post-colonial" and "postcolonial." Appiah is useful here as he tries to distinguish between the post in "postcolonial" versus in "postmodern." He sees the "post" (in both terms) as representing a "space-clearing gesture" and seems to disagree with the notion of the post as "after or beyond" colonialism when he says "many areas of contemporary African cultural life ... are not in this way concerned with transcending, with going beyond coloniality" (Appiah 1991, 348). Quayson is also useful in providing some historical context for the usage of "post-colonial" versus "postcolonial," and it is with the latter termed as "a more wide-ranging culturalist analysis" that I use the unhyphenated version throughout this chapter (Quayson 2000, 1).

4. See McClintock, 1995, for a discussion about why she finds umbrella terms of this sort problematic.
5. This framing from "bondage to freedom" is a nationalist representation of postcoloniality. Anne McClintock finds this notion of progress marked by "post" problematic and outside of academic currency finds little value in its use in postcolonial. She notes "the recurrent, almost ritualistic incantation of the prefix *post* is a symptom, I believe, of a global crisis in ideologies of the future, particularly the ideology of progress" (McClintock 1995, 392). Spivak also links this notion of progress to "epistemic violence" (Spivak 1999). On the other hand, Breckenridge and van der Veer find the term "postcolonial" useful and refer to the postcolonial period "as a framing device to characterize the second half of the twentieth century" and that "to call [this period] postcolonial, then, is to call for reappraisal of the way we frame contemporary world history and to emphasize the rupture in national and global relations created by the urge to forge independent nations—states first in the colonial world..." (Breckenridge and Veer 1993, 1). Commenting on the emergence of colonial studies in anthropology, Asad notes that "fundamental changes have occurred in the world [since World War II] which social anthropology inhabits, changes which have affected the object, the ideological support and the organizational base of social anthropology itself" (Asad 1973a, 12). Although he does not explicitly refer to the postcolonial, his comment, in some sense, may be seen as a precursor to Breckenridge and van der Veer's "the term 'postcolonial' displaces the focus on 'postwar' as a historical marker for the last fifty years" (Breckenridge and van der Veer 1993, 1).
6. See, for example, Mohanty, Russo, and Torres 1991. Sara Suleri has some frustration with this usage of the term "post-colonial" when she notes "where the term once referred exclusively to the discursive practices of the historical fact of prior colonization ... it is now more of an abstraction available for figurative deployment in any strategic redefinition of marginality" (Suleri 1992, 759).
7. In this vein, Quayson talks about the "process of postcolonializing" as "the critical process by which to relate modern-day phenomena to their explicit, implicit or even potential relations to this fraught heritage" (Quayson 2000, 11). Although I find it interesting to think about postcolonialism as a process I am disturbed by his further characterization that a "'postcolonial' project has to be alert to imbalances and injustices wherever these may be found in East and West, North and South" and further that "postcolonialism must be seen as a project to correct imbalances in the world, and not merely to do with specific 'postcolonial' constituencies" (Quayson 2000, 11). Quayson's project here is to bridge what he sees as largely academic debates in postcolonial theory and the "concrete" experiences of postcolonialism. Thus he is less inclined to think about the limits of postcolonial theory and what this may mean for his project.
8. This is not to say that theory is autonomous or independent of the practitioner or that postcolonial theory in particular is a coherent, undifferentiated, unified body of knowledge but rather that it does have an internal logic that together with the historical, geographical, and social conditions in which it is generated and used affect, in important ways, the kinds of questions that may be thought and therefore asked. Vivek Dhareshwar points out that theories that may have been considered marginal have now "become norm, in the sense that [they] now [have] the power to determine contexts of research and set agendas"

(Dhareshwar 1990, 235). Mary John's discussion about partial/composite theories is also instructive here. She notes that although "we need to conceive of theories as already embodying ... both rhetorical and historical dimensions" we must also see them as "compositely structured—made up of networks of assumptions, disciplinary affiliations, historical sediments, and global connections that have never been fixed or uniform but that evolve in an uneven, power-laden flux" (John 1996, 37–38).

9. There is always the problem of language here, and I struggle with this throughout. Referring to groups as nonwhite makes white the referent point, normalizing it in some way and using the term people of color removes whiteness while also naturalizing it, though in a different way. The implication of course being that white is not a color and by extension not a raced position through which people understand and operate in the world. This problem speaks to the mutual constitutiveness of race such that blacknesses and whitenesses do constitute each other. This is not a problem that will be resolved here. For the remainder of the paper I will use "people of color" self-consciously to refer to people and groups who identify or are identified as not white.

10. It is worthwhile here to keep in mind that "history" itself, like anthropology is implicated in colonial projects (see Asad 1973b) and needs (as much as any discipline or discourse can ever "properly" or "fully" be) to be decolonized.

11. On this point, Scott argues for "deconstructive readings" which he sees as necessary for "repositioning [anthropological texts] within their appropriate contexts of argument" (Scott 1997, 520). It is not clear to me what "appropriate context of argument" means nor am I convinced that this is even possible. I take his point about the deconstruction and reconstruction of anthropological objects but the process of going back to discern the original "context" of texts in order to determine whether or not anthropology is responding to "colonial questions" or "reproducing or displacing colonial objects" is fraught with problems of reading, (re)reading, and who gets to determine meaning. This problem has been addressed elsewhere (see, for example, Spivak 1988).

12. Thinking about colonial power as an entity to be overcome denies the ways in which we (scholars, postcolonial people, and postcolonial scholars) are complicit in colonialist projects and gives credence to the idea that it is possible to return to a precolonial space, even theoretically, to speak from. Again, Spivak is useful here in her discussion about the "prepropriative" as a place that cannot be returned to and thus cannot be appropriated (Spivak 1992).

13. See http://www.npr.org/templates/rundowns/rundown.php?prgId=2&prgDate=10-24-2008

14. This is a local term for someone who receives the privileges of whiteness in Jamaica but may not be accorded those privileges outside Jamaica. This is a contested term and though most Jamaicans of all classes and colors know the term and claim to know who it describes there is variation in who the term is used to describe.

15. This may be interpreted as avoiding hooligans but there are definite color/class connotations in the use of the term "nega" which is loosely equivalent to "nigger" in the United States (though with more class overtones than the usage generally allows in the United States).

16. See Smith's discussion about Anglo-Saxon clubs in Virginia in the early twentieth century.

7. ON THE IMPOSSIBILITIES OF A POST-RACIST AMERICA IN THE OBAMA ERA

KARANJA KEITA CARROLL

THIS CHAPTER INTERROGATES THE REALITY OF RACISM AND WHITE SU-
premacy in what some today refer to as "the Obama era" and what others regard as evidence of a "post-racist America." By utilizing an African-centered conceptual framework, centering on culture and worldview, this discourse constitutes a critical examination of the impossibilities of a post-racist America by investigating the lived experiences of African-descended people and other communities of color. Through this analysis, it will be evident that while we may be in "the Obama era," we are far from a post-racist society. Thus, discussions of post-racism are assessed as conceptual masks used to conceal the philosophical and structural realities of global white supremacy as exemplified through continuous racist practices.

The election of Barack Hussein Obama is a significant event in American history. To some, it reflects a new era in the history of American race relations, while to others, the election of President Obama signals the declining significance of race in America; and possibly the "end" of racism (Matt 2008, 34; Romano and Ammah-Tagoe, and No 2009, 42–45; Halewood 2009, 1047–52; Robinson III 2009, 212–23; J. James 2009, 459–81; Staples 2010, 128–44; Ossei-Owusu 2009, 64–75; Gines 2010, 370–84; Thomas 2010, 22–23). Although these interpretations are held valid among pundits, including some within the African American community, both views lack a clear understanding of racism, global white supremacy, and the history of American race relations. These "pundits" are misguided in heralding the "end of race" and fail to take notice of the everyday obstacles to social equality endured by African-descended people and other groups of color. In order to clearly understand the nature of this misreading and lack of fundamental change in the social reality of people of color, it is necessary to investigate the concepts of culture, worldview, race, racism, and global white supremacy. Clarity on these concepts and their impact upon the lived reality of African-descended peoples, and other people of color, sheds a more accurate light on the reality of race and racism within the Obama era.

It is essential to investigate the unique cultural and philosophical foundations that are the basis of this particular thought system and the behavioral tendencies connected to it (i.e., racism and white supremacy). Culture and worldview are essential tools of analysis when attempting to understand human reality as has been the conclusion of numerous scholars. This is especially the case within a culturally diverse environment where certain cultural assumptions, ways of knowing and ways of existing within the world, that are actually cultural particularities, are posed as cultural universals. Following a review of culture and worldview as discussed by African-centered scholars and a discussion of an epistemological investigation of racism, a number of examples are examined that reflect the little changed reality among people of African descent and other people of color. The goal of this chapter is to accentuate the core components of racism and white supremacy that are still found within the Obama era. Rather than looking for the end of racism as linked to the gaining of access to more resources, or to the election of people of color to political office, the demise of racism will only come about with the critical investigation and later destruction of certain culturally specific ways of knowing and being within the world that impose one value system over others.

CULTURE AND WORLDVIEW[1]

African-centered scholars posit that culture and worldview are essential tools in the analysis of human and social relations (Kambon 1992; Kambon 1996, 57–69; Kambon 1998; Kambon 2004, 73–92; Myers 1991, 15–32; Myers 1988; Banks 1992, 262–72; Nobles 1978, 679–88; Richards 1979, 240–55; Azibo 1999, 1–31; Azibo 2001, 420–41; Schiele 1994, 5–25; Graham 1999, 103–22; Semaj 1996, 193–202). These scholars suggest that the cultural variation which is pervasive throughout all of humanity significantly impacts the responses one has to social phenomena. African-centered scholars argue that only by taking into account these varied cultural realities does the social theorist and social scientist truly engage in meaningful social analysis.

Culture, as defined by Wade Nobles, refers to "a general design for living and patterns for interpreting reality" (Nobles 1985, 102). African-centered scholars have relied upon this understanding of culture to generate a model of culture based upon two levels. Nobles and others posit that we can understand culture as it relates to a deep structure and surface structure of culture. From the above definition, the surface structure correlates with "a general design for living," while the deep structure correlates with the "patterns for interpreting reality" (Myers 1987, 72–85; Myers 1991, 15–32; Myers 1993; Azibo 1999, 1–31; Azibo 2001). Together, the deep and surface structures of culture encompass the depth and pervasiveness of culture, especially as it relates to the investigation of social phenomenon.

"A general design for living" or the surface structure of culture refers to any aspect of one's lived reality that is engaged through the five senses. Thus, most aspects that we use to define cultural differences are reflective of the surface structure. Whether we speak of food, dress, or beauty, each aspect is accessible through reliance upon what we can see, touch, taste, hear and, smell. Surface structure manifestations represent culture at its most simplistic level. While cultural variance at the surface level is important, it is also important to recognize variance on other levels.

The "patterns for interpreting reality," or deep structure, of culture provides a more profound understanding of culture and refers to the manner in which we engage social and lived phenomena on a conceptual level. That is, how do we understand that which we engage with the five senses? Noble's understanding of deep structure is interchangeable with the concept of worldview. Both are concerned with philosophical questions that are essential in understanding varied experiences based upon that which is materially apprehensible. Generally speaking, "a worldview refers to the way in which a people make sense of their surroundings; make sense of life and of the universe" (Ani 1980, 4). Mack Jones adds clarity to this definition by stating that all "people have a worldview that is a product of [their] lived experience and that constitutes the lens through which the world of sense perceptions is reduced to described fact" (Jones 1992, 30). However, what exactly is a worldview?

As the above definitions suggest, worldview can be understood on multiple levels, from the simplistic "how one sees the world" to the more complex articulation suggested by Jones. Building upon the work of Vernon Dixon, African-centered scholars (especially those who have been called "Black psychologists") posit that the concept of worldview centers on the role of philosophical assumptions (Dixon 1971, 119–56; Dixon 1976, 51–102). These philosophical assumptions include: cosmology, ontology, axiology, epistemology, teleology, and logic.

Given that African-centered analysis is concerned with accurately interpreting the lived reality of African-descended people, the majority of cultural and worldview analysis within this area of research prioritizes the cultural and worldview distinctions between Africans and Europeans.

This should not negate the potential similarities and differences between non-African and non-European communities. However, given the historical continuous and contentious relationship between global Africans and global Europeans, this relationship is predominant. Furthermore, this does not negate the impact of global European peoples on other non-Europeans. In fact, the analysis that will follow supports the cultural and worldview based response of global European peoples to non-Europeans. However, the current priority focuses on clarifying the cultural and worldview distinctions between African and European peoples.

Some may also question the validity of encapsulating the worldviews of such large and internally diverse populations under the nomenclature of an "African worldview" or "European worldview." This is done with good reason and skepticism. However, neither concept should suggest a static means of interpreting either cultural world. As Kwame Gyekye suggests in regards to traditional African culture and by extension African diasporic culture, "[a] painstakingly comparative study of African cultures leaves one in no doubt that despite the undoubted cultural diversity arising from Africa's ethnic pluralism, threads of underlying affinity do run through the beliefs, customs, value systems, and sociopolitical institutions and practices of the various African societies" (Gyekye 1995, 192). Furthermore, Daudi Ajani ya Azibo, relying upon the arguments of Jacob Carruthers, argues that the African worldview is "the universal and timeless worldview characteristic of African people throughout space and time" (Azibo 2001, 422). While intracultural variance is acknowledged, it is not acknowledged at the expense of unity. Marimba Ani clearly grasps this idea when she argues that

> *our oppressors have emphasized the loss of language, dress, living patterns and other tangible and surface aspects of culture, just as they do in discussions of African culture on the continent. They emphasize difference in language, and customs—even physique—from one society to another. They do this with good reason. It is an emphasis that serves their objectives. Until we learn that it serves our objectives to emphasize the similarities, the ties, the unifying principles, the common threads and themes that bind and identify us all as "African," we will continue to be politically and ideologically confused. (Ani 1980, 1)*

It is with these realities in mind that we now precede with a comparative model of the African and European worldviews.

As previously stated, a worldview consists of concepts such as cosmology, ontology, axiology, epistemology, and other philosophical assumptions.

Together, a cultural group's understanding of the universe (cosmology), nature of being (ontology), values (axiology), and knowledge (epistemology), all contribute to the ways in which a people make sense of reality, i.e., their worldview.

Beginning with the cosmological assumption, the etymological origin of the term cosmology (*cosmos*—Greek, universe) refers to the nature/structure of the universe (Myers 1993; Kambon 1992; Kambon 1996; Kambon 1998). African-centered scholars contend that the African cosmology is based upon "an interconnected and interdependent edifice," where "all things in the universe are interconnected and interdependent" (Azibo 2001, 424). The cosmological assumption of independence and separation is reflective of the European worldview and guides the majority of Western social reality. However, this assumption requires separation between interrelated areas contributing to unnecessary divisions of human and social experiences.

Etymologically, the concept of ontology is rooted in the Greek root *ontos*, referring to being. The ontological assumption of the worldview concept engages questions pertaining to the nature of reality and/or nature of a being. An African ontology suggests that the nature of reality and being is spirit/energy. Dona Richards argues that

> *the essence of the African cosmos is spiritual reality; that is its fundamental nature, its primary essence. But realities are not conceived as being in irreconcilable opposition, as they are in the West, and spirit is not separate from matter. Both spiritual and material being are necessary in order for there to be meaningful reality. While spiritual being gives force and energy to matter, material beings give form to spirit.* (Richards 1990, 210)

Therefore, at the fundamental level of all existence is a spiritual force/energy manifesting itself on all levels of human reality. However, the ontological assumption manifests itself as solely material reality within the European worldview orientation. This reliance solely on material reality to define existence will manifest itself in the predominance of material and physical mechanisms to define self, worth, and beingness.

The concept of axiology is concerned with the nature of values. The etymological origin of the term axiology (*axios*—Greek, values) confirms this understanding. Put another way, axiology addresses the questions: What do you value? What do your values consist of? Linda James Myers argues that the distinctions between axiologies is found within an optimal (African) axiology where the "highest value [is] in positive interpersonal relationships among people," and a suboptimal (European) axiology where the "highest value [is] in objects or acquisition of objects" (Myers 1993, 97). Kambon also distinguishes between values among the two worldviews, by arguing that the African worldview's axiological basis is grounded in cooperation and collective responsibility; corporateness and interdependence; and spiritualism and circularity. This is in contradistinction to the European axiology which is founded on competition and individual rights; separateness and independence; and materialism and ordinality (Kambon 1996, 61).

As the following section will outline, essential to this discussion of worldview and its impact on racism, is the concept of epistemology. Following its etymological origin (*episteme*—Greek, knowledge/to know), epistemology refers to the nature of knowledge, but more importantly, how one knows what s/he knows? It asks the question: What are the processes that are used in order to know something? The central distinction between African and European conceptions of epistemology centers on what Vernon Dixon has referred to as "perceptual space" (Dixon 1976). This refers to the relational distance between that which one is trying to know and the knower. This manifests itself in notions of objectivity, in which the only valid means of knowing within a Western epistemology is through separation, while according to an African epistemology, knowledge comes through positive relational connections.

Objectivity as an outgrowth of the European epistemology determines the manner in which one comes to know and/or attain information about phenomena. In discussing the ideological nature of objectivity, Richards states,

> *The knowing subject must disengage himself from that which he wishes to know. He must become emotionally uninvolved—detached. Indeed, he must become remote from it. By doing this, he successfully controls that which he wishes to know and thereby makes of it an object. The object has been created by the distance of the knowing self from the thing to be known.* (Richards 1989, 24)

By objectivity functioning within this manner, and by it being a key component of Western social reality, it is obvious that this concept is detrimental to accurately and holistically understanding social phenomenon. In reality, the assumption of objectivity is an affront to the African cosmological and epistemological assumptions, as previously mentioned. But more importantly,

> *the African worldview immerses us in a vibrant universe. It seeks to close gaps—to do away with discontinuity—to bring us close to the essence of life. The epistemology it generates does away with distance. Since there is no distance, there are no mediators. The mode of our epistemological method is that of participation, and relationship rather than separation and control. (Richards 1989, 24, 31)*

The epistemological differences between African and European worldviews become another key distinction negatively impacting an accurate assessment of human and social reality.

Together, the cultural and worldview differences of Africans and Europeans leads one to infer that social reality is not only lived differently, but also understood differently. While the African worldview prioritizes an interconnected and interrelated reality that relies upon the immaterial aspects of reality to make sense of the lived experience and favors relations of the whole, the European worldview prioritizes the separation of social reality, only utilizing that which can be apprehended with the five senses to validate and provide meaning for that which we engage through our lived experience. It is these aspects of the European worldview that directly correlate to the development and manifestation of racism and white supremacy. The components of the African worldview suggest a different model of viewing the world that is beyond separation, hierarchy and control, some of the very basic components that are foundational for racism and white supremacy.

This comparative analysis of components of the African and European worldviews implies basic distinctions at their fundamental core. As Kobi Kambon argues,

> *Our worldview system determines our definitions, our concepts and our values; whether we consider events that we experience important, true, good, etc. or whether we attend to them at all. Thus, we make assumptions about events that we experience based on our "predisposed" values, beliefs and attitudes toward the nature of things. These values, beliefs and attitudes comprise an organized body of ideas or a conceptual framework for viewing, defining and experiencing the nature and meaning of events that constitute our phenomenal reality, and even determine what phenomenal reality will in fact be. (Kambon 1992, 4)*

Thus, one's worldview is essential to their very being and the basis of how they come to know, make sense of, and engage their social reality.

Reliance upon the concepts of culture and worldview provide an alternative means of making sense of modern racism. Rather than seeing racism and white supremacy as obscure and abnormal behavioral tendencies, we can in fact see them as realities consistent with a particular cultural and worldview orientation. The following analysis builds upon this discussion through a look at racism as it relates to a culturally specific epistemological framework.

RACISM: AN EPISTEMOLOGICAL BASIS

The epistemological basis of American racism is rooted in a unique western European proclivity toward separation, hierarchy, dominance, and control. This is embedded in the philosophical assumptions which guide the very essence of Western thought. Marimba Ani, in *Yurugu: An African-Centered Critique of European Cultural Thought and Practice*, outlines this framework as the basis of what she refers to as the European utamawazo (Ani 1994, 104–108). This system of logic and epistemology is then extended into areas of race, gender, class, sexual orientation, and a host of other socially constructed and validated components of human existence. While this current application of Ani's model is specific to issues of race and racism, the application is valid beyond race and is essential in understanding the nature of Western thought and those who rely upon this culturally based thought system as they engage "the other."

After a thorough review of some consistent themes in Western epistemological thought, Marimba Ani argues that there are several components that are essential in recognizing the unique cognitive style of western Europeans and their descendents. While Ani outlines nine components which make up the basis of her understanding of the European utamawazo, the very essence of modern day racism and white supremacy becomes self-evident within the first three components. These begin with a process of dichotomization in which "all realities are split into two parts" (Ani 1994, 104–108, 105). As applied to issues of race, rather than acknowledge that the various phenotypical differences across humanity, we must instead make precise lines of demarcation as they relate to so-called races.

Building upon dichotomization is the process of oppositional, confrontational, and antagonistic relationships which takes the originally dichotomized human group and suggests that these separate "races" are in conflict and therefore have a confrontational relationship between one another.

Rather than seeing human variation through a lens of interrelated components, the epistemological assumptions of Western thought automatically construct reality centering on issues of differences as opposed to complementarities. These two components lead into the third component of hierarchical segmentation, in which the varied human groups are then valued in relation to one another along a given hierarchy. Ani clarifies this component by arguing that

> *the original splitting and separating mental process assigns qualitatively different (unequal) value to the opposing realities of the dichotomies and a stratification of value to all realities within a given set or category. This process of valuation and devaluation is accompanied by that of segmentation and compartmentalization of independently derived entities. The effect is to eliminate the possibility of organic or sympathetic relationship, thereby establishing grounds for the dominance of the "superior" form or phenomenon over that which is perceived to be inferior: the power-relationship. (Ani 1994, 104–8)*

Thus, in relation to issues of race and racism, we find that within the Western world the physical differences that distinguish human beings are used as the basis to categorize races. This categorization is then used as the basis for some assumed conflict between these varied human groupings. In a society based upon the assumed dominance of Europe, and her descendants, this valuation system is assigned to those who are phenotypically white with the highest-ranking position in the hierarchy and those labeled as black the lowest-ranking. All other colors are placed within the white-black binary, as Latino/as, Asians, and Native Americans all attempt to position themselves closest to the highest-ranking position (whiteness) and farthest away from the lowest-ranking position (blackness).

Arguably, it is a logic and epistemology of separation, conflict, hierarchy, and control that is unique to Europe and her descendants, which characterizes the reality of racism within the modern world. This reading of racism and white supremacy indicates a cultural foundation, grounded in the worldview and unique philosophical assumptions of Europeans. Thus, racism and white supremacy are culturally specific to people of European ancestry. However, the cultural specificity of racism draws non-European peoples into the discussion determining the manner in which we in fact see, make sense of, and understand racism and white supremacy. Speaking broadly about the far-reaching implications of a worldviews analysis, Kobi

Kambon argues that "every person operates according to some group's conception of reality, whether they are aware of it or not; and it is a conception which they share with their reference group, the group with which they are identified (in terms of values, beliefs, customs, etc.)" (Kambon 2004, 73). Living in a multicultural and multiracial society dominated by the culture and worldview of Euro Americans leads to conceptions of racism and white supremacy on the terms of the dominant group; in fact, it impacts how we define these concepts.

However, an African-centered interpretation of racism stresses the cultural and worldview foundations of this phenomenon. While in agreement with many of the radical interpretations of racism, most deny racism's cultural and worldview basis. In doing so, these readings suggest that anyone can be racist rather than connecting racism with a culturally specific thought system. Seeing racism and white supremacy as a culturally specific phenomena rooted in the unique culture and worldview of European-descended people provides an expansive model of racism and supports a more nuanced explanation of its institutional nature as expounded on by many scholars of racial theory.

An explanation of racism in relation to the European worldview also suggests that the manner by which we determine the end of racism must move beyond mere surface level examples (i.e., an African American president, CEOs of color, etc.). Linda James Myers supports this assessment in her extended explanation of the myth of cultural pluralism and assimilation. She argues that

> *society may espouse a value for cultural pluralism, but at the same time perpetuate institutional structures that prevent it and insure assimilation (Myers, 1981). On a conscious level an individual in that society may say, "I support the right of every ethnic group to participate." Unconsciously they may mean, "as long as they do it my way, like me." The same individual may be unconscious of feelings of insecurity, inferiority, and/or inadequacy surrounding what would happen to his/her own sense of self, if the ethnically different were to be accepted for their difference. Between individuals, continuing the same example, we might find that the nonacceptance of "true" cultural difference is totally outside of the awareness of the dominant cultural group (nonconscious). On a conscious level members of the dominant group are likely not to really know what the "other" culture is like except on a superficial level (i.e., based on the perception and understanding their own cul-*

ture's system allows). Therefore, it will be easy for the dominant group in seeking additional members to make itself more heterogeneous to select those potentially (superficial appearing) different candidates with essential characteristics (i.e., beliefs, world view, conceptual systems) most like themselves. As a consequence, the status quo is reinforced, and no substantive change takes place. Although we may now have added blacks or women to our group, we chose only those blacks or women who think and see the world as we do. (Myers 1991, 18–19)

POST-RACE, POST-RACIAL AND/OR POST-RACISM?

This argument is directly applicable to the current presidency of Barack Hussein Obama and is rather evident as one analyzes the first year of his term, along with other telltale signs prior to his election. Indeed, the concepts of post-race, post-racial, and post-racism have now come into vogue (Matt 2008; Romano, Ammah-Tagoe, and No 2009, 42–45; Halewood 2009, 1047–52; Robinson III 2009, 212–23; James 2009, 459–81; Staples 2010, 128–44; Ossei-Owusu 2009, 64–75; Gines 2010, 370–84; Thomas 2010, 22–23). In doing so, these terms provide the much relied upon terminologies to classify and clarify the current state of race relations within the United States. While on the surface each term seems to suggest we are beyond and done with race and racism in the age of Obama, these terms also support the assumption of colorblindness as an American ideal (Halewood 2009, 1047–52; James 2009, 459–81; Staples 2010, 128–44; Gines 2010, 370–84; Thomas 2010, 22–23).

Race within America is best understood as a social construct with real life consequences. Thus, while race may be biologically questionable, the differences that beset a person of African descent from a person of European descent are in fact real and impact their life chances in the job market, education, healthcare, politics, and so on. The suggestions of a post-racial America fly in the face of the fact that within a society dominated by white supremacy, "race" will always have real life consequences. The only means by which we can undermine this reality is to do away with the concept of race. Yet to deny the reality of race leads to the utter fallacy of colorblindness and suggests an America that is "race-free." As Dawn G. Williams and Roderic R. Land argue, "Non-recognition of race reinforces and reproduces the flawed structure of society because it does not allow for the analysis of social inequality at the core of the problem" (Williams and Land 2006, 579–88). To postulate the existence of a post-race America will only function to maintain the current system of white supremacy without referring to it as "racism" or even considering it as "race-related."

Kathryn T. Gines provides a critical discussion on the current usages of "post-racial," along with all of its variants used within American popular culture today. She argues that "the term gained considerable momentum during Barack Obama's successful presidential campaign—as if the election of President Obama is a singular event of such magnitude that it has altogether ended racism, and further rendered racial categories insignificant and even nonexistent" (Gines 2010, 379). She further adds that all too many times the usage of this term "implies that America is not only post-*racial* but also post-*racist*." While these terms are not interchangeable given the flimsy definitions of "race," "racial," "racism," and "racist" within American popular culture, it is only logical that these terms are used interchangeably and incorrectly. However, Gines provides her most critical insight when she argues that if by "post-racial" people in fact mean "post-white," then this might be a worthy desire. "Post-white" would entail "displacing whiteness as the universal and the presume to be non-raced standard, as well as disrupting the hierarchies that have resulted from the myth of whiteness" (Gines 2010, 379–80). "Post-racial" in this sense "offer[s] a beginning step toward the project of dis-lodging white privilege" (Gines 2010, 379, 380), yet this is not the manner in which "post-racial" is used and thus "post-racial" refers to the all too mythic beliefs that America and American society have moved beyond race and racism as realities that impact the lives of people of color.

While "post-race" and "post-racism" may speak to the intentions of a colorblind America, these terms do nothing in regards to illuminating the continued persistence of race for people of color in a society dominated by white supremacy. As Joy James correctly asserts, "*Postracial* is not synonymous with postwhite supremacy. Whiteness retains its hegemonic normativity" (James 2009, 470). By maintaining systems of white dominance these terms solely help to perpetuate the fallacy of meritocracy and an equal playing field that plays into the current social structure. Instead of finding the systematic means of racial inequality, post-racist logic and terminologies continuously lead to blaming those of African descent and other people of color for not taking advantage of all of their newfound opportunities since race and racism are no longer impediments to their success. In addition, Peter Halewood correctly explains the problematic usage of post-racialist terms and concepts, when he argues that "self-congratulation on having achieved a post-racial society is both premature and suspect, for encoded in claims of post-racialism is a sort of white triumphalism, a sense that race and racism have finally been delegitimized as the basis for black grievance" (Halewood 2009, 1049). However, the current lived realities speak to an accurate picture of the lives of African-descended people and others of color in relation to the realities of racism.

RACISM AND THE LIVED REALITY OF AFRICAN-DESCENDED PEOPLE IN AMERICA

This grasp of racism through the lens of a worldview analysis provides an alternative to most discussions of this topic. Contingent on any discussion of racism is the construct of race. While some argue that race is a social construct, these arguments fail to thoroughly discuss the lived reality connected to race. Race is both a social construct and a *lived* reality. It is this lived reality connected with race and racism that bears the evidentiary fruit of the continued existence of racism within the age of Obama. What follows are exemplary sketches of events that have taken place within the age of Obama that clearly convey that we are not in a post-racism moment.

As Valerie Rawlston Wilson of the National Urban League Policy Institute states in the 2009 Equality Index, "Ironically, even as an African American man holds the highest office in the country, African Americans remain twice as likely as whites to be unemployed, three times more likely to live in poverty and more than six times as likely to be incarcerated" (Wilson 2009, 15). The conclusions of the 2009 and 2010 Equality Index published by the National Urban League still reflect a lived reality which shows minimal changes within the presidency of Barack Obama. The National Urban League's Equality Index "can be interpreted as the relative status of blacks and whites in American society, measured according to five areas—economics, health, education, social justice and civic engagement" (Wilson 2010, 11). Of the five areas which the Equality Index measures, it was only in the realm of civic engagement that we see substantive change for 2010. As Wilson further states, "The [civic engagement] score primarily improved because of the large increase in black voter turnout during the 2008 election season."[2] However, in regards to economics, health, education, and social justice, African Americans lag behind whites at an index rate of 67.2 percent for 2010, which is a decrease of .5 percent from 2009. The findings lead to an overall conclusion that rather than living in a post-racist America, most

African Americans and other people of color have little to no changes in their lived reality. In fact, these findings suggest that their conditions have not improved but have actually worsened. Yet there are other telltale signs regarding the falsity of a post-racist American in the age of Obama.

Educational opportunities function as one of many barometers in determining the continued maintenance of instructional structures that support the existence of race and racism as factors that impact the life chances of people of African ancestry within the United States. With the varied racial makeup of American classrooms, one would think that the teaching force would reflect these realities. Yet this is far from the truth. In fact, since the historic 1954 *Brown v. the Board of Education* decision, teachers within American classrooms have continuously become whiter, further impacting the ways in which students of color construct images of educators, understand education, and realize the sociopolitical function of educational institutions.

While many pride the advances of *Brown*, many do not consider the devastating impact this decision had on the teaching profession for the African American community and by extension communities of color. Prior to 1954, 82,000 African American teachers were responsible for the education of 2 million African American children. Within the first ten years of *Brown*, 38,000 African American teachers in Southern and border states lost their jobs. Between 1975 and 1985, African American students majoring in education declined by 66 percent. Throughout the mid-to-late 1980s, 37,000 teachers, including 21,000 African American teachers, were eliminated due to new teacher education requirements (Hudson and Holmes 1994, 389). In 2006, 87 percent of all teachers were caucasian/white, 6 percent African American, 4 percent Latino/a, 1 percent Asian, 1 percent Native American, 3 percent multiracial, and 3 percent self-indentified as "other." However, while people of color within the U.S. make up over 25 percent of the population, they only make up just around 13 percent of the teaching population. Take the state of Texas, where 62 percent of the student population are students of color yet less than 33 percent of the teaching population are people of color. Or California, where 70 percent of the teaching force is white and female, with close to 65 percent of the teaching force including people of color.[3] Or New York City, we find that in 2008 the rate of African American teachers steadily decreased from its position in 2000. The percentage of African American teachers dropped from 22 percent to 20 percent in 2008 while the rate for white teachers stayed consistent at 60 percent (Green 2008). The examples provided by Texas, California, and New York City support the notion that through the mechanism of education, it is clear that structural inequality continues to persist. Furthermore, this inequality impacts another generation so much so that many of these students question the profession of education as a worthwhile career choice, especially given the fact that they have rarely experienced educators who look like them, think like them, and/or speak like them.

While education can be a factor in determining the future of people of African descent within American society, the conclusions of Algernon Austin suggest that education may not always trump race. In agreement with the conclusions of Michael Brown, et al., in their 2003 text *Whitewashing Race: The Myth of a Color-blind Society* (Brown et al. 2003), Algernon Austin of the Thora Institute concludes that "when one compare blacks and whites with each other, it is clear that whites have a distinct advantage [in regards to employment]. Blacks with high school diplomas have unemployment rates that are equivalent to white high school dropouts. Blacks with college degrees only do modestly better at finding work than whites with high school diplomas."[4]

The structural barriers of advancement in America for people of African descent should be clear, whether in regards to poor educational outcomes, graduation rates, access to higher education, employment, and incarceration, the most recent data on black life in America is replete with examples that we are far from a post-racist America. In fact, the structural barriers to advancement are only coupled with the outright facts of racist and discriminatory acts towards people of African descent. What follows are exemplary sketches of events that have taken place within the age of Obama that clearly convey that we are not in a post-racism moment.

Since the election and subsequent inauguration of President Barack Hussein Obama, we have experienced telltale examples of the reality of racism and white supremacy living and breathing, alive and well in these United States of America, from simple media images that hearken back to America's racist past to continued discrimination or lack of access to public facilities. Even a close reading of discussions centering on President Obama speak to the reality of white supremacy and racism in this "age of Obama."

Historically, the American media has been an outlet through which the foundational beliefs of American society are expressed. Sometimes under the guise of free speech, and other times through claims of ignorance, the American popular press has negatively depicted and stereotyped nonwhite populations. The *New York Post* cartoonist Sean Delanos's February 18, 2009, depiction of a wild and violent chimpanzee being gunned down by two white police officers reflects numerous assumptions regarding authority, power, and control, all placed within the hands of white police officers.[5] In response to the proposed stimulus bill of the Obama administration, the caption from the white police officers states, "They'll have to find someone else to write the next stimulus bill." Given the outcry by both people of color and white readers of the *Post*, along with high-profile community activists such as Al Sharpton, the *New York Post* would eventually apologize for publishing this cartoon. However, any basic knowledge of American race relations would suggest that the problem with this image is its connection to historical representations of African-descended people as primates or the intimidating control of the white power structure of the United States.

Western racial thought has historically connected blackness and people of African origin with being closely connected to primates. The Great Chain of Being exemplified by racial classificatory systems by the likes of Lord Henry H. Kames (1696–1782), Charles Caldwell (1772–1853) and Robert Knox (1791–1862) represent a sprinkling of the earlier presumptions made about African-descended people and primates, which became a foundational assumption of most monogenetic and polygenetic Enlightenment theories of race and racial difference (Jackson, Jr. and Weidman 2004, 39–54). This belief/assumption continued into the modern era with representations of King Kong's capturing of a white woman to the most recent representation found on the April 2008 edition of *Vogue*, depicting former Cleveland Cavaliers forward Lebron James and supermodel Gisele Bundchen.[6] Each representation attempts to connect and establish the assumption that blackness is animalistic and supports racially motivated representations of African-descended people. Thus, when we see Delanos's *New York Post* cartoon, we are clearly aware of the historical development of these images in their connection to African-descended people, and more specifically, Barack Obama, with primates.

There is yet another dimension of racially motivated media representation at play here. The fact that the two officers who shoot this chimpanzee are white men seems to suggest that they are the real power brokers, those who have a final say in how change will actually develop. This unconscious assumption of white men being the final authority that stopped this wild chimpanzee from going out of control merely supports the historical assumption of whiteness being correct and normative, and thus the final word. This reading of Delanos's *New York Post* cartoon suggests that although we may have an African American man in office, the very basic thoughts and assumptions related to race and racism are still alive and well.

However, as previously stated, media becomes a rather straightforward outlet for the expression of unconscious racist thought. We can take, for instance, the recent depiction of Ohio state senator Nina Turner as Aunt Jemima in the November 25, 2009, edition of the *Call & Post*.[7] Walt Carr's racist caricature depicts an older African American women dressed as Aunt Jemima stirring the contents of a mixing bowl, with Nina Turner on her apron. The caption reads: "I be's the new leader." At face value, this may seem like an ordinary racist caricature but when we learn that the *Call & Post* is a predominately African American-read newspaper funded by Don King, we must rethink what is considered simplistic.

Eduardo Bonilla-Silva's model of the racialized social system provides clarity on State Senator Turner's representation in *Call & Post*. According to Bonilla-Silva, dominant racial groups develop a racial ideology that is then taken for granted by all socially constructed racial actors (Bonilla-Silva 2001). Thus, given the black-white binary, you will find African-descended people exhibiting a white racial ideology due to this being the functionally established racial ideology in a predominantly white society. On the surface, finding this racist caricature in a predominately African American publication may be surprising, but it only reflects the reality of white racial ideology and its negative consequences on racialized representations of African-descended people and other people of color.

Moving beyond the media, we can take the case of Omar Edwards, a second-year officer for the New York Police Department (NYPD), who was shot and killed by two fellow police officers (the primary shooter was white) on May 28, 2009 (Kovaleski 2009). Edwards, while off duty, drew his gun as he chased someone he found rummaging through his car and was eventually shot and killed by two NYPD police officers, a few blocks away from the Harlem Police Station where he worked.

The shock and outrage by community members and fellow police officers reflects the concerns about how something like this could have actually happened. How is it possible that an African American man could be shot and killed blocks from his precinct by two fellow NYPD officers? On November 16, 2009, a hearing held by law enforcement officials, scholars, and community activists delved into the topic of racially motivated police-on-police shootings.[8] A similar public hearing took place on December 3, 2009, in Harlem, where Edwards was fatally shot. The shooting and killing of Omar Edwards speaks to the reality of being an African American male within a white dominated society that has historically seen African American men as a threat. Even though two people may both be law enforcers, each has been affected by sociohistorically constructed images of African-descended people and more specifically African-descended males. Thus, in the case of the African-descended male as a threat, it is safer for a white officer to shoot first and ask questions later, even when it comes at the expense of an Africana life and a fellow officer.

Historically, conflict with law enforcement officers has represented an aspect of the lived experiences of African Americans. Juan Nunez, off-duty New York Police Department officer, along with four other Latinos participated in the assault of fifty-two-year old Daryl Jackson (Karoliszyn, et al. 2009). Jackson, who was aggressively panhandling, became the victim of this attack that included severe physical abuse and racial epithets including statements about "going back to Africa," all from law enforcement officers of color. This example clearly supports the internalized racial ideology that people of color have fallen victim to in their attempt to survive in a society based upon white dominance. Latino/as and other people of color are all victims of the dominant racial ideology that has been imposed on them and developed by white Americans. Thus, the actions of Juan Nunez and company only speak to the internalization of white racial ideology among people of color.

Finally, the June 29, 2009, expulsion of over fifty northeast Philadelphia summer campers, from the Valley Swim Club in Huntingdon Valley is reflective of a long history of separate swimming facilities throughout the United States (Nunnally and Tillman 2009). This incident shut down Valley Swim Club for a number of days as they attempted to nullify their rather blatantly racist actions over concerns that these swimmers might "change the complexion" of their facilities. Luckily, in this instance, the U.S. Justice Department accused Valley Swim Club of racism in a federal suit in early January 2010, but the other telltale signs of racism that go uninvestigated suggest the reality of racism and white supremacy in America.

The above-mentioned examples only reflect a sampling of incidents that have taken place within the first 365 days of Obama's presidency. Interestingly, these incidents fly in the face of post-racism and in fact support the reality of racism in the lived experiences of African-descended people and other people of color. Furthermore, these examples support the assumption that the structural nature of racism will be found in the public and private sector, throughout numerous institutions and rather blatantly, in print media. It is primarily through a well-constructed racial ideology used as the basis of a racialized social system that racism and white supremacy are maintained in the face of such assumed racial progress. Numerous examples of racism in America abound. The aforementioned incidents provide evidence to refute the notion that America has entered a post-racial phase in the age of Obama.

CONCLUSION

This chapter has provided the manner by which one can understand the cultural and philosophical foundations of racism that are rooted in a unique European approach to reality. By utilizing an African-centered conceptual framework, centering on culture and worldview, this discourse provided a critical examination of the impossibilities of a post-racist America by investigating the lived experiences of African-descended people and other communities of color. Grasping racism and white supremacy at its cultural and philosophical roots allows for a radical reinterpretation of American racism and global white supremacy. The cultural root of racism institutionally and systematically implicates those of European ancestry. This infers that there is something culturally unique that has allowed a system of thought to develop that is based fundamentally on hierarchy and, more specifically, racial hierarchy. At the same rate, it is the philosophical roots of racism that move the implication of the maintenance of racism and white supremacy beyond white people and pulls people of color into a dialogue of social hierarchy based upon the cultural terms of the socially dominant. Thus, while people of color may be the victims of racism, many of the examples discussed suggest that people of color have internalized the dominant racial ideology and thus work to maintain the racially dominant assumptions developed by people of European ancestry. This analysis attempts to show that while we may be in "the Obama era," we are far from a post-racist society due to the hegemonic nature of the European worldview and its impact upon people of color.

Notes

1. Many of the arguments in this section were previously developed in a previous publication. See Carroll 2008, 4–27.
2. Wilson, "Introduction to the 2010 Equality Index," 12.
3. Educational Data Partnership, http://www.ed-data.k12.ca.us/articles/article.asp?title=teachers%20in%20california.
4. Algernon Austin, "What Obama Did Not Say at Hampton: Education Is Not Enough," http://thorainstitute.blogspot.com/2010_05_01_archive.html.

5. Available online at: http://www.nypost.com/opinion/cartoons/delonas.htm.
6. *Vogue*, April 2008.
7. "Metro Desk," *Call & Post*, November 18, 2009, http://www.cleveland.com/call-and-post/index.ssf/2009/11/an_editorial_frank_sinatra_sai.html.
8. First Deputy Superintendent Pedro J. Perez, *Governor's Task Force on Police-on-Police Shooting*, November 16, 2009.

8. OBAMA, THE INSTABILITY OF COLOR LINES, AND THE PROMISE OF A POSTETHNIC FUTURE

DAVID A. HOLLINGER

THE FOCUS OF MEDIA DEPICTIONS OF BARACK OBAMA AS A "POST-RAcial," "post-black," or postethnic" candidate is usually limited to two aspects of his presidential campaign. First, his self-presentation with minimal references to his color. Unlike Jesse Jackson or Al Sharpton, whose presidential candidacies were more directed at the significance of the color line, Obama has never offered himself as the candidate of a particular ethno-racial group. Second, the press calls attention to the willingness of millions of white voters to respond to Obama. Some of his greatest margins in primary elections and caucuses were in heavily white states like Idaho and Montana. He even won huge numbers of white voters in some states of the old Confederacy, carrying Florida, Virginia, and North Carolina in the November election.

But there is much more to it.

The Obama candidacy was a far-reaching challenge to identity politics, and that challenge will only deepen now that Obama is president. At the center of that challenge is a gradually spreading uncertainty about the significance of color lines, especially the significance of blackness itself. Blackness is the pivotal concept in the intellectual and administrative apparatus used in the United States for dealing with ethno-racial distinctions. Doubts about its basic meaning, boundaries, and social role affected ideas about whiteness, and all other color-coded identities. These uncertainties make it easier to contemplate a possible future in which the ethno-racial categories central to identity politics would be more matters of choice than ascription; in which mobilization by ethno-racial groups would be more a strategic option than a presumed destiny attendant upon mere membership in a group; and in which economic inequalities would be confronted head-on, instead of through the medium of ethno-race.

To denote that possible future, I prefer the term "postethnic" to "post-racial." The former recognizes that at issue is all identity by natal community, including as experienced by, or ascribed to, population groups to whom the problematic term "race" is rarely applied. The reconceptualization affects the status of Latinos and other immigrant-based populations not generally counted as "races." A postethnic social order would encourage individuals to devote as much—or as little—of their energies as they wished to their community of descent, and would discourage public and private agencies from implicitly telling citizens that the most important thing about them was their descent community. Hence, to be postethnic is not to be anti-ethnic, or even colorblind, but to reject the idea that descent is destiny.

Obama's mixed ancestry generates some of the new uncertainty about blackness. The white part of his genetic inheritance is not socially hidden, as it often is for "light-skinned blacks" who descend from black women sexually exploited by white slaveholders and other white males. Rather, Obama's white ancestry is right there in the open, visible in the form of the white woman who, as a single mother, raised Obama after his black father left the family to return to his native Kenya. Press accounts of Obama's life, as well as his own autobiographical writings, render his whiteness hard to miss. No public figure, not even Tiger Woods, has done as much as Obama to make Americans of every education level and social surrounding aware of color-mixing in general and that most of the "black" population of the United States, in particular, are partially white. The "one-drop rule," which denies that color is a two-way street, is far from dead, but not since the era of its legal and social consolidation in the early 1920s has the ordinance of this rule been so subject to challenge.

But even more important to the new instability in the meaning of blackness in American life is the fact that Obama's black ancestry is *immigrant* rather than U.S.-born. The knowledge that Obama's black father came to the United States from Kenya may have done more than anything else to make Americans in general aware of the distinction within the black population of the United States between those who, like Obama's wife, Michelle, are the descendants of men and women who were enslaved in the United States and lived through the Jim Crow era, and those like Obama himself who are the descendants of immigrants from Africa or from the Caribbean.

To understand why the immigrant-originating blackness of Obama is so significant, we need to view it in relation to other happenings. That well over one-third of African Americans doubt that the black population of the United States is any longer a single people was revealed in a

November 2007 report by the Pew Research Center. Although the gap in values between middle-class and poorer African Americans was the focus of the study, black immigrants and their children are especially likely to be identified as middle class. A study by the Princeton University sociologist Douglas S. Massey and his collaborators shows that black immigrants and their children are overrepresented by several hundred percent among the black freshmen at Ivy League colleges. Such statistics are common at many other institutions, including Queens College of the City University of New York, a public university whose campus is located near a large population of African Americans. Many studies tell us that black immigrants and their children do better educationally and economically than do the descendants of American slavery and Jim Crow.

These studies demonstrate that educational and employment opportunities can be available to black people, even in the context of continued white racism. *This reality calls into question the credibility of blackness as our default standard for identifying the worst cases of inequality, and for serving as the focal point of remedies.* Slavery ended in the British Caribbean three decades before it ended in the United States, and black Caribbeans experienced a better post-emancipation educational system than did most black people in the United States. Perhaps the force keeping so many black Americans down is operative not so much in the eye of the empowered white beholder as in that legacy of slavery and Jim Crow, in the form of diminished socioeconomic capacity to take advantage of educational and employment opportunities?

To proceed down the theoretical and policy roads offered by this idea is not to doubt the power of white racism, but to locate more precisely its harmful effects. Our colleges and universities, as well as our remedies for employment discrimination, have generally assumed that white prejudice—a legacy, indeed, of slavery and Jim Crow—is the problem. That black people face prejudice today is beyond doubt, and numerous studies show that darker-skinned black people are more likely to be mistreated than those with lighter skin. But skin color does not tell the whole story. If it did, the immigrant/non-immigrant distinction within the black population would not have shown itself to have such striking consequences.

The African American descendants of slavery and Jim Crow are the only population group in the United States with a multi-century legacy of group-specific enslavement and institutionalized debasement, including hypo-descent racialization ("one drop of blood" makes a person black) and anti-miscegenation laws (black-white marriages were against the law in most states with large black populations until 1967), carried out under constitutional authority. Neither Obama nor any other African American of immigrant background is a member of this population group. The success of Obama in becoming the presidential nominee of one of the nation's two major political parties is, like the success of other black immigrants in other domains, an indication that something other than color-prejudice in the eye of empowered white people is at the root of structural inequality in the United States.

To be sure, many immigrants from the Caribbean have slave ancestors, too, and slavery also has a history in Africa itself. Other groups have been mistreated in other ways, in this country and in the countries of origin of many immigrants. But the segment of the African diaspora enslaved under American constitutional authority has a unique history, the awareness of which was vital in creating the political will in the 1960s and early 1970s to deploy federal power against racism in general, and to produce the concept of affirmative action in particular.

The differences in history and circumstances among various descent groups were largely ignored during the era when our conceptual and administrative apparatus for dealing with inequality was put in place. As John D. Skrentny, a sociologist at the University of California at San Diego, has shown—in his important 2002 book, *The Minority Rights Revolution*—conflating Asian Americans, Latinos, and American Indians with African Americans was a largely unconscious step driven by the unexamined assumption that those groups were "like blacks"; that is, they were functionally indistinguishable from the Americans who experienced slavery and Jim Crow. Such conflation was officially perpetuated as late as 1998, when President Clinton's Initiative on Race, *One America in the 21st Century: Forging a New Future*, systematically and willfully obscured those differences. That was done by burying statistics that disproved the all-minorities-are-alike myth, and by fashioning more than fifty recommendations to combat racism, not a single one of which spoke to the unique claims of black people.

If we are now going to recognize that even some *black* people—people like Obama—are not "like blacks," how can Mexican Americans and Cambodian Americans be "like blacks"? Can the latter be eligible for entitlements that were assigned largely on the basis of a "black model" that suddenly seems not to apply even to all black people? If black people with immigrant backgrounds are less appropriate targets of affirmative action and "diversity" programs than other black people, a huge issue can no longer be avoided: What claims for special treatment can be made for nonblack populations with an immigrant base? Can the genie of the immigrant/non-immigrant distinction be put back in the bottle, or are we to generate new, group-specific theoretical justifications for each group? That prospect is an intimidating one, trapping us by our habit of defining disadvantaged groups ethno-racially.

Employers and educators are asked to treat the Latino population as an ethno-racial group, yet the strongest claim that many of its members have for special protections and benefits is specific to economic conditions. The history of mistreatment of Latinos by Anglos is well documented, but the instances most comparable to anti-black racism predate the migration of the bulk of today's Latino population. One need not deny the reality of prejudicial treatment of Latinos to recognize another reality as more salient: immigration policies and practices that actively encourage the formation of a low-skilled, poorly educated population of immigrant labor from Mexico and other Latin American nations. As the recent debates over immigration confirm, the United States positively demands an underclass of workers and finds it convenient to obtain most of them from nearby Mexico.

But the service institutions obliged to deal with the needs of that population are held accountable on the basis of ethno-racial rather than economic classifications. Colleges and universities are routinely asked to recruit more Latino students and faculty members, and are accused of prejudice if they do not. People who are encouraged to immigrate to this country, legally or illegally, because they are poorly educated, willing to work for low wages and likely to avoid trade unions, do have a powerful claim on our resources, but it is an economic, not an ethno-racial claim. In the Latino case, more than any other, ethno-race is widely used as a proxy for dealing with economic inequality. The widely debated issue of whether Latinos ought to be regarded as a separate "race" would lose much of its point if the economic circumstances of this immigration-based population were confronted honestly rather than through an ethno-racial proxy.

The Asian American section of our color-conscious system is even more anachronistic. There are historical reasons for the relatively weak class position of immigrants from Cambodia and the Philippines, but our category of Asian American conceals the differences between those groups and those who trace their ancestry to Korea, whose adult immigrants to the United States are overwhelmingly college graduates. Institutions eager to assist the poorest immigrants sometimes do so through the hyper-ethnic step of breaking down the Asian category, enabling them to establish programs for Cambodians but not for Japanese. For example, the undergraduate admissions forms for the University of California system will soon ask Asian and Pacific-Islander applicants to classify themselves in twenty-three ethnic categories.

These considerations suggest that a historical approach to understanding the dynamics of inequality in American life has much to recommend it. Obama himself pointed in this direction in his epochal speech on race, delivered in March of 2008 in the wake of publicity given to the inflammatory sermons of his pastor, the Reverend Jeremiah Wright. "Many of the disparities that exist in the African-American community today can be directly traced to inequalities passed on from an earlier generation that suffered under the brutal legacy of slavery and Jim Crow," Obama declared in a crucial turn in that speech.

Before taking that turn, Obama surprised many people by alluding sympathetically to white workers who, damaged by economic turndowns, tended to blame affirmative action for their problems. Even while describing his own childhood pain upon hearing his white grandmother articulate negative stereotypes about black people, Obama turned the spotlight for a few minutes on whites. Obama offered sympathy and legitimacy to a variety of group-specific complaints without fostering an oppression Olympics, and without indulging the sentimental falsehood that all pains are equal. Hence, Obama at once urged Americans to look upon inequality in historical terms, and reached out across the black-white color line, confirming his image as a black politician who did not offer a black-centered message.

Yet we can expect that circumstances will push Obama back and forth between images of "more black than we thought" and "not as black as we thought." When, prior to Wright's having persisted in outrageous public behavior, Obama defended Wright's ministry, there was some buzz that he was farther to the black side of the color spectrum than his previous image had suggested. Once he renounced Wright, exited from Wright's congregation, and increased the frequency with which photographs of his white grandparents were displayed, there was some buzz that he was farther on the white side of that spectrum than some had supposed. These oscillations do not mean that Obama is lacking in authenticity; they mean that once his blackness is destabilized, it can intensify or diminish in a variety of contexts, including trivial ones.

Does the analysis sketched here mean that blackness is no longer relevant to the dynamics of mistreatment in the United States, and is no longer an appropriate basis for solidarity? Of course not. Black people have plenty of reasons to look to each other for mutual support, and to form enclaves strategically, while refusing to have their lives confined by color. The central postethnic principle, after all, is affiliation by revocable consent. But attention to skin color alone will not carry the United States very far toward diminishing the inequalities for which the extraordinary overrepresentation of black men in American prisons is a commanding emblem. A new, more realistic way to distribute resources and energies, calculated to diminish even those inequalities that owe much to a history of prejudice and violence, is needed. Whether it can be created remains to be seen. The Obama phenomenon makes a real conversation more possible than ever before.

The United States is still a long way from the cosmopolitan society that I sketched as an ideal thirteen years ago in my book *Postethnic America: Beyond Multiculturalism*. I have written this essay in response to many suggestions that I address the Obama phenomenon in the context of my ideas about postethnicity. Today we are closer than before to engaging inequalities that are too often understood in ethno-racial rather than economic terms. The energies and ideas flourishing around the Obama presidency may promote a long-overdue breakthrough. Obama's illustration in his own person of the contrast between immigrant and nonimmigrant black people, and of the reality of ethno-racial mixing, presents a compelling invitation to explore the limits of blackness especially, but also of whiteness, and of all color-coded devices for dealing with inequality in the United States. In the long run, the fact that Obama is the son of an immigrant may prove to be almost as important as the fact that he is the son of a black man and a white mother. Obama's destabilization of color lines will be hard to forget. Identity politics in the United States will never be the same again.

Note

The bulk of this essay appeared, in slightly different form, as "Obama, Blackness, and Postethnic America," *Chronicle of Higher Education*, February 29, 2008. For conversations that helped me develop the ideas I emphasize in this essay, I wish to thank Mark Brilliant, Jennifer Hochschild, Kenneth Prewitt, and Kim Williams.

PART III

RACE, GENDER, AND THE OBAMA PHENOMENON

9. FROM CHATTEL TO FIRST LADY

Black Women Moving from the Margins

MARSHA J. TYSON DARLING

ONLY THE BLACK WOMAN CAN SAY, "WHEN AND WHERE I ENTER, IN THE quiet, undisputed dignity of my womanhood, without violence and without suing or special patronage, then and there the whole *Negro race enters with me*" (Cooper 1892, 31).

This quote is taken from a speech delivered to black clergymen by Anna Julia Cooper in 1886, a tumultuous year following the Civil War. In "Womanhood: A Vital Element in the Regeneration and Progress of a Race," Cooper, an admired public speaker, expressed black women's sense of a pursuit of self-discovery. She eloquently captured the relationship between the advancement of *Negro* women and the uplift of the *Negro* race. Cooper, and many other black women, might not have imagined that within two generations of their active agency to transform social relations in America that a majority of the nation's voting electorate would elect and re-elect a black man to lead the United States as its president, and that a black woman from working-class roots would stand and act at his side as First Lady.

INTERSECTIONALITY, COMPOUNDING DISCRIMINATIONS, AND BLACK WOMEN'S "HERSTORY"

This essay is a discourse on the journey of the black woman from chattel to First Lady. The cumbersome, slow, thorny road that black women have traveled from being someone's personal property (chattel) to First Lady has required an active tradition of black women's self-help agency and mutual assistance, and far-reaching social and political changes across the nation.

Indeed, recent surveys of black Americans who lived through or were directly affected by Jim and Jane Crow segregation confirm that few imagined that Americans would elect a black president in their lifetimes. First Lady Michelle Obama is no shadow of her husband. She was an accomplished lawyer before she met Barack Obama, and she continues active personal agency in her work to advance projects that she considers important and socially transformative, especially the crisis of obesity in the nation and the connection between food, diet, and health.

As important as Ivy-educated Michelle Obama is to our nation and to the discourse on black women's "herstory" in this narrative, the opportunities she has acted on were out of reach for most black women in her mother's and grandmother's generations. Indeed, it was the powerful and transformative social forces that reshaped American society that enabled Michelle Obama's self-help aspirations. Because it is important to engage a perspective that assesses intergenerational social transformation of black women's herstory, this essay examines important social thresholds in black women's journey from chattel to First Lady. This chapter begins by examining the manner in which socially constructed ideas and stereotypical stigmas about black women have, over time, become corrosive barriers to the social advancement of black women as a group. Then, it briefly notes the active self-help traditions and transformative social forces that have helped many black women connect upwardly mobile personal aspirations with progressive outcomes. Next, it focuses on First Lady Michelle Obama and the social forces, stereotypes, and personal agency and self-discovery that have enabled a working-class girl to move from the margins toward the center, where life-affirming options, privileges, and immunities exist. And finally, it concludes by situating this historical moment and Michelle Obama in society's larger context.

All women and girls experience their lives through socially constructed multiple and intersecting identities. They belong to more than one community and have more than one identity in their social relationships within various patriarchies. A social science methodology that exposes how multiple and intersecting discriminations affect women's and girls' lived experiences is particularly useful. Intersectional analysis is such a theoretical approach in that it identifies the intersection and operation of the racial, ethnic, economic, sexual, cultural, age, caste, ability, and gendered dimensions of multiple and compounding forms of discriminations against women and girls. Intersectionality also exposes how the convergence of multiple discriminations in the lives of women and girls operates to subjugate and marginalize them (Darling 2010b, 91–106).

Intersectionality is not a new paradigm for delineating multiple, intersecting, and compounding identities, especially identities marked for discrimination, subordination, and marginalization. Over the past several decades, black feminist theorists have enjoined intersectional analyses in providing discourses regarding critical race feminism. Intersectionality emerged as an essential component of the critical race theory discourses espoused by feminist women of color who sought to render the multiple discriminations experienced by indigenous women, women of color, and racialized women more visible. Intersectionality has helped to denote the marginalizing racial, ethnic, class, and sexual aspects of gender discrimination. It has also been instrumental in promoting advancement and equity for marginalized women and girls of color (Collins 2000b, 404–20; Crenshaw 1991, 1241–99).

Considering that black women and girls lead lives at the intersection of blackness, femaleness, and often poverty-all of the time—it is important to keep the theory of intersectionality in the forefront of our thinking and analysis because too often black women's multiple burdens have been missing from public debate and scholarly discourse. It should also be noted that direct and derivative white privilege, patriarchal fundamentalism, and internalized self-hate are among the continuing threats to black women and girls actualizing racial and gender equality and class advancement.[1]

STEREOTYPES OF BLACK WOMEN IN THE AMERICAN CULTURAL IMAGINATION

Although oppressions should not be ranked hierarchically, some burdens are unique to black women in the United States. The multiple, intersecting, and compounding discrimination and marginalization of black women and girls that continue to stymie their social progress derive from powerful racist and misogynist stereotypes and social metaphors that have been repeated intergenerationally.

Some of the derogatory and degrading ideas and stereotypes that have had the greatest impact on black women's lives have become icons in the American cultural imagination. Many have an enduring place in the white imagination, and some, such as "wench," "Jezebel," "Sapphire," and "Welfare Queen," have become part of U.S. popular culture and black vernacular. Beliefs about black women as property, as evil seductresses, as possessing an unrestrained sexuality and unclean genitals, often have been used as a rationale for sexual assault and rape.

Sexualizing black women and girls in racist and overtly misogynist ways assures that some members of dominant groups will target them for sexual assault. It also means that assault on or violence against marginalized black women and girls is often dismissed or excused, and the violated are blamed for "causing" or "deserving" the violence. Such is the power of negative stereotypical stigmas to complement marginalizing private action against black women and girls (Jewell 1993, 35–54).

On the other side of the impact of negative stereotypical stigmas directed toward black women and girls is that notions of white male decency and white female virtue increase. White culture is presented as civilizing, tolerant, and uplifting of black people, even references to white men as rapists (except in abolitionist literature) have been largely muted. A focus on white people's contribution to the moral propriety of black people helps to sustain skin-color privilege for all whites. Hence, white-skin privilege exists in direct proportion to the actions, ideas, and stereotypical images and slogans that are created by white racial and gender dominance.

Stereotypes are powerful servants of thought and action because they pose answers to the unasked queries about social order and ranking. Stereotypes are always offered as an answer and never the question about why social subjugation continues to occur. In reality, racial, gender, class, and ethnic stereotypes almost always serve to camouflage and naturalize social dominance and oppression. While stereotypes can be negative or positive, racist and misogynist stereotypes continue to maintain patriarchal and white-skin privilege in U.S. society. Some stereotypes, often repeated intergenerationally, have assumed a life of their own, and many people hold them as truth. In fact, some stereotypes are so powerful that they function as icons in our culture. As representations of ideas, beliefs, and even stereotypes, icons can appear without an accompanying explanation and still be tremendously effective in conveying social meaning.

Racist and misogynist stereotypes continue to maintain multiple and intersecting racial, gender, and class discriminations against black women and girls and simultaneously posit inferiority and dysfunction as static qualities that are expected of them. So pervasive is this legacy that one frequently hears white people and foreigners express surprise when they interact with a black woman or man who acts outside the learned social boundaries established by racial, gender, and class stereotypes. Furthermore, while such stereotypes blunt the racial and cultural knowledge capacity of many whites, racist, misogynist, and classist stereotypes often operate to undermine and even destroy self-esteem in black females. This is especially true if the stereotype denigrates a black woman's capacity for intelligence and moral sensibility. Hence, such stereotypes help to maintain the discriminations that enable the marginalization of black women and girls.

The stereotypes about black women that are focused on here are derived from historical relationships laden with racial betrayal and sexual exploitation. In that historical narrative, the most destructive stereotypes have reduced black women to an object (or "a thing"). A "thing" is not a sentient human being. Denying black women's humanity while sexually and materially exploiting their persons was a betrayal encoded into the social dominance practiced by many white males. Then, as now, oppressive choices and decisions that created and sustained betrayal, inequality, and marginalization required an explanation. The marginalizing portrayals and representations of black women as "wench," "Jezebel," "Mammy," "Sapphire," or, more recently, "pathological," "Baby Machine," "Welfare Queen," and "whore" have sought to undermine personal agency as well as compassion for black women and girls.

SLAVERY, BLACK WOMEN, AND THE EUROPEAN AMERICAN CULTURAL LANDSCAPE

Discrimination is created by dominant social groups that impose social barriers on black women's lives: poverty, lack of healthcare, poor education, sexual violence, substandard housing, and poor diet, as well as police violence in poor communities. Marginalizing stereotypes are tools for presenting negative images that further the political, economic, social, and even cultural work of opposing social progress and discouraging civil rights agency for certain segments of society; in this chapter, black women. The incongruity between most black women's lives and the stereotypes of passivity, ignorance, uncontrolled anger, and sexual licentiousness endure despite a reality that is far afield of the illusion. While these stereotypes tell us little about the actual lived experiences of most black women, they signal the persistence of significant social barriers to their entitlement in the United States.

One starts with the fact that black women live in a society that values people of Western European descent. Black women occupy a social space at the intersection of blackness and femaleness, and since most have been and continue to be poor; they have been pushed to the margins of society because of the intersection of their race, gender, and class. Perchance, add lesbian or transgender sexual orientation and the stigmatizing discriminations that black women and girls experience are multiple and compounding. Of course, age is always an important qualifier of social status. Hence, since black women derive no skin-color privilege that lifts them beyond the diminished social status accorded to all women under patriarchy, and since most black women are poor, there is little if any social reward accorded black women in a society dominated by all men and light-skinned or white people.

For centuries, the oppression of black women has been intensely physical, psychological, and spiritual as a direct result of chattel slavery. The system of chattel slavery developed in the last half of the seventeenth century by English colonial slaveholders was based on the "absolute authority" of slave owners over the life or death of enslaved women and men. The enslaved had no *human right* to life. A colonial Virginia statute proclaimed that slave owners who killed a "slave" were exempt from felony charges. The argument that planters took care of the enslaved because they had paid money for them has three weaknesses. First, the record shows that some planters also worked white indentured servants to death, so why presume that Africans captured for the taking, or birthed and reared on plantations—and lacking any of the cultural "value" accorded white Christians coming from Europe—would have fared any better? (Heilbroner and Singer 1999, 40).

Second, the fact of the law's passage is instructive, because resistance to enslavement and its arduous labor-intensive work was an ever-present reality, and violence, even death, was a means to control captive African men in particular. Third, the statute unequivocally supported the emerging doctrine of "absolute authority." It is important to note that Atlantic economy slavery developed away from any of the institutions, customs, traditions, or customary obligations formed in Europe's social evolution that might have served as checks and balances, restraining some of the authoritarian excesses of slave owners, who answered to no one. Taking authority a step further, at about the same time that the Virginia House of Burgesses led the way in crafting "absolute authority" as slavery's operating doctrine, slave owners in the British North Atlantic colonies established in law that black enslavement would extend across generations (Higginbotham, Jr. 1978, 19–60).

By law, the bodies of enslaved women, and especially their wombs, were the key to the intergenerational transmission of enslavement for all of the children born to them. Racial and sexual slavery *evolved*—that is, captive black women performed agricultural and reproductive work, as quite literally enslaved women's wombs became *capital.* Enslaved women's wombs were put to "work," undergoing pregnancy for as many of their fertile years as possible. "Breeding babies" reproduced a slave labor force for free, as by law an infant's status rested entirely on the status of one's mother. While the evidence is more scant than the frequency of its occurrence, it is clear that some enslaved black women resisted the intentions of slave owners to treat them as "breeding machines" (Schwartz 2006, 9–32, 67–106).

As students of history know, captive women and rape and coerced sex go hand in hand. Treated as sexual prey from the moment of capture, enslaved women and girls were victims of sexual coercion or violence. Slave owners largely controlled the paternity of pregnancies of enslaved women. The wombs of enslaved black women became part of an agricultural production process—black women were stereotyped as a "wench," which is a tool, a unit of production. Enslaved black women were compelled to bear children sired by captive black men and mulatto children sired by white men. For at least two hundred years, such were the conditions of racial and sexual slavery for black women, puberty-aged girls, and their children (Morgan 2004; Roberts 1997; Jennings 1990, 3, 45–74; 2001, 1619–50; Follet 2003, 510–39).

Of course, there were instances where white males developed genuinely caring relationships with enslaved black women. Some white men who had mixed-race children with enslaved black women, freed the woman, and raised their biracial children. Some white men manumitted and married enslaved black women, and sometimes a white man purchased the freedom of an enslaved woman from another man in order to marry her. However, we should question to what extent consensual relationships between men and women, free and slave, within the context of slavery were ever really possible. It was the power that white males held over black people in such settings that went largely unchecked by other whites. Such a system of extreme social dominance seldom generated consensual relationships.

Even though slave owners crafted a social order that worked to their advantage, moral issues emerged that required a response. The issue of sexual "licentiousness," namely, sex outside Christian marriage, in an age of professed fervent Christian morality disturbed many individuals, especially those in the pulpit. Second, the issue of interracial sex between white men and their "slave" women, evidenced by the increasing numbers of light brown babies being born, also bore directly on Christian marriage. To complicate matters, many of the mulatto babies born to captive black women were sired by white men of property who were married to white women. Some married white Christian women anguished over the threat that the presence of captive African and captivity-born black women posed to their husbands' sexual loyalty. But white women were themselves in no position to curtail male lust for their concubines. Consequently, many white males, both married and single, continued the sexual behaviors that pleased them—after all, white wives and black or mulatto concubines were all white male property (Omolade 1994, 3–18).

Ever accustomed to answering to no one in slavery's system of "absolute authority" over captive Africans, slave owners came under moral pressure from white and free black abolitionists. Abolitionists used every available means: newspapers, broadsides, speeches, books, articles, and by the nineteenth century, autobiographies to attack the institution of slavery. The issue of moral impropriety/fornication emerged as abolitionists began providing the funds to publish the narratives of black women who had escaped slavery. Scathing in their indictment of the rampant sexual abuse of enslaved black women and girls by white men in the South, the few black women's narratives that were published exposed, through first-person accounts, the horrors of the sexual abuse and violence they had experienced and witnessed (Jacobs 1861, 26–29; Sterling 1984, 18–31).

White men were called upon to answer the moral challenge to their virtue. They denied any moral impropriety, insisting that they were governing over Christian wives and promiscuous, sex-crazed slave women who would not let them be good Christian men. They called the enslaved women "Jezebel," an evil seductress invoked from biblical teachings (White 1985/1999, 27–61; Jewell 1993, 55–71). Further seeking to quell allegations of conduct unbecoming of moral Christian men, slave owners offered an image of the quintessential female servant/slave, "Mammy," as a counterpoint to Jezebel. Mammy was a dutiful, hard-working, self-sacrificing black woman who was committed to serving her white "family" at the expense of her own children; even as that "family" maintained its belief in her innate racial inferiority. Asexual, unattractive, and "ugly" by white standards of beauty, never sassy or a seductress, sometimes fat or obese from eating well in the big house, a great cook who toiled without a fret, she was always docile and loyal. Thus, many slave owners sought to assert that her role in their lives posed no threat at all to their moral sensibility or to white Christian marriage.

"Mammy," Jezebel, and Sapphire

"Mammy" has become the dominant racial and sexual stereotype and cultural icon of black women in American society dating from the slavery era. In the early twentieth century, Hollywood films packaged the stereotype of an idyllic slavery South—*Birth of a Nation*, *Song of the South*, *Show Boat*, *Imitation of Life*, and the all-time blockbuster, *Gone with the Wind*, which cast Hattie McDaniel in her Oscar-winning portrayal as Mammy. With the advent of television in the 1950s, Mammy moved into American living rooms. Although "tweaked" a bit, she is still with us on television today. Mammy's pictorial representation—head scarf covering unkempt or "ugly" hair, obese, asexual, and always smiling while cooking—remains as it has been for decades, as "Aunt Jemima" (Bogle 1992, 9–18).

The Jezebel and Mammy stereotypes stood in stark contrast to a system of production based on at times the brutal sexual exploitation of black women's bodies and wombs. During the same decades that black women's slave narratives were published, some Virginia slave owners engaged in the business of "breeding" slaves for sale (Baptist 2001, 1619–50). Mean-spirited measures held slavery in place: physical brutality—whippings which sometimes resulted in death, the withholding of food, especially in relation to obtaining sexual compliance from captive women, selling family members away from each other as punishment, and other controlling behaviors. As the decades passed, the numbers of black captives fleeing into the dark of night increased—though many more black men ran away than black women who would not leave their children behind.

In addition to Jezebel, slave owners invented "Sapphire," the out-of-control, wild-with-anger black "thing," who could only be subdued with physical force. Those outside slavery's domain were shocked and horrified when enslaved black women who had escaped bared their backs to reveal the scars of repeated beatings. The illusion of southern tranquility and docile, primitive slaves ran headlong into the reality that slavery was a system of racial and sexual exploitation held in place by sustained physical and sexual violence.

Black men who watched their mothers, sisters, wives, lovers, daughters, and other female relatives and friends indiscriminately raped or coerced into having sex with white men were not likely to have blamed the black women and girls around them. Indeed, some of these enslaved black men lost their lives, or were crippled or maimed attempting to prevent the sexual abuse of the vulnerable women and girls whom they cared for (Northrup 1853). While enslaved black men scoffed at white men's constructions of Jezebel and Sapphire stereotypes, the persistence of these stereotypes has continued to exert a colonizing influence on black popular culture.

For decades now, stereotypes of an oversexed, uppity, and in-your-face black woman—the "black bitch"—have trickled from the wider American culture into black popular culture and song. The "black bitch" is Sapphire renamed, and she is invoked to explain why black women and girls have to be treated roughly. Only aggression and violence, not compassion or love, works. In real time, misogyny (Jezebel, Sapphire, and the "black bitch"), like racism, provides stereotypes that transfer the blame for group oppression onto the victim. This misogynist message represents black women as fallible, sexually tainted, even fallen women who have made unwise choices based on individual preferences; it is the women who have created their bad situations.

BLACK WOMEN FROM SLAVERY TO FREEDOM-SELF-HELP AND MUTUAL AID

Free black women worked in the only jobs available to them: washing, sewing, cooking, cleaning, nursing, and caring for other people's children. Even during the twentieth century, the majority of black women were relegated to service jobs. More prosperous free black women were able to acquire an education, often at colleges such as Oberlin College in Ohio, which opened its doors to blacks in the nineteenth century. Educated black women worked as teachers, or started businesses, such as catering, bakeries, hair salons, boarding houses, millineries, and dressmaking. Black women also participated in mutual aid societies; they paid dues to benevolent associations for burial benefits and initiated their own educational and benefit organizations. Some supported philanthropic efforts to assist those in need, especially blacks on the run from enslavement. Many were avid antislavery proponents, and some assisted with the Underground Railroad, and many helped to institutionalize independent black churches. Some black women even helped strengthen the development of African Free Schools in northern cities. In some instances, they used their earnings to operate their own businesses, including boarding houses (precursors to inns and motels), and established societies, schools, and colleges to educate black girls and women.[2]

Claiming freedom with the Civil War behind them, black women looked to a future ripe with promise, but soon confronted southern *de jure* (by law) and northern *de facto* (by custom) racial segregation and disfranchisement as white opposition to black progress. A number of middle-class black women mobilized to strengthen black communities and create advancement opportunities for black women and girls. The creation of the organizations and institutions that comprised the black Women's Club Movement:

the Bethel Literary and Historical Association (Washington, D.C.), the Colored Women's League (Washington, D.C., 1892), the New Era Club (Boston, 1895), the National Federation of Afro-American Women (Boston, 1895), the National Association of Colored Women (NACW, Washington, D.C., 1896), the Northeastern Federation of Women's Clubs, the National Council of Negro Women, the Phillis Wheatley clubs and homes, and the Working Girls' Home Association was spearheaded by Ida B. Wells-Barnett, Mary Church Terrell, Josephine St. Pierre Ruffin, Mary McLeod Bethune, Jane Edna Hunter, Margaret Murray Washington, Anna Julia Cooper, and other black women who sought to provide leadership outlets for professional black women and race uplift (Clark-Lewis 1994, 51–95; Giddings 1984, 57–117; Higginbotham 1993, 1–88; Hunter 1997, 74–97; Jones 1985, 142–46; Terborg-Penn 1998, 1–80).

BLACK WOMEN FROM SEGREGATION TO CIVIL RIGHTS

Black women's organizations worked to promote the educational, economic, and social advancement of black people, including women and girls during the very same decades in which racial and sexual segregation were the ugliest (for instance, by 1930 official reports confirmed that over 3,000 black men had been lynched primarily in the South). A generation of young black girls watched their mothers, older sisters, aunts, and older woman friends help sustain and strengthen black institutions and organizations while also promoting self-help goals. Such was the "stuff" of self-discovery that spurred some black women to ask and expect more of American society. The generation of young black women and men who stood with Dr. Martin Luther King, Jr., grew up watching black adults engage in self-help activities as "race uplift." In the post–World War II years, as the Supreme Court's *Brown* decisions in 1954 and 1955 struck a decisive blow at the *Plessy* doctrine of race-based segregation and exclusion, increasing numbers of black women and men dared to act on rising expectations for their lives (Collier-Thomas and Franklin 2001, 21–41; Gilkes 2001, 15–60).

While helping to sustain themselves and their families in the twentieth century, black women confronted pervasive racist and misogynist stereotypes about their bodies—especially their skin color, hair texture, lip shape, buttocks size, sexuality, intelligence, and moral values. Some fell prey to the sustained hate that a virulent racism imposed on black women's lives—what Professor Melissa Harris-Perry describes as the "crooked room," which robbed them of a sense of an affirming set of positive possibilities. Many others found a way to live affirming lives and teach the generation they were rearing to create a better future for themselves and their communities. Many also taught the young that if opportunity presented itself, they should work for change. The black women who predate Michelle Obama were raised by black women and men whose active agency sustained them through poverty, discrimination, and institutional marginalization.[3]

The Obamas, Fruits of the Great Society

Barack and Michelle Obama and their generation are beneficiaries of social transformations that have produced enormously transfiguring changes in American society over the past fifty years. These transformations did not come easily; long-standing barriers to the exercise of civil rights and access to educational, economic, and political opportunities were a constant struggle. Barack and Michelle were children during the tumultuous struggles that created the social changes that in their teenage years enabled both to earn scholarships to attend America's premier educational institutions. This meant access to still greater portals of opportunity for achievement, entitlement, and power.

Barack and Michelle Obama have enjoyed fulfilling work and financial prosperity beyond what their parents might have imagined as possible. They have enjoyed successful professional advancement and upper-middle-class family life in America. Like so many other black folks, who now enjoy the fruits of the great society, Barack and Michelle were able to pass through "opportunity's doors" when those doors swung open.

Barack Obama's parents were privileged in terms of their educational background and as such were part of the middle class. Barack's mother attained a doctoral degree in anthropology and his father earned a master's degree in economics. Yet both Barack and Michelle came from modest economic circumstances and were raised by parents who lived in a generation that witnessed changes in their access to civil rights and social equality. We can be sure that those parents whispered to them, "Yes, you can!," as they began to find their way. Barack and Michelle are among those who have used educational advancement, smart career choices, political savvy, and a changing political climate to fashion a reality for themselves that is hardly reminiscent of America's dark racial past. The ascent of Barack and Michelle to fame, fortune, and real political power suggests a new direction for American race relations. Michelle's place in this new era suggests not just a shift in the gendered dimensions of race relations in the United States, as Michelle's journey from margins to mainstream has been interesting to observe.

MICHELLE OBAMA—BLACK WOMAN FROM THE MARGINS TO THE MAINSTREAM

As Barack Obama sought and achieved the presidency in 2008, many also focused on Michelle Obama. So who is Michelle Obama? How does she represent herself and how is she represented by others? And how much of those representations derive from the legacy of how racism and misogyny have intersected to demean black womanhood in the United States? What has Michelle been up against, especially in terms of the American media, and how has she responded? What has she done to meet customary expectations as First Lady? What is her impact on America and on black women and girls? In what ways has she sought to "connect" children in marginalized communities with powerful people and institutions, and what has been her self-described motivation for attempting to reach black girls?

Born on January 17, 1964, to Fraser Robinson III and Marian Robinson, Michelle LaVaughn Robinson is the younger of two children. Michelle's researched genealogy reveals that she is descended from Melvinia (a mother at the age of fifteen), an enslaved black woman who lived in the mid-nineteenth century and who gave birth to a mulatto child fathered by a white man on a 200-acre plantation in Georgia. Growing up in a working-class family surrounded by an extended kinship network, Michelle and her older brother, Craig, received many of the core values that have remained with them over time: hard work, persistence, stick-togetherness, sacrifice, aspiration, self-help, being charitable, and obligation/reciprocity.

While these affirming self-worth values are not unique to the black working class, it is important to mention them because racist and even classist representations of working-class people of color often deny that these values are important to identity development among those who are poor. In Michelle's words:

> I was raised in a working-class family on the South Side of Chicago, that's how I identify myself, a working-class girl. My mother came home and took care of us through high school. My father was a city shift worker who took care of us all his life. We were so blessed, my brother

and I, because we had everything you needed. It had nothing to do with money, but we had two parents that loved us, a father that had a steady job all of his life. We had a strong external family unit, I grew up with grandparents and uncles and aunts. People didn't go to college, but you had Christmas dinner together. You know, they were just this huge, strong support system. The neighborhood that I lived in wasn't wealthy, but it wasn't crime-ridden, so you could play in the streets, and there were gangs, but there weren't gangs that would keep you from going to school. (Scherer and Gibbs 2009; Newton-Small 2008)

When Michelle reflects on who helped define her other than her quiet, steady father who used family monies to help both Craig and Michelle attend college, she says of her upbringing:

But in terms of whose stories stay in my head, it's my mother's, my aunts', my neighbors', my teachers' from growing up on the South Side of Chicago. I mean the people who really moved me were the people that I knew in my life: my mother, the teachers that I had. I mean, I have real strong memories of great teachers that I had in grammar school, the teachers who told me that I was smart, who pushed me to skip a grade, who challenged me with tough projects. Those are really the people. Those are the stories that really guide me. Those are the folks that I'm trying to make proud. (Scherer and Gibbs 2009)

Michelle graduated from Chicago public schools and went on to undergraduate studies at Princeton, where she graduated with a Bachelor of Arts in Sociology in 1985. Michelle's sixty-four-page senior honors thesis, "Princeton-Educated Blacks and the Black Community," offers insights into being black, female, and working class at a prestigious white university. Michelle noted,

Earlier in my college career, there was no doubt in my mind that as a member of the Black community I was somehow obligated to this community and would utilize all of my present and future resources to benefit this community first and foremost. My experiences at Princeton have made me far more aware of my "Blackness" than ever before. . . . I sometimes feel like a visitor on campus; as if I really don't belong. . . . These experiences have made it apparent to me that the path I have chosen to follow by attending Princeton will likely lead to my further integration and/or assimilation into a white cultural and social structure that will only allow me to remain on the periphery of society; never becoming a full participant. This realization has presently made my goals to actively utilize my resources to benefit the Black community more desirable.

In addition to her studies, Michelle spent time working with kids in a free literacy program (Robinson 1985, 2–3).

Michelle took her interest in progressive social change with her to Harvard Law School, where she participated in demonstrations that pressed Harvard to recruit more minority professors and students. Harvard law professor Charles Ogletree remembers Michelle Robinson as exerting practical energy in working to recruit black undergrads to Harvard Law School. After graduating, Michelle was hired as an intellectual-property lawyer at Sidley Austin, a prestigious Chicago firm. After meeting and falling in love with Barack, a junior lawyer she mentored, Michelle left her position at Sidley Austin to work in public service, initially working for the Chicago mayor's office, followed by working to build Public Allies, a new charity. After successfully helping to anchor the organization financially, Michelle moved on to work as an associate dean of students at the University of Chicago, and then to serving the university as the vice president of external relations. In both positions, she worked to connect the university to its undergraduates and to improve the university's relations with local communities (Wolffe 2008; Newton-Small 2008).

As the quotes above make clear, Michelle Obama sees her past in her personality and makeup. It is a past filled with loving and affirming adults who also challenged her towards high achievement. Michelle recounts how little she knew or understood the world of privilege and opportunity that existed where she grew up on the South Side of Chicago: "There but for fortune go I." A major goal for Michelle Obama is that she has "made" something fine of herself and is ever concerned to promote children's self-discovery. Her self-image is confident, positive, and affirming about being black; she is affectionate and emotionally secure. She is committed to helping her daughters navigate from childhood to young adulthood, and she seeks to empower others, especially children in marginalized communities. That's how Michelle Obama sees and understands herself.

When it comes to how others see and represent Michelle Obama, answers reflect the complicated legacy bearing on black women's lives. The accomplished, professional black woman in American society is not something new. The tradition of black women's active agency outside the confines of family life is long-standing. Professional black women in earlier generations were usually educated at historically black colleges and universities (HBCU). Michelle Obama received her education when the walls of Jane and Jim Crow segregation were beginning to crumble. While Michelle attended Chicago's segregated public schools through high school, unlike her black female predecessors, she received her undergraduate and professional training at Ivy League universities. This allowed her to assume a professional "place" in the white world previously only imagined by black folks accustomed to living professionally active but segregated lives within the confines of black communities.

Despite Michelle's achievements, she still encounters white perceptions of her that harken back to America's legacy of black women-hating. Specifically, her assertiveness—a quality highly prized in her corporate law firm and in her role at the University of Chicago—often has been interpreted as black women's "bitchiness" by some in the white media. There have been several caricatures of Michelle Obama dating to Barack Obama's 2008 bid for the White House. Not surprisingly, a tradition of negative stigmas and hate imaging of black women has also given strength to sustaining hate speech toward black women who step out of "their place." Those voices attack Michelle's *persona* and not just her *ideas*; they represent her as "the bitter, anti-American, ungrateful, rude, crude, ghetto, angry Michelle Obama." These are words that strike not only at Michelle's ideas about what needs to be done in the nation, but also her concern on behalf of those in the United States who have been marginalized or left behind. Depicting her in such a negative light is an attack on *her* working-class roots and her concern for the humble folks who in their poor circumstances are so often invisible and ignored. Reflecting the ways in which many Americans have learned to renounce black women's voices, in 2008 Michelle was dismissed by many as just an *angry black woman* (Gibbs 2008).

Conservatives have accused Michelle Obama of "whining" and preaching a "Gospel of Misery," and radio star Hugh Hewitt noted that when she says that "before we can work on the problems, we have to fix our souls," his response is "whenever someone from the government comes to you and says, 'we have to fix your soul,' be very afraid. No one believes outside of the hard-core left that government can fix your soul." Rejection words have been accompanied by images of Michelle as threatening and out of step with the American character. The "black bitch" is Sapphire descended from her nineteenth-century creation as the aggressive, threatening woman whose person, and not just her ideas, should be assaulted. During the 2008 campaign, the white media wasted no time invoking a menacing image of Michelle Obama. That spring, the *National Review* pictured Michelle Obama on its front cover calling her "Mrs. Grievance," accompanied by the text, "Michelle Obama embodies a peculiar mix of privilege and victimology which is not where most Americans live" (Gibbs 2008).

Then, in July 2008, the cover of *The New Yorker* represented the Obamas as dangerous, flag-burning militants. Michelle is represented with a very large Afro hairstyle, reminiscent of how Angela Davis appeared on FBI wanted posters during the Black Power Movement. Michelle is standing in what appears to be the Oval Office, exchanging fist-banging greetings with Barack under a picture of a much sought after al-Qaeda "terrorist." Michelle is toting a large shell capacity assault weapon strapped to her back, and she is wearing military style pants stuffed into above ankle combat boots. Barack is represented as unbecoming in his place in Western civilization; an "alien," he is clad in the tunic, turban, and sandals easily associated with Muslim men. Decried by some as racist and misogynist, *The New Yorker* cover stirred old portrayals of black women and men as radicals who pose a threat to America. At a time when many Americans wished for Osama Bin Laden's murder, and some questioned Barack's pedigree, to suggest a similarity between al-Qaeda and the Obamas served to intensify not diminish racial and cultural fears of them. The Secret Service reported record numbers of death threats against the Obamas, and some whites brought ropes tied into nooses and explicitly racist posters to political rallies. Melissa Harris-Perry has aptly noted that *The New Yorker*'s representation of Michelle emerged from an ideological perspective about her, in which "anger was an easy default framework for interpreting Michelle."[4]

Amidst the clamor over Michelle's occasional forthrightness during Barack's 2008 campaign, *Time* magazine's Nancy Gibbs commented that Michelle's "speeches can sound stark and stern compared with her husband's roof raisers. He's about the promise; she's more about the problem.... She goes further, worrying out loud about the country's lack of fairness, the corrosive cynicism of its citizens and how Americans spend more time talking about what we won't do, what won't work, what can't change than about what is possible." Gibbs noted that some commentators are uncomfortable and angry at Michelle Obama's concern for the voiceless on the margins. They also seemed angry that Michelle has an assertive voice and uses it, which is something white men and some white women in positions of authority do frequently, but they assert their agency in a society where the legacy of racial stereotypes does not trigger animus towards their assertiveness. So, while Michelle Obama sometimes received praise for her candor in the 2008 campaign she also received opprobrium, especially by the right wing, for stepping out of her "place" as a black woman (Gibbs 2008).

MICHELLE OBAMA AND THE COMPLICATED LEGACY OF BLACK WOMEN'S LIVES

Not surprisingly, a number of black women commentators have focused on the ways in which Michelle Obama will surely challenge the racist and misogynist legacies that have followed black women in America. In *Newsweek* in November 2008, several months after the controversial and negative portrayals of Michelle Obama on the covers of the *National Review* and *The New Yorker*, Allison Samuels, an African American reporter, noted that Michelle has a chance to counter the negative stereotypes about black women:

> *Usually, the lives of Black women go largely unexamined. The prevailing theory seems to be that we're all hot-tempered single mothers who can't keep a man, and according to CNN's* Black in America *documentary, those of us who aren't street-walking crack addicts are on the verge of dying from AIDS. My "sistafriends" are mostly college educated, in healthy, productive relationships and have a major aversion to sassy one-liners. They are teachers, doctors, and business owners.... Yet, pop culture continues to hold a much unevolved view of African-American women. Black women still can't escape the stereotype of being neck-swirling, eye-rolling, oversexed females raised by our never married, alcoholic mothers.... These images have helped define the way all black women are viewed, including Michelle Obama." (Samuels 2008)*

But the nation's First Lady has responded to the racist misogyny that has attacked her persona in at least three significant ways. First, she has challenged and redefined conventional expectations of the First Lady so well that some journalists have taken note: "As a political spouse, she is somewhat unusual. She isn't the traditional Stepford booster, smiling vacantly at her husband and sticking to the script of carefully vetted blandishments.... She travels the country giving speeches and attending events" (Wolffe 2008). Further, Michelle has learned to protect herself by carefully choosing which media outlets she will be interviewed by, photographed by, or profiled by using first-person quotes she supplies.

In an interview in which Michelle was asked about how she felt about public perceptions of her, she reflected: "I'm pretty much who I've been for a long time. So that, I just think that people have the opportunity to see all of who Michelle Obama is over a longer period of time. And, hopefully, they like what they see. And I think they actually—to the extent that they saw all of me—liked what they saw then ... because if it weren't the case, I don't think Barack would be President" (Scherer and Gibbs 2009). Michelle's oversight of the East Wing is vitally important to her sense of connecting vision with action: "I think that's where the relationship between the East and the West Wing matters.... The issues I've selected are important to me personally, which is the start ... it is also important that these are issues that are going to potentially have some kind of traction with the West Wing" (Scherer and Gibbs 2009).

Michelle has become known as a leader in her own right—spearheading Let's Move!, an effort to combat childhood obesity by focusing on healthy eating choices and physical fitness in our schools (M. Obama 2011, 138–40). In addition, the First Lady travels to speak on behalf and advocate for military families, noting "when our troops go to war, our families go to war. We can do a greater service if we can ensure that while those folks are fighting on behalf of our country that their houses aren't being foreclosed on, that they have health care, that their kids have good schools to go to" (Rogak 2009, 100). Further, she cares deeply about supporting and encouraging volunteerism.

In the same interview in which reporters prescreened questions (at her request), Michelle Obama focused on her work to reach out to children, especially girls. Commenting on her decision to invite successful, high-profile women such as Alicia Keys to join her visiting local schools and then having the children at the White House, Michelle Obama has sought to create a bridge that reduces the divide she knows exists between the lives of many children and powerful people and institutions:

> *And I just feel like through the small things that we can do here at the White House with messages of encouragement, we can start exemplifying the importance of building those bridges, in real meaningful ways, so that when young people come here, they don't have to come here and be something they're not. They can come here and be who they are, and the folks here will listen. And we can go out and be ourselves and listen*

in their communities as well. . . . Well, how powerful would it be for young girls to come into this space and hear from other really powerful, impressive, dynamic women and to have that conversation go on here in the White House? (Rogak 2009, 100)

Choosing what she will wear and how she wears it is still another way in which Michelle Obama has chosen to control what happens with her image, while also distinguishing her own sense of style. In the spring of 2009, the *New York Times* reported that contrary to tradition or the expectations of editors-in-chief, Michelle Obama chose what she would wear, how she styled her hair, and what, if any, makeup she used when she appeared for the photo shoots that put her on the covers of *People, Essence, Vogue, More*, and *O Magazine*. A *New York Times* reporter noted the First Lady's efforts at image control:

Vogue Magazine, *the fashion world's chronicler of first ladies, bedecked Hillary Rodham Clinton in black velvet and Laura Bush in blue silk; but not Michelle Obama. She insisted on choosing her own dress (a sleeveless, magenta silk number) and using her own hair and makeup stylists for the glossy photograph which splashed across* Vogue's *March cover. . . . Indeed, the First Lady is methodically shaping her public image, and in ways that extend far beyond fashion. . . . By focusing on her domestic persona and harnessing the fascination with her family, the First Lady and her communications team have emerged as the key architects of one of the most remarkable political transformations in years. Only ten months ago, Mrs. Obama was described as an angry black woman by some conservatives and as a liability to her husband. (Swarns 2009)*

The First Lady has worked assiduously to craft a public persona on her own terms rather than through the lens of those whom she feels may not really understand her. In her comments to MSNBC, Michelle noted, "We certainly don't want to spend the next four or eight years in the White House trying to live up a persona that isn't true. I want to be able to be me." (Rogak 2009, 81). Michelle Obama relates her philosophical view on accessing self-discovery on one's own terms as a woman:

One of my personal philosophies and it didn't come from this experience, it just came over life, is that in life you're got to make choices that make sense for you, because there is always going to be somebody who'll think you should do something differently. So you might as well start with what you like and what you care about, what your passions are, what makes sense. That's my message to women ... find your space. . . . If you're comfortable in the choice and it resonates with you, then all of the other stuff is just conversation. . . . As women we don't make choices that have meaning to us. And when those things fall apart, you have to have yourself to fall back on. . . . You have to own the choices you make. (Scherer and Gibbs 2009)

Embedded in Michelle Obama's statement is a message about her decision to make choices that she finds personally fulfilling regardless of how others attempt to control her. While it is a message that any number of professional women might offer, it is particularly important coming from the most visible woman in the United States—and it is a message coming from a black woman whose sense of self-direction is nothing short of compelling.

While Michelle Obama has had her detractors and critics, she also has millions of admirers, including African American women's blogs such as Black Girls Rock, Sisterlicious, and That Black Girl Group. Contributor Felicia Jones wrote of her: "Michelle Obama will be the hero my little girls have been looking for. The hero doesn't have to shake her booty or point her finger to get noticed and respected. My little girls finally have a 'role model.' Michelle will have to work to please everyone—an impossible task. But, for many African-American women like me, just a little of her poise, confidence and intellect will go a long way in changing an image that's been around for far too long" (Samuels 2008; Harris-Perry 2011, 269–77). Clearly, Michelle Obama is already building her legacy. Whenever and how she enters our lives as Americans, she immediately challenges and helps to transform negative stereotypes of black women because her level of visibility is a beacon to the generation of young girls on their way to womanhood.

PROGRESS AND CONTINUING CHALLENGES FOR BLACK WOMEN

Black women have endured unique burdens, which Harris-Perry describes as occurring in "America's crooked room," a place "for most black women . . . filled with distorted images, presenting many opportunities for shame and disaster" (Harris-Perry 2011, 299). Despite the barriers to self-discovery, notable numbers of black women hail from a tradition of organized self-help, and professional black women like Michelle Obama are not only the beneficiaries of progressive social reforms but are themselves social reformers. Today there are thirteen black women serving in the U.S. House of Representatives, one each representing the District of Columbia and the Virgin Islands, and 240 in state legislatures. Seven black women (Charlene Mitchell in 1968, Shirley Chisholm in 1972, Margaret Wright in 1976, Lenora Fulani in 1988 and 1992, Isabell Masters in 1992 and 1996, Monica Moorehead in 1998 and 2000, and Cynthia McKinney in 2008) have been candidates for presidents; one black woman, Carol Moseley Braun, has served in the Senate; and a black woman, Condoleezza Rice, served as secretary of state in the George W. Bush administration. Clearly a number of professional black women have made gains that have served to fulfill personal aspirations, and at the same time change the face of leadership in the nation. That is the good news: that some black women are able to engage in self-discovery, help empower others, and challenge long-standing, demoralizing negative racial and gender stereotypes (Smooth 2010, 14–18).

Needless to say, the majority of black women remain poor and marginalized. Unwed black mothers are still a target not only of the conservative media, but also of the conservative, largely male-controlled black media. On the one hand, black communities are hard-pressed to help care for the increasing numbers of children being raised by single, poor mothers or grandparents. Nearly 60 percent of black families are headed by black women, and 3.7 million black children live in poverty. On the other hand, with so many absent fathers, poor black mothers and grandparents are the principal resource for their children's survival (Cooper 2008, 83–87).

Many of the absent fathers are incarcerated. As the Bureau of Justice statistics indicate, in 2006 black men comprised 37 percent of the male prison population in the United States (compared to 35 percent of white men and 21 percent of Latino men). Black women are approximately 48 percent of incarcerated women (compared to 33 percent of white women and 15 percent of Latina women) (Johnson 2003, 19–49). In addition, health-care disparities are a significant issue for all women of color. The intersection of race, gender, and class translates into the reality that poor black women are at far greater risk than white women to die from diabetes, AIDS, cancer, cardiovascular disease, and complications in pregnancy. Also, in terms of health insurance, approximately one-third of uninsured black women live below the poverty level and are between the ages of eighteen and twenty-four (Morris 2008, 173–77; Schulz and Mullings 2006, 3–17).

Chattel to First Lady: Black Women Moving from the Margins   199

Black women-hating is too often a theme playing in the background of American society. It has become a hot-selling commodity in which representing black women as a "thing" to be insulted, disrespected, conquered, abused, and abandoned is widespread, especially in much of black male hip-hop music. Black women-hating sells music and enriches primarily white record and music video producers, as well as black male rappers. Presented and often defended as entertainment, this co-optation of black popular culture is a major avenue of oppression. Young black feminists and their male allies are challenging misogynist images and messages aimed at destroying black women, and especially the capacity for working-class black love and black solidarity. Their challenge to internalized hate is to decode the messages that fuel black colonization and oppression. Thus, it is essential that they bring a message that hate is not a sustainable self-determination, especially for a people long colonized by systemic hate (Davis 1995, 127–42; Morgan 1999, 74–78; Pough 2007, 889–92; Rose 1994, 146–85).

CONCLUSION

Black people have been a colonized social group for most of the nation's history. When social groups are oppressed, individual members in those groups are often deprived of human and civil rights and they are often powerless to exercise the few rights that they do have. The intersecting discriminations, particularly those borne by poor black women and girls, compound over time to trap many on the margins of society where their needs for respect, compassion, kindness, and opportunities for personal development and the exercise of meaningful personal agency go unmet. Since those who are physically dominated and marginalized seldom control the production of information, the root causes of their marginalization remains largely invisible.

Self-discovery has never been easily attained for black women in U.S. history. For centuries, colored, Negro, Afro American, African American, and black woman have referred to a quantifiable percentage of blood that comprised one's racial pedigree—the nation's "one-drop rule." "Race" has been powerful in its authority to determine one's relationship to social death (slavery and racial segregation). But it turns out that race is just an *idea*, an illusion that has spawned an ideology that has recently been deprived of any scientific legitimacy. Scientists at the Human Genome Project (HGP) have reported that there is no gene for "race," and further, that we are all descended from an African woman ancestor. It seems quite likely that in time the remarkable findings of the HGP will alter the intellectual and social landscape of our nation. But while "race" is being discounted as a genetic marker transmitted across generations, the reality of racism and the persistence of its impact on many people's lives remains. One can only hope that having elected a black man and black woman to our highest office, U.S. society is signaling that even though the road is long and winding, strewn with impediments and hazards along the way, we are nonetheless moving forward.

Notes

1. Elsewhere, I have written on the statutory, legal, political and social burdens borne by women of the African diaspora, dating from being transported as captives to the North Atlantic British colonies to the present. See Darling, 2010a, 389–402.
2. For example, Francis Jackson Coppin (1836–1913) graduated from Oberlin College and founded the Institute for Colored Youth, later renamed Cheyney State College in Pennsylvania. See Hine, Hine, and Harrold, 2008.
3. See Rodgers-Rose 1980, 15–41, and Harris-Perry 2011, 28–97 on the social construction of a "crooked room" surrounding black women's lives in the United States.
4. See, "Cover," *New Yorker*, July 21, 2008, July 21, 2008, http://archives.newyorker.com/?i=2008-07-21, and Harris-Perry, 2011, 276.

10. THE "OUTSIDER" AND THE PRESIDENCY

Mediated Representations of Race and Gender in the 2008 Presidential Primaries

TESSA DITONTO

INTRODUCTION

"Mr. Obama rarely mentions his race explicitly ... Mrs. Clinton has made more direct appeals to mothers and daughters and 'making history,' but has for the most part predicated her candidacy on the masculine virtues of toughness, resolve and her extensive experience in the (male-dominated) realm of politics and government. (Leibovich 2008)

"While Obama's ascendancy has brought many issues into the spotlight, one of the most confounding—at least for far too many pundits—is the notion of blackness, what defines it and who gets to determine whether the prevailing definition is correct." (Givhan 2008)

"Presaging his recent focus on class, Mr. Obama argued that whites were more likely to join blacks in supporting programs that were not racially based. An emphasis on universal, as opposed to race-specific programs isn't just good policy, Mr. Obama said in his book. 'It's good politics.'" (Swarns 2008)

THE THREE QUOTATIONS ABOVE, TAKEN FROM THE *NEW YORK TIMES* AND *the Washington Post* and chosen from three different points along the campaign timeline of the 2008 Democratic presidential primaries, exemplify the extraordinary nature of this unprecedented race. Not only were the two Democratic front runners a black man and a white woman, but they competed on very similar policy platforms in the closest primary race in recent history. Because of the exceptional nature of a contest in which, for the first time, either a member of a minority racial group or a woman was assured to win their party's nomination, and in which that candidate was considered to have a very real chance of winning the general election, questions of identity for these two candidates were bound to be particularly prevalent in the media. Beneath alternately scathing and glowing editorials, analyses of policy positions, and even articles focused only explicitly on the "horse race"—i.e., which candidate is winning, and where—were questions of identity, advocacy, and each candidate's ability to legitimately represent the interests of the various groups whose votes they hoped to win.

It is in this context that I shall explore questions of representation in the 2008 Democratic primaries. By "representation," I refer here to three distinct but, I argue, increasingly interrelated concepts: representation of the national electorate at the executive level, descriptive representation of historically oppressed, ascriptive social groups, and representations of the candidates themselves in the mass media. This chapter employs a content analysis of newspaper coverage surrounding Hillary Clinton and Barack Obama in the 2008 Democratic primaries in order to begin to explore the complex relationship between these three types of representation, and, specifically, how that relationship was treated in elite national discourse during the primary election contests.

THE OUTSIDER AND THE PRESIDENCY

Both political science and elite political discourse are replete with examples of candidates deemed "outsiders," or candidates that are not considered to be a part of the political mainstream for reasons based on background, ideology, or availability of resources. While outsider status can help a candidate in certain electoral contexts—if it serves to set them apart from what is seen as an entrenched, corrupt, or ineffective governing body (e.g., King 2002)—it can also harm a candidate's perceived viability. Specifically, and at least in the American context, politicians who are social or demographic outsiders, or those who are members of ascriptive groups not considered part of the political status quo (e.g., women and racial/ethnic minorities), may be forced to endure their outsider status whether or not they consider it to be a strategic advantage.

In the context of the 2008 Democratic presidential primary contest, the "outsider" trope is a useful tool for analyzing media portrayals of both Senators Hillary Clinton and Barack Obama. While this label was embraced by both to a certain extent—particularly by Barack Obama, in terms of his "Washington outsider" status—I speak specifically in this case about each candidate's inescapable membership in a historically oppressed subgroup of the population. Because they were both *demographic* outsiders running—with a shot at actually winning, for the first time in history—for the highest elective office in the nation, questions around political legitimacy as a function of their identities were inevitable.

As I shall argue later, these questions were often framed in terms of distinct but related themes: the (in)ability of each to represent his/her own social group (i.e., African Americans and women), and the (in)ability of each to represent the nation as a whole. Both speak to important questions surrounding the nature of executive representation, as well as questions that we can only now begin to explore concerning the role that the president could play as a descriptive representative for "outsider" groups within the political system. Fundamentally, the question is: Who can speak for whom? Obama's eventual election to the presidency shows that the American electorate is willing, at least in this instance, to allow a member of a marginalized racial group to speak for the population as a whole. However, to what extent can an "outsider" candidate simultaneously represent the interests of his or her particular social group? I argue that the combination of the two roles—descriptive representative of an outsider group and national, "universal" representative as president—creates a kind of representational paradox with which outsider presidential candidates must contend.

DESCRIPTIVE REPRESENTATION AND EXECUTIVE REPRESENTATION: COMMON THREADS

In her seminal work on representation, Pitkin (1967) distinguishes between substantive representation, or "acting for," and descriptive representation, or "standing for." The difference between them resides primarily in the role that the identity of a representative does or does not play—substantive representation can arguably be carried out by anyone for anyone else; the personal experiences and characteristics of the representative are unimportant as long as he or she is acting on behalf of the interests of the represented. Descriptive representation, however, requires a representative to share some politically relevant trait with the group(s) being represented.

Despite the fact that Pitkin and other representation scholars have dismissed descriptive representation as unimportant or uninteresting (Swain 1993; Birch 1972; Grofman 1982), others have found evidence for its utility and effectiveness in providing a voice for marginalized groups within the political process (Canon 1999; Bobo and Gilliam 1992; Mansbridge 1999; Dovi 2003). Many of these arguments rest on the assertion that simply electing black or female bodies into office is not enough for representation of groups to be effective, but that, in one way or another, they must be the "right" kind of descriptive representative. Dovi (2003), for example, asserts that "strong, mutual relationships with dispossessed subgroups" is an essential criterion for effective descriptive representation. Similarly, Jane Mansbridge (1999) specifies four instances in which descriptive representation is useful: when it provides "adequate communication in contexts of mistrust"; promotes "innovative thinking in contexts of uncrystalized interests"; creates "social meaning and an 'ability to rule' for oppressed groups"; and/or when it helps to "increase a polity's de facto legitimacy" (Mansbridge 1999, 628–29).

In other words, the importance of descriptive representation is often tied to a candidate's willingness to work toward the interests of those groups, as well. At its best, the presence of a descriptive representative must at least hold the potential for improved substantive representation as well, whether in the legislative, judicial, or executive branch. The relevant question for this chapter, then, becomes whether or not the media has portrayed Senators Clinton and Obama as willing to represent, and/or capable of representing, their female and black constituencies in these ways.

This question speaks to the differences between executive and legislative representation, as well. The majority of the literature on descriptive representation at the national level examines its role in the legislative branch (e.g., Swain 1993; Canon 1999; Tate 2003), and to a lesser extent, the judicial (e.g., Welch, Combs, and Gruhl 1988; Bratton and Spill 2002), both of which are deliberative bodies comprised of multiple members. Unlike in Congress, in the case of the presidency, a black man or a white woman is no longer one representative among many, there to "stand for" a specific subgroup of the population. Rather, the presidency is an office occupied by one individual who is chosen by the entire population and has come to be seen as the popular representative for the entire nation (e.g., Rossiter 1949; Cronin 1975).

I argue that for three reasons a presidential candidate who is also a demographic outsider may have a difficult time balancing his/her roles as a descriptive representative for a particular group and the representative of the national constituency, both in office and in their media portrayals. First, a number of presidency scholars (Neustadt 1960; Tulis 1987; Stuckey 2004;

Dahl 1990) have argued that modern presidents have had to increasingly rely on popular communication to garner public support for an ever-expanding policy agenda. Because presidents increasingly seek to make policy, and have relied on mass approval as a means of achieving their policy objectives, the public has, over time, come to expect the president to act as their popular representative. Because of this, presidential candidates must have the broadest possible appeal. Second, their reliance on popular support often constrains what their agenda can and will include. Riley (1999), for example, argues that, due to popular and constitutional factors, the presidency is inherently a nation-maintaining institution, particularly when it has come to issues of social hierarchy. This has led most presidents to strive for preservation of the status quo. By examining moments in history when membership in American political culture has been challenged, Riley finds that the objectives of most presidents are often fundamentally at odds with any form of significant social change that seeks to include into the political mainstream previously excluded groups. This suggests that the office itself, regardless of the person who occupies it, is an obstacle to effective representation of outsider groups. Finally, the symbolic importance of the president as the foremost representative of the nation as a whole cannot be overstated. As our "first citizen" (Landy and Milkis 2002), the president is looked to not only as a politician, but as leader, educator, and keeper of our "constitutional soul." Thus, the president is a fundamentally different elected official—one that represents not only popular opinion, but the embodiment of our national identity as well.

What does all of this mean for an "outsider" who is also a serious presidential candidate? Is it possible for a woman or an African American to be an effective descriptive representative—one who maintains ties to, and is willing to work toward political gains for, his or her specific group—while at the same time act as the popular representative and identifying symbol of a national constituency? The literature seems to suggest an unavoidable paradox for these candidates, and it is with the objective of determining if and how that paradox was presented during this race that I turn to elite discourse in the media.

While the representation literature and political communication literature have not spoken to each other much, I contend that the media is a useful site for exploring national perceptions of individual representatives, thereby giving us clues as to how Americans think about representation in general, as well. Since we, as an electorate, are "cognitive misers" (e.g., Mclean, Orbell, and Dawes 1991), most casual observers of politics will look to information "shortcuts" when it comes to gaining political knowledge. Among the most prolific of these shortcuts is elite communication (Zaller 1992). It is reasonable to assume, then, that many turned to elite discourse in the media for cues on how to think about the possibility of these two candidates as representatives. The framing of these candidates' identities in the media is a useful proxy for how the national conversation around descriptive representation and the presidency progressed throughout these two campaigns.

This chapter analyzes content of two print media sources—the *New York Times* and the *Washington Post*—to examine what the nature of descriptive representation in the national executive might be, and how elite discourse has treated this new possibility in the contexts of Senators Hillary Clinton and Barack Obama. First, it seeks to explore how the media framed the discussion around the ability of each candidate to represent his/her own group—namely, African Americans and women. Did the media assume that their descriptive representation of these groups would lead to increased substantive representation, as well, and was this framed as a normatively good or bad thing? Second, because the president has such symbolic importance as the national representative, it examines what media said about the possibility of a man or woman, each of whom inevitably represents an "outsider" group, symbolically representing the entire country. Were these two functions portrayed as being mutually exclusive? Finally, it analyzes the differences that emerged between narratives based on gender and those surrounding race.

FRAMING AND REPRESENTATION IN THE MEDIA

While framing as a theoretical construct that has been approached in varied and sometimes conflicting ways, I will use Kinder's (2003) definition of a frame: "a central organizing idea or storyline that provides meaning to an unfolding event." In other words, a given issue is rarely presented in any media source as a simple list of facts or events. Instead, the media present a very specific context in which readers/viewers/listeners are prompted to think about that issue. In this way, media sources also often lead consumers to think about that issue or event in the context of a specific narrative.

When it comes to politicians, there is a host of evidence suggesting that women are framed in certain ways that differ from their male counterparts, and that those frames often put them at a disadvantage. For example, women's viability as candidates is often framed more negatively than men's (Kahn 1996), women are often framed in a classist and biologically essentialized manner (Vavrus 1998), and news reports on women leaders tend to focus on characteristically "feminine" factors, such as clothing and personal demeanor, as opposed to policy substance (Witt, Paget, and Matthews 1994).

Further, because Hillary Clinton was in the news on a regular basis as First Lady from 1992 through 2000, scholars have been able to analyze how she, personally, has been framed. Winfield (1997) has found that, from the beginning, she challenged traditional First-Lady frames and that the media has often portrayed her by questioning "who she really is." Gardetto (1997) offers evidence that she was framed as controversial from the start, and was often portrayed in three related ways: with the "her strength—his weakness" frame, echoing the "double-bind" mentioned above, with the "comparing women/wifestyles" frame, which compared her unfavorably to other political wives, and with the "new kind of marital partnership" frame, emphasizing her independence and careerism.

In the case of African Americans, the use of racialized frames has been more complex. Some scholars have found that the media tend to highlight race in political contexts (e.g., Reeves 1994; Traugott, Price, and Czilli 1993), while others (e.g., Jones and Clemons 1993) have found that candidates themselves tend to "play the race card" before the media. Terkildson and Damore (1999, 681), however, posit that the media actually "shape the racial tone of election coverage by limiting the racial references put forth by candidates while promoting candidate race themselves." This "racial dualism," they argue, is particularly strong in competitive, biracial contests, such as this one.

Similar to Clinton, Obama has been in the media sufficiently long as a senator and presidential candidate for a number of scholars, mostly in the field of communications, to analyze his media portrayals. Like the racial framing literature more generally, the conclusions have been mixed. Garfield (2008) finds that he is often framed as being "acceptably black ... non-threatening to white people ... standard English, clean-cut appearance ... and the most Caucasian features possible." Further, while Jones (2007), suggests that the media have been using Obama's youth as a proxy for his race when questioning his competence, Hart (2007) proclaims that he "transcends racial stereotypes."

Clearly, the media have scrutinized both candidates since the beginning of their public service careers within the context of their group memberships. Clinton has never been seen as a traditionally female persona thanks to her strength and ambition, while Obama is rarely seen as traditionally black due to his various measures of "acceptability" among whites. It is likely that this element of being seen as nontraditional members of these groups has contributed to their presidential viability, but what does this mean for their prospects as effective descriptive representatives? Further, what has it meant for their portrayals as the possible national representative?

HYPOTHESIS AND METHOD

The hypotheses of this chapter rests on the assumption of an uncomfortable merger between the demographic political outsider and the foremost national elective office. An analysis of extant literature suggests that a representational paradox may emerge between his/her responsibility to the national constituency—both substantively and symbolically—and his/her responsibility to the groups he/she represents descriptively. I predict that a content analysis of various media sources will show that this paradox appeared in elite discourse in the mass media throughout the 2008 Democratic primary contest between Hillary Clinton and Barack Obama. Specifically, I look for manifestations of this paradox in three locations: in articles addressing the candidates' positions on group-specific policy issues; in articles about the candidates' positions on "universal" policy issues; and in articles addressing each candidate's group's equal rights movements (feminism and civil rights).

Many political issues in the United States are group-centric; that is, public opinion on those issues is shaped, at least to some extent,[1] by opinions about who is assumed to benefit (or not) from policy surrounding those issues (Nelson and Kinder 1996). In the case of the 2008 Democratic primary, I focus on several issues that "belong" either to African Americans or women. Issues like affirmative action (Kinder and Sanders 1990), poverty (Gilens 1996), school busing (Gilens 1996), and crime (Hurwitz and Peffley 1997) have all been shown to have cognitive links to African Americans, for example, while reproductive rights, pay equity, healthcare, women's health, and child care (e.g., Schaffner 2005; Kahn 1996; Hutchings, Valentino, Philpot, and White 2004) are all considered to be "women's issues." The three specific gender-coded issues used in this analysis are abortion/reproductive rights, pay equity and child care, while race-coded issues include affirmative action, poverty, and urban public education. Issues were chosen in order to examine a range of group-specific policy areas, with different levels of coverage, salience in this election, and relative controversy. Both abortion and affirmative action were chosen to be "hot-button" issues that always tend to be salient and controversial, even within the Democratic Party and the groups they affect. Urban public education and government-funded child care are both social spending issues[2] that received some attention in this election cycle and are similar, yet proved to be two facets of education policy that are often discussed in terms of race and gender, respectively. Poverty and pay equity are both issues that are non-controversial in their relative value judgments (most agree that poverty is bad and equal pay for equal work is good), but controversial in what is seen as the appropriate role of government in addressing them.

Another possible site of elite discussion about Obama and Clinton as representatives is in coverage of their positions on non-group-specific issues. Literature suggests that group-coded issues in general are applicable predominantly (or perhaps exclusively) to outsider groups—there are no "white male issues" in the same sense that affirmative action "belongs" to African Americans or pay equity "belongs" to women, for example. Issues that are not directly applicable to other groups—the mainstream issues that, in one way or another, "belong" to the universal, un-raced, un-sexed electorate—will be referred to as "universal" issues. These include policy areas such as the economy, foreign policy, and budget considerations, and are also considered to be the most important and "prestigious" of all policy issues (e.g., Shepsle 1978; Heberlig 2003). The economy was chosen as the universal issue of analysis in this study because it was a salient political topic throughout the primaries, and eventually overtook even the Iraq War and terrorism as voters' number one concern in many polls.

Many articles were also found to directly discuss the candidates and their relationships to each of their respective group's ongoing struggle for equal rights. I was interested in exploring how Obama was connected to the civil rights movement and Clinton to feminism, because if substantive representation is "acting for" a constituency, and descriptive representation is "standing for" that group, perhaps a useful place to examine the extent to which each is willing to do both is within the context of a candidate's advocacy on behalf of that group's status within the social hierarchy. Strong ties to civil rights or feminism may serve as a useful proxy for measuring not only commitment to each group's political interests, but for evaluating how much each is shown to identify with the group and to what extent each expresses a level of "group consciousness" or "linked fate" with the groups they represent, descriptively (e.g., Dawson 1994; Paolino 1995, 294–313).

I expected to see manifestations of elite discomfort with the candidates when they were portrayed as strong group advocates for group-specific policy issues, due to a widespread expectation that any serious candidate for president will be a representative of the national electorate in its entirety. My first hypothesis, then, is that when attention is drawn to the candidates' race or gender, the overall valence of an article should be more negative. Specifically, candidate coverage in articles related to group-specific policy issues should be more negative overall than in articles covering universal issues (i.e., the economy). Similarly, articles in any issue category that refer to Clinton or Obama as either a woman or an African American, respectively, should be coded as negative more often than those that do not. Further, I expect that when the candidates are portrayed as strong group advocates, coverage should be even more negative, particularly in articles related to the economy. Conversely, I expect candidates to be portrayed more positively when emphasis is placed on their status as a universal representative.

Hypothesis 2 addresses the differences I expect to see in the coverage between the two candidates in both issue-related articles and those addressing feminism/civil rights. In general, because race is "different" in the sense that race issues have proven to be uniquely divisive among the electorate (e.g., Frymer 1999, 34; Mendelberg 2001), I predict that any black candidate who made it to the primaries as a front runner must have done so through a certain distancing of him or herself from race-specific advocacy. As mentioned above, early Communications scholarship on media portrayals of Obama have shown support for this theory, describing him as "acceptably black" and emphasizing his universal appeal. On the other hand, Clinton has been portrayed throughout her career as a feminist and strong advocate for women. Because gender is a crosscutting cleavage—i.e., most women have men in their lives to whom they are close, and vice versa—and because we tend to view groups that we are closer to more favorably (e.g., Gurin, et al. 1980), it follows that there may be more room for a universal representative to also advocate on behalf of women than for a presidential candidate to do so on behalf of African Americans. For these reasons, I expect Clinton to be referred to specifically as a woman more often than Obama is referred to as black, and also to be portrayed as a strong group advocate more often than Obama. It follows from Hypothesis 1, then, that coverage of Clinton should be more negative than that of Obama, overall—both in articles addressing specific policy issues and those discussing feminism.

Finally, a more qualitative analysis of how these candidates and issues are framed should demonstrate a tension between being too explicitly a group member and not enough of a group advocate. Elites focused on the universal, symbolic function of the presidency should either downplay the candidates' race/gender or speak directly to their responsibility as a national representative. Conversely, I expect to see an opposing storyline, as well, that decries each candidate's lack of attention to his/her specific groups. Hypothesis 3, then, is that these competing narratives should result in my ability to identify contrasting, parallel frames for each candidate; one highlighting their responsibility to the national electorate—and thereby either praising their attempts at universal appeal or chastising their outreach to women or African Americans—and another emphasizing their duty to those ascriptive groups while providing positive or negative evaluations of their attempts to do so.

In order to test these hypotheses, I conducted a content analysis of relevant articles in both the *New York Times* and the *Wall Street Journal* during the 2008 Democratic primaries.[3] My method is a combination of both quantitative and qualitative content analysis measuring both content and valence of the articles analyzed. Articles were coded for a number of variables, including specific issue, issue type (race, gender, or universal), valence (scored as either positive, negative, or neutral), whether the candidate was described as a group member (i.e., whether Clinton was referred to specifically as a woman or Obama was described specifically as black or African American), whether she/he was portrayed as a strong group representative,[4] and whether or not the candidate was referred to as a universal representative.[5]

To begin this analysis, I conducted a LexisNexis search and looked at all articles that specifically mention the candidate's position or ability related to each issue. For all race and gender-coded issues, the entire population of news, news analysis, and op-ed articles covering each was used. The same is true for articles on feminism and civil rights. Because of the large number of articles covering the candidates and the economy, a random sample of sixty for each candidate (thirty each, from each paper) was taken.

ISSUE COVERAGE RESULTS

Table 1 shows the initial results of a search for coverage of these issues in the *New York Times* and the *Washington Post*.[6] Articles mentioning the candidates' stance on the economy were by far the most abundant. In terms of gender-coded issues, abortion received the most attention—twenty-seven

Table 1 Issue Count

	Abortion	Pay Equity	Child Care	Affirmative Action	Poverty	Urban Schools	Economy—Clinton	Economy—Obama	Total
Total Articles	27	11	10	21	44	13	60*	60*	246
Candidate Referred to as Group Member	11 40.7%	7 63.6%	3 30%	16 76.2%	10 22.7%	3 23.1%	12 20%	9 15%	71 28.9%
Candidate Position on Universal Issues Mentioned	12 44.4%	4 36.4%	7 70%	9 42.9%	36 81.8%	10 76.9%	-	-	78** 62%
Candidate Portrayed as Strong Group Advocate	22 81.5%	8 72.7%	8 80%	13 14.3%	27 61.4%	9 69.2%	2 3.3%	1 1.7%	80 32.5%

*Economy articles are a random sample of total number of articles mentioning each candidate's position on economic issues.
**Out of 126, excluding 120 economy articles.

articles between the two papers—with both pay equity and child care receiving less than half the coverage of abortion (ten and eleven articles, respectively). Poverty was the most widely covered race-coded issue, with forty-four articles mentioning Obama's stance on poverty issues. Obama's position on affirmative action was mentioned in twenty-one articles, while urban public education was covered in thirteen. Table 2 collapses the three race and three gender issues into two categories, which shows a total of forty-eight articles dealing specifically with gender-coded issues, and seventy-eight focused on race-coded issues.

Both tables also show how often articles about each issue and issue category also refer to the candidate directly as a group member (i.e., articles about Clinton refer to her as a woman and articles about Obama refer to him as black or African American). Some of the most striking findings in these tables center around the differences between coverage of race and gender-coded issues. In articles about Hillary Clinton in the context of both gender-coded and universal issues, she is mentioned as a woman at a higher rate than that at which Obama is described as black or African American. In 43.8 percent of gender-coded articles and 20 percent of economy-related articles, Clinton is described as a member of her ascriptive group, while the

Table 2 Issue Type Percentages

	Gender	Race	Universal—Clinton	Universal—Obama
Total Articles	48	78	60	60
Total Referring to Candidate as Group Member	43.8%*	37.2%*	20%*	15%*
Candidate Position on Universal Issues Mentioned	47.9%*	70.5%	-	-
Candidate Mentioned as Strong Group Advocate	79.2%**	50%**	3.3%**	1.7%**

*Chi-square significant at p<.01
**Chi-square significant at p<.001

same is true of Obama in 37.2 percent of race-coded articles and 15 percent of economy articles. Finally, Obama is described as black or African American most often in affirmative action related articles (76.2 percent) while Clinton is mentioned most frequently as a woman in articles about pay equity (63.6 percent of the time).

By examining how often each candidate's positions on universal issues are mentioned in articles predominantly about race or gender-coded issues, Tables 1 and 2 also shed some light on the extent to which each candidate is considered to be a universal representative and group advocate, simultaneously. Table 2 clearly shows that articles about race-coded issues refer to Obama's position on non-race-coded issues more often than articles about gender-coded issues refer to Clinton's stance on universal issues (70.5 percent to 47.9 percent, respectively). Pay equity articles mention the candidate's stance on universal issues least often of all at 36.4 percent, while affirmative action articles do so least among race-specific issues, at 42.9 percent.

Finally, Tables 1 and 2 show the frequency with which articles about each issue and issue category refer to each candidate as a strong group advocate. Clinton is portrayed as being a strong advocate for women in 79.2 percent of articles about gender-specific topics, and in 3.3 percent of articles about the economy. Obama is shown as a strong group advocate in 50 percent of race-specific articles and only 1.7 percent of economy-related articles. When broken down by issue, Clinton is portrayed as a strong group advocate most often in articles related to abortion (81.5 percent of the time) and least often in articles about pay equity (72.7 percent of the time). Obama, on the other hand, is portrayed as a strong group advocate most often in articles related

Table 3a Candidate Group Member X Valence

	Candidate Mentioned as Group Member?		
	Yes	No	Total
Negative	8 (11%)	48 (27%)	56 (23%)
Neutral	43 (61%)	106 (61%)	149 (61%)
Positive	20 (28%)	21 (12%)	41 (17%)
Total	71 (100%)	175 (100%)	246 (100%)

Pearson chi-square = .137, significant at p<.001.

Table 3b Candidate Group Member X Valence (-1 - +1 Trichotomous Measure)

Candidate Mentioned as Group Member?		N	Mean	Std. Dev.
	Yes	71	.17	.61
	No	175	-.15	.61

F Statistic = 14.186, significant at p<.001

to urban public education (69.2 percent), and least often in coverage of affirmative action (14.3 percent).

Overall, the results from Tables 1 and 2 provide some initial support for my hypotheses. Clinton is more often mentioned specifically as being a woman, is less often portrayed as a universal representative, and is more often described as a strong group advocate than Obama. Unexpectedly, Obama is actually talked about in terms of both group representation and universal issues in articles about race-coded issues more often than not. However, this may lend further support to Hypothesis 2, since he is only portrayed as a strong group advocate on race-related issues half of the time. These initial results do seem to indicate a pattern in which Clinton is shown as a representative for women more often and to a greater degree than Obama is shown as an advocate for African Americans.

I turn now to the tone of the coverage of each candidate. Are the candidates generally portrayed more positively when they are not described as group representatives, as Hypothesis 1 predicts? Table 3a shows a cross-tab and Table 3b a one-way ANOVA between whether or not a candidate is mentioned as a group member and the overall valence of the article, which is measured as a trichotomous variable with values of -1 for a negative valence, 0 for a neutral, and +1 for a positive valence. Surprisingly, a statistically significant relationship between attention to a candidate's group membership and article valence is found in both analyses, but the directionality of

Table 4 Candidate Strong Group Advocate X Valence (-1 - +1 Trichotomous Measure)

Candidate Mentioned as Strong Group Representative?		N	Mean	Std. Dev.
	Yes	80	.05	.65
	No	166	-.11	.57

F-Statistic = 3.765, significant at p<.01.

both is the opposite of what was expected. In other words, articles are actually more likely to portray candidates positively if they also refer to them as either a woman or African American, respectively. The mean valence score for an article that refers to a candidate as a group member is .17, while the mean for articles that do not is -.15 (F-statistic=14.2, significant at p<.001). It is also worth noting that a similar and significant relationship was found for articles about Obama alone, while no significant relationship was found for Clinton, though the directionality remained the same.

Similarly, Table 4 shows a one-way ANOVA between whether or not a candidate is portrayed as a strong group advocate and the same -1 – +1 trichotomous valence measure. Again, a statistically significant, though not quite as robust, relationship appears in the same direction (F-statistic=3.765, significant at p<.01). Articles about these issues are more likely to be positive when candidates are portrayed as strong group advocates, though the mean for each category in this analysis is less positive, overall.

These initial findings suggest that though Clinton is portrayed as a group member and a strong group advocate more often than Obama, this does not necessarily lead to more negative coverage of her in the context of policy issues. To make this comparison directly, Table 5 shows a cross-tabulation of article valence and issue type (with economy coverage separated by candidate). While a X^2 test of difference is not significant here, this table does provide an idea of how negative/positive coverage of each candidate was, in general. Both candidates were portrayed neutrally more often than not in all categories, and negatively more often than positively when discussing the economy. While Obama was portrayed more negatively than positively when discussing race-coded issues, Clinton was actually portrayed positively and negatively with equal frequency (16.7 percent for each). Little support is found for Hypothesis 1 in an analysis of issue-related coverage, then. Mentioning the candidates' race/gender does not necessarily lead to more negative portrayals, and actually seems to coincide with positive portrayals. Some support was confirmed for Hypothesis 2, however. As expected, Clinton is portrayed as a group-specific representative and a strong group

Table 5 Thematic Issue Frames

	Issue In Which Frame Appears	Candidate	Valence	Frequency
"Clinton Owns Economy"	Abortion Child Care Economy	Clinton	Positive	23
"Community Organizer"	Poverty Urban Schools Economy	Obama	Negative	20
"Issue Avoidance"	Abortion Pay Equity Child Care Affirmative Action Poverty Urban Schools	Both	Negative	19
"Obama Vague/Unassertive"	Economy	Obama	Negative	14
"Radical Feminist"	Abortion Child Care Pay Equity	Clinton	Negative	14

advocate more often than Obama, and Obama is portrayed as a universal representative more often, even in the context of articles about race-coded issues. To test Hypothesis 3, I turn to an analysis of commonly used issue frames.

ISSUE FRAMES

I turn now to a more qualitative discussion of several prevalent issue frames that were identified across paper and article type. Table 5 lists the five most common frames found throughout these articles, along with the issues to which they apply, the general valence of each, and the frequency with which each is seen. The frame identified most often is what I will call the "Clinton owns the economy" frame. In twenty-three of the total articles (predominantly those covering the economy, but also in several articles about abortion and child care), Clinton is portrayed as an authority on economic issues. Both in terms of policy and public opinion, Clinton, more than Obama, is seen as the candidate who has a plan and can fix the then-unfolding economic problems. Coverage from the *Washington Post*, for example, claims that "Sen. Hillary Rodham Clinton (D-NY) ... won the Ohio presidential primary this week in part on the strength of support from voters worried about the economy"(Baker 2008) and "offers ... a proven track record and a variety of specific policy prescriptions" on economic issues (Schoen 2008). In contrast, another prevalent frame is the "Obama vague/unassertive" frame. In fourteen of the articles that talk about Obama and the economy, he is described as either unclear or not aggressive enough on economic issues. The *New York Times*, for example, states that "after two straight defeats in presidential elections, Democrats sometimes speak of hungering for a more aggressive standard-bearer to confront Republican attacks" (Powell 2008).

On issues that are specifically coded as belonging to either women or African Americans, three clearly conflicting frames emerge that lend support to my hypotheses. In nineteen of the race and gender-coded issues, the frame of "Issue Avoidance" appears rather strongly. Both candidates are accused of either completely neglecting or not doing enough to address each and every group-specific issue included in this analysis, and the articles that used this frame were overwhelmingly negative. Obama is accused of not "offering anything like a comprehensive vision for urban America,"[7] for example, and of being unaware that[8] Clinton, meanwhile, has been stated to have "shown a predilection for compromise at the expense of the poor" (P. Goodman 2008), and an article in the *Washington Post* accuses her of an "attempt to play down the issue [which] represents a marked change in a party for which abortion rights has been a defining issue" (Murray 2008).

In contrast, a separate frame also emerged for each candidate that emphasized the extent to which each has been a strong advocate for his/her group. The "Community Organizer" frame posits Obama as a radical, left-wing, civil rights advocate, while the "Radical Feminist" frame similarly paints Clinton as a an extreme second-wave feminist, rooted in the women's rights movement of the 1970s. Both frames are overwhelmingly negative. Clinton, for example, is described as "genuinely radical" (Gerson 2008) on issues like abortion, and several articles mention fears that Obama's "days as a community organizer in Chicago ... paint him as a radical who will be unwilling to challenge liberal orthodoxy on social and poverty issues" (Weisman and Murray 2008).

Clearly, this analysis of article content and recurrent issue frames points to a complex portrayal of these candidates and their relationships to their respective group constituencies. While evidence suggests that Clinton was generally seen as a stronger representative for women's interests than Obama was for blacks, both were, at times, chastised for either being too much of a group representative and, at others, not enough of a group advocate. The evidence also suggests a complicated narrative around each

Table 6a Movement by Valence

	Feminism	Civil Rights	Total
Negative	13 (20%)	2 (2%)	15 (10%)
Neutral	28 (43%)	48 (57%)	76 (51%)
Positive	24 (37%)	35 (41%)	59 (39%)
Total	65 (100%)	85 (100%)	150 (100%)

Pearson's chi-square = .129, significant at p<.01.

Table 6b Movement by Valence ANOVA (-1 - +1 Trichotomous Measure)

Movement Label		N	Mean	Std. Dev.
	Feminism	65	.17	.74
	Civil Rights	85	.39	.54

F-Statistic = 4.41, significant at p<.01.

candidate and their positions/authority on universal issues. In articles about race and gender-coded issues, Obama was more often discussed as a universal representative, but an analysis of issue frames shows that Clinton was often portrayed as the candidate most in control of economic issues. In hopes of further parsing these tangled relationships, then, I will now turn to similar analyses of coverage that connects both candidates to their respective equal rights movements.

FEMINISM/CIVIL RIGHTS AND THE MEDIA

Tables 6a and 6b show the results of a cross-tab and analysis of variance between each movement label and the same trichotomous valence score used in the analysis of issue articles. Coverage of each is generally neutral, and more positive than negative. Interestingly, however, and in keeping with Hypothesis 2, coverage of Clinton's relationship to feminism is more negative, overall, than that of Obama and civil rights. While 20 percent of articles that mention Clinton and feminism are negative, only 2 percent of civil rights articles are scored as negative (X^2 = .129, significant at p<.01). Similarly, the mean valence score for feminism is .17, while the mean valence score for civil rights is .39 (F-statistic=4.41 at p<.01). Combined with the findings from the issue data that Clinton was often portrayed as a stronger group advocate than Obama (and therefore a stronger feminist than Obama was

Table 7a Candidate Described as Universal Representative X Valence

	No	Yes
Negative	10 (13%)	5 (7%)
Neutral	44 (58%)	32 (43%)
Positive	22 (29%)	37 (50%)
Total	65 (100%)	85 (100%)

Pearson chi-Square = 7.35, significant at p<.05.

Table 7b Candidate Universal Representative X Valence ANOVA (-1 - +1 Trichotomous Measure)

Candidate Universal Representative?		N	Mean	Std. Dev.
	Yes	74	.43	.63
	No	76	.16	.62

F-Statistic = 7.18, significant at p<.01.

a civil rights advocate), this evidence seems to offer some evidence that a stronger relationship to a group-specific movement may be portrayed more negatively than a weaker relationship.

Tables 7a and 7b examine the relationship between the candidates' ties to their movements, and portrayals of them as universal representatives. The results clearly show that the candidates are portrayed more positively when they are portrayed as universal representatives within these contexts than when they are not. A cross-tab analysis between whether or not a candidate is described as a universal representative and valence scores yields a X^2 value of 7.35, significant at p<.05, while a one-way ANOVA shows that the mean valence score for articles that do mention the candidate as a universal representative is .43, while those that do not average a score of .16. This also lends credence to my contention that portrayals of these candidates as universal representatives are tied to more positive portrayals, overall.

Taken together, the evidence from this movement-related data suggest that Clinton's relatively strong relationship to feminism is regarded less positively, overall, than Obama's relatively weaker relationship to civil rights, and that articles characterizing both candidates as universal representatives result in more positive portrayals. In order to place these findings in a broader context of movement coverage, I now turn to a discussion of how the candidates and the movements they represent have been framed.

Table 8 Movement Frames

	Candidate	Valence	Frequency
"Generation Gap"	Both	Both	37; 13 Clinton, 24 Obama
"Obama Post-Race"	Obama	Positive	28
"Obama Symbol"	Obama	Positive	18
"Race v. Gender"	Both	Negative	13; 7 Clinton, 6 Obama
"Showing Us Sexism"	Clinton	Neutral	10
"Billary"	Clinton	Negative	9

MOVEMENT FRAMES

Table 8 identifies the six most common frames utilized in the narrative surrounding both Hillary Clinton and feminism, and Barack Obama and civil rights. Most prevalent was the "Generation Gap" frame. Articles that utilize this frame posit Clinton as an "old-guard" feminist and, in some, an "old-guard" civil rights advocate, as well. She is seen as belonging to the feminist movement in an often negative, archaic way, unable to transcend the feminist label in a "post-feminist" society. One op-ed columnist in the *Washington Post* talks about a "collective shrug about a woman running for president right now" among young women (Odell 2008), for example, while another blames her losses to Obama directly on her identification with feminism: "At 40-something, organized feminism is having trouble reproducing ... nothing says that more clearly than Clinton's struggle in the primaries" (Hirshman 2008). Maureen Dowd sums up this sentiment nicely when she argues that "women have moved past that men-are-pigs, woe-is-me, sisters-must-stick-together, pantsuits-are-powerful era that Hillary's campaign has lately revived with a vengeance" (Dowd 2008).

Obama, on the other hand, is often portrayed as a product of the civil rights movement, but not "of" it in the same way that Clinton is "of" the women's rights movement. This is often discussed as an asset to Obama who, because of it, is more inspiring to younger, "post-racial," "post-feminist" generations and more electable because he is less explicitly tied to a marginalized group's fight for social equality. A *New York Times* editorial by Nicholas Kristof from early February, for example, states that "Mr. Obama probably has a better chance than a black candidate who emerged from the civil rights movement" (Kristof 2008), and another *Times* article from late January observes that "Mr. Obama has not regularly wrapped himself in the mantle of the civil rights movement, the hallmark of an earlier generation of black politicians" (Toner 2008).

The next two most frequently used frames are related to the "Generation Gap" and both apply to Obama, as well. In articles that use either the "Obama Post-Race" or "Obama As Symbol" frame (or both), Obama is portrayed as simultaneously transcending racial conflict and acting as living proof that we are truly beyond race in this country. Obama must "serve as symbol and trope. He must represent his multiethnic constituency and he must represent" (Givhan 2008). Because Obama is a "candidate who happens to be black" rather than a "black candidate," he is able to unite various constituencies around various universal issues. At the same time, interestingly, many of these articles acknowledge the symbolic importance of possibly electing an African American president without acknowledging any necessity for substantive representation specifically for blacks from Obama. The importance of his being black, then, seems to reside entirely in his role as a symbol of progress and "how far we've come."[9]

Another common frame pits feminism and civil rights against each other, directly. The "Race v. Gender" frame, which appears in thirteen articles, posits the contest between Clinton and Obama as a zero-sum battle between two marginalized groups, in which one must ultimately lose. This theme is echoed in statements such as: "People will have to choose which of America's sins are greater, and which stain will have to be removed first. Is misogyny worse than racism, or is racism worse than misogyny?" (Dowd 2008) Or: "History shows that 'the public mind' is too conservative to accept both a black man and a white woman in the seat of power" (Applegate 2008).

Other clear, widely used frames for Clinton and feminism were not as prevalent. In ten of the articles analyzed, a "Showing Us Sexism" frame did emerge, however. These articles tended to treat Clinton as a representative for women, insofar as she served as a reminder to a largely post-feminist society that sexism and misogyny still exist. Through statements such as, "the politics of the last few months have certainly opened a spigot on the question of where exactly society stands on gender matters" (Zernike 2008), and attention to "the Internet . . . overloaded with message boards full of male chauvinists who believe that Clinton is a candidate only because of her husband, and with Web sites that market a product called the Hillary Nutcracker" (Saslow 2008), a less prevalent but noticeable narrative emerges around the surprising endurance of sexism in our society.

Finally, and perhaps in contrast, nine feminism articles used what I'll call the "Billary" frame, in which Clinton is often chastised for being too "tied up" in her husband's identity and, therefore, not deserving of the nomination. Articles that fall into this thematic category tend to be quite hostile and seem to attempt to undermine her feminist credentials: "Hillary Clinton has 'just under eight years of experience in elective office—one more than John Edwards and four fewer than Obama.' And, to boot, Hillary the Feminist has her man to fight her battles" (King 2008).

DISCUSSION AND CONCLUSIONS

In this chapter, I have argued that a representational paradox exists for presidential candidates who are also members of "outsider" social groups. Hillary Clinton and Barack Obama, as the first major party candidates seriously vying for a nomination that fall into this category, provide scholars with a fascinating case in which to explore the complex relationship between substantive, symbolic, and descriptive representation in the national executive. Similarly, elite discourse in the mass media has served as a useful site in which to examine how national discourse around these questions of representation have progressed throughout the primaries.

A complex picture emerged, with some evidence lending support to my hypotheses and other findings contradicting my expected results. An analysis of group-coded and universal policy issues shows that though Hillary Clinton was largely portrayed as a stronger group advocate for women than Obama was for African Americans, in the context of political issues, this did not lead to more negative coverage of her. However, in the context of articles related to feminism and civil rights, coverage of Clinton was significantly more negative than that of Obama. Also, portrayals of candidates as universal representatives in both contexts led to more positive coverage of each of them, supporting the notion that presidents and presidential candidates need to be viable representatives for the universal, national electorate. A broader analysis of commonly used thematic frames does in fact show contrasting, parallel narratives for each candidate and their relationships to both their outsider groups and the country as a whole—neither seemed to be able to pull off the dual-role of effective descriptive representative for a marginalized group and legitimate universal representative, simultaneously.

Perhaps some of the most intriguing findings of this analysis lie in the differences in candidate coverage in the context of issues vs. that of feminism and civil rights. Though Clinton was more often portrayed as a group member and a strong group advocate for women in coverage of women's issues, she was still covered more positively than Obama, and the prevalence of the "Hillary Owns the Economy" frame suggests that she was even largely considered to have the upper hand on certain universal issues as well. This scenario seemed to change dramatically when her advocacy on behalf of women was tied explicitly to feminism, however. Not only did the overall tone of coverage become significantly more negative, but I was unable to identify a single recurrent frame that portrayed Clinton and her ties to feminism positively.

In contrast, when Obama's relationship to African Americans was couched in terms of civil rights, his coverage became significantly more positive than negative (remember that only 2 percent of articles related to Obama and civil rights were negative in tone). There may be several reasons for this divergence, but theory and evidence taken together suggest that one probable factor may be the very different nature of the relationship Obama had to civil rights versus the relationship Clinton had to feminism. Clinton's history and commitment to women's issues, as well as her age and appeal to older generations of women, seemed to contribute to elite opinion that she was a "traditional" feminist, concerned about women's rights to an extent that was inconsistent with mainstream public opinion. Obama, on the other hand, with his more explicit attempts to downplay race issues and appeal to younger generations in more universal terms, seemed to grow more favorable in the eyes of the media when his willingness to let go of traditional civil rights issues was mentioned explicitly.

Elite emphasis on the interaction of age with both race and gender is another unexpected finding that is worth mentioning here. The marked prevalence of the "Generation Gap" frame seems to indicate a general sentiment that group-specific representation matters to older generations, but that younger voters are more interested in "transcending" group-related strife in favor of a universal candidate. In this case, that universal candidate "happened to be black," but as the "Obama Post-Race" frame exemplifies, Obama's appeal (at least in the minds of elite media) lay in his ability and willingness to remain an explicitly universal candidate.

Similarly, the recurrence of the "Obama As Symbol" frame suggests that elites did admit to a certain importance in Obama's being the first black candidate to come so close (and eventually achieve) a major party nomination, but that importance was allowed only a purely symbolic function. His candidacy was largely portrayed as proof that we are beyond the need for race or gender-specific representation. Such a frame did not emerge for Clinton and women—perhaps indicative of that "collective shrug" regarding a woman running for president mentioned earlier. In fact, the "Generation Gap" frame suggests that it was more symbolically valuable for women not to vote for Clinton. It was a sign of "how far we've come" that women did not have to vote for the female candidate.

Taken together, the evidence from this analysis suggests that a representational paradox did indeed surface in elite discourse surrounding the 2008 Democratic primaries for both Hillary Clinton and Barack Obama. The nature of that paradox, however, is clearly complicated. Other confounding factors such as differences in candidates' ages, personal and political histories, and elite acknowledgement of their ties to their respective groups led to this complex relationship between group and universal representation playing out very differently for each candidate. Whether or not Obama's more universal media portrayals played a role in his eventual victory is beyond the scope of this chapter, but his precedent-setting presidency will certainly provide ample opportunity for scholars to continue to explore the quickly changing relationship between descriptive representation and executive office.

Notes

1. As Nelson and Kinder are quick to remind us in the same article, political attitudes are dependent on many factors, including a specific political context, so the extent to which this is the case is likely to vary from year to year, election to election.
2. Several studies have shown attitudes toward social spending and welfare issues to be a main predictor of both male and female vote choice (e.g., Hutchings, et al. 2004, and Kauffman 2002).
3. In the interest of manageability, I limited my analysis to articles that appeared in either paper from January 1, 2008, through August 28, 2008. This covers the beginning of the first primary contest through the Democratic convention.
4. An article was determined to portray the candidate as a strong group representative/advocate if he or she was mentioned as specifically working for black/women's interests, or paying particular attention to those constituencies.
5. A candidate was considered to be portrayed as a universal representative if reference was made to his/her stance on non-race/gender-coded issues (the economy, foreign policy, taxation, etc.), or if he/she was mentioned directly as a representative of other constituencies.
6. In none of my analyses were systematic, significant differences found by newspaper.
7. "In Search of a Real Urban Policy," *New York Times*, February 19, 2008, http://www.nytimes.com/2008/02/19/opinion/19tue1.html.
8. "An I for Incomplete; Barack Obama and John McCain Have Some Useful Ideas on Education. But Something Bolder Is Needed," *Washington Post*, August 2, 2008.
9. Interestingly, no such frame emerged for women, suggesting that Clinton was not portrayed as an important symbol for women in the same way that Obama was for African Americans. This was mirrored in many of the "Generation Gap"-framed articles as well; young women were portrayed as not seeing the need to vote for women. In fact, younger women were often mentioned as feeling "liberated enough" not to vote for a woman.

11. OBAMA'S "UNISEX" CAMPAIGN

Masculinities, Race, and Law

FRANK RUDY COOPER

DURING THE 2008 DEMOCRATIC PRESIDENTIAL CAMPAIGN, THERE WAS A significant discourse in the media about Senator Barack Obama's femininity. When he faced Senator Hillary Clinton in the primaries, the head of a women's non-profit said, "He's the girl in the race."[1] The idea was that while Clinton was tough and hawkish, Obama was empathetic and inclusive (Linsky 2008). Carol Marin expressed that point of view in an editorial in the *Chicago Sun Times*:

> "If Bill Clinton was once considered America's first black president, Obama may one day be viewed as our first woman president." While Hillary Clinton, the warrior, battles on, talks about toughness, and out loud considers nuking Iran, it is Obama who is full of feminine virtues. Consensus. Conciliation. Peace, not war. (Marin 2008, A170)

For those reasons, some people referred to Obama as potentially our first female president (Lucy Berrington and Jeff Onore 2008).

In order to analyze the significance of Obama's alleged feminine side, I will turn to theories of identity. Critical race theory explores the ways that race is simultaneously nonexistent and materially consequential (Cooper 2006b, 148;). Masculinities studies says that assumptions about the meaning of manhood influence behaviors, ideologies, and institutions (Cooper 2009, 671).[2] Together, these theories will help us analyze how Obama's first presidential campaign influenced popular understandings of femininity and of black male identity.

I argue that Obama was more feminine than most mainstream presidential candidates because he is a black male. I base this argument on my theory of the "bipolarity" of media representations of black men (Cooper 2006a, 853). We are typically described as either the completely threatening Bad Black Man or the fully assimilationist Good Black Man. The Bad Black Man is a criminal you might see on the local news or a race-conscious black leader (Cooper 2006a, 875–79). The Good Black Man is a token member of the corporate world or a conservative post-race spokesman (Cooper 2006a, 879–86).[3] A prime stereotype of the Bad Black Man that Obama must avoid is the stereotype of the angry black man (Milloy 2008, B1).[4] One way to counter this stereotype is to be unusually calm. Obama has that quality, as well as a penchant for negotiation over imposition. Together, those qualities seem to be the source of claims that he would be our first female president (Linsky 2008).

Obama's feminization strategy was potentially dangerous, though, since femininity is still a slur in our male-dominated culture. Obama had to engage in a balancing act. He could not be too masculine because that would trigger the Bad Black Man image but he could not be too feminine because that would have looked unpresidential.

Obama seems to have resolved that conflict by being masculine enough to pass the commander in chief test yet feminine enough to make people comfortable with his blackness.[5] He tried to place himself more toward the middle of the general gender continuum, rather than the masculine end that most presidential candidates frequent, as a means of showing that he was on the good side of the specific black masculinity continuum. The appropriate term for Obama's feminine-but-not-too-much-so style seems to be "unisex."[6] A unisex style is one that is "designed to be suitable for" either gender.[7] A unisex style can swing both ways, creating the overall impression of being in the middle of the gender continuum. Obama's style was unisex in that he moved from more masculine to more feminine depending on the context. Accordingly, I argue that Obama is not our first female presidential candidate, but our first unisex president.

I will make that argument in three stages. First, I will review some tenets of critical race theory and masculinities studies. Next, I will analyze how the discourse on Obama's femininity is related to both the bipolarity of black masculinity and the denigration of femininity within the hegemonic discourse on masculinity. Finally, I will conclude by calling on Obama to use his considerable skills as an initiator of new ways of performing race and gender to help young black men undo their profile as always-already-suspect (Cooper 2013, 1204).

THEORIES OF IDENTITIES

In order to evaluate Obama's status as our first female president, we must ask, what does it mean to say that a presidential candidate acted "feminine" or "masculine" during the campaign? "Masculine" qualities are hardly limited to men and "feminine" qualities are not limited to women (Ehrenreich 2005, 132). Masculine and feminine qualities are nothing more than shared understandings about what it means to act like a man or woman (Kimmel 2005, 26). They are not reflective of stable essences of man or woman as such (Mutua 2006). Their definitions are subject to change over time and in different cultural contexts. Nonetheless, the discourse in the popular media used these concepts to describe the presidential candidates. Consequently, my methodology in this chapter is rather straightforward. I have reviewed the news stories on Lexis/Nexis that discuss Obama's first presidential campaign and femininity. I have analyzed those stories using the lenses of critical race theory and masculinities studies.

The Performative Theory of Identities

Before I describe my theories of race and of masculinities, I need to describe my theory of identities in general. I begin by noting that everybody has a sense of *self identity* (Cooper 2003, note 10, 841–46). This is the sense of self that we carry around inside our own heads. That self-image changes over time, but we could, theoretically, isolate a particular self-image at a particular time (Carbado and Gulati 2000, note 7, 1261, n.2.)

But there are other images of us. Others have theories of who we are. They attribute certain characteristics to us (Carbado and Gulati 2000, 1261, n.2). That *attributed identity* is also a part of an individual's identity because each of us must confront the expectations of others when going about our lives. For instance, let us hypothesize that Obama self-identifies as being as much white as black. The fact that he looks like a fairly typical black man means that he was always likely to be labeled black as a matter of attributed identity. Consequently, one's self identity and attributed identity can be in conflict.

At that point, the individual has some freedom of choice.[8] He could seek to have others fully adopt his self-conception, he could comport himself fully in accordance with his attributed identity, or he could act somewhere along the continuum between those two poles. If Obama does think of himself as being as much white as black, he could have insisted that he is not black, but has a hybrid identity, as Tiger Woods did (May 2008, 7A). Or Obama could have never referred to his whiteness. Or Obama could have generally accepted his attributed blackness, but occasionally reminded people of his white roots, which is what he did. Each of those choices constitutes a particular way of performing his identity. So, in addition to the realms of self-identity and attributed identity, there is a realm of *identity performance*.

The choice of how to perform one's identity is constrained by the intelligibility or unintelligibility of particular performances to the audience and influenced by the incentives or disincentives a cultural context attaches to particular performances (Onwuachi-Willig 2007b, 1917). As legal scholar Athena Mutua declares:

> *Both individuals and groups have some agency in defining masculinity. However, neither groups nor individuals define and construct masculinity in a vacuum. Rather, they draw on other culturally prevalent notions and are constrained by various social structures. (Mutua 2006, 14)*

Given that identity performances are not made in a vacuum, individuals can only signal their identity in terms that will be recognized by their audiences. Meanwhile, as critics of assimilation have shown, society has certain expectations for how particular individuals will act. The expected behaviors are rewarded and unexpected behaviors are often punished (Onwuachi-Willig 2007a, 2393). Society thus steers individuals toward particular identity performances.

In philosopher Judith Butler's view, the possibility of change exists in the form of citing precedent but with a new wrinkle added to the performance (Butler 1997, 147). The early adopters of the metrosexual style revealed that we already had the freedom to be straight-but-gay-acting, but they did not create that performance from the whole cloth. They were citing gay subcultural performances, but with the wrinkle that they were straight men. This is the sense in which we are "free" to make change even under a Butlerian understanding of identity performance.

Shared Tenets of Critical Race and Masculinities Theories

A shared tenet of both critical race theory and masculinities studies is that race and masculinity are not natural but socially constructed.[9] People's identities are socially constructed in that we learn our roles, rather than being born with an essential identity that we merely express (Marc Poirier

2003, 326). Men do not act like men simply because they are biologically male (Levit 1996, 1098). Instead, all men must learn how to act out particular forms of masculinity through social training (Levit 1996, 1062). Because identity is socially constructed, part of what was at stake in the 2008 presidential election was what types of behaviors people would learn to expect of black men.

Another shared tenet of both critical race theory and masculinities studies is that identities are multiple. Critical race theory's concept of intersectionality illustrates this point. Intersectionality refers to the fact that unique identities are formed at the places where categories of identities intersect (Crenshaw 1991, 1241).[10] Men who are black have different attributed identities (and self identities) than men who are white. Likewise, men who are black have different attributed identities (and self identities) than blacks who are also women. Consequently, masculinities studies scholars agree that there is no such thing as a singular masculinity; instead, there are masculinities in the plural.[11] The plurality of masculine identities includes working-class white masculinity, gay black masculinity, and so on.[12] And each of those subgroups is further segmented (Mutua 2006, 20–21).

A third shared tenet of both critical race theory and masculinities studies is that there are hierarchies within identities. The hierarchization of races in the West is so obvious that it does not bear further discussion (West 1993). Similarly, sociologists R. W. (now Raewyn) Connell and James Messerschmidt say that certain forms of masculinities are more honored and wield more power than others (Connell and Messerschmidt 2005, 846).[13] The masculinity traditionally associated with white, Christian, straight upper-class men has been installed as the ideal (Kimmel 2003, 25). Alternative masculinities, such as those associated with black, Jewish, gay, and lower-class men have been denigrated. Those men have been depicted as too masculine or too feminine, or both (Kimmel 2003, 37–38). The tenets that identities are performative, socially constructed, multiple, and hierarchized constitute a shared understanding of how identities work that grounds my explications of critical race theory and masculinities studies.

CRITICAL RACE THEORY

With those shared understandings of identities in mind, I now turn to the task of summarizing critical race theory. Critical race theory is an interdisciplinary field that draws heavily upon ethnic studies, history, and sociology, among other fields. The editors of the legal academy's most important anthology of critical race theory texts define this school of thought as "challeng[ing] the ways in which race and racial power are constructed and represented in American legal culture and, more generally, in American society as a whole" (Crenshaw et al. 1995, xiii).[14] In this section of the chapter, I will review some tenets of critical race theory.[15]

The first tenet of critical race theory is that it is founded on the need to unpack the ways in which race and other identities are both socially constructed and materially consequential (Cooper 2006b, 148). Race and masculinity, and thus black maleness, do not actually exist. Society "forms" the meanings of identity positions, such as heterosexual black maleness, and people then adopt the practices associated with those positions (Smith 1998, 61). However, the status of being black and male is materially consequential in that it triggers a whole host of stereotypes, such as the angry black man stereotype that I discuss further later. Those stereotypes are materially consequential in that they influence the distribution of social goods (Carbado and Gulati 2000, 1267–70).

A second tenet of critical race theory is the critique of colorblindness. As presently used, colorblindness is a perversion of the first Justice Harlan's statement that "our constitution is colorblind"[16] and Martin Luther King, Jr.'s statement that blacks should be judged by the "content of their character" (Crenshaw et al. 1995, xv). Those statements have been translated into the proposition that merely acknowledging someone's race is invidious racism (Crehshaw et al. 1995, xiv). Accordingly, schools cannot consider how a student's racial identity has negatively affected or enriched her experiences (Hunt 2008, A34). Elsewhere, I have noted that accepting colorblindness seems to be an implicit requirement for black men to be able to advance in corporations (Cooper 2006a, 884). Later in this chapter, I will argue that during the campaign Obama was subject to assimilationist pressure to pretend that race does not matter.

As this focus on how identity characteristics matter suggests, a third tenet of critical race theory is that the racial status quo is often perpetuated by bias that is implicit rather than explicit. Accordingly, Jerry Kang and Mahzarin Banaji apply implicit bias theory to argue that, rather than traditional affirmative action, what we need are "debiasing agents" (Kang and Banaji 2006, 1063, 1066). These are people whose identities contradict biases about who would, and would not, hold certain positions (Kang and Banaji 2006, 1109–11). As a black president, Obama could serve as a debiasing agent for the whole country by changing expectations about what types of people can hold that position.

Taken together, the principles of identity theories in general and these three tenets of critical race theory in particular describe a perspective that can be brought to bear on the question of how black men are understood in popular culture. In my article, "Against Bipolar Black Masculinity: Intersectionality, Assimilation, Identity Performance, and Hierarchy," I critically reviewed scholarship on media representations of black men and found that they depict us as either the completely threatening Bad Black Man or the fully assimilationist Good Black Man. The Bad Black Man is animalistic, sexually depraved, and crime-prone. The Good Black Man distances himself from black people and emulates white views. The images are bipolar in that they swing from one extreme to another with little room for nuanced depictions. Threatened with the Bad Black Man image, black men are provided with an "assimilationist incentive" to pursue the Good Black Man image (Cooper 2006a, 857–58).

I identify race consciousness as a trait of the Bad Black Man because the bipolarity of black masculinity has the purpose of forcing assimilation to the mainstream norm. The assimilationist model makes no room for race consciousness, let alone racial loyalty. Since the default position on black men is that we are bad, we must defeat that presumption to gain mainstream acceptance. While the criminal is the paradigmatic Bad Black Man, the race-conscious black man also fails to defeat that presumption.

Because the default position on black men is that we fit the Bad Black Man stereotype, we are incentivized to demonstrate our assimilation (Cooper 2006a, 887). Race-distancing acts, such as adopting the colorblind stance that one does not even notice the color of the people one interacts with, are ways of performing one's identity that respond to the assimilationist incentive. Such race-distancing in order to assimilate is problematic, though, since it suggests that only blacks who act white deserve mainstream success (Cooper 2006a, 893–95). As a mainstream candidate, Obama would seem to have been especially subject to the assimilationist incentive. I will apply this theory of bipolar black masculinity to Obama later in this chapter by arguing that his feminine style was a choice about how to perform his identity that had strategic benefits.

MASCULINITIES STUDIES

We can best define masculinities studies as the interdisciplinary field that describes the ways assumptions about the meanings of manhood are used to justify particular ideas, behaviors, and institutions (Cooper 2009, note 10, 674). Masculinities studies is interdisciplinary in that it draws heavily upon feminist theory, sociology, and queer theory, among other fields. I will describe the contours of this field by reviewing some of masculinities studies basic tenets.[17]

The first tenet of masculinities studies is that the principal message that masculinity norms send is that masculinity is to be privileged over femininity. A book that I co-edited with feminist employment law scholar Ann C. McGinley provides examples. In *Masculinities and the Law: A Multidimensional Approach*, authors discuss the following topics: how norms about who can be a firefighter erase Asian men; the ways that norms of masculinity influence the behavior of policemen and soldiers; employment discrimination against masculine cocktail waitresses and transgendered employees in general; the contradictions of legal treatment of fathers in the United States, as well as the ways unauthorized migrant fathers use the dangers of border crossing to boost their masculine esteem; how Title IX fails to curtail the masculinity of sport; the racist assumptions behind the prison rape debate; the complicated nature of women veiling in Turkey; and the surprising roots of homophobia in Jamaican dancehall music (Cooper and McGinley 2012). Because of the variety of ways that specific forms of masculinities are themselves influenced by the cultural context and the other identities in play, the book calls for a Multidimensional Masculinities Theory. Here, that means not only noting the invisible privileging of certain norms of masculinity in the fact that Obama was often denigrated for having feminine traits but also attending to the ways that race, age, and other factors influenced the discourse on Obama.[18]

A second tenet of masculinities studies is that men have a constant need to prove to other men that they possess the normative masculinity, which leads to an ongoing masculine anxiety (Kimmel 2003, 33).[19] That is so because the rules of the hegemonic, or dominant, form of masculinity[20] are unrealizable (Kimmel 2003, 31). Manhood is a relentless test of how close you are to the ideal. Men must constantly prove and prove again that they possess the hegemonic form of masculinity (Kimmel 2003, 36). We are thus placed in a state of constant anxiety over our masculinity (Kimmel 2003, 36).

A third tenet of masculinities studies is that norms of masculinity constrain men's performances of their identities. The first constraint on men's identity performances is the need to denigrate contrast figures. As Mutua says, "The central feature of masculinity is the domination and oppression of others; namely women, children, and other subordinated men" (Mutua

2006, 5). Since the idealized figure of the powerful white male is the model for hegemonic masculinity, demonstrating that you fit the hegemonic pattern of U.S. masculinity involves a repudiation of that model's contrast figures, most notably, women, gays, and racial minorities (Mutua 2006, 24–25). Accordingly, during the 2008 presidential general campaign, Obama denigrated Senator John McCain as old ("erratic") (Babington 2008, 3; Rhee 2008, A8; Zuckman and McCormick 2008, C1) and McCain denigrated Obama as effete (Lehrer October 5, 2008, K1; Milbank 2008, A3; Zuckman 2008, C1).

A second constraint on men's identity performance stems from the first: a competitiveness reflected in a need to dominate other men. Behaviors that seek to express dominance over other men, such as aggression, are part of the project of establishing that one possesses the hegemonic form of U.S. masculinity (Collins 2006, 86). Given that hegemonic masculinity is associated with professional status, it might seem strange that a lowbrow quality like aggression is so prized. But as Jewel Woods notes,

> *Despite the economic trend away from blue-collar jobs, many of the most powerful expressions of masculinity within contemporary American society continue to be associated with blue-collar imagery....*
>
> *At the very same time society is becoming less reliant on male brawn, the dominant cultural images of masculinity are largely derived from the "traditional" ideas of maleness. (Woods 2008, 25)*

So, there is a nostalgia for blue-collar aggression. The expectation that a man will display an aggressive demeanor is so pervasive that it stands as a second constraint on men's performances of their identities.[21] This fact was reflected in the many criticisms of Obama for not striking back more aggressively when attacked by Hillary Clinton or McCain, which I will analyze later in this chapter (Dowd 2007, B7; Milloy 2008, note 14, B1; Alkon 2008).

ANALYZING OBAMA'S FEMININITY

As sociologist Michael Kimmel has noted, "From the founding of the country, presidents of the United States have seen the political arena as a masculine testing ground" (Kimmel 1997, 181, 183). It is thus appropriate that a letter to the editor in the *Orlando Sentinel* presented the 2008 presidential general election as a referendum on whether we wanted masculine leadership or feminine leadership. It read: "Now that the actual presidential campaign is under way, we have the traditionally 'masculine' style, embodied by John McCain, emphasizing experience, toughness, feistiness, stubbornness, grit, exclusivity, etc., and the newly emergent 'feminine' managerial style practiced by Obama and emphasizing communication, consensus, collegiality and inclusivity" (*Orlando Sentinel* 2008, A18). Prior to that editorial, the *New York Post* ran an editorial suggesting that Obama would be "our first woman president" (Berrington and Onore 2008). There are more examples of the gendered framing of this race in the media, which I will address later (E. Goodman 2008, B7; Milloy 2008, B1).

Obama was called feminine because of his restraint, calm demeanor, collaborative style, willingness to speak with enemies, and finely honed language (E. Goodman 2008, B7). Those characterizations of Obama as feminine, while melodramatic, did seem to capture real differences between Obama and his opponents. The media has recognized that Obama has "an unusual blend of traditionally masculine and feminine skills at work in him" (Parsons 2008, C1). Further, there is reason to believe Obama's feminization was conscious: Obama's feminine style was unlikely to be accidental given the meticulous planning that goes into every move of a presidential candidate.[22] The media's gendered framing of Obama thus had some basis in Obama's actions.

CRITICAL RACE THEORY AND OBAMA AS A GOOD BLACK MAN

Does the bipolar black masculinity thesis that I described earlier in this chapter apply to the 2008 election? Seemingly, yes. The media has sometimes acknowledged Obama's bipolarity problem. In an article in the *Washington Post*, journalist Courtland Milloy says, "You can walk a fine line between being too black for whites and not black enough for blacks" (Milloy 2008, B1). David A. Frank and Mark Lawrence McPhail illustrate the way Obama has been positioned as a Good Black Man in their article, "Barack Obama's Address to the 2004 Democratic National Convention: Trauma, Compromise, Consilience, and the (Im)Possibility of Racial Reconciliation" (Frank and McPhail 2005, 571–93). They note that at the 2004 Democratic convention, the media contrasted Obama as the Good Black Man against the Reverend Al Sharpton as the Bad Black Man (Frank and McPhail 2005, 576–77, 583–85). Sharpton was a Bad Black Man because he was race-conscious rather than race-distancing. Observers agree that during his presidential run Obama distanced himself from both race in general and past racial minority candidates in particular.[23] He could thus be characterized as playing the Good Black Man role.

As the Good Black Man image would dictate, Obama consistently downplayed his race and avoided racial issues (Cooper 2006a, 887). For instance, David Axelrod, a significant Obama campaign official, was quoted as saying that "we're focusing not on his race but the qualities of leadership that he would bring to this country" (Parsons and McCormick 2008, N1; Page and Risser 2008, 1A; Williams 2008, A1). Such statements are problematic because, in the context of Obama's refusal to mention race even as he made racial history, they suggest that he was engaging in the type of race-distancing acts that the Good Black Man model calls for.[24] That conclusion is supported by the fact that Obama seemingly tied himself to colorblindness (Frank and McPhail 2005, 583–84), another characteristic of the Good Black Man (Cooper 2006a, 884). Obama often said things like, "There's not a black America and white America and Latino America and Asian America—there's the United States of America."[25] Those words are more true than ever, but ignore problematic facts, such as the explosion of racialized hyperincarceration. The statement thus served better as a race-distancing wish than as a depiction of the present.

My analysis of Obama as a potential Good Black Man also seems to be supported by his handling of the controversy over his former pastor, Jeremiah Wright. Obama repudiated Wright because Wright is a symbol of the Bad Black Man by virtue of his race-affirming rather than race-distancing acts. Specifically, Wright has said, "The government gives (black men) drugs, builds bigger prisons, passes a three-strike law and then wants us to sing 'God Bless America'" (Szaniszlo, Mar. 16 2008, 14). Because those statements are highly race-affirming, they raise the Bad Black Man association. As journalist Remnick says, the Obama campaign worried that whites were wondering if "underneath his welcoming demeanor, was he [Obama] like a cartoon version of Wright, full of condemnation and loyal only to his race?" (Remnick 2008, 78). The loyalty question is key, as black men are presumed to be completely race loyal (Cooper 2006a, 891). Obama needed to sever his connections to such a speaker more so than a white politician would have had to sever ties to a white supremacist because the bipolarity of black masculinity makes such associations a sign of a completely bad character. If white masculinity were represented in such a bipolar fashion, McCain could have been subjected to claims that he had a completely bad character. But the media hardly mentioned McCain's ties to Reverend John Hagee, who said that Hitler "was fulfilling God's plan for Jews" (Ressner 2008, B2; Rich 2008, WK12; Scherer 2008, 28).

Having seen the applicability of the bipolar black masculinity thesis, we can now see that Obama's post-racial Good Black Man approach is related to his feminine style. The best example of this is the fact that, as a black man, Obama had to soften his approach or be deemed an angry black man. During the campaign, Milloy said that Obama was being called on to prove he was man enough for the presidency, but "without coming off as an angry black man" (Milloy 2008, B1). That stereotype may be related to the image of black men as overly masculine since anger is an extreme form of the aggressiveness expected of men (Kimmel 2003, 38). People fear that black men will easily lose their tempers and become out of control.[26] *Time* magazine made this point a month before the general election (Klein 2008).

I speculate that Obama's preternaturally calm demeanor originated in his need to counter the stereotype of the angry black man. For instance, Remnick concludes that as an undergraduate, "what Obama did learn in those days was the strategic benefit of a calm and inviting temperament" (Remnick 2008, 71). Obama learned that people like a calm black man; "such a pleasant surprise to find a well-mannered young black man who didn't seem angry all the time."[27] Remnick's statements are consistent with what we know about how young black men are raised. We are often warned to be non-threatening in order to avoid police brutality, which is disproportionately visited upon young black males (Carbado 2002, 953–54). Obama was certainly aware that black men are often viewed as threatening since he mentioned his grandmother's fear of black men during his campaign speech on race (McAuliff and Saul 2008, 9).

My argument is not that Obama was, in fact, an angry black man who hid his anger during the campaign. Rather, I argue that Obama became a calm black man much earlier in life because he learned that angry black men are not acceptable in elite mainstream environments. Further, the reason angry black masculinity is unacceptable is because it is associated with a race-affirming position. For example, even when Obama wanted to infuse race into the conversation, he found that whites would not allow him to do so. As Remnick reports, the campaign noted a decline in Obama's poll numbers after he repeatedly stated that he did not look like the other presidents on U.S. currency during his European tour (Remnick 2008, 78). Obama immediately ceased and desisted from race talk (Remnick 2008, 78). Consequently, Obama's refusal to get angry even in the face of attacks, which contradicts hegemonic masculinity's call for aggressiveness and is a primary basis for his being called feminine, should be deemed to be the result of special constraints on the performance of black male identity. The principal reason Obama was more feminine than other presidential candidates was to avoid a pervasive stereotype associated with the Bad Black Man. As I will demonstrate, however, that feminization strategy came with risks.

MASCULINITIES STUDIES AND THE DANGERS OF OBAMA'S FEMINIZATION

Obama's conundrum was that he had to feminize himself in order not to be seen as an angry black man, but femininity is still a slur. People do not fully believe that women can lead or that feminine styles can show strength (Padilla 2007, 443–85; Radford 1990, 490–91; Rhode 2003, 15–17). Despite his masculine traits, such as being an avid sports fan (Martin January 11, 2009), and his seemingly traditional relationship with his wife Michelle (Parsons 2009, A9),[28] Obama had a feminine style. History professor Estelle Freedman fleshed out Obama's gender problem. She said, "Some of the criticism of Obama as being too aloof or not going after red meat enough or not being aggressive enough are really questioning his masculinity in some ways" (Milloy 2008, B1).[29] So, Obama's restrained style could have proven unacceptable to too many people because it was a break with the masculine style traditionally associated with the presidency.

The masculinities studies tenets I noted earlier elucidate the aspects of Obama's feminine style that proved problematic. First, the privileging of masculinity is clearly seen in the denigration of Obama for his feminine style. For example, MSNBC talk show host Joe Scarborough called Obama "prissy" and insinuated that Obama is not "a real man" because he is not good at bowling.[30] That denigration of Obama's perceived feminine qualities was consistent with hegemonic masculinity's privileging of masculinity over femininity. The persistence of associations between the presidency and masculinity suggests that we still have a long way to go on gender.

Second, we see masculine anxiety in the handwringing about the possibility that an Obama presidency might be a feminized presidency. Recall that a need to prove that one is sufficiently masculine is built into the structure of the hegemonic form of U.S. masculinity. Moreover, many people implicitly expect to be able to bask in the nation's reflected masculinity (Ehrenreich 2005, 132). By virtue of his feminine style, Obama risked failing to satisfy people's needs to soothe their anxiety over our nation's masculinity.

His calmness and openness to negotiating rather than imposing his will made some people worry he was not tough enough to be president (Killian 2007). That anxiousness was gendered.

Third, the criticism of Obama's lack of manliness reflects hegemonic masculinity's constraint of requiring the denigration of contrast figures. Given the need to denigrate contrast figures that inheres in hegemonic masculinity, Obama put his masculinity in question when he acted inclusive rather than exclusive. As I suggested when discussing the constraints on the performance of masculinity, hegemonic masculinity calls on men to reject femininity (Capers 1991, 1171–72; Cohen 1998, 106; Stark 1997, 336). Obama's failure to do so may explain why he was often criticized as unmanly.

Fourth, a further constraint on Obama's performance of his identity is that, given the premium that hegemonic masculinity places on aggressiveness, Obama's empathetic style is anti-masculine (Becker 1999, 21–27; Cohen 2003, 169, 173–75; Lindsay 2005, 345–51). This was reflected in the calls for Obama to be tougher in responding to attacks. The title of one editorial captures the spirit of this criticism: "Where's His Right Hook? Barack Obama seems refreshingly decent. Can he survive hardball politics?" (Dowd 2007, B7). That attitude about Obama's candidacy was reflective of the expectation that men will maintain an aggressive demeanor, especially in the face of attacks. Calls for Obama to be more aggressive were also reflective of Democrats' desires to "fight the last war" by not having their candidate get "swift-boated."[31] But the intensity of the calls for aggressiveness, in conjunction with general calls for Obama to be more manly, suggests that gender, and not just political effectiveness, was at issue.[32]

OBAMA HAD TO BE UNISEX

So, why do I suggest that Obama is our first "unisex" president? Because Obama could not be too masculine, even as he had to prove he was not too feminine. Perhaps, then, Obama's masculinity problem is really a refracted version of his bipolar black masculinity problem. Just as Obama had to navigate between the shoals of blackness and whiteness, he had to position himself as feminine, but not too much so. He had to be unisex.

While there is some implication that a unisex style is one that lacks the characteristics of either sex, I am emphasizing the fact that a unisex style is one that a member of either gender can adopt. Often the term applies to clothing that can be worn by either men or women. The example that comes to mind is the blue jean, which can be masculinized or feminized to suit the wearer's needs on the particular occasion. A unisex style fits between the two genders, but not in the sense of being asexual. Obama was more feminine than most presidential candidates, but hardly non-gendered, like "Pat" from the famous *Saturday Night Live* skit.[33] Obama's style ranged from his tough-guy acceptance speech at the Democratic convention (Marinucci Aug. 29, 2008, A1) to his playing of feminist folk songs at his rallies (Scherer 2007).

Use of the term unisex is especially appropriate in this context because it captures the performative nature of race and gender. If Obama was unisex in the sense that blue jeans are unisex, the strategic nature of his choices of when to act more feminine or more masculine comes into high relief. He sometimes chose to be more feminine than other presidential candidates in order to be racially palatable. He sometimes chose to be more masculine in order to project the ability to be commander in chief. The overall effect was to place him more on the feminine side of the gender continuum that we might expect from a presidential candidate rather than on the more masculine end.

Still, he was hardly feminine compared to the general populace. Rather, he was relatively unisex for the context of a presidential campaign. That his gender performance must be contextualized helps us see that all identity performance is limited by what is intelligible and acceptable to the relevant audience. As McGinley points out, Hillary Clinton, Sarah Palin, and Michelle Obama each performed their identities differently because of ways that aspects of their identities, such as age, ideology, and race, made certain identity stances more or less available to them (McGinley, 2009, 710). For Obama, identity factors impelled him toward a certain unisex style.

CONCLUSION: THE POSSIBILITIES OF A UNISEX PRESIDENCY

The potential for Obama to change what is an intelligible performance of black masculinity has been recognized by black men:

> *For African-American men, Obama has accomplished something even more extraordinary. He has arguably single-handedly transformed the black public sphere. In their eyes, it is no longer "easy" to view black men solely through the lens of deficiencies, bad behavior, their bodies or even their relationship to black women. (Woods 2008, 25)*

In the simplest sense, then, black male identity has already been reconstructed by Obama's success since it is now possible to imagine a black man as a president. In addition to that opening up of images of black men, there may also be a shutting down of images. After Obama, many people's dominant image of black men will be of calmness rather than anger. Obama thus has a debiasing effect on racial stereotypes. This is the racial payoff of Obama's success.[34]

The gender payoff of Obama's success is that it could remove some of the stigma from femininity. Taken together, the tenets of masculinity describe a privileged but anxious status that may constrain men nearly as much as it empowers them. This is why men, who are clearly privileged as a group, sometimes feel disempowered as individuals (Kimmel 2003, 40). This creates a tension in masculinity whereby masculinity is both something people expect you to demonstrate and something some people might want to escape. This may be the genius of Obama's feminization: it allows us to have it both ways on masculinity. While Obama is hardly effeminate, he seems unusually non-anxious about his masculinity. As *Ms.* magazine put it on their cover, perhaps Obama is "what a feminist looks like."[35] He certainly seems to be a man who is comfortable with the fact that he has a feminine side. As a result, the potential is there for Obama's example to allow all men greater movement along the gender continuum.

I would have liked to end this chapter on that positive note. I cannot. As Obama said in response to Florida neighborhood watch captain George Zimmerman's acquittal for stalking and slaying unarmed young black male Trayvon Martin, this country struggles to make young black men believe they matter (Huffington Post July 19, 2013).[36] I agree with Obama's tacit acknowledgement that "there is more that we can do to give them the sense that their country cares about them and values them and is willing to invest in them" (Huffington Post July 19, 2013). I thus believe that we need a comprehensive national campaign to change the profile of black men as always-already-suspect (Cooper 2013, 1204). That campaign needs to have a Mothers Against Drunk Driving type of impact. It should aim to overturn legal principles that allow racial profiling of black men, but also realize that changing cultural norms is the best way to accomplish that result. However, this cultural-legal campaign must not repeat the sexism of earlier black civil rights movements. Here is where Obama's unisex style might help us. Conscious of the multidimensionality of masculinities, we might move toward what Mutua calls "progressive black masculinities" that are not based on the denigration of femininity (Mutua 2006, 7.) Former president Jimmy Carter builds houses; might Obama help rebuild black masculinities? Yes, he can.

Notes

Copyright © 2013, Frank Rudy Cooper. All rights reserved. I thank Ann Brown, Rick Buckingham, Devon Carbado, Eddie Crane, Diane D'Angelo, Tamra Lawson, MyungJin Lee, Lia Marino, Ann C. McGinley, Angela Onwuachi-Willig, Andrew Perlman, Song Richardson, and Jessica Silbey. A version of this chapter appears as "'Our First Unisex President?': Black Masculinity and Obama's Feminine Side" in *Denver University Law Review*. Another version also appears as "Our First Unisex President?: Obama, Critical Race Theory, and Masculinities Studies" in *The Obama Effect: Multidiciplinary Renderings of the 2008 Campaign*.

1. Amy Sullivan 2008, at 36 (quoting Marie Wilson).
2. For more on law and masculinities studies, see Cooper and McGinley 2012.
3. Analyzing masculinity in the presidential contest.
4. In this sense, Obama was engaged in what Carbado and Gulati call a "comforting strategy." Carbado and Gulati, 2000, 1301–04.
5. One could suggest that Obama's style was "metrosexual," but I do not believe that label fits. The term is "generally applied to heterosexual men with a strong concern for their appearance, and/or whose lifestyles display attributes stereotypically attributed to gay men." Wikipedia, http://en.wikipedia.org/wiki/Metrosexual.
6. *Shorter Oxford English Dictonary*, 5th ed., 2002, 3447.
7. "Unisex" means different things for people with different identities. Hillary Clinton's version of going unisex was to wear pantsuits with conservative blouses. See Givhan, 2007. For examples of how Clinton and other prominent women had their identity performances constrained during the 2008 campaign, see McGinley, 2009.
8. I mean "freedom of choice" only in the sense that, with one set of assumptions having been broken down, there seems to be more of a possibility that we can break down other assumptions. I do not mean that we are free in a transcendental sense. I agree with Judith Butler that "freedom" is actually obtained through the repetition of what has come before with a slight difference. See Butler 1997.
9. On race as socially constructed, see, for example, Onwuachi-Willig and Mario Barnes 2005, 1283, 1296. On gender as socially constructed, see, for example, Levit 1996, 1037, 1051.
10. For a nice explication of the differences between intersectionality theory and identity performance theory, see Carbado and Gulati 2001.
11. See "Introduction" to Smith 1996, 1, 3 ("[M]asculinity *is not*; rather, there are only *masculinities* in the plural").
12. In keeping with multidimensionality theory's elaboration upon intersectionality theory, we can say that "given the interconnectedness of patriarch/sexism and racism, among other oppressive systems, black men, as a single multidimensional positionality, are in some contexts privileged by gender and sometimes oppressed by gendered racism." See Mutua 2006, 6.
13. Still, hegemonic authority is exercised by co-opting portions of disparate points of view so as to make the dominant view palatable to a wide range of groups. See Connell and Messerschmidt 2005, 844.
14. For a more recent compilation of articles, legal cases, and other materials, see Perera et al. 2007.

15. These are not nearly all of the tenets of critical race theory, but they are the ones that are relevant to this essay. Some additional projects of critical race theory include the critique of the black-white binary paradigm of race, the critique of the intentional model of discrimination, and exploration of the place of autobiography in critique.
16. *Plessy v. Ferguson*, 163 U.S. 537, 559 (1896) (Harlan, J., dissenting).
17. There are other tenets, but these are the ones most useful to my current project.
18. What makes this privileging of masculinity over femininity all the more insidious is the fact that it has been invisible. When I say masculinities have been invisible, I mean this in the way Barbara Flagg talks about "white transparency." Flagg's point is that whites sometimes operate from perspectives that are widely shared by whites but not widely shared by nonwhites without acknowledging that they are utilizing a particular perspective (Flagg 2001). Similarly, men may often operate from a male perspective while thinking they are operating from a neutral perspective; they may suffer from "masculine transparency." Cooper 2009, note 10.
19. Defining masculinity as "homosocial" in this sense.
20. Kimmel's rules of hegemonic masculinity are (1) never act feminine, (2) accrue power, success, wealth, and status, (3) always hold your emotions in check, and (4) always exude an aura of daring and aggression. Kimmel 2003, 30–31.
21. The expectation of aggression can be thought of as stemming from our "culture of honor." See Cohen and Vandello 2004; Cooper 2009, note 10.
22. Obama may have found it strategic to demonstrate a feminine side to the disproportionately female Democratic electorate.
23. Indiana University, "Two Elephants in the Room," IU News Room, April 10, 2008 http://newsinfo.iu.edu/news/page/normal/7542.html ("Obama . . . is trying to avoid being portrayed as the 'black' candidate") (quoting Larry Hanks).
24. *EUR Political Analysis: Obama Hit for not Mentioning Dr. King's Name During Acceptance Speech*, Electronic Urb. Rep., Sept. 2, 2008. http://www.eurweb.com/story/eur46705.cfm.
25. Farrell 2004, A25 (quoting Barack Obama); Wehner 2008, B7.
26. U.S. Glass Ceiling Commission, Good for Business: Making Full Use of the Nation's Human Capital 71 (1995) (documenting stereotypes of black males as "aggressive," "undisciplined," "violent," "confrontational," "emotional," "hostile," and so on). On stereotyping of black males, see generally Weatherspoon 1998.
27. Remnick 2008 (quoting Obama, *Dreams*, 1995).
28. Of course, this is also about Obama's heteronormativity, which is an important subject that I do not address in this essay.
29. Quoting Estelle Freedman, professor of history, Stanford University.
30. *Morning Joe* (MSNBC television broadcast Mar. 31, 2008), available at http://mediamatters.org/items/200803310007.
31. See, for example, E. J. Dionne, "Finally, Jinxed Month of August is Almost Over," *Charleston (W. Va.) Gazette*, Aug. 23, 2008, 4A (raising the issue of Obama's ability to head-off demonizing attacks).
32. Note, however, that Obama's ability to feminize was bolstered by certain stereotypes. As a man, Obama had more room to feminize without seeming too feminine than female politicians. Moreover, the stereotypes of black men as overly masculine meant people still

took Obama to be sufficiently masculine. As a man, and a black man in particular, Obama had more room to negotiate a partly feminized masculinity.
33. See http://en.wikipedia.org/wiki/Pat_(Saturday_Night_Live).
34. A remaining concern, however, is that Obama may be framed as a special case that proves nothing about the abilities and characters of black men in general.
35. See http://www.msmagazine.com/winter2009/ (showing cover of issue with Obama wearing a "This is what a feminist looks like" T-shirt).
36. See http://www.huffingtonpost.com/2013/07/19/obama-trayvon-martin-speech-transcript_n_3624884.html.

12. "EVERYTHING HIS FATHER WAS NOT"

Fatherhood and Father Figures in Barack Obama's First Term

HEIDI ARDIZZONE

[T]he Barack Obama I know today is . . . the same man who drove me and our new baby daughter home from the hospital ten years ago this summer, inching along at a snail's pace, peering anxiously at us in the rearview mirror, feeling the whole weight of her future in his hands, determined to give her everything he'd struggled so hard for himself, determined to give her what he never had: the affirming embrace of a father's love.[1]
—MICHELLE OBAMA, 2008

If I had a son, he would look like Trayvon [Martin].[2]
—BARACK OBAMA, 2012

"ARE YOU OKAY, BABY?" THE FORTY-FOURTH PRESIDENT OF THE UNITED States coos at the baby fussing in his wife's arms; her back is initially to the camera, obscuring her face and the child. "Oh, no! Oh!" he laughs, as the fussing escalates to loud cries. In a video released by the White House just before Father's Day, 2011, the Obamas are chatting with a small group of mostly white families who laugh sympathetically with their attempts to soothe their temporary charge. As the First Lady starts to return the now loudly unhappy infant, the mother asks instead for a photo with the president. He obligingly reaches out to pull the child against him, and she immediately falls silent, much to the delight of onlookers. Michelle Obama turns to stare in half-outrage as her husband smugly grins back, patting the contented baby's back with a practiced hand.

Much circulated on the Internet and boasting over a million views among the top two copies posted to YouTube,[3] this "crying baby" video both

Figure 1. President Obama comforts a crying baby; this still shot taken from a different angle than the video discussed. (Pete Souza, White House Photographer, June 15, 2011.)

captured and reconfigured the baby kissing photo-op that every political campaign seeks for its candidate. Moreover, it featured a twist that made Barack Obama supporters (and some critics) melt: his immediate success, where his wife had failed, in quieting the child. The apparent soothing nature of the president's touch, dubbed "magic" by several news organizations and bloggers, might have reflected the "Magical Negro" critiques of Obama's political opposition.[4] But here it is his fatherhood on view.

This crying baby video is only one of hundreds of stories and images of Barack Obama with children that have circulated in mainstream press and online communities during the four years of his first term in the White House. Obama is particularly adept at interacting with children, comfortable in the modern role of the nurturing father, whether to his own daughters or to the younger members of audiences at political events. Photographers consistently capture him actively engaged with children: crouching down, leaning in close, making faces.

Obama's reputation as a "baby whisperer" is grounded in his own experience as a father. The looks he exchanges with his wife in the "crying baby" video are all too familiar to partnered couples who share, if not completely equally, the burdens of late-night feedings and capriciously fussy babies. Images of him holding, talking with, or otherwise interacting with children evoke his relationship, past and present, with his own children. And actual images of the Obama family were everywhere during his campaign and first years in office. In the vast majority of these family photos, Obama is in close

Figure 2. The Obama family on election night, 2008. (Carol M. Highsmith Archive, Library of Congress, Prints and Photographs Division.)

physical connection with at least one of his daughters: carrying them when they are young, holding a hand, touching a shoulder, bending down to listen or talk. In both contexts he is performing fatherhood: Obama-as-father and Obama-as-symbolic-father are closely linked.

Obama's performance as a father has also played a role in his political career. His public interactions with children are part of his own self-representation and the political image-making of his campaigns and White House press. Although little academic attention has been paid to this aspect of his presidency, media coverage and popular interest place great emphasis on his role as "father in chief." Obama's ability to embody the nurturing father is particularly significant; visual and textual representations of Obama depict a modern father with a deep connection to his own family and a genuine ease with children. At the same time, these images resonate against a complicated pattern of expectations for fatherhood, for black men and their families, and for dual career couples and parenting. Obama's real and symbolic position as the first First African American father evoke the absence of other black men from the (African) American family:[5] absent fathers and endangered (or dangerous) black boys.

Beyond the frames of images of the happy, healthy, functional Obama family stands a crowd of supposedly "dysfunctional" families that they are not and black men whom he is not. The grim statistics of those men and boys disproportionately unemployed, dropped out, imprisoned, or killed, challenge post-election declarations of America as post-racial. Not only has performing fatherhood become a significant aspect of Obama's political identity, then, but his political fatherhood operates in a crossroads of tensions around economic success and family structures, the shifting and contested expectations for American fathers, and the particular pressures on and scrutiny of African American families in the twenty-first century.

AFRICAN AMERICAN FAMILIES AND PHOTOGRAPHY

In a voice-over against photo and video montages of the new First Family, which introduced a 2009 interview with the president, Harry Smith of CBS News summarized the importance of Obama's fatherhood.

Maybe it was on Election Night when we first realized that not only would there be a new president, but also a new First Family ... a family with young children. Along with the role of commander-in-chief and leader of the free world, Barack Obama would be First Dad. So yes, there would be a swing set. And yes, there would be a dog. He is everything his father is not.[6]

This idealized family picture, with the heterosexual, married couple and their two beautiful biological daughters, a swing set in the yard, a dog running around it, is marred only by the shadow presence of the other father Smith evokes: the father who was not there. Similarly, visual studies scholars have argued that photographs and images contain more than the objects and figures they capture. The literal images within the photograph's frame enter into a relationship with memory, identity, and cultural ideologies. They prompt the viewer to think, reminisce, remember, and reimagine both what is inside and outside the boundaries of the image (Barthes 1981, 53–57; Raiford 2011, 1–28; Romano and Raiford 2006, xi–xxiv). It is in this sense that I consider the absent presence of missing fathers, and eventually sons, in visual and other representations of the Obama family, and Obama's symbolic fatherhood especially. Before examining these absent figures, however, I begin with the significance of depictions of the First Family as they are usually defined: father, mother, daughters.

Commentary on Obama's campaign and early presidency has evinced a particularly "deep fascination" with the Obamas (Ogletree 2011, v). More children's books had been written about Obama before the end of his first year in office than about any other recent president (Nel 2010, 334–35).[7] WorldCat lists over 3,000 non-juvenile books with Obama as the subject, virtually all of them published since 2008. The vast majority of adult books examine his political development, emerging policies, and historic significance. Many, however, also or exclusively focus on his personal story and life.[8] Moreover, popular magazine and news stories, photoessays, and interviews provide a collective "celebration of his own role as father and husband" (McElya 2011, 185). The book sales and family focused articles suggest that the U.S. public is eager to know more about the man whose candidacy and presidency seemed so unlikely for so many reasons.

Lisa Belkin, in the *New York Times* magazine, attributes this popular interest to "a generation of parents obsessed with parenting" who would therefore already be interested in parents coming into the White House.

> *We are intrigued by the first family not only because their children are adorable and so excited about getting a puppy and meeting the Jonas Brothers but also because our president seems to be such a good father.* (Belkin 2009, MM9)

For many who praise his parenting, understanding Obama as a "good father" seems to be the key to understanding him as a man and a politician. His family life perhaps promises to reveal more about him than his political actions. Belkin warns here that Obama's political leadership style might also be "fatherly" and Americans' expectations of him might, to their detriment, become more the expectations for a father, not a president. For others, Obama's fatherhood operates on a different plane from politics. As Fox News' Neil Cavuto put it, "Policies can be debated, but this man's commitment to fatherhood cannot" (Cavuto 2012). The implications or contradictions of fatherhood for the president's particular political views or policies is beyond the scope of this essay, other than to note the many, many times he has cited his daughters as the inspiration or motivation for specific legislation, general political statements, or his very decision to enter politics (Sarlin 2012). Here, I focus on the social and cultural ramifications of Obama's performance of fatherhood: What does it mean to be a "good father"? What does it mean for a black, married, heterosexual father of two young black girls? What does it mean for the president for the United States?

These questions have a social history as well as a visual history. They also convey the hope that this American and black family represent for a better racial future for the nation (Schwarz 2011, 138–55).[9] Barack Obama's positioning as the culmination of African American struggles for civil rights is reflected in his own references to the nation's "better history," to his inauguration as representing the "long time coming ... change."[10]

But in the context of a century of African American family portraits, Obama family photographs come into conversation with a longer movement of struggle for upward mobility, inclusion, and equality. Whether created for private display or public exhibition, these portrayals collectively countered popular stereotypes of laziness, sexual deviance, and inferiority. In both historical and contemporary contexts, black fathers and black families have been sites of external criticism, scrutiny, and public policies, as well as internal tensions (Baskerville 2002, 695–99; Connor and White 2007, 2–8). These family photographs presented a silent illustration of the ongoing collective claim to social equality: Americanness without the erasure of blackness. Drawing on middle-class conventions of family structure and gender roles within it, the images highlighted heterosexual married couples and their children (Gaines 1996, 195–213; Mitchell 2004, 108–72, 218–40). Most relevantly, generations of African Americans have used the visual racial text of photography to emphasize their ability to fit American gender and family norms, and therefore their suitability for full citizenship.

At the turn of the twentieth century, W. E. B. Du Bois and Booker T. Washington both used family photographs that conveyed these dynamics in remarkably similar ways, despite these leaders' very different approaches to addressing racial inequities in the U.S. Both Washington's use of photographs in his *A New Negro for a New Century*, and Du Bois's set of albums brought to the 1900 Paris Exhibition's American Negro Exhibit, emphasized heterosexual marriage as the basis of the family unit, women's roles as wives and mothers, and men's ability to provide for their wives and children (Ross 2004, 66–68; Smith 2004, 44–63). As professional photographers, artists, advertisers, social scientists, and activists, African Americans in the early- to mid-twentieth century continued to rely on this particular definition of family, and a presentation of gendered parental and marital roles (Ross 2004, 1–3, 12–13; Summers 2003, 1–15). For these generations, personal presentation through respectable dress and behavior as well as professional and social accomplishments was a political statement.

African American family photographs of the early- to mid-twentieth century also employed similar photographic conventions to those Du Bois and Washington used in their highly public presentations. For example, Caroline Bond Day collected hundreds of family photos throughout the 1920s as part of her data for an anthropological study of "Negro-White Families" (Ardizzone 2006, 106–132; Day 1930, 3–11). Although Day took many individual portraits herself, most of the hundreds of photographs she included in her study were personal family photos her subjects lent to her. Their emphasis on presenting the "functional black American family" followed consistent patterns across generations and families. Women with carefully coiffed hair and stylish gowns or dresses. Mothers holding their children. Fathers standing behind the family unit. Girls and boys in formal dress, clean and unrumpled. Men in military uniform. Backgrounds revealing an ample porch, a well-furnished room, artwork, automobiles, houses. Handsome. Beautiful. American. For Day's families, their black ancestry was not always obvious in their physical appearance, but she claimed political and social identities as "Negroes" for them and for herself.[11]

Like Caroline Bond Day and her subjects, Barack Obama has not always been accepted or recognized as unambiguously black. Throughout his short political career, Obama's public and social identity has been clearly marked, as the essays in this volume attest, by his biracial ancestry and his identification as both black and mixed. He has also been shaped by his experiences as a brown-skinned boy raised by white Americans in Hawai'i, then Indonesia, then as a black man in the United States, and as the husband of Michelle Obama, an African American woman.

Scholars and pundits alike have made much of this slippery, contested terrain of Obama's racial identity, focusing on his own family and background: Obama has been heralded as symbolizing a multicultural global society and a post-racial turn for the United States by virtue of his multiracial ancestry. At the same time, these experiences and connections (the Muslim Kenyan father, an Indonesian stepfather, and a childhood spent mostly in Hawai'i and Indonesia) are seen as incompatible with American citizenship and identity. In this context, Obama's racialization as black places him back within a familiar and very American context. His earlier experiences and writings emphasized his multiracial identity, and he continues to acknowledge this ancestry and celebrate his multiethnic extended family. But he has increasingly identified as black, culminating in the public announcement of his choice to only check "Black, African American or Negro" rather than add one or more additional categories in the 2010 federal census.[12] As black or African American, Obama becomes a more familiar other for white American voters.

While his family of origin has marginalized Barack Obama, the First Family further solidifies his identity as, or at least with, African Americans. His marriage to an African American woman, and their co-parenting of two beautiful young black girls, performs important political work for a candidate and president whose identity is so unexpected and difficult to simplify into a sound bite. Framed together they are a visually black family, and Barack Obama becomes unambiguously black. Their darker, slightly varied skin tones shade his into a shared palette. Beautiful. Handsome. Black. American (Schwarz 2011, 139).[13]

Obama's wife and children further normalize him for some who see his African Muslim father and his Hawaiian birth as marginal or even incompatible with American identity.[14] A descendent of slaves, raised by two black parents in a working-class home in Chicago, Michelle Obama's family background and connections root him, through her, to mainstream African American history and culture. At times, this role became conscious and explicit. In a popular campaign speech, she playfully acknowledged her own doubts about the man who had to ask her out several times before she said yes:

> *I've got nothing in common with this guy. He grew up in Hawaii! Who grows up in Hawaii? He was biracial. I was like, okay, what's that about? And then it's a funny name, Barack Obama. Who names their child Barack Obama? (Slevin 2007, C01)*[15]

By naming all the ways her husband appears outside the frame of Americanness, Michelle Obama consciously sought to address and counter those fears. Also navigating her own path through the images of her as an angry black woman and a radical, she was adept at reassuring her audiences that her husband was worthy of her, and their, attentions, despite his atypical name, his unusual pedigree, and his non-continental American birth. It was the same message that she gave in her speech at the Democratic National Convention, cited at the top of this piece. There she invited the nation to picture her husband slowly driving her and their newborn daughter home for the first time, "feeling the whole weight of her future in his hands . . . determined to give her what he had never had."[16] Sandwiched between a recitation of the campaign's progress from Iowa and the future election, this vignette promised the same concern and determination to the country under the care of Malia and Sasha's father. The girls joined their mother on stage, and their father appeared on a screen behind them. Barack, Michelle, Malia, and Sasha: the ideal American family unit.

NURTURING FATHERS, PRESIDENTIAL FATHERS, AND ABSENT BLACK MEN

Michelle and Barack Obama were hardly the first presidential couple to bring their children to the White House. Fatherhood and the presidency have a long entwined history: most presidents have also been fathers (Quinn-Musgrove and Kanter 1995, xxiii, xxiv). Other presidents married strong women, were closely invested in their children's lives, and struggled with raising children in front of cameras while dealing with overwhelming national crises and international turmoil. First Families—especially those with young children growing up in the White House—have always been a source of interest to the American public.

Nor has Obama been the first sitting president to focus on fathers and fatherhood in politics or in policies. The 1965 Moynihan report famously linked African American urban poverty to the "pathology" of female-headed households and urban violence and crime to fatherless families. In the context of Lyndon Johnson's War on Poverty, extended in many ways by Richard Nixon, national success became linked to family structure and gendered parenting in federal policy and the racial rhetoric surrounding it. Such associations between blackness, poverty, and absent fathers, continued to shape federal welfare policies of the 1990s and early twenty-first century, perhaps most notably the 1996 welfare reforms under the Clinton administration (Cott 2002, 221–23; Roberts 1998, 145–62). Clinton also introduced the President's Fatherhood Initiative, which emphasized the importance of American men as active and present fathers within a "healthy marriage," in order to address poverty, education, and national values. Clinton followed up with a Responsible Fatherhood Initiative in 2000, focused on promoting employment to boost enforcement of child support payments. George W. Bush continued the RFI, building on the Texas Fatherhood Initiative he claimed credit for as governor. During his term as president, Bush's father-focused policies emphasized faith-based and marriage-based initiatives, many of which Obama has continued. These fatherhood initiatives have had explicitly race-based rhetoric and policy goals, often aimed at black families and fathers (Weaver 2012, 297–309). In 2009, Obama also created a Task Force for Responsible Fatherhood and Healthy Families. These programs, part of a growing "fatherhood responsibility" movement of the 1990s (Gavanas 2004, 247–66), signaled a turn for Obama's performance of political and social fatherhood. In this context, Obama's success at fatherhood also serves to further distance himself from the bad fathers that pervade popular images of black men in the United States, including his own absent father.

Over the same four or five decades of increasing federal attention to fathers as a key to solving economic and social problems, the model of the male breadwinner father has declined in American society. In the wake of economic need for most households to have two incomes and feminist shifts in women's roles, the "nurturing father" or the "involved father" has emerged as a new model (Kellan 2008, 1172–75; Lewis 2001, 152–54; Marks and Palkovitz 2004, 113–29). This is not to say that the good provider husband and father, paired with the stay-at-home wife and mother, has disappeared: it still describes the economic division of labor of approximately one quarter of American households since 2000 (Kreider and Elliot 2010, 7–8). Compatible with an array of employment patterns, nurturing fathers might also be breadwinners, part of a dual-career couple, or stay-at-home dads. The expectation that fathers, regardless of their economic role in the household, should see their primary role as the caretaking of their children, prioritizing an emotional relationship with them, emerged in the 1970s and 1980s (Coltrane 1996, 3–7, 51–83; Lamb 1987, 3–17). The male-breadwinner/female-homemaker couple also survives as an ideology: a set of ideas about gender, work, marriage, and parenting, which define an ideal against which other practices might be judged (Cott 2004, 3, 93; Cunningham 2008, 300–302). But recent work emphasizes the increased obstacles posed by labor downturns, even before the 2008 economic crises that preceded Obama's election and quickly eclipsed his campaign priorities to shape his presidency (Williams 2008, 488). The attention to Obama as a father also coincides with the aftermath of an economic crash that led to increased unemployment and underemployment, overrepresented in traditionally male jobs. Regardless of the specific economic and political issues he has faced in office, however, the president sits at the crossroads of rhetoric about the problems of black fatherhood and changing expectations for the behavior of men who are present in their children's lives.

Married in 1992, with their daughters born in 1998 and 2001, Michelle and Barack Obama reflect this shift and the lingering significance of the breadwinner ideal in their co-parenting style. When the girls were very young, Michelle Obama also worked full time and felt the burden of the "second shift" of unpaid domestic and child care work that falls to the vast majority of employed American mothers (Hoshchild and Machung 1989, 238–49, 415–23). And both have been honest about the difficulties she faced, working full time and raising two young girls.

Both Obamas are also unapologetically modern in their understanding of the gendered and ungendered nature of parenting. As his rising political career increased time away from home, she made a series of sacrifices to her career in order to offset his absences. This resulted in a very traditional-looking division of labor, but the meaning they give to it is hardly traditional. While avoiding the label "feminist," Michelle Obama is very clear that she expects her husband to participate in the most mundane aspects of parenting as well as remain emotionally connected to the family despite his grueling schedule. And she understands her willingness to take the role she has as situational, not gender-determined: "someone has to be focusing on the kids—and that's me. But it could easily be him. There's no reason why the nurturing has to come from Mom—it just has to be there" (Salvatore 2008, 3).

While the division of labor with the children is clearly quite traditional, Obama continues the model of the nurturing, involved father. He phones or video-chats with his daughters from the road, schedules family time, even coaches Sasha's soccer team. "The president manages to strike a balance between leading our country and spending time with his family," Ron Kirk told *Jet* magazine, "and that is something we all can learn from."[17] Kirk further specified that Obama's example of "active" fathering was particularly pertinent for African American men, a qualification Obama would probably agree with. "I resolved many years ago that it was my obligation to break the cycle," he explained in his 2008 Father's Day speech. Being "a good father to my girls" would become his priority.[18] And, as we have seen, the definition of good fatherhood has expanded.

During his first term in office, Barack Obama has been very outspoken about the problems he sees facing families in the United States, especially in the black community. While scores of sociological studies challenge a direct association of "single mother" with "dysfunction," Obama himself has been quick to identify "missing" fathers as the source of many other problems. His "More Perfect Union" speech cited "a lack of economic opportunity among black men, and the shame and frustration that came from not being able to provide for one's family" as contributing to "the erosion of black families."[19]

His controversial 2008 Father's Day speech before the African American Apostolic Church of God in Chicago went even further. After praising the important work that fathers were doing, he also chastised the "too many fathers" who were "missing from too many lives and too many homes. They have abandoned their responsibilities, acting like boys instead of men. And the foundations of our families are weaker because of it."[20] Such statements have earned mixed responses. Most criticisms focus on his failure to identify or directly address the contexts for those failures: the sustained patterns of discrimination and racism, poverty and lack of resources, opportunities, and support. And, add Mark and Roger McPhail, "the fundamental contradiction of being on the one hand denied one's personhood, and on the other expected to be a 'man'" (McPhail and McPhail 2011, 680).

Still, Obama's focus on responsible, engaged fatherhood within black communities has also garnered widespread support. *Jet* magazine published a story titled "America's Favorite Family Man: How Obama is Restoring the Image of African American Males," which highlighted Obama's consistent messages to fathers to be more active and more nurturing, but also emphasized the significance of his own marriage and parenting as a model for black men.[21] Juan Williams also wrote approvingly about the speech and praised the father in chief as a "national treasure . . . the fact that he is a good father who leads a black family is even more important because the rate of absentee fathers in the black and Hispanic community amounts to a national crisis (Williams 2011, 488).

His hard stance on absent fathers appealed to conservatives who otherwise found little in his policies to approve of. The *National Review*, for example, praised Obama's Father's Day message the following year. Noting that the president was "now in a unique position to shape black attitudes toward marriage and fatherhood," the magazine cited his speech approvingly: "We need fathers to realize that responsibility does not end at conception. We need them to realize that what makes you a man is not the ability to have a child—it's the courage to raise one" (Currie 2009, 27–28).

Images of Obama as a father also range from neutral to assertively pro-Obama. There is a wealth of negative, anti-Obama imagery, some of it horrifically racist. However, his fatherhood rarely comes up in more mainstream attacks. There are some exceptions, of course. Bishop Harry R. Jackson, for example, criticized Obama's recent public support of same-sex marriage, quite predictably given Jackson's connections to the anti-gay rights Family Research Council. And Jackson particularly scolded Obama for failing to act as a proper father by teaching his daughters the moral arguments against homosexuality. Instead, Obama had allowed the roles to be reversed, letting himself be swayed by the girls' acceptance of their friends' same-sex parents. Despite this criticism of Obama's failure to maintain his most basic "father knows best" authority, Jackson carefully couched his comments in praise for the president "as a family man." He admired the "healthy family practices" that the First Family models, and called Obama "the nation's father in chief!"[22]

It is also worth noting Kevin Williamson's mocking comments that Obama's failure to have biological sons suggested a failure of his masculinity and leadership abilities (Williamson 2012). Written during the second election cycle, Williamson's satirical point was to compare Obama unfavorably to Republican presidential nominee Mitt Romney, who had five sons and far more grandsons than granddaughters. Through a combination of allusion to the biblical patriarchs and evolutionary psychology, Williamson concluded the Romney was clearly biologically the superior man and leader. The target of the joke was not only Obama, who had won the damning label of effeminate before for his quiet tone, his intellectualism, and his liberalism. The target was also femaleness itself. In the logic of the humor, sons were clearly superior to daughters.

But, in the run-up to the 2008 election, the girls' age and their gender probably helped their father's image as safely domesticated husband and father. Sasha (Natasha) and Malia Obama were seven and ten, respectively, when they attended their father's 2008 inauguration. In a gender analysis of presidential children from Lyndon Johnson to Chelsea Clinton, Lori Cox Han concluded that daughters garnered "an overwhelming amount" of the media coverage, relative to sons (Han 2004, 160). Those daughters, however, were significantly younger than the sons and six of them married while their fathers were in office. As many news reports noted, Amy Carter at nine and Chelsea Clinton at twelve were the closest in age to the Obama daughters in recent history. In the twentieth century, only the Kennedys had younger children when they moved into the White House.[23]

Sasha is now eleven; her father recently won a new round of praise when he announced he is assistant coach for her basketball team (Cavuto 2012; Simon 2011). Malia has since reached fourteen, a tall slender athletic girl who is not yet allowed to date. Nor is she likely to, if her father follows through on his recent jokes that a second term in the White House will allow him to keep her surrounded by "men with guns" and allow him to intimidate prospective dates by meeting them in the Oval Office.[24] Video and photographs of the family at their late-hour 2012 election night appearance provided visual evidence of how much the younger Obamas had grown in the four years of their father's first term.

On a personal level, Barack Obama does not seem to experience his lack of sons as a lack at all. When asked about the possibility of sons, which he has been on several occasions, he has never expressed a desire for one, although he acknowledges that boys are "generally" different from girls "in some ways."[25] The question implies the same assumption as the Williamson piece: that sons are better than daughters, or at least preferred by men. In public statements, Obama has made it clear that he could envision one of his daughters following in his footsteps and having a political career. Given his understanding of gender, there is not much that a son could do that a daughter might not do as well.

In many ways, images of Sasha and Malia have continued the political work of literature and iconography of the black girl as the innocent, non-threatening representative of her race. Numerous scholars have highlighted the real and imagined dangers of sexuality, especially vulnerability to violence that haunt cultural images of black girls (Collins 2002, 112–17). But the Obama girls "carry us forward to a promise . . . which encompasses hope, not only for black America but for all of us" (Schwarz 2011, 144).

But let's consider Obama's shadow sons. If his daughters are the most visible promise of a better America, then where are black boys in that imagined future? How would a fourteen-year-old son in the White House fit into the visual text of the First (African American) Family? Into the acceptance of them as beautiful? Black? American? Neither Obama nor the scholars, journalists, political pundits, and other onlookers have had nearly as much to say about these missing boys as they have the missing fathers. But on a few well-publicized occasions, Obama has reached out to a symbolic son: several times captured in a photograph or video, the other posthumously in the midst of national debate. These moments do not seem to have captured public attention to the same extent as the crying baby video did. They are harder to watch and hear, demand more difficult reckonings then watching the Obamas compete to quiet a white female infant.

Just a few months before the crying baby video, White House photographer Pete Souza caught another image that was both official and spontaneous. It is tradition for departing staff members to bring their families for an introduction and photograph with the president. Five-year-old Jacob Philadelphia took advantage of the opportunity to ask a question that surprised his parents. He wanted to know "if my hair is just like yours." In reply, Obama bent his head down to the boy and invited him to "touch it and see for yourself ... Touch it, dude!" In the image, the president appears to be bowing down to the child who reaches up gingerly to touch his head. Despite the snapshot-like composition of the photograph, Souza chose it to display in the administrative offices. "That one became an instant favorite of the staff. I think people are struck by the fact that the president of the United States was willing to bend down and let a little boy feel his head."[26] Souza's interpretation of this image's popularity speaks to the significance of Obama's ability to extend his fatherhood to other people's children, here putting aside the formality of his position to invite the intimacy of a touch on the head.[27] As a black man, such intimacies must be carefully negotiated, and both Obamas are practiced at doing just that. But in this context Obama is authenticating his blackness to a child who needs to know that "his" hair could grow on the head of the president. For Jacob and his parents, the experience was undoubtedly about affirming that the president was black, like him, and therefore that his accomplishments were possible for other black children. Three years later, the boy reported that he wanted to be president when he grew up—or fly. Becoming an astronaut was a close second option.[28]

The second example is far more devastating. In February 2012, a self-assigned neighborhood watchman shot and killed an unarmed seventeen-year-old black boy he believed was "up to no good." When reports started circulating a few weeks later that police had not brought charges against George Zimmerman, outrage began to mount. Trayvon Martin's death, in his own neighborhood, on his way home from buying candy and a soft drink, came on the heels of too many stories and personal experiences of official and unofficial harassment of young black men.[29]

Obama had not been very successful in his previous attempts to comment on examples of racial discrimination during his first term in office.[30] He had made no comments on New York City police's "stop and frisk" practices, which studies had shown predominantly targeted young black men. He had not addressed the heightened scrutiny of black communities that contributed to higher rates of traffic stops, arrests for petty crimes. As we have seen, his more recent speeches about missing fathers had glossed over or ignored the systemic "whys" often behind their absence. But when he made a statement on the Trayvon Martin case, he connected himself directly to the situation by claiming Martin as symbolic family. After expressing condolences to Martin's parents, Obama somberly stated, "If I had a son, he would look like Trayvon Martin."[31] Amidst official scrutiny into how local Florida police had handled the case, this read to some activists as far too weak a statement. The wave of hooded protesters taking to the literal and social media streets demanding justice for Martin wanted more from the first black father in chief. But Obama's simple statement had complicated, and potentially transformative implications.

Obama's absent sons are the canaries in the coal mine of American racialism. It is to the statistical fates of black boys and young men that scholars turn first to when countering the hopeful claims that Obama's election marked a national turn to a "post-racial." The high school dropouts, the murdered, the imprisoned, the African American boys and young men "missing" from society: these are the brutal facts that remind us how far from post-racial we are (Neal 2005, 1–3; Gaines 2010, 197–99; Sugrue 2010, 83–91; Joseph 2010, 213–22). In the controversy that developed around the Martin-Zimmerman case two very different images of the young boy emerged: in one he was a violent young thug, exactly the sort of delinquent or criminal that Zimmerman was justified in targeting as suspicious. In the other he was a victim of the racialization of criminality as black, of the systematic hyperscrutiny and policing of young black men: a middle-class kid with no serious trouble or record.[32]

Obama's interactions with black boys and his statement on Trayvon Martin's death have not translated into policy changes, nor were they likely ever intended to.[33] Still, by simply inviting Americans to imagine Trayvon as his son (Handsome, Beautiful, Black, American), Obama invited young black men into the imagined framework of his family—a family he defines as representing our whole nation. In short, he invited us to do the same for all young black boys who could be seen as dangerous and threatening simply by being who they were.[34] For some of us, of course, those children are our literal sons. For Obama's employment of political fatherhood and family, they belong to all of us, and we to them.

This, I would argue, is the more realistic hope then "post-racialism" for what might emerge in the aftermath of the Obama administration. New definitions of racial and ethnic categories have come and gone before. Immigration and intermixing have shaped and reshaped seemingly consistent categories like "white" and "black" for generations. Racism has proven its ability to outlast legalized segregation and structures of overt discrimination. Collapsing the "double consciousness" of Du Bois is not a matter of African Americans coming to see themselves as simultaneously black and American: that is not new either. Rather, it is this ability to see each other as family, as connected, especially the ability of whites to simultaneously acknowledge race and make those connections across it.

For now, however, this inclusive reframing of the nation-family has not happened. So far Obama has only brought missing black boys and fathers back in rhetorical and limited ways. Furthermore, as Obama would have learned from some of his Harvard law school training at the height of the development of critical race theory, legal systems cannot control racism. Nor can presidents.

Notes

My thanks to all my students at Saint Louis University, but especially to Mark Koschmann, Jacqueline Kutnik-Bauder, Melissa Ford, Maya Rao, and Chelsea Jaeger for discussions of scholarship on and writings by Barack Obama in spring 2012. Alan Blair assisted with references and photographs; colleagues Lorri Glover, Nadia Brown, and especially Torrie Hester provided helpful critiques of drafts.

1. Michelle Obama, speech given at the Democratic National Convention, August 25, 2008.
2. Barack Obama, statement on Trayvon Martin, March 23, 2012, http://whitehouse.blogs.cnn.com/2012/03/23/president-obama-statement-on-trayvon-martin-case/.
3. "Crying Baby No Match for Obama," CNN, June 22, 2011, http://www.youtube.com/watch?v=l6k6kIrTAGk. The high-volume posts of the video include http://www.youtube.com/watch?v=uqhzWlqN3uc (over 975,000 by November 10, 2012); http://www.youtube.com/watch?v=-uNoNnoKjZA (over 700,000 by November 10, 2012).
4. The "Magical Negro" trope was first applied to Obama by black liberal columnist David Ehrenstein (Ehrenstein 2007). But it was immediately taken up by political opposition, most notably with Rush Limbaugh's repeated airing of a song parody "Barack the Magical Negro," which was included in a campaign CD by would-be Republican Party National Chair Chip Saltsman. In the weeks following its release, copies of this thirty-second clip circulated on blogs, online news, and social media. It was also featured on major network newscasts and became the zen moment at the end of Jon Stewart's *Daily Show*. "Moment of Zen: Barack Obama Calms a Crying Baby, June 21, 2011; abcnews.com, June 21, 2011; "President Obama Can Charm Even a Hysterically Crying Baby," http://www.huffingtonpost.com/2011/06/21/obama-baby-crying_n_881288.html
5. Although I will use these terms largely interchangeably in this essay, they are not synonymous. Obama's own parentage does not fit the primary definition of African Americans as those Americans descended from West African slaves who arrived in the colonial or early United States by the early nineteenth century. This discrepancy, along with his mixed ancestry, fueled debates early in his campaign over his "legitimacy" as either black or African American.
6. "Father-in-Chief," Harry Smith interview with Barack Obama, *The Early Show*, CBS, June 22, 2009.
7. Philip Nel's analysis of these books compared to those of previous, recent presidents concludes that books about Obama for children are measurably more positive and embracing:

all but one "embrace him as 'ours.'" Furthermore, "attempts to reify Obama as an ideal American collide with his more complex history, sometimes even effacing his race."
8. No one has yet taken on the massive study these books would require, although analyses of individual and groups of them abound. John Avlon of *The Daily Beast* has been tracking Obama-hating books and counts eighty-nine "obsessively anti-Obama books" published by fall 2012, from a previous count of 46 in 2010. "The Obama-Haters Bookclub: The Canon Swells," *Daily Beast*, October 26, 2012, http://www.thedailybeast.com/articles/2012/10/26/the-obama-haters-book-club-the-canon-swells.html.
9. Schwarz is the only example I have found of a scholar analyzing Obama family photographs. He does so against a remembered past of African American disenfranchisement and activism, especially children's activism, in the mid-twentieth century.
10. Barack Obama, inauguration speech, January 2, 2009.
11. Day was the first African American woman to get a graduate degree in anthropology at Harvard University. Because of Day's focus on mixed-race families, the visual representation of blackness was not always obvious. Although none of the families she depicted were passing as white, about a third of them had relatives who did, and many had physical features that were ambiguous. In their dress, posture, tableaus, and use of middle-class possessions in the background, however, there was no difference between darker and lighter African American families' self-portrayals.
12. This was almost certainly the first time a sitting president has ever made a public statement regarding how he filled out personal demographic information on a federal census. The fact that the White House issued such a statement reflects the continued debate over the relationship between Obama's ancestry and his identity.
13. Schwarz also notes the close gradations of skin tone among the Obamas, but not in the context of Obama's contested blackness.
14. It is not within the scope of this chapter to consider the range and scale of racist and other negative images of Barack Obama that have circulated before and during his first term. Here, I am interested in his ability to be accepted as both African American and American enough to win two elections despite his outsiderness, both real and imagined, and despite very strong economic and political criticism from both the left and the right.
15. Slevin is quoting from a campaign speech in Iowa.
16. Michelle Obama, speech given at the Democratic National Convention, August 25, 2008.
17. Ron Kirk (U.S. trade representative) quoted in Chapell 2009, 8.
18. Obama, Father's Day Speech, Apostolic Church of God on Chicago's South Side, June 22, 2008.
19. Obama, "A More Perfect Union," March 2008.
20. Obama, June 22, 2008.
21. *Jet*, June 22, 2009, Cover.
22. Harry R. Jackson, "Father in Chief—Or Just Another Politician," June 19, 2012, http://www.thetruthinblackandwhite.com/Weekly_Column/?Father_in_Chief_Or_Just_Another_Politician&year=2012. While it is beyond the scope of this chapter to analyze comments on the many online newstories, photoessays, and videos I examined, I will note that it was quite common to find responses that stated both an opposition to Obama's politics, but an admiration for either him as a father or with children in general.

23. Political pundits made many comparisons between Obama and Kennedy during the 2008 election campaign, their youth and young families being just one of them. Just as they had during the Kennedy administration, White House and media photographers delight in finding formal and informal opportunities to catch the First Couple in their role as parents. Caroline Kennedy was three and her brother John, Jr., an infant at their father's inauguration, making them a truly unique First Family. Amy Carter and Chelsea Clinton would make better potential comparisons, particularly considering Obama's second term. Such an analysis, however, would have to take into account changes in both media technologies and behaviors as well as shifting and racialized expectations for girls and young women. Very few non-fathers have served as U.S. President, and none since the Kennedy administration. Johnson, Ford, and G. W. Bush had older teenagers or young adults; Nixon, Reagon, and G. H. W. Bush had adult children who were no longer living with them.
24. Obama, *Good Morning America*, June 16, 2011, http://abcnews.go.com/Politics/president-obama-opens-fatherhood-anthony-weiner-scandal-american/story?id=13862014.
25. Ibid. This question came from a "Little League Father" of two boys.
26. Quotes from "Indelible Image of a Boy's Pat on the President's Head," *New York Times*, May 23, 2012. See also Stebner 2012.
27. Jonathan Capehart wrote about this image in the context of African American experiences of their hair and white curiosity and interest in it. *Washington Post*, May 42, 2012.
28. *New York Times*, May 24, 2012, http://www.nytimes.com/2012/05/24/us/politics/indelible-image-of-a-boys-pat-on-obamas-head-hangs-in-white-house.html.
29. For summaries of the Martin case see Blow 2012; Macky 2012.
30. The most famous of these was the "Beergate" episode prompted by the arrest of Harvard scholar Henry Louis Gates. (Ogletree, vii, Joseph, 8).
31. Barack Obama, Statement on Trayvon Martin, March 23, 2012.
32. Elspeth Reeve offers a comparison of the photographs of Trayvon (or initially reported to be of him) on liberal and conservative blogs in the weeks after the case went national. "What Did Trayvon Look Like? That Depends on Your Politics," *The Atlantic Wire*, March 30, 2012, http://www.theatlanticwire.com/politics/2012/03/what-did-trayvon-look-depends-your-politics/50570/.
33. As I was completing final edits on this essay, the Sandy Hook shootings have prompted a renewed attempt at federal reforms to gun control.
34. At the time of this writing, the Zimmerman case is pending trial and much conflicting information about what happened that night has emerged. Zimmerman claims Martin attacked him, and there is some physical evidence that the two fought. But there is no doubt that Zimmerman followed Martin for blocks before the physical confrontation, frightening the teenager, and ignoring police requests to stop tailing his "suspect."

PART IV

RACE, POLITICS, AND THE OBAMA PHENOMENON

13. BARACK OBAMA'S ADDRESS TO THE 2004 DEMOCRATIC NATIONAL CONVENTION

Trauma, Compromise, Consilience, and the (Im)Possibility of Racial Reconciliation

DAVID A. FRANK AND MARK LAWRENCE McPHAIL

The two authors of this chapter offer alternative readings of Barack Obama's July 27, 2004, address to the 2004 Democratic National Convention (DNC) as an experiment in interracial collaborative rhetorical criticism, one in which they "write together separately." David A. Frank judges Obama's speech a prophetic effort advancing the cause of racial healing. Mark Lawrence McPhail finds Obama's speech, particularly when it is compared to the Reverend Al Sharpton's DNC speech of July 28, 2004, an old vision of racelessness. Despite their different readings of Obama's address, both authors conclude that rhetorical scholars have an important role to play in cultivating a climate of racial reconciliation.

ILLINOIS STATE SENATOR BARACK OBAMA'S KEYNOTE ADDRESS TO THE 2004 Democratic National Convention marked an important moment in the trajectory of African American rhetoric. His speech earned two reasonable responses, one upward-inflected and the other downward-inflected (Robeson, Jr. 2004, 13; Kaplan 2004; Tilove 2004a; Tilove 2004b). For one of the authors of this essay, David A. Frank, Obama articulates a post–civil rights rhetoric intended to bring the various components of his composite audience (an audience "embracing people differing in character, loyalties, and functions") into rapprochement (Perelman and Olbrechts-Tyteca 1969, 21).[1] The core value at the center of Obama's speech is the essential equality of created individuals, and the mood he sought to cultivate is one of "audacious hope." Working from these foundations, Obama nests the traumas of slavery and racism with those suffered by American workers lacking a living wage and affordable healthcare, the bigotry faced by gays and Arab Americans, and an America in the wake of 9/11. Commencing from these disparate traumas, Obama encourages his composite audience to walk the path of commonality, and in the process, offers a *rhetoric of consilience*, an approach in which disparate members of a composite audience are invited to "jump together" out of their separate experiences in favor of a common set of values or aspirations.[2]

Obama's *rhetoric of consilience* can foster reconciliation. It also is the symbolic strategy of what Mark Lawrence McPhail terms "coherence" (a conscious understanding and integration of difference in order to transform division) because it acknowledges that many members of his composite audience have and are suffering from shared and unique traumas that can be worked through with multiracial and class coalitions appealing to the ideal of justice. In contrast to the Reverend Al Sharpton's speech, which emphasized the African American trauma, Obama's rhetoric of *consilience* offers an effective discursive strategy for working through the trauma of slavery and segregation, emphasizing the essential nature of human equality and the need for multiple agencies of responsibility and action.[3] It thus has the potential of moving Americans beyond the complicity of racial division and toward coherent reconciliation.[4]

For author Mark Lawrence McPhail, Obama's speech offers little hope for reconciling an America divided by racial difference and indifference. Compared to the Reverend Sharpton's speech, Obama's message ignored and obscured America's racial realities, and even though both men expressed faith in an idealized America, just the mention of racial issues earned Sharpton the dubious (dis)honor of "having hijacked the convention" (Crenshaw 2004). Both speeches reflect, albeit differently, what W. E. B. Du Bois described as the *twoness* of black discourse and identity: the double consciousness of being both African and American (Du Bois 1982, 45), and each reveals the tension between believing in the "promise" of American ideals and the knowledge of the broken promises of America's racial realities. Obama's "post-racial" rhetoric was celebrated and embraced as a "transcendence of the very concerns that minority politicians have championed in the Party for decades" (Crenshaw 2005). Juxtaposed against Sharpton's address, Obama's rhetoric reveals "a troubling public expectation . . . that yearns for a denial of America's racial history as well as its contemporary consequences" (Crenshaw 2005). Indeed, the response to Sharpton's address suggests that even the indirect referencing of racism continues to traumatize many white Americans, and it is their trauma that must be addressed if we are to consider seriously the possibility of coherent racial reconciliation.

For McPhail, the positive response to Obama's address should then be read not as a new vision of race, but as an old vision of racelessness that warrants a critical response comparable to that offered by Socrates in the dialogue *Menexenus*: "there is no difficulty in a man's winning applause when he is contending for fame among the persons whom he is praising."[5] Obama's speech appeals to those ideological impulses at work in the rhetoric of white racial recovery (Gresson III 1995) and the conception of equality he embraces reifies the ideologies of innocence and positive self-presentation that characterize contemporary rhetorics of whiteness and modern racism.[6] Obama appeals to the abstractions and ideals of a transcendent social contract while obscuring or ignoring altogether the traumatic causes and consequences of America's racial past: what Charles W. Mills calls the "Racial Contract" (Mills 1997, 3). In contrast to the rhetorical strategy of re-signing the racial contract, Obama *resigns* race for his audience, and eliminates any need for Americans to address the symbolic and social pathologies of white privilege and power.

We approach these two reasonable responses to Obama's speech as an experiment in rhetorical criticism, David A. Frank as a white American of Jewish and Quaker heritage, and Mark Lawrence McPhail as an African American influenced by Eastern spiritual philosophies. As rhetorical scholars we share both an interest in collaboration and a willingness to weave together voices that have different interpretations of Obama's address into a narrative that results in what Chaïm Perelman and Lucie Olbrechts-Tyteca call a "contact of minds."[7] We acknowledge that our judgments of the Obama address are influenced by our ethnic and cultural backgrounds, and accordingly we "write together separately."[8] Ultimately, we see our effort as both a problematic and a potentially fruitful endeavor to address rhetorical theory and public discourse as they deal with issues of race. While we disagree on many points about Obama's speech, we nonetheless agree on the importance of, and need for, racial reconciliation.

Toward this end, we have divided the paper into three sections. In the first section, David Frank offers an upward-inflected assessment of Obama's speech as an act of "working through" trauma with a rhetoric of *consilience*. Mark McPhail responds by countering that the Obama speech compromises its rhetorical coherence by maximizing the abstract ideals of the social contract while minimizing the concrete realities of the racial contract. Obama's address does indeed signal a "post-racial" rhetorical shift toward coherence, yet the degree to which this shift can move African and European Americans beyond the divisions of historic and contemporary racial traumas constitutes the *stasis* of our debate. In order to move beyond debate and toward dialogue, we conclude by considering the possibilities that our alternative readings of Obama's address might offer for enriching rhetorical studies of racial reconciliation, and the challenges and opportunities that our collaboration presents for studying the rhetoric of racism.

DAVID A. FRANK:
IN CELEBRATION OF OBAMA'S RHETORIC OF CONSILIENCE

The speeches Obama and Sharpton delivered to the convention represent two narrative responses to the traumas suffered by African Americans. These speeches, I believe, illustrate the intertwining of psychology and rhetoric; the continuing legacy of rhetoric, particularly when cast to persuade the composite audience, in affecting material, legal, and cultural change for African Americans; and the power of Obama's speech as a prophetic multiracial narrative. Rhetoric, and in particular narratives, are critically important in managing trauma. Jerome D. Frank and Julia B. Frank observe in their definitive *Persuasion and Healing*: "rhetoric and a related discipline, hermeneutics, may prove to have more in common with psychotherapy than either religion or empiricism" (Frank and Frank 1991, 3). Dominick LaCapra, in a series of books, explains how narratives can "act out" and "work through" the consequences of trauma.[9] The perceived absence of metaphysical foundations for justice and value choice and such historical losses as slavery, the Holocaust, and other traumas can provoke "acting out" (the repetitive rehearsal of a past trauma) and invite "working through" (an act of analysis producing interpretations allowing for responsible control of trauma) through symbolic and nonsymbolic action. Reading African American discourse through the prism of trauma studies weds psychology and rhetoric. This reading begins with the pathologies left in the wake of slavery and segregation, the primary exigence inviting the discursive responses of African Americans, and, I believe, the key roles played by social movement rhetoric, oratory, and argument in the dismantlement of slavery and legal segregation, striking achievements that must be yoked to the traumatic aftershocks that these two institutions created.

These aftershocks, and continuing de facto racism, help to explain the plight faced by African Americans in this century (Forde-Mazrui 2004,

683–753). With the fall of institutionalized slavery in the nineteenth century and legal segregation in the twentieth century, blacks made significant progress. I acknowledge that this progress should be read contrapuntally with trends of resegregation and the continuing disparities between whites and African Americans. While pointing to the significant progress that African Americans have made since the civil rights era in income, ownership of homes, voting, and education, Lee A. Daniels and Rose Jefferson-Frazier, in their National Urban League report, nonetheless observe that "there are still notable gaps between African Americans and whites, especially in the area of economics that reveal major challenges in the pursuit of equality and opportunity" (Daniels and Jefferson-Frazier, and the National Urban League, 2004). Their report documents evidence of progress *and* regress, a warrant for both optimism and skepticism. The progress that has been made is due, in part, to the construction and reconstruction of narratives and an adroit use of the symbol, a legacy justifying some hope for the present and future.

The institution of slavery, which endured for over 244 years, eventually yielded to the Quaker-inspired abolition movement, reflecting the historical reality that "abolitionism was born with the American republic" (Newman 2002, 2). Abolitionists did not give up as they "worked consistently to destroy slavery and racial injustice in these years [1776–1864], their strategy and tactics constantly evolved" (Newman 2002, 2). The antislavery advocates made use of a host of discursive acts and appeals, including nonviolent resistance, petitions, legal briefs, and rational and emotional arguments, and drew upon the religious and Enlightenment principles that many of their audience members found persuasive. David Zarefsky has detailed how the Lincoln-Douglas debates functioned as "both agent and index of social and cultural change" (Zarefsky 1990, xii), and Garry Wills's close reading of Lincoln's Gettysburg Address illustrates how the speech "*makes* history" (Wills 1992, 174) by "impos[ing] a symbol" to "effect an intellectual revolution. No other words could have done it" (Wills 1992, 174–75). Lincoln, Wills concludes, used the speech to call "up a new nation out of the blood and trauma" with a revolutionary reading of the Declaration of Independence and the notion of equality. In this speech, Lincoln creates a nation out of the states and demolishes the justification for slavery.

One hundred years later, legal segregation fell to the civil rights movement, which also deployed a sophisticated nonviolent strategy consisting of powerful rhetorical appeals and found support in an emerging progressive political agenda. According to Cornel West, a legacy of success can be claimed from the twentieth-century labor and civil rights movements:

> Under Roosevelt the organized power of working people was made legitimate, and under Johnson one-half of all black people and elderly (of all colors) were lifted out of poverty. These achievements—resulting from intense organized struggle—may feel so far away, in both time and possibility, that holding them up as models may seem pointless. But reclaiming this powerful democratic legacy is precisely the mission before the Democratic Party today. (West 2004, 34)

With the assassinations of minister Malcolm X, the Reverend Martin Luther King, Jr., and Robert Kennedy, the fragmentation of progressive movements in the late 1960s, and the rise of the New Right, the Roosevelt-Johnson model withered. The failure of the Old and New Left, and of the larger progressive movement to cultivate common ground, identity, and values expressed in a cogent narrative explains, in part, why the progress made during the civil rights era has crested, and in some ways, regressed (Gitlin 1995). In the late 1960s, the progressive narrative dissolved into a mélange of competing identity groups, each with its own trauma, grievance, and demand. The southern strategy of the Republicans complemented the splintering of the left into "identity groups." This combination produced a conservative majority that divided blacks and whites, many of whom shared economic deprivation.

Lacking a narrative that could braid the ethnic groups around a shared purpose, neoliberals appeased blacks and appealed to whites, playing both sides against the other. Clinton's "Sister Souljah strategy," in which he directly confronted Jesse Jackson to secure a greater share of the Southern white vote, is a prime illustration (Germond and Witcover 1993, 300–305). Al Gore sought but did not achieve a similar opportunity in the 2000 election to distance himself from the Reverend Sharpton. Some believe Gore lost because he was perceived to be "an Al Sharpton Democrat" (Mayer 2002, 291). In the wake of King's death, the civil rights movement, led by men such as Jesse Jackson and Al Sharpton, has failed to craft an effective multiracial narrative.

This history forms the backdrop of the Sharpton and Obama speeches to the 2004 Democratic Convention. Sharpton presented a narrative that invoked the material realities of the racial contract, one that featured African American trauma with a narrative that rehearsed traditional themes, reinforcing the values of those who attended the convention and other like-minded observers, but not reaching beyond them. In contrast, Obama's narrative harkened back to the Roosevelt-Johnson legacy of shared purpose and coalition, and embraced a vision of America grounded in the enlightened ideals of a social contract that espoused human equality, dignity, and justice regardless of race, class status, or ethnic origin.

Sharpton and Obama at the 2004 DNC

In his address, Al Sharpton reminded his audience that Abraham Lincoln signed the Emancipation Proclamation, and that blacks were promised forty acres and a mule, which they did not receive. Sharpton recounted the failure of America to live up to its promise to black America. He did weave into this thesis references to other ethnic groups, but the speech centered on the civil rights movement and the reparations owed to African Americans. The speech climaxes with this declaration to George Bush:

> *You said the Republican Party was the party of Lincoln and Frederick Douglass. It is true that Mr. Lincoln signed the Emancipation Proclamation, after which there was a commitment to give 40 acres and a mule. That's where the argument, to this day, of reparations starts. We never got the 40 acres. We went all the way to Herbert Hoover, and we never got the 40 acres. We didn't get the mule. So we decided we'd ride this donkey as far as it would take us.*[10]

Sharpton's narrative casts Bush as the obstacle to, and the Democratic Party as a tool for, reparations. His speech fails to sufficiently acknowledge that many whites in the audience were suffering from the aftershocks of their own traumas. The speech also does not grant blacks the agency to deal with the conditions they face nor allow that Democrats and John Kerry needed the adherence of some white southerners to win the White House. While it may be noble and cathartic to speak unvarnished truths, reinforcing the values of those who already agree, African Americans have made the most progress when they have nested their politics and fate in multiracial movements, casting rhetorical visions designed to persuade a composite audience.

Accordingly, Kim Forde-Mazrui argues with great force that the traditional moral claim for reparations, which Sharpton's speech represents, must be recast (Forde-Mazrui 2004). She marshals evidence that opponents and supporters of affirmative action and reparations can be bridged by rooting the issues in conservative moral terms: "a constructive discourse ... [which] draw[s] upon principles that are either accepted by opponents of affirmative action or are widely accepted by American society as relevant to questions of attributing collective responsibility for the harmful effects of wrongful conduct" (Forde-Mazrui 2004, 693). These principles would draw from universal values and set forth a language of justice that transcends race. First, she identifies the need to emphasize corrective justice as a principle, one that applies to all those who have experienced historical injustice. Second, she argues that society and the American nation should be the agent identified as both the cause of the injustice and the source of rectification. Forde-Mazrui's impulse to seize conservative values and use them to ground arguments in favor of reparations and affirmative action represents a constructive alternative to Sharpton's rehearsal.

Using an approach similar to that of Forde-Mazrui, Obama's speech drew from his multiracial background to craft a speech designed to bridge the divides between and among ethnic groups. He writes in *Dreams from My Father*, "I learned to slip back and forth between my black and white worlds, understanding that each possessed its own language and customs and structures of meaning, convinced that with a bit of translation on my part the two worlds would eventually cohere" (Obama 1995, 82). Coherence, Obama writes, is a function of translation and the capacity to move between and among worlds. He was repulsed by whites who used racist language, and could not use the phrase "white folks" as a synonym for bigot as it was undercut by the memories of the love and nonracist impulses of his white mother and grandfather (Obama 1995, 81). His speech at the convention reflects, as McPhail notes, an ability to integrate competing visions of reality. Obama did so by using a rhetorical strategy of *consilience*, where understanding results through translation, mediation, and an embrace of different languages, values, and traditions. This embrace was intended to inspire a "jumping together" toward common principles.

His political success in Illinois is due to the use of consilience in search of coherence: Obama devised a narrative approach that acknowledged the traumas experienced by nonblacks, doing so without diminishing the need to address African American exigencies. In the process, he enacts consilience, beginning with the multiple traumas affecting the broader community and bridging them to the transcendent value of justice. In his extended *New Republic* profile, Noam Scheiber observes:

> *Whereas many working-class voters are wary of African American candidates, whom they think will promote black interests at the expense of their own, they simply don't see Obama in these terms. This*

allows him to appeal to white voters on traditional Democratic issues like jobs, health care, and education—just like a white candidate would. (Scheiber 2004)

Obama, by all reports, appeals to audiences of mixed racial and economic backgrounds. A close reading of his speech to the Democratic convention reveals his use of *consilience* to achieve coherence.

Obama refers to Lincoln in the beginning and celebrates Jefferson's notion in the Declaration of Independence that "we hold these truths to be self-evident, that all men are created equal, that they are endowed by their Creator with certain unalienable rights." By using Jefferson as a touchstone, one observer noted, "Obama also broke the mold; African-American politicians have not cited those words without sarcasm and qualification for many years." (Malcomson 2004, sec. 4, 5). The choice to feature the value of equality, of course, begins with Jefferson in the eighteenth century, is redefined by Lincoln in the nineteenth to include blacks, and is made urgent by King in the twentieth century. Here, Obama calls for a reaffirmation of American values of equality and liberty, all the while indicating that such precepts have not been fulfilled, and that the country has not lived up to this creed. His use of consilience is in evidence when he includes issues of class, civil liberties, and race in his argument, appealing to a composite audience including Arab Americans, gays, and other identity groups to make use of their shared American values in making their claims.

In addition to reaffirming a commitment to equality, Obama also repeated the word hope eleven times, and the mood of the speech is crystallized by his affirmation of the "audacity of hope." He then inoculates against the response that he was naïve of the need for material change:

I'm not talking about blind optimism here—the almost willful ignorance that thinks unemployment will go away if we just don't think about it, or the health care crisis will solve itself if we just ignore it. (Obama 2004)[11]

Without the possibility of hope, there can be no coherence. In turn, Obama roots this call for hope in an "awesome God," one that he was quick to praise as a bridge between blue and red states, and to acknowledge "things unseen." The strategy of consilience is given concrete form when he links members of the composite audience, divided by historical trauma, class, and race, to the values of equality and hope.

The most striking section of the speech is devoted to an elegant paring of contraries (red and blue states, Democrats and Republicans, gay and straight, prowar and antiwar Americans). In so doing, he challenges the binary thinking at the root of racism and other pathologies. He acknowledges the geographical, racial, political, and sexual differences in the United States and situates them in what they share in common:

> *The pundits like to slice and dice our country into Red States and Blue States; Red States for Republicans, Blue States for Democrats. . . . We worship an awesome God in the Blue States, and we don't like federal agents poking around in our libraries in the Red States. We coach Little League in the Blue States . . . we've got some gay friends in the Red States. There are patriots who opposed the war in Iraq, and there are patriots who supported the war in Iraq.*

The nuance inviting attention is his refusal to obliterate difference or put the individual in service to the many. Most importantly, he links the suffering of others to his own fate, displaying a rhetorical model of empathy necessary for transformation. There is a sense of the universal that serves the interests of all individuals. Indeed, for progress to be made in this country there is an implicit recognition in Obama's speech that God and the universal principle of equality are necessary.

While he does not feature African American trauma, he does make two comments directly about blacks. First, he challenges the identity politics that undermined the progressive movement in the 1960s by declaring invalid the division of the country by race: "There's not a black America and white America and Latino America and Asian America; there's the United States of America." Second, he presents an expansive sense of agency by pairing actions taken by the government to better secure the welfare of its people with individual initiative. Obama stated that "children can't achieve unless we raise their expectations and turn off the television sets and eradicate the slander that says a black youth with a book is acting white." Here, he suggests that blacks themselves have some choice in the values they pursue and their own material fate.

As an Illinois legislator, he consistently voted for governmental programs designed to provide economic protection for the poor, and thus the primary agent of structural change in his speech is the government. He gives credit to the GI Bill for the education of his parents, and the Federal Housing Authority for the purchase of their home. Inoculating against the claim that people become dependent on federal assistance, Obama notes, "people don't expect government to solve all their problems. But they sense, deep in their bones, that with a slight change in priorities, we can make sure that every child in America has a decent shot at life." Indeed, Obama's economic policies recall the Roosevelt-Johnson legacy of government activism, one that effectively reduced black poverty and abolished de jure racial discrimination. As one strand of a larger rhetoric of *consilience*, Obama assumes the government can work in concert with other agents to achieve reconciliation and coherence.

In conclusion, a strong case can be made that the frame used to justify reparations and an apology to blacks for their time in slavery should draw on the template displayed in this speech. To effectively work through the traumas faced by blacks, Obama features the "American nation" and the "American society" as the agent of rectification rather than "white people." This distinction becomes critical both in a case for reparations and in a post-racial rhetorical theory as it shifts responsibility from the nonessential category of race to that of the American people, a construct with history and legal standing, and commanding the capacity for responsibility. Ultimately, Obama's speech may open up the possibility of an authentic dialogue about race, and provide the narrative necessary for multiracial coalitions and the contact of minds necessary for progressive change. It does so through using a strategy of *consilience* to achieve reconciliation and coherence.

MARK LAWRENCE McPHAIL: OBAMA'S MENEXENUSIAN MESSAGE

David Frank's foregoing characterization of Barack Obama's address to the 2004 National Democratic Convention is certainly consistent with my own conceptualization of coherence as a discursive strategy that seeks identification in the face of division. Obama's appeal to "what Lincoln called the better angels of our nature" (*Charlie Rose Show* November 23, 2004)[12] draws upon the resources of rhetorical coherence in numerous ways: it embraces the ideals of American culture instead of rejecting them; it focuses on those commonalities that connect us instead of invoking the differences that divide us; and it resists argumentative essentialism and oppositionality and invokes instead discursive appeals that might reasonably be read as a "strategy for construction of a new order." Obama's speech can, as Frank suggests, be read as a shift away from complicity and toward coherence in African American discourse, and as a post-racial or post-oppositional rhetoric of *consilience* that could reconcile the traumatic histories of slavery and segregation and move Americans more effectively toward racial reconciliation. I wish to argue, however, that while Obama's rhetoric of *consilience* approximates dialogic coherence, it nonetheless falls short of the discursive demands of racial reconciliation.

Obama weaves a therapeutic narrative of opportunity for all, where the "blessed" African (the name "Barak," we are told, means "blessed") is *blessed* with opportunity in a "tolerant" and "generous" America, where "you don't have to be rich to achieve your potential." Obama breaks down binary oppositions when he contends that "there's not a liberal America and a conservative America—there's the United States of America. There's not a black America and white America and Latino America and Asian America; there's the United States of America." As such, we "are one people, all of us pledging allegiance to the stars and stripes, all of us defending the United States of America." Obama's appeal to identification and unity illustrates the use of consilience, the linking of diverse voices and values, to achieve coherence, the finding of similarity in difference, of *unum* in *pluribus*.

Indeed, Obama draws upon the resources of empathy and identification to envision an undifferentiated America, an America in which "we can tuck our children in at night and know they are fed and clothed and safe from harm," one where we can believe in the "inescapable network of mutuality" dreamt of four decades earlier by another eloquent African American. Obama envisions an America grounded in the belief that we're all connected as one people.

> *If there's a child on the South Side of Chicago who can't read, that matters to me, even if it's not my child. If there's a senior citizen somewhere who can't pay for their prescription drugs and has to choose between medicine and the rent, that makes my life poorer, even if it's not my grandparent. If there's an Arab American family being rounded up without benefit of an attorney or due process, that threatens my civil liberties. It is that fundamental belief... that I am my brother's keeper, I am my sisters' keeper—that makes this country work. It's what allows us to pursue our individual dreams yet still come together as one American family.*

John W. Rogers, Jr., CEO of Ariel Capital Management, compares Obama to Martin Luther King, Jr., arguing that he has the potential to "fill an enormous void with his extraordinary gifts," and serve as "a voice for the voiceless" (Meeks 2004, 95). Like King, Obama draws upon coherent principles of identification and empathy that address "the social and psychological divisions that undermine human unity and cooperation" (McPhail 1996, 87). Obama's speech does, as Frank suggests, invoke *consilience* to achieve coherence by transforming his diverse audiences into one composite audience. Unlike King, however, Obama's ultimately fails to translate *consilience* into coherence.

While King understood the salience and centrality of race, Obama invites the erasure of race instead of its re-signing, and this is where his oratory departs most radically and most unfortunately from the African American rhetorical tradition of "spiritually inspired militancy" (McPhail 2002a, 77–95). Some who praise Obama argue that "he represents a new form of leadership," one that departs from the traditional concerns of civil rights rhetoric, rhetoric marked by "a willingness to agitate with firebrand conviction and the ability to mobilize large groups of blacks around a common cause." Obama's rhetoric, however, is "less about equal access and more about education and economic opportunities," and Obama aligns his politics with those African American leaders who view "themselves as coalition builders and economic developers seeking to appeal to broad constituencies and abandoning rhetoric that would tag them as liberals" (Meeks 2004, 95). While there are certainly similarities between Obama and King in terms of rhetorical style, their substantive views on America's racial legacy reveal important differences between King's achievement of coherence and Obama's attempt to reach it through *consilience*.

While King saw the ideals of democracy and equality as possibilities, Obama idealizes them as actualities. While King called upon America to "be true to what you said on paper," Obama invests the paper declarations of the past with an authority of self-evidence that has yet to be fully realized in the present. While King was powerfully aware of the traumatic histories of slavery, segregation, and white supremacy and the need for the nation as a whole to consciously and conscientiously acknowledge and attend to these histories, Obama conflates these traumas with those of other Americans in a manner that undermines their historical specificity in order to construct a "politics of hope." Obama explains:

> *I'm not talking about blind optimism here—the almost willful ignorance that thinks unemployment will go away if we just don't think about it, or the health care crisis will solve itself if we just ignore it. I'm*

> talking about something more substantial. It's the hope of slaves sitting around a fire singing freedom songs; the hope of immigrants setting out for distant shores; the hope of a young naval lieutenant bravely patrolling the Mekong Delta; the hope of a millworker's son who dares to defy the odds; the hope of a skinny kid with a funny name who believes that America has a place for him, too.... The audacity of hope!

Obama's reduction of black trauma to "slaves sitting around a fire singing freedom songs" romanticizes the historical realities of black suffering and borders on the stereotypical image of the "happy darkie" of traditional racism. His lack of any discussion of race, except to illustrate the ways in which black people are implicated in racism when expressing the belief that "a black youth with a book is acting white," is troubling for much the same reason: it ignores the structural and historical conditions that gave rise to such attitudes. And if one substitutes "race" for either "unemployment" or "healthcare crisis" in Obama's speech, the silences of "blind optimism" and "willful ignorance" seemingly become acceptable.

In short, Obama's "politics of hope" might be read alternately as what Matthew Frye Jacobson describes as a "politics of disavowal," the rhetorical strategy of conflating the experiences of white ethnics with persons of African descent, and of denying the role of white power and privilege on the demoralizing conditions that continue to disproportionately affect the lives of black folk in America (Jacobson 1998, 279–80). Obama's rhetoric, while stylistically appealing, nonetheless ignores the historical and social realities of American racism, realities that Sharpton had the audacity to invoke in his address. Obama's "audacious hope" then, when juxtaposed against Sharpton's audacious truth, leans more toward compromise than either *consilience* or coherence. And it is this discursive compromise, I believe, that undermines the transformative and emancipatory possibilities of Obama's rhetoric, and limits its potential for achieving coherent reconciliation. Coherence requires connections between principles and practices to create the social transformations it envisions.

Reconciliation similarly requires the creation of "a new common history" and not simply the rehearsal of an old mythology. "It is earned through a sequence of personal acts: of apology, remorse, and restitution, on one side, and by positive forgiveness on the other" (Clark 2002, 364). As Mary E. Clark explains, reconciliation involves a very specific set of actions: "first, to address the past as seen by each side; second, to identify common goals for the future; third, to develop concrete projects to meet these goals and begin together to implement them" (Clark 2002, 368). Obama's speech fails to address the first of these, and instead embraces a mythological American monologue, a narrative grounded in the ideals of the social contract and painfully ignorant of the realities of the racial contract. By ignoring the concrete social and material realities of America's racial history, and instead invoking the enlightenment ideals of its abstract social mythology, Obama's speech offers a *Menexenusian* message that, while presented as a praising of *all* Americans, draws heavily upon the resources of whiteness and its dominant rhetorical tropes: innocence, race neutrality, and positive self-presentation. It articulates well with white racial recovery narratives that silence serious discussions about race in this country.

Read this way, Obama's speech does not reveal a new trajectory within African American discourse, but a compromise between the acquiescence of assimilationist rhetorics and the oppositionality of revolutionary rhetoric. The public space between these has been inhabited by the integrationist rhetorics of civil rights and social justice, the concerns and themes of which were expressed clearly in Sharpton's speech. Unlike Obama, Sharpton views race as deeply implicated in what the former terms the "long political darkness," but which the latter decries as "a vicious spirit in the body politic." In contrast to Obama's narrative of an idealized America in which race is never mentioned, Sharpton tells the story of America's racial realities, a story in which black men and women crafted the abstractions of freedom, justice, and democracy into lived realities. Sharpton reminds his readers that "a Black man from Barbados named Crispus Attucks" was the first to die in the fight for freedom; a black woman—Fannie Lou Hamer—led the fight for equal political representation; and it was the "firebrand convictions" of a Jesse Jackson that mobilized a victory for the Democratic Party twenty years earlier. Sharpton's speech embodied the very best of the African American tradition of civil rights discourse, oppositional yet inclusive, affirming of fundamental values yet agitating uncompromisingly for their achievement in practice as well as principle.

Indeed, Sharpton's speech is ultimately a call for coherence, one fundamentally grounded in the tradition of spiritually inspired militancy that articulates a strategy of reconstruction for the transformation of race in America. Sharpton's speech also coheres more closely with the rhetorical practices and principles necessary for reconciliation. He explicitly notes the need for an acknowledgment and clarification of history when he counters Bush's attempt to align the Republican Party of the present with "the party of Lincoln and Frederick Douglass." Sharpton iterates, "We got the

Civil Rights Act under a Democrat. We got the Voting Rights Act under a Democrat. We got the right to organize under a Democrat." He also demands atonement for the long and sordid history of African American disenfranchisement, enthymemically indicting Bush by invoking the 2000 election: "Mr. President, the reason we are fighting so hard, the reason we took Florida so seriously, is our right to vote wasn't gained because of our age. Our vote was soaked in the blood of martyrs, soaked in the blood of Goodman, Chaney and Schwerner, soaked in the blood of four little girls in Birmingham. This vote is sacred to us. This vote can't be bargained away. This vote can't be given away." Finally, Sharpton's explicit call for reparations fulfills the requirements for reconciliation, and his eloquent observation "we decided we'd ride this donkey as far as it would take us" evokes applause from the audience—almost a full minute—that far surpasses even the most enthusiastic response elicited by Obama.

Therefore, whether viewed from the perspective of coherent or classical rhetorical principles, Sharpton's speech is far superior to Obama's. Like King's, it draws on the resources of an African American tradition of spiritually inspired discourse, and is more concerned with speaking truth to power than praising Athenians in Athens. And like King, Sharpton does not reject the ideals of American history and society, but instead demands that its guardians "be true to what you said on paper." His discourse is dialogic and inclusive, and his invocation of Ray Charles's rendition of "America the Beautiful" is an amazingly powerful and eloquent peroration that re-signs, in the best tradition of black rhetoric, the racial contract: "Mr. President, we love America, not because all of us have seen the beauty all the time. But we believed if we kept on working, if we kept on marching, if we kept on voting, if we kept on believing, we would make America beautiful for everybody." Sharpton tells the unspoken story of American equality, the story in which people of African descent have been instrumental in crafting America's abstract ideals into social realities (Condit and Lucaites 1993).

Yet many white commentators demonized Sharpton, and denounced his address as "off message" and "incendiary" (Condit and Lucaites 1993). Kimberle Williams Crenshaw reads these criticisms as a troubling example of a larger white recovery project: "One can't help but infer that the media and perhaps some in the Democratic Party just want race to go away. So significant is this sentiment that even Sharpton's act of telling a story of democratic redemption in the face of repressive antidemocratic forces is seen as divisive, off-message and demogogic" (Crenshaw 2004). The response to Sharpton's call for a continuing commitment to racial justice and social equality might suggest that "America . . . doesn't want to hear about it anymore. Al Sharpton's telling of civil history violates their sense of civility, even though everything he said was absolutely true, and to millions of Americans, absolutely relevant" (Crenshaw 2004). Crenshaw's analysis offers a powerful commentary on the motives underlying the news media's demonizing of Sharpton and praising of Obama, and its potential consequences. She asserts, "The zeal to get beyond race will hasten efforts to drive wedges between black politicians—a move already afoot in the effort to hold up Barack Obama as 'the good black' and Sharpton, Jackson and others as the 'bad blacks'"(Crenshaw 2004). This characterization of African Americans in essentialist terms is particularly problematic, Crenshaw notes, because it implies that "the failure to achieve unity on civil rights is the natural consequence of the black discursive tradition, 'I Have a Dream' notwithstanding" (Crenshaw 2004). While Obama's speech simply *resigned* the need to address race in any substantive way, Sharpton's speech *re-signed* the racial contract, and signified a tradition of spiritually inspired militancy that has called consistently for coherence and been instrumental in concretizing the equalities and freedoms idealized in the social contract.

Thus, while Crenshaw suggests that the difference between the rhetorics and politics of Sharpton and Obama is "far more a difference of style than substance" (Crenshaw 2004), I would counter that their rhetorics are substantively different in terms of their conceptions of race. Indeed, to the extent that Obama departs from this tradition of spiritually inspired militancy that consciously re-signs the racial contract, it is unlikely that his voice will contribute productively to a dialogue about race that can move us closer to reconciliation and transformation. This is, ultimately, what any coherent rhetoric must achieve if it is to be anything more than "mere" rhetoric. It must address the history of traumatic betrayals endured by "every generation of African Americans since the white founders of the U.S. agreed to write a compromise in the Constitution of 1789 to keep African Americans in slavery" (Alan 2004), and it must move white Americans to acknowledge that history, atone for it, and seek to repair the damage that it has done to the American mind and spirit.

Obama's departure from this tradition and his move toward racelessness will do little to inspire white Americans toward a resigning of the racial contract. While he acknowledges that "we have more work to do," this work consists essentially of "measuring up to the legacy of our forbearers" and "reclaiming" the vision of an idealized America. Obama here imagines an

America freed from the traumas of racial history by the "promise" of equality. Yet, as Stephen L. Carter explains, this is a vision of America that

> *almost nobody really believes in but almost everybody desperately wants to. In this vision, we are united in a common enterprise and governed by common consent. Although the nation has problems, some of them caused by racism, we are people of good will, aiming at a fairer, more integrated society, which we will achieve through the actions of our essentially fair institutions. (Carter 1994, xiii)*

Carter is responding to the failed nomination of Lani Guinier, another African American rhetor whose discourse embraced the principles of coherence and who attempted to translate them into social practice. Gunier's analysis of America's racial realities was based not only on idealized representations of American democracy, but on empirical evidence of the dismantling of the Voting Rights Act, largely engineered under President Ronald Reagan,[13] who, according to Aaron David Gresson III, was the principal architect of the contemporary white recovery project (Gresson 1995, 10).

Reagan's speech at the Neshoba County Fair in Philadelphia, Mississippi, in 1980, where he unambiguously expressed his support for "state's rights," employed a southern strategy that has been exploited by Republican politicians since Goldwater, "all of whom used coded racial messages to lure disaffected blue collar and Southern white voters away from the Democrats" (White 2005). The politics of white racial recovery gave rise to the anti-affirmative action and civil rights legislation that shaped the post–civil rights era, undermining racial justice and equality by proclaiming that they had already been achieved: that America was a "color blind" nation, in which African Americans who continued to call for racial justice were asking only for "special privileges," and were guilty of "reverse racism."

Obama's address, and the rhetorical situation that elicited it, must be read against this history of racial recovery in order to accurately assess its potential for racial reconciliation and its potential to persuade white Americans to resign the racial contract. Once weighed against the empirical and material realities of the racial contract, Obama's "audacious hope" seems at best naïve, and at worst opportunistic. On the one hand, it employs a conception of "equality" that is abstract and revisionist, and on the other hand, it fails to address in substantive terms the material realities of African American trauma. Indeed, studies of trauma within the African American context similarly call into question the possibility of Obama's rhetoric successfully reconciling America's racial divisions.

Timothy Brown's exploration of black American trauma can be fruitfully applied to the analysis of Obama's rhetoric. "The production of cultural works that have the potential to address our common humanity is very important, but a political response forces us to see how our cultural productions are implicated in the perpetuation of traumatic violence" (Brown 2004). Psychotherapist Dee Watts-Jones suggests that these cultural productions must be part of an open and honest dialogue that involves both black and white Americans:

Healing from internalized racism eventually includes the freedom to share the pain and shame across groups, because continuing to bear it as our shame alone reinforces oppression. The shame of internalized racism among people of African descent does not belong to us. It is the shame of oppression, and needs to be shared by whites as well. This is part of our healing, and the healing work that whites need to do. (Watts-Jones 2002, 595–96)

Watts-Jones's insights are particularly important for our discussion of the potential that a rhetoric of *consilience* holds for the re-signing of the racial contract by African Americans, and its resigning by white Americans. While African Americans will need to continue to cultivate inclusive and affirmative discourses about race, unless white Americans are willing to become part of an honest dialogue about racism that will lead to its resignation, it is unlikely that a coherent understanding of our common humanity can be achieved. Indeed, when just the mention of race leads to demonizing and denial as it did in the case of Al Sharpton, it is difficult to believe that any rhetorical strategy that even touches on the subject will lead to productive conversation about race, much less racial reconciliation.

Thus, I continue to believe that the greatest impediment to racial reconciliation is an unwillingness, largely on the part of people of European descent, to talk openly and honestly about America's long and troubling legacy of racism. Obama's rhetoric of *consilience* will not, in my view, move us any closer to this much-needed conversation. Because Obama celebrates the abstractions of the social contract while ignoring the realities of the racial contract, his message is unlikely to affect in practice the values it embraces in principle. The connection between these is ultimately the best indication of rhetoric's transformative power, and the greatest impediment to that power is the silence of self-interest and the absence of dialogue. In concluding, we reflect on the ways in which we might transform these impediments into opportunities to move beyond complicity and toward coherent reconciliation in the rhetoric of racism, and perhaps transform our different readings of Obama's speech into a more productive conversation about the problems and possibilities of racial reconciliation.

WRESTLING WITH OUR BETTER ANGELS: COHERENCE AND CONSILIENCE AT THE RENDEZVOUS OF HISTORY

Barack Obama's invocation of Lincoln's reference to "the better angels of our nature" offers a starting point for exploring the commitment to faith that connects the theoretical and critical impulses of both coherence and *consilience*. Both coherence and *consilience* are committed to finding a way to wrestle with the painful realities that separate us so that we might better understand the audacious hopes that can bring us together. Like Jacob, whose wrestling with an angel ended in both trauma and transformation, we have sought to examine the ways in which discourse could address deep and painful divisions to, in the words of Aimé Césaire, make "room for all at the meeting-place of conquest" (Césaire 1969, 85). Like Obama, we agree that there is a foundational decency in the American people that we often fail to recognize. With regard to rhetoric, that decency has often been conceived in abstract terms, as a principled commitment to freedom, justice, and equality. With regard to both race and culture, however, those same principles have been realized in practice only after prolonged struggle and sacrifice, and have revealed the limits of both reason and persuasion as they have been conceived in the West. Such limits point to the need for an enlarged conception of rhetoric, one that addresses spirituality as well as rationality, appeals to *pathos* as well as *logos*, and celebrates empathy as much as material evidence.

Such a rhetoric also recognizes the importance of understanding human psychology and spirituality for addressing the causes and consequences of trauma. Rhetoric is, at its best, a *pietho*, a talking cure that can facilitate healing when, as James Hillman suggests, it involves "discovering instruments for moving ideas, beliefs, feelings, images, and fantasies. Then rhetoric, persuasion, holds major importance. Through words we can alter reality; we can bring into being and remove from being; we can shape and change the very structure of what is real. The art of speech becomes the primary mode of moving reality" (Hillman, 1980, 21). Within the context of the traumatic history of race in America, a re-signed rhetoric would address directly the spiritual and material incoherence of white supremacy and black inferiority, and reshape the contours of interest convergence that have thus far limited the possibilities of racial reconciliation.[14]

With Césaire's vision as a polar star, we believe that rhetorical critics in this country can begin to do the hard work necessary to acknowledge that the American problem of the twentieth century, which Du Bois presciently identified as the "color line," has now become a problem of conscience. And even though Barack Obama's rhetoric of *consilience* is a call to conscience, its resigning of race nonetheless limits its potential for coherent reconciliation. A truly powerful and redemptive narrative would recognize and challenge the separation between an idealized social contract and a realized racial contract, and would interrogate the complicities of whiteness as vigorously as those of blackness. It would decry, in prophetic terms, our mixed record in dealing with race, and issue a clarion call for an unambiguous commitment to racial justice and reparations. One example of this rhetorical ideal is seen in former Mississippi secretary of state Richard Molpus, whose speech at the fortieth anniversary of the deaths of James Chaney, Andrew Goodman, and Michael Schwerner reflected powerfully principles of rhetorical coherence and *consilience*. Molpus offers a coherent acknowledgment of racial reality, and its audaciously hopeful belief in the possibilities of racial reconciliation (Molpus 2004). The Molpus address exemplifies an understanding that our "common humanity" is something still to be constructed, not only in symbolic action but in social action as well. It invokes the redemptive possibilities of reason and argumentation as agents of change, which Du Bois affirms in the neglected "Afterthought" of the *Souls of Black Folk*: "Thus in Thy good time may infinite reason turn the tangle straight, and these crooked marks on a fragile leaf be not indeed" (Du Bois 1982, 278).

Du Bois, whose American dream was situated at the intersection of the historical, the rhetorical, and the poetic, recognized that our reconciliation of racial difference would require a willingness to acknowledge the ways in which the color line has shaped not only the souls of black folk, but the souls of white folk as well.[15] This recognition is compromised when we assume or assert that our collective dreams of freedom and justice have been achieved, when in reality they remain, for too many, unrealized. Barack Obama's speech before the 2004 Democratic National Convention reveals this tension between a dream idealized and a dream deferred, between compromise and coherent *consilience*. It thus provides us with an important opportunity to explore the potential for racial reconciliation from both sides of the color line, to confront the dark angel of race and through the courageous expression of conviction in action, strive to overcome it. It invites us to conceive of a re-signed rhetoric and to dream of the resigning of race. To that end, we conclude in the spirit of audacious hope with the words of Robert Penn Warren, who though positioned on the other side of the color line from Du Bois, was similarly situated at the intersection of history, rhetoric, and poetry:

> *For the dream is only a self of yourself—and Jacob once wrestled, nightlong, his angel, though with wrenched thigh, had blackmailed a blessing, by dawn. (Warren 1987, 29)*

Notes

1. On Obama's intentions, see Scheiber 2004; and his autobiography, Obama, *Dreams*, 1995.
2. On the rhetoric of *consilience*, see Perelman and Olbrechts-Tyteca 1969, 472.
3. Numerous transcripts of both speeches are available. The most accurate reproductions of the speeches are the videos found at America 2004, the Democratic National Convention Web site, http://www.dems2004.org/site. A version also is also available of Obama's speech in *Dreams*, 445–53.
4. Frank's argument is offered in response to McPhail's pessimistic assessment of contemporary race relations outlined in McPhail 2002b, and McPhail's response to John B. Hatch's essay see McPhail 2003, 737–64. See also McPhail 2004, 391–403.
5. *Menexenus by Plato*, translated with an introduction by Benjamin Jowett, *eBooks @ Adelaide*, August 10, 2004, http://ebooks.adelaide.edu.au/p/plato/p71mx/index.html.
6. For a discussion of the ideological foundation of whiteness and modern racism, see McPhail 2002b, 185–99.
7. On this notion, see Perelman and Olbrechts-Tyteca 1969, 14–18.
8. See Newman 1996, 1–12 on the difficulties of interethnic scholarly collaboration.
9. See especially LaCapra 2004.
10. Sharpton DNC speech. All quotations are taken from the transcript citation listed in note 4.
11. Obama DNC speech. All quotations are taken from the transcript cited in note 4.
12. "Interview with Barack Obama," *Charlie Rose Show*, November 23, 2004.
13. For a rhetorical analysis of Guinier's critique of Reagan's attack on Voting Rights Act and her resulting demonization in the media, see Kañas and McPhail 2004, 223–44.
14. Kirt Wilson argues that interest convergence has functioned to sustain white privilege while creating the illusion of black progress. See Wilson 2004, 367–77.
15. For a consideration of connections between double consciousness and rhetoric, see McPhail 2001.

14. BARACK OBAMA'S WHITE APPEAL AND THE PERVERSE RACIAL POLITICS OF THE POST-CIVIL RIGHTS ERA

PAUL STREET

Editor's Note: This chapter has four components: an essay (bearing the same name as this chapter) originally published in June of 2007, more than a year before Barack Obama's election to the presidency; an initial postscript on the "post-racial" politics of the Obama administration written in late December of 2009; a second and much shorter postscript on the same topic written in April of 2012; a very brief postscript written in the wake of President Obama's re-election.

I ONCE GAVE A TALK ABOUT RACISM THAT WAS FOLLOWED BY AN INTERESTING COMMENT FROM A MIDDLE-AGED WHITE MAN. "You can't seriously imagine that racism is still a big problem in the United States," this man said, "when millions of white Americans are ready to vote for Barack Obama, a black man, for president."

I wrote an article on Obama that elicited the following response from a white Republican science professor in a Detroit suburb: "If Obama gets elected president, it would be a big—probably the biggest since the Emancipation Proclamation—step toward race equality in the U.S. If a half-black man gets elected president," the professor elaborated, "we could stop focusing so much on race in this country and focus on other things."

A different essay critical of Obama provoked an angry response from a black man who thought I was African American. "How can you betray your race like this?" this individual asked. "Why are you undermining a brother with a shot at the most powerful job in the world?" By this writer's estimation, Obama's black identity was in itself sufficient reason for a responsible black journalist to swallow any criticisms of the junior senator from Illinois.

The racial meaning of "the Obama phenomenon" is an interesting question that merits careful consideration. It is significantly more complicated than my three commentators grasped.

Is there anything positive about the fact that droves of whites are willing to embrace a black presidential candidate? Sure. Forty years ago, as the United States entered the racially turbulent summer of 1967 and the movie *Guess Who's Coming to Dinner* disturbed conventional racial norms by portraying a black doctor (played by Sidney Poitier) dating a white woman (Katharine Houghton), it would have been impossible for a black politician to become a viable presidential contender. Nothing a black candidate could have done or said would have prevented him from being excluded on the basis of the color of his or her skin. The fact that this is no longer true is a sign of some (admittedly slow) racial progress more than fifty years after the Civil Rights Act and Voting Rights Act. But there are at least three reasons not to get overly excited about Obama's cross-racial appeal from a racial justice perspective.

"HE'S NOT ALL THAT BLACK"

The first difficulty is that part of Obama's appeal to white America has to do with the widespread Caucasian sense that Obama "isn't all that black." Many whites who roll their eyes at the mention of the names of Jesse Jackson or Al Sharpton—former presidential candidates who behave in ways that many whites find too African American—are soothed by the cool, underplayed blackness and ponderous, quasi-academic tone of the half-white, Harvard-educated Obama. Obama doesn't shout, chant, holler, or drawl. He doesn't rail against injustice, bring the parishioners to their feet and threaten delicate white suburban and middle-class sensibilities. He stays away from the sort of angry confrontations with concentrated wealth and power that are becoming the staple of John Edwards's quest for the Democratic nomination. To use Joe Biden's revealing terminology, Obama strikes many whites as "clean" and "articulate"—something different from their unfortunately persistent image of blacks as dirty, dangerous, and unintelligible.

Obama has no obligation to shed his biracial identity, "multicultural" background and elite education to "act [more stereotypically] black." But whites' racial attitudes are less progressive than might be assumed when their willingness to embrace a black candidate is conditioned by their requirement that his or her "blackness" be qualified. When ingrained sensibilities lead you (other things being equal) to prefer your "straight-acting" gay uncle over your outwardly "effeminate" gay nephew, your tolerance for non-traditional sexual orientations might be less enlightened than you think.

"WHAT AILS BLACKS IS NOT FUNDAMENTALLY DIFFERENT"

A second and related reason not to do racial justice cartwheels over Obama's popularity with whites is the candidate's deep willingness to accommodate white supremacy. In his tedious, power-worshipping, and badly titled campaign book *The Audacity of Hope*, Obama ignores elementary U.S. social reality and strokes the master race by claiming that "what ails working- and middle-class blacks is not fundamentally different from what ails their white counterparts." Equally calming to the white majority is Obama's argument that "white guilt has largely exhausted itself in America" as "even the most fair-minded of whites . . . tend to push back against suggestions of racial victimization and race-based claims based on the history of racial discrimination in this country" (Obama 2006, 247). Part of the reason for this "push back"—also known as backlash and denial—is, Obama claims, the bad culture and poor work ethic of the inner city black poor (Obama 2006, 245, 254–56).

White fears that Obama will reawaken the tragically unfinished revolutions of Reconstruction and civil rights are further soothed by his claim that most black Americans have been "pulled into the economic mainstream" (Obama 2006, 248–49). During a speech marking the anniversary of the Selma, Alabama, voting-rights march, Obama claimed that 1950s and 1960s civil rights activists—who he referred to as "the Moses Generation"—had brought black America "90 percent of the way" to racial equality. It's up to Obama and his fellow "Joshua generation" members to get past "that 10 percent in order to cross over to the other side" (Obama 2007c).

Then there's Obama's claim that "conservatives and Bill Clinton were right about welfare." The abolished Aid for Families with Dependent Children (AFDC) program, Obama claims, "sapped" inner-city blacks of their "initiative" and detached them from the great material and spiritual gains that flow to those who attach themselves to the capitalist labor market, including "independence," "income," "order, structure, dignity and opportunity for growth in peoples' lives." He argues that encouraging black girls to finish high school and stop having babies out of wedlock is "the single biggest thing that we could do to reduce inner-city poverty" (Obama 2006, 256).

Never mind that blacks are afflicted with a shocking racial wealth gap that keeps their average net worth at one eleventh that of whites and an income structure starkly and persistently tilted towards poverty (Loewen 2005, 130; Shapiro 2005). Never mind that lower-, working-, and middle-class blacks continue to face numerous steep and interrelated white-supremacist barriers to equality. Or that multidimensional racial discrimination is still rife in "post–civil rights America," deeply woven into the fabric of the nation's social institutions and drawing heavily on the living and unresolved legacy of centuries of not-so "past" racism (Feagin 2000; Brown et al. 2003; Street 2005; Street 2007g).

Never mind that the long centuries of slavery and Jim Crow are still quite historically recent and would continue to exercise a crippling influence on black experience even if the dominant white claim that black "racial victimization" is a "thing of the past" was remotely accurate (Brown et al. *Whitewashing Race*; Feagin, *Racist America*; Street, *Racial Oppression*). Never mind the existence of numerous left Caucasians (e.g., Joe Feagin, Tim Wise, Michael Albert, Stephen Steinberg, yours truly, and many more), not to mention a large number of black Americans, who support not simply the "race-based" claims of affirmative actions but the demand for reparations to address the living and powerful legacy of slavery and Jim Crow.

And never mind the absence of social-scientific evidence for the "conservative" claim that AFDC destroyed inner city work ethics or generated "intergenerational poverty." Forget the existence of numerous studies showing that the absence of decent, minimally well-paid, and dignified work has always been the single leading cause of black inner-city poverty and "welfare dependency" (Handler 1995, 32–55; Jencks 1992, 204–35; Stier and Tienda 2001). Disregard research showing that high black teenage pregnancy rates reflect the absence of meaningful long-term life and economic opportunities in the nation's hyper-segregated inner-city and suburban ring ghettos. Forget that the single biggest thing that could be done to reduce inner city poverty would be to make the simple and elementary moral decision to abolish it through the provision of a decent guaranteed income—something once advocated by Martin Luther King, Jr., and that other dangerous left "moral absolutist" (Obama's description of 1960s New Left peace and justice activists), Richard Nixon.

Racial hierarchy isn't the only oppression structure that Senator Obama is willing to accommodate. As I've been arguing for some time now he plays the same essential opportunistic and power-worshipping game in relation to related inequality structures of class and empire (Street 2004a; Street

2004b; Street 2006; Street 2007e; Street 2007d; Street 2007f; Street 2007h; Street 2007b). Beneath peaceful and populist sounding claims to the contrary, he's largely on the dark and neoliberal side of power when it comes to each of what the democratic socialist and anti-imperialist Martin Luther King, Jr., called "the triple evils that are interrelated": racism, economic exploitation/inequality (capitalism), and militarism (King, Jr. 1991, 250–51; Garrow 1986, 546). It's not for nothing that Obama was recently described as "deeply conservative" in a flattering *New Yorker* write-up titled "The Conciliator" (MacFarquar 2007).

THE POST–CIVIL RIGHTS ERA

In accommodating white supremacy, Obama is playing to the perverse racial politics of the post–civil rights era, wherein the leading architects of policy and opinion have declared "race" over as a barrier to black advancement. It is a time when a large number of Americans, including many blacks, claim "exhaustion" with race issues. Race- and racism-avoidance have become the orders of the day in an officially "colorblind" neoliberal age when conventional wisdom ascribes people's status and wealth to purely private and personal success or failure in adapting to the permanent, inherently human realities of inequality in a "free market" system of reactionary corporate rule to which "there is no alternative." In the dominant public discourse of this era, the nation's "pervasive racial hierarchies collapse," in the words of Henry A. Giroux, "into power-evasive strategies such as blaming minorities of class and color for not working hard enough, refusing to exercise individual initiative, or practicing reverse racism." Even as an enveloping, increasingly invisible racism "functions" as "one of the deep and abiding currents in everyday [American] life," this discourse works "to erase the social from the language of public life as to reduce all racial problems to private issues [of] . . . individual character and cultural depravity."

This "neoliberal racism," as Giroux calls it, "can imagine public issues only as private concerns." It sees "human agency as simply a matter of individualized choices, the only obstacle to effective citizenship being the lack of principled self-help and moral responsibility" on the part of those most victimized by structural oppression and the amoral agency of those superempowered actors who stand atop the nation's steep and interrelated hierarchies of class and race. Under its rule, "human misery is largely defined as a function of personal choices," consistent with "the central neoliberal tenet that all problems are private rather than social in nature" (Giroux 2003; Giroux 2004).

The technically biracial Obama's campaign and persona are perfectly calibrated for this era of victim-blaming neoliberal racism. He allows whites to assuage their racial guilt and feel non-racist by liking and perhaps even voting for him while signaling that he won't do anything to tackle and redress the steep racial disparities and systemic racial oppression that continue to deeply scar U.S. life and institutions. "What . . . me and my country racist? You can't be serious: we're thinking seriously about voting for a black man as president. My wife and son just love Oprah and Jamie Foxx."

RACISM'S DIFFERENT LEVELS: "STATE OF BEING" V. "STATE OF MIND"

This brings me to the third reason not to sing racial-justice hosannas over the sudden rise of Obama. His election could actually worsen racism's power in ways that are unintentionally suggested at the end of the professor's comment given at the beginning of this chapter. The main problem with the conventional white wisdom holding that racism no longer poses relevant barriers to black advancement and black-white equality in post–civil rights America is a failure to distinguish adequately between overt "state-of-mind" racism and covert institutional, societal, and "state-of-being" racism (Street 2002; Street 2004a; Street 2004b; Street 2007g).

The first variety of racism has a long and sordid history. It includes such actions, policies and practices as the burning of black homes and black churches, the murder of "uppity" blacks and civil rights workers, the public use of derogatory racial slurs and epithets, the open banning of blacks from numerous occupations, the open political disenfranchisement of blacks and the open segregation of public facilities by race. It is largely defeated, outlawed, and discredited in the "politically correct" environment created partly by the victories of the civil rights movement.

The second variety lives on, with terrible consequences. It involves the more impersonal operation of social, economic, and institutional forces and processes that both reflect and shape the related processes of capitalism in ways that "just happen" but nonetheless serve to reproduce black disadvantage in numerous interrelated key sectors of American life. It includes racially segregating real estate and home-lending practices, residential "white flight" (from black neighbors), statistical racial discrimination in hiring and promotion, the systematic underfunding and under-equipping of schools predominately attended by blacks relative to schools predominately attended by whites, the disproportionate surveillance, arrest, and incarceration of blacks, and much more.

Richly enabled by policymakers who commonly declare allegiance to antiracist ideals, this deeper racism has an equally ancient history that has outlived the explicit, open, and public racism of the past and the passage of justly cherished civil rights legislation. It does not necessarily involve individual white bigotry or even subtly prejudiced "ill will" against blacks. Consciously or even unconsciously prejudiced white actors are not required and black actors are more than welcome to help enforce the new age societal racism of the post-King era. This entrenched, enduring, and more concealed societal racism does not depend on racist intent in order to exist as a relevant social and political phenomenon. The racism that matters most today does not require a large portion of the white population to be consciously and willfully prejudiced against blacks or any other racial minority. It only needs to produce racially disparate outcomes through the operation of objectively racialized processes. It critically includes a pivotal failure and/or refusal to acknowledge, address, and reverse the living (present and future) windfall bestowed on sections of the white community by "past" racist structures, policies, and practices that were more willfully and openly discriminatory toward blacks.

"State-of-being" or structural racism generates racially disparate results even without racist intent—"state-of-mind" racism—on the part of white actors. It oppresses blacks with objectively racialized social processes that work in "routine" and "ordinary" fashion to sustain racial hierarchy and white supremacy often and typically without white racist hostility or purpose (Carmichael and Hamilton 1967, 4; Steinberg 1995, 68–78: Feagin, *Racist America*; Brown et al., *Whitewashing Race*; Street, *Racial Oppression*).

JANUS-FACED VICTORIES

Sadly, the fact that level-one (overt) racism has been defeated while the deeper (level-two) racism survives is not just a matter of the social and racial justice glass being half-full. It's more darkly complicated than that. The second and deeper level of racial oppression's power may actually be more firmly entrenched by celebrated civil rights victories and related black upward mobility into the middle and upper classes insofar as those victories and achievements encourage the illusion that racism has disappeared and that the only obstacles left to African-American success and equality are internal to individual blacks and their community—the idea that, in Derrick Bell's phrase, "the indolence of blacks rather than the injustice of whites explains the socioeconomic gaps separating the races" (Bell 2004, 77–78). "It's hard," Leonard Steinhorn and Barbara Diggs-Brown have noted, "to blame people" for believing (falsely in Steinhorn and Diggs-Brown's view) that racism is dead in America "when our public life is filled with repeated affirmations of the integration ideal and our ostensible progress towards achieving it" (Steinhorn and Diggs-Brown 1999, 6–7).

In a similar vein, Sheryl Cashin notes that "there are [now] enough examples of successful middle-class African-Americans to make many whites believe that blacks have reached parity with them. The fact that some blacks now lead powerful mainstream institutions offers evidence to whites that racial barriers have been eliminated; the issue now is individual effort" (Cashin 2004, xi).

The white-run culture's regular rituals of self-congratulation over the defeat of overt, level-one racism—the Martin Luther King national holiday, the playing of King's "I Have a Dream" speech over school sound systems and on television, the demotion of Trent Lott, the routine reference to integrationist ideals in political speeches, and now the presidential viability of the "conservative" Obama—reinforce the dominant white sentiment that the United States no longer has much of anything to answer for in regard to its treatment of black America and the ubiquitous white American notion that racism is something only from the now relatively irrelevant and distant "past." "Now we can finally forget about race completely" is the basic white wish-seeking fulfillment in the election of someone like Obama.

This is a problem that Martin Luther King, Jr., anticipated. By the middle 1960s, King and other civil rights leaders were most concerned about the deeper institutional and societal racism that existed across the entire United States. King and others feared that the defeat of open segregation and racial terrorism in the South would reinforce the majority white nation's tendency to avoid more covert, established, invisible and nationwide forms of racial oppression while encouraging whites to falsely conclude that all the nation's racial problems have been "automatically solved" (King 1969/1991).

King also worried that early civil rights victories over level-one racism would encourage white Americans to deny the powerful and living legacy and material relevance of "past racism." As he knew and as is still true today, the older, more open racism of the long pre-civil rights past continues to cast more than just an incidental shadow over contemporary racial inequalities. Most white Americans object strenuously to the idea that "past racial discrimination matters in the present" (Feagin 2000, 261). But anyone who examines capitalism in an honest way knows that what people get from the present and future so-called "free market" is very much about what and how much they bring to that present and future market from the past. "Long ago" racism continues to exact a major cost on current-day black Americans, raising the question of whether unresolved historical inequity is really "past." Slavery and then Jim Crow segregation in the South—and the racial terrorism, discrimination and apartheid imposed on black northerners in places like Chicago and Detroit and the thousands of northern all-white "Sundown towns" that were formed between 1890 and 1968 (see James Loewen's masterly study *Sundown Towns: A Hidden Dimension of American Racism*)—"long ago" continue to shape present-day racial inequality.

As Michael K. Brown and his colleagues note in their study, *Whitewashing Race: The Myth of a Color-Blind Society* (2003), racial "inequalities are cumulative, a fact adherents of the new public wisdom on race ignore in their rush to celebrate [racial] progress." Because the "inequalities accumulate over time," the authors argue, the distinction frequently made by "racial conservatives" between "past and present racism" is often inadequate and deceptive" (Brown et al. 2003, 24–25). The ongoing need for historical acknowledgement and correction, commonly called reparations, is developed quite well in the following useful analogy advanced by political scientist Roy L. Brooks:

> Two persons—one white and the other black—are playing a game of poker. The game has been in progress for some 300 years. One player—the white one—has been cheating during much of this time, but now announces: "from this day forward, there will be a new game with new players and no more cheating." Hopeful but suspicious, the black player responds, "That's great. I've been waiting to hear you say that for 300 years. Let me ask you, what are you going to do with all those poker chips that you have stacked up on your side of the table all these years?" "Well," said the white player, somewhat bewildered by the question, "they are going to stay right here, of course." "That's unfair," snaps the black player. "The new white player will benefit from your past cheating. Where's the equality in that?" "But you can't realistically expect me to redistribute the poker chips along racial lines when we are trying to move away from considerations of race and when the future

offers no guarantees to anyone," insists the white player. *"And surely,"* he continues, *"redistributing the poker chips would punish individuals for something they did not do. Punish me, not the innocents!"* Emotionally exhausted, the black player answers, *"but the innocents will reap a racial windfall."* (Brooks 1996, ix)

Seen against the backdrop of Brooks's living "racial windfall," there is something significantly racist about the widespread white assumption that the white majority society owes African Americans nothing in the way of special, ongoing compensation for singular black disadvantages resulting from past explicit racism. Brooks's surplus "chips" are not quaint but irrelevant hangovers from "days gone by." They are weapons of racial oppression in the present and future. Given what is well known about the relationship between historically accumulated resources and current and future success, the very distinction between past and present racism ought perhaps to be considered part of the ideological superstructure of contemporary white supremacy functioning as an ongoing barrier to black advancement and equality.

It is important to remember that the explicit and overt racism that made it impossible for a black man to seriously consider running for higher office in the not-so-distant past was about more than the sadistic infliction of racial terror in and of itself. That racism served and enforced the economic exploitation and material subordination of black Americans. That long exploitation gave rise to a steep, living and historically cumulative racial wealth and power gap whereby stark contemporary disparities are deeply fed by past inequalities. Such is the deep and dark reality behind what Barack "The Conciliator" Obama (MacFarquhar, 2007) calmly terms the tendency of "even the most fair-minded of whites . . . to push back against suggestions of racial victimization and race-based claims based on the history of racial discrimination in this country."

THE WHITE-SUPREMACIST FUNCTIONAL UTILITY OF BLACK SUCCESS STORIES

Thinking about white America's superficial "post-racism" and the related distinction between level-one and level-two racism, a left black political writer recently told me that the election of a black Democrat like Obama would be a "disaster" for the cause of black equality. It would be a big negative from a racial-justice perspective, this writer feels, because it would deeply reinforce the pervasive majority white notion that racism is essentially over as a relevant barrier to black equality in the U.S. The writer was thinking also about the perverse role that the related success of a minority of privileged blacks and the related class bifurcation of the black community has long played in the preservation of white privilege. As Stephen Steinberg noted in his important book:

> *The success of the black middle-class [since the Civil Rights Movement is not] proof of . . . a more favorable opportunity structure for blacks. After all, racism has never been indifferent to class distinctions, and it may well be that blacks who have acquired the "right" status characteristics are exempted from stereotypes and behaviors that continue to be directed at less privileged blacks. [But] there is nothing new in this phenomenon. Even in the worst days of Jim Crow, there were blacks who owned land, received favored treatment from whites and were held forth as "success stories" to prove that lower-class blacks had only themselves to blame for their destitution . . . The existence of this black elite did not prove that racism was abating (though illusions to this effect were common even among blacks). On the contrary, the black elite itself was a vital part of the system of [racial] oppression, serving as a buffer between the [ruling white] oppressor and [most truly black] oppressed and furthering the illusion that blacks could surmount their difficulties if only they had the exemplary qualities of the black elite. (Steinberg 1995, 149–50)*

The remarkable success of power-respectful, bourgeois, non-threatening (to whites) and (in short) "good" blacks like Barack Obama, Oprah Winfrey, and Colin Powell helps white Americans believe that blacks have only themselves to blame on the whole for black America's persistently separate and unequal status in the United States. For many whites, loving national black bourgeois media stars like Winfrey and Obama is the nice reverse side of hating poor inner-city black Americans.

The sophisticated and opportunistic Obama knows this very well. He's not going to complicate his comfortable funding relationships with the likes of Goldman Sachs, Morgan Stanley, Henry Crown and Co., and General Dynamics (Street 2007h; Street 2007b) by substantively criticizing empire and/or class inequality at home and abroad. In a similarly calculating and power-seeking vein, he's not about to undermine his favorable post–civil rights situation with the white electoral majority by making strong public reference to the persistently powerful and pervasive role of anti-black racism in U.S. life. He's going to try to ride white America's self-serving racial confusion and denial as far as he can—all the way, he hopes, to the White House.

POSTSCRIPT 1 (DECEMBER 2009) THE POST-RACIAL PRESIDENCY

As I detailed at length in my book *Barack Obama and the Future of American Politics* (2008),[1] presidential candidate Obama bent over backwards to demonstrate his "black but not like Jesse" (Jackson) safety to white America during the year that followed the publication of the above essay. As part of that project, he worked hard to distance himself as much as a potential "first black president" could from identification with the race issue and from the traditional black political charge—some (including this writer) might prefer to say "observation"—that the U.S. is a racist society. Expressing what *Newsweek* reporters Richard Wolffe and Darren Briscoe called in the summer of 2007 a "surprising lack of [racial] grievance" (Wolffe and Briscoe 2007), candidate Obama was less than eager to challenge reigning white wisdom on the "over"-ness of anti-black racial oppression in post–civil rights America. As *Black Agenda Report* executive director Glen Ford noted after Obama's critical victory in the Democratic presidential caucus in the predominantly white state of Iowa, the Obama campaign was "relentlessly send[ing] out signals to white people that a vote for Barack Obama, an Obama presidency, would signal the beginning of the end of black-specific agitation, that it would take race discourse off of the table. Barack Obama," Ford explained, "does not carry [black peoples'] burden, in addition to other burdens. He in fact promises to lift white-people-as-a-whole's burden, the burden of having to listen to these very specific and historical black complaints, to deal with the legacies of slavery. That is his promise to them" (*Democracy Now*, January 9, 2008).[2]

Obama's carefully calibrated response to the assault of the right-wing, the media, and Hillary Clinton on his longstanding relationship with his former pastor, the explicitly antiracist Reverend Jeremiah Wright, was consistent with that "promise." In his instantly famous and widely lauded "Philadelphia Race Speech" of March 18, 2008, Obama portrayed the racism that created the preacher's (supposedly) dysfunctional "anger" as a function mainly of *the past*. As *Black Commentator*'s Bill Fletcher noted, Obama "attributed much of the anger of Rev. Wright to the past, as if Rev. Wright is stuck in a time warp, *rather than the fact that Rev. Wright's anger about the domestic and foreign policies of the USA are well rooted—and documented-in the current reality of the USA* [emphasis added]" (Fletcher 2008).[3] Obama's speech bought heavily into the "past" versus "present racism" narrative that is common among those seeking to downplay the continuing power and relevance of racial oppression in American life.

"One Common Danger"

The post-racialist "promise" to post–civil rights white America has been kept during the Obama presidency. In his inaugural address, Obama proclaimed a "new era of responsibility," saying that "God calls on us to shape an uncertain destiny." He asked Americans to remember how

> *in the year of America's birth, in the coldest of months, a small band of patriots huddled by dying campfires on the shores of an icy river. The capital was abandoned. The enemy was advancing. The snow was stained with blood. At a moment when the outcome of our revolution was most in doubt, the father of our nation ordered these words be read to the people: "Let it be told to the future world . . . that in the depth of winter, when nothing but hope and virtue could survive . . . that the city and the country,* alarmed at one common danger, *came forth to meet (it) [emphasis added]."*

It was interesting and, for some (this writer included), disturbing to hear the nation's first black president citing the white founders' rebellion against England (1763–83) as an example of how "we" Americans need to stand together "against one common enemy." The early republic's many black chattel did not merit recognition as part of "the people" as far as the white U.S. majority was concerned. Many American slaves and indigenous people found and acted on good reasons to favor the British over the colonists in the war between England and the rising new racist and settler-imperialist slave state (Berlin 1976, 16–20; Foner 2005, 217–26). The new republic's snows and soils and forests and tobacco, rice, and cotton and killing fields had long been stained with the blood and tears of Native Americans and of a growing population of black chattel slaves. The fate and struggle of the early republic's black and red victims foretold the future struggles of Asians, Latin

Americans, and Middle Easterners caught on the wrong side of "freedom"-loving America's imperial guns, alliances, and doctrines.

There was nothing in Obama's inaugural address about rising poverty (a growing national problem with particularly harsh manifestations in the nation's persistently segregated minority communities) and stunning socioeconomic and racial inequality in the "homeland." His opening oration did, however, focus heavily on the predominantly white United States' supposed God-given right and duty to lead and run the mainly nonwhite world. After lecturing the Muslim world to "unclench its fist" (in what most have struck many Middle East and South Asia residents on the wrong side of the United States' guns as an ironic and offensive statement), Obama said that "we [the United States] will not apologize for our way of life," failing to mention that extreme racial (and related class and gender) disparities (along with many other unpleasant facts) remained a core aspect of the U.S. national experience and "way of life."

The Gates Incident

President Obama seemed to briefly break "post-racial" character when, during a mid-July 2009 press conference dedicated mainly to health reform, he responded angrily to a recent incident in which white Cambridge, Massachusetts, police officers had clumsily and unnecessarily arrested the celebrated black Harvard literature professor Henry Louis Gates, Jr., in Gates's home. But Obama quickly backed off his stance as the right-wing talk radio cadres and Fox News had a field day claiming that Obama had been unfair to the Caucasian cops, as the brouhaha over the Gates-Cambridge incident stole the thunder of the president's healthcare message, and as it became clear that Gates was not without a measure of blame for the incident.[4] Revealingly enough, the Gates-Cambridge-Obama episode came to a conclusion not with any White House effort to tackle the widespread problem of racial bias in the criminal justice system but rather with the officer who arrested Gates being invited to "have a beer" with the professor and the president in the White House's rose garden.

"If Racists Can Ostensibly Lose an Election..."

The Obama administration has demonstrated its willingness to accommodate white sentiments in other ways. It offered no defense of the largely minority-based urban activist organization ACORN when right-wing media and leading Republicans launched a neo-McCarthyite smear campaign against that group over the spring and summer of 2009. It asked for, and received, the resignation of the brilliant, highly qualified African America "green jobs czar" Van Jones, preposterously smeared as a "communist" and "black nationalist" reparations advocate by Fox News television host Glenn Beck in the same season. By the perceptive account of the black Pennsylvania death row inhabitant and political commentator Mumia Abu-Jamal, "Jones resigned, to protect a President who wouldn't protect him." Abu-Jamal was "reminded ... of Lani Guinier, another brilliant Yale trained Black lawyer, who got left hanging when racists dubbed her 'quota queen' when she was nominated for a post in the Clinton administration's Justice Dept."—a very apt analogy. "If racists can ostensibly lose an election, and still dictate policy," Abu-Jamal added, "then, have they really lost?" (Abu-Jamal 2009).

"President Says He Shouldn't Put Focus on Blacks' Troubles"

In early December 2009, the nation's first black president received some interesting criticism from the Congressional Black Caucus (CBC). Accusing the White House of ignoring the specific economic plight of minorities, ten members of the caucus boycotted a key House committee vote on financial regulations. The group expressed frustration at the White House and Congress' failure to tackle minority-specific economic problems including an official black unemployment rate of 16 percent, higher than the national rate of 10 percent. "We can no long afford for our public policy to be defined by the world view of Wall Street," the caucus announced, adding that "policy for the least of these must be integrated into everything we do."

Obama flatly rejected the criticism in a special interview with *USA Today* and the *Detroit Free Press* prior to a White House "jobs summit" in early December. "It's a mistake," Obama told the newspapers, "to start thinking in terms of particular ethnic segments of the United States rather than to think that we are all in this together and we are all going to get out of this together" (Hyde and Wolf 2009, 4A). Just because he happened to be black, Obama was announcing, black Americans should not think that he would be any more willing than George W. Bush or Bill Clinton to acknowledge and act upon the distinctive oppression and inequality still experienced by many in the United States' still highly segregated and relatively impoverished black population. The title of the *USA Today* article reporting Obama's response to the caucus' criticism was on point: "President Says He Shouldn't Put Focus on Blacks' Troubles."

Meanwhile, as the caucus knew, many in the black working and lower classes fell all too invisibly into ever-deeper material misery. Following the standard racial pattern in the history of American business cycles, the Great Recession that Obama inherited from the Bush years hit people of color harder than whites. The rising official black poverty and unemployment rates continued (as usual) to hover around double that of whites. Black and Latino communities already struggling with poverty and a shortage of affordable housing were pushed into shocking levels of destitution, joblessness, and foreclosure, experiencing a degree of concentrated misery before which the very real economic discomfort of white communities seemed mild by comparison. In a 2009 report titled "The Silent Depression: State of the Dream 2009," the progressive social research organization United for a Fair Economy noted that 10 percent of U.S. whites were living in official poverty, as compared to 24 percent of U.S. blacks and 21 percent of the nation's Latinos (Pascale and Beran 2009, 31).[5]

Olympic "One City" Silence

Another example comes from late September 2009. That's when Michelle Obama and then the president himself flew to Copenhagen to join Oprah Winfrey in high-profile lobbying of the International Olympic Committee (IOC) in support of Chicago's corporate, Democratic mayor Richard M. Daley's failed bid to make Chicago home for the 2016 Olympics. As progressive social-justice and civil rights activists and community organizers across the city had been pointing out for years, a Chicago Olympics would have primarily benefited the city's downtown business elite at the expense of city taxpayers. The city's plans particularly targeted inner-city black city residents on Chicago's South Side for clearance and removal, escalating an ongoing urban gentrification project that was pushing hundreds of thousands of impoverished African Americans out of black neighborhoods and to the margins of the metropolis and its glittering, ever-expanding corporate downtown (Zirin 2009; ABC 7 News 2009; Street 2007g, 51, 107, 164, 172, 260, 293, 296). As the black Chicago superstars, the Obamas and Winfrey, joined the city's white mayor in pitching the Midwestern metropolis as a glorious global city, hundreds of South Side residents planned to attend the funeral of a young black teenager, Derrion Albert, an honor student and innocent bystander who had recently been clubbed to death in a videotaped gang melee outside his South Side high school (CNN 2009). "Chicago," the president told the IOC, "is that most American of American cities, but one where citizens from more than 130 nations inhabit a rich tapestry of distinctive neighborhoods." Further:

Each one of those neighborhoods ... has its own unique character, its own unique history, its songs, its language. But each is also part of our city—one city—a city where I finally found a home.

Chicago is a place where we strive to celebrate what makes us different just as we celebrate what we have in common....

Chicago is a city where the practical and the inspirational exist in harmony ... It's a bustling metropolis with the warmth of a small town; where the world already comes together every day to live and work and reach for a dream—a dream that no matter who we are, where we come from; no matter what we look like or what hand life has dealt us; with hard work, and discipline, and dedication, we can make it if we try.

That's not just the American Dream. That is the Olympic spirit.[6]

City public schools' staffers noted that bloody battles were common in and around schools set in black Chicago's desperately impoverished neighborhoods, including communities where real unemployment had certainly climbed to 40 percent and higher. As the nation's first black president trumpeted his "home city" as a fit setting for the global games, the reality of black living conditions in that city's highly segregated ghetto communities spoke to the persistence and deepening of the concentrated urban misery that Dr. Martin Luther King, Jr., tried without success to overcome in black Chicago in the mid-1960s (Palmer 2009, Street 2007g).

Significantly, Derrion Albert's murder took place outside one of the Chicago Public Schools' (CPS) "turnaround schools." As part of the aggressive schools privatization ("reform") agenda pursued by former CPS CEO and Obama's corporatist education secretary Arne Duncan, Fenger High School (the scene of Albert's brutal murder) was "subjected," in the words of Chicago Teachers Union activist Deborah Lynch, "to the CPS' latest attack on struggling schools by dumping all the staff, even the engineers, and keeping the same students. The 'reform' was after probation, restructuring, reconstitution, and a host of other unsuccessful Daley-team draconian, top-down efforts"—efforts that stripped Fenger's highly troubled and poor, black student population of its connection to its teachers and other staff who had known them for years, "No one at Fenger this year has known their kids for more than three weeks," Lynch noted, adding that "this is a tragedy for all the students, not to mention the effects of the staff elimination on the staff."(Lynch 2009, 1, 13).

Revealingly enough, the best that the Olympics-focused White House could do in responding to news of Albert's murder was a weak comment from White House Press Secretary Gibbs. President Obama found the video of Albert's beating "chilling," Gibbs assured the nation. This comment came only in response to a reporter's question and not as part of any formal statement. The irony of the first black president and self-declared South Side Chicagoan Barack Obama's silence on the widely watched fatal beating as he sold his ghetto-ridden "home" metropolis' "small town" warmth to the IOC was not lost on some black citizens, including one who commented as follows in a blog discussion on the class difference between the Gates incident and the Derrion Albert killing: "u all think that Derrion Albert's mother will be invited to the White House for beer?"(Navarette, Jr. 2009).

"We've Got to Go Through Procedures"

Two weeks later, President Obama made his belated first presidential visit to New Orleans, site of Hurricane Katrina and the disastrous August 2005 hurricane and federal fiasco that left tens of thousands of disproportionately black and poor inner-city residents trapped by deadly floodwaters. Seeking to deflect criticism claiming that he had not paid sufficient attention to the city and the broader Mississippi Delta region, Obama appeared to overwhelming applause at a town-hall meeting to claim that "progress is being made" with federal recovery efforts. But the event's happy feeling was interrupted when a local resident asked, "Why is it, four years after Katrina, we're still fighting for money to repair our devastated city?" The questioner added, "I expected as much from the Bush administration. But why are we still being nickeled and dimed?"

Obama's response was less than impressive. It waxed dry, wonkish and technocratic as he referred to "complications between the state, the city, and the feds in making assessments of the damages."[7] According to the *New York Times*:

> *The president, in a rare moment on the defensive in a format that is usually friendly to him, said many people in New Orleans were "understandably impatient" and said he had inherited a backlog of problems.*
>
> *"These things were not going to be fixed tomorrow," Mr. Obama said. "So we are working as hard as we can, as quickly as we can." He added, "I wish I could just write a check."*
>
> *When some shouted "Why not?"' Mr. Obama replied, "There's this whole thing about the Constitution."*
>
> *He added that "We've got to go through procedures." (Baker and Robertson 2009, A16)*

Surely many in the town hall were well aware that the new president, the Democratic-majority Congress, and their constitutionally encoded "procedures" had managed to quickly grant trillions of taxpayer dollars to the nation's predominantly white financial barons and to the Pentagon and thus to the nation's powerful "defense" contractors. Some certainly reflected on the fact that Obama, the House of Representatives, and the Senate were spending vast federal resources on overseas wars of occupation while black ghettos, Latino barrios, and working-class communities of all races and ethnicities deteriorated across what Obama had joined George W. Bush in calling "the [imperial] homeland."

Tellingly enough, Obama the senator and presidential candidate made five visits to New Orleans after Katrina—a great symbol of Republican and Bush administration incompetence and callousness towards the poor. After waiting nine months to visit the devastated majority-black city he'd found so politically useful to speak from during his campaign, President Obama now stayed for only a few hours before jetting off to a posh and predominantly white-bourgeois Democratic Party fundraiser in San Francisco. During his short stop in New Orleans, Obama did manage to promote his and Arne Duncan's corporate-crafted schools privatization agenda by visiting the oxymoronically named "Martin Luther King Jr. Charter School" in the city's predominantly black, flood-ravaged Lower Ninth Ward. "The school," *Times* reporters Peter Baker and Campbell Robertson noted, was "surrounded by boarded-up houses, empty lots with overgrown grass and dilapidated storefronts with for-rent signs" (Baker and Robertson October 16, 2009, A16). Baker and Robertson might have noted that corporate education forces had seized on Katrina as a great opportunity, using the crisis to advance their privatization model on the reconstitution of New Orleans' school system (Klein 2007, 5). As *Times* columnist Maureen Dowd noted three days after Obama's brief stopover, the White House Web site that went up during Obama's first week in office boasted of four trips to New Orleans as senator. It pledged to "keep the broken promises made by President Bush to re-build New Orleans" (Dowd 2009).

"A Nation of Cowards"

In February of 2009, in a speech to his new employees at the Justice Department, the United States' first black attorney general Eric Holder caused a momentary media stir by saying that the U.S. "is a nation of cowards on race." Most Americans, Holder argued, avoid honest and serious discussion of the nation's continuing racial problems. Sadly enough, the administration in which Holder has served has done little indeed to move itself or the nation past "racial cowardice" beyond the simple fact of being headed by an African American.

There was no "betrayal" on this score, however. Obama's political team has always taken an official position of cowardice on race, generally refusing to seriously engage the volatile question of racism beyond the simple and admittedly symbolically powerful fact of advancing a black candidate for the presidency. The refusal is of course politically astute given "post–civil rights" white America's majority sentiment that racism no longer poses significant obstacles to black American advancement and racial equality, a sentiment that is sadly but unavoidably furthered by Obama's historic election.

"The Final Piece of Evidence That America Has Reached Full Racial Equality"

In one key sense at least, it seems possible that Obama's ascendancy heralded not simply "no change" for poor blacks but perhaps even—cruelly enough—change for the worse. I am referring to the significant extent to which the election of a technically black president reinforces the longstanding conventional white illusion that racism has disappeared and that the only obstacles left to African American success and equality are internal to individual blacks and their community—the aforementioned idea that, in "the indolence of blacks rather than the injustice of whites explains the socioeconomic gaps separating the races" (Bell 2004, 77–78). And what could trump the attainment of the U.S. presidency—the most powerful office on Earth—in feeding and locking in that belief? The black urban studies professor Marc Lamont Hill said it well in an important *CounterPunch* critique in early February of 2008:

> *After Obama's recent success with white voters, particularly his win in Iowa, many have announced America's transition into a post-racial moment. Even Obama himself has claimed that race will no longer prevent the fair-minded citizenry from supporting his bid. In reality, however, an Obama presidency is already being treated as a racial talisman that would instantly heal the scars of a nation wounded by racism.*
>
> *For whites, an Obama victory would serve as the final piece of evidence that America has reached full racial equality. Such a belief allows them to sidestep mounds of evidence that shows that, despite Obama's*

claims that "we are 90 percent of the way to equality," black people remain consistently assaulted by the forces by white supremacy. For many black people, Obama's success would provide symbolic value by showing that the black man (not woman!) can make it to the top. Although black faces in high places may provide psychological comfort, they are often incorporated into a Cosbyesque gospel of personal responsibility ("Obama did it, so can you!") that allows dangerous public policies to go unchallenged. (Hill 2008)

As one white Obama supporter told the *Washington Post* at a campaign event, he hoped that an Obama presidency would help America "erase all this nonsense about race."[8] How nice to imagine that racial oppression is something so nonsensical and superficial that it could be expunged by the mere act of putting into the White House a technically half-black politician who has gone out of his way not to threaten majority white cultural and ideological sensibilities surrounding race.

As some racial justice activists and intellectuals feared from the beginning of the Obama phenomenon, the ascendancy of Obama has not been an unmixed blessing for the cause of racial progress in America.

POSTSCRIPT 2 (JUNE 2012)
"IF I HAD A SON, HE'D LOOK LIKE TRAYVON"

Already terrible under George W. Bush, black economic circumstances worsened in the Age of Obama. As CBS reported in June of 2011, official unemployment had recently risen to 9.1 percent for the general U.S. population but surged to 16.2 percent for black Americans and 17.5 percent for black males. "Historically, the unemployment rate for African Americans has always been higher than the national average," CBS noted. "However, now it's at Depression-era levels" (Miller 2011). The official black unemployment measure rose considerably since Obama took office, when it stood at 12.6.[9] The black poverty rate reached 27 percent in 2010, nearly three times the white poverty rate (Tavernise 2011).

The foreclosure crisis disproportionately damaged black homeowners. As *Washington Post* reporters Michael Fletcher and John Cohen observed in February of 2011, it was "particularly devastating to African American and Latino families." In the transition from Bush to Obama, Fletcher and Cohen noted, black economic prospects deteriorated markedly: "Wages, homeownership rates and employment levels all grew worse for African-Americans between 2000 and 2007, a time in which the overall economy expanded. . . . African-Americans and Hispanics were more likely to be left broke, jobless and concerned that they lack the skills needed to shape their economic futures." Elaborating on the Great Recession's heavier toll on blacks, Fletcher and Cohen added that:

> *The downturn obliterated years of African-American economic progress—strides that were on shaky ground even before the recession . . . At the same time, some of the most reliable paths for blacks to ascend to the middle class are in danger of being narrowed . . . Federal, state and local governments, which employ a disproportionate share of African-Americans, are shedding jobs, a trend expected to continue in coming years. Meanwhile, the auto industry, long a bastion of high-paying, stable jobs that helped sustain many black middle-class families throughout the industrial Midwest, has been significantly downsized. (Fletcher and Cohen 2011)*

And Obama offered no real help, consistent with his earlier and repeated statements to the effect that he held no special concern for the plight of black Americans.

"If I had a son," the president of the United States said in March of 2012, "he'd look like Trayvon." It was hard to know exactly what to make of Obama's curiously narcissistic and identity-based comment on the chase and murder of seventeen-year-old Trayvon Martin by a white neighborhood watch captain in the central Florida town of Sanford a few weeks before. It was clear, however, that Obama had no intention of using the nationally prominent Martin incident (which sparked large black and black-led demonstrations across the country) as an occasion to put his administration behind a serious investigation of the many ways in which anti-black racism remains deeply entrenched in the American system he nominally headed—certainly not in an election year.

For what it's worth, Obama's rather vapid observation on what a son of his would look like was not the oddest thing he initially said about the Martin killing. His strangest remark was that he was "glad that the Justice Department was looking into it." That was a curious act of dissociation: the former constitutional law professor in the Oval Office certainly knew that he directed the Department of Justice from the White House.

POSTSCRIPT 3 (DECEMBER 2012)

National race cowardice in the Age of Obama remained alive and well during the 2012 presidential campaign and the re-election of the nation's first black president. Racism deeply understood remains firmly embedded in the U.S., where black median household wealth is equivalent now to 7 cents on the median white household wealth dollar; where black unemployment and poverty rates remain double those of whites; where blacks and Latinos together make up more than two thirds of the country's unmatched prison population; where one in three black male adults is saddled with the crippling mark of a felony record; and where millions of black children are stuck in highly segregated, inadequately funded, and standardized test score-obsessed schools

The problem was essentially nonexistent in the 2012 presidential race. It was more invisible than ever, cloaked in part by the deadly notion that the predominantly white electorate's willingness to elect a certain kind of black ("but-not-like-Jesse") candidate to the White House four years ago proves that racism is over as a barrier to black advancement and equality. Neither official candidate raised a peep about racially disparate mass incarceration or segregated schools or black inner city neighborhoods with unemployment and poverty rates over 40 percent.

Notes

From *Dissident Voice* 2007.

1. See Street 2008, 73–121. For more on Obama's race neutralism, during the campaign, see my following essays: Street 2007f; Street 2008).
2. "Barack Obama and the African American Community: A Debate with Michael Eric Dyson and Glen Ford," *Democracy Now*, January 9, 2008. http://www.democracynow.org/2008/1/9/barack_obama_and_the_african_american.
3. I had a very similar response. As I noted in a commentary that appeared two days after Obama's Philadelphia oration, "The oppression that angers Wright and other black Americans oppose is more than an overhang from the bad old past. The humiliation and hopelessness felt by millions of those Americans are being reinforced, generated, and expanded anew on a daily basis right now ... in the *21st century*. Black 'anger and bitterness' is being generated within the U.S. by racist policies and practices in *these* 'Joshua Generation' years as well as in '*those*' ('Moses Generation') years. New 'memories' of racial tyranny are being created *right now* beneath the national self congratulation over the defeat of level-one racism." See Paul Street, "Obama's Latest 'Beautiful Speech,'" *ZNet Magazine*, March 20, 2008, http://www.zcommunications.org/znet/viewArticle/16947.

4. As no mainstream reporters or commentators noted, moreover, Gates (described by the president as "a personal friend" from Harvard) was a curious martyr in the struggle against racial oppression. He had made something of a career on the Public Broadcasting System (PBS) arguing (in a sophisticated, Ivy League version of the well-known black-bourgeois Bill Cosby argument) that lower- and working-class blacks needed to stop pointing to racism and other forms of oppression as an explanation for their position at the bottom of the nation's hierarchies, arguing in a 2004 PBS special (titled *Beyond the Color Line*) for blacks to "master the ABCs, stay in school, work hard, defer gratification. What's happened to these values?" asked Gates, adding that "my father always said, and it's true, if we studied calculus like we studied basketball, we'd be running MIT. It's true and there's no excuse." This was the key theme in a previous PBS special narrated by Gates. In that documentary, titled *Two Nations*, Gates proclaimed that black poverty was pretty much about poor decisions: "deciding to get pregnant or not to have protected sex. Deciding to do drugs. Deciding not to study. Deciding, deciding, deciding." "The Two Nations of Black America: Interview with Henry Louis Gates, Jr.," *Frontline*, PBS, http://www.pbs.org/wgbh/pages/frontline/shows/race/interviews/gates.html; Street 2004; Johnson 2004.
5. Pascale and Beran noted that "Native Americans who live in circumstances that rival those of the poorest countries often do not even appear in government statistics."
6. "Remarks by the President and First Lady to the International Olympic Committee," Copenhagen, Denmark, October 2, 2009, http://www.whitehouse.gov/the_press_office/Remarks-By-the-President-And-the-First-Lady-to-the-International-Olympic-Committee.
7. Quoted in Maureen Dowd 2009, 9.
8. Quoted in Judis, March 12, 2008, 24.
9. "Black Unemployment Soared in January," *Daily Voice*, February 6, 2009, http://thedailyvoice.com/voice/2009/02/black-unemployment-soars-001583.php.

15. BARACK OBAMA'S (IM)PERFECT UNION

An Analysis of the Strategic Successes and Failures in His Speech on Race

EBONY UTLEY AND AMY L. HEYSE

IN MARCH 2008, PRESIDENTIAL CANDIDATE BARACK OBAMA WAS EN-gulfed in political controversy. Video recordings of his pastor and spiritual advisor, the Reverend Jeremiah Wright, Jr., were broadcast on every news channel and widely circulated on the Internet. The recordings featured snippets from Wright's most provocative sermons. One of those sermons, originally titled "Confusing God and the Government," delivered on April 13, 2003, was retitled "God Damn America" on YouTube. Wright preached that the United States government enacted genocide against Native Americans and African Americans, helped imprison Nelson Mandela, and manipulated God's word and will to sanction slavery and segregation. Wright implied that a racist government supported the infusion of drugs into black communities, frequently planted evidence against people of color, and preferred to imprison African Americans rather than provide them with the best education. Wright was also quoted repeatedly exclaiming, "God damn America" (Wright 2003).

On March 18, 2008, Obama issued a statement denouncing his longtime pastor's proclamations: "I vehemently disagree and strongly condemn the statements that have been the subject of this controversy. I categorically denounce any statement that disparages our great country or serves to divide us from our allies" (Obama 2008b). In that statement, Obama also described a personal relationship with Wright and explained that Wright "has never been my political advisor; he's been my pastor" (Obama 2008b). These clarifications, however, failed to satiate the news media and skeptical American voters. Obama hoped to finally put the issue to rest by directly addressing the controversy in a speech delivered in Philadelphia on March 18, 2008, titled "A More Perfect Union."

In this chapter, we argue that Barack Obama's "A More Perfect Union" was an appropriate and successful response to a political-personal crisis. Obama negotiated the controversy surrounding his personal relationship with the Reverend Wright by acknowledging racial disparities in the United States without placing blame for those disparities. Through this approach, Obama successfully maintained a post-racial rhetorical stance that appealed to extremely diverse audiences. We further argue, however, that the speech failed to accurately represent a racially differentiated United States of America. By sanitizing the country's histories of chattel slavery and racism, Obama's speech reified many harmful racial tropes. Our essay exposes the potentially damaging strategies Obama employed to resolve his political-personal crisis and considers the rhetorical implications of a post-racial discourse.

The chapter proceeds in four sections. In the first section, we explain the rhetorical situation and consider historical and rhetorical antecedents of political-personal crises for African American candidates. The second section is an analysis of the speech for Obama's successful post-racial strategies in addressing the Wright controversy. The third section examines the potentially harmful tropes Obama employed as he addressed the larger issue of American race relations. The essay's discussion of implications concludes with a contribution to the study of post-racial rhetoric.

THE RHETORICAL SITUATION AND POLITICAL-PERSONAL CRISIS

Barack Obama entered the political limelight in 2004 with his keynote address to the Democratic National Convention. Since then, the man and his messages have become popular subjects of academic study and critique (Asante 2007, 105–15; Burnside and Whitehurst 2007, 75–89; Clayton 2007, 52–63; Dorsey and Díaz-Barriga 2007, 90–104; Dumm 2008, 317–20; Frank and McPhail 2005, 571–94; Fraser 2009, 17–40; Harris 2009, 41–49; Harris-Lacewell and Junn 2007, 30–50; Hill 2009, 60–78; S. James 2009, 51–59; Marable 1990, 22–31; Marable 2009, 1–15; Mazama 2007, 3–6; McIlwain 2007, 64–74; Rowland and Jones 2007, 425–48; Walters 2007, 7–29). Some rhetorical scholars credit Obama's ecumenical discourse for its ability to "recast the American dream from a conservative to a liberal story" (Rowland and Jones 2007, 425), while others fault him for "ignor[ing] the historical and social realities of American racism" (Frank and McPhail 2005, 583). Obama's

"A More Perfect Union" speech offers rhetorical critics the opportunity to study his response to a pressing and pivotal rhetorical situation.

The rhetorical situation involving Reverend Wright was a political-personal crisis for Obama. According to Bitzer, a rhetorical situation is "a complex of persons, events, objects, and relations presenting an actual or potential exigence which can be completely or partially removed [by] discourse" (Bitzer 1968, 6). In March 2008, Obama's "exigence"—or the "imperfection marked by urgency"—was a political-personal crisis ignited by the circulation of Wright's incendiary remarks about the government (Bitzer 1968, 6). Candidates and incumbents encounter political-personal crisis situations when a personal event, association, or statement becomes a concern for the public; that is, when the populous becomes skeptical of a politician's ability to govern, lead, or faithfully execute their positions because of a personal happening. Candidates responding to a political-personal crisis may choose to ignore the situation, deny the situation, briefly address and then attempt to move away from the crisis, or appear open and willing to answer all questions and concerns (Tuman 2008).

The historical and rhetorical antecedents that are most informative for our analysis are those involving raced candidates whose political-personal crisis was related to their visible identification as nonwhite, an exigence that can be neither ignored nor denied (Hill 2009, 61). Successful raced candidates have dissolved voter concerns about their race and have been elected into office by employing rhetorical patterns of direct addresses in the form of the Jackson model, a neo-accomodationist approach, or a post-racial approach.

Speaking about race in frank yet non-confrontational terms is often referred to as the "Jackson model" and most closely aligns with the political-personal crisis strategy of appearing open and willing to answer difficult questions and concerns (Walters 2007, 16). Jesse Jackson ran for the Democratic nomination for president in 1984 and 1988, and although he did not win, he did succeed in gaining widespread support, especially with middle-class blacks who considered Jackson "a symbolic advocate of their own interests" (Marable 1990, 23). Jackson's now famous appeal to "the real rainbow coalition" (Jackson 1988) allowed him to address tough moral issues like racial equality because he believed that they were the keys to political success and equality for all (Jackson 1988, 9). Walters argues that Jackson's two campaigns were "the most important mobilizations of the black community in presidential politics to date," modeling a serviceable rhetorical strategy for raced candidates who followed (Walters 2007, 16).

Another observable rhetorical strategy of raced candidates is the neo-accommodationist approach (Marable 1990, 25). Accommodation is a strategy that black politicians from Booker T. Washington in the Reconstruction era to contemporaries like Douglas Wilder and David Dinkins employ to appear "non-threatening" and thereby electable to the white middle class (Marable 1990, 24). The cases of Douglas Wilder, the first black governor of Virginia, and David Dinkins, the first black mayor of New York City, are especially significant because they illuminate this rhetorical practice at work: "rather than denying the reality of race, Wilder and Dinkins sought to 'transcend' the color line, offering generous platitudes of how racism had supposedly declined in significance during the 1980s" (Marable 1990, 25, 28). While both of these men won their positions, Marable cautions that the accommodation strategy may do more harm than good: "the strategy of declaring victory against racial prejudice may produce some short-term victories, but it will only reinforce white supremacy within the electoral process in the long run" (Marable 1990, 25).

The final rhetorical strategy of raced candidates is the post-racial approach. Harris best explains this "race-neutral" rhetoric: "Fearful that white voters would be turned off by policy positions that steered too closely to black interests, black candidates running before majority or near-majority white constituencies have to adopt campaign strategies that deemphasize race. These strategies deemphasize or neglect discussions about racism but take up the banner of racial unity and public policies that appeal to all citizens as a way to allay the concerns of white voters" (Harris 2009, 43). Political agents like Harold Washington, Chicago's first black mayor in 1983, Cory Booker, mayor of Newark, New Jersey in 2006, and Deval Patrick, governor of Massachusetts in 2006, have successfully employed this strategy to win their offices. In his inaugural address, after a viscous campaign season (Davis 1983), Washington announced, "Racial fears and divisiveness have hurt us in the past. But I believe that this is a situation that will and must be overcome" (Washington April 29, 1983). Similarly, Booker adopted a post-racial perspective in his State of the City address in which he repeatedly declared, "we will rise" to the residents of Newark, New Jersey (Booker February 9, 2009). Patrick summed up his post-racial position in his campaign slogan, "together we can."[1] However, just as Marable warns about the long-term impact of a neo-accommodationist perspective, Harris cautions that "while [the post-racial approach] can be a winnable strategy for black candidates running in state-wide and national campaigns, it often leaves issues that are specific to the concerns of black voters off the public agenda"

(Harris 2009, 43). Unlike the Jackson model, post-racial political rhetoric does not outwardly address the role of race in politics and society, and unlike the neo-accommodationist angle, post-racial discourse does not declare racism defeated. However, both the neo-accomodationist and post-racial approaches mimic the political-personal crisis resolution strategy of briefly addressing race and attempting to transcend it.

It has been widely argued that Barack Obama is a post-racial candidate who speaks in universal terms so as to have the greatest rhetorical appeal.[2] Obama himself affirmed this perspective. In an interview on National Public Radio, Obama explained that "there has always been some tension between speaking in universal terms and speaking in very race-specific terms about the plight of the African American community. By virtue of my background, I am more likely to speak in universal terms."[3] When describing how Obama addressed his background, journalist Gwen Ifill notes, "He did not deny his race, but he generally didn't bring it up either" (Ifill 2009, 54). In 2007, another reporter, Tom Baldwin for the *Times of London*, observes that Obama "did not make a single reference to the color of his skin.... Not once did the words 'black' or 'African-American' pass Mr. Obama's lips" in his announcement of candidacy speech.[4] Perhaps best summing up the perspectives on Obama as a post-racial candidate, though, was a black Obama pollster who once mused, "A *black man* can't be president of America. However, an extraordinary, gifted, and talented young man who happens to be black can be president."[5]

While effective in some spheres, the post-racial approach is roundly criticized in other camps because the perspective ignores the unique concerns of the black community. It attempts to transcend race without transcending racial inequality (Roediger 2008). Mazama argues that the notion of transcending race may be inherently racist because non-raced candidates are never asked or expected to do so (Mazama 2007, 3). Frank and McPhail read Obama's 2004 conciliatory Democratic National Convention (DNC) speech, for example, as "an old vision of racelessness" that appealed to "rhetorics of whiteness and modern racism" (Frank and McPhail 2005, 572–73. Professor of religion and African American studies Eddie Glaude is also disappointed with Obama's stance: "Why is it the case that he can't simply say, when we talk about health care, we know it disproportionately affects poor people and black people? Why can't he begin to talk about these issues in ways that identify black communities, without trying to sound like Jesse Jackson and Al Sharpton? The thing is, the very way that Jesse and Al have exploited the theater of racial politics, he's doing it from a different vantage point. We haven't changed the game. That's what makes me so angry. He hasn't stepped outside of the game."[6] The rhetorical situation of the political-personal crisis presents an opportunity to step outside of the game. A measured and appropriate response that addresses the exigence (seemingly) divulges all information, and satisfies all concerned audiences, then, could take the form of the Jackson model, accommodation, or a post-racial position.

Shortly after winning the Iowa caucus in January 2008, "the Wright controversy brought race to the forefront" and challenged Obama's post-racial rhetoric (Fraser 2009, 31). In what has now been dubbed "the race speech," Obama was forced to openly and directly discuss race relations with the American public rather than in one of his carefully edited autobiographies (Dumm 2007, 317–20). While directly speaking about race, Obama remarkably managed to retain his post-racial stance. As Darsey observes, "Obama's 'race speech' . . . one of the most important and most highly publicized speeches of the campaign, illuminates the nexus at which Obama seeks to transcend the limits of racial identification and to identify his narrative with the American narrative" (Darsey 2009, 98). Similarly, Fraser adds that, "while to many academics and liberals the issues Obama raised were not groundbreaking, the speech was remarkable in its ability to speak to those white voters in Middle America, who may not have given serious thought to racial inequalities before, while maintaining his postracial message of unity" (Fraser 2009, 32). Even though Obama has been cast by others and often casts himself as a post-racial candidate who transcends race, he acknowledges racial divides. When, how, and why he acknowledges race issues are important to scholars of race during the post-racial Obama presidency because Obama's discourse paradigmatically represents conversations about race and racism in our society. In the following section, we posit specific ways that the post-racial rhetorical strategy was successful in gaining political power for Barack Obama.

THE RHETORICAL SUCCESSES OF A POST-RACIAL CANDIDATE

After Wright's incendiary indictments of the government became public, Obama's exigence was his relationship with Wright. Wright's discourse threatened Obama's favor with voters, particularly independent voters, who might have associated his politics and decision making with Wright's perceived racism. Openly admitting his relationship with Wright, Obama asked for the public's understanding and their continued support of his candidacy. To ultimately regain favor with the voting public, Obama employed a master strategy of identification that included 1) directly asking and answering questions, 2) situating Wright as a member of the Obama family, the community, and the American people, and 3) limning Wright within the parameters of the civil rights movement of the 1950s and 1960s.

Rhetorical theorist Kenneth Burke describes identification as a strategy of building common ground between individuals in order to reduce the division amongst them (Burke 1969). This strategy is a hallmark of postracial rhetoric as the rhetor attempts to unite his/her listeners and move them past race. Obama attempted to bridge the racial divide by asserting that "working together, we can move beyond some of our old racial wounds, and that in fact we have no choice if we are to continue on the path of a more perfect union" (Obama 2008b, 5). Calling for all Americans to "find that common stake we all have in one another," Obama asked his diverse audiences to band together, put race aside, and work towards common goals (Obama 2008b, 6). Implicit in his appeal was the suggestion that voters also "move beyond" the Wright controversy and elect Barack Obama president (Obama 2008b, 6).

Obama first attempted to build identification with his audience by directly asking and answering questions about his relationship with Wright. These were questions he imagined still remained in the minds of skeptical Americans even after the release of his statement. Such a strategy cast the rhetor as open and honest, as someone who seriously considered tough questions and answered them plainly. In other words, Obama did not avoid or ignore the concerns of voters; he directly addressed them: "I supposed the politically safe thing to do would be to move on from this episode and just hope that it fades into the woodwork" (Obama 2008b, 4). But Obama would not do that; instead, he would stay and answer the tough questions. Obama explained, "For some, nagging questions remain. Did I know him to be an occasionally fierce critic of American domestic and foreign policy? Of course. Did I ever hear him make remarks that could be considered controversial while I sat in church? Yes. Did I strongly disagree with many of his political views? Absolutely—just as I'm sure many of you have heard remarks from your pastors, priests, or rabbis with which you strongly disagree" (Obama 2008b, 3). Obama's answers were simple—"of course," "yes," and "absolutely"—which are uncommon and perhaps refreshing responses from a political rhetor. Obama appeared to fully disclose his knowledge of Wright by bluntly responding to the doubts against himself. It could be argued, though, that Obama's answers were *too* simple. Perhaps this is why the next part of his speech was devoted to elaborate and detailed responses.

While the next questions were not so simply answered, Obama presented himself up to that point as someone who frankly replies to tough questions, so his listeners were more likely to trust and believe his longer and more in-depth responses. Put simply, his straightforward responses to the previous questions boosted his ethos. Now imagining what his inquisitors would like to know, Obama queried, "Why associate myself with Reverend Wright in the first place, they may ask? Why not join another church?" (Obama 2008b, 3). Obama began his response by building identification with his inquisitors: "I confess that if all that I knew of Reverend Wright were the snippets of those sermons that have run in an endless loop on the television sets and YouTube, or if Trinity United Church of Christ conformed to the caricatures being peddled by some commentators, there is no doubt that I would react in much the same way" (Obama 2008b, 5). This statement presented the concerns of his skeptics as valid and worthy of serious attention, and therefore deserving of thoughtful, honest answers.

Once identification with his audience had been solidified through the construction of his ethos, Obama attempted to transfer positive credibility to Wright. Obama explained that judging Wright based on the media representations of him was a mistake, especially because Wright "is a man who helped introduce me to my Christian faith, a man who spoke to me about our obligations to love one another, to care for the sick and lift up the poor" (Obama 2008b, 3). Obama further explained that Wright "is a man who served his country as a United States Marine; who has studied and lectured at some of the finest universities and seminaries in the country, and who for over 30 years has led a church that serves the community by doing God's work here on Earth—by housing the homeless, ministering to the needy, providing day care services and scholarships and prison ministries, and reaching out to those suffering from HIV/AIDS" (Obama 2008b, 3). Obama answered the question—why associate myself with Reverend Wright—by presenting comparable ethos for both men. They associated because they shared the same faith and the same passion for their country and their communities.

Obama's second identification strategy situated Wright within the Obama family, the black community, and the American family. By placing Wright within these groups, Obama reframed the image of Wright as a demagogue into a family man/community member/typical American. This strategy is characteristically post-racial as Obama attempted to transcend

Wright's racial identity into universal terms. Obama explained, "As imperfect as he may be, he has been like family to me. He strengthened my faith, officiated my wedding, and baptized my children" (Obama 2008b, 4). Obama expounded in greater detail his familial relationship to Wright: "I can no more disown him than I can disown the black community. I can no more disown him than I can disown my white grandmother" (Obama 2008b, 4). Obama could not disown Wright who was part of the Obama family and an important member of the larger black community. Obama took the next step and rhetorically identified his family, his pastor, and the black community within the larger American public: "These people are a part of me. And they are part of America, this country that I love" (Obama 2008b, 4). Because his audience was also "part of America," Obama could no less disown Wright as he could disown any American.

The third identification strategy Obama utilized in his speech associated Wright with not just a group of people, but with an important period of time in U.S. history. Wright's connection with the civil rights movement helped Obama explain the mindset of a generation who "came of age in the late '50s and early '60s, a time when segregation was still the law of the land and opportunity was systematically constricted" (Obama 2008b, 5). Wright was not the only black man to feel angry about injustices such as racism. In fact, "for those blacks who did make it, questions of race and racism continue to define their worldview in fundamental ways. For the men and women of Reverend Wright's generation, the memories of humiliation and doubt and fear have not gone away; nor has the anger and the bitterness of those years" (Obama 2008b, 6). In other words, Wright was just one of many black people who still felt angry about the violent racism they endured in the 1950s and 1960s; therefore, the American public should not single him out and scapegoat him for merely identifying with what so many others had felt.

The rhetorical choices Obama made in "A More Perfect Union" appropriately addressed the biggest rhetorical crisis of his campaign by promoting identification with and among his audiences. By directly asking and answering the questions of concerned voters, Obama painted himself as an open and honest candidate who was unwilling to ignore or skirt past the controversy in front of him. Obama also chose to identify Wright with the Obama family, the community, and the American people, effectively explaining why Obama could not completely extricate himself from their relationship. Also, by associating Wright with the civil rights movement, Obama argued that Wright was consubstantial with the numerous African Americans who remembered racist policies like segregation.

Taken together, these identification strategies helped Obama maintain his post-racial stance, appropriately address the concerns of the American people, and ultimately transform the rhetorical situation from a specific controversy about Wright to a larger discussion about U.S. race relations and the role of race in American politics. Identification, however, is a Janus-faced rhetorical strategy. It is always accompanied by division (Burke 1969, 22). The following section on Obama's strategic failures addresses how his identification strategies held the potential to progressively alienate black audiences.

THE STRATEGIC FAILURES OF A POST-RACIAL PERSPECTIVE

Obama's post-racial stance ostensibly increased identification among his non-African American audiences but potentially failed to maintain commensurate identification among his black audiences by 1) de-emphasizing his African influences, 2) eliding African American rhetorical traditions, 3) sanitizing the United States' history of racial injustice, and 4) problematically representing black and white Americans' experiences. Careful to not disturb the racial hierarchy, Obama failed to engage serious discussions of race relations in the United States partially by alienating himself from African and African American history and also by reifying revisionist versions of race talk that hegemonically maintain the status quo.

Obama's first strategic failure was the de-emphasis of his African influences. He began his racial genealogy by describing himself as "the son of a black man from Kenya and a white woman from Kansas" (Obama 2008b, 2). He did not identify his father as an African man; neither did he geographically situate Kenya in Africa. By describing his father as a black man, Obama extracted him from an African heritage. Furthermore, when he described his wife as a "black American," instead of an African American, he removed her from African influences as well (Obama 2008b, 2). He admitted that she "carries within her the blood of slaves and slave owners," but at no point in the speech were these slaves referred to as Africans (Obama 2008b, 2). Obama emphasized Michelle Obama's mixed ancestry in order to dilute her experiences as a black woman of African ancestry. By acknowledging the slave owner ancestors in her bloodline, Obama simultaneously acknowledged the unique aspects of the black American experience, celebrated the diversity of mixed black ancestry, and distanced himself and his wife from African influences by choosing not to use the term. Obama used his personal history to create identification between himself and his diverse audiences, but by understating his and his family's African heritage, he ignored the horrors of the African slave trade and the beauty of the linguistic, spiritual, and cultural African diaspora that has contributed to diversity around the globe.

Obama's second strategic failure of his post-racial perspective was his elision of African American rhetorical religious traditions. Obama chastised Wright for expanding the racial lacuna without considering whether there was some measure of truth to some of his words. By refusing to cite anything spoken by Wright, audiences could not be sure which of Wright's inflammatory comments Obama condemned. One might assume that all of them should be condemned. Wright was certainly controversial, but his subject position was rooted in a black liberation preaching tradition that condemns injustice in society and urges God's people to resist it. Obama ignored what Frank and McPhail called a "spiritually inspired militancy" (Frank and McPhail 2005, 582) when he described Trinity United Church of Christ's virtues in terms of social welfare projects like "housing the homeless, ministering to the needy, providing day care services and scholarships and prison ministries, and reaching out to those suffering from HIV/AIDS" (Obama 2008b, 3) and not identifying the church with social justice projects like boycotting discriminatory establishments, protesting police brutality, and holding one's elected officials accountable for their misrepresentation and misdeeds.

Obama further depoliticized black religious rhetoric by downplaying the struggles between the oppressed and their oppressors. He ironically cited the stories of David and Goliath, Moses and Pharaoh, and the Christians in the lion's den without identifying David, Moses, and the Christians as the oppressed populations persecuted by a power structure that discriminated against them because of their difference. This religious history has been adopted by African Americans primarily because it mimics their social position and the potential for the pursuit of justice. Obama appreciated the Biblical stories yet failed to historically situate them within black liberation traditions to maintain the division from the concept of an oppressive power structure from which blacks must be liberated.

In addition to Obama's lack of recognition for black speaking traditions, his third strategic failure was including a sanitized version of the United States' history of racial injustice. Marable praised Obama for "refusing to be defined or restricted by that history," but we argue that historical omissions compromised Obama's pleas for racial unity (Marable 2009, 9). For instance,

Obama opened the speech with a reference to the U.S. Constitution and described its preamble as "ultimately unfinished" but answering "the slavery question" by promising a more perfect union of liberty and justice for all American people (Obama 2008b, 1). Obama neglected to mention that all American people have not wholeheartedly embraced the Constitution as an antislavery document. Garrisonian abolitionists refused to abide by the Constitution because they believed it to be inherently flawed as a proslavery document (Schrader 1999, 85–99). Contemporary philosophers are still debating whether or not the intent behind the Constitution will allow it to truly benefit black Americans, but Obama adduced a foregone conclusion (Mills 1999, 100–42).

Obama continued to champion the decency, generosity, greatness, and goodness of the American people without acknowledging their less charitable characteristics. If the country is indeed great and good, one must consider the unpaid labor and lives of those whose were sacrificed for it to become that way. Obama wanted to celebrate and identify with what is great about the United States of America without accounting for the exploitation of American Indian, African American, and immigrant populations who made it that way. His nods to "inferior education," "legalized discrimination," and "a lack of economic opportunity" for African Americans were depicted as unfortunate consequences of a bygone era of segregation that is steadily improving and not the result of centuries of oppression and power distributions that remain unchanged despite his mantras of hope and change (Obama 2008b, 5). Obama criticized Wright for describing our country as "still irrevocably bound to a tragic past" without considering how traces of this tragic past shape reality for many of the country's citizens. Obama maintained his post-racial stance by not mentioning how whites benefit from racism (Obama 2008b, 7).

Racism includes institutional forms of discrimination against a group of people based upon their physical characteristics—primarily their skin color. Hill describes racism as "[giving] framework to the superstructural, substructural, and infrastructural processes and institutions that practice racial exclusion, circumscription, and proscription" (Hill 2009, 62). Racism is a privilege of those with power and access to resources. African Americans cannot be racist in the way whites have the potential to be racist because they do not control the institutions that maintain systematic privileges for whites (Asumah 2004, 501–10; Hill 2009). Obama described how the Reagan coalition, politicians, and media personalities wielded their power at the expense of the black community, but failed to identify those actions as legitimate, sanctioned forms of institutionalized racism. Every individual harbors prejudices. Any individual can discriminate against another, but racism is connected to power. Obama's grandmother's racial stereotypes cannot be equated with Wright's identification of how privileges continue to benefit those in power. His grandmother most likely harbored prejudices and spoke out of ignorance. Wright spoke about power in his articulation of the ways in which blacks have systematically been exploited by their government's racist practices.

Similar to his comparison of his grandmother and Wright, Obama's fourth strategic failure was a problematic representation of black and white Americans' experiences by equating their frustrations and reifying racial stereotypes. Frank and McPhail note Obama's penchant for conflation in his 2004 DNC speech when he used "the rhetorical strategy of conflating the experiences of white ethnics with persons of African descent, and of denying the role of white power and privilege on the demoralizing conditions that continue to disproportionately affect the lives of black folk in America. Obama's rhetoric, while stylistically appealing, nonetheless ignores the historical and social realities of American racism" (Frank and McPhail 2005, 583).

Specifically in his "race speech," when Obama equated black and white frustrations, he effectively likened apples to apple pickers. African Americans who are struggling are not frustrated because they haphazardly fell on hard times. These individuals are oftentimes frustrated because many white Americans have benefited from their misfortune. A white American who loses a job today is not equally frustrated as the African American who has been discriminated against for years and was never able to work a job commensurate with her skills and education simply because of the color of her skin. An immigrant who is disappointed by the lack of opportunities is not on equal footing with an African American who is not considered equal even though his stolen, traded, and purchased ancestors made this country prosperous.

Obama also equated the black and white "middle-class squeeze" experience, but the facts belied his optimism. According to the most recent calculation, the median household income for blacks is $33,916 whereas the median income for whites is $52,115 (Orozco and Tomarelli 2009, 26). United for a Fair Economy reports that "existing trends would not equalize black and white median household wealth for more than half a millennium."[7] Despite talk of economic parity, Patillo describes the white and black middle class as two separate and unequal entities (Patillo-McCoy 2000).

Despite his tendency to gloss over the differences in black and white lived experiences, Obama was not ignorant of the historical discrimination against African Americans. He conceded: "Legalized discrimination, where blacks were prevented, often through violence, from owning property, or loans were not granted to African American business owners, or black homeowners could not access FHA mortgages, or blacks were excluded from unions, or the police force, or the fire department meant that black families could not amass any meaningful wealth to bequeath to future generations" (Obama 2008b, 5). Unfortunately, Obama's description of discriminatory effects in his "race speech" paralleled Frank and McPhail's prior observation of his DNC speech: that is, Obama's rhetoric "fail[ed] to address in *substantive* [italics added] terms the material realities of African American trauma" (Frank and McPhail 2005, 587). Some of those substantive distinctions included the facts that "African Americans remain twice as likely as whites to be unemployed, three times more likely to live in poverty and more than six times as likely to be incarcerated. (Wilson 2009, 15). Wilson continues, stating that "an economic downturn only amplifies the existing gaps between black and white America" (Wilson 2009, 15). Nearly twice as many African Americans lack health insurance compared to whites (Orozco and Tomarelli 2009, 31). Smith reports: "Over fifty years after *Brown v. Board of Education*, nearly half of our nation's African-American students, nearly 40 percent of Latino students and 11 percent of white students attend high schools in which graduation is not the norm" (H. F. Smith 2009, 45–46). Additionally, Obama limned injustice to "the reality in which Reverend Wright and other African Americans of his generation grew up ... in the late '50s and early '60s, a time when segregation was still the law of the land and opportunity was systematically constricted" (Obama 2008b, 5). In his attempt to envision a better future, Obama strategically regulated the non-specific racial disparities he did mention to a distant past.

Obama further misrepresented black and white frustrations by reifying racial stereotypes. He sanitized the conditions in which many blacks live by characterizing the problems as "injustice and inequality" instead of oppression, exploitation, and degradation. Furthermore, Obama perpetuated a bias when he depicted blacks as charismatic, emotional, bawdy, bitter, biased, and angry. Whites were not characterized in similarly unflattering terms. They merely "have ... resentments" (Obama 2008b, 6). Since Obama was advocating for equality, both blacks and whites should "have resentments," but instead he depicted blacks as stereotypically angry, emotional, and bitter. Obama also seemed comfortable perpetuating the stereotype of black "economic dependency and laziness" as often portrayed in the welfare recipient (Mendelberg 2001, 29). When explaining to his listeners how Trinity United Church of Christ "embodied the black community in its entirety," Obama listed the "welfare mom" alongside "the doctor" and the "former gang banger" (Obama 2008b, 3). Hardly a passing mention, Obama went on to cite "welfare and affirmative action" as sources of white anger (Obama 2008b, 5), "welfare policies" as a problem for black families (Obama 2008b, 4), and the myth about "blacks who were on welfare and too lazy to work" as potentially infecting the mindset of a white woman (Obama 2008b, 7). Racist depictions of black welfare recipients have been perpetuated in this country from the individual to the halls of congress as warrants for welfare reform (Collins 2000a; Gring-Pemble 2001, 341–66; Gring-Pemble 2003, 473–98). Obama's use of the welfare trope brought him into a potentially racist realm of political discourse. Despite acknowledging the "complexities of race in this country that we've never really worked through," Obama's speech made clear that he was not going to heal that divide at the expense of his more perfect union (Obama 2008b, 5).

In addition, Obama's general tendency was to hold blacks responsible for racial progress. When he described Americans who were willing to "do their part," protesting and struggling "on the streets and in the courts, through a civil war and civil disobedience," images of primarily African Americans likely came to mind (Obama 2008b, 2). Those who risked their lives for equality and justice during the civil rights and Black Power movements were primarily young black people. Throughout U.S. history, the oppressors—that is, the slave owners, the slave traders, the segregationists, and the variously biased representatives of the government—were not part of this power struggle. They were not identified and they were not held accountable here. The responsibility for justice continues to lie with those who have been oppressed. Obama actually urged the African American population to "bind our particular grievances ... to the larger aspirations of all Americans" (Obama 2008b, 7). Does that mean racial injustice should be overlooked for the greater good? Is racism less important than the concerns of all Americans? Obama suggested that focusing on better healthcare, schools, and jobs was more important than the racial divisions that create disparities in healthcare, education, and employment.

Although Obama depicted blacks as primarily responsible for righting racial wrongs, in his final anecdote, the powerful dénouement of the speech, Obama portrayed whites as overseers of the struggle. According to Davis, the trope of white liberal saviors who sacrifice themselves to help blacks become more like whites is legendary in African American literature and in practice (Davis 2000). Obama revived this trope as he told the story of Ashley's commitment "to organize a mostly African American community" and narrated her struggles against injustice (Obama 2008b, 9). After privileging Ashley's lived experiences, Obama included the response of a nameless elderly black man to her plight. The man said, "I am here because of Ashley" (Obama 2008b, 9). Obama's more perfect union was premised upon a nameless subservient black man who shared the desires of his white female organizer. Historically black men were conditioned to acquiesce to white women out of fear of being lynched. For fifty years, black men were systematically murdered for infractions as slight as preparing to glance in the direction of a white woman. The racial paranoia of the black brute's "sexual retribution" for victimizing pure white womanhood was the foundation for Restoration, mob violence, de facto, and de jure segregation and yet Obama proudly alluded to it within the context of a more perfect union (Mendelberg 2001). Obama urged his audiences to move beyond race "in the same direction: towards a better future for our children and our grandchildren" (Obama 2008b, 2). We urge our audiences to understand that this better future was compromised by Obama's perpetuation of racist tropes.

Despite his attempts at unity and universality, Obama's speech ultimately failed to build a more perfect racial union because of his over-identification with non-African American audiences through the elision of black history and the use of raced stereotypes at the expense of black audiences. As a raced candidate running a post-racial campaign, Obama may have resolved his personal crisis but the perpetual sociopolitical crisis surrounding race and racism remained unresolved in his speech and possibly in his presidency.

Public discussions of race in the United States are rarely afforded the wide exposure or support that Obama's speech has enjoyed. In fact, the speech was instantly lauded as "perhaps the most important political speech since John Kennedy's in the 1960 presidential campaign, when he took on the issue of his Catholic faith before an audience of Protestant ministers" (Dumm 2008, 318). The speech has received many accolades for meeting its rhetorical exigencies and effectively calming the nation's fears about Obama's potential racialized radicalism. A *New York Times* editorial states, "It is hard to imagine how he could have handled it better" (*New York Times* March 18, 2008)." James Fallow of *The Atlantic* asserts, "It was a moment that Obama made great through the seriousness, intelligence, eloquence, and courage of what he said. I don't recall another speech about race with as little pandering or posturing or shying from awkward points, and as much honest attempt to explain and connect, as this one" (Fallow March 18, 2008). Andrew Sullivan of *The Daily Dish* similarly celebrates the speech: "I do want to say that this searing, nuanced, gut-wrenching, loyal, and deeply, deeply Christian speech is the most honest speech on race in America in my adult lifetime. It is a speech we have all been waiting for for a generation. Its ability to embrace both the legitimate fears and resentments of whites and the understandable anger and dashed hopes of many blacks was, in my view, unique in recent American history" (A. Sullivan March 18, 2008). And yet this masterfully given speech belied the contours of race and the effects of racism in the United States.

A speech of this caliber deserves careful critical interrogation because of its rarity and because of its impact on how the country will address issues of social justice. Can we assume that those voters and political pundits who gushed over the speech are also gushing over the idea of a post-racial society? Are they comfortable with erasing African influences from the black American experience? Are all black people who talk about endemic racism and social justice merely angry people from the civil rights era? Do they believe that all Americans share the same frustrations? Do they expect black men to remain subservient to white women? Answers to these questions lie in an analysis of reactions to the speech, which is outside of the scope of this essay. We can conclude from our analysis, however, that these perspectives are possible and permissible within the context of the speech.

CONCLUSION

Obama's political-personal crisis was colored by race, but his response failed to include a productive analysis of race and that absence may have contributed to the text's success. A speech this effective at negotiating a political-personal crisis is misleading because it looks, on its surface, as if it met all of its goals. This is not the case. Obama's more perfect union was peppered with imperfections in its sanitized history of race and racism in the United States. The speech failed to equally identify with the distinct experiences of black and white Americans. It is impossible to be fully post-racial in a society with such stark racial disparities. Although scholars have cautioned against the negative effects of race-neutral discourse, this essay contributes to the conversation by showing which aspects of post-racial rhetoric may help the rhetor but be detrimental to a productive discussion about race.

"A More Perfect Union" was not the incontrovertible word on race but a significant contribution towards understanding the role of identification in discourse about race to mixed-race audiences. Specifically, we find that identification can be an invaluable rhetorical resource for raced candidates as they seek to build racial unity as long as they do not over-identify with select audiences. Our balanced reading of Obama's successes and failures provides an alternative perspective on the speech that contributes to more complex analyses of the merits and disadvantages of post-racial discourse.

Notes

1. Quoted in Ifil 2009, 194.
2. See, for example, Burnside and Whitehurst 2007, Frank and McPhail 2005, Fraser 2009; Hill 2009; Ifill 2009; Mazama 2007; Roediger 2008; Rowland and Jones 2007; Walters 2007.
3. Barack Obama, "Obama to Attend Selma March Anniversary." Interview by Steve Inskeep, *National Public Radio*, February 28, 2007, http://www.npr.org/templates/story/story.php?storyId=7630250, quoted in Walters, "Barack Obama," 13–14.
4. Tom Baldwin, "Obama Seeks 'Stay Fresh' Formula as He Tries to Widen Appeal," *(London) Times*, February 12, 2007, http://www.timesonline.co.uk/tol/news/world/us_and_americas/article1368652.ece, quoted in Walters, "Barack Obama," 19.
5. Quoted in Ifill 2009, 54.
6. Ibid., 69.
7. Rivera, Cotto-Escalera, Desai, Huezo, and Muhammad 2008 quoted in Roediger, "Race Will Survive," 2.

EPILOGUE

Obama, Race, and the 2012 Presidential Election

PAUL SPICKARD

IN THE WAKE OF THE 2012 PRESIDENTIAL ELECTION, PAUL WEST WROTE in the *Los Angeles Times* that "even more than the election that made Barack Obama the first black president, the one that returned him to office sent an unmistakable signal that the hegemony of the straight white male in America is over" (West 2012). Well, maybe not so much.

It is true that President Obama was elected to a second term, and in no small part because he possesses a remarkable set of racial skills. He grew up in a polyglot international world. He was born to a White American mother and a Black Kenyan father, raised in Hawai'i, then in Indonesia, and finally back in that little bit of Kansas that his grandparents created for him in Honolulu (Obama 1995). He went off to college and then to law school. He learned to see himself and to be accepted as a Black American when he was a community organizer in Chicago, in much the same way that a small-town New England boy of mixed ancestry, W. E. B. Du Bois, learned to be Black when he went to Fisk University nearly a century before.[1]

Obama has always performed Whiteness perfectly, and he has usually performed Blackness pretty convincingly—these are among the skills that have been crucial to his success. His breakthrough moment came at the 2004 Democratic National Convention in Boston, where he delivered the keynote speech. Showing promise of a future as healer-in-chief, he proclaimed:

> *There is not a liberal America and a conservative America—there is the United States of America. There is not a Black America and a White America and Latino America and Asian America—there's the United States of America....*

> We worship an "awesome God" in the blue states, and we don't like federal agents poking around in our libraries in the red states. We coach Little League in the blue states and yes, we've got some gay friends in the red states. There are patriots who opposed the war in Iraq and there are patriots who supported the war in Iraq. We are one people, all of us pledging allegiance to the stars and stripes, all of us defending the United States of America.[2]

Not everyone caught it, but in that speech Obama marked himself as an evangelical Christian. His "God" remark strummed the chords of "Awesome God," which was then the most popular praise song being sung in White evangelical churches across the nation.[3]

Obama performed racial legerdemain once again four years later when he won the Iowa Democratic Party caucuses—a first, surprising victory in his meandering path to the Democratic nomination and later the presidency. Iowans are a churchy lot, Democrats nearly as much as Republicans. They are good neighbors and family folk. Most of them are sincerely good, Christian, White people who want to do a good, generous thing when they can. They believe in hard work and—the Democrats among them at least—believe that it is important for people to work together and take care of one another. In Barack Obama, Iowa caucusers rightly perceived one of their own. He was that nice, clean-cut, well-spoken Negro young man who knew all the words to the hymns they sang on Sunday. It made them feel good to vote for someone Black who was like them in so many ways.

In that first campaign and as president, Obama performed his Blackness only sporadically, though with considerable fluency when he chose to do so. He was a Black man, but he was a particular kind of Black man, one whose story we knew. His father was not a descendant of American slaves but an apparently elite international student from Kenya, and in any case he didn't stay around for long. Young Barack was raised not in Detroit or Newark but in exotic Hawai'i and Indonesia by his White hippie mother and his working-class White grandparents. Politicians like Jesse Jackson and Charlie Rangel were not the sort of Black men who could get elected to the presidency, for as smart, driven, and well-connected as they were, they could not perform Whiteness the way that Obama could. In office, Obama chose to perform simply as president, seldom as an explicitly racialized figure, despite some opponents' attempts to paint him as one (Peck 2012).

Does Obama's double election to the presidency mean that America has arrived at a post-racial moment in our history? Hardly (Sugrue 2010;

Kinder and Dale-Riddle 2012; Tesler and Sears 2010; King and Smith 2011). The enthusiasm for Obama among American voters (and those millions in other countries who celebrated with us in November 2008) was racialized. Liberals—and a lot of non-liberals who were people of good will—applauded Obama's ascendancy as a partial fulfillment of the promise of the civil rights movement. I confess that I did not think I would see a Black president in my lifetime, and I was pretty jazzed when it happened. The historic nature of this election was felt around the globe. On election night 2008 I was in a small city in Germany where 500 university students took over an entire restaurant and stayed through the night until five o'clock in the morning, awaiting the final news that Obama had been elected. Part of the enthusiasm, in the United States and abroad, was generated by Obama's political skills, his positions on issues, and the respite he promised from George Bush's mistakes. But much of it was that a Black man could be elected to America's highest office.

Likewise, opposition to President Obama was and remains racialized. Tea Party rally signs regularly depicted the president as a witch doctor with a bone through his nose or in other dehumanizing disguises that had African themes. On April 19, 2010, White gun-rights activists brought loaded weapons and fiery rhetoric to two small national parks—Gravelly Point and Fort Hunt—in Virginia just across the Potomac from the White House. Can you imagine the outcry if Black loudmouths had brought guns and made threatening speeches across from the White House while a White president was in residence? Conservative commentators, from Fox News and elsewhere, piled on Michelle Obama. They objected to Barack and Michelle exchanging a congratulatory fistbump, calling their gesture gangland thuggery. They made demeaning comments about Mrs. Obama's arms, implying she lacked femininity, and the shape of her buttocks, suggesting she was no person to be lecturing the nation's youth on weight and diet. And they tried to make her out to be an Angry Black Woman, rather than a warm, intelligent, articulate First Lady (Fantz 2012; Kunkle and Gerhart 2010; Stodghill 2012).

The president was repeatedly racialized as Other. It began during the Democratic primary campaign in 2008, with Hillary Clinton's reference to "real Americans, White Americans" not supporting Obama, implying that her opponent, because he was not fully White, was not a real American and not fit to lead Americans. When some ignorant critics contended that the Protestant Obama was a Muslim (and Muslims have come in for a lot of hate in the last decade), Clinton did not correct them. Instead, responding to a Steve Croft question on CBS's *60 Minutes*, she stared into the camera and said merely, "I take him on the basis of what he says"—that he is a Christian—"and, you know, there isn't any reason to doubt that." She knew better, but she wanted the top job and so was willing to say pretty much anything to get it.[4]

Then there were the contentions about the president's place of birth, which escalated as the 2012 election approached. Donald Trump and other birthers contended that Obama was not an American citizen because he was born, they said, in Kenya. Hence, he was not legitimately president. They had no evidence for their claim about his birthplace, but that did not stop them from declaring him illegitimate.[5] Orly Taitz, while a 2012 birther candidate for U.S. senate from California, promised that if elected she would "demand investigation and prosecution of governmental officials who are aiding and abetting Barack Obama in his occupation of the position of the U.S. President without any valid identification papers."[6]

President Obama produced his 1961 Honolulu birth certificate, and the Republican governor of Hawai'i pronounced it authentic. But Trump insisted that "a lot of people do not think it was an authentic certificate" (Peoples 2012). Yes, it was authentic. But it doesn't matter. Article 2 of the Constitution declares: "No person except a natural-born citizen . . . shall be eligible to the office of President." It does not say the person has to be born in the United States.

Since the founding of the nation, U.S. law has always recognized two ways to be a "natural-born citizen." One can be born on U.S. soil (the law of *jus soli*) or one can be born to a parent who is a U.S. citizen (*jus sanguinis*). U.S. law in this matter follows English Common Law, which has recognized both principles for many centuries. The first U.S. Congress in 1790 passed a law declaring that "the children of citizens of the United States that may be born beyond the sea, or outside the limits of the United States, shall be considered as natural-born citizens of the United States" (LeMay and Barkan 1999, 17).

No one is arguing that President Obama's mother, Stanley Ann Dunham, was not a U.S. citizen in 1961. Therefore, it doesn't matter if Barack Obama was born in Hawai'i, in Kenya, or in a rocket ship on the way to Mars. He still is a natural-born U.S. citizen.

In 2008, no one questioned John McCain's eligibility to hold the office of president. Yet McCain was born in—wait for it—Panama. He was born in a U.S. naval hospital in the Canal Zone, territory that the U.S. controlled in much the same way that it controls Guantanamo Bay today. If the birthers want to argue that the Panama Canal Zone was U.S. soil, then they will have to concede that Guantanamo Bay is U.S. soil and subject to the rule of U.S. law—hardly a position they are likely to advocate. Then there is the citizenship status of George Romney, Mitt's father. The elder Romney was born in Mexico and came to the United States with his U.S.-citizen parents when he was a small boy, apparently without papers. When George Romney ran for president in 1967, no one seriously questioned his citizenship status. Nor, to my knowledge, has anyone questioned the U.S. citizenship of Mitt Romney.[7]

It is worth pointing out that some of the people who questioned President Obama's citizenship, like Senator Dean Heller (R-NV) and presidential candidate Ron Paul (a Republican congressman from Texas), also said they wanted to end *jus soli*—citizenship for immigrants' children by virtue of their birth on U.S. soil. They really can't have it both ways. Without both *jus sanguinis* and *jus soli*, we would not have any natural-born citizens at all, and no one would be eligible to run for president.[8]

This is all about race, not about citizenship or personal history. Questioning President Obama's U.S. citizenship, like suggesting he is a secret Muslim, is thinly veiled code. What the conspiracy theorists really mean is that President Obama is not legitimately president because he is Black. It is long past time to end this birther nonsense. It does not matter where President Obama was born (it was in Hawai'i, but it doesn't matter). He is a U.S. citizen, and he is president. He has been elected twice, and he has been exercising the powers of the office for over four years. The birthers need to get over it, but they show no signs of getting that message.

In his 2012 campaign stump speech, Governor Romney tried to repeat the same refrain with his frequent complaint that "President Obama doesn't understand America." His campaign co-chairman, John Sununu, opined: "I wish this president would learn how to be an American. . . . He has no idea how the American system functions." In addition, he called President Obama "babbling," "lazy," "disengaged," and "not that bright." Neither Romney, nor Sununu, nor the right-wing incendiaries who fed them lines understood that they could not prevail based on coded racial attacks on the president.[9]

In the end, Obama's performance as president and the superior organization of his campaign carried him to victory. Killing Osama bin Laden took away the tough-on-foreign-policy issue from the Republicans. The more-or-less ending of two wars in Iraq and Afghanistan played well with the American public. President Obama demonstrated a steady, effortless command of relations with foreign countries that neither Governor Romney nor any other Republican candidate could match. Indeed, Obama's easy way with foreign leaders and foreign publics stood out in stark contrast to both George W. Bush's clumsiness (as in trying to give German Chancellor Angela Merkel an unwanted massage) and Mitt Romney's fecklessness (his insult to London on its conduct of the 2012 Olympics, or his one-note, all-Israel-all-the-time approach to international affairs). The bailout of Chrysler and General Motors (which did amount to socialism, more or less) won Obama Ohio, Michigan, and Wisconsin—and the election. The president's handling of Hurricane Sandy on election eve made a sharp contrast to the cluelessness of Bush in the wake of Hurricane Katrina. It also was a winning contrast to Romney, who had promised to privatize the Federal Emergency Management Agency. That Obama's response to the hurricane also won him key endorsements from New Jersey Republican governor Chris Christie and New York City mayor Michael Bloomberg was frosting on Obama's cake. Romney had a huge edge in money, most of it in unaccounted-for SuperPACs, but in the end that money only proved the Whitman Rule. As with the 2010 California gubernatorial campaign of mega-millionaire Meg Whitman and two campaigns for a senate seat in Connecticut by the similarly wealthy huckster Linda McMahon, Romney's presidential run proved that you can buy familiarity, but you can't buy love. Spending a ton of money on a campaign can make it so that people get to know you, but it can't make them like you (Applebome 2012).

President Obama won the 2012 election, despite the racialized abuse he endured, in large part because more Americans thought he was their kind of guy.[10] *USA Today*'s voter exit polls showed Governor Romney with double-digit leads over Obama among voters who said the most important quality for a candidate was "Has a vision of the future," "Strong leader," or "Shares my values." By contrast, "Cares about people like me" won Obama the job—81 percent of people who thought this was the most important quality of a candidate voted for President Obama. That is saying something, when even White people in large numbers can identify with and feel protected by a Black man.

Much of the problem, as conservative columnist David Brooks put it after the election, was that the Republicans had a bad product to sell (Brooks 2012). Voters (except for suburban White men and some among the elderly) just never warmed to Mitt Romney. He seemed ever-adjustable in his approach to issues and disingenuous about his own past positions. He was hamstrung by a party platform that kowtowed to the extreme right wing of the Republican Party and simply did not appeal to a lot of Americans.

Part of what drove many voters away was the pandering to racist and anti-immigrant wackos that not only Romney but almost all major Republican leaders performed. Retired Army colonel Lawrence Wilkerson, a Republican and former chief of staff to Secretary of State Colin Powell, said shortly before the election:

> *My party, unfortunately, is the bastion of those people—not all of them, but most of them—who are still basing their positions on race. Let me just be candid: My party is full of racists, and the real reason a considerable portion of my party wants President Obama out of the White House has nothing to do with the content of his character, nothing to do with his competence as commander-in-chief and president, and everything to do with the color of his skin, and that's despicable. (Finocchiaro 2012)*

The Obama team managed to capitalize on a certain revulsion at such naked racism without addressing race directly. They successfully painted Romney as a rich guy who was out of touch with the American people, and Obama as the defender of the middle class and working poor. On raising taxes on the wealthy, on maintaining Medicare and Social Security in their current form, on the virtues of the auto industry bailout, on the conduct of foreign affairs, on the way toward a brighter future, 92 percent of Democrats stood behind the president. Ninety-three percent of Republicans stood with Romney. Independents broke for Obama 52 to 44 percent, and that was the ball game (Banks 2012).

Put these advantages—Obama's attractive personality versus Romney's stiffness, a Republican platform that a majority of Americans just did not want—together with a superb county-by-county, neighborhood-by-neighborhood, precinct-by-precinct organization and computer-assisted voter analysis (far more sophisticated than any national race has ever seen), and the table was set for an Obama victory.

The president's people were able as no candidate before to turn out their vote. Part of this was racially energized. In Pennsylvania, Ohio, Florida, and other key swing states, Republican election officials did their best to limit the Democratic turnout, especially by Blacks and Latinos. They restricted the days and hours for early voting, which disproportionately hindered working-class people from voting. They passed laws requiring state-issued picture identification cards for voting; these had not previously been required, and many young, old, and poor people did not possess them. They purged the voter rolls of many people who were long-standing voters—and this tactic fell disproportionately on voters of color. And they made it harder for new voters to register (Kam and Lantigua 2012).

This barrage of attempts to restrict the Democratic vote seems to have backfired on the Republicans. Exit polls suggest that a lot of poor people, Blacks, and Latinas/os were angered, not discouraged, by the attempts to keep them from voting. Key institutions like Black churches organized voter-registration and get-to-the-polls efforts, and the numbers of Democratic voters remained high. Even those African Americans who did not feel that President Obama had done enough for Black Americans felt protective of Obama on racial grounds and made the extra effort to vote despite the hurdles placed in front of them (Bronner 2012; La Ganga 2012; Reid and Rendell 2012).

It was not just the Black vote that put Obama over the top. The fastest-rising segment of the electorate—Latinas/os—gave Obama more than two-thirds of their votes. The president had not delivered on promises to fix the economy and pass comprehensive immigration reform, including a path to citizenship for immigrants who came without papers. But he had issued an executive decree that provided a window for undocumented young people who had been brought to the U.S. as children to normalize their status. Latinos were turned off by the incessant, racially tinged immigrant bashing of Romney and other Republicans—the exhortations to "self-deportation" and the like. They seem to have concluded that they had a better chance of a fair shake with Obama in the White House. This was even true among Cuban Americans, who had been a reliably Republican voting bloc since the 1960s: they broke 49 to 47 percent for President Obama in Florida. The decline of Fidel Castro, gradual loosening of restrictions on travel between the U.S. and Cuba, and the rise of a second and third generation of Cuban Americans who had less strong anti-Castro feelings than their parents and grandparents all contributed to the shift (McGregor 2012; González and Nowicki 2012; Fabian 2012; Lillis 2012).

Other key groups who contributed to Obama's new coalition included gays (76 percent voted for Obama), single women, and Asian Americans, who voted for Obama at a 74 percent clip (Lee and Ramakrishnan 2012). So maybe Paul West is right in a sense. Race and racism have surely not gone away. But it might just be the case that the Democratic Party's victory in 2012 heralds the founding of a new, durable governing coalition of Blacks, Latinas/os, Asians, gays, single people, and women.

If that be true, what is the future of the Republican Party? It is hard to tell. There have been many occasions when one party or the other has been written off as about to go the way of the Whigs, yet each time they have managed to come back from the dead. Remember, it was just a decade ago that Karl Rove was talking about establishing a "permanent Republican majority"; his dream does not seem to have come to pass. Neither should we assume that the current disarray on the Republican side cannot be overcome.

But if the Republicans are to become again a party capable of winning national elections with any regularity, they are going to have to moderate their stances on racial and cultural issues. Stuart Spencer, a top campaign strategist for Ronald Reagan, said: "You have to have a come-to-Jesus meeting at all levels, both state and national." He called on party leaders to abandon their anti-immigrant stance. He said that, to win, a party must reflect the diverse character of the electorate. Another longtime Republican strategist, John Weaver, was pungent in his assessment: "If we're going to be anything but a regional, middle-aged white-man party, we have to do the obvious thing, which is, first, accept the reality that America is a diverse nation and we need to start selling to those people. There is climate change. Accept that. There are gay people in our midst, marrying one another. Get over it. . . . The government isn't going to deport 15 million [unauthorized immigrants], and they're not going to deport themselves" (Barabak 2012).

The Republican Party's leaders, and their recent standard bearer, do not seem to have gotten the message yet. Fox News pundit Bill O'Reilly and Governor Romney himself have put down their loss to President Obama having bribed voters with gifts from the public treasury, not to the content of their message or the ineptitude of their candidate. But it is still early days. Perhaps they will yet find a way back from their 2012 debacle. If they are to do that, they will have to deal differently with the issue of race than they have ever done before (Hulse 2012; Lizza 2012; Preston 2012).

In the meantime, Barack Obama is president for a second term. What his achievements and failures in office over the next four years may be, and what may be their racial dimension, we will have to wait and see. Surely, his presidency thus far has begun to change the racial calculus in American politics.

Notes

I am grateful to G. Reginald Daniel for inviting me to make these reflections; to Rubén Rumbaut and Berndt Ostendorf for sending me reams of data on the election; and to Anna L. L. Spickard for enduring thousands of hours of election coverage and discussion with me.

1. See any of Du Bois's autobiographies, but especially *Dusk of Dawn* 1940.
2. Barack Obama, Keynote Speech, Democratic National Convention, Fleet Center, Boston (July 27, 2004). http://www.americanrhetoric.com/speeches/convention2004/barack obama2004dnc.htm.
3. Smith, November 21, 2001. The refrain goes: "Our God is an awesome God, He reigns from Heaven above. With wisdom, power and love, Our God is an awesome God."
4. "Clinton Says Obama Muslim Rumor Not True 'As Far as I Know,'" ABC News blog *Political Punch*.
5. This section appeared in another form on the op-ed page of the *San Jose Mercury News* under the title, "'Birthers' Attack on Obama Is Not Only Bogus, It's Irrelevant" (June 16, 2012). I am grateful to Salim Yaqub for hounding me until I wrote it.
6. See http://orlytaitzforussenate2012.com/platform.html.
7. Apparently there was some question raised by the American Independent Party about the elder Romney's citizenship, but the matter went nowhere. In his 2012 stump speech, Mitt Romney frequently alluded to his birth in Michigan and that of his wife as proof of their U.S. citizenship, and contrasted that to the birthers' questioning Obama's citizenship.
8. See http://deanheller.com; http://www.ronpaul.com/on-the-issues/border-security.
9. See "Sununu: Obama Should 'Learn How to Be an American.'" http://www.politico.com/blogs/burns-haberman/2012/07; Volsky 2012: http://thinkprogress.org/election/2012/10/04/963501. Samples of the work of ideologues who fed strategy to the Romney campaign: Coulter 2012; D'Souza 2010b; D'Souza 2012.
10. Except where otherwise noted, the following analysis is based on the November 7, 2012, post-election special issues of the *New York Times*, the *Los Angeles Times*, and *USA Today*; as well as detailed exit polls published online by the *New York Times* (http://elections.nytimes.com/2012/results/president/exit-polls).

REFERENCES

ABC 7 News. 2009. "Michelle, Oprah Arrive in Copenhagen." September.
Abel, Elizabeth, Barbara Christian, and Helene Moglen, eds. 1997. *Female Subjects in Black and White: Race, Psychoanalysis, Feminism*. Berkeley and Los Angeles: University of California Press.
Abu-Jamal, Mumia. 2009. "Imagine Being Van Jones." *ZNetMagazine*, September 22. http://axisoflogic.com/artman/publish/article_57003.shtml.
Advisory Board for the President's Initiative on Race. 1998. *One America in the 21st Century: The President's Initiative on Race*. Washington, D.C.
Alan, John. 2004. "Kerry Misquotes Hughes." *News and Letters*, August-September. http://www.newsandletters.org/Issues/2004/August-September/BRV_August2004.htm.
Alkon, Amy. 2008. "The Self-help President." *Advice Goddess Blog*, August 26. http://www.advicegoddess.com/archives/2008/08/26/the_selfhelp_pr.html.
Alter, Jonathan. 2013. *The Center Holds: Obama and His Enemies*. New York: Simon and Schuster.
Altman, Micah, and Philip A. Klinkner. 2006. "Measuring the Difference between White Voting and Polling on Interracial Marriage." *Du Bois Review* 3(2)(September): 299–315.
Alvarado, Leticia. 2013. "Zimmerman, Whiteness, and Latinos: Zimmerman and Latinos' Overvaluation of Whiteness." ABC News Internet Ventures, July 18. http://abcnews.go.com/ABC_Univision/News/zimmerman-trial-latinos-overvaluation-whiteness/print?id=19701774.
Andrade, Roy D. 1984. "Cultural Meaning Systems." In *Culture Theory: Essays on Mind, Self, and Emotion*, ed. Richard A. Shedder and Robert A. Levine, 88–119. Cambridge: Cambridge University Press.
Ani, Marimba. 1980. *Let the Circle Be Unbroken: The Implications of African Spirituality in the Diaspora*. New York: Nkominfo.
———. 1994. *Yurugu: An African Cultural Critique of European Cultural Thought and Behavior*. Trenton, NJ: Africa World Press.
Anzaldúa, Gloria. 1987. *Borderlands: La Frontera—The New Mestiza*. San Francisco: Spinsters/Aunt Lute.
Apollon, Dominique. 2011. "Don't Call Them 'Post-Racial.' Millennials' Attitudes on Race, Racism, and Key Systems in Our Society." Applied Research Center. June 7. http://www.racialequitytools.org/resourcefiles/ARC_Millennials_Report_June_2011.pdf.
Appiah, K. Anthony, and Amy Gutmann. 1996. *Color Conscious: The Political Morality of Race*. Princeton, NJ: Princeton University Press.

Appiah, Kwame Anthony. 1991. "Is the Post- in Postmodernism the Post- in Postcolonial?" *Critical Inquiry* 17(2)(Winter): 336–57.

Applebome, Peter. 2012. "Democrat Is Elected to U.S. Senate After a Bitter Race in Connecticut." *New York Times*, November 7.

Applegate, Debby. 2008. "Two Can Make History." *New York Times*, May 25. http://www.nytimes.com/2008/05/25/opinion/25applegate.html?pagewanted=all&gwh=92E3ADDB07C2944154A7984CC74CA2B8.

Arce, Carlos, Edward Murguia, and W. Parker Frisbie. 1987. "Phenotype and Life Chances Among Chicanos." *Hispanic Journal of Behavioral Sciences* 9(1): 19–33.

Ardizzone, Heidi. 2006. "'Such Fine Families': Photography and Race in the Work of Caroline Bond Day." *Visual Studies* 21(2)(October): 106–32.

Asad, Talal. 1973a. "Introduction." In *Anthropology and the Colonial Encounter*, ed. Talal Asad, 9–24. New York: Humanities Press.

———. 1973b. "Two European Images of Non-European Rule." In *Anthropology and the Colonial Encounter*, ed. Talal Asad, 103–18. New York: Humanities Press.

Asante, Molefi K. 2007. "Barack Obama and the Dilemma of Power: An Africological Observation." *Journal of Black Studies* 38(1): 105–15.

Associated Press. 2007. "Lynne Cheney: VP, Obama Are Eighth Cousins." MSNBC, October 17. http://www.msnbc.msn.com/id/21340764/.

———. 2008a. "Monkey Doll Named for Obama Called Racist." MSNBC, June 14. http://www.msnbc.msn.com/id/25163827/.

———. 2008b. "What Bradley Effect? No Hidden Bias Seen in '08." MSNBC, November 7. http://www.msnbc.msn.com/id/27589729/from/ET/.

———. 2009a. "Ali Visiting Irish Home of His Ancestors, Boxing Legend Meets Distant Relatives During Celebrations." MSNBC, September 1. http://nbcsports.msnbc.com/id/32640853/ns/sports-other_sports/.

———. 2009b. "Challenge to Obama Is Dismissed." *New York Times*, March 6. http://www.nytimes.com/2009/03/06/us/06brfs-LAWSUITOVERC_BRF.html?_r=0.

———. 2010a. "Chris Matthews on Obama: 'I Forgot He Was Black.'" *San Francisco Chronicle*, January 28. http://www.sfgate.com/cgi-bin/article.cgi?file=/n/a/2010/01/28/entertainment/e073429S30.DTL.

———. 2010b. "Reid: Sorry for 'Negro' Remark About Obama: Top Democrat Says He Used 'Poor Choice of Words' During 2008 Campaign." MSNBC, January 9. www.msnbc.msn.com/id/34783136/ns/politics-capitol_hill.

Asumah, Seth N. 2004. "Racial Identity and Policy Making: Redefining Whiteness." *Western Journal of Black Studies* 28(4): 501–10.

Austin, Algeron. 2006. "Are Africans in America African Americans?" *Black Directions* 2(2): May 8. http://www.thorainstitute.com/2006/05/black-directions-vol-2-no-2.html.

Avila, Oscar. 2010. "Obama's Census Form choice: Black." *Los Angeles Times*, April 4. http://articles.latimes.com/2010/apr/04/nation/la-na-obama-census4-201.

Avlon, John. 2012. "The Obama-Haters Bookclub: The Canon Swells." *Daily Beast*. October 26. http://www.thedailybeast.com/articles/2012/10/26/the-obama-haters-book-club-the-canon-swells.html.

Azibo, Daudi Ajani Ya. 1999. "Africentric Conceptualizing as the Pathway to African Liberation." *International Journal of Africana Studies* 5:1–31.

———. 2001. "Articulating the Distinction between Black Studies and the Study of Blacks: The Fundamental Role of Culture and the African-centered Worldview." In *The African American Studies Reader*, ed. Nathaniel Norment, 420–41. Durham: Carolina Academic Press.

Babington, Charles. 2008. "Mortgage Plan Called Raw Deal." *Star Ledger*, October 10, sec. 3.

Bai, Matt. 2008. "Post-Race." *New York Times*, August 10, sec. MM8.

Baker, Peter. 2008. "Debate on Economy Grows More Urgent Job-Loss Report Is Worst in 5 Years." *Washington Post*, March 3. http://newsgroups.derkeiler.com/Archive/Alt/alt.politics.bush/2008-03/msg00402.html.

Baker, Peter, and Campbell Robertson. 2009. "Obama Tells New Orleans Progress Is Being Made." *New York Times*, October 16, A16.

Banks, Sandy. 2012. "Reality Crashes This Party." *Los Angeles Times*, November 10.

Banks, William Curtis. 1992. "The Theoretical and Methodological Crisis of the Africentric Conception." *Journal of Negro Education* 61(3): 262–72.

Baptist, Edward E. 2001. "'Cuffy,' 'Fancy Maids,' and 'One-Eyed Men': Rape, Commodification, and the Domestic Slave Trade in the U.S." *American Historical Review* 106(5)(December): 1619–50.

Barabak, Mark Z. 2012. "Republicans in Disarray over How to Fix Damage." *Los Angeles Times*, November 12.

Barthé, Darryl G., Jr. 2012. "Racial Revisionism, Caste Revisited: Whiteness, Blackness, and Barack Obama." In *Obama and the Biracial Factor: The Battle for a New American Majority*, ed. Andrew J. Jolivétte, 81–98. Bristol, UK: Policy Press.

Barthes, Roland. *Camera Lucida: Reflections on Photography*. Trans. Richard Howard. New York: Hill and Wang.

Baskerville, Stephen. 2002. "The Politics of Fatherhood." *Political Science and Politics*. December: 695–699. www.apsanet.org.

Becker, Mary. 1999. "Patriarchy and Inequality: Towards a Substantive Feminism." *University of Chicago Legal Forum* 1999: 21–88.

Belkin, Lisa. 2009. "Father in Chief." *New York Times Magazine*, February 19.

Bell, Derrick. 2004. *Silent Covenants: Brown v. Board of Education and the Unfulfilled Hopes for Radical Reform*. New York: Oxford University Press.

Benjamin, Rich. 2013. "Obama's Safe, Overrated, and Airy Comments on the Trayvon Martin Affair." *Alternet*, July 19. http://www.alternet.org/civil-liberties/obamas-safe-overrated-and-airy-comments-trayvon-martin-affair.

Berger, John. 1973. *Ways of Seeing*. New York: Viking Press.

Berlin, Ira. 1976. "The Revolution in Black Life." In *The American Revolution: Explorations in the History of American Radicalism*, ed. Alfred Young, 349–82. Dekalb: Northern Illinois University Press.

Berman, Ari. 2012. "Tea Party and the Right, the GOP's Voter Suppression Strategy." *Alternet*, November 26. http://www.alternet.org/tea-party-and-right/gops-voter-suppression-strategy?akid=9721.3701.g43T5R&rd=1&src=newsletter750513&t=14.

Berman, Douglas, and Harlan Protass. 2013. "Obama Can Do More to Ease Disparities in US Sentencing." *Slate*, July 29. http://www.slate.com/articles/news_and_politics/jurisprudence/2013/07/obama_needs_to_fix_the_crack_cocaine_sentencing_gap.html?wpisrc =newsletter_jcr:content.

Berrington, Lucy, and Jeff Onore. 2008. "Bam: Our 1st Woman Prez?" *New York Post*, January 7. http://www.nypost.com/seven/01072008/postopinion/opedcolumnists/bam __our_1st_woman_prez__2 46772.htm.

Bhabha, Homi K. 1990. "The Third Space." In *Identity, Community, Culture, Difference*, ed. Jonathan Rutherford, 207–21. New York: Lawrence Wishart.

———. 1994a. *The Location of Culture*. New York: Routledge.

———. 1994b. "Frontliners/borderposts." In *Displacements: Cultural Identity in Question*, ed. Angelika Bammer, 269–72. Bloomington: Indiana University Press.

Binning, Kevin R., Miguel M. Unzueta, Yuen J. Huo, and Ludwin E. Molina. 2009. "The Interpretation of Multiracial Status and Its Relation to Social Engagement and Psychological Well-being." *Journal of Social Issues* 65(1): 35–49.

Birch, Anthony Harold. 1972. *Representation*. MacMillan Press: London.

Bitzer, Lloyd. 1968. "The Rhetorical Situation." *Philosophy and Rhetoric* 1(1)(January): 1–14.

Blackmon, Douglas A. 2008. "Two Families Named McCain: Candidate's Kin Share a History with Descendants of Slaves." *Wall Street Journal*, October 17. http://online.wsj .com/article/SB122419511761942501.html.

Bloom, Lisa. 2013. "Zimmerman Prosecutors Duck the Race Issue." *New York Times*, July 15. http://www.nytimes.com/2013/07/16/opinion/zimmerman-prosecutors-duck-the-race -issue.html?pagewanted=all&_r=2&.

Blow, Charles M. "The Curious Case of Trayvon Martin." *New York Times*, March 16. http:// www.nytimes.com/2012/03/17/opinion/blow-the-curious-case-of-trayvon-martin .html?pagewanted=all&_r=0.

Boardman, William. 2013. "Did the Prosecutor Screw Up in the Zimmerman Case?" *Alternet.org*, July 23. http://www.alternet.org/civil-liberties/listening-lead-prosecutors -final-argument-against-zimmerman-its-hard-believe-he?akid=10724.3701.p5c9MU&r d=1&src=newsletter872869&t=9&paging=off.

Bobo, L., and F Gilliam. 1992. "Race, Sociopolitical Participation, and Black Empowerment." *American Political Science Review* 84(2): 377–393.

Bogado, Aura. 2013a. "Obama, Trayvon and the Problem That Won't Be Named." *Colorlines*, July 22. http://colorlines.com/archives/2013/07/obama_and_the_problem_that_cannot _be_named.html.

———. 2013b. "Putting Racism on Trial." *Colorlines*, July 16. http://colorlines.com/ar chives/2013/07/racist-without-even-knowing-it.html.

Bogle, Donald. 1992. *Toms, Coons, Mulattoes, Mammies, and Bucks: An Interpretive History of Blacks in American Films*. New York: Continuum International.

Bonilla-Silva, Eduardo, 2001. *White Supremacy and Racism in the Post–Civil Rights Era*. Boulder, CO: Lynne Rienner.

———. 2006. *Racism Without Racists: Color-Blind Racism and the Persistence of Racial Inequality in the United States*. Lanham, MD: Rowman & Littlefield.

Bonilla-Silva, Eduardo, and Tukufu Zuberi, eds. 2008. *White Logic, White Methods: Racism and Methodology*. Lanham, MD: Rowman and Littlefield.

Booker, Cory. 2009. "2009 State of the City Address." *City of Newark New Jersey On-Line*, February 9. http://www.ci.newark.nj.us/userimages/downloads/home_MAYOR_CORY_A_BOOKER_STATE_OF_CITY_ADDRESS_2009_AS_DELIVERED.pdf: 1–25.

Bourdieu, Pierre. 1977. *Outline of a Theory of Practice*. Trans. Richard Nice. New York: Cambridge University Press.

Bradshaw, Carla K. 1992. "Beauty and the Beast: On Racial Ambiguity." In *Racially Mixed People in America*, ed. Maria P. P. Root, 77–88. Newbury Park, CA: Sage.

Bratton, Kathleen, and Rorie Spill. 2002. "Existing Diversity and Judicial Selection: The Role of the Appointment Method in Establishing Gender Diversity in State Supreme Courts." *Social Science Quarterly*. 83(2): 504–18.

Bratu, Becky. 2013. "From Scorn to Gratitude, Mixed Reactions to Obama's Remarks on Zimmerman." NBC News, July 19. http://usnews.nbcnews.com/_news/2013/07/19/19564830-from-scorn-to-gratitude-mixed-reactions-to-obamas-remarks-on-zimmerman-verdict.

Breckenridge, Carol, and Peter van der Veer. 1993. "Orientalism and the Postcolonial Predicament." In *Orientalism and the Postcolonial Predicament: Perspectives on South Asia*, ed. Carol Breckenridge and Peter van der Veer, 1–22. Philadelphia: University of Pennsylvania Press.

Bronner, Ethan. 2012. "Long Lines, Demands for ID and Provisional Ballots Mar Voting for Some." *New York Times*, November 7.

Brooks, David. 2012. Interview with E. J. Dionne. *All Things Considered*, National Public Radio, November 9.

Brooks, Ray. 1996. *Integration or Separation: A Strategy for Racial Equality*. Cambridge: Harvard University Press.

Brown, Michael, Martin Carnoy, Elliott Currie, Troy Duster, David B. Oppenheimer, Marjorie Shultz, and David Wellman. 2003 *Whitewashing Race: The Myth of a Color-Blind Society*. Berkeley and Los Angeles: University of California Press.

Brown, Timothy. 2004. "Revisiting the Subject of Trauma." *Global Black News*, October 11. http://www.globalblacknews.com/brown-trauma.html.

Brunsma, David L. 2006. "Public Categories, Private Identities: Exploring Regional Differences in the Biracial Experiences." *Social Science Research* 35:555–76.

Bureau of the Census. 2000. "Population by Race and Hispanic or Latino Origin, for the United States, Regions, Divisions, and States, and for Puerto Rico: 2000. U.S. Department of Commerce," http://factfinder.census.gov/home/en/datanotes/expplu.html.

Burghart, Devin, and Leonard Zeskind. 2010. *Tea Party Nationalism: A Critical Examination of the Tea Party Movement and the Size, Scope, and Focus of Its National Factions*. Kansas City, MO; Institute for Research and Education on Human Rights http://www.irehr.org/the-report.

Burke, Kenneth. 1969. *A Rhetoric of Motives*. Berkeley and Los Angeles: University of California Press.

Burnside, Randolph, and Kami Whitehurst. 2007. "From the Statehouse to the White House?: Barack Obama's Bid to Become the Next President." Journal of Black Studies 38(1), The Barack Obama Phenomenon (Sept. 2007): 75–89.

Butera, Jeff. 2012. "Zimmerman: Dad Worked as Magistrate." ABC Action News, March 28. http://www.abcactionnews.com/dpp/news/crime/zimmerman-dad-worked-as-magistrate.

Butler, Judith. 1997. *Excitable Speech: A Politics of the Performative*. New York: Routledge.

Cañas, Kathryn, and Mark Lawrence McPhail. 2004. "Demonizing Democracy: The Strange Career of Lani Guinier." In *New Approaches to Rhetoric*, ed. Patricia A. Sullivan and Steven R. Goldzwig, 223–44. Thousand Oaks, CA: Sage.

Canon, David. 1999. *Race, Redistricting, and Representation*. Chicago: University of Chicago Press.

Capehart, Jonathan. 2012. "Photo Speaks Volumes About Obama Race." *Washington Post*, May 24.

Capers, I. Bennett. 1991. "Sex(ual) Orientation and Title VII." *Columbia Law Review* 91(5) (June): 1158–87. http://www.washingtonpost.com/blogs/post-partisan/post/photo-speaks-volumes-about-obama-and-race/2012/05/24/gJQA2T2lmU_blog.html.

Carbado, Devon W. 2002. "(E)Racing the Fourth Amendment." *Michigan Law Review* 100 (March): 946–1004.

Carbado, Devon W., and Mitu Gulati. 2000. "Working Identity." *Cornell Law Review* 85:1259–1308.

———. 2001. "The Fifth Black Woman." *Journal of Contemporary Law Issues* 11: 701–29.

Carmichael, Stokely, and Charles V. Hamilton. 1967. *Black Power: The Politics of Liberation in America*. New York: Vintage.

Carrera, Magali Marie. 2003. "*Imagining Identity in New Spain: Race, Lineage, and the Colonial Body in Portraiture and Casta Paintings*." Austin: University of Texas Press.

Carroll, Karanja Keita. 2008. "Africana Studies and Research Methodology: Revisiting the Centrality of the Afrikan Worldview." *Journal of Pan African Studies* 2(2): 4–27.

Carson, Clayborne. 2009, "King, Obama, and the Great American Dialogue: What Would Martin Luther King Jr.—Had He Been Alive Today—Have Thought of Our Latest President's Oratory?" *American Heritage People*, May 25. http://www.americanheritage.com/articles/web/20090525-President-Civil-Rights-Martin-Luther-King-Jr-Barack-Obama-Speech-I-Have-A-Dream.shtml>.

Carter, Stephen L. 1994. "Foreword." In *The Tyranny of the Majority: Fundamental Fairness in Representative Democracy*, edited by Lani Guinier, vii–xx. New York: Free Press.

Caruso, Eugene M., Nicole L. Mead, and Emily Balcetis. 2009. "Political Partisanship Influences Perception of Biracial Candidates' Skin Tone." *PNAS* 106(48)(December): 20168–73. http://www.pnas.org_cgi_doi_10.1073_pnas.0905362106.

Caruth, Cathy. 1996. *Unclaimed Experience: Trauma, Narrative, and History*. Baltimore, MD: Johns Hopkins University Press.

Cashin, Sheryll. 2004. *The Failures of Integration: How Race and Class Are Undermining the American Dream*. New York: Public Affairs.

Castle, W. E. 1903. "Mendel's Law of Heredity." *Science* 18(456): 396–506.

———. 1926. "The Explanation of Hybrid Vigor." *Proceedings of the National Academy of Sciences of the United States of America* 12(1): 16–19.

Cavuto, Neil. 2012. "Salute to the Father in Chief." *Your World*, Fox News, June 15. http://www.foxnews.com/on-air/your-world-cavuto/2012/06/15/salute-father-chief#ixzz22dXZxV00.

CBS. 2007a. "Candidate Obama's Sense of Urgency." *60 Minutes*, February 11.

———. 2007b. "Roots." *60 Minutes*, October 7.

———. 2011. "African-American Unemployment at 16 Percent." June 19. http://www.cbsnews.com/stories/2011/06/19/eveningnews/main20072425.shtml.

———. 2013. "Zimmerman Juror: Half of Us at First Voted to Convict." July 16. http://www.cbsnews.com/8301-201_162-57593887/zimmerman-juror-half-of-us-at-first-voted-to-convict/.

Chapell, Kevin. 2009. "Role Model for a Nation." *Jet*, June 22, 8.

Childress, Sarah. 2013. "With Voting Rights Act Out, States Push Voter ID Laws." *Frontline*, June 26. http://www.pbs.org/wgbh/pages/frontline/government-elections-politics/with-voting-rights-act-out-states-push-voter-id-laws/.

Christopher, Tommy. 2009. "'Cracker' Means Something Entirely Different in Florida: A Source of 'Pride.'" Mediate, June 27. http://www.mediaite.com/online/cracker-means-something-entirely-different-in-florida-a-source-of-pride/

Clark, Mary E. 2002. *In Search of Human Nature*. London: Routledge.

Clark-Lewis, Elizabeth. 1994. *Living in, Living out: African American Domestics in Washington, DC 1910–1940*. Washington, D.C.: Smithsonian Institution Press.

Clayton, Dewey. 2007. "The Audacity of Hope." *Journal of Black Studies* 38(1)(September): 51–63.

CNN. 2005. "Reaction to Katrina Split on Racial Lines." September 13. http://www.cnn.com/2005/US/09/12/katrina.race.poll/index.html.

———. 2007. "Poll: Presidential Races Tighten on Both Sides." April 27. http://www.cnn.com/2007/POLITICS/04/16/poll.2008/index.html.

———. 2011. "Crying Baby No Match for Obama." June 22. http://www.youtube.com/watch?v=l6k6kIrTAGk.

CNN.com. 2008. "Election Center 2008, President Full Results." November 17. http://www.cnn.com/ELECTION/2008/results/president/.

———. 2009. "Police Seek 3 More in Teen's Death." September 29. http://www.cnn.com/2009/CRIME/09/29/chicago.teen.beating/.

Coates, Ta-Nehisi Paul. 2007. "Is Obama Black Enough?" *Time*, February 1. http://www.time.com/time/nation/article/0,8599,1584736,00.html.

———. 2013. "Trayvon Martin and the Irony of American Justice." *Atlantic*, July 15. http://www.theatlantic.com/ta-nehisi-coates/.

Cohen, Amy. 2003. "Gender: An (Un)useful Category of Prescriptive Negotiation Analysis?" *Texas Journal of Women and Law* 13(1)(Fall): 169–96.

Cohen, Dova, and Joe Vandello. 2004. *When Believing is Seeing: Sustaining Norms of Violence in Cultures of Honor*." In *The Psychologial Foundations of Culture*, ed. M. Schaller and C. Crandall, 281–304. New York: Lawrence Erlbaum.

Cohen, Jane Maslow. 1998. "Equality for Girls and Other Women: The Built Architecture for the Purposive Life." *Journal of Contemporary Legal Issues* 9:103–106.

Cohen, Jon. 2013. "Zimmerman Verdict: 86 Percent of African Americans Disapprove." *Washington Post*, July 22. http://www.washingtonpost.com/blogs/post-politics/wp/2013/07/22/zimmerman-verdict-86-percent-of-african-americans-disapprove/.

Cohn, Marjorie. 2013. "Key Mistakes Sway Jury in Zimmerman Trial." *Truthout*, July 17. http://www.truth-out.org/news/item/17620-zimmerman-vs-martin-racial-profiling-and-self-defense.

Coleman, Will. 2002. "'Amen' and 'Ashe': African American Protestant Worship and its West African Ancestor." *Cross Currents: Liturgy and Its Discontents* 52(2)(Summer): 158–64. http://findarticles.com/p/articles/mi_m2096/is_2_52/ai_92285031/.

Colker, Ruth. 1996. *Hybrid: Bisexuals, Multiracials, and Other Misfits under American Law.* New York: New York University Press.

Collier-Thomas, Bettye, and V. P. Franklin, eds. 2001. *Sisters in the Struggle: African American Women in the Civil Rights—Black Power Movement.* New York: New York University Press.

Collins, Lisa Gail. 2002. *The Art of History: African American Women Engage the Past.* New Brunswick: Rutgers University Press.

Collins, Patricia Hill. 2000a. "Black Feminist Thought." In *Theories of Race and Racism: A Reader*, ed. Les Back and John Solomos, 404–20. New York: Routledge.

———. 2000b. *Black Feminist Thought: Knowledge, Consciousness, and the Politics of Empowerment.* 2nd ed. New York: Routledge.

———. 2006. "A Telling Difference: Dominance, Strength, and Black Masculinities." In *Progressive Black Masculinities*, ed. Athena D. Mutua, 73–98. New York: Routledge.

Collins, Robert Keith. 2012. "A Different Kind of Blackness: The Question of Obama's Blackness and Intraracial Variation Among African Americans." In *Obama and the Biracial Factor: The Battle for a New American Majority*, ed. Andrew J. Jolivétte, 169–90. Bristol, UK: Policy Press.

Coltrane, Scott. 1996. *Family Man: Fatherhood, Housework, and Gender Equity.* New York: Oxford University Press.

Connell, R. W., and James W. Messerschmidt. 2005. "Hegemonic Masculinity: Rethinking the Concept." *Gender and Society* 19(6)(December): 829–59.

Connor, Michael E., and Joseph L White. "Fatherhood in Contemporary Black America, an Invisible Presence." *Black Scholar* 37(2): 2–8.

Cooper, Anna Julia. 1892. *A Voice From the South.* Xenia, OH: Aldine Printing House.

Cooper, Frank Rudy. 2003. "Cultural Context Matters: Terry's 'Seesaw effect.'" *Oklahoma Law Review* 56(4): 833–77.

———. 2006a. "Against Bipolar Black Masculinity: Intersectionality, Assimilation, Identity Performance, and Hierarchy." *UC-Davis Law Review* 39:853–903.

———. 2006b. "The 'Seesaw Effect' from Racial Profiling to Depolicing: Toward Critical Cultural Theory." In *The New Civil Rights Research: A Constitutive Approach*, ed. Benjamin Fleury-Steiner and Laura Beth Neilsen, 139–55. Burlington, VT: Ashgate.

———. 2009. "'Who's the Man?'": Masculinities Studies, *Terry* Stops, and Police Training." *Columbia Journal of Gender and Law* 18(3): 671–742.

———. 2011. "Masculinities Studies, Post-racialism, and the Gates Controversy." *Nevada Law Journal* 11:1–43.

Cooper, Frank Rudy, and Ann C. McGinley, eds. 2012. *Masculinities and the Law: A Multidimensional Approach.* New York: New York University Press.

Cooper, Maudine R. 2008. "The Invisibility Blues of Black Women in America." In *The State of Black America in 2008: In the Black Woman's Voice*, ed. Amy J. Schulz and Leith Mullings, 83–87. New York: National Urban League.

Cornell, Stephen, and Douglas Hartmann. 1998. *Ethnicity and Race: Making Identities in a Changing World.* Thousand Oaks, CA: Pine Forge Press

Costa, Robert. 2010. "Gingrich: Obama's 'Kenyan, Anti-colonial' Worldview." *National Review Online*, September 11. http://www.nationalreview.com/corner/246302/gingrich-obama-s-kenyan-anti-colonial-worldview-robert-costa.

Cott, Nancy. 2002. *Public Vows: A History of Marriage and the Nation.* Cambridge: Harvard University Press.

Coulter, Ann. 2012. *Mugged: Racial Demagoguery from the Seventies to Obama.* New York: Sentinel/Penguin.

Crenshaw, Kimberlé. 1991. "Mapping the Margins: Intersectionality, Identity Politics, and Violence Against Women of Color." *Stanford Law Review* 43(6): 1241–99.

——. 1995. "Introduction." In *Critical Race Theory: The Key Writings that Formed the Movement*, ed. Kimberlé Crenshaw, Neil Gotanda, Garry Peller, and Kendall Thomas, xii–xxxii. New York: New Press.

——. 2004. "Sharp Tongues for Sharpton." *Nation*, August 16. http://www.thenation.com/doc.mhtml/6=20048816&s=crenshaw.

——. 2005. "Sharpton Sharpens the Challenge with An Overtime Victory." *Common Dreams Newscenter,* January 23. http://commondreams.org/views04/0730-12.htm.

Cronin, Thomas. 1975. *The State of the Presidency.* Boston: Little Brown.

Crouch, Stanley. 2006. "What Obama Isn't: Black Like Me on Race." *(New York) Daily News*, November 2. http://www.nydailynews.com/opinions/2006/11/02/2006-11-02_what_obama_isnt_black_like_me_on_race.html.

Cunningham, Mick. 2008. "Changing Attitudes Toward the Male Breadwinner, Female Homemaker Family Model: Influences of Women's Employment and Education over the Lifecourse." *Social Forces* 87(1): 299–323.

Curiel, Jonathan. 2007. "The Year of Keeping Up with Obama: Democrat Candidates Courting Black Voters." *San Francisco Chronicle*, March 11. http://www.sfchroniclemarketplace.com/cgi-bin/article.cgi?f/c/a/2007/03/11/ING1IOH2Q11.DTL.

Currie, Duncan. 2009. "The Parent Problem: On the Persistent Link between Family Structure and Black Poverty." *National Review*, June 8.

DaCosta, Kimberly McClain. 2007. *Making Multiracials: State, Family, and Market in the Redrawing of the Color Line.* Palo Alto: Stanford University Press.

——. 2009. "Interracial Intimacies, Barack Obama, and the Politics of Multiracialism." *Black Scholar* 39(3–4)(September): 4–12.

Dahl, Julia. 2012. "Trayvon Martin Shooting: What Do We Know?" Crimesider, CBS News, March 30. http://www.cbsnews.com/8301-504083_162-57407115-504083/trayvon-martin-shooting-what-do-we-know-/.

Dahl, Robert. 1990. "The Myth of the Presidential Mandate." *Political Science Quarterly* 105(3)(Autumn): 355–72.

The Daily Show. 2011. "Moment of Zen: Barack Obama Calms a Crying Baby." June 21. http://www.thedailyshow.com/watch/tue-june-21-2011/moment-of-zen---barack-obama-calms-a-crying-baby.

Daily Voice. 2009. "Black Unemployment Soared in January." February 6. http://thedailyvoice.com/voice/2009/02/black-unemployment-soars-001583.php.

Daniel, G. Reginald. 2002. *More Than Black?: Multiracial identity and the New Racial Order.* Philadelphia: Temple University Press.

———. 2006. *Race and Multiraciality in Brazil and the United States: Converging Paths?* University Park: Pennsylvania State University Press.

———. 2012. *Machado de Assis: Multiracial Identity and the Brazilian Novelist.* University Park: Pennsylvania State University Press.

Daniel, G. Reginald, and Hettie V. Williams. 2011. "Barack Obama and Multiraciality." In *Encyclopedia of African American History*, ed. Joe Trotter, 20. New York: Facts on File, 2011.

Daniels, Lee A., and Rose Jefferson Frazier. 2004. *The State of Black America.* New York: National Urban League.

Daniels, Ron. 2009. "The State of Black Progress in America." *ZNet*, May 12. http://www.zcommunications.org/zspace/commentaries/3861.

Dariotis, Wei Ming, and Grace J. Yoo. 2012. "Obama Mamas and Mixed Race: Hoping for 'A More Perfect Union.'" In *Obama and the Biracial Factor: The Battle for a New American Majority*, ed. Andrew J. Jolivétte, 99–112. Bristol, UK: Policy Press.

Darling, Marsha J. Tyson. 2012a. "Burdened Intersections: Black Women and Race, Gender and Class." In *Color Struck: Essays on Race and Ethnicity in Global Perspective*, ed. Julius O. Adekunle and Hettie V. Williams, 389–402. New York: University Press of America.

———. 2012b. "Gender Intersectionality: The Unfinished Business of Justice Advocacy." In *Women of Color in Leadership: Taking Their Rightful Place*, ed. Greggory Johnson III and G. L. A. Harris, 91–106. San Diego: Birkdale Publishers.

Darsey, James. 2009. "Barack Obama and America's Journey." *Southern Communication Journal* 74(1): 88–103.

Davenport, Charles Benedict. 1928. "Race Crossing in Jamaica." *Scientific Monthly* 27(3): 225–38.

———. 1930. "Some Criticisms of 'Race Crossing in Jamaica.'" *Science* 72(1872): 501–502.

Davenport, Charles Benedict, and Florence Harris Danielson. 1913. *Heredity of Skin Color in Negro-White Crosses.* Washington, D.C.: Carnegie Institution of Washington.

Davis, Eisa. 1995. "Sexism and the Art of Feminist Hip-hop Maintenance." In *To Be Real: Telling the Truth and Changing the Face of Feminism*, ed. Rebecca Walker, 127–41. New York: Anchor Books.

Davis, F. James. 1991. *Who is Black? One Nation's Definition.* University Park: Pennsylvania State University Press.

Davis, Jane. 2000. *The White Image in the Black Mind: A Study of African American Literature.* Westport, CT: Greenwood.

Davis, John. 2011. *The Barack Obama Presidency: A Two Year Assessment.* New York: Palgrave Macmillan.

Davis, Robert. 1983. "The Election of Harold Washington, the First Black Mayor of Chicago." *Chicago Tribune*, April 12. http://www.chicagotribune.com/news/politics/chi-chicago days-haroldwashington-story,0,6299016.story.

Dawson, Michael C. 1994. *Behind the Mule: Race and Class in African American Politics.* Princeton, NJ: Princeton University Press.

Day, Caroline Bond. 1930. *A Study of Some Negro-White Families.* Cambridge: Harvard University Press.

Dedman, Bill. 2008. "Historians Write 1st Draft on Obama Victory." MSNBC, November 5. http://www.msnbc.msn.com/id/27539416/from/ET.

Democracy Now. 2008. "Barack Obama and the African American Community: A Debate with Michael Eric Dyson and Glen Ford." January 9. http://www.democracynow.org/2008/1/9/barack_obama_and_the_african_american.

Derrida, Jacques. 1998. *Of Grammatology.* Trans. Gayatri Chakravorty Spivak. Baltimore, MD: Johns Hopkins University Press.

Dhareshwar, Vivek. 1990. "The Predicament of Theory." In *Theory Between the Disciplines: Authority, Vision, Politics*, ed. Martin Kreiswirth and Mark A. Cheetham, 231–50. Ann Arbor: University of Michigan Press.

Dickerson, Debra. 2004. *The End of Blackness: Returning the Souls of Black Folk to Their Rightful Owners.* New York: Pantheon Books.

Dionne, Eugene Joseph. 2008. "Finally, Jinxed Month of August is Almost Over." *Charleston Gazette*, August 23, sec. 4A.

Dixon, Vernon J. 1971. "African-oriented and Euro-American Methodologies and Economics." *Review of Black Political Economy* 7(2): 119–56.

———. 1976. "Worldviews and Research Methodology." In *African Philosophy: Assumption and Paradigms for Research on Black Persons*, ed. Lewis King, 51–102. Los Angeles: Fanon R and D Center.

Do It Yourself Barack Obama Poster. http://www.pentdego.com/obama.aspx.

Dolan, Eric. 2010. "NAACP Exposes Ties Between Tea Party and Racist Extremist Groups." *Alternet*, October 21. http://www.alternet.org/story/148569/naacp_exposes_ties_between_tea_party_and_racist_extremist_groups?paging=off&current_page=1#bookmark.

Dorsey, Margaret E., and Miguel Díaz-Barriga. 2007. "Senator Barack Obama and Immigration Reform." *Journal of Black Studies* 38(2007): 90–104.

Douglass, Frederick. 1845. *Narrative of the Life of Frederick Douglass: An American Slave.* Boston: Anti-Slavery Office.

Douglass, Lisa. 1992. *The Power of Sentiment: Love, Hierarchy, and the Jamaican Family Elite.* San Francisco: Westview.

Dovi, Suzanne. 2003. "Preferable Descriptive Representatives: Will Just any Woman, Black, or Latino Do?" *American Political Science Review* 96(4)(December): 729–43.

Dowd, Maureen. 2007. "Where's His Right Hook? Barack Obama Seems Refreshingly Decent. Can He Survive Hardball Politics?" *Pittsburgh Post-Gazette*, March 5, sec. B7.

———. 2008. "Duel of Historical Guilts." *New York Times*, March 5. http://www.nytimes.com/2008/03/05/opinion/05dowd.html?gwh=D95044BC87B284F50380BFC561D4B5AE.

———. 2009. "Fie, Fatal Flaw!" *New York Times* October 17. http://www.nytimes.com/2009/10/18/opinion/18dowd.html?_r=0.

D'Souza, Dinesh. 2010a. "Obama's Problem with Business." *Fortune*, September 27, 84–94.

———. 2010b. *The Roots of Obama's Rage*. Washington, D.C.: Regnery.

———. 2012. *Obama's America: Unmaking the American Dream*. Washington: Regnery.

Du Bois, W. E. B. 1940. *Dusk of Dawn: An Essay Toward an Autobiography of a Race Concept*. New York: Harcourt, Brace, and World.

———. 1982. *The Souls of Black Folk*. New York: New American Library.

Dumm, Thomas L. 2008. "Barack Obama and the Souls of White Folk." *Communication and Critical/Cultural Studies* 5(3): 317–20.

Duster, Troy. 2003. "Buried Alive: The Concept of Race in Science." In *Genetic Nature/Culture: Anthropology and Science Beyond the Two-Culture Divide*, ed. Alan H. Goodman, Deborah Heath, and Susan Lindee, 258–77. Berkeley and Los Angeles: University of California Press.

Ehrenreich, Nancy. 2005. "Disgusting Empire: Racialized Masculinity and the 'Civilizing' of Iraq." *Cleveland State Law Review* 52(1): 131–38.

Ehrenstein, David. 2007. "Obama the Magical Negro." *Los Angeles Times*, March 19.

Elam, Michele. 2011. *The Souls of Mixed Folk: Race, Politics, and Aesthetics in the New Millennium*. Palo Alto, CA: Stanford University Press.

Electronic Urban Rep. 2008. "EUR Political Analysis: Obama Hit for Not Mentioning Dr. King's Name During Acceptance Speech." September 2, sec. 1.

Eyes on the Prize; America's Civil Rights Years. Blackside, Inc. Produced and Directed by Judith Vecchione; Executive Producer, Harry Hampton; Series writer, Steve Fayer, video cassette. vol. 1: "Awakenings: 1954–1956."

Fabian, Jordan. 2012. "Analysis: Romney Done in by GOP's Latino Problem." ABC News, November 7. http://abcnews.go.com

Fallow, James. 2008. "Instant Reaction to Obama's Speech from Other Side of the World." *Atlantic*, March 18. http://www.theatlantic.com/technology/archive/2008/03/instant-reaction-to-obama-apos-s-speech-from-other-side-of-the-world/7973/.

Fantz, Ashely. 2012. "Obama as Witch Doctor: Racist or Satirical?" CNN.com, September 18.

Farrell, John Aloysius. 2004. "Obama Revives MLK's Dream." *Denver Post*, August 1, sec. A25.

Fausset, Richard. 2012. "Trayvon Martin Case: George Zimmerman Quietly Pleaded Not Guilty." *Los Angeles Times*, April 24. http://articles.latimes.com/2012/apr/24/nation/la-na-nn-zimmerman-not-guilty-plea.

Feagin, Joe. 2000. *Racist America: Roots, Current Realities, and Future Reparations*. New York: Routledge.

———. 2012. *White Party, White Government: Race, Class, and U.S. Politics*. New York: Routledge.

Fears, Darryl. 2003. "Latinos or Hispanics? A Debate About Identity." *Washington Post*, August 25, Page A01.

Feldman, Stanley. 2008. "Why Obama Won." CBS News, November 5. http://www.cbsnews.com/stories/2008/11/05/politics/main4572555.shtml.

Figueroa, Alyssa, and Alana de Hinojosa. 2013. "8 Signs the Zimmerman Verdict May Have Big Ramifications." *Alternet*, July 24. http://www.alternet.org/activism/8-signals-zimmerman-verdict-will-have-big-ramifications.

Finocchiaro, Peter. 2012. "Lawrence Wilkerson, Former Colin Powell Aide, Blasts Sununu, GOP, as 'Full of Racists.'" *Huffington Post*, October 26. http://www.huffingtonpost.com/2012/10/26.

Fissell, Mary. 2003. "Hairy Women and Naked Truths: Gender and the Politics of Knowledge in Aristotle's Masterpiece." *William and Mary Quarterly* 60(1)(January): 43–74.

Fitzgerald, F. Scott. 1925. *The Great Gatsby*. New York: Charles Scribners' Sons.

Fitzgerald, Sandy. 2013. "Oprah Tells Obama 'No' for Obamacare Help." *Newsmax*, November 22. http://www.newsmax.com/Newsfront/oprah-obama-no-support/2013/10/20/id/532037.

Flagg, Barbara J. 2001. "'Was Blind, But Now I See': White Race Consciousness and the Requirement of Discriminatory Intent." In *A Reader on Race, Civil Rights, and American Law: A Multiracial Approach*, ed. Timothy Davis, Kevin R. Johnson, and George A. Martinez, 33–40. Durham: Carolina Academic Press.

Flatow, Nicole. 2013. "Why Stand Your Ground Is Central to George Zimmerman's Case After All." *ThinkProgress*, July 15. http://thinkprogress.org/justice/2013/07/15/2301621/why-stand-your-ground-is-central-to-george-zimmermans-case-after-all/.

Fletcher, Bill. 2008. "Obama Race Speech Analysis." *Black Commentator*, March 20. http://www.blackCommentator.com/269/_cover_obama_race_speech_analysis_ed_bd.html.

Fletcher, Michael, and Jon Cohen. 2011. "Poll Finds Minorities More Optimistic About Economy Despite Losses." *Washington Post*, February 20. http://www.postandcourier.com/news/2011/feb/20/21econ/.

Florida Senate, The. 2011a. "Florida Statutes, Title XLVI (Crimes), Chapter 776 (Justifiable Use of Force), 776.013a."

———. 2011b. "Florida Statutes, Title XLVI (Crimes), Chapter 776 (Justifiable Use of Force), 776.041."

Follet, Richard. 2003. "Heat, Sex, and Sugar: Pregnancy and Childbearing in the Slave Quarters." *Journal of Family History* 28:510–39.

Foner, Eric. 2005. *Give Me Liberty! An American History, Volume I: To 1877*. New York: Norton.

Ford, Clyde. 1994. *The Hero with an African Face*. New York: Bantam Books.

Ford, Glen. 2009. "Obama Preserves Entrenched Power, Sidesteps Racial Disparities." *Black Agenda Report: The Journal of African American Thought and Action*, May 6. http://www.blackagendareport.com/?q=content/obama-preserves-entrenched-power-sidesteps-racial-disparities.

Forde-Mazrui, Kim. 2004. "Taking Conservatives Seriously: A Moral Justification for Affirmative Action and Reparations." *California Law Review* 92(3): 683–753.

Foucault, Michel. 1983. "Afterword: The Subject and Power." In *Michel Foucault: Beyond Structuralism and Hermeneutics*, ed. Herbert L. Dreyfus and Paul Rainbow, 208–26. Chicago: University of Chicago Press.

Fram, Alan. 2008. "'Mutts Like Me' Shows Obama's Racial Comfort." *MSNBC*, November 8. http://www.msnbc.msn.com/id/27606637/.

Frank, David A., and Mark Lawrence McPhail. 2005. "Barack Obama's address to the 2004 Democratic National Convention: Trauma, Compromise, Consilience, and the (Im)possibility of Racial Reconciliation." *Rhetoric and Public Affairs* 8(4): 571–94.

Fraser, Carly. 2009. "Race, Post-Black Politics, and the Democratic Presidential Candidacy of Barack Obama." *Souls* 11(1): 17–40.

Frymer, Paul. 1999. *Uneasy Alliances: Race and Party Competition in America*. Princeton, NJ: Princeton University Press.

Fuentes, Carlos. 2009. "Obama: The First Mestizo Leader North of the Border." *NPQ: New Perspectives Quarterly* 26(1)(Winter): 34. http://www.digitalnpq.org/archive/2009_winter/13_fuentes.html.

Gaines, Kevin. 1996. *Uplifting the Race: Black Leadership, Politics and Culture in the Twentieth Century*. Chapel Hill: The University of North Carolina Press.

———. 2010. "Of Teachable Moments and Specters of Race." *American Quarterly* 62(2) (June): 195–213.

Gamboa, Suzanne. 2012. "Trayvon Martin Case: George Zimmerman's Race Is a Complicated Matter." *Huffington Post*, March 29. http://www.huffingtonpost.com/2012/03/29/trayvon-martin-case-georg_n_1387711.html.

García Saiz, María Concepción. 1989. *Las Castas Mexicanas: Un Género Pictórico Americano*. Torino: Olivetti.

Gardetto, Darleine. 1997. "Hillary Rodham Clinton, Symbolic Gender Politics, and the New York Times: January-November 1992." *Political Communication* 14(2): 225–40.

Garfield, Bob. 2008. "Why Even Hardened Racists Will Vote for Obama." *Advertising Age* 79(9): 25–25.

Gaskins, Pearl Fuyo, ed. 1999. *What Are You?: Voices of Mixed-Race Young People*. New York: Henry Holt.

Gasper, Kevin. 2012. "I Have a Somewhat Different Take on the Zimmerman Shooting." *Plusgoogle.com*, March 28. https://plus.google.com/115585398292418640701/posts/HArFnjsFxag#115585398292418640701/pos ts/HArFnjsFxag.

Gavanas, Anna. 2004. "Domesticating Masculinity and Masculinizing Domesticity in Contemporary US Fatherhood Politics." *Social Politics* 11(2)(Summer): 247–66.

Germond, Jack W., and Jules Witcover. 1993. *Mad as Hell: Revolt at the Ballot Box*. New York: Warner Books.

Gerson, Michael. 2008. "The Incumbent." *Washington Post*, February 25. http://www.washingtonpost.com/wp-dyn/content/article/2008/01/24/AR2008012402797.htm.

Gibbs, Nancy. 2008. "The War over Michelle Obama." *Time*, May 22. http://www.time.com/time/printout/0,8816,1808642,00.html.

Giddings, Paula. 1984. *When and Where I Enter: The Impact of Black Women on Race and Sex in America*. New York: William Morrow.

Gikandi, Simon. 2002. "Race and Cosmopolitanism." *American Literary History* 14(3): 593–615.

Gilens, Martin. 1996. "Race Coding and White Opposition to Welfare." *American Political Science Review:* 90(3): 593–604.

Giles, Nancy. 2007. "What Exactly Is 'Black Enough?' Nancy Giles Ponders the Question Everyone Seems to Asking." CBS News, March 4. http://www.cbsnews.com/stories/2007/03/04/sunday/main2534119.shtml.

Gilkes, Cheryl Townsend. 2001. *If It Wasn't for the Women: Black Women's Experience and Womanist Culture in Church and Community*. Maryknoll, NY: Orbis Books.

Gines, Kathryn. T. 2010. "From Color-Blind to Post-Racial: Blacks and Social Justice in the Twenty-First Century." *Journal of Social Philosophy* 41(3): 370–84.

Giroux, Henry A. 2003. *The Abandoned Generation: Democracy Beyond the Culture of Fear*. New York: Palgrave-Macmillan.

Gitlin, Aaron David. 1995. *The Twilight of Common Dreams: Why America Is Wracked by Culture Wars*. New York: Metropolite Books.

Givhan, Robin. 2007. "The Frontrunners: Fashion Sense." *Washington Post*, December 18. http://www.washingtonpost.com/wpdyn/content/discussion/2007/12/16/DI2007121601778.html.

———. 2008. "Plunging into Blackness." *Washington Post*, July 20. http://articles.washingtonpost.com/2008-07-20/news/36876456_1_barack-obama-matter-of-skin-tone-black-culture.

Goff, Keli. 2013. "Obama Fails Black America and Trayvon." *Root*, July 14. http://www.theroot.com/blogs/blogging-beltway/obama-fails-black-america-and-trayvon.

Gómez, Christina. 2008. "Brown Outs: The Role of Skin Color and Latinas." In *Racism in the 21st Century: An Empirical Analysis of Skin Color*, ed. Ronald Hall, 193–204. New York: Springer.

González, Daniel, and Dan Nowicki. 2012. "Latino Votes Key to Obama's Victory." *Arizona Republic*, November 7. http://www.azcentral.com/arizonarepublic/news/articles/20121107latino-votes-key-obamas-win.html.

"Good for Business: U.S. Glass Ceiling Common Good for Business: Making Full Use of the Nation's Human Capital." 1995. The Environmental Scan. The Fact-Finding Report of the Federal Class Ceiling Commission. Washington, D.C., 71.

Goodman, Ellen. 2008. "Trading Places; Obama is the Woman." *Pittsburgh Post-Gazette*, February 22, sec. B7.

Goodman, Peter. 2008. "From Welfare Shift in '96, '08 Reminder for Clinton." *New York Times*, April 4. http://www.nytimes.com/2008/04/11/us/politics/11welfare.html?pagewanted=all&gwh=441587B5AB7DE50706D07F9CFAD6E85F.

Gordy, Cynthia. 2011. "Defending Obama's Drug Policy." *Root*, Novemner 2011. http://www.theroot.com/blogs/blogging_the_beltway/2011/11/drug_czar_gil_kerlikowske_interview_new_strategies_in_the_war_on_drugs.html.

Gossett, Thomas F. 1997. *Race: The History of an Idea in America*. New York: Oxford University Press.

Graham, Susan. 2008. "Dogs Are Mutts; People Are Multiracial." November 21. http://www.projectrace.com/fromthedirector/archive/112108_obama_mutt_multiracial.php.

Gramsci, Antonio. 1971. *Selections from the Prison Notebooks*, ed. Quentin Hoare and Geoffrey Nowell Smith. New York: International.

Greenwald, Glen. 2013. "NSA Collecting Phone Records of Millions of Verizon Customers Daily." *Guardian*, June 5. http://www.guardian.co.uk/world/2013/jun/06/nsa-phone-records-verizon-court-order.

Gregory, David. 2007. "Sen. Biden Apologizes for Remarks on Obama." MSNBC, January 31. http://www.msnbc.msn.com/id/16911044/.

Gresson, Aaron David. 1995. *The Recovery of Race in America*. Minneapolis: University of Minnesota Press.

Gring-Pemble, Lisa M. 2001. "'Are We Going to Now Govern by Anecdote?' Rhetorical Constructions of Welfare Recipients in Congressional Hearings, Debates, and Legislation, 1992–1996." *Quarterly Journal of Speech* 87(4): 341–66.

———. 2003. "Legislating a 'Normal, Classic Family': The Rhetorical Construction of Families in American Welfare Policy." *Political Communication* 20(4): 473–98.

Grofman, Bernard. 1982. *Representation and Redistricting Issues*. Lexington: Lexington Books.

Gurin, Patricia, Arthur Miller, and Gerald Gurin. 1980. "Stratum Identification and Consciousness." *Social Psychology Quarterly* 43: 30–47.

Gyekye, Kwame. 1995. *African Philosophical Thought: The Akan Conceptual Scheme*. Philadelphia: Temple University Press.

Hagiwara, Nao, Deborah A. Kashy, and Joseph Cesario. 2012. "The Independent Effects of Skin Tone and Facial Features on Whites' Affective Reactions to Blacks." *Journal of Experimental Psychology* 48:892–98.

Hale, Dorothy. 1994. "Bakhtin in African American Literary Theory." *English Literary History* 61(2)(Summer): 445–71.

Halewood, Peter. 2009. "Laying Down the Law: Post-Racialism and the Deracination Project." *Albany Law Review* 72(4): 1047–52.

Hall, Ronald E., ed. 2003. *Discrimination among Oppressed Populations*. Lewiston, NY: Edwin Mellen Press.

Halperin, Mark, and John Heilemann. 2012. *Double Down: Game Change*. New York: The Penguin Press.

Han, Lori Cox. 2004. "First Sons versus First Daughters: A Gender Bias in News Media Coverage?" In *Life in the White House: A Social History of the First Family and the President's House*, ed. Robert P. Watson, 143–64. Albany: SUNY Press.

Handler, Joel. 1995. *The Poverty of Welfare Reform*. New Haven, CT: Yale University Press.

Haney López, Ian. 2014. *Dog Whistle Politics: How Coded Racial Appeals Have Reinvented Racism and Wrecked the Middle Class*. New York: Oxford University Press.

Hannaham, James. 2008. "Multiracial Man: The Obama Campaign's Deft Use of the Candidate's Mixed Heritage Is Making It Harder to Read His Candidacy in Terms of Race." *Salon.com*, February 2. http://www.salon.com/opinion/feature/2008/02/02/biracial_obama/print.html.

Haraway, Donna. 1991. "A Cyborg Manifesto: Science, Technology, and Socialist Feminism in the Late Twentieth Century." In *Simians, Cyborgs, and Women: The Reinvention of Nature*, ed. Donna Haraway, 141–81. New York: Routledge.

———. 2003. "Race: Universal Donors in a Vampire Culture. It's All in the Family: Biological Kinship Categories in the Twentieth-century United States." In *The Haraway Reader*, ed. Donna Haraway, 251–94. New York: Routledge.

Harris, Cheryl L. 1993. "Whiteness As Property." *Harvard Law Review* 106(8): 1707–91.
Harris, Fredrick. 2009. "Toward a Pragmatic Black Politics?" *Souls* 11: 41–49.
Harris-Lacewell, Melissa, and Jane Junn. "Old Friends and New Alliances: How the 2004 Illinois Senate Race Complicates the Study of Race and Religion." *Journal of Black Studies* 38(2007): 30–50.
Harris-Perry, Melissa. 2011. *Sister Citizen: Shame, Stereotypes, and Black Women in America*. New Haven, CT: Yale University Press.
Hart, Peter. 2007. "Obamamania: How Loving Barack Obama Helps Pundits Love Themselves." *Extra!*, March/April. http://fair.org/extra-online-articles/obamamania/.
Healy, Patrick. 2008. "Two Conventions with No Shortage of Contrasts." *New York Times*, September 3. http://www.nytimes.com/2008/09/04/us/politics/04compare.html.
Heberlig, Eric. 2003. "Congressional Parties, Fundraising and Political Ambition." *Political Research Quarterly*: 56(2): 151–61.
Heilbroner, Robert, and Aaron Singer. 1999. *The Economic Transformation of America: 1600 to the Present*. 4th ed. Boston, MS: Wadsworth.
Heilemann, John, and Mark Halperin. 2010. *Game Change: Obama and the Clintons, McCain and Palin, and the Race of a Lifetime*. New York: Harper.
Higginbotham, A. Leon, Jr. 1978. *In the Matter of Color: Race and the American Legal Process: The Colonial Period*. New York: Oxford University Press.
Higginbotham, Evelyn Brooks. 1993. *Righteous Discontent: The Women's Movement in the Black Baptist Church, 1880–1920*. Cambridge: Harvard University Press.
Hightower, Kyle, and Mike Schneider. 2013a. "George Zimmerman Jury Selected: All Women Jurors Chosen in Trial of Trayvon Martin Killer." *Huffington Post*, June 20. http://www.huffingtonpost.com/2013/06/20/george-zimmerman-jury-_n_3474181.html.
———. 2013b. "Selene Bahadoor, First Eyewitness, Testifies in George Zimmerman Trial." *Huffington Post*, June 27. http://www.huffingtonpost.com/2013/06/26/selene-bahadoor_n_3502071.html.
Hill, Marc Lamont. 2008. "Not My Brand of Hope: Obama's Politics of Cunning, Compromise, and Consilience." *Counter Punch*, February 11. http://www.counterpunch.org/2008/02/11/not-my-brand-of-hope/
Hill, Mike. 2004. *After Whiteness: Unmaking an American Majority*. Cultural Front (Series). New York: New York University Press.
Hill, Rickey. 2009. "The Race Problematic, the Narrative of Martin Luther King Jr., and the Election of Barack Obama." *Souls* 11(1): 60–78.
Hillman, James. 1980. "On the Necessity of Abnormal Psychology: Ananke and Athena." *Facing the Gods*, ed. James Hillman, 1–38. Irving: University of Dallas Press.
Hine, Darlene Clark, William C. Hine, and Stanley Harrold. 2008. *The African-American Odyssey*. 4th ed. Upper Saddle River, NJ: Pearson Prentice Hall.
Hirshman, Linda. 2008. "When Dreams Collide; Looking to the Future, Feminism Has to Focus . . ." *Washington Post*, June 8. http://www.washingtonpost.com/wp-dyn/content/article/2008/06/06/AR2008060603494.html.
Hislop, Stehpen G. 2009. "Florida Crackers: America's Tropical Cowboys." The History Channel Club, June 26. http://www.thehistorychannelclub.com/articles/articletype/articleview/articleid/239/florida-crackers-americas-tropical-cowboys.

Hochschild, Arlie, and Anne Machung. 1989. *The Second Shift: Working Parents and the Revolution at Home.* New York: Viking Penguin.

Hochschild, Jennifer L., and Vesla Weaver. 2007. "The Skin Color Paradox and the American Racial Order." *Social Forces* 86(2): 643–70.

Hodes, Martha. 1997. *White Women, Black Men: Illicit Sex in the Nineteenth-Century South.* New Haven: Yale University Press.

Hollinger, David A. 2008. "Obama, the Instability of Color Lines, and the Promise of a Postethnic Future." *Callaloo* 31(4): 1033–37.

Holloway, Lynette. 2013. "Cornel West: MSNBC Is a 'Rent-a-Negro' Phenomenon." *Root*, July 24. http://www.theroot.com/buzz/cornel-west-msnbc-rent-negro-phenomenon.

hooks, bell. 1992. *Black Looks: Race and Representation.* Boston: South End Press.

Hotline. 2007. "The Field; What's Your Campaign A-Gender?" July 12.

Howard, Sheena C. 2009. "Facility of Nommo: Afrocentric Rhetorical Analysis of Barack Obama." Paper presented at the National Association of African American Studies Conference, February, Baton Rouge, Louisiana.

Huckabee, Charles. 2008. "U. of Kentucky Apologizes after Obama Effigy Is Found on Its Campus." *Chronicle of Higher Education*, October 29. http://chronicle.com/news/article/5415/u-of-kentucky-apologizes-after-obama-effigy-is-found-on-its-campus.

Hudson, Adam. 2013. "The Astonishing Collapse of Black and Latino Household Wealth." *Alternet*, May 13. http://www.alternet.org/economy/black-and-latino-household-wealth-has-collapsed.

Hudson, Mildred J., and Barbara J. Holmes. 1994. "Missing Teachers, Impaired Communities: The Unanticipated Consequences of *Brown v. Board of Education* on the African American Teaching Force at the Precollegiate Level." *Journal of Negro Education* 63(3): 388–93.

Hughes, Michael, and Bradley R. Hertel. 1990. "The Significance of Color Remains: A Study of Life Chances, Mate Selection, and Ethnic Consciousness among Black Americans." *Social Forces* 68(4): 1105–20.

Hulse, Carle. 2012. "Republicans Face Struggle Over Party's Direction." *New York Times*, November 7.

Humes, Karen R., Nicholas A. Jones, and Roberto R. Ramirez. 2011. "Overview of Race and Hispanic Origin: 2010." 2010 Census Briefs. Washington, D.C.: U.S. Census Bureau, March 2011. http://www.census.gov/prod/cen2010/briefs/c2010br-02.pdf.

Hunt, Darnell M. 2008. "UCLA's Process Rights a Wrong." *Los Angeles Times*, September 7, sec. A34.

Hunter, Margaret L. 2005. *Race, Gender, and the Politics of Skin Tone.* New York: Routledge.

———. 2011. "Buying Racial Capital: Skin-Bleaching and Cosmetic Surgery." *Journal of Pan African Studies.* 4(4)(June): 142–61.

Hunter, Tera W. 1997. *To 'Joy My Freedom: Southern Black Women's Lives and Labors after the Civil War.* Cambridge: Harvard University Press.

Hutchings, Vincent, Nicholas Valentino, Tasha Philpot and Ismail White. 2004. "The Compassion Strategy." *Public Opinion Quarterly* 68(4): 512–41.

Hutchins, Loriane, and Lani Kaahumanu. 1991. "Bicoastal Introduction." In *Bi Any Other Name: Bisexual People Speak Out*, ed. Loriane Hutchins and Lani Kaahumanu, xxii–xxiv. Boston: Alyson Publications.

Hutchinson, Darren Lenard. 2012. "Trayvon Martin: 'Stand Your Ground' Rule Has NOTHING To Do With This Case." *Dissenting Justice*, March 21. http://dissentingjustice.blogspot.com/2012/03/trayvon-martin-stand-your-ground-rule.html.

———. 2013. "Race, Justice, and Trayvon Martin." MSNBC.com, July 15. http://tv.msnbc.com/2013/07/15/race-justice-and-trayvon-martin/.

Hyde, Justin, and Richard Wolf. 2009. "President Says He Shouldn't Put Focus on Blacks Troubles." *USA Today*, December 4, 4A.

Hyde, Lewis. 1998. *Trickster Makes This World*. New York: North Point Press.

Ifill, Gwen. 2009. *The Breakthrough: Politics and Race in the Age of Obama*. New York: Doubleday.

IMDb. 2009. "Obama: Heated Debate Is on Role of Government." September 18. http://www.imdb.com/video/hulu/vi930415129/.

Inskeep, Steve. 2007. "Obama to Attend Selma March Anniversary." National Public Radio, February 28. http://www.npr.org/templates/story/story.php?storyId.

Isikoff, Michael. 2013. "Exclusive: Justice Department Memo Reveals Legal Case for Drone Strikes on Americans." MSNBC, February 5. http://openchannel.nbcnews.com/_news/2013/02/04/16843014-exclusive-justice-department-memo-reveals-legal-case-for-drone-strikes-on-americans?lite.

IU News Room. 2008. "Two Elephants in the Room." April 10. http://newsinfo.iu.edu/news/page/normal/7542.html.

Iweala, Uzodinma. 2008. "Racism in 'Post-Racial' America: Silence About Race in the Presidential Campaign Underscores the Problem." *Los Angeles Times*, January 23. http://articles.latimes.com/2008/jan/23/opinion/oe-iweala23.

Jackson, Harry. 2012. "Father in Chief—Or Just Another Politician." June 19. http://www.thetruthinblackandwhite.com/Weekly_Column/?Father_in_Chief_Or_Just_Another_Politician&year=2012.

Jackson, Jesse. 1988. "1988 Democratic National Convention Speech." *American Rhetoric*, July 19. http://www.americanrhetoric.com/speeches/PDFFiles/Jesse%20Jackson%20%201988%20DNC%20Address.pdf: 1–12.

Jackson, John P., Jr., and Nadine M. Weidman. 2004. *Race, Racism, and Science: Social Impact and Interaction*. Santa Barbara, CA: ABC-Clio.

Jacobs, Harriet Brent. 1861. *Incidents in the Life of a Slave Girl Written by Herself: Documenting the American South*. Boston: Harvard University Press

Jacobson, Matthew Frye. 1998. *Whiteness of a Different Color: European Immigrants and the Alchemy of Race*. Cambridge: Harvard University Press.

James, Joy. 2009. "The Dead Zone: Stumbling at the Crossroads of Party Politics, Genocide, and Postracial Racism." *South Atlantic Quarterly* 108(3): 459–81.

James, Stanlie M. 2009. "Barack Obama: Coalitions of a Purple Mandate." *Souls* 11(1): 51–59.

Jeffries, Michael P. 2013. *Paint the White House Black: Barack Obama and the Meaning of Race in America*. Palo Alto, CA: Stanford University Press.

Jennings, Thelma. 1990. "Us Colored Women Had to Go Through a Plenty: Sexual Exploitation of African American Slave Women." *Journal of Women's History* 1(3) (Winter): 45–74.

Jewell, K. Sue. 1993. *From Mammy to Miss America and Beyond: Cultural Images and the Shaping of U.S. Social Policy*. New York: Routledge.

John, Mary E. 1996. *Discrepant Dislocations: Feminism, Theory, and Postcolonial Histories*. Berkeley and Los Angeles: University of California Press.

Johnson, Glen. 2010. "President Obama, Scott Brown Related, Genealogists Say." *Huffington Post*, January 29. http://www.huffingtonpost.com/2010/01/29/president-obama-scott-bro_n_441754.html.

Johnson, L. A. 2008. "Obama Candidacy Raises Old Questions about What Is Black." *Pittsburgh Post-Gazette*, March 8. http://www.post-gazette.com/pg/08129/879988-176.stm.

Johnson, Paula C. 2003. *Inner Lives: Voices of African American Women in Prison*. New York: New York University Press.

Johnson, Steve. 2004. "Behind Gates: How the Harvard Scholar Is Using His 'Color-Line' PBS as a Wake-Up Call." *Chicago Tribune*, February, sec. 5, 1.

Johnston, Marc P., and Kevin L. Nadal. 2010. "Multiracial Microaggressions: Exposing Monoracism." In *Microaggressions and Marginality: Manifestation, Dynamics, and Impact*, ed. Derald Wing Sue, 123–44. Hoboken, NJ: John Wiley and Sons.

Jolivétte, Andrew J. "Obama and the Biracial Factor: An Introduction." In *Obama and the Biracial Factor: The Battle for a New American Majority*, ed. Andrew J. Jolivétte, 3–30. Bristol, UK: Policy Press.

Jones, Jacqueline. 1985. *Labor of Love, Labor of Sorrow: Black Women, Work, and the Family from Slavery to the Present*. New York: Basic Books.

Jones, Keith Walters. 2009. "Obama and Buffett: Six Degrees of Barack Includes Billionaire, Angelina Jolie Beau?" *National Ledger*, December 16. http://www.nationalledger.com/artman/publish/article_272629527.shtml.

Jones, Mack. 1992. "Political Science and the Black Political Experience: Issues in Epistemology and Relevance." *National Political Science Review: Ethnic Politics and Civil Liberties* 3:25–39.

Jones, Nicholas A. 2005. "We the People of More Than One Race in the United States." Census 2000 Special Reports, CENSR-22. Washington, D.C.: U.S. Census Bureau, April. http://www.census.gov/prod/2005pubs/censr-22.pdf.

Jones, Stephanie J., ed. 2009. *The State of Black America 2009: Message to the President*. New York: National Urban League.

Jones, Terry. 2007. "Diversity Meets National Politics: Only White Males Need Apply." *St. Louis Journalism Review* 37(295): 9–19.

Jones, Trina. 2000. "Shades of Brown: The Law of Skin Color." *Duke Law Journal* 49:1487–1557.

Jordan, Winthrop D. 2014. "Historical Origins of the One-Drop Racial Rule in the United States." *Journal of Critical Mixed Race Studies* 1(1): 98–132.

Joseph, Peniel. 2010. *Dark Days, Bright Nights: From Black Power to Barack Obama*. New York: Basic Civitas Books.

Judis, John B. 2008. "American Adam: Obama and the Cult of the New." *New Republic*, March 12, 24.

Kahn, Kim Fridkin. 1996. *The Political Consequences of Being a Woman*. New York: Columbia University Press.

Kam, Dara, and Jon Lantigua. 2012. "Former Florida GOP Leaders Say Voter Suppression Was Reason They Pushed New Election Law." *Palm Beach Post*, November 25. http://www.palmbeachpost.com/news/news/state-regional-govt-politics/early-voting-curbs-called-power-play/nTFDy/.

Kambon, Kobi. 1992. *The African Personality in America: An African Centered Framework*. Tallahassee, FL: Nubian Nation.

———. 1996. "The Africentric Paradigm and African-American Psychological Liberation." In *African Psychology in Historical Perspective and Related Commentary*, ed. Daudi Ajani Ya Azibo, 57–69. Trenton, NJ: Africa World Press.

———. 1998. *African/Black Psychology in the American Context: An African Centered Approach*. Tallahassee, FA: Nubian Nations.

Kane, Paul, 2010. "'Tea Party' Protesters Accused of Spitting on Lawmaker, Using Slurs." *Washington Post*, March 20. http://www.washingtonpost.com/wp-dyn/content/article/2010/03/20/AR2010032002556.html.

Kang, Jerry. 2005. "Trojan Horses of Race." *Harvard Law Review* 118(5): 1489–1593.

Kang, Jerry, and Mahzarin R. Banaji. 2006. "Fair Measures: A Behavioral Realist Revision of "Affirmative Action." *California Law Review* 94(4): 1063–1118.

Kaplan, Erin Aubry. 2004. "Bringin' Da Funk." *LA Weekly*, August 6.

Kaplan, Rebecca. 2013. "Gingrich Defends Criticism of Obama's Trayvon Martin Comments." CBS News, July 24. http://www.cbsnews.com/8301-503544_162-57404856-503544/gingrich-defends-criticism-of-obamas-trayvon-martin-comments/.

Karoliszyn, Henrick, et al. 2009. "Off-duty Cop Was Part of a Racist Gang that Beat a Long Island Black Man Say Police." *(New York) Daily News*, March 10.

Katzew, Ilona. 2004. *Casta Painting: Images of Race in Eighteenth-Century Mexico*. New Haven, CT: Yale University Press.

Kauffman, Karen. 2002. "Culture Wars, Secular Realignment, and the Gender Gap in Party Identification." *Political Behavior* 24(3): 283–307.

Keith, Verna, and Cedric Herring. 1991. "Skin Tone and Stratification in the Black Community." *American Journal of Sociology* 97(3): 760–78.

Kennedy, Randall. 2011. *The Persistence of the Color Line: Racial Politics and the Obama Presidency*. New York: Pantheon.

Kevles, Daniel J. 1995. *In the Name of Eugenics: Genetics and the Uses of Human Heredity*. Cambridge: Harvard University Press.

Keys, Alexa. 2012. "'Don't Re-Nig in 2012': Maker of Racist Anti-Obama Sticker Shuts Down Site." ABC News, May 16. http://abcnews.go.com/blogs/politics/2012/03/dont-re-nig-in-2012-maker-of-racist-anti-obama-sticker-shuts-down-site/.

Khanna, Nikki. 2010. "'If You're Half Black, You're Just Black': Reflected Appraisals and the Persistence of the One-drop Rule.'" *Sociological Quarterly* 51(1): 96–121.

Killian, Linda. 2007. "Obama's Tough Talk Falls Short." *Politico*, August. 2. http://www.politico.com/news/stories/0807/5222.html.

Kim, Claire Jean. 2000. *Bitter Fruit*. New Haven, CT: Yale University Press.

Kimmel, Michael S. 1997. "Integrating Men into the Curriculum." *Duke Gender Law and Policy* 4(1): 181–83.

———. 2003. "Masculinity as Homophobia." In *Reconstructing Gender: A Multicultural Anthology*, 3rd ed, ed. Estelle Disch, 103–109. New York: McGraw-Hill.

———. 2005. *The Gender of Desire: Essays on Male Sexuality*. Albany: State University of New York Press.

Kinder, Donald. 2003. "Communication and Politics in the Age of Information." In *Oxford Handbook of Political Psychology*, ed. David O. Sears, Leonie Huddy, and Robert Jervis, 357–93. Oxford: Oxford University Press.

Kinder, Donald R., and Allison Dale-Riddle. 2012. *The End of Race Obama, 2008, and Racial Politics in America*. New Haven and London: Yale University Press.

Kinder, Donald, and L. Sanders. 1990. "Mimicking Political Debate with Survey Questions: The Case of White Opinion on Affirmative Action for Blacks." *Social Cognition* 8(1): 73–103.

King, Anthony. 2002. "The Outside as Political Leader: The Case of Margaret Thatcher." *British Journal of Political Science* 32(3): 435–54.

King, Colbert I. 2008. "Billary's Adventures in Primaryland." *Washington Post*, January 26. http://www.washingtonpost.com/wp-dyn/content/article/2008/01/25/AR2008012502780.html.

King, Desmond S., and Rogers Smith. 2011. *Still a House Divided: Race and Politics in Obama's America*. Princeton, NJ: Princeton University Press.

King, Martin Luther, Jr. 1969/1991. "Where Do We Go From Here: Chaos or Community." In *A Testament of Hope: The Essential Writings and Speeches of Martin Luther King, Jr.*, ed. James M. Washington, 567–78. New York: HarperCollins.

King-O'Riain, Rebecca Chiyoko. 2012. "Is 'No One as Irish as Barack O'Bama?'" In *Obama and the Biracial Factor: The Battle for a New American Majority*, ed. Andrew J. Jolivétte, 113–28. Bristol, UK: Policy Press.

Klare, Michael T. 2009. "Welcome to 2025: American Preeminence is Disappearing Fifteen Years Early." *TomDispatch.com*, October 26, http://www.tomdispatch.com/post/175131/michael_klare_the_great_superpower_meltdown.

Klein, Joe. 2006. "The Fresh Face." *Time*, October 23. http//www.time.com/time/magazine/article/0,9171,1546302,00.html.

———. 2008. "Anger vs. Steadiness in the Crisis." *Time*, October 2.

Klein, Naomi. 2007. *The Shock Doctrine: The Rise of Disaster Capitalism*. New York: Metropolitan.

———. 2009. "Obama's Big Silence: The Race Question." *Guardian*, September 11.

Koppelman, Alex. 2009. "Carter: Animosity Towards Obama Based Mostly on Race." *Salon.com*, September 15. http://www.salon.com/politics/war_room/2009/09/15/carter_race/index.html?source=newsletter.

Korgen, Kathleen O. 1998. *From Black to Biracial: Transforming Racial Identity Among Americans*, Westport, CT: Praeger.

Korgen, Kathleen O., and David L. Brunsma. 2013. "Avoiding Race or Following the Racial Scripts? Obama and Race in the Recessionary Part of the Colorblind Era." In *Obama and the Biracial Factor: The Battle for a New American Majority*, ed. Andrew J. Jolivétte, 191–204. Bristol, UK: Policy Press.

Kornreich, Lauren. 2008. "Obama: New Dog Could Be Mutt Like Me." Politicker.blogs.cnn.com, November 7, http://politicker.blogs.cnn.com/2008/11/07/obama-new-dog-could-be-mutt-like-me/?fbid=6ya-SUWVgiG.
Kovaleski, Serge F. 2009. "Two Officers Paths to Fatal Encounter in Harlem." *New York Times*, May 29.
Kovel, Joel. 1907. *White Racism: A Psychohistory*. New York: Columbia University Press.
Kreider, Rose M., and Diana B. Elliott. 2010. "Historical Changes in Stay-at-Home Mothers: 1969 to 2009." Paper presented to the American Sociological Association, 7–8. http://www.census.gov/population/www/socdemo/ASA2010_Kreider_Elliott.pdf.
Kristof, Nicholas D. 2008. "Who Is More Electable?" *New York Times*, February 2. http://www.nytimes.com/2008/02/07/opinion/07kristof.html?gwh=F34549CBFD2DF80E131A72C59 2E2C411.
Kunkle, Fredrick, and Ann Gerhart. 2010. "Gun-Rights Advocates Gather in Va. and D.C. to Celebrate 'Historic Moment.'" *Washington Post*, April 20.
La Ganga, Maria L. 2012. "Where Obama Pride Abides." *Los Angeles Times*, November 8.
Lacan, Jacques. 2005. *Ecrits*. Trans. Heloise Fink and Russell Grigg. New York: Norton.
Lakin, Max. 2008. "The Question: Do You Think 'Brand America' Will Bounce Back with the Obama Administration?; 78% Said Barack Obama Can Bring Back Brand America." *Advertising Age*, November 17.
Lamb, Michael E. 1987. "Introduction: The Emergent American Father." In *The Fathers Role: Cross-cultural Perspectives*, ed. Michel E. Lamb, 3–17. Hillsdale, NJ: Lawrence Erlbaum Associates.
Landy, Marc, and Sidney M. Milkis. 2000. *Presidential Greatness*. Lawrence: University of Kansas Press.
Lavoie, Denise. 2008. "Barack Obama and Brad Pitt Are Cousins, Hillary Clinton and Angelina Jolie Are Also Cousins, Study Says." *Huffington Post*, March 25. http://www.huffingtonpost.com/2008/03/25/barack-obama-and-brad-pit_n_93356.html.
Lawrence, Jill. 2013. "Why Obama's White-Guy Problem Seems Worse Than It Is." *National Journal*, May 30. http://www.nationaljournal.com/whitehouse/why-obama-s-white-guy-problem-seems-worse-than-it-is-20130109.
Lee, Robert G. 1999. *Orientals: Asian Americans in Popular Culture*. Philadelphia: Temple University Press.
Lee, Taeku, and Karthick Ramakrishnan. 2102. "Turning Blue: Asian American Voters' Support for Obama Caught Most Pundits by Surprise." *Los Angeles Times*, November 23.
Leibovich, Mark. 2008. "Rights vs. Rights: An Improbable Collision Course." *New York Times*, January 13. http://www.nytimes.com/2008/01/13/weekinreview/13leibovich.html?pagewanted=all.
Leitsinger, Miranda. 2013. "Supreme Court Ruling Encourages Supporters—and Opponents—of Affirmative Action." NBCNews.com, June 24. http://usnews.nbcnews.com/_news/2013/06/24/19119553-supreme-court-ruling-encourages-supporters-and-opponents-of-affirmative-action?lite&ocid=msnhp&pos=1.
Leksander, Susan. 2007. *Psychosynthesis and Multiracial Clients: Diversity and Integration of Multiple Selves*. San Francisco: California Institute of Integral Studies.
Leland, John, and Gregory Beals. 1997. "In Living Colors." *Newsweek*, May 5, 58–60.

LeMay, Michael, and Elliott Robert Barkan, eds. 1999. *U.S. Immigration and Naturalization Laws and Issues*. Westport, CT: Greenwood.

Levit, Nancy. 1996. "Feminism for Men: Legal Ideology and the Construction of Maleness." *UCLA Law Review* 43(4): 1037–51.

Lewis, Jane. 2001. "The Decline of the Male Breadwinner Model: Implications for Work and Care." *Social Politics* 8(2): 152–69.

Life at the Edge of the World. 2008. "Donna Brazile Isn't Going to the Back of the Bus." October 31, http://lestyoubejudged.wordpress.com/2008/10/31/vote-for-the-issues-donna-brazile-isnt-going-to-the-back-of-the-bus/.

Lillis, Mike. 2012. "Immigration Reformers See Obama Win, Hispanic Turnout as 'Game-Changer.'" *Hill*, November 7. http://thehill.com/homenews/administration/266709.

Lindsay, Emma. 2005. "Lysistrata, Women, and War: International Law's Treatment of Women in Conflict and Post-Conflict Situations." *Texas Wesleyan Law Review* 12(1) (Fall): 345–76.

Linsky, Martin. 2008. "The First Woman President? Obama's Campaign Bends Gender Conventions." *Newsweek*, February 26. http://www.newsweek.com/id/115397/page/1.

Lipsitz, George. 1998. *The Possessive Investment in Whiteness: How White People Profit from Identity Politics*. Philadelphia: Temple University Press.

———. 2011. *How Racism Takes Place*. Philadelphia: Temple University Press.

Liptak, Adam. 2013. "Supreme Court Invalidates Key Part of Voting Rights Act." *New York Times*, June 25. http://www.nytimes.com/2013/06/26/us/supreme-court-ruling.html?pagewanted=all&_r=0.

Liptak, Kevin. 2013. "Obama Urges Patience to Critics of White Male Nominees." *Politicalticker*, January 14. http://politicalticker.blogs.cnn.com/2013/01/14/obama-urges-patience-to-critics-of-white-male-nominees/.

Lipton, Eric. 2013. "With Criminal Case Closed, Justice Department Will Restart Hate Crime Inquiry." *New York Times*, July 14. http://www.nytimes.com/2013/07/15/us/justice-department-to-restart-hate-crime-investigation-in-trayvon-martins-death.html?_r=0.

Livingston, Robert W., and Nicholas A. Pearce. 2009. "Teddy-bear Effect: Does Having a Baby-face Benefit Black Chief Executive Officers?" *Psychological Science* 20(10): 1229–36.

Lizza, Ryan. 2012. "The Party Next Time: As Immigration Turns Red States Blue, How Can Republicans Transform Their Platform?" *New Yorker*, November 19.

Loewen, James. 2005. *Sundown Towns: A Hidden Dimension of American Racism*. New York: Touchstone.

Logan, Enid Lynette. 2011. *At This Defining Moment: Barack Obama's Presidential Candidacy and the New Politics of Race*. New York and London: New York University Press.

Low, Setha M. 2001. "The Edge and the Center: Gated Communities and the Discourse of Urban Fear." *American Anthropologist* 103(1): 45–58.

Lubin, Alex. 2005. *Romance and Rights: The Politics of Interracial Intimacy, 1945–1954*. Jackson: University Press of Mississippi.

Lynch, Deborah. 2009. "Turnaround: The Deadliest Reform of All." *Substance: The Newspaper of Public Education in Chicago* (October): 1, 13.

MacAskill, Ewen. 2008. "US Election: Buffett Joins Obama to Solve Economic Crisis." *Guardian*, July 29. http://www.guardian.co.uk/world/2008/jul/29/barackobama.uselections2008.
MacFarquar, Lisa. 2007. "The Conciliator: Where is Barack Obama Coming From?" *New Yorker*, May 7.
MacGillis, Alec. 2008. "Obama Recalls a Fuller History." *Washington Post*, April 4. http://blog.washingtonpost.com/the-trail/2008/04/04/obama_recalls_a_fuller_history.html.
Macky, Robert. 2012. "'If I Had a Son, He Would Look Like Trayvon,' Obama Says." *New York Times*, March 23.
Mansbridge, Jane. 1999. "Should Blacks Represent Blacks and Women Represent Women? A Contingent 'Yes.'" *Journal of Politics* 61(3): 628–57.
Marable, Manning. 1990. "Black Politics and the Challenges for the Left." *Monthly Review* 41(11): 22–31.
———. 2009. "Racializing Obama: The Enigma of Post-Black Politics and Leadership." *Souls* 11(1): 1–15.
Marger, Martin M. 1994. *Race and Ethnic Relations: American and Global Perspectives*. Belmont, CA: Wadsworth Publishers.
Marin, Carol. 2008. "Thanks to Hillary for Being a Winner at Heart." *Chicago Sun Times*, May 11, sec. A17.
Marinucci, Carla. 2008. "Obama Promises to Restore Promise of the U.S." *San Francisco Chronicle*, August 29, sec. A1.
Marks, Loren, and Ron Palkovitz. 2004. "American Fatherhood Types: The Good, the Bad, and the Uninterested." *Fathering* 2(2)(Spring): 113–29.
May, Clifford. 2008. "The Wright Stuff vs. the Woods Model." *Mississippi Press*, April 3, sec. 7A.
Mayer, Jeremy D. 2002. *Running on Race: Racial Politics in Presidential Campaigns, 1960–2000*. New York: Random House.
Mazama, Ama. 2007. "The Barack Obama Phenomenon." *Journal of Black Studies* 38(1) (September): 3–6.
Mboya, Tom. 1963. *Freedom and After*. Boston: Little Brown.
McAuliff, Michael, and Michael Saul. 2008. "Bam Jam over 'Typical White' Folk Talk in Philly." *(New York) Daily News*, March 21, sec. 9.
McClintock, Anne. 1995. *Imperial Leather: Race, Gender, and Sexuality in the Colonial Contest*. New York: Routledge.
McCoy, Alfred. 2013. "Tomgram: Alfred W. McCoy, Obama's Expanding Surveillance Universe." TomDispatch.com, July 14. http://www.tomdispatch.com/...omDispatch&utm_campaign=f7fb1e61ac-TD_McCoy7_14_2013&utm_medium=email&utm_term=0_1e41682ade-f7fb1e61ac-308757869#more.
McElya, Micki. 2011. "To 'Choose Our Better History': Assessing the Obama Presidency in Real Time." *American Quarterly* 63(1)(March): 179–89.
McGinley, Ann C. 2004. "Masculinities at Work." *Oregon Law Review* 83(2): 359–433.
———. 2009. "Hillary Clinton, Sarah Palin, and Michelle Obama: Performing Gender, Race, and Class on the Campaign Trail." *Denver University Law Review* 86: 709–25.

McGregor, Richard. 2012. "Cuban Americans Stun Republicans as Memories of Castro Rule Fade." *Financial Times*, November 8.

McIlwain, Charlton D. 2007. "Perceptions of Leadership and the Challenge of Obama's Blackness." *Journal of Black Studies* 38: 64–74.

McIntosh, Peggy. 1995. "White Privilege and Male Privilege: A Personal Account of Coming to See Correspondences Through Work in Women's Studies." In *Race, Class, and Gender: An Anthology*, ed. Margaret Anderson and Patricia Hill Collins, 76–87. New York: Wadsworth.

McLean, I., J. M. Orbell, and R. M. Dawes. 1991. "What Should Rational Cognitive Misers Do?" *American Political Science Review* 85(4): 1417–20.

McNally, Joel. 2013. "'They Always Get Away.'" *Express Milwaukee*, July 17. http://express milwaukee.com/article-21473-%25E2%2580%2598they-always-get-away%25E2%2580 %2599.html.

McNally, Terrence. 2009. "Always Controversial Cornel West Disses Obama, Survives Cancer and Almost Spent His Life in Prison." *Alternet*, December 18. www.alternet .org/rights/144569/always_controversial_cornel_west_disses_obama%2C_survives_ca ncer_and_almost_spent_his_life_in_prison?page=entire.

McPhail, Mark Lawrence. 1996. *Zen in the Art of Rhetoric: An Inquiry into Coherence*. Albany: State University of New York Press.

——. 2001. "Double Consciousness in Black and White: Identity, Difference, and the Rhetorical Ideal of Life." Van Zelst Lecture in Communication, Northwestern University School of Speech, Evanston, IL.

——. 2002a. "Dessentializing Difference: Transformative Visions in Contemporary Black Thought." *Howard Journal of Communications* 13: 77–95.

——. 2002b. *The Rhetoric of Racism Revisited: Reparations or Separation?* Lanham, MD: Rowman and Littlefield.

——. 2003. "Reconciliation: Building a Bridge from Complicity to Coherence in the Rhetoric of Race Relations." *Rhetoric and Public Affairs* 6(4): 737–64.

——. 2004. "A Question of Character: Re-Signing the Racial Contract." *Rhetoric and Public Affairs* 7(3)(February): 391–403.

McPhail, Mark Lawrence, and Roger McPhail. 2011. "(E)raced Men: Complicity and Responsibility in the Rhetorics of Barack Obama." *Rhetoric & Public Affairs* 14(4), 673–92.

McTaggart, Lynne. 2007. *The Intention Experiment: Using Your Thoughts to Change Your Life and the World*. New York: Free Press.

Mears, Bill 2012. "Judge Apologizes for Forwarding a Racist E-mail Aimed at Obama." CNN. com, March 1. http://www.cnn.com/2012/03/01/justice/montana-judge-racist-message.

Meeks, Kenneth. 2004. "Favorite Son." *Black Enterprise* 35 (October): 95.

Mendelberg, Tali. 2001. *The Race Card: Campaign Strategy, Implicit Messages, and the Norm of Equality*. Princeton, NJ: Princeton University Press.

Mercurio, John. 2008. "The Final Surprise: Obama's Key Groups." MSNBC, November 5. http://www.msnbc.msn.com/id/27557327/.

Metro Desk. 2009. *Call & Post*. November 18.

Milbank, Dana. 2008. "For Obama and McCain the Bitter and the Sweet." *Washington Post*, April 15, sec. A3.
Miletsky, Zebulon Vance. 2013. "Mutt Like Me: Barack Obama and the Mixed Race Experience in Historical Perspective." In *Obama and the Biracial Factor: The Battle for a New American Majority*, ed. Andrew J. Jolivétte, 141–68. Bristol, UK: Policy Press.
Miller, Michelle. 2011. "African American Unemployment at 16 Percent." *CBS Evening News*, June 19. http://www.cbsnews.com/8301-18563_162-20072425.html.
Milloy, Courtland. 2008. "Maybe It's Time We Redefined Manliness." *Washington Post*, September 10, sec. B1.
Mills, Charles W. 1997. *The Racial Contract*. Ithaca, NY: Cornell University Press.
———. 1999. "Whose Fourth of July? Frederick Douglass and 'Original Intent.'" In *Frederick Douglass: A Critical Reader*, ed. Bill E. Lawson and Frank M. Kirkland, 100–42. Malden, MA: Blackwell.
Mitchell, Mary. 2008. "Discussions Across the Racial Divide." *Chicago Sun-Times*, February 14. http://blogs.suntimes.com/mitchell/2008/02/sen_barack_obamas_letter_to_ta_1.html.
Mitchell, Michelle. 2004. *Righteous Propagation: African Americans and the Politics of Racial Destiny After Reconstruction*. Chapel Hill: The University of North Carolina Press.
Mock, Brentin. 2013. "How Zimmerman's Colorblind Trial Helps the Justice Dept.'s Case." *Colorlines*, July 17. http://colorlines.com/archives/2013/07/justice_department_hate_crime_case_zimmerman.htm.
Mohanty, Chandra Talpade. 1991. "Under Western Eyes: Feminist Scholarship and Colonial Discourses." In *Third World Women and the Politics of Feminism*, ed. Chandra Talpade Mohanty, Ann Russo, and Lourdes Torres, 51–80. Bloomington: Indiana University Press.
Molpus, Richard. 2004. "40th Commemoration Speech. Coliseum." Philadelphia, Mississippi, June 20.
Moore, Jacqueline. 1999. *Leading the Race: The Transformation of the Black Elite in the Nation's Capital, 1880–1920*. Charlottesville: University of Virginia Press.
Moran, Rachel F. 2001. *Interracial Intimacy: The Regulation of Race and Romance*. Chicago: University of Chicago Press.
———. 2007. "*Loving* and the Legacy of Unintended Consequences." *Wisconsin Law Review* 2: 239–81.
Morgan, Jennifer L. 2004. *Laboring Women: Reproduction and Gender in New World Slavery*. Philadelphia: University of Pennsylvania Press.
Morgan, Joan. 1999. *When Chickenheads Come Home to Roost: My Life as a Hip-Hop Feminist*. New York: Simon & Schuster.
Morgenstern, Madeleine. 2013. "Juan Williams on Obama's Trayvon Martin Remarks: 'The Risk . . . Is That It Will Stoke Racial Tension.'" *Blaze*, July 19. http://www.theblaze.com/stories/2013/07/19/juan-williams-on-obamas-trayvon-martin-remarks-the-risk-is-that-he-will-stoke-racial-tension/.
Mörner, Magnus. 1967. *Race Mixture in the History of Latin America*. Boston: Little, Brown.
Morning Joe. 2008. MSNBC. March 31. http://mediamatters.org/items/200803310007.

Morris, Eboni. 2008. "By the Numbers: Uninsured African American Women." In *The State of Black America 2008: In the Black Woman's Voice*, ed. Stephanie J. Jones and Julianne Malveaux, 173–78. New York: National Urban League.

Morton, Samuel. 1847. "Hybridity in Animals, Considered in Reference to the Question of the Unity of the Human Species." *American Journal of Science* 3: 39–50, 203–12.

Moten, Fred. 2003. *In the Break: The Aesthetics of the Black Radical Tradition*. Minneapolis: University of Minnesota Press.

Moynihan, Daniel P. 1967. "The Negro Family: The Case for National Action." In *The Moynihan Report and the Politics of Controversy*, ed. Lee Rainwater and William L. Yancey, 41–124. Cambridge: MIT Press.

MSNBC. 2008. "How Much Will Obama's Race Matter." Decision 08, September 21. www.mefeedia.com/entry/how-much-will-obamas-race-matter/11664714.

———. 2013a. "Prosecution Begins Closing Arguments." *Politics Nation, Lead Forward*, July 11. http://www.nbcnews.com/id/45755884/vp/52454880#52592448.

———. 2013b. "Prosecution Gets Final Word in Zimmerman Trial." *Verdict Watch*, July 12. http://video.msnbc.msn.com/msnbc/52465384#52465384.

Mulvey, Laura. 1977. "Visual Pleasure and Narrative Cinema." *Screen* 16(3): 6–18.

Murray, Mark. 2012. "One Month Later, Republicans Find Plenty of Blame for Election Loss." MSNBC, December 4. http://firstread.nbcnews.com/_news/2012/12/04/15677908-one-month-later-republicans-find-plenty-of-blame-for-election-loss?lite&ocid=msnhp&pos=1.

Murray, Shailagh. 2008. "For Obama, Unexpected Support; Antiabortion Lawmakers' Backing May Help in Pa., Ind." *Washington Post*, April 14. http://www.washingtonpost.com/wp-dyn/content/story/2008/04/13/ST2008041302552.html.

Muskal, Michael. 2013. "George Zimmerman Prosecution Faced Hurdles It Couldn't Clear." *Los Angeles Times*, July 14. http://www.latimes.com/news/nation/nationnow/la-na-nn-george-zimmerman-acquittal-analysis-20130714,0,4007527.

Muskal, Michael, and Molly Hennessy-Fiske. 2013. "Zimmerman Trial: Jurors Seek Definition of Manslaughter." *Los Angeles Times*, July 13. http://www.latimes.com/news/nation/nationnow/la-na-nn-zimmerman-jury-question-manslaughter-20130713,0,2195595.story.

Mutua, Athena D. 2006. "Theorizing Progressive Black Masculinities." In *Progressive Black Masculinities*, ed. Athena D. Mutua, 3–42. New York: Routledge.

Myers, Linda James. 1987. "The Deep Structure of Culture: The Relevance of Traditional African Culture in Contemporary Times." *Journal of Black Studies* 18(1): 72–85.

———. 1991. "Expanding the Psychology of Knowledge Optimally: The Importance of Worldview Revisited." In *Black Psychology*, ed. Reginald Jones, 15–32. Berkeley: Cobb & Henry Publishers.

———. 1993. *Understanding an Afrocentric Worldview: Introduction to an Optimal Psychology*. Dubuque, IA: Kendall/Hunt.

Nadal, Kevin L. 2011. "Microaggressions and the Multiracial Experience." *International Journal of Humanities and Social Science* 1(7)(June): 36–44.

Nakashima, Cynthia L. 2001. "Servants of Culture: The Symbolic Role of Mixed-Race Asians in American Discourse." In *The Sum of our Parts: Mixed-Heritage Asian Americans*, ed. Teresa Williams-León and Cynthia L. Nakashima, 35–57. Philadelphia: Temple University Press.

Nash, Gary B. 1995. "The Hidden History of Mestizo America." *Journal of American History* 82(3): 941–64.

Nation. "No Games Chicago, Press Release." September 22, 2009. http://nogames.files.word press.com/2009/03/rally_press_release.pdf.

National Association for the Advancement of Colored People. 2007. "How Congress Voted: Civil Rights Federal Legislative Report Card; 109th Congress 2005 and 2006: January 4, 2005 through December 9, 2006." http://www.naacp.org/pdfs/109th_final_report _card3.pdf.

Nava, Mica. 2007. *Visceral Cosmopolitanism: Gender, Culture, and the Normalization of Difference.* New York: Berg.

Navarette, Rubin, Jr. 2009. "Commentary: Obama's Silence on Chicago Crime." CNN, October 2. http://www.cnn.com/2009/POLITICS/10/02/navarrette.chicago.obama .olympics/index/html#cnnSTC Text.

Neal, Mark Anthony. 2005. *New Black Man.* New York: Routledge.

Nel, Philip. 2010. "Obama Fiction for Children: Imagining the Forty-Fourth U.S. President." *Children's Literature Association Quarterly* 35(4)(Winter): 334–56.

Nelson, Thomas, and Donald Kinder. 1996. "Issue Frames and Group-Centrism in American Public Opinion." *Journal of Politics* 58(4): 1055–78.

Neumeister, Larry. 2010, "Rev. Wright: 'Obama Threw Me Under the Bus' President's Former Pastor Complains He Is Being Ignored by the White House." MSNBC, May 18. http:// www.nbcnews.com/id/37208439/ns/politics-white_house/

Neustadt, Richard E. 1960. *Presidential Power: The Politics of Leadership.* New York: John Wiley and Sons.

New York Times. 2008. "Mr. Obama's Profile in Courage." March 18. http://www.nytimes .com/2008/03/19/opinion/19wed1.html.

Newman, David. 1996. "Writing Together Separately: Critical Discourse and the Problems of Cross-ethnic Co-authorship." *Area* 28: 1–12.

Newman, Richard S. 2002. *The Transformation of American Abolitionism: Fighting Slavery in the Early Republic.* Chapel Hill: University of North Carolina Press.

Newton-Small, Jay. 2008. Michelle Obama's Savvy Sacrifice. *Time*, August 25. http://www .time.com/time/printout/0,8816,1835686,00.html.

Niesse, Mark. 2011. "Hawaii Government Hands over Obama's Birth Records." *Huffington Post*, April 27. http://www.huffingtonpost.com/huff-wires/20110427/us-obama-birth -hawaii/.

Nobles, Wade. 1985. *Africanity and the Black Family.* Oakland, CA: Black Family Institute.

Norris, Pippa. 1997. *Women, Media, and Politics.* New York: Oxford University Press.

———. 1978. Toward an Empirical and Theoretical Framework for Defining Black Families." *Journal of Marriage and the Family* 40(4): 679–88.

Northrup, Solomon. 1853. *Twelve Years a Slave, the Narrative of Solomon Northrop.* London, UK: Sampson Low, Son & Company.

Nott, Josiah Clark. 1843. "The Mulatto a Hybrid: Probable Extinction of the Two Races If the Whites and Blacks Are Allowed to Intermarry." *American Journal of the Medical Sciences* 6(11): 249–55.

Novogrod, James, Tom Winter, and Tracy Connor. 2013. "Essential or Irrelevant? Zimmerman Prosecutor Fights to Reveal Previous Calls to Cops." NBC News, June 24. http://usnews.nbcnews.com/_news/2013/06/24/19116607-essential-or-irrelevant-zimmerman-prosecutor-fights-to-reveal-previous-calls-to-cops?lite.

Nunnally, Derrick, and Zoe Tillman. 2009. "Agency Investigating Alleged Discrimination at Pool." *Philadelphia Inquirer*, July 10.

Obama, Barack. 1995. *Dreams from My Father: A Story of Race and Inheritance*. New York: Times Books.

———. 2004. "Keynote Speech, Democratic National Convention." Fleet Center, Boston, July 27. http://www.americanrhetoric.com/speeches/convention2004/barackobama2004dnc.htm.

———. 2005. "Statement of Senator Barack Obama on Hurricane Katrina Relief Efforts." September 6. http://obama.senate.gov/statement/050906-statement_of_senator_barack_obama_on_hurricane_katrina_relief_efforts/index.html.

———. 2006. *The Audacity of Hope: Thoughts on Reclaiming the American Dream*. New York: Crown.

———. 2007a. "Full Text of Senator Barack Obama's Announcement for President." February 10.

———. 2007b. "Obama to Attend Selma March Anniversary." Interview by Steve Inskeep. National Public Radio, February 28. http://www.npr.org/templates/story/story.php?storyId=7630250.

———. 2007c. "Selma Voting Rights Commemoration." Brown Chapel A.M.E. Church, Selma, Alabama, March 4. http://obamiconme.pastemagazine.com/.

———. 2008a. "Iowa Caucus Victory Speech." *American Rhetoric*, January 3. www.americanrhetoric.com.

———. 2008b. "A More Perfect Union." *American Rhetoric*, March 18. http://www.americanrhetoric.com/speeches/barackobamaperfectunion.htm.

———. 2008c. "Obama Victory Speech." video text. *Huffington Post*, November 4. http://www.huffingtonpost.com/2008/11/04/Obama-victory-speech_n_141191.html.

———. 2009a. "Commencement Address at the University of Notre Dame." *American Rhetoric*, May 18. www.americanrhetoric.com.

———. 2009b. "First Speech Before the United Nations General Assembly." September 23, www.americanrhetoric.com.

———. 2009c. "Inauguration Speech, January 20, 2009." http://www.whitehouse.gov/blog/inaugural-address.

———. 2009d. "A New Beginning: Speech at Cairo University." *American Rhetoric*, June 4. www.americanrhetoric.com.

———. 2009e. "Speech to the NAACP." July 17. http://www.whitehouse.gov/.

———. 2010. "Nobel Prize for Peace Lecture." *American Rhetoric*, December 10. www.americanrhetoric.com. http://www.barackobama.com/2007/02/10/remarks_of_senator_barack_obam_11.php.

———. 2011a. *Watch President Obama's Full Speech at Tucson Memorial*. video, 34:18. January 12. http://www.youtube.com/watch?v=ztbJmXQDIGA.

———. 2011b. *White House Correspondents' Dinner*. video, 18:54. April 30. http://www.youtube.com/watch?v=n9mzJhvC-8E.

———. 2012. "Statement on Trayvon Martin." March 23. http://whitehouse.blogs.cnn.com/2012/03/23/president-obama-statement-on-trayvon-martin-case/.

Obama, Michelle. 2011. "Healthier Schools." In *The State of Black America 2011: Jobs Rebuild America*, ed. Chanelle P. Hardy, Lisa Bland Malone, and Valerie Rawlston Wilson, 138–41. New York: The National Urban League.

"Obamaicon.Me." 2008. Paste Media Group.

O'Brien, Michael. 2013. "Obama: 'Trayvon Martin Could Have Been Me 35 Years Ago.'" MSNBC, July 19. http://nbcpolitics.nbcnews.com/_news/2013/07/19/19563211-obama-trayvon-martin-could-have-been-me-35-years-ago?lite.

Odell, Sarah. 2008. "Clinton's Run; My Seminar on Sexism." *Washington Post*, June 8. http://articles.washingtonpost.com/2008-06-08/opinions/36898723_1_wellesley-students-clinton-s-run-college-schedule.

Ogbonnaya, A. Okechukwu. 1994. "Person as Community: An African Understanding of the Person as an Intrapsychic Community." *Journal of Black Psychology* 20(1): 75–87.

Ogletree, Charles J. 2011. "Foreword." In *The Obamas and a (Post) Racial America?*, ed. Gregory S. Parks and Matthew W. Hughey, i–viii. New York: Oxford University Press.

O'Hearn, Claudine C. 1998. *Half and Half: Writers on Growing Up Biracial and Bicultural*. New York: Pantheon Books.

Olson, Steve 2002. *Mapping Human History: Discovering the Past through Our Genes*. New York: Houghton Mifflin.

———. 2006. "We Are All Jesus' Children: Go Back a Few Millenniums, and We've All Got the Same Ancestors." *Slate*, March 15. http://www.slate.com/id/2138060.

Omi, Michael, and Howard Winant. 1994. *Racial Formation: From the 1980s to the 1990s*. 2nd ed. New York: Routledge.

Omolade, Barbara. 1994. *The Rising Song of African American Women*. New York: Routledge.

Onwuachi-Willig, Angela. 2007a. "A Beautiful Lie: Exploring *Rhinelander v. Rhinelander* as a Formative Lesson on Race, Identity, Marriage, and Family." *California Law Review* 95(6): 2393–2458.

———. 2007b. "Volunteer Discrimination." *UC-Davis Law Review* 40: 1895–1917.

Onwuachi-Willig, Angela, and Mario Barnes. 2005. "By Any Other Name? On Being 'Regarded As' Black, and Why Title VII Should Apply Even If Lakisha and Jamal Are White." *Wisconsin Law Review* 5: 1283–1343.

Orlando Sentinel. 2008. "The Macho Factor." September 1.

Orozco, Ana, and Robert Tomarelli. 2009. "National Urban League Equality Index 2009." In *The State of Black America 2009: Message to the President*, ed. Stephanie Jones, 25–41. New York: National Urban League.

Ostroy, Andy. 2010. "The Tea Party Movement Isn't About Racism? Read This . . ." *Huffington Post*, April 15. http://www.huffingtonpost.com/andy-ostroy/the-tea-party-movement-is_b_538750.html.

Pabst, Naomi. 2009. "An Unexpected Blackness: Musings on Diasporic Encounters and Hybrid Engagements." *Transition* 100: 112–32.

Padilla, Laura. 2007. "A Gendered Update on Women Law Deans: Who, Where and Why Not?" *American University Journal on Gender, Social Policy and Law* 15(3): 443–546.

Page, Susan, and William Risser. 2008. "Beyond Black and White; Obama's Rise Spotlights Gains in Race Relations and How Ethnicity Remains a Dividing Line on Some Issues. *USA Today*, September 23, sec. 1A.

Palmer, J. Coyden. 2009. "Are Chicago Public School Policies to Blame for Melee That Killed Derrion Albert?" *Chicago Crusader*, October 5. http://www.theskanner.com.

Paolino, Philip. 1995. "Group-Salient Issues and Group Representation: Support for Women Candidates in the 1992 Elections." *American Journal of Political Science* 39(2): 294–313.

Parker, Christopher, and Matt A. Barreto. 2013. *Change They Can't Believe In: The Tea Party and Reactionary Politics in America*. Princeton, NJ: Princeton University Press.

Parker, Kathleen. 2013. "The Road to Bedlam." *Brainerd Dispatch*, July 19. http://brainerd dispatch.com/opinion/guest-columns/2013-07-19/road-bedlam.

Parsons, Christi. 2008. "Women Lean Toward Obama; But McCain Fights for Clinton Backers." *Chicago Tribune*, June 18, sec. C1.

———. 2009. "The Nation: Michelle Obama—In the Kitchen, Her Early Appearances Suggest a Traditional First Lady Role. It Seems Unlikely to Last, But She's Playing It Cautious for Now." *Los Angeles Times*, February 23, sec. A9.

Parsons, Christi, and John McCormick. 2008. "Obama, Huckabee Strike First with Iowa Victories; Edwards Ekes by Clinton for 2nd Amid Huge Turnout." *Chicago Tribune*, January 4, sec. N1.

Pascale, Celine Marie, and Katie Beran. 2009. "Nowhere to Fall." *Z Magazine*, October, 31–34. http://www.zcommunications.org/nowhere-to-fall-by-katie-beran.

Patillo-McCoy, Mary. 2000. *Black Picket Fences: Privilege and Peril among the Black Middle Class*. Chicago: University of Chicago Press.

Patterson, Nathaniel. 2012. "The Most Threatened President in History." *RSN*, November 27. http://readersupportednews.org/news-section2/318-66/14744-focus-the-most-threat ened-president-in-history.

Peck, Patrick. 2012. "Biracial Versus Black: Thought Leaders Weigh in on the Meaning of President Obama's Biracial Heritage." *Grio*, November 19. http://thegrio.com/2012/11/19.

Pelton, Robert. 1980. *Trickster in West Africa*. Berkeley: University of California Press.

Peoples, Steve. 2012. "Trump Overshadows Romney with 'Birther' Talk." *Associated Press*, May 29. http://bigstory.ap.org/content/trump-overshadows-romney-birther-talk.

Perelman, Chaim, and Lucie Olbrechts-Tyteca. 1969. *The New Rhetoric: A Treatise on Argumentation*. Notre Dame, IN: University of Notre Dame Press.

Peters, Justin. 2013. "George Zimmerman Is Probably Going to Walk, and That's Not a Bad Thing." *Slate*, July 10, 2013. http://www.slate.com/blogs/crime/2013/07/10/george_zim merman_trial_trayvon_martin_s_shooter_is_probably_going_to_walk.html.

Pew Research. 2011a. "Beyond Red vs. Blue Political Typology." March 4. http://www.peo ple-press.org/2011/05/04/section-3-demographics-and-news-sources/.

———. 2011b. "Wealth Gaps Rise to Record Highs Between Whites, Blacks, and Hispanics." July 26.

———. 2012. "Partisan Polarization Surges in Bush, Obama Years." June 4, 14.
———. 2013. "Big Racial Racial Divide over Zimmerman Verdict." July 22, 1.
Pitkin, Hannah. 1967. *The Concept of Representation*. Berkeley: University of California Press.
Plank, Elizabeth. 2013. "New Study Finds More Than Half of Female Voters Are Feminist." *Policymic*, March 19. http://www.policymic.com/articles/30270/new-study-finds-more-than-half-of-female-voters-are-feminists.
Plato. 2004. *Menexenus, Translated with an Introduction by Benjamin Jowett*. eBooks @ Adelaide. The University of Adelaide Library. http://ebooks.adelaide.edu.au/p/plato/p71mx/index.html.
Plessy v. Ferguson, 163 U.S. 537, 559 (1896).
Pogatchnik, Shawn. 2009. "Boxing Legend Ali Traces Roots to Irish Town Ali the Irishman: Fans Cheer Boxing Icon as He Finds Irish Roots in Great-Granddad's Hometown." Associated Press, September 1. http://abcnews.go.com/International/wireStory?id=8460201.
Poirier, Marc. 2003. "Hastening the *Kulturkampf*: Boy Scouts of America v. Dale and the Politics of American Masculinity." *Law and Sexuality* 12:271–326.
Political Blind Spot. 2013. "George Zimmerman's Old MySpace Surfaces: Full of Racist Comments and Admissions of Criminal Activity." July 15. http://politicalblindspot.org/george-zimmermans-old-myspace-surfaces-full-of-racist-statements-and-admissions-of-criminal-activity/.
Ponder, Justin. 2012. "'A Patchwork Heritage': Multiracial Citation in Barack Obama's *Dreams from My Father*." In *Obama and the Biracial Factor: The Battle for a New American Majority*, ed. Andrew J. Jolivétte, 61–80. Bristol, UK: Policy Press.
Pough, Gwendolyn D. 2007. "Love Feminism But Where Is My Hip Hop?" In *Women's Lives: Multicultural Perspectives*, 4th ed., ed. Gwyn Kirk, 85–95. New York: McGraw-Hill.
Powell, Michael. 2008. "With Genie out of Bottle, Obama Treads Carefully on Race." *New York Times*, August 2. http://www.nytimes.com/2008/08/02/us/politics/02obama.html?pagewanted=all&_r=0.
Preston, Julia. 2012. "Republicans Reconsider Positions on Immigration." *New York Times*, November 9.
Price, Gregory N., and Kwabena Gyimah-Brempong. 2006. "Black, Dark, Disadvantaged: Crime, Punishment and Skin Hue in Mississippi." *Murc Digest* 2(2)(April): 2–3.
Prieto, Bianca. 2012. "Trayvon Martin: 'We Are Gathered Here Today to Demand Justice' in Teen's Fatal Shooting." *Orlando Sentinel*, March 14. http://articles.orlandosentinel.com/2012-03-14/news/os-trayvon-martin-shooting-death-rally-20120314_1_shooting-death-bryant-chief-bill-lee.
Prince, Richard. 2013. "Obama Speech Came After Black Prodding: President Obama's Surprise Remarks on Trayvon Came After Public Criticism by Black Commentators." *Root.com*, July 21. http://www.theroot.com/blogs/journalisms/obama-talk-verdict-followed-black-prodding?wpisrc=root_lightbox.
Quayson, Ato. 2000. *Postcolonialism: Theory, Practice or Process*. Cambridge: Policy Press.
Quinn-Musgrove, Sandra L., and Sanford Kanter. 1995. *America's Royalty: All the Presidents' Children*. Westport, CT: Greenwood Press.

Radford, Mary. 1990. "Sex Stereotyping and the Promotion of Women to Positions of Power." *Hastings Law Journal* 41(March): 471–535.

Raiford, Leigh, and Renee C. Romano. 2006. "Introduction: The Struggle over Memory." In *The Civil Rights Movement in American Memory*, ed. Renée Christine Romano and Leigh Raiford, xi–xxiv. Athens: University of Georgia.

———. 2011. *Imprisoned in a Luminous Glare: Photography and the African American Freedom Struggle*. Chapel Hill: University of North Carolina Press.

Rawick, George P. 2010. "Radical Sociology or Marxism? Some Comments." In *Listening to Revolt: Selected Writings*, ed. David Roediger with Martin Smith, 65–69. Chicago: Charles H. Kerr.

"Rebirth of a Nation, Computer Style." 1993. *Time*, Fall, 66–67.

Reeve, Elspeth. 2012. "What Did Trayvon Look Like? That Depends on Your Politics." *Atlantic Wire*, March 30. http://www.theatlanticwire.com/politics/2012/03/what-did-trayvon-look-depends-your-politics/50570/.

Reeves, Keith. 1994. *Race as a Determinant of White Vote Choice in Biracial Election Campaigns*. Ann Arbor: University Microfilms International.

Reid, Joy, and Ed Rendell. 2012. *NOW with Alex Wagner*, MSNBC. November 8.

Reid, Joy-Ann. 2013. "Even after the Verdict, Legal Action May Continue in Zimmerman Case." *Grio*, July 13. http://thegrio.com/2013/07/13/op-ed-even-after-the-verdict-legal-action-could-continue-in-zimmerman-case/.

Remnick, David. 2008. "The Joshua Generation." *New Yorker*, November 17, sec. 68.

———. 2014. "Going the Distance: On and Off the Road with Barack Obama." *New Yorker*, January 27.

Renn, Kristin A. 2004. *Mixed Race Students in College: The Ecology of Race, Identity, and Community on Campus*. Albany: State University of New York Press.

Ressner, Eric. 2008. "Associations: Tit for Tat." *St. Louis Post-Dispatch*, October 19, sec. B2.

Rhee, Foon. 2008. "Candidates Step Up Battle over Mortgage Crisis, Ailing Economy." *Boston Glove*, October 10, sec. A8.

Rhode, Deborah L. 2003. "The Difference 'Difference' Makes." *Maine Law Review* 55(1): 15–21.

Rich, Frank. 2008. "If Terrorists Rock the Vote in 2008." *New York Times*, June 29, sec. WK12.

Riley, Russell L. 1999. *The Presidency and the Politics of Racial Inequality: Nation-Keeping from 1831–1965*. New York: Columbia University Press.

Rivera, Amaad, Brenda Cotto-Escalera, Anisha Desai, Jeannette Huezo, and Derick Muhammad. "Foreclosed: State of the Dream 2008." Boston: United for a Fair Economy. http://www.faireconomy.org/files/pdf/StateOfDream_01_16_08_Web.pdf.

Roberts, Dorothy. 1997. *Killing the Black Body: Race, Reproduction, and the Meaning of Liberty*. New York: Pantheon Books.

———. 1998. "The Absent Black Father." In *Lost Fathers: The Politics of Fatherlessness in America*, ed. Cynthia Daniels, 145–62. New York: St. Martin's Press.

Roberts, Sam, and Peter Baker. 2010. "Asked to Declare His Race, Obama Checks 'Black.'" *New York Times*, April 2. http://www.nytimes.com/2010/04/03/us/politics/03census.html?_r=0.

Robeson, Paul, Jr. 2004. "Election 2004: Hope Is on the Way." *New York Amsterdam News*, August 5, 13.

Robinson J., III. 2009. "Coloring the Blind Spot: The Urban Black Community As an Object of Racial Discourse in the Age of Obama." *Western Journal of Black Studies* 33(3): 212–23.

Robinson, Michelle LaVaughn. 1985. "Princeton Educated Blacks and the Black Community." Unpublished senior honors thesis. Princeton University, Princeton, NJ.

Rockquemore, Kerry Ann, and David L. Brunsma. 2002. *Beyond Black: Biracial Identity in America*. Thousand Oaks, CA: Sage.

Rockquemore, Kerry Ann, David L. Brunsma, and Daniel J. Delgado. 2009. "Racing to Theory or Retheorizing Race? Understanding the Struggle to Build a Multiracial Identity Theory." *Journal of Social Issues* 65(1): 13–34.

Rodgers-Rose, LaFrances, ed. 1980. *The Black Woman*. Beverly Hills, CA: Sage.

Roediger, David R. 2002. *Colored White: Transcending the Racial Past*. Berkeley and Los Angeles: University of California Press.

———. 2008. "Race Will Survive the Obama Phenomenon." *Chronicle of Higher Education*, October 10. http://chronicle.com/article/Race-Will-Survive-the Obama/21983.

Rogak, Lisa, ed. 2009. *Michelle Obama in Her Own Words: The Views and Values of America's First Lady*. New York: Public Affairs.

Roman, John K. 2013. "Race, Justifiable Homicide, and Stand Your Ground Laws: Analysis of FBI Supplementary Homicide Report Data." Washington, D.C.: Urban Institute

Romano, Andrew, Ammah-Tagoe, Aku, and No, Brian. 2009. "Black in the Age of Obama." *Newsweek*, April 27.

Rondilla, Joanne L., and Paul R. Spickard, eds. 2005. *Is Lighter Better? Skin-tone Discrimination among Asian Americans*. New York: Routledge.

Root, Maria P. P. 1996. "A Bill of Rights for Racially Mixed People." In *The Multiracial Experience: Racial Borders as the New Frontier*, ed. Maria P. P. Root, 3–14. Thousand Oaks, CA: Sage.

Rose, Adam. 2010. "Obama and Palin Related? Website Claims President Also Has Ties to Limbaugh, Bush Family." *Huffington Post*, September 13. http://www.huffingtonpost.com/2010/10/13/obama-and-palin-related-w_n_760689.html.

Rose, Tricia. 1994. *Black Noise: Rap Music and Black Culture in Contemporary America*. Hanover, CT: Wesleyan University Press.

Rosenfeld, Steven. 2013. "10 Reasons Lawyers Say Florida Law Enforcement Threw Away George Zimmerman Case." *Alternet*, August 6. http://www.alternet.org/civil-liberties/10-reasons-lawyers-say-floridas-law-enforcement-threw-ryan-zimmermans-case-away.

Ross, Brian, and Rehab el-Buri. 2008. "Obama's Pastor: God Damn America, U.S. to Blame for 9/11." ABC News, March 13. http://abcnews.go.com/Blotter/story?id=4443788.

Ross, Marlon. 2004. *Manning the Race: Reforming Black Men in the Jim Crow Era*. New York: New York University Press.

Rossiter, Clinton. 1949. "The Political Philosophy of FD Roosevelt: A Challenge to Scholarship." *Review of Politics* 11(1): 87–95.

Rowe, Aimee Carrillo. 2008. *Power Lines: On the Subject of Feminist Alliances*. Duke University Press.

Rowland, Robert C., and John M. Jones. 2007. "Recasting the American Dream and American Politics: Barack Obama's Keynote Address to the 2004 Democratic National Convention." *Quarterly Journal of Speech* 93(4): 425–48.

Russell, Kathy Y., Midge Wilson, and Ronald Hall. 1992. *The Color Complex: The Politics of Skin Color among African Americans*. New York: Harcourt Brace Jovanovich.

Salon.com. 2008. "What Should Obama Do About Rev. Jeremiah Wright?" April 29. http://www.salon.com/2008/04/29/obama_wright/.

Salvatore, Diane. 2008. "Barack and Michelle Obama: The Full Interview." *Ladies Home Journal*, August 3. http://www.lhj.com/style/covers/barack-and-michelle-obama-the-full-interview/.

Samuels, Allison. 2008. "What Michelle Can Teach Us." *Newsweek*, November 1. http://www.newsweek.com/2008/10/31/what-michelle-can-teach-us.print.html.

Samuels, Allison, and Jerry Adler. 2010. "The Reinvention of the Reverend." *Newsweek*, July 25. http://www.newsweek.com/2010/07/25/the-reinvention-of-the-reverend.html.

Santos, Juan. 2008. "Barack Obama and the End of Racism." *Countercurrents.com*, February 12. http://www.countercurrents.org/santos120208.htm.

Sarlin, Benjy. 2012. "The President Gets Personal." *Talking Points Memo*, March 23. http://2012.talkingpointsmemo.com/2012/03/obamas-american-family-how-the-president-gets-personal.php.

Saslow, Eli. 2008. "To Women, So Much More Than Just a Candidate." *Washington Post*, March 4, A01. http://www.washingtonpost.com/wp-dyn/content/story/2008/03/03/ST2008030303087.html.

Schaffner, Brian. 2005. "Priming Gender: Campaigning on Women's Issues in U.S. Senate Elections." *American Journal of Political Science* 49(4): 803–17.

Schapiro, Rich. 2010. "Rev. Jeremiah Wright Claims President Obama 'Threw Me Under the Bus' in Letter to African Aid Group." *New York Daily News*, May 18. http://www.nydailynews.com/news/politics/rev-jeremiah-wright-claims-president-obama-threw-bus-letter-african-aid-group-article-1.447986#ixzz2ZMIg5fon.

Scheiber, Noam. 2004. "Race Against History." *New Republic*, May 31. http://www.countercurrents.org/santo/20208.htm.

Scherer, Michael. 2007. "Hillary Is from Mars, Obama Is from Venus." *Salon.com*, July 12. http://www.salon.com/news/feature/2007/07/12/obama_hillary/print.html

Scherer, Michael, and Nancy Gibbs. 2009. "Interview with the First Lady." *Time*, May 21. http://www.time.com/time/printout/0,8816,1899741,00.html.

Schoen, Douglas E. 2008. "The Disaffected Voters Who'll Decide 2008." *Washington Post*, February 10. http://articles.washingtonpost.com/2008-02-10/opinions/36769061_1_angry-voters-bloc-presidential-race.

Schorr, Daniel. 2008. "A New 'Post-Racial' Political Era in America." January 28. http://www.npr.org/templates/story/story.php?storyId=18489466.

Schmalfeldt, Bill. 2012. "Killer of Trayvon Martin Is Son of Retired Virginia State Supreme Court Judge." *Examiner.com*, March 27. http://www.examiner.com/article/killer-of-trayvon-martin-is-son-of-retired-virginia-state-supreme-court-judge.

Schneider, Mike, and Kyle Hightower. 2013a. "George Zimmerman Jury Selected: All Women Jurors Chosen in Trial of Trayvon Martin Killer." *Huffington Post*, June 20.

http://www.huffingtonpost.com/2013/06/20/george-zimmerman-jury-_n_3474181.html?view=print&comm_ref=false.

———. 2013b. "Jury Could Begin Deliberations in Zimmerman Trial." *Huffington Post*, July 12. http://www.huffingtonpost.com/2013/07/12/jury-deliberation-zimmerman_n_3585297.html.

Schrader, David. 1999. "Natural Law in the Constitutional Thought of Frederick Douglass." In *Frederick Douglass: A Critical Reader*, ed. Bill E. Lawson and Frank M. Kirkland, 85–99. Malden, MA: Blackwell.

Schulz, Amy J., and Leith Mullings, eds. 2006. *Gender, Race, Class and Health: Intersectional Approaches*. San Francisco: Jossey Bass.

Schwartz, Marie Jenkins. 2006. *Birthing a Slave: Motherhood and Medicine in the Antebellum South*. Cambridge: Harvard University Press.

Schwarz, Bill. 2011. "'Our Unadmitted Sorrow': the Rhetorics of Civil Rights Photography." *History Workshop Journal* 72(1)(Autumn): 138–55.

Schwarz, David. 1997. *Listening Subjects: Music, Psychoanalysis, Culture*. Durham: Duke University Press.

Scocca, Tom. 2012. "Eighty-Eight Percent of Romney Voters Were White: The GOP Candidate's Race-based, Monochromatic Campaign Made Him a Loser." *Salon.com*, November 7. http://www.slate.com/articles/news_and_politics/scocca/2012/11/mitt_romney_white_voters_the_gop_candidate_s_race_based_monochromatic_campaign.html

Scott, David. 1997. "Colonialism: Anthropology and Criticism." *International Social Science Journal* 49(4): 517–26.

Sen, Rinku. 2013. "The Racist Mind." *Colorlines*, July 31. http://colorlines.com/archives/2013/07/rinku_sen_thinking_through_racism.html.

Senna, Marta de. 2005. "Strategies of Deceit: *Dom Casmurro*." *Portuguese Literary and Cultural Studies* 13–14(Fall-Spring): 407–18.

Serwer, Adam. 2008. "He's Black, Get Over It." *American Prospect*, December 5. http://www.prospect.org/cs/articles?article=hes_black_get_over_it.

Shafer, Jack. 2008. "How Obama Does that Thing He Does: A Professor of Rhetoric Cracks the Candidate's Code." *Slate*, February 14. http://www.slate.com/id/2184480/.

Shepsle, Kenneth. 1978. *The Giant Jigsaw Puzzle: Democratic Committee Assignments in the Modern House*. Chicago: University of Chicago Press.

Simon, Jeff. 2011. "Lessons this Father's Day from the Father-in-chief." CNN, *Politicalticker*, June 18. http://politicalticker.blogs.cnn.com/2011/06/18/lessons-this-father%E2%80%99s-day-from-the-father-in-chief/.

Sinclair-Chapman, Valeria, and Melanye Price. 2008. "Black Politics, the 2008 Election, and the (Im)possibility of Race Transcendence." *Political Science and Politics* 41(4): 739–45.

Skrentny, John. 2002. *The Minority Rights Revolution*. Cambridge: Harvard University Press.

Slevin, Peter. 2007. "Her Heart's in the Race: Michelle Obama on the Campaign Trail and Her Life's Path." *Washington Post*, November 28, C01.

Smith, Anne Marie. 1998. *Laclau and Mouffe: The Radical Democratic Imaginary*. New York: Routledge.

Smith, Hal F. 2009. "The Questions Before Us: Opportunity, Education and Equity." In *The State of Black America 2009: Message to the President*, ed. Stephanie Jones, 45–55. New York: National Urban League.

Smith, Harry. 2009. "Father-in-Chief: Interview with Barack Obama." *The Early Show*, CBS, June 22.

Smith, Michael W. 2011. "Awesome God." http://www.sing365.com.

Smith, Paul. 1996. "Introduction." In *Boys: Masculinities in Contemporary Culture*, ed. Paul Smith, 1–8. New York: HarperCollins.

Smith, Shawn Michelle. 2004. *Photography on the Color Line: W. E. B. Du Bois, Race, and Visual Culture*. Durham: Duke University.

Smith, Terry. 2012. *Barack Obama, Post-Racialism, and the New Politics of Triangulation*. New York: Palgrave Macmillan.

Smith, Zadie. 2009. "Speaking in Tongues." *New York Review of Books*, February 26. http://www.nybooks.com/articles/archives/2009/feb/26/speaking-in-tongues-2/.

Smolenyak, Megan. 2009. "Michelle Obama's Roots." *Megan TV*, August. http://www.honoringourancestors.com/megan-tv.html.

Smooth, Wendy. 2010. "Standing at the Crossroads." *Crisis (Special Issue: Black Women and the Future of Politics)* 117(2)(Spring): 14–18.

Sollors, Werner. 1997. *Neither Black nor White Yet Both: Thematic Explorations of Interracial Literature*. New York: Oxford University Press.

Solomon, Deborah. 2008. "All in the Family." *New York Times*, January 20. http://nytimes.com/2008/01/20/magazine/20wwln-Q4-t.html_r=1&pagewanted=print.

Spencer, Rainier. 2006. *Challenging Multiracial Identity*. Boulder, CO: Lynne Rienner.

Spickard, Paul. 1989. *Mixed Blood: Intermarriage and Ethnic Identity in Twentieth-Century America*. Madison: University of Wisconsin Press.

———. 2012. "'Birthers' Attack on Obama Is Not Only Bogus, It's Irrelevant." *San José Mercury News*, June 16.

Spickard, Paul, and Rowena Fong. 1995. "Pacific Islander Americans and Multiethnicity: A Vision of America's Future?" *Social Forces* 73(4): 1365–83.

Spillers, Hortense J. 2003. *Black, White, and in Color: Essays on American Literature and Culture*. Chicago: University of Chicago Press.

Spivak, Gayatri Chakravorty. 1988. "Can the Subaltern Speak?" In *Marxism and Interpretation of Culture*, ed. Cary Nelson and Lawrence Grossberg, 271–313. Urbana: University of Illinois Press.

———. 1992. "French Feminism Revisited: Ethics and Politics." In *Feminists Theorize the Political*, ed. Judith Butler and Joan W. Scott, 54–85. New York: Routledge.

———. 1999. *A Critique of Postcolonial Reason: Toward a History of the Vanishing Present*. Cambridge: Harvard University Press.

Stan, Adel. 2008. "Christian Right Voter Summit Sells Racist 'Obama Waffles.'" *Alternet*, September 15. http://www.alternet.org/election08/98908/christian_right_voter_summit_sells_racist_'obama_waffles'/.

Staples, Robert. 2010. "The Post Racial Presidency: The Myths of a Nation and Its People." *Journal of African American Studies* 14(1): 128–44.

Stark, Barbara. 1997. "Guys and Dolls: Remedial Nurturing Skills in Post-Divorce Practice, Feminist Theory, and Family Law Doctrine." *Hofstra Law Review* 26(2): 293–376.

Stebner, Beth. 2012. "Obama's Human Touch: Heartwarming Story Behind Picture of Young Boy Feeling the President's Hair . . . and How the Image Has Become a West Wing Favourite." *Daily Mail*, May 24.

Steele, Shelby. 1990. *The Content of Our Character: A New Vision of Race in America*. New York: St. Martin's Press.

———. 2004. *Bound Man: Why We Are Excited about Obama and Why He Can't Win*. New York: Free Press.

———. 2007. "The Identity Card." *Time*, November 30. http://www.time.com/time/print out/0,8816,1689619,00.html.

Stein, Jeff. 2009. "Obama, Racism, and Jimmy Carter: Nearly 30 Years Ago, Carter Team Kept Quiet on Race and Reagan Campaign." MSNBC, September 17. http://www.msnbc.msn.com/id/32895021/ns/politics-cq_politics/.

Steinberg, Steven. 1995. *Turning Back: The Retreat from Racial Justice in American Thought and Policy*. Boston: Beacon Press.

Stickmon, Janet C. Mendoza. 2007. *Trickster as Decolonizer: An Empowering Role for African American and Filipina(o)-American Young Adults*. San Francisco: San Francisco State University.

Stanton, William. 1960. *The Leopard's Spots: Scientific Attitudes Toward Race in America, 1815–59*. Chicago: University of Chicago Press.

Steinhorn, Leonard, and Barbara Diggs-Brown. 1999. *By the Color of Our Skin: The Illusion of Integration and the Reality of Race*. New York: Dutton.

Sterling, Dorothy, ed. 1984. *We Are Your Sisters: Black Women in the Nineteenth Century*. New York: W. W. Norton.

Stodghill, Alexis Garrett. 2012. "Tea Party Group Makes Racially-Tinged Obama Skunk Reference." *Grio*, December 12. http://thegrio.com/2011/12/12.

Stolberg, Sheryl Gay. 2012. "Obama Has Ties to Slavery Not by His Father but His Mother, Research Suggests." *New York Times* July 30. http://www.nytimes.com/2012/07/30/us/obamas-mother-had-african-forebear-study-suggests.html?pagewanted=all.

Street, Paul. 2002. "A Whole Lott Missing: Rituals of Purification and Deep Racism Denial." *Black Commentator*, December 22. http://blackagendareport.com/content/barack-obama%E2%80%99s-white-appeal-and-perverse-racial-politics-post-civil-rights-era.

———. 2004a. "Keynote Reflections." *ZNet Magazine*, July 29.

———. 2004b. "Skipping Past Structural Racism: Center Trumps Left in Recent PBS Series in Race in America." *Black Commentator*, April 8. http://www.blackcommentator.com/85/85_think_street.html.

———. 2005. *Still Separate, Unequal: Race, Place, Policy and the State of Black Chicago*. Chicago: Chicago Urban League.

———. 2006. "Obama's Path to Hell," *ZNet Sustainers' Commentary*, June 18.

———. 2007a. "Barack Obama's White Appeal and the Perverse Racial Politics of the Post–Civil Rights Era." *Dissident Voice*, June 16. http://dissidentvoice.org/2007/06/barack-obama%E2%80%99s-white-appeal-and-the-perverse-racial-politics-of-the-post-civil-rights-era/. http://www.zmag.org/content/showarticle.cfm?ItemID=12336.

———. 2007b. "'He's a Mouse:' Russell Simmons' Speaks Some Truth on Obama." *Black Agenda Report*, May 9. http://www.zmag.org/content/showarticle.cfm?ItemID=12336;;
———. 2007c. "The Meaning of the Black Revolution." *ZNet Magazine*, March 16.
———. 2007d. "Obama's Audacious Deference to Power: A Critical Review of Barack Obama's Audacity of Hope." *Black Agenda Report*, January 31.
———. 2007e "The Obama Illusion." *Z Magazine*, February, 29–33.
———. 2007f. "The Pale Reflection: Barack Obama, Martin Luther King, Jr. and the Meaning of the Black Revolution." *ZNet Magazine*, March 16.
———. 2007g. *Racial Oppression in a Global Metropolis: A Living Black Chicago History.* New York: Rowman and Littlefield.
———. 2007h. "Sitting Out the Obama Dance in Iowa City." *ZNet Magazine*, April 28.
———. 2008. *Barack Obama and the Future of American Politics.* Boulder, CO: Paradigm Publishers.
———. 2008a. "Race and Class in the Democratic Primaries." *ZNet Magazine*, April 25. http://www.zcommunications.org/znet/viewArticle/17509.
Streeter, Caroline A. 2003. "The Hazards of Visibility: 'Biracial' Women, Media Images, and Narratives of Identity." In *New Faces in a Changing America: Multiracial Identity in the 21st Century*, ed. Loretta I. Winters and Herman L. DeBose. 201–322. Thousand Oaks, CA: Sage.
Stephens-Davidowitz, Seth. 2012. "How Racist Are We? Ask Google." *New York Times*, June 9. http://campaignstops.blogs.nytimes.com/2012/06/09/how-racist-are-we-ask-google/?_php=true&_type=blogs&_r=0.
Stuckey, Mary. 2004. *Defining Americans: The Presidency and National Identity.* Lawrence: University of Kansas Press.
Stuckey, Mike. 2008. "Multiracial Americans Surge in Number, Voice: Obama Candidacy Focuses New Attention on Their Quest for Understanding." MSNBC, May 28. http://www.msnbc.msn.com/id/24542138/.
Sugrue, Thomas. 2010. *Not Even Past: Barack Obama and the Burden of Race.* Princeton, NJ: Princeton University Press.
Suleri, Sara. 1992. "Woman Skin Deep: Feminism and the Postcolonial Condition." *Critical Inquiry* 18(4): 756–69.
Sullivan, Amy. 2008. "Gender Bender." *Time*, June 16, 36.
Sullivan, Andrew. 2008. "The Speech." *Atlantic*, March 18. http://andrewsullivan.theatlantic".com/the_daily_dish/2008/03/the-speech.html.
Sullivan, Eileen. 2008. "Obama Faces More Personal Threats Than Other Presidents-Elect." *Huffington Post*, November 14. http://www.huffingtonpost.com/2008/11/14/obama-faces-more-personal_n_144005.html?page=3.
Sullivan, Patricia A. 1993. "Signification and African-American Rhetoric: A Case Study of Jesse Jackson's 'Common Ground and Common Sense' Speech." *Communication Quarterly* 41(1): 1–15.
Summers, Martin. 2003. *Manliness and Its Discontents: The Black Middle Class and the Transformation of Masculinity, 1900–1930.* Chapel Hill: University of North Carolina Press.

SuzeNYC. 2008. "How We Are Getting Racists to Vote for Obama." *Daily Kos*, November 4. http://www.dailykos.com/story/2008/11/5/11149/2882/55/652861.
Swain, Carol. 1993. *Black Faces, Black Interests*. Lanham, MD: University Press of America.
Swarns, Rachel L. 2008. "Obama Walks a Delicate Path on Class and Race Preferences." *New York Times*, August 3. http://www.nytimes.com/2008/08/03/us/politics/03affirmative.html?ref=opinion&gwh=4671D50CE2 0FC05A1081AD8E071642B6.
———. 2009. "First Lady in Control of Image Building." *New York Times*, April 25. http://www.nytimes.com/2009/04/25/us/politics/25michelle.html?_r=1&emc=eta1&pagewa.
———. 2012. *American Tapestry: The Story of the Black, White, and Multiracial Ancestors of Michelle Obama*. New York: Amistad.
Swarns, Rachel L., and Jodi Kantor. 2009. "In First Lady's Roots, a Complex Path from Slavery." *New York Times*, October 7. http://www.nytimes.com/2009/10/08/us/politics/08genealogy.html?_r=1.
Swerdlick, David. 2013. "Obama's Response to the Verdict Was Right." *Root*, July 15. http://www.theroot.com/print/73709.
Szaniszlo, Marie. 2008. "Race for White House Impacted by Freedom of Preach. *Boston Herald*, March 16, sec. 14.
Tate, Katherine. 2003. *Black Faces in the Mirror*. Princeton, NJ: Princeton University Press.
Tate, Shirley Ann. 2005. *Black Skins, Black Masks: Hybridity, Dialogism, Performativity*. Burlington, VT: Ashgate.
Tavernise, Sabrina. 2011. "Soaring Poverty Casts Spotlight on 'Lost Decade.'" *New York Times*, September 13. http://www.nytimes.com/2011/09/14/us/14census.html?pagewanted=all.
Taylor, G. Flint. 2013. "Racism, the U.S. Justice System, and the Trayvon Martin Verdict." *Huffington Post*, July 18. http://www.huffingtonpost.com/g-flint-taylor/racism-the-u-s-justice-sy_b_3612241.html.
Telles, Edward E., and Edward Murguia. 1990. "Phenotypic Discrimination and Income Differences Among Mexican Americans." *Social Science Quarterly* 7(4): 682–96.
Tenzer, Laurence R. 1990. *A Completely New Look at Interracial Sexuality: Public Opinions and Select Commentaries*. Manahawkin, NJ: Scholar's Publishing House.
Terborg-Penn, Rosalyn. 1998. *African American Women in the Struggle for the Vote, 1850–1920*. Bloomington: Indiana University Press.
Terkildson, Nayda, and David Damore. 1999. "The Dynamics of Racialized Media Coverage in Congressional Elections." *Journal of Politics* 61(3): 680–99.
Tesler, Michael, and David O. Sears. 2010. *Obama's Race: The 2008 Election and the Dream of a Post-Racial America*. Chicago: University of Chicago Press.
Thomas, Sheila. 2010. "Debunking the Myth of a Post-Racial Society." *Human Rights* 37(4): 22–25.
Thompson, Maxine S., and Verna M. Keith. 2001. "The Blacker the Berry: Gender, Skin Tone, Self-Esteem, and Self-Efficacy." *Gender and Society* 15 (3): 336–57.
Thuman, Scott. 2012. "Zimmerman Publicly Accused Sanford Police of Corruption in 2011." WJLA-TV, Washington, D.C., May 24. http://www.wjla.com/articles/2012/05/zimmerman-publicly-accused-sanford-police-of-corruption-in-2011-76322.html.

Tilove, Jonathan. 2004a. "Boston Events May Be Changing of the Guard in Black Politics." *Newhouse News Service*, July 27.

———. 2004b. "The Politics of Tokenism." *Economist*, August 14. http://www.lexisnexis.com/hottopics/lnacademic.

Times Wires. 2007. "Obama Comes to Tampa." *St. Petersburg (Fla.) Times*, March 19. http://sptimes.com/2007/03/19/Hillsborough/Obama_comes_to_Tampa.shtml.

Toner, Robin. 2008. "Separated by a Quarter-Century of Change, but Linked by Race." *New York Times*, January 25. http://www.nytimes.com/2008/01/25/washington/25jackson.html?gwh=8D66CE2FC8496891A389AE C3A85B9949&_r=0.

Traugott, Michael, Vincent Price, and Edward Czilli. 1993. "Polls Apart: Race, Polls and Journalism in Mayoral and Gubernatorial Election Campaigns." Presented at the Annual Meeting of the Association for American Public Opinion, St. Charles, IL.

Trinko, Katrina. 2013. "David Brooks Praises Obama's Martin Speech as 'Highlight' of Presidency." *National Review Online*, July 21. http://www.nationalreview.com/corner/354014/david-brooks-praises-obamas-martin-speech-highlight-presidency-katrina-trinko.

Tseng, Thomas. 2008. "Millennials: Key to Post-Ethnic America?" *New Geography*, July 30. http://www.newgeography.com/content/00137-millennials-key-post-ethnic-america.

Tucker, Cynthia. 2013. "Tea Partiers React with Fury to World They Can't Control." *National Memo*, October 12. http://www.nationalmemo.com/tea-partiers-react-with-fury-to-world-they-cant-control/2/.

Tulis, Jeffrey. 1987. *The Rhetorical Presidency*. Princeton, NJ: Princeton University Press.

Tuman, Joseph S. 2008. *Political Communication in American Campaigns*. Los Angeles: Sage.

Turner, Victor W. 1969. *The Ritual Process: Structure and Anti-structure*. New York: Cornell University Press.

Turow, Scott. 2004. "The New Face of the Democratic Party—and America." *Salon.com*, March 30. http://dir.salon.com/story/news/feature/2004/03/30/obama/index.html.

U.S. Bureau of the Census. 2008. Table 6: Resident Population by Sex, Race, and Hispanic-origin Status. In *Annual Estimates of the Population by Sex, Race, and Hispanic Origin for the United States: April 1, 2000 to July 1, 2007* (NC-EST2007-03), Population Division. Washington, D.C.: U.S. Government Printing Office.

U.S. Congress Votes Database. 2007. "Members of Congress: Barack Obama." http://projects.washingtonpost.com/congress/members/0000167/.

USA Today. 2008. "Obama's Historic Journey Shows How Far U.S. Has Come." November 5, 22A.

Vandello, Joseph A., and Dov Cohen. 2004. "When Believing Is Seeing: Sustaining Norms of Violence in Cultures of Honor." In *The Psychological Foundations of Culture*, ed. M. Schaller and C. Crandall, 281–304. Mahwah, NJ: Lawrence Erlbaum Associates.

Vavrus, Mary Douglas. 1998. "Working the Senate from the Outside in the Mediated Construction of a Feminist Political Campaign." *Critical Studies in Mass Communications* 15(3): 213–35.

Viglione, Jill, Lance Hannon, and Robert DeFina. 2011. "The Impact of Light Skin on Prison Time for Black Female Offenders." *The Social Science Journal* 48(1)(January): 250–58.

Volsky, Igor. 2012. "Romney Campaign Chair on Obama: 'When You're Not That Bright You Can't Get Better Prepared.'" *Thinkprogress*, October 4. http://thinkprogress.org/election/2012/10/04/962501/romney-campaign-chair-on-obama-when-youre-not-that-bright-you-cant-get-better-prepared/

———. 2013. "McCain Praises Obama's Race Speech: 'We've Still Got a Long Way to Go' on Race Relations." *Thinkprogress*, July 21. http://thinkprogress.org/politics/2013/07/21/2333201/mccain-praises-obamas-race-speech-weve-still-got-a-long-way-to-go-on-race-relations/.

Voorhees, Josh. 2013. "Second Juror Comes Forward, Says 'George Zimmerman Got Away With Murder.'" *Slate*, July 25. http://www.slate.com/blogs/the_slatest/2013/07/25/juror_b29_mandy_zimmerman_juror_tells_abc_that_george_zimmerman_got_away.html.

Wade, T. Joel, Melanie Judkins Romano, and Leslie Blue. 2004. "The Effect of African American Skin Color on Hiring Preferences." *Journal of Applied Social Psychology* 34(12): 2550–58.

Waggenspack, Beth M. 2010. "Deceptive Narratives in the 2008 Presidential Campaign." In *Studies of Identity in the 2008 Presidential Campaign*, ed. Robert E. Denton, Jr., 155–200. Lanham, MD: Lexington Books.

Wallace, Kendra R. 2001. *Relative/Outsider: The Art and Politics of Identity among Mixed Heritage Students*. Westport, CT: Greenwood.

Wallis, William. 2008. "Dodging the Ballot: How Stolen Votes Are Testing Africa's Faith in Democracy." *Financial Times*, January 15.

Walters, Ronald. 2005. *Freedom Is Not Enough: Black Voters, Black Candidates and American Presidential Politics*. Lanham, MD: Rowman & Littlefield.

———. 2007. "Barack Obama and the Politics of Blackness." *Journal of Black Studies* 38(1): 7–29.

Warren, Robert Penn. 1987. *Now and Then Poems, 1976–1978*. New York: Random House.

Washington, Harold. 1983. "Inaugural Address of Mayor Harold Washington," April 29. *Chicago Public Library*. http://www.chipublib.org/cplbooksmovies/cplarchive/mayors/washington_inaug01.php.

Watkins, Boyce. 2013. "President Obama Lacks the Moral Authority to Give His Lopsided Speech at Morehouse." *Black and Blue Dog*, May 20. http://www.blackbluedog.com/2013/05/news/dr-boyce-president-obama-lacks-the-moral-authority-to-give-his-lopsided-speech-at-morehouse.

Watkins, Mel. 1994. *On the Real Side*. New York: Simon and Schuster.

Watts-Jones, Dee. 2002. "Healing Internalized Racism: The Role of Within-group Sanctuary among People of African Descent." *Family Process* 41(4): 595–601.

Weatherspoon, Floyd D. 1998. *African-American Males and the Law: Cases and Materials*. Lanham, MD: University Press of America.

Weaver, Jessica Dixon. 2012. "The First Father: Perspectives on the President's Fatherhood Initiative." *Family Court Review* 50(2)(April): 297–309.

Wehner, Peter. 2008. "Why Republicans Like Obama." *Washington Post*, February 3, sec. B7.

Weisman, Jonathan, and Shailagh Murray. 2008. "OBAMA: In the Weeks to Come, a Costly Battle on Two Fronts." *Washington Post*, March 3. http://articles.washingtonpost.com/2008-03-05/politics/36836426_1_obama-aides-obama-supporter-clinton-supporter.

Welch, Susan, Michael Combs, and John Gruhl. 1988. "Do Black Judges Make a Difference?" *American Journal of Political Science* 32(1): 126–36.

Wenner, Jann S. 2010. "Obama in Command." *Rolling Stone*, October 14.

———. 2012. "Ready for the Fight: Rolling Stone Interview with Barack Obama." *Rolling Stone*, April 25. http://www.rollingstone.com/politics/news/ready-for-the-fight-rolling-stone-interview-with-barack-obama-20120425#ixzz1t9JA0THw.

West, Paul. 2012. "Obama's Victory Demonstrates Fundamental Shift in Electorate," *Los Angeles Times*, November 8.

White, Deborah G. 1985. *Ar'n't I a Woman?: Female Slaves in the Plantation South*. New York: W. W. Norton & Company.

White, Jack. 2005. "Lott, Reagan, and Republican Racism." *Time*, December 14. http://www.time.com/time/nation/article/ 0,8599,399921,00.html.

White House. 2011. *The President's Agenda and the African American Community*. Washington, D.C. http://www.whitehouse.gov/sites/default/files/af_am_report_final.pdf.

Wilber, Ken. 1997. "An Integral Theory of Consciousness." *Journal of Consciousness Studies* 4(1)(February): 71–92.

———. 1998. *The Marriage of Sense and Soul: Integrating Science and Religion*. New York: Random House.

———. 2000. *Integral Psychology: Consciousness, Spirit, Psychology, Therapy*. Boston: Shambhala Publications.

Will Durant Foundation. http://www.willdurant.com/interdependence.htm.

Williams, Dawn G., and Roderic R. Land. 2006. "The Legitimization of Black Subordination: The Impact of Color-blind Ideology on African American Education." *Journal of Negro Education* 75(4): 579–88.

Williams, Joseph. 2008. "Changing of the Guard: New Generation Replaces Past Civil Rights Leaders." *Boston Globe*, August 28, sec. A1.

Williams, Juan. 2011. "Obama as Dad—a National Treasure and Role Model." Fox News, June 19. http://www.foxnews.com/opinion/2011/06/19/obama-as-dad-national-treasure-and-role-model/.

Williams, Karn. 2002. "Hollywood Action Star and Sex Symbol Remains a Modest Guy from New York." *Afro-American*, August 23, B1.

Williams, Kimberly M. 2008. *Mark One of More: Civil Rights in Multiracial America*. Ann Arbor: University of Michigan Press.

Williams, Mark. 2006. "Williams Identity Survey 11/1/06 thru 11/2/06." Zogby International.

Williams, Pete. 2013. "Holder: Justice Dept. Will Contest Texas Redistricting." NBC News, July 25. http://firstread.nbcnews.com/_news/2013/07/25/19678352-holder-justice-dept-will-contest-texas-redistricting?lite&ocid=msnhp&pos=1.

Williams, Stephan. 2008. "What is Fatherhood? Searching for the Reflexive Father." *Sociology* 42(3): 487–502.

Williams, Teresa K., Cynthia L. Nakashima, George Kitahara Kich, and G. Reginald Daniel. 1996. "Being Different Together in the University Classroom: Multiracial Identity as Transgressive Education." In *The Multiracial Experience: Racial Borders as the New Frontier*, ed. Maria P. P. Root, 359–79. Thousand Oaks, CA: Sage Publications.

Wills, Gary. 1992. *Lincoln at Gettysburg: The Words That Remade America*. New York: Simon and Schuster.
Wilson, Valerie R. 2009. "Introduction to the 2009 Equality Index." In *The State of Black America 2009: Message to the President*, ed. Stephanie Jones, 15–24. New York: National Urban League.
Winfield, Betty Houchin. 1997. "The Making of an Image: Hillary Rodham Clinton and American Journalists." *Political Communication* 14(2): 241–53.
Wingfield, Adia Harvey, and Joe R. Feagin. 2009. *Yes We Can: White Racial Framing and the Obama Presidency Campaign*. First edition. New York: Routledge.
———. 2012. *Yes We Can: White Racial Framing and the Obama Presidency Campaign*. Second edition. New York: Routledge.
Winograd, Morley, and Michael D. Hais. 2008. *Millennial Makeover: MySpace, YouTube, and the Future of American Politics*. Piscataway, NJ: Rutgers University Press.
Witt, Linda, Karen Paget, and Glenna Matthews. 1994. *Running as a Woman: Gender and Power in American Politics*. New York: The Free Press.
Wolfe, Richard, and Darren Briscoe. 2008. "Across the Divide: Barack Obama's Road to Racial Reconstruction." *ZNet Magazine*, April 25. http://www.zcommunications/org/Znet/view/article/17509.
Wolffe, Richard. 2008. "Barack's Rock." *Newsweek*, February 16. http://www.newsweek.com/2008/02/16/barack-s-rock.print.html, accessed 7/9/2010.
Woods, Jewel. 2008. "Why Guys Have a Man-Crush on Obama; Sure Women Swoon, But Modern Men Seem Weak-kneed, Too." *Chicago Sun-Times*, July 24, sec. 25.
Wright, Jeremiah. 2003. "Confusing God and Government." *Black Past*, April 13. http://www.blackpast.org/?q=2008-rev-jeremiah-wright-confusing-god-and-government.
Yager, Jordy, and Daniel Strauss. 2013. "Holder Attacks 'Stand Your Ground' Laws for Sowing 'Dangerous Conflict.'" *Hill*, July 13. http://thehill.com/video/administration/311461-holder-slams-stand-your-ground-law-in-wake-of-zimmerman-ruling.
Yawson, Ama. 2013. "I Am George Zimmerman." *Huffington Post*, August 8. http://www.huffingtonpost.com/ama.
Yilma, Teklehaymanot. 2013. "George Zimmerman Manslaughter Charge Wouldn't Bring Justice." *Policymic*, July. http://www.policymic.com/articles/54227/george-zimmerman-manslaughter-charge-wouldn-t-bring-justice.
York, Byron. 2011. "Black Caucus: Tired of Making Excuses for Obama." *Washington Examiner*, August 17. http://campaign2012.washingtonexaminer.com/blogs/beltway-confidential/black-caucus-tired-making-excuses-obama.
Zack, Naomi. 1994. *Race and Mixed Race*. Philadelphia: Temple University Press.
Zaller, John. 1992. *The Nature and Origins of Mass Opinion*. Cambridge: Cambridge University Press.
Zarefsky, David. 1990. *Lincoln, Douglas, and Slavery: In the Crucible of Public Debate*. Chicago: University of Chicago Press.
Zelney, Jeff 2005. "When It Comes to Race, Obama Makes His Point—with Subtlety." *Chicago Tribune*, June 26. http://www.chicagotribune.com/news/nationworld/chi-050626obama-race-archive,0,4277361.story.

Zernike, Kate. 2008. "Postfeminism and Other Fairy Tales." *New York Times*, March 16. http://www.nytimes.com/2008/03/16/weekinreview/16zern.html?pagewanted=all&gwh=A95F4D711284CB1287FAAC83D04B8173.

Zirin, David. 2009. "Olympics in Chicago: Obama's Folly?" *Nation*, September 22. http://nogames.files.wordpress.com/2009/03/rally_press_release.pdf.

Zogby, John. 2009. "Barack Obama: America's First Global President." *Politics* 30(3)(March): 45.

Zuckman, Jill. 2008. "Obama's 2-front Battle Has Given McCain an Edge." *Chicago Tribune*, May 11, sec. C1.

Zuckman, Jill, and John McCormick. 2008. "Fighting to the Finish." *Chicago Tribune*, October 16, sec. C1.

CONTRIBUTORS

LISA ANDERSON-LEVY is a professor in the Department of Anthropology, Beloit College, and is an affiliated faculty in Critical Identities Studies. Her areas of interest include feminist anthropology and methodologies, ethnographic methods, critical race theory, citizenship and nationalism, transnational whitenesses, postcolonial theory, sexuality and the state, color/race, gender, and class in the Caribbean and United States. Her research examines the reproduction of whitenesses through everyday practices in Jamaica.

HEIDI ARDIZZONE is a professor in American Studies at Saint Louis University. She is currently working on a book manuscript on the significance of the black-white multiracial figure for civil rights movements from abolition through the early twentieth century. Her previous publications include *An Illuminated Life: Belle da Costa Greene's Journey from Prejudice to Privilege*, W. W. Norton and Co. (2007) and *Love on Trial: An American Scandal in Black and White*, W. W. Norton and Co. (2001).

KARANJA KEITA CARROLL is a professor in Black Studies at the State University of New York at New Paltz. His teaching and research interests include intellectual history within Africana Studies, the disciplinary structure of Africana Studies, the contributions of Cheikh Anta Diop to African-centered thought, African/Black Psychology, African-centered Social Theory and African-centered Theory and Methodology. He is also associate editor of the *Journal of Pan African Studies*.

GREG CARTER is a professor in the Department of History at the University of Wisconsin, Milwaukee. His research and teaching interests include mixed-race identity and representation, racial science, popular culture, and the civil rights movement in U.S. history. He has taught courses on civil rights, hip-hop, race relations, and mixed-race identity. Carter's work has appeared in Ethnic Studies Review and the edited volume *Mixed Race in Hollywood Film and Television* (2008). His most recent book is entitled *The United States of United Races: A Utopian History of Racial Mixing* (2013).

FRANK RUDY COOPER is a professor at Suffolk University Law School in Boston, Massachusetts. He has also taught at Villanova University School of Law. He teaches Criminal Procedure (Police), Constitutional Law (Powers and Rights), Criminal Law, Civil Rights, and Critical Race Theory (Race, Gender, and Law). His writings have utilized the perspectives of cultural studies, critical race theory, criminal procedure theory, and masculinities studies. His topics have included police stop and frisk practices, racial profiling, images of black masculinity, and the television show *The Wire*. He has been a leader in national law professor organizations, including the Association of American Law Schools Law and Humanities Section, the Society of American Law Teachers, and Latina/o Critical Legal Theory, Inc. He is the co-editor (with Ann C. McGinley) of *Masculinities and the Law: A Multidimensional Approach* (2012).

G. REGINALD DANIEL is a professor in the Department of Sociology, University of California, Santa Barbara. Since 1989, he has taught "Betwixt and Between," which is one of the first and longest-standing university courses to deal specifically with the question of multiracial identity comparing the U.S. with various parts of the world. He is co-founding editor and editor-in-chief of the *Journal of Critical Mixed Race Studies*. Daniel has published numerous articles and chapters that cover this topic, including his books entitled *More Than Black? Multiracial Identity and the New Racial Order* (2002), *Race and Multiraciality in Brazil and the United States: Converging Paths?* (2006), and *Machado de Assis: Multiracial Identity and the Brazilian Novelist* (2012).

MARSHA J. TYSON DARLING is a professor in history and interdisciplinary studies and the director of the center for African, Black, and Caribbean Studies at Adelphi University located in Garden City, New York. She is the editor of the multivolume work *Race, Voting, Redistricting and the Constitution: Sources and Explorations on the Fifteenth Amendment* (2001) and the journal *Political Environments: A Publication of the Committee on Women, Population, and the Environment* (2007). She has published articles on gender and race intersectionality, Black women's herstory, the civil rights movement, the nation's Eugenics legacy, and in recent years, bioethics, justice, and governance issues related to assisted reproductive technologies and various forms of surrogacy.

TESSA DITONTO is a professor in the Department of Political Science at Iowa State University. Her research focuses on political psychology, American political behavior, race, and politics, as well as gender and politics. Her doctoral dissertation examined the effects of candidate race and gender on voters' information search patterns and candidate evaluations during political campaigns. Her work has recently been published in the journals *Political Psychology* and *Political Behavior*.

DAVID A. FRANK is Dean of the Robert D. Clark Honors College at the University of Oregon. He is the author of six books and twenty-three articles in the leading journals in his field, Frank's most recent publication *Frames of Evil: The Holocaust as Horror in American Film*, co-authored with Caroline J. S. Picart, critiques the use of visual rhetoric and narrative devices in Schindler's List and other popular films to explain evil in the world. In February 2008, during the height of the Democratic election primaries, Frank, who is also the director of the UO forensics program, was interviewed on National Public Radio about Barack Obama's rhetoric of consilience.

AMY L. HEYSE is a professor in the Department of Communication Studies at California State University, Long Beach. Her research focuses on political rhetoric and women's rhetoric. Her most recent journal articles appear in the *Southern Communication Journal, Communication Quarterly, Women and Language, The Western Journal of Black Studies, Rhetoric Society Quarterly*, and on-line at the Voices of Democracy oratory project. Professor Heyse teaches courses in rhetorical criticism, campaign persuasion, gender and communication, and American public address.

DAVID A. HOLLINGER is Preston Hotchkis Professor of History at the University of California, Berkeley. He is an elected fellow of the American Academy of Arts and Sciences and was president of the Organization of American Historians in 2010–2011. His books include *Postethnic America: Beyond Multiculturalism* (2006), *Cosmopolitanism and Solidarity* (2006), and *Science, Jews, and Secular Culture* (Princeton University Press, 1996). His recent essays include "The Concept of Post-Racial: Why Its Easy Dismissal

Obscures Important Questions," *Daedalus* (Winter 2011). His other recent essays have appeared in *London Review of Books, Representations, Journal of American History, American Jewish History, Church History,* and *Pacific Historical Review.*

GEORGE LIPSITZ is a professor in the Departments of Black Studies and Sociology at the University of California, Santa Barbara. His interests encompass studies of social movements, urban culture, and inequality. His books include *Midnight at the Barrel House, Footsteps in the Dark, The Possessive Investment in Whiteness, A Life in the Struggle, Time Passages,* and *How Racism Takes Place.* Lipsitz serves as chairman of the board of directors of the African American Policy Forum and is a member of the board of directors of the National Fair Housing Alliance.

MARK LAWRENCE MCPHAIL is Dean of the College of Arts and Communication at the University of Wisconsin-Whitewater. He is the author of *Zen in the Art of Rhetoric: An Inquiry into Coherence,* and *The Rhetoric of Racism Revisited: Reparations or Separation?* His research has been published in numerous scholarly journals, including *The Quarterly Journal of Speech, Critical Studies in Mass Communication,* the *Howard Journal of Communications,* and *Rhetoric and Public Affairs.*

TAVIA NYONG'O is a professor in Performance Studies at New York University. His book *The Amalgamation Waltz: Race, Performance and the Ruses of Memory* (2009) won the 2010 Errol Hill Award of the American Society for Theatre Research. His essays have appeared in *Theatre Journal, GLQ, Radical History Review, Social Text, Journal of Popular Music Studies, Criticism, TDR, Performance Research,* and the *Spike Lee Reader.* He is the co-editor of *Social Text.*

DAVID ROEDIGER is a professor in history and African American Studies at the University of Illinois. Roediger has taught labor and Southern history at Northwestern, University of Missouri, and University of Minnesota. He has also worked as an editor of the Frederick Douglass Papers at Yale University. His books include *The Wages of Whiteness* (1990), *How Race Survived U.S. History* (2008), and *Towards the Abolition of Whiteness* (1994) and *Working Toward Whiteness* (2005). Among his edited books include an edition of *Covington Hall's Labor Struggles in the Deep South* (1999) and one of *W. E. B.*

Du Bois's John Brown (2001), as well as *Black on White: Black Writers on What It Means to Be White* (1998).

PAUL SPICKARD is a professor in the Department of History at the University of California, Santa Barbara. He is author or editor of sixteen books and seventy-odd articles on race, migration, and related topics in the United States, the Pacific, Northeast Asia, and Europe, including: *Multiple Identities: Migrants, Ethnicity, and Membership* (2013); *Almost All Aliens: Immigration, Race, and Colonialism in American History and Identity* (2007); *Race and Nation: Ethnic Systems in the Modern World* (2005); and *Mixed Blood: Intermarriage and Ethnic Identity in Twentieth-Century America* (1989).

JANET C. MENDOZA STICKMON is a professor of Humanities at Napa Valley College and currently teaches Africana Studies, Filipina/o-American Heritage, and two ethnic studies-oriented humanities courses called American Mind I and II. She is the founder and facilitator of Broken Shackle Developmental Training—a series of workshops designed to promote the use of healing techniques to reduce the effects of internalized racism. She is author of *Crushing Soft Rubies* (2003) and *Midnight Peaches, Two O'Clock Patience* (2012), is a teacher, writer, and performer. Her memoir, *Crushing Soft Rubies*, has been used as a course textbook at several colleges and universities across the country.

PAUL STREET is the author of *Racial Oppression in the Global Metropolis: A Living Black Chicago History* (2007); *Segregated Schools: Educational Apartheid in the Post–Civil Rights Era* (2005); *Empire and Inequality: America and the World Since 9/11* (2004); *Barack Obama and the Future of American Politics* (2008); *The Empire's New Clothes: Barack Obama in the Real World of Power* (2010); *Crashing the Tea Party* (2011); and *They Rule: The 1% v. Democracy* (2014). Street was the Director of Research at The Chicago Urban League from 2000 to 2005.

EBONY UTLEY is a professor in the Department of Communication Studies at California State University, Long Beach. She is an expert in hip-hop, race, and love relationships. Her book, *Rap and Religion: Understanding the Gangsta's God*, reveals how a God-sanctioned gangsta identity empowers young black people facing declining economic opportunities. In her other research, Utley examines how Americans talk about race and racism, asks probing questions about black women's experiences with infidelity, investigates African American beliefs about marriage, and explores the tenuous relationship between hip-hop and love. Her work has appeared in *Black Women, Gender and Families, Critical Studies in Media Communication, Rhetoric and Public Affairs, The Journal of Men's Studies, The Western Journal of Black Studies, Women and Language, Ms. Magazine,* and *Religion Dispatches.* Utley resides on the web at http://theutleyexperience.com.

HETTIE V. WILLIAMS is a professor in African American history in the Department of History and Anthropology at Monmouth University. Her research interests include race, identity, and the cultural history of African Americans; recent American history; studies in the African Diaspora; and gender. She has taught survey courses in U.S. history, world history, Western civilization, and upper division courses on the history of African Americans. She has published more than thirty entries and essays for several encyclopedias and edited volumes and written a text entitled *We Shall Overcome to We Shall Overrun: The Collapse of the Civil Rights Movement and the Black Power Revolt* (1962–1968) and an edited volume with Julius O. Adekunle titled *Color Struck: Essays on Race and Ethnicity in Global Perspective.* She is completing a book titled *There is Confusion: Black Identity in the African Diaspora* (forthcoming).

INDEX

Page numbers in *italics* indicate illustrations.

Abernathy, Ralph, xli–xlii
abolitionism, 184, 186, 269
abortion, and 2008 election, 208–9, 211–12, 213
absolute authority doctrine, 182, 184
Abu-Jamal, Mumia, 301
accommodation, 314; in neo-accommodationist approach to rhetoric, 314–15; of structural inequalities and racism by Obama, 289–92, 300–301
ACORN, 300–301
affirmative action: class-based vs. race-based, xxix; Obama on, xxix–xxx, 212; as reverse racism, 19; successful blacks as evidence of end of need for, xxiii, 19, 135; Supreme Court on, xxii–xxiii, 20; and 2008 election, 208–9, 212, 213, 214
Afghanistan war: Cairo speech on, 72; end of, 333; vs. Iraq war, 72
Africa: black immigrants from, 168–71; culture and worldview of, 149–53; human origins in, 35, 200; Obama's de-emphasis of influence of, 320–21; Obama's pre-presidential visit to, 131n7; as unclaimed paternity of Obama, 120–23
African Americans. *See* black Americans
African-centered analysis of culture and worldview, 148–54, 156, 165
African Free Schools, 186
"Against Bipolar Black Masculinity" (Cooper), 231

Agassiz, Louis, 45
age: of Obama as proxy for race, 207; of Obama's daughters, 256
aggression in performance of masculinity, 233, 236, 238, 242n21
Aid for Families with Dependent Children (AFDC), 289, 290
Akan people, 69, 83n9
Albert, Derrion, 302, 303–4
Al Fayed, Dodi, 106–7
Ali, Muhammad, 12
Allred, Frances, 13
All Things Considered, 139
Alter, Jonathan, *The Promise*, xv
Alvarado, Leticia, 25
ambiguity: of Ananse (trickster), 68; in physical appearance of multiracial individuals, 48–49, 52; of "postcolonial," 134; in visual representations of multiracial individuals, 41; vs. certainty, public preference for, 42, 48, 49, 52, 60–61
American Civil Rights Institute, xxiii
American Independent Party, 338n7
American Jobs Act, 30, 40n30
American Renaissance (white supremacist group), xiii
American Revolution, 299
Ananse (trickster), 66–69; characteristics and responsibilities of, 68–69; multi-ethnic individuals relating to, 62–63; parallels between Obama and, 64, 78, 80–82, 82n2

ancestral guardian soul, 68
Ancestry.com, 11, 13
Anderson-Levy, Lisa, xxxiv–xxxv
angry black man/woman stereotype: Michelle Obama as, 192, 193, 196, 331; Obama's avoidance of, xxxv, 226, 236–37; Obama's use in Philadelphia speech, 324; Wright as, 110, 298–99
Ani, Marimba, 150; *Yurugu*, 154–55
Another Country (Baldwin), 96, 112n8
anthropology: colonial studies in, 145n5; postcolonial theory in, 135–36, 146n11
anti-miscegenation laws: end of, 4, 9–10; one-drop rule and, 3–4
Appiah, Kwame Anthony, 144n3
Arab Americans, racial profiling of, xxiii
Arab Peace Initiative, 73
Ardizzone, Heidi, xxxv
art, regulation of, in colonial Mexico, 43. See also visual representations
Asad, Talal, 145n5
asexual style vs. unisex style, 239
Ashanti people, 68–69, 83n9. See also Ananse
Asian Americans: on black identity of Obama, xxvi, 14; collective identity of, 48; conflation with blacks, in policies, 170; current population of, xii; diversity among groups of, 171–72; future population of "pure" vs. mixed, xxv; in 2008 election, xxvi, 14; in 2012 election, 15, 336; support for Obama among, lack of, xxvi
assimilation, myth of, 156–57
assimilationist incentive, 230, 231
Association of MultiEthnic Americans (AMEA), 91, 92
Atlantic, The, 326–27
attributed identity, 227–28
Audacity of Hope, The (Obama): accommodation of white supremacy in, 289; cosmopolitanism in, 108; heteroglossia in, 104; on multiracial experience vs. black experience, 112n27; on racial identity formation, 103; timing of publication of, xv
audience: of DNC speech, 265–66, 273, 277; of Philadelphia speech, 317–20
"Aunt Jemima" stereotype, 185
Austin, Algernon, 161
autobiographies, ethnic fluidity of identity in, 84–85. See *Dreams from My Father*
auto industry bailout, 334
Avlon, John, 261n8
"Awesome God," 330, 338n3
Axelrod, David, 235
axiology, 151; in worldviews, 149, 150–52
Azibo, Daudi Ajani ya, 150

Bachmann, Michele, 79
Bad Black Man stereotype, 226, 231; Obama's avoidance of, 234, 235, 237; Sharpton as, 234, 281; Wright as, 235
Bai, Matt, 144n2
Baker, Houston, 36n2
Baker, Peter, 305
Bakhtin, Mikhail, 85, 86, 103–4, 111n2, 113n28
Balcetis, Emily, 33
Baldwin, James, xxv; *Another Country*, 96, 112n8
Baldwin, Tom, 315
Bambara people, 82
Banaji, Mahzarin, 230
Barack Obama and African American Empowerment (Marable and Clarke), xvii
Barack Obama and the Future of American Politics (Street), 298
Barack Obama's America (White), xvi
"Barack the Magical Negro," 260n4
bargaining, 7–8; Obama's use of, 7–8, 55; racial diplomacy by black candidates as, 7–8; vs. challenging, 8, 37n7, 55
basketball, and Obama, 98
Bassard, Katherine, 128
Beck, Glenn, 301
Beinart, Peter, 54, 102

Belkin, Lisa, 248
Bell, Derrick, 294
Benveniste, Emile, 103
Beran, Katie, 310n5
Berger, John, 51
Berlin speech by Obama (2008), 107
Berry, Halle, 20
Bethel Literary and Historical Association, 187
Bethune, Mary McLeod, 187
Between Barack and a Hard Place (Wise), xvi
Beyond the Color Line, 310n4
Bhabha, Homi K., 86, 101, 102, 111n2, 112n26
biases: debiasing agents and, 230, 240; regarding skin color and tone, 16–18, 19–20, 33, 38n18
bias theory, 230
Biden, Joseph, 16, 102, 288
"Billary" frame, 220, 221–22
Bill Moyers Journal, 8
Bill of Rights, in Philadelphia speech, 7
binary oppositions: in European epistemology, 154; Obama's challenge to, 64, 274, 276; in scholarship, xxxviii–xxxix
bin Laden, Osama, 333
biology, of race, 89–90, 199–200
bipolarity, in representations of black masculinity, 226, 231, 234–36
Biracial Family Network (BFN), 91
birth certificate of Obama: release of, 28–29, 332; in White House Correspondents' Dinner speech, 78–79
"birthers," 28–29, 332–33; claims of, xii, 28, 332; lawsuits by, 119; Obama's sense of humor about, 78–79; in 2012 election, 332–33; Trump as, 79–80, 332; U.S. citizenship of Obama's mother and, 40n28, 131n4, 332; white anxiety of, xii–xiii, 28–29, 110; xenophobia of, 119–20
bitch stereotype of black women, 185–86, 192–93
Bitzer, Lloyd, 313
Black Agenda Report, 298

black Americans: current population of, xii; DNC speech on trauma of, 266, 268–71, 275, 277–78, 282–83, 324; economic policies targeting, 30, 301–2, 308; election of Obama as symbolic victory, 40n27, 60; future population of "pure" vs. mixed, xxv–xxvi; genealogy of, 11–13, 168; Great Recession's impact on, 30, 301–2, 307–8; policy issues of, 208–9; Hispanic, 38n18; homeownership by, xiv, xxx–xxxi; immigrant unity with, xxv–xxviii; immigrant vs. descendants of slaves, 168–71; linguistic identity of, 104; lived reality of, 147, 157, 159–65; "Obama effect" on, xvii; poverty rates among, 302, 307; on racial identity of Obama, 14, 38n13; rhetorical religious traditions of, 321; successes of, 18–19, 135, 293–94, 296–98; in 2008 election, xxiii–xxiv, 14, 28; in 2012 election, 15, 336; typical experience vs. multiracial experience of Obama, 54–55, 84, 112n27; as violating traditional U.S. values, 29; voting rights for, 20, 280, 282; vs. African Americans, Obama's use of terms, 320; on Zimmerman trial, 26. *See also* black men; black women
Blackapina, 62
"black bitch" stereotype, 185–86, 192–93
Black Commentator, 299
black community, 110
Black Entertainment Television (BET), 30
blackface minstrelsy, 59
black families: absent fathers in, 198, 247, 252–55; fatherhood initiatives aimed at, 252–53; gender hierarchy in, 125–27; Moynihan report on, 125–27, 252; Philadelphia speech on, 254, 325; photographs of, 249–50
black feminist theory, 118, 120, 125–30, 179
black identity: linguistic, 104; one-drop rule in, 3–6. *See also* racial identity of Obama
black liberation theology, xxix, 321

black men: as absent fathers, 198, 247, 252–55; as always-already-suspect, 226, 240; bipolarity in representations of masculinity of, 226, 231, 234–36; Obama on perils of being, 32; Obama's impact on perceptions of, 239–40, 243n34, 255; in prison system, xiv, xxi, 198, 309; racial profiling of, 240; white fear of, 139, 236

Black Orpheus, 129–30

black political candidates: Bradley effect on, xvii, 14, 38n14; connections to black community, 110; framing in media of, 207; Latino support for, xxvi, xxvii; "Obama effect" on, xvii; old vs. new, 133, 144n2; racial diplomacy by, 7–8; racial transcendence strategy used by, 110, 314; racist depictions of, 163; rhetorical strategies of, 313–15; skin color, biases regarding, 20, 33; vs. white candidates, 138; women as, 198

Black psychology, 149

Black Scholar, xiv–xv

Black Skins, Black Masks (Tate), 86, 100, 101, 111n2, 113n28

black women, 177–200; club movement among, 186–87; challenges facing, 198–99; educational and employment opportunities for, 186, 200n2; herstory of, 178; legacy of slavery for, 181–86; Michelle Obama's impact on, 189, 194–97; multiple discriminations against, 178–79, 181–82, 199; multiple identities of, 178–79; as political candidates, 198; poverty among, 179, 181–82, 198; progress and successes of, 197–98; self-help traditions of, 177, 178, 186–87, 198; as single mothers, 198, 289

blackness: essentialist, 35, 85; experience of slavery in, 54–55, 102; functional, 100–103; instability of meaning and significance of, 167–73; of Obama, 54–55; one-drop rule in, 4, 46; as paradigmatic of race, 138; in preservation of slavery, 4, 45–46; variation in legal, 4; white fear of, 139–40

Blitt, Barry, 59–60

Bloomberg, Michael, 334

blue jeans, 239

Blue Skies, No Fences (Cheney), 11–12

Bonet, Lisa, 49

Bonilla-Silva, Eduardo, xxxviii, 34, 42, 163

Booker, Cory, 314

bootstraps narrative, 18

Bourdieu, Pierre, 5

Boyd, Todd, 37n4

Bradley, Tom, 38n14; effect, xvii, 14, 38n14

Braun, Carol Moseley, 198

Brazile, Donna, 15–16

breadwinner ideal, 253–54

Breakthrough, The (Ifill), xv

Breckenridge, Carol, 145n5

Bridge, The (Remnick), xv

Briscoe, Darren, 298

Brooke, Edward W., 20

Brooks, David, 334

Brooks, Roy L., 295–96; *Racial Justice in the Age of Obama*, xvi

Brown, Michael, *Whitewashing Race*, 161, 295

Brown, Scott, 12

Brown, Timothy, 283

Brown v. Board of Education, 160, 187

Brunsma, David, 93

Buchenwald concentration camp, 73, 83n11

Buffett, Warren, 12

Bunch, Anna, and family, 13

Bundchen, Gisele, 162

Bureau of Justice, 198

Burke, Kenneth, 317

burqa, 74

Bush, George H. W.: children of, 262n23; as distant cousin of Obama, 12

Bush, George W.: children of, 262n23; on cloning, 58–59; as distant cousin of Obama, 12; fatherhood initiatives of, 252; foreign relations under, 334; response to hurricanes Katrina and

Rita, 80, 304, 305, 334; in Sharpton's 2004 DNC speech, 271, 279–80; spread of democracy by, 73
Bush, Laura, 196
Butler, Judith, 228, 241n8

Cairo speech by Obama (2009), 70–75; cosmopolitanism in, 109; messages of, 64, 70–75; Obama as mediator in, 70, 73, 81–82
Caldwell, Charles, 162
California: immigrant-rights demonstrations of 2006 in, xxvii–xxviii; population of, xii; race of teachers in, 160; 2008 primary in, xxvi
Call & Post, 163
Cambodian Americans, 170, 171
Camus, Marcel, 129
Capehart, Jonathan, 262n27
capitalism, legacy of racism in, 295
Carbado, Devon W., 241n4
Carey, Mariah, 49
Caribbean: black immigrants from, 168–71; end of slavery in, 169
carjackings, 39n23
Carr, Walt, 163
Carroll, Karanja Keita, x, xxxiv–xxxv, xxxviii
Carruthers, Jacob, 150
Carter, Amy, 256, 262n23
Carter, Greg, xxxiv
Carter, Jimmy, 31, 240
Carter, Stephen L., 282
Caruso, Eugene M., 33
Cashin, Sheryl, 294
casta paintings: functions of, 43; mannerisms, 44; origins of, 43; Spanish collectors of, 41, 43; visual and verbal conventions of, 43–45
Castle, William E., 46
Castle Doctrine, 23–24, 39n23
Castro, Fidel, 336
Cavuto, Neil, 248
Cebull, Richard, 28

celebrities, multiracial, 49
census, U.S.: Hispanic as ethnic category in, 21; immigrants in, xi; multiracial individuals in, xi–xii, xxiv, 11; Obama's selection of race in, 9, 92, 251, 261n12; selection of multiple races in, xi, xxiv, 10, 92
certainty, public preference for, 42, 48, 49, 52, 61
Césaire, Aimé, 284, 285
challenging vs. bargaining, 8, 37n7, 55
Chaney, James, 285
change: government as agent of, 274–75; Obama as catalyst for, 64, 82; tricksters as catalyst for, 66
Charles, Ray, 280
"Chasing Day Break," 9
chattel slavery. *See* slavery
Cheney, Dick, 11–12
Cheney, Lynne, *Blue Skies, No Fences*, 11–12
Cheyney State College, 200n2
Chicago: Michelle Obama's career in, 191; Michelle Obama's childhood in, 189–90, 192; Obama's move to, 98; as proposed site for Olympics, 302–4; in racial identity formation of Obama, 98, 100
Chicago Sun Times, 225
child care, as policy issue in 2008 election, 208–9, 212
childhood of Obama: black friends in, 98; overview of, 53, 87, 96–98; in racial identity, 8–9, 86, 97–98, 250
children: of immigrants, citizenship for, 333; Michelle Obama's advocacy for, 195–96; Obama's interactions with, 245, 245–46, 257–58; of presidents, 252, 256, 262n23; of slaves, 45–46, 126–27, 128, 182–83. *See also* daughters of Obama
children's books, about Obama, 248, 260n7
child support, 252
Child Tax Credit, 30
Chin, Vincent, xxviii
Chisholm, Shirley, 110, 198

choice: in Iraq war vs. Afghanistan war, 72; in racial identity, xxiv–xxv, 3, 167, 227–28
Christianity: in DNC speech, 330, 338n3; and moral issues of slavery, 183–84
Christie, Chris, 334
Chrysler, 334
Churchill, Winston, 12
citizenship, U.S.: for immigrants, x, 333; of Obama, mother as U.S. citizen and, 40n28, 131n4, 332; of Romney, 333, 338n7. *See also* "birthers"
City University of New York, Queens College of, 169
civility in politics, xiii, 29
civil rights movement: challenging vs. bargaining as tactic in, 8; legacy of success of, 269–70; and *Loving v. Virginia*, 9–10; mass participation in success of, xxxvii, xli–xlii; mobilization of apolitical individuals in, xxxvii; multiracial movement as outgrowth of, 91; Obama as product of, 220; Obama on racial equality achieved by, 289; repudiation of aims and ideals of, xl–xli; rhetoric of, 269–70, 277, 279; in 2008 Democratic primaries, 209, 210, 218–20, 218–23; Wright's connection with, 319. *See also* post–civil rights era
Clark, Mary E., 278–79
Clarke, Kristen, *Barack Obama and African American Empowerment*, xvii
class, social: affirmative action based on, xxix; of black immigrants, 169; black vs. white middle class, 323; of Michelle Obama's family, 188, 189–90; social inequalities attributed to, 19
Cleaver, Emanuel, 31
Clinton, Bill: economy in elections of, xxx; fatherhood initiatives of, 252; Initiative on Race under, 170; "Sister Souljah strategy" of, 270; welfare reform under, 252, 289
Clinton, Chelsea, 256, 262n23

Clinton, Hillary: Asian American support for, xxvi; black support for, xxiii; framing in media of, 207–8; Latino support for, xxvi, xxvii; media coverage as First Lady, 207; Obama depicted as "other" by, 331–32; performance of identity by, 239; "red phone" campaign ad by, xxii; and subprime mortgage crisis, xxxi; unisex style of, 241n7; on *Vogue* cover as First Lady, 196; vs. Obama, 225. *See also* Democratic primaries of 2008
"Clinton Owns Economy" frame, 216, 216–17, 222–23
cloning research, 58–59
clothing: in *casta* paintings, 44; of Hillary Clinton, 241n7; of Muslim women, 74; of Michelle Obama, 196; unisex, 238–39, 241n7
cocaine, 30, 40n32
Cohen, John, 307–8
Cohen, Rob, 52
coherence: in DNC speech, 266–68, 273, 275–85; Obama's search for, 8, 103, 272; strategy of, 266
Colbert, Stephen, 54–55
Colbert Report, The, 54–55
Coleman, Marshall, 38n14
collective identities, 47–48
colonial America, slavery in, 182, 185
colonial Kenya, independence for, 119, 131n5
colonial Mexico, *casta* paintings in, 41, 42–45
colonial studies, in anthropology, 145n5
colorblind antiracism, 34
colorblind racism, 34, 42
colorblind rhetoric: conservatives' use of, 18–19; critical race theory's critique of, 230; denial of reality of race in, 157–58; Obama's use of, 235; politicians embracing, xli; selective nature of integration masked by, 18–19; and shooting of Trayvon Martin, 20–23
Colored Women's League, 187

color lines: Du Bois on, 285; Obama in destabilization of, 167, 172, 173
Columbia University, 53, 99–100
comforting strategy, 241n4
commander in chief test, 226
common law: Castle Doctrine in, 24; citizenship in, 332
community, Obama's search for, 98–100
"Community Organizer" frame, 216, 217
composite audience of DNC speech, 265–66, 273, 277
composite identity of Obama, 84, 86, 93, 94, 97, 103
compromise in DNC speech, 278–79
Congress, U.S.: black women in, 198; legislative representation in, 204; on natural-born citizenship, 332; Obama in, 53, 54; racial epithets in protests at, 31; "You lie" outburst by Joe Wilson at Obama's speech to, 30–31, 33
Congressional Black Caucus (CBC), 30, 40n31, 301–2
Connecticut, Sandy Hook shootings in, 262n33
Connell, R. W., 229
consciousness: double, 104, 259, 266; race, 231, 234
consensual relationships, in slavery, 183
conservatives: bootstraps narrative of, 18; colorblind rhetoric of, 18–19; "Magical Negro" trope used by, 245; on Michelle Obama, 192–93; Obama as, 291; on Obama's middle name, xxiii; on Obama's position on absent fathers, 255; on welfare, 289, 290
consilience, rhetoric of, 266; in DNC speech, 266, 267, 272–78, 283–85; in Philadelphia speech, 7
conspiracy theories, 79
Constitution, U.S.: on citizenship, 119; Obama's use of rhetoric of, ix; in Philadelphia speech, 7, 322; slavery in, 281, 322
control, in European epistemology, 154–55

Cooper, Anna Julia, 177, 187
Cooper, Frank Rudy, xxxv; "Against Bipolar Black Masculinity," 231; *Masculinities and the Law*, 232
Coppin, Frances Jackson, 200n2
cosmology, 151; in worldviews, 149, 150–51
cosmopolitanism, 106; forms of, 106–7; in hybrid fluidity, 85–86; of Obama, 86–87, 88–89, 101, 105–9, 111n2, 113n28
Council of Conservative Citizens, 143
CounterPunch, 306–7
cowardice, racial, 305–6, 309
crack cocaine, 30, 40n32
"cracker" epithet, 22–23
Crenshaw, Kimberlé, xl, 280–81
crime, 140–42
criminality: racial profiling and, 39n22; skin color and, 16
criminal trials, 26, 39n26. *See also* Zimmerman trial
critical multiraciality, 34–36; as antiracist strategy, 34; and colorblind antiracism, 34; contrasted with colorblind racism, 34; contrasted with hypocritical multiraciality, 34
critical race theory, 228–31; bipolar black masculinity in, 231, 234–36; and femininity of Obama, 225, 230, 234–37; in feminism, 179; multiethnic/multiracial individuals' understanding of, 62; and Obama as Good Black Man, 234–37; tenets of, 228–29, 230–31, 242n15; tenets shared with masculinities studies, 228–29
Croft, Steve, 332
Crouch, Stanley, 54, 102
"crying baby" video, 244–45, 245, 257, 260n4
Cuban Americans, 336
Cultural Cosmopolitanism (Nava), 106–7
cultural pluralism, 156–57
culture, 148–49; African vs. European, 149–50; deep and surface structures of, 148–49; of ethnicity, 82n1; in epistemological basis of racism, 155–56, 165; and

impossibility of post-racist America, 147–54, 165; social inequalities attributed to, 19; stereotypes of black women in, 179–81; as tool in analysis of human relations, 148. *See also* popular culture
Current Population Survey, 14
"Cyborg Manifesto" (Haraway), 111n1

Daily Dish, The, 327
Daily Show, 260n4
Daley, Richard M., 302
Damon, Matt, 79
Damore, David, 207
D'Andrade, Roy, xxxvi
Daniel, G. Reginald, x, xxxiv, xxxvi, 82n1, 112n9, 112n22, 113n30; *More Than Black,* 91, 113n30
Daniels, Lee A., 269
Darsey, James, 316
Darwinism, social, 46
Davenport, C. B.: *Heredity of Skin Color in Negro-White Crosses,* 46–47; visual representations of multiracial individuals by, 41, 45–47
Davis, Angela, 193
Davis, Darrin, xxix–xxx
Davis, Jane, 325–26
Dawn, Marpessa, 130
Dawson, Michael, xxvii
Day, Caroline Bond, 250, 261n11
death panels, xii–xiii
debiasing agents, 230, 240
Declaration of Independence: in DNC speech, 273; in Philadelphia speech, 7
Declaration of Interdependence, 7, 37n3
De Genova, Nicholas, xxviii
Delanos, Sean, 161–62
de la Rionda, Bernie, 22
democracy: participatory, xxxvii; as source of tension between U.S. and Muslim world, 72, 73–74; U.S. in spread of, 73
Democratic National Convention (1967), 37n6

Democratic National Convention (2004), Obama's speech at, 265–86; coherence in, 266–68, 273, 275–85; composite audience of, 265–66, 273, 277; consilience in, 266, 267, 272–78, 283–85; debate over significance of, xxxiv, 265–68; Good Black Man stereotype in, 234; on government as agent of change, 274–75; on multiracial background, 53, 272; on one America, 29, 274, 276, 329–30; origins of Obama phenomenon in, xv, 312, 329–30; racelessness in, old vision of, 265, 267, 315; transcripts of, 286n3; on traumas of blacks, 266, 268–71, 275, 277–78, 282–83, 324; on traumas of nonblacks, 266, 272, 277–78, 323; vs. Sharpton's speech, 265, 266–67, 268, 270–72, 278, 279–81
Democratic National Convention (2008): daughters of Obama at, 252; diversity at, 29; humor about Obama's name at, 123; Michelle Obama's speech at, 244, 251; Obama's white relatives at, 15
Democratic National Convention (2012), diversity at, 29
Democratic Party: on affirmative action, xxix; racial composition of, 29
Democratic primaries (2008): Asian American voters in, xxvi; black voters in, xxiii; closeness of outcome, 201–2; in Iowa caucuses, 298, 330; Latino voters in, xxvi, xxvii; Obama depicted as "other" in, 331–32; "red phone" campaign ad in, xxii; similarities between policy platforms in, 201–2; subprime mortgage crisis in, xxxi. *See also* election of 2008; media coverage of Democratic primaries
demographic outsiders, 202, 203, 204–5
Derrida, Jacques, 121–22, 124, 130
descriptive representation of social groups, 202–6; in conflict with executive representation, 204–6, 208, 222–24; by outsiders, 204–5, 222; utility and

effectiveness of, 203–4; vs. substantive representation, 203–4
Detroit Free Press, 301
Deukmejian, George, 38n14
Dhareshwar, Vivek, 145n8
dialogism, 103
Diana, Princess of Wales, 106–7
dichotomization, in European epistemology, 154
Dickerson, Debra, 54–55, 102; *The End of Blackness*, 54
Diesel, Vin, 52
Diggs-Brown, Barbara, 34, 294
Dinkins, David, xxvii, 20, 314
Diogenes, 106
discrimination, facing black women, 178–79, 181–82, 199. *See also* racism
Ditonto, Tessa, xxxv
Dixon, Vernon, 149, 152
domestic surveillance, 40n27
domestic work, by black women, 186
domination, in performance of masculinity, 232–33
double consciousness, 104, 259, 266
double voice, 85
Douglas, Stephen, 269
Dovi, Suzanne, 204
Dowd, Maureen, 220, 305
doxa, 5
Dragon in Dream, 56
Dreams from My Father (Obama): as coming of age story, 85; cosmopolitanism in, 107, 108; on death of father, 120–21; dreams of the mother in, 120, 122, 128–30; heteroglossia in, 104; on inheritance of racial identity, 96, 121; as "many-voiced," 85, 105; meaning of title, 96, 121; on multiracial experience vs. black experience, 84, 112n27; multiracial identity rejected in, 93–94; on nickname Barry, 122–23; on outsider experience, 94; on parents' marriage, 88; on racial identity formation, 90, 96, 97–100, 103; on relationship with white woman, 94; Zadie Smith on, 85, 105, 112n8; on straddling multiple worlds, 8, 103, 272; timing of publication of, xv, 120

Du Bois, W. E. B.: on color line, 285; on double consciousness, 104, 259, 266; and family photographs, 249; Obama compared to, 329; *Souls of Black Folk*, 285; on the veil, 47
Duncan, Arne, 303, 305
Dunham, Stanley Ann (mother): birth of, 13; black ancestry of, 13; dreams of, 120, 122, 128–30; education of, 188; Irish ancestry of, 63; marriage to Obama Sr., 53, 88; marriage to Soetoro, 96–97; slave and slaveholding ancestors of, 13, 119; U.S. citizenship of, 40n28, 131n4, 332; whiteness of, xi, 8, 15, 63, 87, 96, 168
Durant, Will, 37n3
Duster, Troy, 89–90
Dyson, Michael Eric, xvi

Earned Income Tax Credit, 30
East-West Center of the University of Hawai'i, 96–97
Eastwood, Clint, xiii
economic cosmopolitanism, 106
economic crisis of 2008: impact on blacks and Latinos, 30, 301–2, 307–8; on Obama's response to, 40n27; Stimulus Program response to, 30; subprime mortgages in, xxx–xxxi
economic development, as source of tension between U.S. and Muslim world, 72
economic inequalities, vs. racial inequalities, 171, 173. *See also* structural inequalities
economic policies, under Obama, 30, 301–2, 308
economy: as dominant issue in 2008 election, xxvi, xxx, 14, 57; legacy of racism in, 295; as policy issue in 2008 Democratic primaries, 209, 211, 213, 216–17

Edmonston, Barry, xxv
education: for Asian Americans, 171–72; for black Americans, 159, 160–61, 169; for black immigrants vs. descendants of slaves, 169; black teachers in, 160–61; for black women, 186, 192, 200n2; as policy issue in 2008 election, 208–9, 212, 214; high school dropout rates, xiii–xiv; for Latinos, 171; of Michelle Obama, 190–91, 192; racial segregation in, end of, 160, 187. *See also* public schools
education of Obama: college, 53, 98–100; in Hawai'i, 53, 122; in Indonesia, 97; law school, 63
Edwards, John, 288
Edwards, Omar, 163–64
egalitarian integration, *17*, 19
egalitarian pluralism, *17*, 38n17
Ehrenstein, David, 260n4
either/or thinking, 5–6, 9
election of 1984, Jesse Jackson in, 7, 313
election of 1988, Jesse Jackson in, 7, 313
election of 1992, Clinton's "Sister Souljah strategy" in, 270
election of 2000: Gore's distance from Sharpton in, 270; in Sharpton's 2004 DNC speech, 280
election of 2004, white voters in, 271
election of 2008: affirmative action as issue in, xxix–xxx; Asian American voters in, xxvi, 14; black voters in, xxiii–xxiv, 14, 28; and claims about end of race, xxiii–xxiv; and the economy, xxvi, xxx, 14, 57; international reactions to, xi, 331; journalistic literature on, xv; Latino voters in, xxvi–xxvii, 14; masculinity of candidates in, 233, 234; Michelle Obama's role in, 192–94; Obama depicted as "other" in, 331–32; Obama's campaign staff in, 110; Obama's middle name in, 79; photographs of Obama family in, 245–46, *246*; popular vote in, 14; race-neutrality of Obama in, 6, 31; racially-charged Google searches and, 27; racist depictions of Obama in, 28, 193; racist depictions of Michelle Obama in, 193; scholarship on, xvi–xvii; whiteness of Obama in, 15–16; white voters in, 14, 15–16, 138, 167. *See also* Democratic primaries
election of 2012, 329–37; Asian American voters in, 15, 336; "birthers" in, 332–33; black voters in, 15, 336; exit polls on, 334, 336; foreign policy and relations in, 333–34; and future of Republican Party, 336–37; Latino voters in, 15, 336; Obama depicted as "other" in, 332–33; Obama's election night speech after win, ix; racial cowardice in, 309; racist depictions of Obama in, xiii, 28; reasons for Obama's victory in, 333–35, 337; Tea Party in, 28; voter suppression in, 15, 335–36; weaknesses of Romney in, 333–35; white voters in, xii, 15
Election of Barack Obama, The (Porterfield), xvii
election of Obama: changes in national racial order in, xxxix; debate over significance of, xxxiii–xxxiv, xxxvi, 147; deniers of legitimacy of, xiii, 119–20; as first black president, xi–xiv, 117–18; as first postcolonial president, 117; as first post-racial president, 117, 133, 167, 298–300, 315–16; as first unisex president, 226, 238–40; as first woman president, 225, 227, 234; international reactions to, xi, 331; and one-drop rule, 6; post-racial society achieved through, 27, 60, 158, 259, 287, 330–31; power of racism worsened by, 292–93, 306–7; racial skills of Obama in, 329–30; as resolution of slavery, 60; structural inequalities after, xiii–xiv, 159–65, 309; as symbolic victory for blacks, 40n27, 60; white anxiety in response to, xii–xiii, 27–29, 110–11; white fear in response to, 138–40; white support for, 287–93, 306–7; white supremacy challenged by,

xii–xiii. *See also* election of 2008; election of 2012
empathy, in DNC speech, 276–77
employment opportunities, for black women, 186. *See also* unemployment rate
End of Blackness, The (Dickerson), 54
English, Ron, 59
epistemology: in African vs. European worldviews, 152–53; in concept of worldview, 149, 150–51; European, as basis for racism, 154–57, 165; European, in scholarship, xxxviii
equality, Obama on: and civil rights movement, 289; in DNC speech, 273, 282. *See also* racial inequalities; structural inequalities
Equality Index, 159
equal rights movements, in media coverage, 208–11, *218–20*, 218–23. *See also* civil rights movement; feminism
Eshu (trickster), 66–69; characteristics and responsibilities of, 66–68; multiethnic/multiracial individuals relating to, 62–63; parallels between Obama and, 64, 71–73, 77, 81–82, 82n2
essentialism, racial, 35, 85
essentialist hybridity, in multiracial movement, Obama's rejection of, 88–89
ethnic autobiographies, fluidity of identity in, 84–85
ethnic diversity. *See* racial and ethnic diversity
ethnicity, 82n1; in Kenya, 118; of Pacific Islander Americans, 97; race and culture as part of, 82n1
eugenics: role of scholarship in, xxxviii; in visual representations of multiraciality, 41, 45–47
Europe, culture and worldview of, 149–53
evangelical Christianity, in DNC speech, 330, 338n3
executive representation of national electorate, 202–6; in conflict with descriptive representation, 204–6, 208, 222–24; vs. legislative representation, 204; by outsiders, 204–5

Fairey, Shepard, "Hope" poster by, 41, 57–58
Fair Sentencing Act of 2010, 30
Fallow, James, 326–27
family of Obama: campaign emphasis on whiteness in, 15–16; genealogy of, 6, 11–13, 119; negative views about black people in, 172, 236, 323; overview of, 53, 87–88, 96–98; photographs of, 245–49, *246*, 256–57, 261n9; siblings, 87–88, 96, 97; visibility of whiteness in, 88, 168. *See also* daughters of Obama; parents of Obama
Family Research Council, 255
Fanon, Franz, 111n2
father, Obama as, 244–60; absent black fathers and, 247, 252–55; absent sons and, 256–59; in co-parenting style, 253–54; critics of, 255–56; in "crying baby" video, 244–45, *245*, 257, 260n4; in family photographs, 245–49, *246*; and fatherhood initiatives, 252–53; media coverage of, 245, *246*, 248; nurturing, 245–46, 254; in political image and identity, 246–47, 248–49; symbolic, 246–47
fatherhood initiatives, 252–53
fathers: absence in black families, 198, 247, 252–55; real, 131n7; symbolic vs. imaginary, 121
Father's Day speech by Obama (2008), 254, 255
Federal Bureau of Investigation (FBI), 25
Federal Emergency Management Agency (FEMA), 334
femininity, 227; of Hillary Clinton, 225; vs. masculinity, 232, 237, 242n18
femininity, of Barack Obama, 233–40; bipolar black masculinity and, 226, 231, 234–36; characteristics of, 234; critical race theory and, 225, 230, 234–37; Good Black Man stereotype and, 226; masculinities studies and, 225, 232, 233, 237–38;

media coverage of, 225, 227, 234–35; performance of masculinity and, 228, 232–33, 236, 238–39; as political strategy, 226, 234, 238–39, 242n22; risks of revealing, 237–38, 242n32; in unisex style, 226, 238–40

feminism: black, 118, 120, 125–30, 179; in 2008 Democratic primaries, 209, 210, *218–20*, 218–23; on 2012 election, 15; in post-feminist society, 220, 221; Standpoint, 111n1

Filipino Americans, 171

films, stereotypes of black women in, 184–85

First Black President, The (Hill), xvi

Fischer, Michael M. J., 84–85

fist-bump, 59–60, 193, 331

Fitzgerald, F. Scott, *The Great Gatsby*, 46

Flagg, Barbara, 242n18

Flatow, Nicole, 24

Fletcher, Bill, 299

Fletcher, Michael, 307–8

Florida: "stand your ground" law in, 23–25; use of term "cracker" in, 23. *See also* Zimmerman trial

fluidity: of identity in ethnic autobiographies, 84–85; of race, xxiv–xxv. *See also* hybrid fluidity

Ford, Gerald, 12, 262n23

Ford, Glen, 298

Forde-Mazrui, Kim, 271–72

foreclosure crisis, xxx, 30, 307

foreign policy, U.S.: Obama's, 333–34; Wright's critique of, 6, 299, 317

Foucault, Michel, xxxvii–xxxviii, 86

Fox News, 79

framing, 206–8; in 2008 Democratic primaries, 207–8, *216*, 216–18, *220*, 220–23

Frank, Barney, 31

Frank, David A., xxxiv, xxxv, 7, 234, 315, 321, 323, 324

Frank, Jerome D., and Julia B. Frank, *Persuasion and Healing*, 268

Fraser, Carly, 103, 316

Freedman, Estelle, 237

Fuentes, Carlos, 107

Fulani, Lenora, 198

functional blackness, 100–103

Funko, 56

Galton, Francis, 46

Game Change (Heilemann and Halperin), xv

Gardetto, Darleine, 207

Garfield, Bob, 207

Gasper, Kevin, 24

Gates, Henry Louis, Jr., 262n30, 300, 304, 310n4

gay communities: as postcolonial, 134; white privilege in, 137

gay marriage, Obama's position on, 255–56

gender, in the media, 206–7

gender hierarchy: in black families, 125–27; of sons vs. daughters, 256, 257

genealogy, 11–13; of Michelle Obama, 6, 12–13, 168, 189, 320; of Obama, 11–13, 119

General Motors, 334

"Generation Gap" frame, 220, 220–21, 223, 224n9

Generation Mix, 92, 112n6

genetics, 35; of race, 35–36, 89–90, 199–200; of skin color, 46–47, 89–90

Gennep, Arnold Van, *Les Rites de Passage*, 113n30

Gettysburg Address (Lincoln), ix, 269

Gibbs, Nancy, 193–94

Gibbs, Robert, 304

Giffords, Gabrielle, xiii, 75, 76

Gilroy, Paul, xxv, 111n2

Gines, Kathryn T., 158

Giroux, Henry A., 291

Givhan, Robin, 201

Glaude, Eddie, 315

Gone with the Wind, 185

Good Black Man stereotype, 226, 231; Obama as, 226, 234–37, 281

Goodman, Andrew, 285

Good Morning America, 25

Gordon, Ed, 16
Gore, Al, 270
government, as agent of change, 274–75
Grady, Abe, 12
Gramsci, Antonio, 19
Grant, Madison, *The Passing of the Great Race*, 46
Great Chain of Being, 162
Great Gatsby, The (Fitzgerald), 46
Great Recession of 2007–2009, 30, 301–2, 307–8
Greece, ancient, 106
Green, Christina, 75
Gresson, Aaron David, III, 282
Grutter v. Bollinger, xxii–xxiii
Guantanamo Bay detention camp, 73, 332–33
Guess Who's Coming to Dinner, 288
Guinier, Lani, 282, 301
Gulati, Mitu, 241n4
gun control, 262n33
gun-rights activists, 331
gun violence: Obama on, 32, 75–77; at Sandy Hook, 262n33. *See also* Tucson shooting
Guy, John, 22
Gyekye, Kwame, 150

Hagee, John, 235–36
hair, of Obama, 257–58
Hale, Dorothy J., 84, 104
Halewood, Pater, 158–59
Hall, Stuart, 111n2
Halperin, Mark, 40n31; *Game Change*, xv
Han, Lori Cox, 256
Haney López, Ian, 27
Hannaham, James, 55
Haraway, Donna, 51; "Cyborg Manifesto," 111n1
Harlan, J., 230
Harris, Cheryl, 137
Harris, Fredrick, 314
Harris, Patricia, 20
Harris-Perry, Melissa, 187–88, 193, 197

Hart, Peter, 207
Hart-Celler Act of 1965. *See* Immigration and Nationality Act
Hartman, Saidiya, 120
Hartsock, Nancy, 111n1
Harvard Law School: Michelle Obama at, 191; Obama at, 63
hate groups, 29
Hawai'i: birth of Obama in, 53, 96; childhood of Obama in, 8, 53, 86, 87, 97–98, 122, 250; population of, xii; Obama's birth certificate in, 28–29; Pacific Islander Americans of, 97
healthcare: death panels in, xii–xiii; disparities for women of color, 198; undocumented immigrants in, 31
hegemonic masculinity, 232–33, 236–38, 242n20
hegemony, white, 19–20
Heilemann, John, 40n31; *Game Change*, xv
Heller, Dean, 333
Heredity of Skin Color in Negro-White Crosses (Davenport), 46–47
hermeneutics, 268
Hernandez, Daniel, 76
Hernandez, Tanya, 95
Herring, Cedric, 18
herstory, of black women, 178
Hertel, Bradley R., 17–18
heteroglossia, 103–4
heteronormativity, of Obama, 237, 242n28
Hewitt, Hugh, 192
Heyse, Amy L., xxxv–xxxvi, 36n2
hierarchies: in European epistemology, 155; within identities, 229; within masculinities, 229; of masculinity and femininity, 232, 237, 242n18. *See also* gender hierarchy; racial hierarchies
high school dropout rates, xiii–xiv
hijab, 74
Hill, John Bernard, *The First Black President*, xvi
Hill, Marc Lamont, 306–7
Hill, Rickey, 322

Hillman, James, 284
Hispanic Americans: skin color of, 38n18; as white, xxii, 21, 38n18. *See also* Latinas/os
historically black colleges and universities (HBCU), 192
Hitler, Adolf, 46, 236
Hochschild, Jennifer L., 16
Holder, Eric, 26, 305–6
Hollinger, David A., x, 88; *Postethnic America*, 173
homeownership: black rates of, xiv; foreclosure crisis and, xxx, 30, 307; subprime mortgages in, xxx–xxxi
hooks, bell, 140
hope, in DNC speech, 273, 277–78, 282
"Hope" poster (Fairey), 41, 57–58
Houghton, Katharine, 288
household wealth, racial differences in, xxi, xxiii, 323
Hughes, Michael, 17–18
Hughey, Matthew, *The Obamas and a (Post) Racial America?*, xviii
Human Genome Project (HGP), 199–200
human rights, Obama on, 74
humans: and genes shared by all, 35; history of migration of, 35; origins in Africa, 35, 200
humor: Ananse's use of, 69, 80, 81; Obama's use of, 78–82, 123
Hunter, Jane Edna, 187
Huntsman, Jon, 79
hurricanes, 80, 304–5, 334
Hussein, Saddam, 79
Hutchinson, Darren Lenard, 24, 33
hybrid degeneracy, 45–46
hybrid fixity, 92; in multiracial identity, 84, 92; in multiracial movement, 88–89, 92–95; Obama's rejection of, 88–89; vs. hybrid fluidity, 84
hybrid fluidity: cosmopolitanism in, 85–86; multiraciality in, 85–86; Obama's self-identity as, 84–86, 88; vs. hybrid fixity, 84; in writings of Obama, 84–86

hybridity: essentialist, 88–89; of Obama, xxiv; and parallels with tricksters, 64; in population projections, xxv; as rooted in blackness, 9, 112n22; as "third space," 101–2, 112n26
hypocritical multiraciality, 34; and colorblind racism, 34; contrasted with critical multiraciality, 34

identification, 317; in DNC speech, 276–77; in Philadelphia speech, 317–21, 328
identity: fluidity of, 84–85; as fragmented, 84, 111n1; hierarchies within, 229; language in, 103–5; performance of, 228, 239; postcolonial, 134; self vs. attributed, 227–28; theories of, 225, 227–29
identity politics: Obama candidacy as challenge to, 167, 274; rise of, 270, 274
Ifa (deity), 67–68
Ifill, Gwen, 315; *The Breakthrough*, xv
"I Have a Dream" (King), 7
imaginary father, 121
immigrant rights movement, xxvii–xxviii
immigrants: black, 168–71; black unity with, xxv–xxviii; citizenship for, x, 333; deportations under Obama, 38n15; in end of race, xxii; in ethno-racial composition of population, x–xi; in healthcare reform, 31; legislation on, x–xi, xxvii; Obama as second-generation, xxiv, xxvi, 168–69, 173; Obama's policies on, 336; in postethnic vs. post-racial society, 168; poverty among, xxvii; quotas on, xxvii; racism against, xxviii; Republican policies on, 336, 337
Immigration and Nationality Act of 1965, x–xi, xxvii
implicit bias theory, 230
inaugural address (2008), 299–300
indentured servants, 3–4
Indonesia, childhood of Obama in, 8, 53, 86, 87, 97, 250
inegalitarianism, 17, 19
inner-city poverty, 289–90

Institute for Colored Youth, 200n2
intergenerational poverty, 290
International Olympic Committee (IOC), 302–4
Interracial Family Alliance (IFA), 91
interracial marriages and unions: anti-miscegenation laws on, 3–4, 9–10; and end of race, xxii, xxiv; and ethnic diversity of U.S., xii; in genealogical research, 11–13; increase in prevalence of, xi, xii; one-drop rule in, 3–4, 36n1; slaves in, 3–4, 45–46, 183–84; Supreme Court on, 4, 9–10, 42
intersectionality, 229; in critical race theory, 229; multiethnic individuals' experience of, 62–63; women's experience of, 178–79
invagination, 124–27
Invasion of the Body Snatchers, 95
Iowa, Obama's 2008 victory in, 298, 330
I-Pride, 91
Iraq, war in: vs. Afghanistan war, 72; Cairo speech on, 72–73; end of, 333
Irish Republican Army (IRA), xiii
Islam, Obama's knowledge about, 70–71. *See also* Muslims
Islamophobia, xiii
Israel, 72, 73
"Issue Avoidance" frame, *216*, 217

Jackson, Daryl, 164
Jackson, Harry R., 255–56
Jackson, Jesse: as antecedent to Obama's Philadelphia speech, 7, 313; as Bad Black Man, 281; black community in campaigns of, 110; blackness of, 288, 330; Clinton's "Sister Souljah strategy" and, 270; color line in campaign of, 167; in 1984 election, 7, 313; in 1988 election, 7, 313; vs. Obama as post-racial candidate, 133; Obama distancing from, 7, 37n4; Sharpton on, 279
Jackson, Michael, 58
Jacobson, Matthew Frye, 278

Jailbreak Toys, 56
Jamaica, 140–42, 146nn14–15
James, Joy, 158
James, Lebron, 162
Jealous, Ben, 37n5
Jeantel, Rachel, 22–23
Jefferson, Thomas, 273
Jefferson-Frazier, Rose, 269
Jeffries, Michael P., 37n10
Jeter, Mildred, 10
Jet magazine, 254, 255
"Jezebel" stereotype of black women, 179, 181, 184, 185
Jim Crow segregation. *See* racial segregation
Jindal, Bobby, 131n2
John, Mary, 146n8
Johnson, Lyndon B.: children of, 262n23; as distant cousin of Obama, 12; immigration legislation under, x–xi; legacy of, 270, 275; War on Poverty by, 252, 270
Johnston, Marc P., 5
jokester, Obama as, 78–82
Jolivétte, Andrew J., *Obama and the Biracial Factor*, xiv
Jones, Felicia, 197
Jones, Mack, 149
Jones, Terry, 207
Jones, Van, 301
Jordan, Barbara, 37n6
"Joshua Generation," 289, 309n3
Journal of Black Studies, xiv–xv
jus sanguinis, 332–33
jus soli, 332–33
Justice, Department of (DOJ): Holder's 2009 speech, 305–6; on racism at Valley Swim Club, 164; in Zimmerman case, 25–26, 308

Kambon, Kobi, 152, 153, 155–56
Kames, Henry H., 162
Kang, Jerry, 230
Kant, Immanuel, *Perpetual Peace*, 106
Katrina, Hurricane, 80, 304–5, 334

Keith, Verna, 18
Kelley, Matt, 91
Kennedy, Caroline, 256, 262n23
Kennedy, John F., 256, 262n23, 326
Kennedy, John F., Jr., 256, 262n23
Kennedy, Robert, 270
Kenya: as British colony, 119, 131n5; ethnicity in, 118; Obama in favor of, 320–21; Obama Sr. from, 118–20
Kerry, John, xxix, 271
Keys, Alicia, 195
Kimmel, Michael S., 233, 242n20
Kinder, Donald, 206, 224n1
King, Don, 163
King, Martin Luther, Jr.: assassination of, 270; black women influenced by, 187; in Chicago, 303; and colorblindness, 230; on guaranteed income, 290; "I Have a Dream," 7; on mobilization of apolitical individuals, xxxvi–xxxvii; Obama compared to, 276–77; on overt vs. covert racism, 294–95; Sharpton compared to, 280; on triple evils, 291; 2008 anniversary of assassination of, 8; *Where Do We Go From Here?*, xxxvii; Wright and, xxix
King, Peter, xiii
King Kong, 162
Kirk, Ron, 254
Kitwana, Bakari, xvii
Klein, Joe, 53
Klein, Naomi, 110–11
Knox, Robert, 162
Korean Americans, 171
Kravitz, Lenny, 49
Kristof, Nicholas, 220

Lacan, Jacques, 117–18, 120, 121, 131n1, 131n6
LaCapra, Dominick, 268
Laing, Sandra, 90, 112n4
Land, Roderic R., 157–58
Latin America: multiracial matrix in, 95; white supremacy in colonies, 43

Latinas/os: black candidates supported by, xxvi, xxvii; on black identity of Obama, xxvi, 14; collective identity of, 48; conflation with blacks, 170; current population of, xii; economic challenges facing, 171; as ethno-racial group, 171; future population of, xxv–xxvi; Great Recession's impact on, 30, 302, 308; history of prejudice against, 171; in postethnic vs. post-racial society, 168; poverty rates among, 302; quotas on immigration by, xxvii; support for Obama among, xxvi–xxvii; in 2008 election, xxvi–xxvii, 14; in 2012 election, 15, 336; as white, 39n21
lazy stereotype of blacks, 325
leadership style, 233–34, 237
Lee, Robert E., 12
Lee, Sharon M., xxv
legislation: anti-miscegenation, 3–4, 9–10; immigration, x–xi, xxvii
Leibovich, Mark, 201
Leksander, Susan, 64–65, 66
lesbian communities: as postcolonial, 134; white privilege in, 137
Let's Move!, 195
Lewis, John, 31
Limbaugh, Rush, 12, 260n4
liminality, 9, 105, 113n30
Lincoln, Abraham: on "better angels of our nature," 275, 284; debates with Douglas, 269; Gettysburg Address, ix, 269; in Obama's 2004 DNC speech, 273; Obama's image mixed with image of, 59; in Sharpton's 2004 DNC speech, 271
linguistic identity, 103–5
linguistic subject, Obama as, 103–5
Lion King, The, 78–79
Lipsitz, George, 4, 137
Livingston, Robert W., 18
Los Angeles, 2006 demonstrations, xxvii–xxviii
Los Angeles Times, 329
Loughner, Jared Lee, xiii

Loving, Richard, 10
Loving v. Virginia, 4, 9–10, 42
Low, Setha, 142
loyalty, racial, 231, 235
Luo people, 117, 118, 121, 122
Lynch, Deborah, 303
lynching, xiii, 28, 187, 326

Mackey, Nathaniel, 124
Madison, James, 12
Mad magazine, 59
magazine covers: Michelle Obama on, 56, 60, 193, 196; Obama on, 56–57, 59–60, 193
"Magical Negro" trope, 245, 260n4
Maisch, Patricia, 76
majority-minority party, Democratic Party as, 29
majority-minority populations, xii, xxii
male gaze, 51
"Mammy" stereotype of black women, 181, 184–85
Mansbridge, Jane, 204
Mantei, Richard, 22
Marable, Manning, xvi, 314, 321; *Barack Obama and African American Empowerment*, xvii
Marin, Carol, 225
marriage: Christian, 183–84; interracial, 255–56
marriage, of Barack and Michelle Obama: co-parenting in, 253–54; masculinity of Barack in, 237; Michelle's career after, 191; in racial identity of Barack, 56, 100, 251
Marshall, Thurgood, 20
Martin, Trayvon: "cracker" epithet used by, 22–23; description of shooting of, 20–21; DOJ investigation into shooting of, 25–26, 308; Obama's response to death of, 32–33, 244, 258–59, 308. *See also* Zimmerman trial
masculine anxiety, 232

Masculinities and the Law (Cooper and McGinley), 232
masculinities studies, 231–33; and femininity of Obama, 225, 232, 233, 237–38; tenets of, 228–29, 232–33
masculinity, 227; of black men, 226, 231, 234–36; hegemonic, 232–33, 236–38, 242n20; hierarchies of, 229, 237, 242n18; multiple identities in, 229; norms of, 232–33; of Obama, 226, 237–38; Obama's impact on perceptions of, 239–40; performance of, 228, 232–33, 236, 238–39; social construction of, 228–29, 230
masses: in Obama's speeches, 64; in success of civil rights movement, xxxvii, xli–xlii
Massey, Douglas S., 169
Masters, Isabell, 198
matriarchy, black, 125–26
Matthews, Chris, 40n33
MAVIN, 9, 91, 92
Mazama, Ama, 315
Mboya, Tom, 119
McCain, John: black ancestors of, 12, 38n12; citizenship of, 131n4, 332–33; masculine leadership of, 234; on Obama's masculinity, 233; on "stand your ground" laws, 32; and subprime mortgage crisis, xxxi; ties to Hagee, 235–36; white voters support, 14. *See also* election of 2008
McCarren-Walter Act of 1952, x
McClintock, Anne, 145n5
McDaniel, Hattie, 185
McGinley, Ann C., 239; *Masculinities and the Law*, 232
McIntosh, Peggy, 143
McKinney, Cynthia, 198
McMahon, Linda, 334
McPhail, Mark Lawrence, xxxiv, xxxv, 7, 234, 255, 315, 321, 323, 324
McPhail, Roger, 255
McTaggart, Lynne, *The Power of Intention*, 83n8
Mead, Nicole L., 33

media coverage: of children of presidents, 256; on femininity of Obama, 225, 227, 234–35; framing in, 206–8; of Hillary Clinton as First Lady, 207; lived reality of racism in, 161–63; of masculinity of black men, 226, 231; of Michelle Obama, 56, 60, 192–97; of Obama as father, 245, 246, 248; of Obama as senator, 53; of Philadelphia speech, 326–27; racist depictions of Obama in, xiii, 162, 193; of storms, Obama on, 80; of Zimmerman case and trial, 21. *See also* magazine covers

media coverage, of 2008 Democratic primaries, 201–24; on black identity of Obama, 54–55; conflict between descriptive and executive representation in, 204–6, 208, 222–24; descriptive representation of social groups in, 202–6; end of race predicted in, xxiii–xxiv; equal rights movements in, 208–11, *218–20*, 218–23; executive representation of national electorate in, 202–6; on femininity of Obama, 225, 227; framing in, 207–8, *216*, 216–18, *220*, 220–23; policy issues in, 208–18, *212–16*, 222; on outsider status of candidates, 202–3, 222; on race of voters, xxiii–xxiv

mediator, Obama as, 70, 73, 81–82

men: absent sons and, 256–59; as breadwinners, 253–54. *See also* black men

Mendel, Gregor, 46

Mendoza Stickmon, Janet C., xxxiv

Menexenus (Plato), 267, 279

Merkel, Angela, 334

Messerschmidt, James, 229

mestizos: "21st-century," xxvi; in colonial Mexico, 45

metaracism, 20

metrosexual style, 228, 241n5

Mexico: *casta* paintings, 41, 42–45; on immigration from, xxvii; regulation of religious art, 43

middle class, 323

Millennials: diversity of, 14; self-identified as multiracial, xi; support for Obama among, xii, 14

Milloy, Courtland, 234, 236

Mills, Charles W., xxxviii, 27, 267

Milton Bradley color wheel, 46–47

minister, Obama as, 75–77, 81–82

minorities, 170; as majority in Democratic Party, 29; in populations, xii, xxii

Minority Rights Revolution, The (Skrentny), 170

minstrelsy, 59

Minutemen Civil Defense Core, 143

misogyny, 179–80, 186

Mitchell, Charlene, 198

Molpus, Richard, 285

monoraciality: critique of, 5–6; and monological thinking, 5; one-drop rule in, 5

Montgomery Bus Boycott, xli–xlii

Moorehead, Monica, 198

Moraga, Cherrie, xxvi

moral cosmopolitanism, 106–8

morality, of interracial unions in slavery, 183–84

"More Perfect Union, A." *See* Philadelphia speech by Obama

More Than Black (Daniel), 91, 113n30

Morning Edition, 139

Morph 2.0 software, 41, 49, 50

Morton, Samuel, 45

"Moses Generation," 289, 309n3

Moten, Fred, 124

mothers, 198, 289

MoveOn.org, 26

Moynihan, Daniel Patrick, 125–27, 252

Ms. magazine, 240

mulattoes: in colonial Mexico, 45; identification of, 45–46

multiculturalism, 19

Multidimensional Masculinities Theory, 232

multiethnic individuals, 82n1; identities of, 62, 97; vs. multiracial individuals, 82n1; Pacific Islander Americans as, 97; tricksters and, 62–63

multiple identities: in critical race theory and masculinities studies, 229; of multiethnic individuals, 62, 97; of women, 178–79
Multiracial Americans of Southern California (MASC), 91
multiracial background of Obama: in DNC speech, 53, 272; experience of, 8, 63–64, 65–66, 81, 103–5, 272; genealogical research on, 11–13; Obama's comfort with, 11, 87–88; Obama's de-emphasis of Africa in, 320–21; overview of, 53, 87–88, 96–100, 329; political method as product of, 53; in racial identity of Obama, 8–9, 86–87, 93, 101–2, 250; vs. typical black American experience, 54–55, 84, 112n27
Multiracial Experience, The (Root), 91
multiracial identity, 92; in end of race, xxii; hybrid fixity in, 84, 92; liminality of, 9; Obama's lack of self-identification with, 9, 10, 87, 92–96; one-drop rule and, 10; rise of post–civil rights era, 10
multiracial individuals: ambiguity of, 48–49, 52; average age of, xi; on black self-identity of Obama, 9, 37n10; census options for, xi, xxiv, 10, 92; current population of, xi–xii, 11; future population of, xxv–xxvi; genealogical research on, 11–13; vs. multiethnic individuals, 82n1; psychosynthesis on, 64–66, 82
multiraciality: critical, 34–36; in hybrid fluidity, 85–86; hypocritical, 34; in "more perfect union," ix; Philadelphia speech on, 6; ubiquity of, 11–13, 35–36
multiracial movement, 91–96; hybrid fixity in, 88–89, 92–95; Obama's rejection of, 88–89, 92–93; organizations associated with, 91–92
Mulvey, Laura, 51
music, stereotypes of black women in, 199
Muslims: beliefs about Obama as, 110, 331–32; racial profiling of, xxiii; U.S. population of, 71; and women, 74

Muslim world: history of U.S. and, 70–75; Obama on misconceptions about, 70–75, 81; sources of tension between U.S. and, 72–74; 2008 inaugural address on, 300
"mutt," Obama as self-described, 11, 38n11, 87, 104
Mutua, Athena, 228, 232–33, 240
Myers, Linda James, 151–52, 156–57

Nadal, Kevin L., 5
Nakashima, Cynthia L., 51–52
Name-of-the-Father, 120–21, 131n6
Nash, Gary, 42
National Association for the Advancement of Colored People (NAACP): Obama administration's work with, 37n5; Obama speech, 8; scope of, 39n25; on Zimmerman, 25–26
National Association of Colored Women (NACW), 187
National Council of Negro Women, 187
National Federation of Afro-American Women, 187
National Press Club, speech by Obama at, 8
National Public Radio, 139, 315
National Review, 193, 255
National Urban League, 159, 269
Native Americans: in American Revolution, 299; conflation with blacks, 170; poverty among, 310n5
Nava, Mica, *Cultural Cosmopolitanism*, 106–7
nega, 142, 146n15
"Negro-White Families" (Day), 250
Nel, Philip, 260n7
Nelson, Debra, 22
Nelson, Thomas, 224n1
neo-accommodationist approach to rhetoric, 314–15
neoliberalism, 270
neoliberal racism, 291–92
"New Beginning, A." *See* Cairo speech by Obama

New Era Club, 187
New Left, 270
Newman, Alfred E., 59
New Mexico, population of, xii
New Negro for a New Century, A (Washington), 249
New Orleans: Hurricane Katrina in, 80, 304–5, 334; Obama's visits to, 304–5
New Republic, The, xxii, 54, 272–73
New Right, rise of, 270
Newsweek, 194, 298
New York City: Obama's move to, 99–100; police in, 163–64, 258; race of teachers in, 160
New York Daily News, 102
New Yorker, 31–32, 60, 193, 291
New York Magazine, 56
New York Police Department (NYPD), 163–64, 258
New York Post, xiii, 161–62, 234
New York Times: on end of race, xxii; on Michelle Obama, 196; on Obama in New Orleans, 304, 305; on Philadelphia speech, 326; on 2008 Democratic primaries, 201, 206, 211, 217, 220
New York Times magazine, 248
Nixon, Richard, 37n6, 252, 262n23, 290
Nobel Peace Prize lecture by Obama (2009), 109
Nobles, Wade, 148–49
nommo, 101
norm: of masculinity, 232–33; whiteness as, 16, 138, 162
Northeastern Federation of Women's Clubs, 187
Nott, Josiah, 45
nuclear weapons, 72
Nunez, Juan, 164
nurturing father: emergence of, 253; Obama as, 245–46, 254
Nyong'o, Tavia, xxxiv–xxxv

Obama, Barack: action figures, 56; birth of, 53, 96, 119, 131n5; calmness, 226, 236–37, 238, 240; conservatives' use of name, xxiii; as first post-racial president, 117, 133, 167, 298–300, 315–16; as first woman president, 225, 227, 234; linguistic origins of name, 117, 121–23; Michelle Obama on, 123, 251; middle name Hussein, xxiii, 79; nickname Barry, 122–23; pragmatism of, 109–10; sense of humor about name, 79, 123; openness to negotiation, 226, 238; life story of, 53, 87–88, 96–100; psychoanalytic theory on name, 120–27; as senator, 53, 54; on torture, 73
Obama, Barack Hussein, Sr. (father), 118–23; blackness of, 8, 96; correspondence with Obama, 97, 98; death of, 97, 120–21; education of, 188; as immigrant, 118–19; as "Kenyan father," 118–20; last visit with Obama, 97; marriage to Dunham, 53, 88, 96; and Obama as second-generation immigrant, xxiv, xxvi, 168–69, 173; Obama on racial identity, 96, 121; other marriages of, 96
Obama, Malia (daughter), 256–57; age of, 256; co-parenting of, 253–54; lack of sons and, 256–59; photographs with Obama, 245–46, 246; skin tone of, 251, 261n13; at 2008 DNC, 252; in White House, 256–57
Obama, Michelle (wife), 188–200; advocacy as First Lady, 178, 194–96; assertiveness of, 192–94; birth of, 189; on black identity of Obama, 56, 100, 251; career of, 178, 191, 192, 254; childhood of, 188, 189–90, 192; co-parenting style of, 253–54; education of, 190–91, 192; fist-bumps with Obama, 59–60, 193, 331; genealogy of, 6, 12–13, 168, 189, 320; impact on black girls and women, 189, 194–97; and masculinity of Obama, 237; media coverage of, 56, 60, 192–97; on Obama as father, 244, 251, 254; on Obama's name, 123, 251; parents of, 188, 189–90; performance of identity by,

239; Philadelphia speech on family of, 6, 320; physical appearance of, critics of, 331; public perceptions of, 191–94, 195–96; self-image of, 191, 196–97; and "State of the Black Union" symposium, 37n9; visual representations of, 56, 60, 192–93; working-class background of, 188, 189–90

Obama, Sasha (daughter), 256–57; age of, 256; co-parenting of, 253–54; lack of sons and, 256–59; photographs with Obama, 245–46, 246; skin tone of, 251, 261n13; at 2008 DNC, 252; in White House, 256–57

Obama and the Biracial Factor (Jolivétte), xiv

"Obama as Symbol" frame, 220, 221, 223, 224n9

Obama era, 147–48, 165

Obama phenomenon: debate over meaning, x, xxxvi; journalistic literature on, xv; origins before presidency, xv, 312, 329–30; scholarship on, ix–x, xiv–xvii

"Obama Post-Race" frame, 220, 220–21, 223

Obamas and a (Post) Racial America?, The (Hughey and Parks), xviii

Obama's Race (Tesler and Sears), xvi

Obama's War (Woodward), xv

"Obama Vague/Unassertive" frame, 216, 217

Oberlin College, 186, 200n2

objectivity, in European epistemology, 152–53

Occidental College, 53, 98–99

O'Connor, Sandra Day, xxii–xxiii

Ogletree, Charles, 191

Olbrechts-Tyteca, Lucie, 267

Old Left, failure of, 270

Olurun (deity), 68

Omi, Michael, 19; *Racial Formation in the United States*, 89, 90

One America in the 21st Century, 170

one-drop rule, 3–6; and black women, 199; current status of, 4–5, 168; decline of, 10, 19, 95, 168; election of Obama and, 6; embraced by blacks, 5; in multiracial identity formation, 10; in preservation of slavery, 4, 46; and racial identity of Obama, 95; in unions between blacks and other groups of color, 36n1

On the Real Side (Watkins), 78–79

ontology, 151; in worldviews, 149, 150–51

O'Reilly, Bill, 337

Orlando Sentinel, 233–34

Ossorio, Pilar, 89–90

"other," Obama as: in 2008 and 2012 elections, 331–33; white anxiety about, 110–11; white fear of, 139

"other black," 86–89, 111n2, 113n28; vs. essentialist notions of blackness, 85; Obama as, 86–87, 100–101, 111n2, 113n28

Our Nig (Wilson), 128

outsiders: demographic, 202, 203, 204–5; descriptive and executive representation by, 204–5, 222; media coverage of Obama and Clinton as, 202–3; Obama on experience as, 94; Washington, 203

Pabst, Naomi, 101, 102–3

Pacific Islander Americans, 97, 172

Palestinians, 72, 73

Palin, Sarah, 239; as cousin of Obama, 12

parents of Obama, 117–18; educational background, 188; marriage, 53, 88, 96; in Philadelphia speech, 6; and racial identity of Obama, 8–9, 88, 96. *See also* Dunham, Stanley Ann; Obama, Barack Hussein, Sr.

Paris Exhibition of 1900, 249

Parks, Gregory S., *The Obamas and a (Post) Racial America?*, xviii

partus sequitur ventrem, 126–27, 128

Pascale, Celine Marie, 310n5

Passel, Jeffrey S., xxv

passing as white, 12, 89–90

Passing of the Great Race, The (Grant), 46

Paste magazine, 57

"past" racism, 294–96, 298–99, 309n3

Patillo-McCoy, Mary, 323

Patrick, Deval, 314
Patriot Freedom Alliance, 28
patronymic, 123–26
Patterson, Orlando, xxii
Paul, Ron, 333
Pawlenty, Tim, 79
pay equity, as policy issue in 2008 election, 208–9, 212, 213
Pearce, Nicholas A., 18
Pelton, Robert, 66–68, 69; *The Trickster of West Africa*, 80
people of color, use of term, 135, 146n9
Perelman, Chaïm, 267
performative theory of identities, 227–28
Perpetual Peace (Kant), 106
Persuasion and Healing (Frank and Frank), 268
Pew Research Center, xi, 26, 169
phenotypes: biases based on, 18, 9–20; of Obama, 96. See also physical appearance
Philadelphia, Jacob, 257–58
Philadelphia speech by Obama (2008), 311–28; on affirmative action, xxix; antecedents and precursors to, 7, 37n6, 313–15; bargaining vs. challenging tactics in, 7–8; on black families, 254, 325; consilience in, 7; on context for Wright's remarks, 6–7, 8, 318–19; on economy, xxx; founding documents in, 7, 322; on history and legacy of racism, 172, 298–99, 309n3, 312, 319, 321–24; identification strategy in, 317–21, 328; and Latino support for Obama, xxvi; media reactions to, 326–27; on Michelle Obama's genealogy, 6, 320; on multiraciality, 6; pragmatism of, 109–10; racial stereotypes in, 312, 324–27; on relationship with Wright, 317–19; as response to political-personal crisis, 36n2, 312–16, 327; strategic failures of post-racial rhetoric of, 37n2, 312, 320–28; strategic successes in post-racial rhetoric of, 312,
316–20; vagueness of, xxix; on white resentment, xxix, 6–7, 110, 172, 323, 324
Philippines, immigrants from, 171
Phillis Wheatley clubs and homes, 187
philosophical assumptions, of worldview, 149, 150–53
photographs: absent figures in, 247; of black families, 249–50; of Obama family, *245*, 245–49, *246*, 256–58, 261n9
physical appearance: biases based on, 18, 19–20; black hair in, 257–58; of Michelle Obama, 331; of multiracial individuals, 48–49, 52; racial traits in, 35–36. *See also* skin color
Pitkin, Hannah, 203
Pitt, Brad, 12
Plato, *Menexenus*, 267, 279
Plessy doctrine, 187
pluralism: cultural, 156–57; in cultural cosmopolitanism, 106; egalitarian, *17*, 38n17; inegalitarian, *17*, 19
Poitier, Sidney, 288
police: and Latinos as white, 39n21; in lived reality of blacks, 163–64; "stop and frisk" practices of, 258; in Trayvon Martin shooting, 21
political candidates: outsider, 202–3; skin color of, 33; white, 133, 138; women, 206–7
political cosmopolitanism, 106–8
political identity of Obama, fatherhood in, 246–47, 248–49
political parties, diversity of, 29
political-personal crisis, 313; Philadelphia speech on, 36n2, 312–16, 327
politics: and speaking on race, xxv, xxviii–xxxi; colorblindness in, xli; lack of civility in, xiii, 29; of post-civil rights era, 291–92; racial diplomacy in, 7–8
popular culture: colorblind racism in, 42; stereotypes of black women in, 179, 185–86, 199; visual representations of multiracial individuals in, 42

population, U.S.: future of ethno-racial, xxii, xxv–xxvi; immigrants in, x–xi; majority-minority, xii, xxii; multiracial, xi–xii; "pure" vs. mixed, xxv–xxvi; recent changes in ethno-racial, x–xi

Porterfield, Jason, *The Election of Barack Obama*, xvii

post–civil rights era, 291–92; African American firsts in, 19–20; multiracial identity in, 10; racial politics of, 291–92; racism in, xii–xiii, 19, 290, 291–92; rhetoric in DNC speech, 265; selective nature of racial integration in, 18–19; structural inequalities after, xiii–xiv, 159–65, 309; white domination in, 19

postcolonial as term: debate over meaning and use of, 134, 145nn5–7; emergence of, 144; progress in concept of, 134, 145n5; vs. postcolonial, 144n3; vs. postmodern, 144n3; vs. post-racial, 134–37, 144

Postethnic America (Hollinger), 173

postethnic society, 168, 173

post-feminist society, 220, 221

postmodern, vs. postcolonial, 144n3

post-racial as term, 133–44; common perception of meaning of, 40n33; current usages of, 158–59; differences in understanding of, 133; geographic element of, 134–35; popularity of, 157; vs. postcolonial, 134–37, 144; vs. postethnic, 168; vs. post-racist, 158; as post-white, 158; white fear and, 139–43; white privilege in discussions of, 133–34, 137–39, 142–44

post-racial rhetoric: black candidates' use of, 314–15; critics of, 315–16; in 2008 Democratic primaries, 220–21; identification strategy in, 317–21, 328; Obama's rejection of, 27; in Philadelphia speech, 37n2, 312, 316–28

post-racial society: arrival of, 27, 60, 158, 259, 287, 330–31; critical multiraciality in, 35; multiracial identity in, 34–35; vs. postethnic society, 168

post-racism: popularity of, 157; vs. post-racial, 158

post-racist America, xxi–xxxi, 147–65; culture and worldview in, 147–54, 165; epistemological basis of racism and, 154–57, 165; lived reality of racism and, 147, 157, 159–65; problems with terminology and, 157–59; white support for Obama and, 287–93, 306–7

poverty: affirmative action based on, xxix; among black women, 179, 181–82, 198; as policy issue in 2008 election, 208–9, 212; among immigrants, xxvii; Obama on causes of, 289–90; racial differences in rates of, 302, 307; single mothers in, 198, 289; war on, 252, 270

Powell, Colin, 20

power, blacks in, 139–40

Power of Intention, The (McTaggart), 83n8

Preacher and the Politician, The (Walker and Smither), xvi

"President's Agenda and the African American Community, The," 30

President's Fatherhood Initiative, 252

Price, Melanye, 87

primates, 161–62

"Princeton-Educated Blacks and the Black Community" (Obama), 190–91

Princeton University, Michelle Obama at, 190–91

prison system: light- vs. dark-skinned blacks in, 16; number of black men in, xiv, xxi, 198, 309; sentencing for cocaine in, 30, 40n32

private sphere, interracial marriage in, 9–10

progress, in concept of postcolonialism, 134, 145n5

progressive movements in 1960s, 270

Project RACE, 91, 92

Promise, The (Alter), xv

psychoanalytic theory, on Obama's name, 120–27

psychology: Black, 149; ties between rhetoric and, 268, 284

psychosynthesis, 64–65; and multiraciality, 64–66, 82
Public Allies, 191
Public Broadcasting System (PBS), 310n4
public opinion: on ambiguity in racial identity, 42, 48, 49, 52, 60–61; on group-centric political issues, 208; on Zimmerman trial, 26
public schools: black teachers in, 160–61; in Chicago, 303, 304–5; in New Orleans, 305; racial segregation in, 160, 187; urban, 208–9, 212, 214
public service, Michelle Obama's work in, 191
public sphere, interracial marriage in, 9–10
Punch, John, 13

Qaeda, al-, 193
quadroon, 45
Quayson, Ato, 144n3, 145n7
Queens College, 169

race: biology of, 89–90, 199–200; blackness as paradigmatic of, 138; choice in, xxiv–xxv, 3, 167, 227–28; claims about end of, xxi–xxxi, 147; in definition of ethnicity, 82n1; fluidity of, xxiv–xxv; in framing in media, 207; genetics of, 35–36, 89–90, 199–200; Latinos as separate, 171; lived reality of, 147, 157, 159–65; origins of concept, xxi, 89; scholarship on, xxxviii–xxxix; social construction of, 157, 159, 228–29, 230; social inequalities based on, 19; at social level, 89, 90–91
race-affirming, 235, 236
"race card," 31, 207
race consciousness, in Bad Black Man stereotype, 231, 234
race-distancing, 231, 234–35
racelessness: in DNC speech, 265, 267, 281–82, 315; of multiracial individuals, 60; of Obama, xxvi; whiteness as, 133, 136, 138

race-neutrality of Obama: in bargaining tactic, 7–8, 314; critics of, 30; in Philadelphia speech, 7; and post-racial fantasy, 27; in response to Joe Wilson's outburst, 30–31; in 2008 election, 6, 31; white anxiety in spite of, 110
race uplift, 177, 187
"Race v. Gender" frame, 220, 221
racial and ethnic diversity, in U.S.: future of, xxii, xxv–xxvi; of Millennials, 14; rise of, xi–xii; of teachers, lack of, 160–61; at 2008 and 2012 national conventions, 29
racial capital, 19–20
racial contract, 27; in Obama's 2004 DNC speech, 267, 279, 281–83; in Sharpton's 2004 DNC speech, 270, 280, 281; vs. social contract, 27, 267
racial cowardice, 305–6, 309
racial diplomacy, in politics, 7–8
racial divide, Obama's ability to bridge, 15, 26–27, 53, 317
racial epithets: "cracker" as, 22–23; in protests against Congress, 31
racial essentialism, 35, 85
Racial Formation in the United States (Omi and Winant), 89, 90
racial formation theory, 89; origins of, 89. *See also* racial identity
racial hierarchies: in *casta* paintings, 43–45; speaking out against in politics, xxv, xxviii–xxxi
racial identity: choice in, xxiv–xxv, 3, 167, 227–28; creation of collective, 47–48; one-drop rule in, 3–6, 10; public acceptance of, 42, 48, 49, 52, 60–61; of siblings of Obama, 87–88, 96. *See also* black identity; multiracial identity; white identity
racial identity of Obama: Asian American views on, xxvi, 14; black critics of, 54–55, 102; as "black enough," xxiii, 6, 55, 64, 234; black views on, 14, 38n13; in census, 9, 92, 251, 261n12; as composite, 84, 86, 93, 94, 97, 103; cosmopolitanism

in, 86–87, 88–89, 101, 105–9, 111n2; *Dreams from My Father* on, 90, 93, 94, 96, 97; formation of, 90, 96–100, 103; as fragmented vs. unitary, 84; framing in media of, 207–8; functional blackness of, 100–103; hybrid fluidity of, 84–86, 88; inheritance of, 96, 121; lack of experience of slavery in, 54–55; in language, 100–105; Latino views on, xxvi, 14; marriage to Michelle in, 56, 100, 251; media coverage of, 54–55; multiracial background in, 8–9, 86–87, 93, 101–2, 250; multiracial individuals' views on, 9, 37n10; as "not all that black," 288–89; as not multiracial, 9, 10, 87, 92–96; as "other black," 86–87, 100–101, 111n2, 113n28; Pacific Islanders' identities and, 97; parents of Obama in, 8–9, 88, 96; performance of, 100–101, 228, 329–30; as reaction to racism, 95; self-awareness of, 85–87; self-identification as black, 9, 84, 86, 94–95, 250–51; self vs. attributed, 227–28; siblings on, 87–88, 96; as "too black," 6, 64, 234; views on, 14; white views on, 14, 288–89
racial ideology, white, 163–65
racial inequalities: claims about end of, xxiii, 306–7; as cumulative, 295; eradication of racism, 34; lived reality of, 159–65; Obama's accommodation of, 289–92; vs. economic inequalities, 171, 173. *See also* structural inequalities
racial integration: egalitarian vs. inegalitarian, 17, 19; of schools, 160, 187; selective nature of, 18–19
racialization, 48
racial justice: Obama on black responsibility for, 325; Obama's DNC speech and, 281, 282, 285; Obama's version of history of, 321–23; white support for Obama and, 288–93, 307
Racial Justice in the Age of Obama (Brooks), xvi
racial loyalty, 231, 235

Racially Mixed People in America (Root), 91
racial order, U.S.: anxieties underlying, 120; changes in and election of Obama, xxxix; racial contract in, 27; ternary, 91; white domination in, 19
racial profiling, 39n22; of black men, 240; of voters, xxiv; in war on terror, xxiii; in Zimmerman trial, 22, 23
racial purity: in colorblind racism, 42; one-drop rule in, 3, 5; in U.S. population, xxv–xxvi
racial reconciliation: Obama's 2004 DNC speech and, 265, 266, 276, 278–79, 282–86; rhetorical scholars' role in, 265; Sharpton's 2004 DNC speech and, 279–80
racial segregation: black women's experience of, 186–87; one-drop rule in, 4; as overt state-of-mind racism, 292; rhetoric on trauma of, 266–67, 268–69, 277–78; in schools, 160, 187; time between election of Obama and, 178; at swimming facilities, 164
racial spoils system, 19
racial traits, 35–36
racial transcendence: black candidates' use of, 110, 314; Obama's use of, 110, 315–16
racism, 322; anti-immigrant, xxviii; against black immigrants, 169–70; claims about end of, xxi–xxxi; colorblind, 34, 42; covert, 292–95; critical multiraciality against, 34; culture and worldview in, 147–57; cumulative effects of, 295–96; in depictions of Obama, xiii, 28, 162; epistemological basis of, 154–57, 165; eradication of, 34; European worldview in, 153, 154–57; lived reality of, 147, 157, 159–65; metaracism, 20; monoracism, 5; neoliberal, 291–92; new vs. old-fashioned, 29; Obama's accommodation of, 300–301; Obama's experiences with, 32, 108, 323; overt, 292, 293, 294; "past," 294–96, 298–99, 309n3; persistence of, xii–xiii, 19, 290, 291–92; Philadelphia

speech on, 172, 298–99, 309n3, 312, 319, 321–24; power of, 292–93, 306–7; in racial transcendence, 315; in Republican Party, 335; in response to election of Obama, xii–xiii; reverse, 19, 322; successful blacks as evidence of end of, 18–19, 135, 293–94, 296–98; in 2012 election, xii, xiii; unconscious, 18, 33, 163
"Radical Feminist" frame, 216, 217
Rangel, Charlie, 330
rap music, stereotypes of black women in, 199
Rawick, George P., xxxix
raza, 43
Reagan, Ronald, 262n23, 282, 337
reasonable doubt, 26, 39n26
"red phone" campaign advertisement, xxii
Reeve, Elspeth, 262n32
Reid, Harry, xv, 16, 102
religious art, in Mexico, 43
religious freedom, 72, 74
religious rhetoric, African American traditions of, 321
Remnick, David, 31–32, 60, 235, 236; *The Bridge*, xv
reparations: effects of racism and, 295–96; Obama's 2004 DNC speech and, 275; in Sharpton's 2004 DNC speech, 271–72, 280; white support for, 290
representation: by outsiders, 204–5; substantive, 203–4. *See also* descriptive representation; executive representation; visual representations
reproductive rights, 208–9, 211–12, 213
Republican National Convention (2008), 29
Republican National Convention (2012), xiii, 29
Republican Party: future of, 336–37; immigration policy of, 336, 337; racial composition of, 29, 337; racism in, 335; southern strategy of, 270, 282; and voter suppression, 15, 335–36
Responsible Fatherhood Initiative (RFI), 252

reverse racism: affirmative action as, 19; impossibility of, 322
rhetoric: African American religious traditions of, 321; black candidates' and, 313–15; of civil rights movement, 269–70, 277, 279; in management of traumas, 268; psychology and, 268, 284
rhetorical situation, 313; in Philadelphia speech, 312–16
rhetoric of Obama: colorblindness in, 235; "more perfect union" in, ix; power of, 66, 82; in racial identity, 100–105; racial transcendence in, 110, 315–16; strategic failures in, 320–28; use in speeches, 104–5. *See also* post-racial rhetoric
Rice, Condoleezza, 198
Richards, Dona, 151, 152
Riley, Russell L., 205
Riley, Steven F., xvii
Rising Tide of Color, The (Stoddard), 46
Rita, Hurricane, 80
Rites de Passage, Les (Gennep), 113n30
Robertson, Campbell, 305
Robinson, Craig, 189–90
Robinson, Fraser, III, 189–90
Robinson, Marian, 189–90
Rockquemore, Kerry Ann, 93
Roediger, David, x, 51
Rogers, John W., Jr., 276–77
Roll, John, xiii, 75
Rolling Stone, 27
Roman, John K., 25
Romney, George, 333, 338n7
Romney, Mitt: campaign money of, 334; citizenship of, 333, 338n7; foreign relations skills of, 334; Obama depicted as "other" by, 333; in Obama's White House Correspondents' Dinner speech, 79; on reasons for 2012 loss, 337; sons of, 256; weaknesses of, 333–35; white voters supporting, xii, 15. *See also* election of 2012
Roosevelt, Franklin Delano, 59, 270, 275
Root, Maria P. P.: *The Multiracial Experience*, 91; *Racially Mixed People in America*, 91

Rose, Charlie, 102
Rosenfeld, Steven, 23
Rove, Karl, 337
Rowe, Aimee Carrillo, 137
Ruffin, Josephine St. Pierre, 187
Ryan, Paul, 79

Saltsman, Chip, 260n4
same sex marriage, 255–56
Samuels, Allison, 194
Sandoval, Chela, 111n1
Sandy, Hurricane, 334
Sandy Hook shootings, 262n33
"Sapphire" stereotype of black women, 179, 181, 185, 186, 192–93
Scarborough, Joe, 237
Scheiber, Noam, 272–73
scholarship: differences in, xxxviii–xxxix; mixed-race studies in, 91; on Obama phenomenon, ix–x, xiv–xvii; on 2008 presidential election, xvi–xvii; white supremacy in, xxxviii
Schwarz, Bill, 261n9, 261n13
Schwerner, Michael, 285
Scott, David, 135–37, 144, 146n11
Scott, Rick, 22
Sears, David O., *Obama's Race*, xvi
Secret Service, 40n29, 193
security threats, against Obama, 29, 40n29, 193
self-awareness, Obama's sense of, 85–87, 93, 94
self-defense, in Zimmerman case, 21, 23–25
self-deportation, 336
self-discovery, for black women, 177, 187, 197–98, 199
self-help traditions, among black women, 177, 178, 186–87, 198
self-identity: vs. attributed identity, 227–28; as multiracial, xi; in one-drop rule, 3. *See also* identity
Selma, Alabama, Obama's speech in, 289
separation, in European epistemology, 154–55

September 11, 2001, attacks: and claims about end of race, xxiii; Obama on U.S. response to, 72–73; racial profiling after, xxiii
Serwer, Adam, 61n1
sexual assault: stereotypes of black women and, 179–80; of women slaves, 183–84, 185
sexuality, in stereotypes of black women, 179–80
sexual slavery, 182–84, 185
Sharpley-Whiting, Denean, xvi; *The Speech*, xvii
Sharpton, Al: as Bad Black Man, 234, 281; blackness of, 288; as challenger vs. bargainer, 55; color line in campaign of, 167; Obama's relationship with, 7, 37n4; race consciousness of, 234; on racist depictions of Obama, 162; on reparations, 271–72, 280; speech at 2004 DNC by, 265, 266–67, 268, 270–72, 278, 279–81, 286n3; in 2000 election, 270
Sherrod, Shirley, 109, 110
Shields, Dolphus T., 12
Shields, Melvina, 12
"Showing Us Sexism" frame, *220, 221*
siblings of Obama, 96, 97; racial identity of, 87–88, 96
Sidley Austin, 191
Sikhs, xxviii
"Silent Depression, The," 302
Sinclair-Chapman, Valeria, 87
single mothers, 198, 289
"Sister Souljah strategy," 270
60 Minutes, 332
skin color: biases regarding, 16–18, 19–20, 33, 38n18; in *casta* paintings, 44; genetics of, 46–47, 89–90; of Hispanics, 38n18; of Obama family, 251, 261n13
Skrentny, John D., *The Minority Rights Revolution*, 170
slavery, in U.S.: abolitionists on, 184, 186, 269; absolute authority doctrine in, 182, 184; black women's legacy of, 181–86;

and election of Obama of, 60; experience of, 54–55, 102; legalization of, 13; origins of, 182; *partus sequitur ventrem* doctrine in, 126–27, 128; preservation of, 4, 45–46; reparations for, 271–72, 275, 280, 290; rhetoric on trauma of, 266, 268–69, 277–78; slave resistance to, 182, 183; time between election of Obama and, 177–78; vs. Caribbean, 169
slaves: in American Revolution, 299; children of, 45–46, 126–27, 128, 182–83; descendants of, 168–71; gender hierarchy of, 125–27; in genealogy of Obama family, 6, 12–13, 119, 189, 320; in interracial unions, 3–4, 45–46, 183–84; owners' mistreatment of, 182–84, 185; resistance to slavery by, 182, 183; women, 182–86
Smiley, Tavis, 8, 39n27
Smith, Adam, 106
Smith, Hal F., 324
Smith, Harry, 247
Smith, Michael W., 143
Smith, Zadie, 85, 105, 112n8
Smither, Gregory D., *The Preacher and the Politician,* xvi
social construction: of masculinity, 228–29, 230; of race, 157, 159, 228–29, 230; of whiteness, 5, 140–42
social contract: in Obama's DNC speech, 267, 271, 279, 283; vs. racial contract, 27, 267
social Darwinism, 46
social spending issues, 209, 224n2
Socrates, 267
Soetoro, Lolo (stepfather), 96–97
Soetoro-Ng, Maya (sibling), 87–88, 96, 97
Sollors, Werner, 47
Solomon, Deborah, 87–88
Souls of Black Folk (Du Bois), 285
Soul Train, 97–98
Southern Poverty Law Center, xiii
Souza, Pete, 257–58
Speech, The (Sharpley-Whiting), xvii
Spencer, Stuart, 337

Spickard, Paul, xxxvi, 40n28, 97
Spillers, Hortense, 120, 125–27, 128
Spivak, Gayatri Chakravorty, 111n2, 145n5, 146n12
"stand your ground" laws, 23–25, 32
"State of the Black Union" symposium (2008), 8, 37n9
State of the Union address (2010), 40n33
Steele, Shelby, 7–8, 55
Steinberg, Stephen, 297
Steinhorn, Leonard, 34, 294
Stephens-Davidowitz, Seth, 27
stereotypes, racial: held by family of Obama, 172, 236, 323; in Philadelphia speech, 312, 324–27
stereotypes of black men: Bad Black Man, 226, 231, 234, 235, 237, 281; countered by Obama, 240; Good Black Man, 226, 231, 234–37, 281; material consequences of, 230. *See also* angry black man/woman stereotype
stereotypes of black women, 179–81, 184–86; applied to Michelle Obama, 192–93; countered by Michelle Obama, 194; in popular culture, 179, 185–86, 199. *See also* angry black man/woman stereotype
Stewart, Jon, 260n4
Stimulus Program, 30
Stoddard, Lothrop, *The Rising Tide of Color,* 46
"stop and frisk" practices, 258
Street, Paul, x, xxxv; *Barack Obama and the Future of American Politics,* 298
Streeter, Caroline, 52
structural inequalities: in covert racism, 292–95; lived reality of, 159–65; Obama's accommodation of, 289–92; Obama's awareness of, 99–100; persistence of, xiii–xiv, xxi, 159–65, 269, 309
subprime mortgage crisis, xxx–xxxi
substantive representation, 203; vs. descriptive representation, 203–4

successes of blacks, as evidence of end of racism, 18–19, 135, 293–94, 296–98
Sugrue, Thomas J., xvi
Suleri, Sara, 145n6
Sullivan, Andrew, 327
Sununu, John, 333
Supreme Court, U.S.: on affirmative action, xxii–xxiii, 20; on interracial marriage, 4, 9–10, 42; on school segregation, 160, 187; on Voting Rights Act, 20
surveillance policies, 40n27
Swarns, Rachel L., 201
Sykes, Wanda, 117, 118, 123
symbolic father: Obama as, 246–47; vs. imaginary father, 121

Taitz, Orly, 332
Task Force for Responsible Fatherhood and Healthy Families, 253
Tate, Shirley Ann, 85–86; *Black Skins, Black Masks,* 86, 100, 101, 111n2, 113n28
teachers: Michelle Obama influenced by, 190; race of, 160–61
Tea Party movement: racism in, 331; white anxiety in, 28; white fear in, 143
teenage pregnancy, 289, 290
teleology, in worldviews, 149
Terkildson, Nayda, 207
Terminator 2, 58
Terrell, Mary Church, 187
Tesler, Michael, 29; *Obama's Race,* xvi
Texas: population of, xii; race of teachers in, 160; 2008 election of, xxvi–xxvii
threats, against Obama, 29, 40n29, 193
Time: on changing face of America, x; on fear of black men, 236; on Michelle Obama, 193; on Obama as senator, 53; Obama on cover of, 56–57, 59; visual representation of multiraciality on cover of, xxii, 41, 49–51, 58
Times of London, 315
transference, 124–25
traumas: acting out, 268; DNC speech on black, 266, 268–71, 275, 277–78, 282–83, 324; DNC speech on nonblack, 266, 272, 277–78, 323; rhetoric in management of, 268, 284; working through, 266, 267, 268
Trickster of West Africa, The (Pelton), 80
tricksters, West African, 66–69. *See also* Ananse; Eshu
Truman, Harry S., 12
Trump, Donald, 79–80, 332
Tucson shooting (2011): casualties of, xiii, 75–76; memorial service speech by Obama, 64, 75–77, 81–82; white rage in, xiii
Turner, Nina, 163
Turner, Victor, 113n30
Turow, Scott, 53
Two Nations, 310n4
Tyson Darling, Marsha J., xxxv

Underground Railroad, 186
unemployment rate: among blacks, xiv, 30, 161, 301–2, 307–8; in Great Recession, 30, 301–2, 307–8; among Latinos, 30
unisex style: of Barack Obama, 226, 238–40; of Hillary Clinton, 241n7
United for a Fair Economy, xxiii, 302, 323
universal policy issues, 208–18, *212–13,* 222
University of Chicago, 191
University of Michigan Law School, xxiii
University of Notre Dame, 108–9
urban areas: fear of crime in, 142; inner-city poverty in, 289–90; public education in, 208–9, 212, 214
USA Today, 301, 334
utamawazo, European, 154
Utley, Ebony, xxxv–xxxvi, 36n2

Valley Swim Club, 164
values: traditional U.S., 29; of black working class, 189–90; of U.S., 273; in worldviews, 150–52
van der Veer, Peter, 145n5
videos: "crying baby," 244–45, *245,* 257, 260n4; of Wright's sermons, 6, 110, 172, 311

Villaraigosa, Antonio, xxvii
violent extremism, 72–73
Virginia, slavery in, 182, 185
visceral cosmopolitanism, 106–8
visual representations: of Michelle Obama, 56, 60, 192–93; of Obama family, in photographs, 245–49, *246*, 256–57
visual representations of multiracial individuals, 41–61; in *casta* paintings, 41–45; by Davenport, 41, 45–47; in popular culture, 42; in *Time* magazine, xxii, 41, 49–51, 58
visual representations of Obama, 56–60; with children of others, 244–45, *245*, 257–58; by Fairey, 41, 57–58; in family photographs, 245–49, *246*; on magazine covers, 56–57, 59–60, 193; mixed with someone else, 58, *59*; racist depictions in, xiii, 28, 162, 193, 331
Vogue, 162, 196
voice, in identity, 103–4
voters: Obama's success in turning out, 335; racial profiling of, xxiv; suppression in 2012 election, 15, 335–36
voting rights, 20, 280, 282
Voting Rights Act of 1965: dismantling of, 282; implications for minorities in, 20, 39n19; Supreme Court on, 20

Walker, Clarence E., *The Preacher and the Politician*, xvi
Wall Street Journal, xxiii
Walters, Ronald, 313
War on Poverty, 252, 270
war on terror: extrajudicial killings in, 40n27; racial profiling in, xxiii
Warren, Robert Penn, 286
Washington, Booker T., 314; *A New Negro for a New Century*, 249
Washington, D.C., population, xii
Washington, Harold, xxvi, 110, 314
Washington, Margaret Murray, 187
Washington Post: on Great Recession, 307–8; on 2008 Democratic primaries, 201, 206, 211, 216–17, 220; on 2008 presidential election, 234, 307
Watergate Hearings, 37n6
Waters, Maxine, 30
Watkins, Mel, *On the Real Side*, 78–79
Watts-Jones, Dee, 283
wealth: household, xxi, xxiii, 323; racial gap in, 290
Weaver, John, 337
Weaver, Vesla, 16
welfare policies: absent fathers and, 252; under Clinton, 252, 289; conservatives on, 289, 290; in Philadelphia speech, 325
Wells-Barnett, Ida B., 187
"wench" stereotype of black women, 179, 181, 183
West, Cornel, 39n27, 269–70
West, Don, 23
West, Paul, 329, 336
Where Do We Go From Here? (King), xxxvii
white: passing as, 12, 89–90; post-, 158
White, John Kenneth, *Barack Obama's America*, xvi
white Americans: and affirmative action, 19; "cracker" epithet, 22–23; future population of "pure" vs. mixed, xxv; Hispanic, xxii, 21, 38n18; Latinos as, 39n21; and light- vs. dark-skinned blacks, 18; as minority, xxii; in 1992 election, 270; nonwhite identifications of, xxiv–xxv; party affiliation of, 29; stereotypes of, 180; poverty rates among, 302, 307; on racial identity of Obama, 14, 288–89; support for Obama, 287–93, 306–7; in 2004 election, 271; in 2008 election, 14, 15–16, 138, 167; in 2012 election, xii, 15
white anxiety, xii–xiii, 27–29, 110–11
white domination, after civil rights movement, 19
white fear, 138–43; of black men, 139, 236; in construction of whiteness, 140–42; of crime, 140–42; in response to Obama's

election, 138–40; in white privilege, 134, 138–43
"white folks," Obama's use of term, 104, 108, 272
white hegemony, 19–20
White House Correspondents' Association Dinner (2011), Obama's speech at, 77–81; humor in, 78–82; messages of, 64, 78–81; visual media, 78–79
white identity: desirability of, xxi; future of, xxii; of Hispanics, xxii
white indentured servants, 3–4
white liberal savior trope, 325–26
whiteness: fear in construction of, 140–42; as norm, 16, 138, 162; one-drop rule in, 5; as racelessness, 133, 136, 138
whiteness of Obama: campaign emphasis on, 15–16; performance of, 329–30; visibility of, 88, 168
white privilege, 133–44; ability to ignore race as, 133, 135; benefits of, 143; effects of, 137; fear in, 134, 138–43; one-drop rule in, 3, 5; in post-racial concept, 133–34, 137–39, 142–44; and racelessness, 133, 136; stereotypes of, 180
white racial ideology, 163–65
white racial recovery project, 267, 279, 280, 282
white rage, in response to Obama's election, xii–xiii, 27
white resentment, xxix, 6–7, 110, 172, 323, 324
white supremacy: and Europe, 43, 153–56; Hagee's and McCain's ties to, 235–36; lived reality of, 161–65; Obama influenced by, 63–64; Obama's accommodation of, 289–92; and Obama's election, xii–xiii; in scholarship, xxxviii
Whitewashing Race (Brown), 161, 295
Whitman, Meg, 334
Whitman Rule, 334
Wilder, L. Douglas, 20, 38n14, 314
Wilkerson, Lawrence, 335
Williams, Dawn G., 157–58
Williams, Hettie V., xxxiv

Williams, Juan, 255
Williams, Mark, 14
Williams, Vanessa, 20
Williamson, Kevin, 256, 257
Wills, Garry, 269
Wilson, Harriet, *Our Nig*, 128
Wilson, Joe, 30–31, 33
Wilson, Kirt, 286n14
Wilson, Valerie Rawlston, 159, 324
Wilson, William Julius, xvii
Winant, Howard, 19; *Racial Formation in the United States*, 89, 90
Winfield, Betty Houchin, 207
Winfrey, Oprah, 39n27, 55, 297, 302
Wise, Tim, *Between Barack and a Hard Place*, xvi
Wolffe, Richard, 298
women: framing in media of, 206–7; identities of, 178–79; policy issues of, 208–9; Muslim, 74; in Obama administration, 38n15; in 2012 election, 15; white privilege in, 137. *See also* black women
Women's Club Movement, 186–87
women's rights, 72, 74
Woods, Jewel, 233
Woods, Tiger, 51–52, 168, 228
Woodward, Bob, *Obama's War*, xv
working class, Michelle Obama's family as, 188, 189–90
Working Girls' Home Association, 187
worldview: and analysis of human relations, 148; European, 154–57; European vs. African, 149–53; and impossibility of post-racist America, 147–54, 165; philosophical assumptions in, 149, 150–53; and structure of culture, 149
Wright, Jeremiah, Jr.: black liberation theology and, xxix, 321; challenging as tactic of, 8; on domestic and foreign policy, 6, 299, 317; on Obama, 37n8; Obama as Good Black Man, 235; Obama's break with, xxix, 8, 109–10, 172, 235; Obama's first statement on, 311; and "past" racism, 298–99, 309n3, 319;

as race-affirming, 235; scholarship on context for, xvi; sermons of, 6, 110, 172, 311; vs. Hagee, 235–36
Wright, Margaret, 19

X, Malcolm, xxix, 270
xenophobia, 119–20

Yoruba people, 66–68, 82. *See also* Eshu
Yurugu (Ani), 154–55

zambo, 45
Zarefsky, David, 269
Zeno of Citium, 106

Zimmerman, George, 20–26; DOJ investigation of, 25–26, 308; civil suit against, 39n26; racial bias of, 25, 39n24; racial heritage of, 20–21, 25, 39n24; as white vs. Hispanic, 21
Zimmerman trial, 20–26; colorblind rhetoric and, 20–23; jury instructions in, 24–25; Obama's response to, 32–33, 240; on outcome of, 26; race and gender of jurors in, 20, 39n20; "stand your ground" law and, 23–25; verdict in, 20, 22, 25
Zogby, John, 107
Zuberi, Tukufu, xxxviii

www.ingramcontent.com/pod-product-compliance
Lightning Source LLC
Chambersburg PA
CBHW030330240426
43661CB00052B/1587